# Great Conversations

# 6

SELECTED AND EDITED BY
Donald H. Whitfield

CONTRIBUTORS
James A. Barham
Kristine Bergman
Nancy Carr
Allie Hirsch
Mary Klein
Dylan Nelson
Donald C. Smith
Mary Williams

# Great Conversations

6

## THE GREAT BOOKS FOUNDATION
*A nonprofit educational organization*

The Great Conversations series receives generous support from
Harrison Middleton University, a Great Books distance-learning college.

**Published and distributed by**

THE GREAT BOOKS FOUNDATION
*A nonprofit educational organization*

35 E. Wacker Drive, Suite 400
Chicago, IL 60601
www.greatbooks.org

With generous support from
Harrison Middleton University,
a Great Books distance-learning college
www.chumsci.edu

First printing
9 8 7 6 5 4 3 2 1

Library of Congress Cataloging-in-Publication Data
Great conversations 6 / selected and edited by Donald H. Whitfield.
    pages cm
  ISBN 978-1-933147-88-8
  1. Literature--Collections. 2. Literature, Modern--History and criticism. I. Whitfield, Donald, editor of compilation. II.. Title: Great conversations six.
  PN6012.G773 2013
  808.8--dc23
                                                                    2012041925

Series book cover and interior design:
Judy Sickle, Forward Design
Chicago, Illinois

# CONTENTS

*Great Conversations 6* brings together selections representing a wide range
of genres, including fiction, essays, drama, poetry, and philosophy. Each was
chosen not only because of its intrinsic excellence but also because of its rich
connections with many of the ideas and issues raised by other selections in the
book. Each of these selections exemplifies one of the primary criteria for a Great
Book: that it is part of a tradition of ongoing intellectual dialogue, responding
to the insights and claims of other writings and contributing its own distinctive
voice to the conversation. The authors of these selections, whether expressing
their ideas through the craft of imaginative literature or the logic of expository
argument, raise an array of stimulating topics for discussion, addressing many of
the perennial questions that people everywhere have grappled with.

Though drawn from different disciplines, the selections in *Great Conversations 6*
do not demand that a reader have any specialized expertise or background
information to fully engage with the content. The selections speak for
themselves and provide readers with much of the guidance necessary to begin
to explore their many levels of meaning. In addition, these selections exemplify
yet another criterion for a Great Book: even though it may be linked to the
particular circumstances in which it was written, it nevertheless addresses
universal concerns with a sense of freshness and immediacy.

This volume is intended for use in book groups that are serious about
discovering the ideas and authors that have shaped our culture and ourselves.
It is also meant for college humanities courses in which students and teachers
seek together, through discussion and writing, to answer the great questions
that have driven human thought throughout history.

Questions follow each of the selections. The first group ("Questions") is designed
to open up specific passages of the text to close reading and interpretation.
These questions ask readers to consider evidence within the selection itself
when seeking answers. Answers are likely to be multiple and complex.

The second group of questions ("For Further Reflection") invites readers to evaluate the claims made by the text in light of their own and others' experience, as well as additional reading. It is one thing to understand what an author is trying to say, but it is just as important to ascertain to what extent the author's claims are accurate or true. To evaluate an author's work, it is essential to put that work into the larger framework of our own thinking and experience. One strong caution: keep discussion of a particular text tethered to the words of the selection for a reasonable amount of time before jumping to the evaluative questions. Determining the value of a work without first fully examining and understanding it gets the two-step process backward.

Book groups or classes can choose to read this book straight through, but there is also the option to organize the reading sequence by theme. Some thematic groupings are provided in the back of this book.

Briefly, these are the guidelines for Shared Inquiry,™ a text-based Socratic method of discussion that the Great Books Foundation has successfully developed over more than six decades of work with educators of all kinds. We recommend these guidelines for users of this book:

1. **Read the selection carefully before participating in the discussion.** This ensures that all participants are equally prepared to talk about the ideas in the work and helps prevent talk that would distract the group from its purpose.

2. **Support your ideas with evidence from the text.** This keeps the discussion focused on understanding the selection and enables the group to weigh textual support for different answers and to choose intelligently among them.

3. **Discuss the ideas in the selection and try to understand them fully before exploring issues that go beyond the selection.** Reflecting on the ideas in the text and the evidence to support them makes the exploration of related issues more productive.

4. **Listen to other participants and respond to them directly.** Shared Inquiry is about the give-and-take of ideas and the willingness to listen to others and talk with them respectfully. Directing your comments and questions to other group members, not always the leader, will make the discussion livelier and more dynamic.

5. **Expect the leader to only ask questions.** Effective leaders help participants develop their own ideas, with everyone gaining a new understanding in the process. When participants hang back and wait for the leader to suggest answers, discussion tends to falter.

The fifteen selections in this volume, plus the discussion guides for two longer works not included in the anthology itself (Edith Wharton's *The Age of Innocence* and Andreï Makine's *Confessions of a Fallen Standard-Bearer*), make it compatible with semester-long offerings in the humanities, where writing assignments can further develop interpretation. The headnote preceding each selection provides a brief biographical and historical context for the author.

*Footnotes by the author are not bracketed; footnotes by the
Great Books Foundation, an editor, or a translator are [bracketed].*

*Spelling and punctuation have been
modernized and slightly altered for clarity.*

Lucius Annaeus Seneca (ca. 4 BCE–65 CE), statesman, philosopher, orator, and playwright, was born in the Roman province of Spain to a wealthy rhetorician. Taken to Rome at a young age to prepare for political life, Seneca was trained in public speaking and philosophy. His career was hindered by ill health and then curtailed in 41 CE when, accused of adultery with a member of the imperial family, he was banished to Corsica by the emperor Claudius. There, he occupied his time studying philosophy and writing the consolations to Helvia and Polybius. These works, addressed to particular individuals, embody the core of Seneca's philosophy.

Seneca's writings reflect the doctrines of Stoicism, a school of thought that originated in Greece and was widely popular during the Roman imperial period. In the perennially turbulent world of Rome, the Stoics' advocacy for a way of life based on moral virtues and emotional balance found ready acceptance. Although many of his principal philosophical ideas are not original but rather transmitted from those of his Greek predecessors, Seneca's subtle restatement of Stoic philosophy and his insight into human emotions are distinctive to his personality and style. Typical of Seneca's attitude are the words he wrote to his mother in the "Consolation to Helvia." Describing his feelings about his exile, he writes, "I am as happy and cheerful as when circumstances were best. Indeed, they are now best, since my mind, free from all other engrossment, has leisure for its own tasks, and now finds joy in lighter studies, now, being eager for the truth, mounts to the consideration of its own nature and the nature of the universe."

In 49, Claudius's wife, Agrippina, recalled Seneca to Rome. Soon, he became tutor to Nero, Agrippina's son, and when Claudius died and Nero ascended the throne, Seneca became one of his chief advisors, along with the prefect of the guard, Sextus Afranius Burrus. During this period, Seneca and Burrus held considerable influence in the governance of Rome. Seneca wrote speeches for the young emperor and took an active part in the administration of the empire. Many historians believe that his essay "On Clemency" was an attempt to encourage Nero, who would prove to be an increasingly volatile ruler, to be just and temperate. In 59, Seneca and Burrus became unwillingly involved in Nero's murder of Agrippina. After Burrus's death in 62, Seneca, no longer able to maintain his compromised position and strained relationship with Nero, withdrew from politics. He devoted himself to the study of philosophy and to writing, producing his major work, the *Letters to Lucilius*. In 65 Seneca was accused of participating in a conspiracy to kill Nero and was ordered by the emperor to commit suicide. True to the tenets of Stoicism, Seneca complied by severing his veins and slowly bleeding to death, surrounded by his friends and dictating his last thoughts to a scribe, events later described in detail by the Roman historian Tacitus in his *Annals*.

Seneca wrote in a number of forms, including dialogues, letters, and longer treatises, and on a range of topics, including politics, natural science, and daily life, though his predominant concern was with ethics. Many of his writings, such as "On Tranquility of Mind," are addressed to an inquirer who asks a question about a philosophical problem; Seneca then replies with a lengthy discourse on the issue raised. This format emphasizes the personal and practical over the formal and logical, a tendency typical of his thought. In addition to philosophy, Seneca was famous for his tragedies, many of which were adapted from Greek models. Seneca's works were seen to have Christian affinities by the early Christian church; he was read by St. Augustine, St. Jerome, and the philosopher Boethius, who found his writings a comfort during his years of imprisonment. Later writers admired not only his philosophy but also his refined writing style, and he was admired and imitated by Petrarch, Erasmus, Montaigne, and other humanists during the Renaissance. Perhaps the greatest literary tribute to Seneca was given by Dante, who placed him in *The Divine Comedy* among the virtuous pagans in a state of eternal happiness, falling short of heaven only because he was not a Christian.

# On Tranquility of Mind

S ERENUS: When I made examination of myself, it became evident, Seneca, that some of my vices are uncovered and displayed so openly that I can put my hand upon them, some are more hidden and lurk in a corner, some are not always present but recur at intervals; and I should say that the last are by far the most troublesome, being like roving enemies that spring upon one when the opportunity offers, and allow one neither to be ready as in war, nor to be off guard as in peace.

Nevertheless the state in which I find myself most of all—for why should I not admit the truth to you as to a physician?—is that I have neither been honestly set free from the things that I hated and feared, nor, on the other hand, am I in bondage to them; while the condition in which I am placed is not the worst, yet I am complaining and fretful—I am neither sick nor well. There is no need for you to say that all the virtues are weakly at the beginning, that firmness and strength are added by time. I am well aware also that the virtues that struggle for outward show, I mean for position and the fame of eloquence and all that comes under the verdict of others, do grow stronger as time passes—both those that provide real strength and those that trick us out with a sort of dye with a view to pleasing must wait long years until gradually length of time develops color—but I greatly fear that habit, which brings stability to most things, may cause this fault of mine to become more deeply implanted. Of things evil as well as good long intercourse induces love.

The nature of this weakness of mind that halts between two things and inclines strongly neither to the right nor to the wrong, I cannot show you so well all at once as a part at a time; I shall tell you what befalls me—you will find a name for my malady. I am possessed by the very greatest love of frugality, I must confess; I do not like a couch made up for display, nor clothing brought forth from a chest or pressed by weights and a thousand mangles to make it glossy, but homely and cheap, that is neither preserved nor to be put on with anxious care; the food that I like is neither prepared nor watched by a household of slaves, it does not need to be ordered many days before nor to be served by many hands, but is easy to get and abundant; there is nothing far-fetched or costly about it, nowhere will there be any lack of it, it is burdensome neither to the purse nor to the body, nor will it return by the way it entered; the servant that I like is a young home-born slave without training or skill; the silver is my country-bred father's heavy plate bearing no stamp of the maker's name, and the table is not notable for the variety of its markings or known to the town from the many fashionable owners through whose hands it has passed, but one that stands for use, and will neither cause the eyes of any guest to linger upon it with pleasure nor fire them with envy. Then, after all these things have had my full approval, my mind is dazzled by the magnificence of some training school for pages, by the sight of slaves bedecked with gold and more carefully arrayed than the leaders of a public procession, and a whole regiment of glittering attendants; by the sight of a house where one even treads on precious stones and riches are scattered about in every corner, where the very roofs glitter, and the whole town pays court and escorts an inheritance on the road to ruin. And what shall I say of the waters, transparent to the bottom, that flow around the guests even as they banquet, what of the feasts that are worthy of their setting? Coming from a long abandonment to thrift, luxury has poured around me the wealth of its splendor and echoed around me on every side. My sight falters a little, for I can lift up my heart toward it more easily than my eyes. And so I come back, not worse, but sadder, and I do not walk among my paltry possessions with head erect as before, and there enters a secret sting and the doubt whether the other life is not better. None of these things changes me, yet none of them fails to disturb me.

I resolve to obey the commands of my teachers and plunge into the midst of public life; I resolve to try to gain office and the consulship, attracted of course, not by the purple or by the lictor's rods, but by the desire to be more serviceable and useful to my friends and relatives and all my countrymen and then to all mankind. Ready and determined, I follow Zeno, Cleanthes, and Chrysippus, of whom nonetheless not one entered upon public life, and not one failed to urge others to do so. And then, whenever something upsets my mind, which is unused to meeting shocks, whenever something happens that is either unworthy of me, and many such occur in the lives of all human beings, or that does not proceed very easily, or when things that are not to be accounted of great value demand much of my time, I turn back to my leisure, and just as wearied flocks too do, I quicken my pace toward home. I resolve to confine my life within its own walls: "Let no one," I say, "who will make me no worthy return for such a loss rob me of a single day; let my mind be fixed upon itself, let it cultivate itself, let it busy itself with nothing outside, nothing that looks toward an umpire; let it love the tranquility that is remote from public and private concern." But when my mind has been aroused by read-ing of great bravery, and noble examples have applied the spur, I want to rush into the forum, to lend my voice to one man; to offer such assistance to another as, even if it will not help, will be an effort to help; or to check the pride of someone in the forum who has been unfortunately puffed up by his successes.

And in my literary studies I think that it is surely better to fix my eyes on the theme itself, and, keeping this uppermost when I speak, to trust meanwhile to the theme to supply the words so that unstudied language may follow it wherever it leads. I say: "What need is there to compose something that will last for centuries? Will you not give up striving to keep posterity from being silent about you? You were born for death; a silent funeral is less troublesome! And so to pass the time, write some-thing in simple style, for your own use, not for publication; they that study for the day have less need to labor." Then again, when my mind has been uplifted by the greatness of its thoughts, it becomes ambitious of words, and with higher aspirations it desires higher expression, and language issues forth to match the dignity of the theme; forgetful then of my rule and of my more restrained judgment, I am swept to loftier heights by an utterance that is no longer my own.

Not to indulge longer in details, I am in all things attended by this weakness of good intention. In fact I fear that I am gradually losing ground, or, what causes me even more worry, that I am hanging like one who is always on the verge of falling, and that perhaps I am in a more serious condition than I myself perceive; for we take a favorable view of our private matters, and partiality always hampers our judgment. I fancy that many men would have arrived at wisdom if they had not fancied that they had already arrived, if they had not dissembled about certain traits in their character and passed by others with their eyes shut. For there is no reason for you to suppose that the adulation of other people is more ruinous to us than our own. Who dares to tell himself the truth? Who, though he is surrounded by a horde of applauding sycophants, is not for all that his own greatest flatterer? I beg you, therefore, if you have any remedy by which you could stop this fluctuation of mine, to deem me worthy of being indebted to you for tranquility. I know that these mental disturbances of mine are not dangerous and give no promise of a storm; to express what I complain of in apt metaphor, I am distressed, not by a tempest, but by seasickness. Do you, then, take from me this trouble, whatever it be, and rush to the rescue of one who is struggling in full sight of land.

SENECA: In truth, Serenus, I have for a long time been silently asking myself to what I should liken such a condition of mind, and I can find nothing that so closely approaches it as the state of those who, after being released from a long and serious illness, are sometimes touched with fits of fever and slight disorders, and, freed from the last traces of them, are nevertheless disquieted with mistrust, and, though now quite well, stretch out their wrist to a physician and complain unjustly of any trace of heat in their body. It is not, Serenus, that these are not quite well in body, but that they are not quite used to being well, just as even a tranquil sea will show some ripple, particularly when it has just subsided after a storm. What you need, therefore, is not any of those harsher measures that we have already left behind, the necessity of opposing yourself at this point, of being angry with yourself at that, of sternly urging yourself on at another, but that which comes last—confidence in yourself and the belief that you are on the right path and have not been led astray by the many cross-tracks of those who are roaming in every direction, some of whom are wandering very near the path itself. But what you desire is something great and supreme and very near to being a god—to be unshaken.

This abiding stability of mind the Greeks call *euthymia*, "well-being of the soul," on which there is an excellent treatise by Democritus; I call it tranquility. For there is no need to imitate and reproduce words in their Greek shape; the thing itself, which is under discussion, must be designated by some name that ought to have, not the form, but the force, of the Greek term. What we are seeking, therefore, is how the mind may always pursue a steady and favorable course, may be well-disposed toward itself, and may view its condition with joy, and suffer no interruption of this joy, but may abide in a peaceful state, being never uplifted nor ever cast down. This will be "tranquility." Let us seek in a general way how it may be obtained; then from the universal remedy *you* will appropriate as much as you like. Meanwhile we must drag forth into the light the whole of the infirmity, and each one will then recognize his own share of it; at the same time you will understand how much less trouble *you* have with your self-depreciation than those who, fettered to some showy declaration and struggling beneath the burden of some grand title, are held more by shame than by desire to the pretense they are making.

All are in the same case, both those, on the one hand, who are plagued with fickleness and boredom and a continual shifting of purpose, and those, on the other, who loll and yawn. Add also those who, just like the wretches who find it hard to sleep, change their position and settle first in one way and then in another, until finally they find rest through weariness. By repeatedly altering the condition of their life they are at last left in that in which, not the dislike of making a change, but old age, which shrinks from novelty, has caught them. And add also those who by fault, not of firmness of character, but of inertia, are not fickle enough, and live, not as they wish, but as they have begun. The characteristics of the malady are countless in number, but it has only one effect—to be dissatisfied with oneself. This springs from a lack of mental poise and from timid or unfulfilled desires, when men either do not dare, or do not attain, as much as they desire, and become entirely dependent upon hope; such men are always unstable and changeable, as must necessarily be the fate of those who live in suspense. They strive to attain their prayers by every means, they teach and force themselves to do dishonorable and difficult things, and, when their effort is without reward, they are tortured by the fruitless disgrace and grieve, not because they wished for what was wrong, but because they wished in vain. Then regret for what they have begun lays hold upon them, and the fear of beginning again, and then creeps in the agitation of a mind that can find no issue, because they can neither rule nor obey their desires, and the hesitancy of a life that fails to find its way clear, and then the dullness of a soul that lies torpid amid abandoned hopes. And all these tendencies are aggravated when from hatred of their laborious ill-success men have taken refuge in leisure and in solitary studies, which are unendurable to a mind that is intent upon public affairs, desirous of action, and naturally restless, because assuredly it has too few resources within itself; when, therefore, the pleasures have been withdrawn that business itself affords to those who are busily engaged, the mind cannot endure home, solitude, and the walls of a room, and sees with dislike that it has been left to itself.

From this comes that boredom and dissatisfaction and the vacillation of a mind that nowhere finds rest, and the sad and languid endurance of one's leisure, especially when one is ashamed to confess the real causes of this condition and bashfulness drives its tortures inward; the desires pent up within narrow bounds, from which there is no escape, strangle one another. Thence comes mourning and melancholy and the thousand waverings of an unsettled mind, which its aspirations hold in suspense and then disappointment renders melancholy. Thence comes that feeling which makes men loathe their own leisure and complain that they themselves have nothing to be busy with; thence too the bitterest jealousy of the advancements of others. For their unhappy sloth fosters envy, and, because they could not succeed themselves, they wish everyone else to be ruined; then from this aversion to the progress of others and despair of their own their mind becomes incensed against fortune, and complains of the times, and retreats into corners and broods over its trouble until it becomes weary and sick of itself. For it is the nature of the human mind to be active and prone to movement. Welcome to it is every opportunity for excitement and distraction, and still more welcome to all those worst natures that willingly wear themselves out in being employed. Just as there are some sores that crave the hands that will hurt them and rejoice to be touched, and as a foul itch of the body delights in whatever scratches, exactly so, I would say, do these minds upon which, so to speak, desires have broken out like wicked sores find pleasure in toil and vexation. For there are certain things that delight our body also while causing it a sort of pain, as turning over and changing a side that is not yet tired and taking one position after another to get cool. Homer's hero Achilles is like that—lying now on his face, now on his back, placing himself in various attitudes, and, just as sick men do, enduring nothing very long and using changes as remedies.

Hence men undertake wide-ranging travel, and wander over remote shores, and their fickleness, always discontented with the present, gives proof of itself now on land and now on sea. "Now let us head for Campania," they say. And now when soft living palls, "Let us see the wild parts," they say, "let us hunt out the passes of Bruttium and Lucania." And yet amid that wilderness something is missing—something pleasant wherein their pampered eyes may find relief from the lasting squalor of those rugged regions: "Let us head for Tarentum with its famous harbor and its mild winter climate, and a territory rich enough to have a horde of people even in antiquity." Too long have their ears missed the shouts and the din; it delights them by now even to enjoy human blood: "Let us now turn our course toward the city." They undertake one journey after another and change spectacle for spectacle. As Lucretius says:

Thus ever from himself doth each man flee.

But what does he gain if he does not escape from himself? He ever follows himself and weighs upon himself as his own most burdensome companion. And so we ought to understand that what we struggle with is the fault, not of the places, but of ourselves; when there is need of endurance, we are weak, and we cannot bear toil or pleasure or ourselves or anything very long. It is this that has driven some men to death, because by often altering their purpose they were always brought back to the same things and had left themselves no room for anything new. They began to be sick of life and the world itself, and from the self-indulgences that wasted them was born the thought: "How long shall I endure the same things?"

You ask what help, in my opinion, should be employed to overcome this tedium. The best course would be, as Athenodorus says, to occupy oneself with practical matters, the management of public affairs, and the duties of a citizen. For as some men pass the day in seeking the sun and in exercise and care of the body, and as athletes find it is most profitable by far to devote the greater part of the day to the development of their muscles and the strength to which alone they have dedicated themselves; so for you, who are training your mind for the struggle of political life, by far the most desirable thing is to be busy at one task. For, whenever a man has the set purpose to make himself useful to his countrymen and all mortals, he both gets practice and does service at the same time when he has placed himself in the very midst of active duties, serving to the best of his ability the interests both of the public and of the individual. "But because," he continues, "in this mad world of ambition where chicanery so frequently twists right into wrong, simplicity is hardly safe, and is always sure to meet with more that hinders than helps it, we ought indeed to withdraw from the forum and public life, but a great mind has an opportunity to display itself freely even in private life; nor, just as the activity of lions and animals is restrained by their dens, is it so of man's, whose greatest achievements are wrought in retirement. Let a man, however, hide himself away bearing in mind that, wherever he secretes his leisure, he should be willing to benefit the individual man and mankind by his intellect, his voice, and his counsel. For the man that does good service to the state is not merely he who brings forward candidates and defends the accused and votes for peace and war, but he also who admonishes young men, who instills virtue into their minds, supplying the great lack of good teachers, who lays hold upon those that are rushing wildly in pursuit of money and luxury, and draws them back, and, if he accomplishes nothing else, at least retards them—such a man performs a public service even in private life. Or does he accomplish more who in the office of praetor, whether in cases between citizens and foreigners or in cases between citizens, delivers to suitors the verdict his assistant has formulated, than he who teaches the meaning of justice, of piety, of endurance, of bravery, of contempt of death, of knowledge of the gods, and how secure and free is the blessing of a good conscience? If, then, the time that you have stolen from public duties is bestowed upon studies, you will neither have deserted, nor refused, your office. For a soldier is not merely one who stands in line and defends the right or the left wing, but he also who guards the gates and fills, not an idle, but a less dangerous, post, who keeps watch at night and has charge of the armory; these offices, though they are bloodless, yet count as military service. If you devote yourself to studies, you will have escaped all your disgust at life, you will not long for night to come because you are weary of the light, nor will you be either burdensome to yourself or useless to others; you will attract many to friendship and those that gather about you will be the most excellent. For virtue, though obscured, is never concealed, but always gives signs of its presence; whoever is worthy will trace her out by her footsteps. But if we give up society altogether and, turning our backs upon the human race, live with our thoughts fixed only upon ourselves, this solitude deprived of every interest will be followed by a want of something to be accomplished. We shall begin to put up some buildings, to pull down others, to thrust back the sea, to cause waters to flow despite the obstacles of nature, and shall make ill disposition of the time that nature has given us to be used. Some use it sparingly, others wastefully; some of us spend it in such a way that we are able to give an account of it, others in such a way—and nothing can be more shameful—that we have no balance left. Often a man who is very old in years has no evidence to prove that he has lived a long time other than his age."

To me, my dearest Serenus, Athenodorus seems to have surrendered too quickly to the times, to have retreated too quickly. I myself would not deny that sometimes one must retire, but it should be a gradual retreat without surrendering the standards, without surrendering the honor of a soldier; those are more respected by their enemies and safer who come to terms with their arms in their hands. This is what I think virtue and virtue's devotee should do. If fortune shall get the upper hand and shall cut off the opportunity for action, let a man not straightway turn his back and flee, throwing away his arms and seeking some hiding place, as if there were anywhere a place where fortune could not reach him, but let him devote himself to his duties more sparingly, and, after making choice, let him find something in which he may be useful to the state. Is he not permitted to be a soldier? Let him seek public office. Must he live in a private station? Let him be a pleader. Is he condemned to silence? Let him help his countrymen by his silent support. Is it dangerous even to enter the forum? In private houses, at the public spectacles, at feasts let him show himself a good comrade, a faithful friend, a temperate feaster. Has he lost the duties of a citizen? Let him exercise those of a man. The very reason for our magnanimity in not shutting ourselves up within the walls of one city, in going forth into intercourse with the whole earth, and in claiming the world as our country, was that we might have a wider field for our virtue. Is the tribunal closed to you, and are you barred from the rostrum and the hustings? Look how many broad stretching countries lie open behind you, how many peoples; never can you be blocked from any part so large that a still larger will not be left to you. But take care that this is not wholly your own fault; you are not willing to serve the state except as a consul or prytanis or herald or sufete. What if you should be unwilling to serve in the army except as a general or a tribune? Even if others shall hold the front line and your lot has placed you among those of the third line, from there where you are do service with your voice, encouragement, example, and spirit; even though a man's hands are cut off, he finds that he can do something for his side in battle if he stands his ground and helps with the shouting. Some such thing is what you should do. If fortune has removed you from the foremost position in the state, you should, nevertheless, stand your ground and help with the shouting, and if someone stops your throat, you should, nevertheless, stand your ground and help in silence. The service of a good citizen is never useless;

by being heard and seen, by his expression, by his gesture, by his silent stubbornness, and by his very walk he helps. As there are certain salutary things that without our tasting and touching them benefit us by their mere odor, so virtue sheds her advantage even from a distance, and in hiding. Whether she walks abroad and of her own right makes herself active, or has her appearances on sufferance and is forced to draw in her sails, or is inactive and mute and pent within narrow bounds, or is openly displayed, no matter what her condition is, she always does good. Why, then, do *you* think that the example of one who lives in honorable retirement is of little value? Accordingly, the best course by far is to combine leisure with business, whenever chance obstacles or the condition of the state shall prevent one's living a really active life; for a man is never so completely shut off from all pursuits that no opportunity is left for any honorable activity.

Can you find any city more wretched than was that of the Athenians when it was being torn to pieces by the Thirty Tyrants? They had slain thirteen hundred citizens, all the best men, and were not for that reason ready to stop, but their very cruelty fed its own flame. In the city in which there was the Areopagus, a most god-fearing court, in which there was a senate and a popular assembly that was like a senate, there gathered together every day a sorry college of hangmen, and the unhappy senate-house was made too narrow by tyrants! Could that city ever find peace in which there were as many tyrants as there might be satellites? No hope even of recovering liberty could offer itself, nor did there seem to be room for any sort of help against such mighty strength of wicked men. For where could the wretched state find enough Harmodiuses? Yet Socrates was in their midst and comforted the mourning city fathers; he encouraged those that were despairing of the state, reproached the rich men that were now dreading their wealth with a too-late repentance of their perilous greed, while to those willing to imitate him he carried round with him a great example, as he moved a free man amid thirty masters. Yet this was the man that Athens herself murdered in prison, and freedom herself could not endure the freedom of one who had mocked in security at a whole band of tyrants. And so you may learn both that the wise man has opportunity to display his power when the state is torn by trouble, and that effrontery, envy, and a thousand other cowardly vices hold sway when it is prosperous and happy. Therefore we shall either expand or contract our effort according as the state shall lend herself to us, according as fortune shall permit us, but in any case we shall keep moving, and shall not be tied down and numbed by fear. Nay, he will be truly a man who, when perils are threatening from every side, when arms and chains are rattling around him, will neither endanger, nor conceal, his virtue; for saving oneself does not mean burying oneself. Curius Dentatus said, truly as I think, that he would rather be a dead man than a live one dead; for the worst of ills is to leave the number of the living before you die. But if you should happen upon a time when it is not at all easy to serve the state, your necessary course will be to claim more time for leisure and for letters, and, just as if you were making a perilous voyage, to put into harbor from time to time, and, without waiting for public affairs to release you, to separate yourself from them of your own accord.

Our duty, however, will be, first, to examine our own selves, then, the matters that we shall undertake, and lastly, those for whose sake or in whose company we are undertaking them.

Above all it is necessary for a man to estimate himself truly, because we commonly think that we can do more than we are able. One man blunders by relying upon his eloquence, another makes more demand upon his fortune than it can stand, another burdens a weakly body with laborious tasks. Some men by reason of their modesty are quite unsuited to civil affairs, which need a strong front; some by reason of their stubborn pride are not fitted for court; some do not have their anger under control, and any sort of provocation hurries them to rash words; some do not know how to restrain their pleasantry and cannot abstain from dangerous wit. For all these retirement is more serviceable than employment; a headstrong and impatient nature should avoid all incitements to a freedom of speech that will prove harmful.

Next, we must estimate the matters themselves that we are undertaking, and must compare our strength with the things that we are about to attempt; for the doer must always be stronger than his task; burdens that are too heavy for their bearer must necessarily crush him. There are certain undertakings, moreover, that are not so much great as they are prolific, and thus lead to many fresh undertakings. Not only ought you to avoid those that give birth to new and multifarious employment, but you ought not to approach a task from which you are not free to retreat; you must put your hand to those that you can either finish, or at least hope to finish, leaving those untouched that grow bigger as you progress and do not cease at the point you intended.

And we must be particularly careful in our choice of men, and consider whether they are worthy of having us devote some part of our life to them, or whether the sacrifice of our time extends to theirs also; for certain people actually charge against us the services we do them. Athenodorus says that he would not go to dine with a man who would not feel indebted to him for doing so. You understand, I suppose, that much less would he go to dinner with those who recompense the services of friends by their table, who set down the courses of a meal as largesses, as if they were being intemperate to do honor to others. Take away the spectators and witnesses, and solitary gluttony will give them no pleasure.

You must consider whether your nature is better adapted to active affairs or to leisurely study and contemplation, and you must turn toward that course to which the bent of your genius shall direct you. Isocrates laid hands upon Ephorus and led him away from the forum, thinking that he would he more useful in compiling the records of history; for inborn tendencies answer ill to compulsion, and where nature opposes labor is in vain.

Nothing, however, gives the mind so much pleasure as fond and faithful friendship. What a blessing it is to have those to whose waiting hearts every secret may be committed with safety, whose knowledge of you you fear less than your knowledge of yourself, whose conversation soothes your anxiety, whose opinion assists your decision, whose cheerfulness scatters your sorrow, the very sight of whom gives you joy! We shall of course choose those who are free, as far as may be, from selfish desires; for vices spread unnoticed, and quickly pass to those nearest and do harm by their contact. And so, just as in times of pestilence we must take care not to sit near those whose bodies are already infected and inflamed with disease, because we shall incur risks and be in danger from their very breath, so, in choosing our friends, we shall have regard for their character, so that we may appropriate those who are marked with fewest stains; to combine the sick with the sound is to spread disease. Yet I would not lay down the rule that you are to follow, or attach to yourself, none but a wise man. For where will you find him whom we have been seeking for so many centuries? In place of the best man take the one least bad! Opportunity for a happier choice scarcely could you have, were you searching for a good man among the Platos and the Xenophons and the rest of that glorious company of the Socratic breed, or, too, if you had at your command the age of Cato, which bore many men who were worthy to be born in Cato's time, just as it also bore many that were worse than had ever been known, and contrivers of the most monstrous crimes; for both classes were necessary in order that Cato might be understood—he needed to have good men that he might win their approval, and bad men that he might prove his strength. But now, when there is such a great dearth of good men, you must be less squeamish in making your choice. Yet those are especially to be avoided who are melancholy and bewail everything, who find pleasure in every opportunity for complaint. Though a man's loyalty and friendliness be assured, yet the companion who is always upset and bemoans everything is a foe to tranquility.

Let us pass now to the matter of fortunes, which are the greatest source of human sorrow; for if you compare all the other ills from which we suffer—deaths, sicknesses, fears, longings, the endurance of pains and labors—with the evils that our money brings, this portion will far outweigh the other. And so we must reflect how much lighter is the sorrow of not having money than of losing it; and we shall understand that, the less poverty has to lose, the less chance it has to torment us. For you are wrong if you think that the rich suffer losses more cheerfully; the pain of a wound is the same in the largest and smallest bodies. Bion says neatly that it hurts the bald-head just as much as the thatched-head to have his hairs plucked. You may be sure that the same thing holds for the poor and the rich, that their suffering is just the same; for their money has a fast grip on both, and cannot be torn away without their feeling it. But, as I have said, it is more endurable and easier not to acquire it than to lose it, and therefore you will see that those whom fortune has never regarded are more cheerful than those whom she has forsaken. Diogenes, that high-souled man, saw this, and made it impossible for anything to be snatched from him. Do *you* call such a state poverty, want, need; give this security any disgraceful name you please. I shall not count the man happy, if you can find anyone else who has nothing to lose! Either I am deceived, or it is a regal thing to be the only one amid all the misers, the sharpers, the robbers, and plunderers who cannot be harmed. If anyone has any doubt about the happiness of Diogenes, he may likewise have doubt about the condition of the immortal gods as well—whether they are living quite unhappily because they have neither manors nor gardens nor costly estates farmed by a foreign tenant, nor a huge yield of interest in the forum. All ye who bow down to riches, where is your shame? Come, turn your eyes upon heaven; you will see the gods quite needy, giving all and having nothing. Do you think that he who stripped himself of all the gifts of fortune is a poor man or simply like the immortal gods? Would you say that Demetrius, the freedman of Pompey, who was not ashamed to be richer than Pompey, was a happier man? He, to whom two underlings and a roomier cell would once have been wealth, used to have the number of his slaves reported to him every day as if he were the general of an army! But the only slave Diogenes had ran away from him once, and, when he was pointed out to him, he did not think it worth while to fetch him back. "It would be a shame," he said, "if Diogenes is not able to live without Manes when Manes is able to live without Diogenes." But he seems to me to have cried: "Fortune, mind your own business; Diogenes has now nothing of yours. My slave has run away—nay, it is I that have got away free!" A household of slaves requires clothes and food; so many bellies of creatures that are always hungry have to be filled, we have to buy clothing for them, and watch their most thievish hands, and use the services of people weeping and cursing. How much happier is he whose only obligation is to one whom he can most easily refuse—himself! Since, however, we do not have such strength of character, we ought at least to reduce our possessions, so as to be less exposed to the injuries of fortune. In war those men are better fitted for service whose bodies can be squeezed into their armor than those whose bodies spill over, and whose very bulk everywhere exposes them to wounds. In the case of money, an amount that does not descend to poverty, and yet is not far removed from poverty, is the most desirable.

Moreover, we shall be content with this measure if we were previously content with thrift, without which no amount of wealth is sufficient, and no amount is not sufficiently ample, especially since the remedy is always near at hand, and poverty of itself is able to turn itself into riches by summoning economy. Let us form the habit of putting away from us mere pomp and of measuring the uses of things, not their decorative qualities. Let food subdue hunger, drink quench thirst; let lust follow the course of nature; let us learn to rely upon our limbs and to conform our dress and mode of life, not to the new fashions, but to the customs our ancestors approved; let us learn to increase our self-control, to restrain luxury, to moderate ambition, to soften anger, to view poverty with unprejudiced eyes, to cultivate frugality, even if many shall be ashamed, all the more to apply to the wants of nature the remedies that cost little, to keep unruly hopes and a mind that is intent upon the future, as it were, in chains, and to determine to seek our riches from ourselves rather than from fortune. It is never possible that all the diversity and injustice of mischance can be so repulsed that many storms will not sweep down upon those who are spreading great sail. We must draw in our activities to a narrow compass in order that the darts of fortune may fall into nothingness, and for this reason exiles and disasters have turned out to be benefits, and more serious ills have been healed by those that are lighter. When the mind is disobedient to precepts and cannot be restored by gentler means, why should it not be for its own good to have poverty, disgrace, and a violent overthrow of fortune applied to it—to match evil with evil? Let us then get accustomed to being able to dine without the multitude, to being the slave of fewer slaves, to getting clothes for the purpose for which they were devised, and to living in narrower quarters. Not only in the race and the contests of the circus, but also in the arena of life we must keep to the inner circle.

Even for studies, where expenditure is most honorable, it is justifiable only so long as it is kept within bounds. What is the use of having countless books and libraries, whose titles their owners can scarcely read through in a whole lifetime? The learner is, not instructed, but burdened by the mass of them, and it is much better to surrender yourself to a few authors than to wander through many. Forty thousand books were burned at Alexandria; let someone else praise this library as the most noble monument to the wealth of kings, as did Titus Livius, who says that it was the most distinguished achievement of the good taste and solicitude of kings. There was no "good taste" or "solicitude" about it, but only learned luxury—nay, not even "learned," since they had collected the books, not for the sake of learning, but to make a show, just as many who lack even a child's knowledge of letters use books, not as the tools of learning, but as decorations for the dining room. Therefore, let just as many books be acquired as are enough, but none for mere show. "It is more respectable," you say, "to squander money on these than on Corinthian bronzes and on pictures." But excess in anything becomes a fault. What excuse have you to offer for a man who seeks to have bookcases of citrus wood and ivory, who collects the works of unknown or discredited authors and sits yawning in the midst of so many thousand books, who gets most of his pleasure from the outsides of volumes and their titles? Consequently it is in the houses of the laziest men that you will see a full collection of orations and history with the boxes piled right up to the ceiling; for by now among cold baths and hot baths a library also is equipped as a necessary ornament of a great house. I would readily pardon these men if they were led astray by their excessive zeal for learning. But as it is, these collections of the works of sacred genius with all the portraits that adorn them are bought for show and a decoration of their walls.

But it may be that you have fallen upon some phase of life which is difficult, and that, before you are aware, your public or your private fortune has you fastened in a noose that you can neither burst nor untie. But reflect that it is only at first that prisoners are worried by the burdens and shackles upon their legs; later, when they have determined not to chafe against them, but to endure them, necessity teaches them to bear them bravely, habit to bear them easily. In any sort of life you will find that there are amusements and relaxations and pleasures if you are willing to consider your evils lightly rather than to make them hateful. On no score has nature more deserved our thanks, who, since she knew to what sorrows we were born, invented habit as an alleviation for disasters, and thus quickly accustoms us to the most serious ills. No one could endure adversity if, while it continued, it kept the same violence that its first blows had. All of us are chained to fortune. Some are bound by a loose and golden chain, others by a tight chain of baser metal; but what difference does it make? The same captivity holds all men in its toils, those who have bound others have also been bound—unless perhaps you think that a chain on the left hand is a lighter one. Some are chained by public office, others by wealth; some carry the burden of high birth, some of low birth; some bow beneath another's empire, some beneath their own; some are kept in one place by exile, others by priesthoods. All life is a servitude. And so a man must become reconciled to his lot, must complain of it as little as possible, and must lay hold of whatever good it may have; no state is so bitter that a calm mind cannot find in it some consolation. Even small spaces by skillful planning often reveal many uses; and arrangement will make habitable a place of ever so small dimensions. Apply reason to difficulties; it is possible to soften what is hard, to widen what is narrow, and burdens will press less heavily upon those who bear them skillfully.

Moreover, we must not send our desires upon a distant quest, but should permit them to have access to what is near, since they do not endure to be shut up altogether. Leaving those things that either cannot be done, or can be done only with difficulty, let us pursue what lies near at hand and allures our hope, but let us be aware that they all are equally trivial, diverse outwardly in appearance, within alike vain. And let us not envy those who stand in higher places; where there appeared heights, there are precipices.

Those, on the other hand, whom an unkind lot has placed in a critical position, will be safer by reducing their pride in the things that are in themselves proud and lowering their fortune, so far as they shall be able, to the common level. While there are many who must necessarily cling to their pinnacle, from which they cannot descend without falling, yet they may bear witness that their greatest burden is the very fact that they are forced to be burdensome to others, being not lifted, but nailed on high. By justice, by kindness, by courtesy, and by lavish and kindly giving let them prepare many safeguards against later mishaps, in hope whereof they may be more easy in their suspense. Yet nothing can free us from these mental waverings so effectively as always to establish some limit to advancement and not leave to fortune the decision of when it shall end, but halt of our own accord far short of the limit that the examples of others urge. In this way there will be some desires to prick on the mind, and yet, because bounds have been set to them, they will not lead it to that which is unlimited and uncertain.

These remarks of mine apply, not to the wise man, but to those who are not yet perfect, to the mediocre, and to the unsound. The wise man does not need to walk timidly and cautiously; for so great is his confidence in himself that he does not hesitate to go against fortune, and will never retreat before her. Nor has he any reason to fear her, for he counts not merely his chattels and his possessions and his position, but even his body and his eyes and his hand and all else that makes life very dear to a man, nay, even himself, among the things that are given on sufferance, and he lives as one who has been lent to himself and will return everything without sorrow when it is reclaimed. Nor is he therefore cheap in his own eyes, because he knows that he does not belong to himself, but he will perform all his duties as diligently and as circumspectly as a devout and holy man is wont to guard the property entrusted to his protection. When, however, he is bidden to give them up, he will not quarrel with fortune, but will say: "I give thanks for what I have possessed and held. I have managed your property to great advantage, but, since you order me, I give it up, I surrender it gratefully and gladly. If you still wish me to have anything of yours, I shall guard it; if your pleasure is otherwise, I give back and restore to you my silver, both wrought and coined, my house, and my household." Should nature recall what she previously entrusted us with, we shall say to her also: "Take back the spirit that is better than when you gave it. I do not quibble or hang back; of my own free will I am ready for you to take what you gave me before I was conscious—away with it!" What hardship is there in returning to the place from which you came? That man will live ill who will not know how to die well. Therefore we must take from the value we set upon this thing, and the breath of life must be counted as a cheap matter. As Cicero says, we feel hostility to gladiators if they are eager to save their life no matter how; if they display contempt for it, we favor them. The same thing, you may know, applies to us; for often the cause of death is the fear of dying. Mistress fortune, who uses us for her sport, says: "Why should I save you, you base and cowardly creature? You will be hacked and pierced with all the more wounds, because you do not know how to offer your throat. But you, who receive the steel courageously and do not withdraw your neck or put out your hands to stop it, shall both live longer and die more easily." He who fears death will never do anything worthy of a man who is alive. But he who knows that these were the terms drawn up for him at the moment of his conception will live according to the bond, and at the same time will also with like strength of mind guarantee that none of the things that happen shall be unexpected. For by looking forward to whatever can happen as though it would happen, he will soften the attacks of all ills, which bring nothing strange to those who have been prepared beforehand and are expecting them; it is the unconcerned and those that expect nothing but good fortune upon whom they fall heavily. Sickness comes, captivity, disaster, conflagration, but none of them is unexpected—I always knew in what disorderly company nature had confined me. Many times has wailing for the dead been heard in my neighborhood; many times have the torch and the taper led untimely funerals past my threshold; often has the crash of a falling building resounded at my side; many of those whom the forum, the senate-house, and conversation had bound to me a night has carried off, and the hands that were joined in friendship have been sundered by the grave. Should I be surprised if the dangers that always have wandered about me should at some time reach me? The number of men that will plan a voyage without thinking of storms is very great. I shall never be ashamed to quote a bad author if what he says is good. Publilius, who, whenever he abandoned the absurdities of farce and language directed to the gallery, had more vigor than the writers of comedy and tragedy, among many other utterances more striking than any that came from the buskined—to say nothing of the comic curtain's—stage, has also this:

Whatever can one man befall can happen just as well to all.

If a man lets this sink deep into his heart, and, when he looks upon the evils of others, of which there is a huge supply every day, remembers that they are free to come to him also, he will arm himself against them long before they attack him. It is too late to equip the soul to endure dangers after the dangers have arisen. You say: "I did not think this would happen," and "Would you have believed that this would happen?" But why not? Where are the riches that do not have poverty and hunger and beggary following close behind? What rank is there whose bordered robe and augur's wand and patrician bootlaces do not carry in their train rags and branded disgrace—a thousand stigmas and utter disrepute? What kingdom is there for which ruin and a trampling underfoot and the tyrant and the hangman are not in store? Nor are such things cut off by long intervals, but between the throne and bending at another's knees there is but an hour's space. Know, then, that every lot in life is changeable, and that whatever befalls any man can befall you also. You are rich; but are you any richer than Pompey? Yet he lacked even bread and water when Gaius, an old kinsman but a new sort of host, had opened to him the house of Caesar in order that he might have a chance to close his own! Though he owned so many rivers that had their source within his own lands and their mouth within his own lands, he had to beg for drops of water. In the palace of his kinsman he perished from hunger and thirst, and, while he was starving, his heir was arranging to give him a state funeral! You have held the highest offices; but have you held any as great, as unlooked for, as comprehensive as those of Sejanus? Yet on the day on which the senate played the escort, the people tore him to pieces! Of the man who had had heaped upon him all that gods and men were able to bestow nothing was left for the executioner to drag to the river! You are a king: It will not be Croesus to whom I shall direct you, who lived to see his own pyre both lighted and extinguished, who was forced to survive, not his kingdom only, but even his own death, nor Jugurtha, whom the Roman people gazed upon as a captive in less than a year after he had made them afraid. We ourselves have seen Ptolemy, king of Africa, and Mithridates, king of Armenia, under the charge of Gaius's guards; the one was sent into exile—the other was anxious to be sent there in better faith! In view of this great mutability of fortune, that moves now upward, now downward, unless you consider that whatever can happen is likely to happen to you, you surrender yourself into the power of adversity, which any man can crush if he sees her first.

Our next concern will be not to labor either for useless ends or uselessly, that is, not to desire either what we are not able to accomplish, or what, if attained, will cause us to understand too late and after much shame the emptiness of our desires. In other words, neither should our labor be in vain and without result, nor the result unworthy of our labor; for as a rule sadness attends upon it, if there has been either lack of success or shame for success. We must curtail the restlessness that a great many men show in wandering through houses and theaters and forums; they thrust themselves into the affairs of others, and always appear to be busily engaged. If you ask one of these as he comes out of the house: "Where are you going? What have you in mind?" he will reply to you: "Upon my word, I really do not know; but I shall see some people, I shall do something." They wander without any plan looking for employment, and they do, not what they have determined to do, but whatever they have stumbled upon. Their course is as aimless and idle as that of ants crawling among bushes, which idly bustle to the top of a twig and then to the bottom; many men are like these in their way of life, which one may not unjustly call "busy idleness." When you see some of them running as if they were going to a fire, you will be sorry for them; so often do they collide with those they meet and send themselves and others sprawling, though all the while they have been rushing to pay a call to someone who will not return it, or to attend the funeral of a man they do not know, or the trial of someone who is always having a suit, or the betrothal of some woman who is always getting married, and, having attached themselves to some litter, have in some places even carried it. Afterward, when they are returning home wearied to no purpose, they swear that they themselves do not know why they left home, or where they have been, and on the next day they will wander over the selfsame track. And so let all your effort be directed toward some object, let it keep some object in view! It is not activity that makes men restless, but false conceptions of things render them mad. For even madmen do not become agitated without some hope; they are excited by the mere appearance of some object, the falsity of which is not apparent to their afflicted mind. In the same way every one of those who go forth to swell the throng is led around the city by worthless and trivial reasons; dawn drives a man forth though he has no task to do, and, after he has been crushed in many men's doorways, all in vain, and has saluted their nomenclators one after another, and has been shut out by many, he finds that, of them all, not one is more difficult to catch at home than himself. From this evil is derived that most disgusting vice of eavesdropping and prying into public and secret matters and learning of many things that it is neither safe to tell nor safe to listen to.

I fancy that Democritus was thinking of this when he began: "If a man shall wish to live tranquilly, let him not engage in many affairs either public or private," referring of course to useless affairs. For if necessity demands, we must engage in many, even countless, affairs both public and private; but when there is no call from sacred duty, we must restrain our activities. For if a man engages in many affairs, he often puts himself in the power of fortune, while his safest course is rarely to tempt her, always to be mindful of her, and never to put any trust in her promises. Say, "I will set sail unless something happens," and "I shall become praetor unless something hinders me," and "My enterprise will be successful unless something interferes." This is why we say that nothing happens to a wise man contrary to his expectations—we release him, not from the accidents, but from the blunders of mankind, nor do all things turn out as he has wished, but as he has thought; but his first thought has been that something might obstruct his plans. Then, too, the suffering that comes to the mind from the abandonment of desire must necessarily be much lighter if you have not certainly promised it success.

We ought also to make ourselves adaptable lest we become too fond of the plans we have formed, and we should pass readily to the condition to which chance has led us, and not dread shifting either purpose or positions—provided that fickleness, a vice most hostile to repose, does not get hold of us. For obstinacy, from which fortune often wrests some concession, must needs be anxious and unhappy, and much more grievous must be a fickleness that nowhere shows self-restraint. Both are foes to tranquility—both the inability to change and the inability to endure. Most of all, the mind must be withdrawn from external interests into itself. Let it have confidence in itself, rejoice in itself, let it admire its own things, let it retire as far as possible from the things of others and devote itself to itself, let it not feel losses, let it interpret kindly even adversities. Zeno, our master, when he received news of a shipwreck and heard that all his property had been sunk, said: "Fortune bids me to follow philosophy with fewer encumbrances." A tyrant was threatening the philosopher Theodorus with death and even with lack of burial: "You have the right," he replied, "to please yourself, you have within your power only a half pint of my blood; for as to burial, you are a fool if you think it makes any difference to me whether I rot above ground or beneath it." Julius Canus, a rarely great man, whom even the fact that he was born in our own age does not prevent our admiring, had had a long dispute with Gaius, and when, as he was leaving, Phalaris said to him: "That you may not by any chance comfort yourself with a foolish hope, I have ordered you to be executed," he replied: "Most excellent prince, I tender you my thanks." I am not sure what he meant, for many explanations occur to me. Did he wish to be insulting and show him how great his cruelty must be if it made death a kindness? Or was he taunting him with the everyday proofs of insanity?—for those whose children had been murdered and whose property had been confiscated used to thank him—or was it that he accepted death as a happy escape? However it may be, it was a high-souled reply. But someone will say: "There was a possibility that after this Gaius might order him to live." Canus had no fear of that; it was well known that in orders of this sort Gaius was a man of his word! Will you believe that Canus spent the ten intervening days before his execution in no anxiety of any sort? What the man said, what he did, how tranquil he was, passes all credence. He was playing chess when the centurion who was dragging off a whole company of victims to death ordered that he also be summoned. Having been called, he counted the pawns and said to his partner: "See that after my death you do not claim falsely that you won"; then nodding to the centurion, he said: "You will bear witness that I am one pawn ahead." Do you think that at that board Canus was playing a game? Nay, he was making game! His friends were sad at the thought of losing such a man; but "Why," said he, "are you sorrowful? You are wondering whether our souls are immortal; but I shall soon know." Nor up to the very end did he cease to search for truth and to make his own death a subject for debate. His own teacher of philosophy was accompanying him, and, when they were not far from the low hill on which the daily sacrifice to Caesar, our god, was made, said: "What are you thinking of now, Canus, or what state of mind are you in?" And Canus said: "I have determined to watch whether the spirit will be conscious that it is leaving the body when that fleetest of moments comes," and he promised that, if he discovered anything, he would make the round of his friends, and reveal to them what the state of the soul really is. Here is tranquility in the very midst of the storm, here is a mind worthy of immortality—a spirit that summons its own fate to the proof of truth, that, in the very act of taking that one last step, questions the departing soul, and learns, not merely up to the point of death, but seeks to learn something even from death itself. No one has ever played the philosopher longer. Not hastily shall so great a man be abandoned, and he must be spoken of with respect. O most glorious soul, chief victim of the murders of Gaius, to the memory of all time will I consign thee!

But it does no good to have got rid of the causes of individual sorrow; for one is sometimes seized by hatred of the whole human race. When you reflect how rare is simplicity, how unknown is innocence, and how good faith scarcely exists, except when it is profitable, and when you think of all the throng of successful crimes and of the gains and losses of lust, both equally hateful, and of ambition that, so far from restraining itself within its own bounds, now gets glory from baseness—when we remember these things, the mind is plunged into night, and as though the virtues, which it is now neither possible to expect nor profitable to possess, had been overthrown, there comes overwhelming gloom. We ought, therefore, to bring ourselves to believe that all the vices of the crowd are, not hateful, but ridiculous, and to imitate Democritus rather than Heraclitus. For the latter, whenever he went forth into public, used to weep, the former to laugh;

to the one all human doings seemed to be miseries, to the other follies. And so we ought to adopt a lighter view of things, and put up with them in an indulgent spirit; it is more human to laugh at life than to lament over it. Add, too, that he deserves better of the human race also who laughs at it than he who bemoans it; for the one allows it some measure of good hope, while the other foolishly weeps over things that he despairs of seeing corrected. And, considering everything, he shows a greater mind who does not restrain his laughter than he who does not restrain his tears, since the laugher gives expression to the mildest of the emotions, and deems that there is nothing important, nothing serious, nor wretched either, in the whole outfit of life. Let a man set before himself the causes, one by one, that give rise to joy and sadness, and he will learn that what Bion said is true, that all the doings of men are just like their beginnings, and that their life is no more respectable or serious than their conception, that born from nothingness they go back to nothingness. Yet it is better to accept calmly the ways of the public and the vices of man, and be thrown neither into laughter nor into tears; for it is unending misery to be worried by the misfortunes of others, and unhuman pleasure to take delight in the misfortunes of others, just as it is a useless show of humanity to weep and pull a long face because someone is burying a son. In the matter of one's own misfortunes, too, the right way to act is to bestow on them the measure of sorrow that nature, not custom, demands; for many shed tears in order to make a show of them, and, whenever a spectator is lacking, their eyes are dry, though they judge it disgraceful not to weep when everyone is doing it. This evil of depending on the opinion of others has become so deeply implanted that even grief, the most natural thing in the world, becomes now a matter of pretense.

I come now to a class of cases that is wont with good cause to sadden and bring us concern. When good men come to bad ends, when Socrates is forced to die in prison, Rutilius to live in exile, Pompey and Cicero to offer their necks to their own clients, and great Cato, the living image of all the virtues, by falling upon his sword to show that the end had come for himself and for the state at the same time, we needs must be distressed that fortune pays her rewards so unjustly. And what hope can anyone then have for himself when he sees that the best men suffer the worst fate? What then is the answer? See the manner in which each one of them bore his fate, and if they were brave, desire with your heart hearts like theirs, if they perished like a woman and a coward, then nothing perished; either they deserve that you should admire their virtue, or they do not deserve that you should desire their cowardice. For if the greatest men by dying bravely make others cowards, what could be more shameful? Let us praise those deserving of praise over and over and say: "The braver a man is, the happier he is! You have escaped from all accident, jealousy, and sickness;

you have gone forth from prison; it was not that you seemed to the gods to be worthy of evil fortune, but unworthy of being subject any longer to the power of fortune." But those who draw back and on the very threshold of death look back toward life—there is need to lay hands on these! I shall weep for no one who is happy, for no one who weeps; the one with his own hand has wiped away my tears, the other by his tears has made himself unworthy of having any of mine. Should I weep for Hercules because he was burned alive, or for Regulus because he was pierced by so many nails, or for Cato because he wounded his own wounds? All these by a slight sacrifice of time found out how they might become eternal, and by dying reached immortality.

And this, too, affords no small occasion for anxieties—if you are bent on assuming a pose and never reveal yourself to anyone frankly, in the fashion of many who live a false life that is all made up for show; for it is torturous to be constantly watching oneself and be fearful of being caught out of our usual role. And we are never free from concern if we think that every time anyone looks at us he is always taking our measure; for many things happen that strip off our pretense against our will, and, though all this attention to self is successful, yet the life of those who live under a mask cannot be happy and without anxiety. But how much pleasure there is in simplicity that is pure, in itself unadorned, and veils no part of its character! Yet even such a life as this does run some risk of scorn, if everything lies open to everybody; for there are those who disdain whatever has become too familiar. But neither does virtue run any risk of being despised when she is brought close to the eyes, and it is better to be scorned by reason of simplicity than tortured by perpetual pretense. Yet we should employ moderation in the matter; there is much difference between living naturally and living carelessly.

Moreover, we ought to retire into ourselves very often; for intercourse with those of dissimilar natures disturbs our settled calm, and rouses the passions anew, and aggravates any weakness in the mind that has not been thoroughly healed. Nevertheless the two things must be combined and resorted to alternately—solitude and the crowd. The one will make us long for men, the other for ourselves, and the one will relieve the other; solitude will cure our aversion to the throng, the throng our weariness of solitude.

And the mind must not be kept invariably at the same tension, but must be diverted to amusements. Socrates did not blush to play with little children, and Cato, when he was wearied by the cares of state, would relax his mind with wine, and Scipio would disport his triumphal and soldierly person to the sound of music, moving not with the voluptuous contortions that are now the fashion, when men even in walking squirm with more than a woman's voluptuousness, but in the manly style in which men in the days of old were wont to dance during the times of sport and festival, risking no loss of dignity even if their own enemies looked on. The mind must be given relaxation; it will arise better and keener after resting. As rich fields must not be forced—for their productiveness, if they have no rest, will quickly exhaust them—so constant labor will break the vigor of the mind, but if it is released and relaxed a little while, it will recover its powers; continuous mental toil breeds in the mind a certain dullness and languor.

Nor would the desire of men tend so much in this direction unless sport and amusement brought a sort of pleasure that was natural, but the frequent use of these will steal all weight and all force from the mind; for sleep also is necessary for refreshment, nevertheless if you prolong it throughout the day and night, it will be death. There is a great difference between slackening and removing your bond! The founders of our laws appointed days of festival in order that men might be forced by the state into merrymaking, thinking that it was necessary to modify their toil by some interruption of their tasks; and among great men, as I have remarked, some used to set aside fixed days every month for a holiday, some divided every day into play time and work time. Asinius Pollio, the great orator, I remember, had such a rule, and never worked at anything beyond the tenth hour; he would not even read letters after that hour for fear something new might arise that needed attention, but in those two hours laid aside the weariness of the whole long day. Some break off in the middle of the day, and reserve some task that requires lighter effort for the afternoon hours. Our ancestors, too, forbade any new motion to be made in the senate after the tenth hour. The soldier divides his watches, and those who have just returned from an expedition have the whole night free. We must be indulgent to the mind, and from time to time must grant it the leisure that serves as its food and strength.

And, too, we ought to take walks out-of-doors in order that the mind may be strengthened and refreshed by the open air and much breathing; sometimes it will get new vigor from a journey by carriage and a change of place and festive company and generous drinking. At times we ought to reach the point even of intoxication, not drowning ourselves in drink, yet succumbing to it; for it washes away troubles, and stirs the mind from its very depths, and heals its sorrow just as it does certain ills of the body; and the inventor of wine is not called the Releaser on account of the license it gives to the tongue, but because it frees the mind from bondage to cares and emancipates it and gives it new life and makes it bolder in all that it attempts. But, as in freedom, so in wine there is a wholesome moderation. It is believed that Solon and Arcesilaus were fond of wine, and Cato has been reproached for drunkenness; but whoever reproaches that man will more easily make reproach honorable than Cato base. Yet we ought not to do this often, for fear that the mind may contract an evil habit, nevertheless there are times when it must be drawn into rejoicing and freedom, and gloomy sobriety must be banished for a while. For whether we believe with the Greek poet that "sometimes it is a pleasure also to rave," or with Plato that "the sane mind knocks in vain at the door of poetry," or with Aristotle that "no great genius has ever existed without some touch of madness"—be that as it may, the lofty utterance that rises above the attempts of others is impossible unless the mind is excited. When it has scorned the vulgar and the commonplace, and has soared far aloft fired by divine inspiration, then alone it chants a strain too lofty for mortal lips. So long as it is left to itself, it is impossible for it to reach any sublime and difficult height; it must forsake the common track and be driven to frenzy and champ the bit and run away with its rider and rush to a height that it would have feared to climb by itself.

Here are the rules, my dearest Serenus, by which you may preserve tranquility, by which you may restore it, by which you may resist the vices that steal upon it unawares. Yet be sure of this—none of them is strong enough to guard a thing so frail unless we surround the wavering mind with earnest and unceasing care.

## QUESTIONS

1. Why does Seneca compare Serenus's condition to that of recently-cured men who "complain unjustly of any trace of heat in their body"? (12)

2. Why does Seneca say that being "entirely dependent upon hope" leads to dissatisfaction with life? (13)

3. Why does Seneca say that each person is "his own most burdensome companion"? (14)

4. Why does Seneca consider fortune the greatest cause of human sorrow?

5. What does it mean to "seek our riches from ourselves"? (21)

6. What does Seneca mean when he says, "All life is a servitude"? (22)

7. In what sense are we to understand acceptance when Seneca advises us "to accept calmly the ways of the public and the vices of man, and be thrown neither into laughter nor into tears"? (29)

8. Why does Seneca end his advice to Serenus by recommending sport, amusement, and even intoxication?

9. For Seneca, which is more disruptive to tranquility, anxiety or melancholy?

10. Why does Seneca say that the rules for tranquility are not "strong enough . . . unless we surround the wavering mind with earnest and unceasing care"? (32)

## FOR FURTHER REFLECTION

1. Has Seneca successfully provided Serenus with a way of ridding himself of anxiety?

2. Is tranquility of mind, as Seneca understands it, ever achievable?

3. How important do you think the exercise of reason is to achieving tranquility?

4. To what extent and in what way is the tranquility of mind that Seneca recommends compatible with an active, public life?

F rancis Bacon (1561–1626) was born at York House, London, the youngest son of Sir Nicholas Bacon and Lady Anne Cooke, a renowned classicist. At age twelve, Bacon enrolled in Trinity College, Cambridge, where he studied philosophy and first found fault with the prevailing Aristotelian framework for explaining the natural world, judging it to be "barren of the production of works for the benefit of the life of man." He began to conceive a new approach to natural philosophy that would lay the foundations of modern science. However, much of Bacon's life was not to be dedicated to scholarly pursuits but rather to an ambitious striving for political power and influence.

After graduating, Bacon went to Paris on a diplomatic mission with the English ambassador but cut short his visit to return to England after the sudden death of his father. Finding himself financially insolvent, he applied to study law at Grey's Inn and passed the bar in 1582. Despite the early promise of his legal career, the next two decades of Bacon's life were marked by political failures. Bacon's efforts to win favor with Queen Elizabeth were unsuccessful, and he found himself in frequent debt. His chief rival, Sir Edward Coke, had successfully garnered the queen's favor. Bacon befriended and aligned himself with the Earl of Essex, whom the queen also favored, but the earl was never able to obtain an office for Bacon. Ironically, it wasn't until the earl's career went awry and he was tried for treason that Bacon was finally appointed to the royal counsel—he wrote the official report on the proceedings.

During these years, Bacon began to formulate a new philosophy of science, and in 1605 he published *The Advancement of Learning*, which established new areas of focus for scientific investigation. It was published two years after the accession of James I to the throne, and two years afterward, having gained the new king's favor, Bacon was appointed solicitor general. The second part of Bacon's project, the *Novum Organum*, or *The New Organon* (1620), was published at the height of his political power and captured the attention of scholars in England and abroad.

The reign of James I allowed Bacon to rise in political power and he was promoted to attorney general in 1613 and Lord Chancellor in 1618. The main reason for his progress was his unstinting service in Parliament, but Bacon was not above forging shrewd alliances to gain power, befriending a future duke of Buckingham for his influence with the king and benefiting from his 1605 marriage to Alice Barnham, the daughter of a prominent alderman. As a result, Bacon became wealthy and was respected as the chief advisor to the king. But Bacon's fall, in 1621, was swift: he was convicted of accepting bribes, briefly imprisoned in the Tower of London, and banned from all centers of royal power. He spent his last years writing scientific treatises, poetry, translations of biblical Psalms, and a utopian romance, *New Atlantis* (1624). In late March of 1626, after conducting an experiment on refrigeration that involved stuffing a dead chicken with snow, Bacon became ill and died of bronchitis shortly afterward.

Bacon was a major influence on the modern approach to studying the natural world that emphasizes direct observation, carefully constructed experiments, and the use of instruments to aid and augment the senses. The precepts laid down in *The New Organon* (from which the following aphorisms are reprinted) and the new divisions of human knowledge established in *The Advancement of Learning* were intended to provide "true directions concerning the interpretation of nature," and to set out a new system of logic for organizing knowledge. A true politician, Bacon had tried to flatter King James I by asking him to make modifications to *The New Organon*, hoping for royal patronage. However, Bacon's ideas were too complex for the king; upon reading the work, the king remarked, "His last book is like the peace of God, that passeth all understanding." Little did the king who had commissioned a new translation of the Bible realize that Bacon's work would powerfully influence the coming split between theology and science and profoundly reshape the way in which we strive to understand the natural world.

.

# The New Organon (selection)

## 1

Man, being the servant and interpreter of nature, can do and understand so much and so much only as he has observed in fact or in thought of the course of nature; beyond this he neither knows anything nor can do anything.

## 2

Neither the naked hand nor the understanding left to itself can effect much. It is by instruments and helps that the work is done, which are as much wanted for the understanding as for the hand. And as the instruments of the hand either give motion or guide it, so the instruments of the mind supply either suggestions for the understanding or cautions.

## 3

Human knowledge and human power meet in one, for where the cause is not known the effect cannot be produced. Nature to be commanded must be obeyed, and that which in contemplation is as the cause is in operation as the rule.

## 4

Towards the effecting of works, all that man can do is to put together or put asunder natural bodies. The rest is done by nature working within.

## 5

The study of nature with a view to works is engaged in by the mechanic, the mathematician, the physician, the alchemist, and the magician, but by all (as things now are) with slight endeavour and scanty success.

## 6

It would be an unsound fancy and self-contradictory to expect that things which have never yet been done can be done except by means which have never yet been tried.

## 7

The productions of the mind and hand seem very numerous in books and manufactures. But all this variety lies in an exquisite subtlety and derivations from a few things already known, not in the number of axioms.

## 8

Moreover, the works already known are due to chance and experiment rather than to sciences; for the sciences we now possess are merely systems for the nice ordering and setting forth of things already invented, not methods of invention or directions for new works.

## 9

The cause and root of nearly all evils in the sciences is this, that while we falsely admire and extol the powers of the human mind we neglect to seek for its true helps.

## 10

The subtlety of nature is greater many times over than the subtlety of the senses and understanding, so that all those specious meditations, speculations, and glosses in which men indulge are quite from the purpose, only there is no one by to observe it.

## 11

As the sciences which we now have do not help us in finding out new works, so neither does the logic which we now have help us in finding out new sciences.

## 12

The logic now in use serves rather to fix and give stability to the errors which have their foundation in commonly received notions than to help the search after truth. So it does more harm than good.

## 19

There are and can be only two ways of searching into and discovering truth. The one flies from the senses and particulars to the most general axioms, and from these principles, the truth of which it takes for settled and immovable, proceeds to judgment and to the discovery of middle axioms. And this way is now in fashion. The other derives axioms from the senses and particulars, rising by a gradual and unbroken ascent, so that it arrives at the most general axioms last of all. This is the true way, but as yet untried.

## 22

Both ways set out from the senses and particulars, and rest in the highest generalities, but the difference between them is infinite. For the one just glances at experiment and particulars in passing, the other dwells duly and orderly among them. The one, again, begins at once by establishing certain abstract and useless generalities, the other rises by gradual steps to that which is prior and better known in the order of nature.

## 23

There is a great difference between the idols of the human mind and the ideas of the divine. That is to say, between certain empty dogmas and the true signatures and marks set upon the works of creation as they are found in nature.

## 26

The conclusions of human reason as ordinarily applied in matters of nature, I call for the sake of distinction anticipations of nature (as a thing rash or premature). That reason which is elicited from facts by a just and methodical process, I call interpretation of nature.

## 31

It is idle to expect any great advancement in science from the superinducing and engrafting of new things upon old. We must begin anew from the very foundations, unless we would revolve forever in a circle with mean and contemptible progress.

## 32

The honour of the ancient authors, and indeed of all, remains untouched, since the comparison I challenge is not of wits or faculties, but of ways and methods, and the part I take upon myself is not that of a judge, but of a guide.

## 33

This must be plainly avowed: no judgment can be rightly formed either of my method or of the discoveries to which it leads, by means of anticipations (that is to say, of the reasoning which is now in use), since I cannot be called on to abide by the sentence of a tribunal which is itself on its trial.

## 36

One method of delivery alone remains to us, which is simply this: we must lead men to the particulars themselves, and their series and order, while men on their side must force themselves for a while to lay their notions by and begin to familiarize themselves with facts.

## 37

The doctrine of those who have denied that certainty could be attained at all has some agreement with my way of proceeding at the first setting out, but they end in being infinitely separated and opposed. For the holders of that doctrine assert simply that nothing can be known; I also assert that not much can be known in nature by the way which is now in use. But then they go on to destroy the authority of the senses and understanding; whereas I proceed to devise and supply helps for the same.

## 38

The idols and false notions which are now in possession of the human understanding, and have taken deep root therein, not only so beset men's minds that truth can hardly find entrance, but even after entrance obtained, they will again in the very instauration of the sciences meet and trouble us, unless men being forewarned of the danger fortify themselves as far as may be against their assaults.

## 39

There are four classes of idols which beset men's minds. To these for distinction's sake I have assigned names, calling the first class *idols of the tribe*; the second, *idols of the cave*; the third, *idols of the marketplace*; the fourth, *idols of the theatre*.

## 40

The formation of ideas and axioms by true induction is no doubt the proper remedy to be applied for the keeping off and clearing away of idols. To point them out, however, is of great use, for the doctrine of idols is to the interpretation of nature what the doctrine of the refutation of sophisms is to common logic.

## 41

The idols of the tribe have their foundation in human nature itself and in the tribe or race of men. For it is a false assertion that the sense of man is the measure of things. On the contrary, all perceptions as well of the sense as of the mind are according to the measure of the individual and not according to the measure of the universe. And the human understanding is like a false mirror, which, receiving rays irregularly, distorts and discolours the nature of things by mingling its own nature with it.

## 42

The idols of the cave are the idols of the individual man. For everyone (besides the errors common to human nature in general) has a cave or den of his own, which refracts and discolours the light of nature, owing either to his own proper and peculiar nature, or to his education and conversation with others, or to the reading of books, and the authority of those whom he esteems and admires, or to the differences of impressions, accordingly as they take place in a mind preoccupied and predisposed or in a mind indifferent and settled, or the like. So that the spirit of man (according as it is meted out to different individuals) is in fact a thing variable and full of perturbation, and governed as it were by chance. Whence it was well observed by Heraclitus that men look for sciences in their own lesser worlds and not in the greater or common world.

## 43

There are also idols formed by the intercourse and association of men with each other, which I call idols of the marketplace on account of the commerce and consort of men there. For it is by discourse that men associate, and words are imposed according to the apprehension of the vulgar. And therefore the ill and unfit choice of words wonderfully obstructs the understanding. Nor do the definitions or explanations wherewith in some things learned men are wont to guard and defend themselves, by any means set the matter right. But words plainly force and overrule the understanding, and throw all into confusion, and lead men away into numberless empty controversies and idle fancies.

## 44

Lastly, there are idols which have immigrated into men's minds from the various dogmas of philosophies and also from wrong laws of demonstration. These I call idols of the theatre, because in my judgment all the received systems are but so many stage plays, representing worlds of their own creation after an unreal and scenic fashion. Nor is it only of the systems now in vogue or only of the ancient sects and philosophies that I speak, for many more plays of the same kind may yet be composed and in like artificial manner set forth, seeing that errors the most widely different have nevertheless causes for the most part alike. Neither again do I mean this only of entire systems, but also of many principles and axioms in science, which by tradition, credulity, and negligence have come to be received.

But of these several kinds of idols I must speak more largely and exactly, that the understanding may be duly cautioned.

## 45

The human understanding is of its own nature prone to suppose the existence of more order and regularity in the world than it finds. And though there be many things in nature which are singular and unmatched, yet it devises for them parallels and conjugates and relatives which do not exist. Hence the fiction that all celestial bodies move in perfect circles, spirals and dragons being (except in name) utterly rejected. Hence too the element of fire with its orb is brought in, to make up the square with the other three which the sense perceives. Hence also the ratio of density of the so-called elements is arbitrarily fixed at ten to one. And so on of other dreams. And these fancies affect not dogmas only, but simple notions also.

## 49

The human understanding is no dry light, but receives an infusion from the will and affections; whence proceed sciences which may be called "sciences as one would." For what a man had rather were true he more readily believes. Therefore he rejects difficult things from impatience of research; sober things because they narrow hope; the deeper things of nature from superstition; the light of experience for arrogance and pride, lest his mind should seem to be occupied with things mean and transitory; things not commonly believed, out of deference to the opinion of the vulgar. Numberless, in short, are the ways, and sometimes imperceptible, in which the affections colour and infect the understanding.

## 50

But by far the greatest hindrance and aberration of the human understanding proceeds from the dulness, incompetency, and deceptions of the senses; in that things which strike the sense outweigh things which do not immediately strike it, though they be more important. Hence it is that speculation commonly ceases where sight ceases; insomuch that of things invisible there is little or no observation. Hence all the working of the spirits inclosed in tangible bodies lies hid and unobserved of men. So also all the more subtle changes of form in the parts of coarser substances (which they commonly call alteration, though it is in truth local motion through exceedingly small spaces) is in like manner unobserved. And yet, unless these two things just mentioned be searched out and brought to light, nothing great can be achieved in nature as far as the production of works is concerned. So again, the essential nature of our common air and of all bodies less dense than air (which are very many) is almost unknown. For the sense by itself is a thing infirm and erring; neither can instruments for enlarging or sharpening the senses do much; but all the truer kind of interpretation of nature is effected by instances and experiments fit and apposite, wherein the sense decides touching the experiment only, and the experiment touching the point in nature and the thing itself.

## 51

The human understanding is of its own nature prone to abstractions and gives a substance and reality to things which are fleeting. But to resolve nature into abstractions is less to our purpose than to dissect her into parts, as did the school of Democritus, which went further into nature than the rest. Matter rather than forms should be the object of our attention, its configurations and changes of configuration, and simple action, and law of action or motion, for forms are figments of the human mind, unless you will call those laws of action forms.

## 52

Such then are the idols which I call *idols of the tribe*, and which take their rise either from the homogeneity of the substance of the human spirit, or from its preoccupation, or from its narrowness, or from its restless motion, or from an infusion of the affections, or from the incompetency of the senses, or from the mode of impression.

## 53

The *idols of the cave* take their rise in the peculiar constitution, mental or bodily, of each individual, and also in education, habit, and accident. Of this kind there is a great number and variety, but I will instance those the pointing out of which contains the most important caution, and which have most effect in disturbing the clearness of the understanding.

## 54

Men become attached to certain particular sciences and speculations, either because they fancy themselves the authors and inventors thereof, or because they have bestowed the greatest pains upon them and become most habituated to them. But men of this kind, if they betake themselves to philosophy and contemplations of a general character, distort and colour them in obedience to their former fancies, a thing especially to be noticed in Aristotle, who made his natural philosophy a mere bondservant to his logic, thereby rendering it contentious and well nigh useless. The race of chemists again out of a few experiments of the furnace have built up a fantastic philosophy, framed with reference to a few things, and Gilbert also, after he had employed himself most laboriously in the study and observation of the loadstone, proceeded at once to construct an entire system in accordance with his favourite subject.

## 55

There is one principal and as it were radical distinction between different minds in respect of philosophy and the sciences, which is this: that some minds are stronger and apter to mark the differences of things, others to mark their resemblances. The steady and acute mind can fix its contemplations and dwell and fasten on the subtlest distinctions; the lofty and discursive mind recognizes and puts together the finest and most general resemblances. Both kinds however easily err in excess, by catching the one at gradations, the other at shadows.

## 58

Let such then be our provision and contemplative prudence for keeping off and dislodging the *idols of the cave*, which grow for the most part either out of the predominance of a favourite subject, or out of an excessive tendency to compare or to distinguish, or out of partiality for particular ages, or out of the largeness or minuteness of the objects contemplated. And generally let every student of nature take this as a rule, that whatever his mind seizes and dwells upon with peculiar satisfaction is to be held in suspicion, and that so much the more care is to be taken in dealing with such questions to keep the understanding even and clear.

## 59

But the *idols of the marketplace* are the most troublesome of all—idols which have crept into the understanding through the alliances of words and names. For men believe that their reason governs words, but it is also true that words react on the understanding, and this it is that has rendered philosophy and the sciences sophistical and inactive. Now words, being commonly framed and applied according to the capacity of the vulgar, follow those lines of division which are most obvious to the vulgar understanding. And whenever an understanding of greater acuteness or a more diligent observation would alter those lines to suit the true divisions of nature, words stand in the way and resist the change. Whence it comes to pass that the high and formal discussions of learned men end oftentimes in disputes about words and names, with which (according to the use and wisdom of the mathematicians) it would be more prudent to begin, and so by means of definitions reduce them to order. Yet even definitions cannot cure this evil in dealing with natural and material things; since the definitions themselves consist of words, and those words beget others, so that it is necessary to recur to individual instances, and those in due series and order, as I shall say presently when I come to the method and scheme for the formation of notions and axioms.

## 60

The idols imposed by words on the understanding are of two kinds. They are either names of things which do not exist (for as there are things left unnamed through lack of observation, so likewise are there names which result from fantastic suppositions and to which nothing in reality corresponds), or they are names of things which exist, but yet confused and ill defined and hastily and irregularly derived from realities. Of the former kind are *fortune*, the *prime mover, planetary orbits, element of fire*, and like fictions which owe their origin to false and idle theories. And this class of idols is more easily expelled, because to get rid of them it is only necessary that all theories should be steadily rejected and dismissed as obsolete.

But the other class, which springs out of a faulty and unskilful abstraction, is intricate and deeply rooted. Let us take for example such a word as *humid*, and see how far the several things which the word is used to signify agree with each other; and we shall find the word *humid* to be nothing else than a mark loosely and confusedly applied to denote a variety of actions which will not bear to be reduced to any constant meaning. For it both signifies that which easily spreads itself round any other body; and that which in itself is indeterminate and cannot solidize; and that which readily yields in every direction; and that which easily divides and scatters itself; and that which easily unites and collects itself; and that which readily flows and is put in motion; and that which readily clings to another body and wets it; and that which is easily reduced to a liquid, or being solid easily melts. Accordingly when you come to apply the word, if you take it in one sense, flame is humid; if in another, air is not humid; if in another, fine dust is humid; if in another, glass is humid. So that it is easy to see that the notion is taken by abstraction only from water and common and ordinary liquids without any due verification.

There are however in words certain degrees of distortion and error. One of the least faulty kinds is that of names of substances, especially of lowest species and well deduced (for the notion of *chalk* and of *mud* is good, of *earth* bad); a more faulty kind is that of actions, as *to generate*, *to corrupt*, *to alter*; the most faulty is of qualities (except such as are the immediate objects of the sense) as *heavy*, *light*, *rare*, *dense*, and the like. Yet in all these cases some notions are of necessity a little better than others, in proportion to the greater variety of subjects that fall within the range of the human sense.

## 61

But the *idols of the theatre* are not innate, nor do they steal into the understanding secretly, but are plainly impressed and received into the mind from the playbooks of philosophical systems and the perverted rules of demonstration. To attempt refutations in this case would be merely inconsistent with what I have already said, for since we agree neither upon principles nor upon demonstrations there is no place for argument. And this is so far well, inasmuch as it leaves the honour of the ancients untouched. For they are no wise disparaged, the question between them and me being only as to the way. For as the saying is, the lame man who keeps the right road outstrips the runner who takes a wrong one. Nay, it is obvious that when a man runs the wrong way, the more active and swift he is the further he will go astray.

But the course I propose for the discovery of sciences is such as leaves but little to the acuteness and strength of wits, but places all wits and understandings nearly on a level. For as in the drawing of a straight line or a perfect circle much depends on the steadiness and practice of the hand, if it be done by aim of hand only, but if with the aid of rule or compass, little or nothing; so is it exactly with my plan. But though particular confutations would be of no avail, yet touching the sects and general divisions of such systems I must say something; something also touching the external signs which show that they are unsound; and finally something touching the causes of such great infelicity and of such lasting and general agreement in error: that so the access to truth may be made less difficult, and the human understanding may the more willingly submit to its purgation and dismiss its idols.

## 62

Idols of the theatre, or of systems, are many, and there can be and perhaps will be yet many more. For were it not that now for many ages men's minds have been busied with religion and theology, and were it not that civil governments, especially monarchies, have been averse to such novelties, even in matters speculative, so that men labour therein to the peril and harming of their fortunes, not only unrewarded but exposed also to contempt and envy, doubtless there would have arisen many other philosophical sects like those which in great variety flourished once among the Greeks. For as on the phenomena of the heavens many hypotheses may be constructed, so likewise (and more also) many various dogmas may be set up and established on the phenomena of philosophy. And in the plays of this philosophical theatre you may observe the same thing which is found in the theatre of the poets, that stories invented for the stage are more compact and elegant, and more as one would wish them to be than true stories out of history.

In general however there is taken for the material of philosophy either a great deal out of a few things, or a very little out of many things, so that on both sides philosophy is based on too narrow a foundation of experiment and natural history, and decides on the authority of too few cases. For the rational school of philosophers snatches from experience a variety of common instances, neither duly ascertained nor diligently examined and weighed, and leaves all the rest to meditation and agitation of wit.

There is also another class of philosophers, who having bestowed much diligent and careful labour on a few experiments, have thence made bold to educe and construct systems, wresting all other facts in a strange fashion to conformity therewith.

And there is yet a third class, consisting of those who out of faith and veneration mix their philosophy with theology and traditions, among whom the vanity of some has gone so far aside as to seek the origin of sciences among spirits and genii. So that this parent stock of errors—this false philosophy—is of three kinds: the sophistical, the empirical, and the superstitious.

# 63

The most conspicuous example of the first class was Aristotle, who corrupted natural philosophy by his logic: fashioning the world out of categories; assigning to the human soul, the noblest of substances, a genus from words of the second intention; doing the business of density and rarity (which is to make bodies of greater or less dimensions, that is, occupy greater or less space) by the frigid distinction of act and power; asserting that single bodies have each a single and proper motion, and that if they participate in any other, then this results from an external cause; and imposing countless other arbitrary restrictions on the nature of things—being always more solicitous to provide an answer to the question and affirm something positive in words than about the inner truth of things; a failing best shown when his philosophy is compared with other systems of note among the Greeks. For the homoeomera of Anaxagoras, the atoms of Leucippus and Democritus, the heaven and earth of Parmenides, the strife and friendship of Empedocles, Heraclitus's doctrine how bodies are resolved into the indifferent nature of fire, and remoulded into solids—have all of them some taste of the natural philosopher, some savour of the nature of things, and experience, and bodies; whereas in the physics of Aristotle you hear hardly anything but the words of logic, which in his metaphysics also, under a more imposing name, and more forsooth as a realist than a nominalist, he has handled over again. Nor let any weight be given to the fact that in his books on animals and his problems and other of his treatises there is frequent dealings with experiments. For he had come to his conclusion before; he did not consult experience, as he should have done, in order to the framing of his decisions and axioms; but having first determined the question according to his will, he then resorts to experience, and bending her into conformity with his placets leads her about like a captive in a procession, so that even on this count he is more guilty than his modern followers, the schoolmen, who have abandoned experience altogether.

## 64

But the empirical school of philosophy gives birth to dogmas more deformed and monstrous than the sophistical or rational school. For it has its foundations not in the light of common notions (which though it be a faint and superficial light, is yet in a manner universal, and has reference to many things) but in the narrowness and darkness of a few experiments. To those therefore who are daily busied with these experiments, and have infected their imagination with them, such a philosophy seems probable and all but certain; to all men else incredible and vain. Of this there is a notable instance in the alchemists and their dogmas, though it is hardly to be found elsewhere in these times, except perhaps in the philosophy of Gilbert. Nevertheless with regard to philosophies of this kind there is one caution not to be omitted; for I foresee that if ever men are roused by my admonitions to betake themselves seriously to experiment and bid farewell to sophistical doctrines, then indeed through the premature hurry of the understanding to leap or fly to universals and principles of things, great danger may be apprehended from philosophies of this kind, against which evil we ought even now to prepare.

## 65

But the corruption of philosophy by superstition and an admixture of theology is far more widely spread, and does the greatest harm, whether to entire systems or to their parts. For the human understanding is obnoxious[1] to the influence of the imagination no less than to the influence of common notions. For the contentious and sophistical kind of philosophy ensnares the understanding; but this kind, being fanciful and tumid and half poetical, misleads it more by flattery. For there is in man an ambition of the understanding, no less than of the will, especially in high and lofty spirits.

Of this kind we have among the Greeks a striking example in Pythagoras, though he united with it a coarser and more cumbrous superstition; another in Plato and his school, more dangerous and subtle. It shows itself likewise in parts of other philosophies, in the introduction of abstract forms and final causes and first causes, with the omission in most cases of causes intermediate, and the like. Upon this point the greatest caution should be used. For nothing is so mischievous as the apotheosis of error; and it is a very plague of the understanding for vanity to become the object of veneration. Yet in this vanity some of the moderns have with

---

1. [Archaic: susceptible.]

extreme levity indulged so far as to attempt to found a system of natural philosophy on the first chapter of Genesis, on the book of Job, and other parts of the sacred writings, seeking for the dead among the living; which also makes the inhibition and repression of it the more important, because from this unwholesome mixture of things human and divine there arises not only a fantastic philosophy but also an heretical religion. Very meet it is therefore that we be sober-minded, and give to faith that only which is faith's.

## 68

So much concerning the several classes of idols, and their equipage: all of which must be renounced and put away with a fixed and solemn determination, and the understanding thoroughly freed and cleansed; the entrance into the kingdom of man, founded on the sciences, being not much other than the entrance into the kingdom of heaven, whereinto none may enter except as a little child.

## QUESTIONS

1.  What does Bacon mean when he refers to "instruments of the mind"? (2)[2]

2.  Why does Bacon assert, "Nature to be commanded must be obeyed"? (3)

3.  Why is Bacon confident that the way of discovering truth that "dwells duly and orderly" among experiments and particulars is superior? (22)

4.  What does Bacon mean by "interpretation of nature" as opposed to "anticipations of nature"? (26)

5.  Why does Bacon refer to the false notions that "beset men's minds" as idols? (39)

6.  If in interpreting nature through scientific experiments, "the sense decides touching the experiment only," does Bacon think humans can know the things themselves that experiments touch? (50)

7.  In Bacon's method of interpreting nature, which emphasizes the central importance of paying attention to "matter," how does Bacon allow for powerful generalities and abstractions such as scientific laws and theories? (51)

8.  Does Bacon think that words, the basis of the idols of the marketplace, can ever adequately assist in the interpretation of nature?

9.  How does Bacon's "course . . . for the discovery of sciences" place "all wits and understandings nearly on a level"? (61) Does this course allow for individual genius in advancing scientific knowledge?

10. Why does Bacon equate the "kingdom of man, founded on the sciences" and the "kingdom of heaven, whereinto none may enter except as a little child"? (68)

---

2. [Numbers refer to the aphorism number.]

## FOR FURTHER REFLECTION

1. Can scientific knowledge itself eliminate the influence of the four idols Bacon describes?

2. Can scientific investigation of the natural world ever be completely objective?

3. Is the pursuit of scientific knowledge for its own sake worthwhile, without any practical application in mind?

4. On what basis should we accept or deny scientific knowledge that appears to contradict religious beliefs?

The philosopher John Locke (1632–1704) was born in Somerset, England, to Puritan parents. His father, a lawyer, had fought for the parliamentary forces in the English Civil Wars, and he used his influence to secure Locke a spot at Westminster School in London. After several years there, he was chosen as a King's Scholar, an academic honor that entitled him to seek admission to England's most prestigious universities. In 1652 he was admitted to Christ Church, the largest college of the University of Oxford. Unimpressed with Oxford's Aristotelian curriculum, Locke studied the works of philosophers Francis Bacon and Rene Descartes and got to know many advocates of the new science. After obtaining bachelor's and master's degrees, he remained at Oxford as a lecturer in Greek and rhetoric, giving a series of talks that later became his *Essays on the Law of Nature*, an early statement of his empiricist philosophy. He also began to study medicine. In 1666 he had occasion to meet Lord Anthony Ashley Cooper (later First Earl of Shaftesbury), leader of the Whigs and one of the most powerful men in post-Restoration England, and the following year, Locke was asked to take up residence at Ashley's house in London, acting as his personal physician (though Locke hadn't completed his degree) and assisting him in his affairs.

In London, Locke found himself at the center of English politics and became involved in drafting the constitution for the English colonies in the Carolinas. He became a fellow of the Royal Society, which had been founded by the Oxford new scientists, and conducted medical research with Thomas Sydenham, the most distinguished physician of the age, eventually returning to Oxford to get his bachelor's degree in medicine. When Ashley fell out of favor with Charles II in 1675, Locke fled to France and continued his medical studies in Montpelier. He returned in 1679 to an England in turmoil, with Ashley and his supporters in peril as a result of their efforts to pass a law excluding the Roman Catholic brother of Charles II from succeeding to the throne. In 1683 Locke and Ashley went into exile in Holland, where Ashley would soon die and Locke would remain for six years.

During the winter of 1685, Locke wrote a letter in Latin to his friend Philip von Limborch, which was translated into English and published anonymously as *A Letter Concerning Toleration* (1689). Locke argued for a renewed understanding of the relationship between religion and civil government. He denounced forceful conversion and argued against Thomas Hobbes's assertion that a nation must have a uniform religion in order to function successfully. Locke's religious beliefs guided the rest of his philosophy, including his political beliefs. Humans were created with the capacity for intellect, Locke contended, and therefore it was their responsibility to create just governments that would allow humans to flourish spiritually.

Locke returned to England in 1689 and took up residence in the home of his friend Lady Damaris Masham, a philosopher in her own right. The two had been romantically involved before Damaris's marriage to Sir Francis Masham, but remained close friends afterward. While living at Oates, the Mashams' house in Essex, Locke published his two most important philosophical tracts in quick succession. *An Essay Concerning Human Understanding* (1689) is a direct attack on Aristotelianism, and the essay would become a cornerstone of the empiricist philosophy that succeeded it. He addresses the capacity of the human mind for knowledge and proposes that knowledge is not innate but acquired through sense impressions and reflection. In *Two Treatises on Government* (1690), his greatest work of political philosophy, Locke first discredits the validity of a monarch's divine right of rule and then outlines a theory of civil society based on equality under the law and the protection of private property. His ideas strongly influenced both the American and French revolutions and the new governments that followed. His ideas particularly influenced Thomas Jefferson when he was writing the Declaration of Independence. During this period Locke also published *Some Thoughts on Education* (1693) and *The Reasonableness of Christianity* (1695). In the last decade of his life, he joined the Board of Trade, which oversaw a large range of issues, including the suppression of piracy and the governance of the American colonies. After retiring in 1700, Locke spent his last years revising his work. His death, in 1704, was "like his life, truly pious, yet natural, easy and unaffected," wrote Lady Masham.

# A Letter Concerning Toleration

Honored Sir,

Since you are pleased to inquire what are my thoughts about the mutual toleration of Christians in their different professions of religion, I must needs answer you freely that I esteem that toleration to be the chief characteristic mark of the true church. For whatsoever some people boast of the antiquity of places and names, or of the pomp of their outward worship; others, of the reformation of their discipline; all, of the orthodoxy of their faith—for everyone is orthodox to himself—these things, and all others of this nature, are much rather marks of men striving for power and empire over one another than of the church of Christ. Let anyone have never so true a claim to all these things, yet if he be destitute of charity, meekness, and goodwill in general toward all mankind, even to those that are not Christians, he is certainly yet short of being a true Christian himself. "The kings of the Gentiles exercise lordship over them," said our Saviour to His disciples, "but ye shall not be so" (Luke 22:25). The business of true religion is quite another thing. It is not instituted in order to the erecting of an external pomp, nor to the obtaining of ecclesiastical dominion, nor to the exercising of compulsive force, but to the regulating of men's lives, according to the rules of virtue and piety. Whosoever will list himself under the banner of Christ must in the first place, and above all things, make war upon his own lusts and vices. It is in vain for any man to usurp the name of Christian without holiness of life, purity of manners, benignity and meekness of spirit. "Let everyone that nameth the name of Christ, depart from iniquity" (2 Tim. 2:19). "Thou, when thou art converted, strengthen thy brethren," said our Lord to Peter (Luke 22:32). It would, indeed, be very hard for one that appears careless about his own salvation to persuade me that he were extremely concerned for mine. For it is impossible that those should sincerely and heartily apply themselves to make other people Christians, who have not really embraced the Christian religion in their own hearts. If the Gospel and the apostles may be credited, no man can be a Christian without charity, and without that faith which works, not by force, but by love. Now I appeal to the consciences of those that persecute, torment, destroy, and kill other men upon pretense of religion, whether they do it out of friendship and kindness toward them or no? And I shall then indeed, and not until then, believe they do so, when I shall see those fiery zealots correcting, in the same manner, their friends and familiar acquaintance for the manifest sins they commit against the precepts of the Gospel; when I shall see them persecute with fire and sword the members of their own communion that are tainted with enormous vices, and without amendment are in danger of eternal perdition; and when I shall see them thus express their love and desire of the salvation of their souls by the infliction of torments and exercise of all manner of cruelties. For if it be out of a principle of charity, as they pretend, and love to men's souls, that they deprive them of their estates, maim them with corporal punishments, starve and torment them in noisome prisons, and in the end even take away their lives—I say, if all this be done merely to make men Christians and procure their salvation, why then do they suffer whoredom, fraud, malice, and suchlike enormities, which (according to the apostle [Rom. 1]) manifestly relish of heathenish corruption, to predominate so much and abound amongst their flocks and people? These, and suchlike things, are certainly more contrary to the glory of God, to the purity of the church, and to the salvation of souls, than any conscientious dissent from ecclesiastical decisions, or separation from public worship, whilst accompanied with innocence of life. Why then does this burning zeal for God, for the church, and for the salvation of souls—burning I say, literally, with fire and faggot—pass by those moral vices and wickednesses, without any chastisement, which are acknowledged by all men to be diametrically opposite to the profession of Christianity, and bend all its nerves either to the introducing of ceremonies, or to the establishment of opinions, which for the most part are about nice and intricate matters that exceed the capacity of ordinary understandings? Which of the parties contending about these things is in the right, which of them is guilty of schism or heresy, whether those that domineer or those that suffer, will then at last be manifest when the causes of their separation comes to be judged of. He, certainly, that follows Christ embraces his doctrine and bears his yoke, though he forsake both father and mother, separate from the public assemblies and ceremonies of his country, or whomsoever or whatsoever else he relinquishes, will not then be judged a heretic.

Now, though the divisions that are amongst sects should be allowed to be never so obstructive of the salvation of souls; yet, nevertheless, adultery, fornication, uncleanliness, lasciviousness, idolatry, and suchlike things, cannot be denied to be works of the flesh, concerning which the apostle has expressly declared (Gal. 5) that "they who do them shall not inherit the kingdom of God." Whosoever, therefore, is sincerely solicitous about the kingdom of God, and thinks it his duty to endeavor the enlargement of it amongst men, ought to apply himself with no less care and industry to the rooting out of these immoralities than to the extirpation of sects. But if anyone do otherwise, and whilst he is cruel and implacable toward those that differ from him in opinion, he be indulgent to such iniquities and immoralities as are unbecoming the name of a Christian, let such a one talk never so much of the church, he plainly demonstrates by his actions that it is another kingdom he aims at, and not the advancement of the kingdom of God.

That any man should think fit to cause another man—whose salvation he heartily desires—to expire in torments, and that even in an unconverted state, would, I confess, seem very strange to me and I think to any other also. But nobody, surely, will ever believe that such a carriage can proceed from charity, love, or goodwill. If anyone maintain that men ought to be compelled by fire and sword to profess certain doctrines, and conform to this or that exterior worship, without any regard had unto their morals; if anyone endeavor to convert those that are erroneous unto the faith, by forcing them to profess things that they do not believe and allowing them to practice things that the Gospel does not permit, it cannot be doubted indeed but such a one is desirous to have a numerous assembly joined in the same profession with himself; but that he principally intends by those means to compose a truly Christian church, is altogether incredible. It is not, therefore, to be wondered at if those who do not really contend for the advancement of the true religion, and of the church of Christ, make use of arms that do not belong to the Christian warfare. If, like the captain of our salvation, they sincerely desired the good of souls, they would tread in the steps and follow the perfect example of that Prince of Peace, who sent out his soldiers to the subduing of nations, and gathering them into his church, not armed with the sword or other instruments of force, but prepared with the Gospel of peace and with the exemplary holiness of their conversation. This was his method. Though if infidels were to be converted by force, if those that are either blind or obstinate were to be drawn off from their errors by armed soldiers, we know very well that it was much more easy for him to do it with armies of heavenly legions than for any son of the church, how potent soever, with all his dragoons.

The toleration of those that differ from others in matters of religion is so agreeable to the Gospel of Jesus Christ, and to the genuine reason of mankind, that it seems monstrous for men to be so blind as not to perceive the necessity and advantage of it in so clear a light. I will not here tax the pride and ambition of some, the passion and uncharitable zeal of others. These are faults from which human affairs can perhaps scarce ever be perfectly freed; but yet such as nobody will bear the plain imputation of, without covering them with some specious color; and so pretend to commendation, whilst they are carried away by their own irregular passions. But, however, that some may not color their spirit of persecution and un-Christian cruelty with a pretense of care of the public weal and observation of the laws; and that others, under pretense of religion, may not seek impunity for their libertinism and licentiousness—in a word, that none may impose either upon himself or others by the pretenses of loyalty and obedience to the prince, or of tenderness and sincerity in the worship of God; I esteem it above all things necessary to distinguish exactly the business of civil government from that of religion, and to settle the just bounds that lie between the one and the other. If this be not done, there can be no end put to the controversies that will be always arising between those that have, or at least pretend to have, on the one side, a concernment for the interest of men's souls, and, on the other side, a care of the commonwealth.

The commonwealth seems to me to be a society of men constituted only for the procuring, preserving, and advancing their own civil interests.

Civil interests I call life, liberty, health, and indolency of body; and the possession of outward things, such as money, lands, houses, furniture, and the like.

It is the duty of the civil magistrate, by the impartial execution of equal laws, to secure unto all the people in general, and to every one of his subjects in particular, the just possession of these things belonging to this life. If anyone presume to violate the laws of public justice and equity, established for the preservation of those things, his presumption is to be checked by the fear of punishment consisting of the deprivation or diminution of those civil interests or goods which otherwise he might and ought to enjoy. But seeing no man does willingly suffer himself to be punished by the deprivation of any part of his goods, and much less of his liberty or life, therefore is the magistrate armed with the force and strength of all his subjects, in order to the punishment of those that violate any other man's rights.

Now that the whole jurisdiction of the magistrate reaches only to these civil concernments; and that all civil power, right, and dominion is bounded and confined to the only care of promoting these things; and that it neither can nor ought in any manner to be extended to the salvation of souls, these following considerations seem unto me abundantly to demonstrate.

First, because the care of souls is not committed to the civil magistrate any more than to other men. It is not committed unto him, I say, by God; because it appears not that God has ever given any such authority to one man over another, as to compel anyone to his religion. Nor can any such power be vested in the magistrate by the consent of the people, because no man can so far abandon the care of his own salvation as blindly to leave to the choice of any other, whether prince or subject, to prescribe to him what faith or worship he shall embrace. For no man can, if he would, conform his faith to the dictates of another. All the life and power of true religion consist in the inward and full persuasion of the mind; and faith is not faith without believing. Whatever profession we make, to whatever outward worship we conform, if we are not fully satisfied in our own mind that the one is true, and the other well pleasing unto God, such profession and such practice, far from being any furtherance, are indeed great obstacles to our salvation. For in this manner, instead of expiating other sins by the exercise of religion, I say, in offering thus unto God Almighty such a worship as we esteem to be displeasing unto him, we add unto the number of our other sins those also of hypocrisy and contempt of His Divine Majesty.

In the second place, the care of souls cannot belong to the civil magistrate because his power consists only in outward force; but true and saving religion consists in the inward persuasion of the mind, without which nothing can be acceptable to God. And such is the nature of the understanding that it cannot be compelled to the belief of anything by outward force. Confiscation of estate, imprisonment, torments, nothing of that nature can have any such efficacy as to make men change the inward judgment that they have framed of things.

It may indeed be alleged that the magistrate may make use of arguments, and thereby draw the heterodox into the way of truth and procure their salvation. I grant it; but this is common to him with other men. In teaching, instructing, and redressing the erroneous by reason, he may certainly do what becomes any good man to do. Magistracy does not oblige him to put off either humanity or Christianity; but it is one thing to persuade, another to command; one thing to press with arguments, another with penalties. This civil power alone has a right to do; to the other, goodwill is authority enough. Every man has commission to admonish, exhort, convince another of error, and, by reasoning, to draw him into truth; but to give laws, receive obedience, and compel with the sword, belongs to none but the magistrate. And upon this ground I affirm that the magistrate's power extends not to the establishing of any articles of faith or forms of worship by the force of his laws. For laws are of no force at all without penalties, and penalties in this case are absolutely impertinent, because they are not proper to convince the mind. Neither the profession of any articles of faith, nor the conformity to any outward form of worship (as has been already said), can be available to the salvation of souls unless the truth of the one, and the acceptableness of the other unto God, be thoroughly believed by those that so profess and practice. But penalties are no way capable to produce such belief. It is only light and evidence that can work a change in men's opinions; which light can in no manner proceed from corporal sufferings or any other outward penalties.

In the third place, the care of the salvation of men's souls cannot belong to the magistrate; because, though the rigor of laws and the force of penalties were capable to convince and change men's minds, yet would not that help at all to the salvation of their souls. For there being but one truth, one way to heaven, what hope is there that more men would be led into it if they had no rule but the religion of the court, and were put under the necessity to quit the light of their own reason, and oppose the dictates of their own consciences, and blindly to resign themselves up to the will of their governors and to the religion which either ignorance, ambition, or superstition had chanced to establish in the countries where they were born? In the variety and contradiction of opinions in religion, wherein the princes of the world are as much divided as in their secular interests, the narrow way would be much straitened; one country alone would be in the right, and all the rest of the world put under an obligation of following their princes in the ways that lead to destruction; and that which heightens the absurdity, and very ill suits the notion of a deity, men would owe their eternal happiness or misery to the places of their nativity.

These considerations, to omit many others that might have been urged to the same purpose, seem unto me sufficient to conclude that all the power of civil government relates only to men's civil interests, is confined to the care of the things of this world, and hath nothing to do with the world to come.

Let us now consider what a church is. A church, then, I take to be a voluntary society of men, joining themselves together of their own accord in order to the public worshipping of God in such manner as they judge acceptable to him, and effectual to the salvation of their souls.

I say it is a free and voluntary society. Nobody is born a member of any church; otherwise the religion of parents would descend unto children by the same right of inheritance as their temporal estates, and everyone would hold his faith by the same tenure he does his lands, than which nothing can be imagined more absurd. Thus, therefore, that matter stands. No man by nature is bound unto any particular church or sect, but everyone joins himself voluntarily to that society in which he believes he has found that profession and worship which is truly acceptable to God. The hope of salvation, as it was the only cause of his entrance into that communion, so it can be the only reason of his stay there. For if afterwards he discover anything either erroneous in the doctrine or incongruous in the worship of that society to which he has joined himself, why should it not be as free for him to go out as it was to enter? No member of a religious society can be tied with any other bonds but what proceed from the certain expectation of eternal life. A church, then, is a society of members voluntarily uniting to that end.

It follows now that we consider what is the power of this church, and unto what laws it is subject.

Forasmuch as no society, how free soever, or upon whatsoever slight occasion instituted, whether of philosophers for learning, of merchants for commerce, or of men of leisure for mutual conversation and discourse, no church or company, I say, can in the least subsist and hold together, but will presently dissolve and break in pieces, unless it be regulated by some laws, and the members all consent to observe some order. Place and time of meeting must be agreed on; rules for admitting and excluding members must be established; distinction of officers, and putting things into a regular course, and suchlike, cannot be omitted. But since the joining together of several members into this church society, as has already been demonstrated, is absolutely free and spontaneous, it necessarily follows that the right of making its laws can belong to none but the society itself; or, at least (which is the same thing), to those whom the society by common consent has authorized thereunto.

Some, perhaps, may object that no such society can be said to be a true church unless it have in it a bishop or presbyter, with ruling authority derived from the very apostles, and continued down to the present times by an uninterrupted succession.

To these I answer: in the first place, let them show me the edict by which Christ has imposed that law upon his church. And let not any man think me impertinent if in a thing of this consequence I require that the terms of that edict be very express and positive; for the promise he has made us (Matt. 18:20), that wheresoever two or three are gathered together in his name he will be in the midst of them, seems to imply the contrary. Whether such an assembly want anything necessary to a true church, pray do you consider. Certain I am that nothing can be there wanting unto the salvation of souls, which is sufficient to our purpose.

Next, pray observe how great have always been the divisions amongst even those who lay so much stress upon the divine institution and continued succession of a certain order of rulers in the church. Now their very dissension unavoidably puts us upon a necessity of deliberating and, consequently, allows a liberty of choosing that which upon consideration we prefer.

And, in the last place, I consent that these men have a ruler in their church, established by such a long series of succession as they judge necessary, provided I may have liberty at the same time to join myself to that society in which I am persuaded those things are to be found which are necessary to the salvation of my soul. In this manner ecclesiastical liberty will be preserved on all sides, and no man will have a legislator imposed upon him but whom himself has chosen.

But since men are so solicitous about the true church, I would only ask them here, by the way, if it be not more agreeable to the church of Christ to make the conditions of her communion consist in such things, and such things only, as the Holy Spirit has in the Holy Scriptures declared, in express words, to be necessary to salvation; I ask, I say, whether this be not more agreeable to the church of Christ than for men to impose their own inventions and interpretations upon others as if they were of divine authority, and to establish by ecclesiastical laws, as absolutely necessary to the profession of Christianity, such things as the Holy Scriptures do either not mention or at least not expressly command? Whosoever requires those things in order to ecclesiastical communion, which Christ does not require in order to life eternal, he may, perhaps, indeed constitute a society accommodated to his own opinion and his own advantage; but how that can be called the church of Christ which is established upon laws that are not his, and which excludes such persons from its communion as he will one day receive into the kingdom of heaven, I understand not. But this being not a proper place to inquire into the marks of the true church, I will only mind those that contend so earnestly for the decrees of their own society and that cry out continually, the church! the church! with as much noise, and perhaps upon the same principle, as the Ephesian silversmiths did for their Diana; this, I say, I desire to mind them of, that the Gospel frequently declares that the true disciples of Christ must suffer persecution; but that the church of Christ should persecute others, and force others by fire and sword to embrace her faith and doctrine, I could never yet find in any of the books of the New Testament.

The end of a religious society (as has already been said) is the public worship of God and, by means thereof, the acquisition of eternal life. All discipline ought therefore to tend to that end, and all ecclesiastical laws to be thereunto confined. Nothing ought nor can be transacted in this society relating to the possession of civil and worldly goods. No force is here to be made use of upon any occasion whatsoever. For force belongs wholly to the civil magistrate, and the possession of all outward goods is subject to his jurisdiction.

But, it may be asked, by what means then shall ecclesiastical laws be established if they must be thus destitute of all compulsive power? I answer: they must be established by means suitable to the nature of such things, whereof the external profession and observation—if not proceeding from a thorough conviction and approbation of the mind—is altogether useless and unprofitable. The arms by which the members of this society are to be kept within their duty are exhortations, admonitions, and advices. If by these means the offenders will not be reclaimed and the erroneous convinced, there remains nothing further to be done but that such stubborn and obstinate persons who give no ground to hope for their reformation, should be cast out and separated from the society. This is the last and utmost force of ecclesiastical authority. No other punishment can thereby be inflicted than that, the relation ceasing between the body and the member which is cut off. The person so condemned ceases to be a part of that church.

These things being thus determined, let us inquire, in the next place: How far the duty of toleration extends, and what is required from everyone by it?

And, first, I hold that no church is bound, by the duty of toleration, to retain any such person in her bosom as, after admonition, continues obstinately to offend against the laws of the society. For these being the condition of communion and the bond of the society, if the breach of them were permitted without any animadversion the society would immediately be thereby dissolved. But, nevertheless, in all such cases care is to be taken that the sentence of excommunication, and the execution thereof, carry with it no rough usage of word or action whereby the ejected person may anywise be damnified in body or estate. For all force (as has often been said) belongs only to the magistrate, nor ought any private persons at any time to use force unless it be in self-defense against unjust violence. Excommunication neither does, nor can, deprive the excommunicated person of any of those civil goods that he formerly possessed. All those things belong to the civil government and are under the magistrate's protection. The whole force of excommunication consists only in this: that the resolution of the society in that respect being declared, the union that was between the body and some member comes thereby to be dissolved; and that relation ceasing, the participation of some certain things which the society communicated to its members, and unto which no man has any civil right, comes also to cease. For there is no civil injury done unto the excommunicated person by the church minister's refusing him that bread and wine, in the celebration of the Lord's Supper, which was not bought with his but other men's money.

Secondly, no private person has any right in any manner to prejudice another person in his civil enjoyments because he is of another church or religion. All the rights and franchises that belong to him as a man or as a denizen are inviolably to be preserved to him. These are not the business of religion. No violence nor injury is to be offered him, whether he be Christian or pagan. Nay, we must not content ourselves with the narrow measures of bare justice; charity, bounty, and liberality must be added to it. This the Gospel enjoins, this reason directs, and this that natural fellowship we are born into requires of us. If any man err from the right way, it is his own misfortune, no injury to thee; nor therefore art thou to punish him in the things of this life because thou supposest he will be miserable in that which is to come.

What I say concerning the mutual toleration of private persons differing from one another in religion, I understand also of particular churches which stand, as it were, in the same relation to each other as private persons among themselves: nor has any one of them any manner of jurisdiction over any other; no, not even when the civil magistrate (as it sometimes happens) comes to be of this or the other communion. For the civil government can give no new right to the church, nor the church to the civil government. So that whether the magistrate join himself to any church, or separate from it, the church remains always as it was before—a free and voluntary society. It neither requires the power of the sword by the magistrate's coming to it, nor does it lose the right of instruction and excommunication by his going from it. This is the fundamental and immutable right of a spontaneous society—that it has power to remove any of its members who transgress the rules of its institution; but it cannot, by the accession of any new members, acquire any right of jurisdiction over those that are not joined with it. And therefore peace, equity, and friendship are always mutually to be observed by particular churches, in the same manner as by private persons, without any pretense of superiority or jurisdiction over one another.

That the thing may be made clearer by an example, let us suppose two churches—the one of Arminians, the other of Calvinists—residing in the city of Constantinople. Will anyone say that either of these churches has right to deprive the members of the other of their estates and liberty (as we see practised elsewhere), because of their differing from it in some doctrines and ceremonies, whilst the Turks in the meanwhile silently stand by and laugh to see with what inhuman cruelty Christians thus rage against Christians? But if one of these churches hath this power of treating the other ill, I ask which of them it is to whom that power belongs, and by what right? It will be answered, undoubtedly, that it is the orthodox church which has the right of authority over the erroneous or heretical. This is, in great and specious words, to say just nothing at all. For every church is orthodox to itself; to others, erroneous or heretical. For whatsoever any church believes it believes to be true; and the contrary unto those things it pronounces to be error. So that the controversy between these churches about the truth of their doctrines and the purity of their worship is on both sides equal; nor is there any judge, either at Constantinople or elsewhere upon earth, by whose sentence it can be determined. The decision of that question belongs only to the Supreme Judge of all men, to whom also alone belongs the punishment of the erroneous. In the meanwhile, let those men consider how heinously they sin, who, adding injustice, if not to their error, yet certainly to their pride, do rashly and arrogantly take upon them to misuse the servants of another master, who are not at all accountable to them.

Nay, further: if it could be manifest which of these two dissenting churches were in the right, there would not accrue thereby unto the orthodox any right of destroying the other. For churches have neither any jurisdiction in worldly matters, nor are fire and sword any proper instruments wherewith to convince men's minds of error, and inform them of the truth. Let us suppose, nevertheless, that the civil magistrate inclined to favor one of them and to put his sword into their hands, that (by his consent) they might chastise the dissenters as they pleased. Will any man say that any right can be derived unto a Christian church over its brethren from a Turkish emperor? An infidel, who has himself no authority to punish Christians for the articles of their faith, cannot confer such an authority upon any society of Christians, nor give unto them a right which he has not himself. This would be the case at Constantinople; and the reason of the thing is the same in any Christian kingdom. The civil power is the same in every place. Nor can that power, in the hands of a Christian prince, confer any greater authority upon the church than in the hands of a heathen; which is to say, just none at all.

Nevertheless, it is worthy to be observed and lamented that the most violent of these defenders of the truth, the opposers of errors, the exclaimers against schism do hardly ever let loose this their zeal for God, with which they are so warmed and inflamed, unless where they have the civil magistrate on their side. But so soon as ever court favor has given them the better end of the staff, and they begin to feel themselves the stronger, then presently peace and charity are to be laid aside. Otherwise they are religiously to be observed. Where they have not the power to carry on persecution and to become masters, there they desire to live upon fair terms and preach up toleration. When they are not strengthened with the civil power, then they can bear most patiently and unmovedly the contagion of idolatry, superstition, and heresy in their neighborhood; of which on other occasions the interest of religion makes them to be extremely apprehensive. They do not forwardly attack those errors which are in fashion at court or are countenanced by the government. Here they can be content to spare their arguments; which yet (with their leave) is the only right method of propagating truth, which has no such way of prevailing as when strong arguments and good reason are joined with the softness of civility and good usage.

Nobody, therefore, in fine, neither single persons nor churches, nay, nor even commonwealths, have any just title to invade the civil rights and worldly goods of each other upon pretense of religion. Those that are of another opinion would do well to consider with themselves how pernicious a seed of discord and war, how powerful a provocation to endless hatreds, rapines, and slaughters they thereby furnish unto mankind. No peace and security, no, not so much as common friendship, can ever be established or preserved amongst men so long as this opinion prevails that dominion is founded in grace and that religion is to be propagated by force of arms.

In the third place, let us see what the duty of toleration requires from those who are distinguished from the rest of mankind (from the laity, as they please to call us) by some ecclesiastical character and office; whether they be bishops, priests, presbyters, ministers, or however else dignified or distinguished. It is not my business to inquire here into the original of the power or dignity of the clergy. This only I say, that whencesoever their authority be sprung, since it is ecclesiastical, it ought to be confined within the bounds of the church, nor can it in any manner be extended to civil affairs, because the church itself is a thing absolutely separate and distinct from the commonwealth. The boundaries on both sides are fixed and immovable. He jumbles heaven and earth together, the things most remote and opposite, who mixes these two societies, which are in their original, end, business, and in everything perfectly distinct and infinitely different from each other. No man, therefore, with whatsoever ecclesiastical office he be dignified, can deprive another man that is not of his church and faith either of liberty or of any part of his worldly goods upon the account of that difference between them in religion. For whatsoever is not lawful to the whole church cannot by any ecclesiastical right become lawful to any of its members.

But this is not all. It is not enough that ecclesiastical men abstain from violence and rapine and all manner of persecution. He that pretends to be a successor of the apostles, and takes upon him the office of teaching, is obliged also to admonish his hearers of the duties of peace and goodwill toward all men, as well toward the erroneous as the orthodox; toward those that differ from them in faith and worship as well as toward those that agree with them therein. And he ought industriously to exhort all men, whether private persons or magistrates (if any such there be in his church), to charity, meekness, and toleration, and diligently endeavor to ally and temper all that heat and unreasonable averseness of mind which either any man's fiery zeal for his own sect or the craft of others has kindled against dissenters. I will not undertake to represent how happy and how great would be the fruit, both in church and state, if the pulpits everywhere sounded with this doctrine of peace and toleration, lest I should seem to reflect too severely upon those men whose dignity I desire not to detract from, nor would have it diminished either by others or themselves. But this I say, that thus it ought to be. And if anyone that professes himself to be a minister of the word of God, a preacher of the gospel of peace, teach otherwise, he either understands not or neglects the business of his calling, and shall one day give account thereof unto the Prince of Peace. If Christians are to be admonished that they abstain from all manner of revenge, even after repeated provocations and multiplied injuries, how much more ought they who suffer nothing, who have had no harm done them, forbear violence and abstain from all manner of ill usage toward those from whom they have received none! This caution and temper they ought certainly to use toward those who mind only their own business, and are solicitous for nothing but that (whatever men think of them) they may worship God in that manner which they are persuaded is acceptable to him, and in which they have the strongest hopes of eternal salvation. In private domestic affairs, in the management of estates, in the conservation of bodily health, every man may consider what suits his own convenience, and follow what course he likes best. No man complains of the ill management of his neighbor's affairs. No man is angry with another for an error committed in sowing his land or in marrying his daughter. Nobody corrects a spendthrift for consuming his substance in taverns. Let any man pull down or build or make whatsoever expenses he pleases, nobody murmurs, nobody controls him; he has his liberty. But if any man do not frequent the church, if he do not there conform his behavior exactly to the accustomed ceremonies, or if he brings not his children to be initiated in the sacred mysteries of this or the other congregation, this immediately causes an uproar. The neighborhood is filled with noise and clamor. Everyone is ready to be the avenger of so great a crime, and the zealots hardly have the patience to refrain from violence and rapine so long till the cause be heard, and the poor man be, according to form, condemned to the loss of liberty, goods, or life. Oh, that our ecclesiastical orators of every sect would apply themselves with all the strength of arguments that they are able to the confounding of men's errors! But let them spare their persons. Let them not supply their want of reasons with the instruments of force, which belong to another jurisdiction, and do ill become a churchman's hands. Let them not call in the magistrate's authority to the aid of their eloquence or learning, lest perhaps, whilst they pretend only love for the truth, this their intemperate zeal, breathing nothing but fire and sword, betray their ambition and show that what they desire is temporal dominion. For it will be very difficult to persuade men of sense that he who with dry eyes and satisfaction of mind can deliver his brother to the executioner to be burnt alive, does sincerely and heartily concern himself to save that brother from the flames of hell in the world to come.

In the last place, let us now consider what is the magistrate's duty in the business of toleration, which certainly is very considerable.

We have already proved that the care of souls does not belong to the magistrate. Not a magisterial care, I mean (if I may so call it), which consists in prescribing by laws and compelling by punishments. But a charitable care, which consists in teaching, admonishing, and persuading, cannot be denied unto any man. The care, therefore, of every man's soul belongs unto himself, and is to be left unto himself. But what if he neglect the care of his soul? I answer: What if he neglect the care of his health or of his estate, which things are nearlier related to the government of the magistrate than the other? Will the magistrate provide by an express law that such a one shall not become poor or sick? Laws provide, as much as is possible, that the goods and health of subjects be not injured by the fraud and violence of others; they do not guard them from the negligence or ill husbandry of the possessors themselves. No man can be forced to be rich or healthful whether he will or no. Nay, God himself will not save men against their wills. Let us suppose, however, that some prince were desirous to force his subjects to accumulate riches or to preserve the health and strength of their bodies. Shall it be provided by law that they must consult none but Roman physicians, and shall everyone be bound to live according to their prescriptions? What, shall no potion, no broth, be taken but what is prepared either in the Vatican, suppose, or in a Geneva shop? Or, to make these subjects rich, shall they all be obliged by law to become merchants or musicians? Or shall everyone turn victualler or smith because there are some that maintain their families plentifully and grow rich in those professions? But, it may be said, there are a thousand ways to wealth, but one only way to heaven. It is well said, indeed, especially by those that plead for compelling men into this or the other way. For if there were several ways that led thither, there would not be so much as a pretense left for compulsion. But now if I be marching on with my utmost vigor in that way which, according to the sacred geography, leads straight to Jerusalem, why am I beaten and ill used by others because, perhaps, I wear not buskins; because my hair is not of the right cut; because, perhaps, I have not been dipped in the right fashion; because I eat flesh upon the road, or some other food which agrees with my stomach; because I avoid certain byways, which seem unto me to lead into briars or precipices; because, amongst the several paths that are in the same road, I choose that to walk in which seems to be the straightest and cleanest; because I avoid to keep company with some travelers that are less grave, and others that are more sour than they ought to be; or, in fine, because I follow a guide that either is, or is not, clothed in white or crowned with a mitre? Certainly, if we consider right, we shall find that, for the most part, they are such frivolous things as these that (without any prejudice to religion or the salvation of souls, if not accompanied with superstition or hypocrisy) might either be observed or omitted. I say they are suchlike things as these which breed implacable enmities amongst Christian brethren, who are all agreed in the substantial and truly fundamental part of religion.

But let us grant unto these zealots, who condemn all things that are not of their mode, that from these circumstances are different ends. What shall we conclude from thence? There is only one of these which is the true way to eternal happiness: but in this great variety of ways that men follow, it is still doubted which is the right one. Now, neither the care of the commonwealth nor the right enacting of laws does discover this way that leads to heaven more certainly to the magistrate than every private man's search and study discovers it unto himself. I have a weak body, sunk under a languishing disease, for which (I suppose) there is one only remedy, but that unknown. Does it therefore belong unto the magistrate to prescribe me a remedy, because there is but one and because it is unknown? Because there is but one way for me to escape death, will it therefore be safe for me to do whatsoever the magistrate ordains? Those things that every man ought sincerely to inquire into himself, and by meditation, study, search, and his own endeavors attain the knowledge of, cannot be looked upon as the peculiar possession of any sort of men. Princes, indeed, are born superior unto other men in power, but in nature equal. Neither the right nor the art of ruling does necessarily carry along with it the certain knowledge of other things, and least of all of true religion. For if it were so, how could it come to pass that the lords of the earth should differ so vastly as they do in religious matters? But let us grant that it is probable the way to eternal life may be better known by a prince than by his subjects, or at least that in this incertitude of things the safest and most commodious way for private persons is to follow his dictates. You will say, what then? If he should bid you follow merchandise for your livelihood, would you decline that course for fear it should not succeed? I answer: I would turn merchant upon the prince's command, because in case I should have ill success in trade, he is abundantly able to make up my loss some other way. If it be true, as he pretends, that he desires I should thrive and grow rich, he can set me up again when unsuccessful voyages have broken me. But this is not the case in the things that regard the life to come; if there I take a wrong course, if in that respect I am once undone, it is not in the magistrate's power to repair my loss, to ease my suffering, nor to restore me in any measure, much less entirely to a good estate. What security can be given for the kingdom of heaven?

Perhaps some will say that they do not suppose this infallible judgment, that all men are bound to follow in the affairs of religion, to be in the civil magistrate, but in the church. What the church has determined, that the civil magistrate orders to be observed; and he provides by his authority that nobody shall either act or believe in the business of religion otherwise than the church teaches. So that the judgment of those things is in the church; the magistrate himself yields obedience thereunto, and requires the like obedience from others. I answer: Who sees not how frequently the name of the church, which was venerable in time of the apostles, has been made use of to throw dust in the people's eyes, in the following ages? But, however, in the present case it helps us not. The one only narrow way which leads to heaven is not better known to the magistrate than to private persons, and therefore I cannot safely take him for my guide who may probably be as ignorant of the way as myself, and who certainly is less concerned for my salvation than I myself am. Amongst so many kings of the Jews, how many of them were there whom any Israelite, thus blindly following, had not fallen into idolatry, and thereby into destruction? Yet nevertheless, you bid me be of good courage, and tell me that all is now safe and secure, because the magistrate does not now enjoin the observance of his own decrees in matters of religion, but only the decrees of the church. Of what church? I beseech you. Of that, certainly, which likes him best. As if he that compels me by laws and penalties to enter into this or the other church, did not interpose his own judgment in the matter. What difference is there whether he lead me himself or deliver me over to be led by others? I depend both ways upon his will, and it is he that determines both ways of my eternal state. Would an Israelite that had worshipped Baal upon the command of his king have been in any better condition because somebody had told him that the king ordered nothing in religion upon his own head, nor commanded anything to be done by his subjects in divine worship but what was approved by the counsel of priests and declared to be of divine right by the doctors of their church? If the religion of any church become therefore true and saving because the head of that sect, the prelates and priests, and those of that tribe, do all of them, with all their might, extol and praise it, what religion can ever be accounted erroneous, false, and destructive? I am doubtful concerning the doctrine of the Socinians, I am suspicious of the way of worship practiced by the Papists or Lutherans; will it be ever a jot safer for me to join either unto the one or the other of those churches, upon the magistrate's command, because he commands nothing in religion but by the authority and counsel of the doctors of that church?

But, to speak the truth, we must acknowledge that the church (if a convention of clergymen, making canons, must be called by that name) is for the most part more apt to be influenced by the court than the court by the church. How the church was under the vicissitude of orthodox and Arian emperors is very well known. Or if those things be too remote, our modern English history affords us fresh examples in the reigns of Henry VIII, Edward VI, Mary, and Elizabeth, how easily and smoothly the clergy changed their decrees, their articles of faith, their form of worship, everything according to the inclination of those kings and queens. Yet were those kings and queens of such different minds in point of religion, and enjoined thereupon such different things, that no man in his wits (I had almost said none but an atheist) will presume to say that any sincere and upright worshipper of God could, with a safe conscience, obey their several decrees. To conclude, it is the same thing whether a king that prescribes laws to another man's religion pretend to do it by his own judgment or by the ecclesiastical authority and advice of others. The decisions of churchmen, whose differences and disputes are sufficiently known, cannot be any sounder or safer than his; nor can all their suffrages joined together add a new strength to the civil power. Though this also must be taken notice of—that princes seldom have any regard to the suffrages of ecclesiastics that are not favorers of their own faith and way of worship.

But, after all, the principal consideration and which absolutely determines this controversy is this: although the magistrate's opinion in religion be sound, and the way that he appoints be truly evangelical, yet, if I be not thoroughly persuaded thereof in my own mind, there will be no safety for me in following it. No way whatsoever that I shall walk in against the dictates of my conscience will ever bring me to the mansions of the blessed. I may grow rich by an art that I take not delight in, I may be cured of some disease by remedies that I have not faith in; but I cannot be saved by a religion that I distrust and by a worship that I abhor. It is in vain for an unbeliever to take up the outward show of another man's profession. Faith only and inward sincerity are the things that procure acceptance with God. The most likely and most approved remedy can have no effect upon the patient if his stomach reject it as soon as taken; and you will in vain cram a medicine down a sick man's throat which his particular constitution will be sure to turn into poison. In a word, whatsoever may be doubtful in religion, yet this at least is certain that no religion which I believe not to be true can be either true or profitable unto me. In vain, therefore, do princes compel their subjects to come into their church communion, under pretense of saving their souls. If they believe, they will come of their own accord; if they believe not, their coming will nothing avail them. How great soever, in fine, may be the pretense of goodwill and charity, and concern for the salvation of men's souls, men cannot be forced to be saved whether they will or no. And therefore, when all is done, they must be left to their own consciences.

Having thus at length freed men from all dominion over one another in matters of religion, let us now consider what they are to do. All men know and acknowledge that God ought to be publicly worshipped; why otherwise do they compel one another unto the public assemblies? Men, therefore, constituted in this liberty, are to enter into some religious society, that they meet together, not only for mutual edification, but to own to the world that they worship God, and offer unto His Divine Majesty such service as they themselves are not ashamed of, and such as they think not unworthy of him, nor unacceptable to him; and finally, that by the purity of doctrine, holiness of life, and decent form of worship, they may draw others unto the love of the true religion, and perform such other things in religion as cannot be done by each private man apart.

These religious societies I call churches; and these, I say, the magistrate ought to tolerate, for the business of these assemblies of the people is nothing but what is lawful for every man in particular to take care of—I mean the salvation of their souls; nor in this case is there any difference between the national church and other separated congregations.

But as in every church there are two things especially to be considered—the outward form and rites of worship, and the doctrines and articles of faith—these things must be handled each distinctly that so the whole matter of toleration may the more clearly be understood.

Concerning outward worship, I say, in the first place, that the magistrate has no power to enforce by law, either in his own church or much less in another, the use of any rites or ceremonies whatsoever in the worship of God. And this, not only because these churches are free societies, but because whatsoever is practised in the worship of God is only so far justifiable as it is believed by those that practise it to be acceptable unto him. Whatsoever is not done with that assurance of faith is neither well in itself, nor can it be acceptable to God. To impose such things, therefore, upon any people, contrary to their own judgment, is in effect to command them to offend God, which, considering that the end of all religion is to please him, and that liberty is essentially necessary to that end, appears to be absurd beyond expression.

But perhaps it may be concluded from hence that I deny unto the magistrate all manner of power about indifferent things, which, if it be not granted, the whole subject matter of lawmaking is taken away. No, I readily grant that indifferent things, and perhaps none but such, are subjected to the legislative power. But it does not therefore follow that the magistrate may ordain whatsoever he pleases concerning anything that is indifferent. The public good is the rule and measure of all lawmaking. If a thing be not useful to the commonwealth, though it be never so indifferent, it may not presently be established by law.

And further, things never so indifferent in their own nature, when they are brought into the church and worship of God, are removed out of the reach of the magistrate's jurisdiction, because in that use they have no connection at all with civil affairs. The only business of the church is the salvation of souls, and it no way concerns the commonwealth, or any member of it, that this or the other ceremony be there made use of. Neither the use nor the omission of any ceremonies in those religious assemblies does either advantage or prejudice the life, liberty, or estate of any man. For example, let it be granted that the washing of an infant with water is in itself an indifferent thing; let it be granted also that the magistrate understand such washing to be profitable to the curing or preventing of any disease the children are subject unto, and esteem the matter weighty enough to be taken care of by a law. In that case he may order it to be done. But will anyone therefore say that a magistrate has the same right to ordain by law that all children shall be baptized by priests in the sacred font in order to the purification of their souls? The extreme difference of these two cases is visible to everyone at first sight. Or let us apply the last case to the child of a Jew, and the thing speaks itself. For what hinders but a Christian magistrate may have subjects that are Jews? Now, if we acknowledge that such an injury may not be done unto a Jew as to compel him, against his own opinion, to practice in his religion a thing that is in its nature indifferent, how can we maintain that anything of this kind may be done to a Christian?

Again, things in their own nature indifferent cannot, by any human authority, be made any part of the worship of God—for this very reason: because they are indifferent. For, since indifferent things are not capable, by any virtue of their own, to propitiate the Deity, no human power or authority can confer on them so much dignity and excellence as to enable them to do it. In the common affairs of life that use of indifferent things which God has not forbidden is free and lawful, and therefore in those things human authority has place. But it is not so in matters of religion. Things indifferent are not otherwise lawful in the worship of God than as they are instituted by God himself, and as he, by some positive command, has ordained them to be made a part of that worship which he will vouchsafe to accept at the hands of poor sinful men. Nor, when an incensed Deity shall ask us, "Who has required these or suchlike things at your hands?" will it be enough to answer him that the magistrate commanded them? If civil jurisdiction extend thus far, what might not lawfully be introduced into religion? What hodgepodge of ceremonies, what superstitious inventions, built upon the magistrate's authority, might not (against conscience) be imposed upon the worshippers of God? For the greatest part of these ceremonies and superstitions consists in the religious use of such things as are in their own nature indifferent; nor are they sinful upon any other account than because God is not the author of them. The sprinkling of water, and the use of bread and wine, are both in their own nature and in the ordinary occasions of life altogether indifferent. Will any man therefore say that these things could have been introduced into religion, and made a part of divine worship, if not by divine institution? If any human authority or civil power could have done this, why might it not also enjoin the eating of fish and drinking of ale in the holy banquet as a part of divine worship? Why not the sprinkling of the blood of beasts in churches, and expiations by water or fire, and abundance more of this kind? But these things, how indifferent soever they be in common uses, when they come to be annexed unto divine worship, without divine authority, they are as abominable to God as the sacrifice of a dog. And why is a dog so abominable? What difference is there between a dog and a goat, in respect of the divine nature, equally and infinitely distant from all affinity with matter, unless it be that God required the use of one in his worship, and not of the other? We see, therefore, that indifferent things, how much soever they be under the power of the civil magistrate, yet cannot, upon that pretense, be introduced into religion and imposed upon religious assemblies because, in the worship of God, they wholly cease to be indifferent. He that worships God does it with design to please him and procure his favor. But that cannot be done by him who, upon the command of another, offers unto God that which he knows will be displeasing to him, because not commanded by himself. This is not to please God, or appease his wrath, but willingly and knowingly to provoke him by a manifest contempt, which is a thing absolutely repugnant to the nature and end of worship.

But it will be here asked: "If nothing belonging to divine worship be left to human discretion, how is it then that churches themselves have the power of ordering anything about the time and place of worship, and the like?" To this I answer that in religious worship we must distinguish between what is part of the worship itself and what is but a circumstance. That is a part of the worship which is believed to be appointed by God and to be well pleasing to him, and therefore that is necessary. Circumstances are such things which, though in general they cannot be separated from worship, yet the particular instances or modifications of them are not determined, and therefore they are indifferent. Of this sort are the time and place of worship, habit and posture of him that worships. These are circumstances, and perfectly indifferent, where God has not given any express command about them. For example: amongst the Jews the time and place of their worship, and the habits of those that officiated in it, were not mere circumstances, but a part of the worship itself, in which if anything were defective or different from the institution, they could not hope that it would be accepted by God. But these, to Christians under the liberty of the Gospel, are mere circumstances of worship, which the prudence of every church may bring into such use as shall be judged most subservient to the end of order, decency, and edification. But, even under the Gospel, those who believe the first or the seventh day to be set apart by God, and consecrated still to his worship, to them that portion of time is not a simple circumstance, but a real part of divine worship, which can neither be changed nor neglected.

In the next place: as the magistrate has no power to impose by his laws the use of any rites and ceremonies in any church, so neither has he any power to forbid the use of such rites and ceremonies as are already received, approved, and practised by any church; because if he did so, he would destroy the church itself; the end of whose institution is only to worship God with freedom after its own manner.

You will say, by this rule, if some congregations should have a mind to sacrifice infants, or (as the primitive Christians were falsely accused) lustfully pollute themselves in promiscuous uncleanliness, or practice any other such heinous enormities, is the magistrate obliged to tolerate them because they are committed in a religious assembly? I answer, No. These things are not lawful in the ordinary course of life, nor in any private house; and therefore neither are they so in the worship of God, or in any religious meeting. But, indeed, if any people congregated upon account of religion should be desirous to sacrifice a calf, I deny that that ought to be prohibited by a law. Meliboeus, whose calf it is, may lawfully kill his calf at home, and burn any part of it that he thinks fit. For no injury is thereby done to anyone, no prejudice to another man's goods. And for the same reason he may kill his calf also in a religious meeting. Whether the doing so be well pleasing to God or no, it is their part to consider that do it. The part of the magistrate is only to take care that the commonwealth receive no prejudice, and that there be no injury done to any man, either in life or estate. And thus what may be spent on a feast may be spent on a sacrifice. But if peradventure such were the state of things that the interest of the commonwealth required all slaughter of beasts should be forborne for some while, in order to the increasing of the stock of cattle that had been destroyed by some extraordinary murrain, who sees not that the magistrate, in such a case, may forbid all his subjects to kill any calves for any use whatsoever? Only it is to be observed that, in this case, the law is not made about a religious, but a political matter; nor is the sacrifice, but the slaughter of calves, thereby prohibited.

By this we see what difference there is between the church and the commonwealth. Whatsoever is lawful in the commonwealth cannot be prohibited by the magistrate in the church. Whatsoever is permitted unto any of his subjects for their ordinary use neither can nor ought to be forbidden by him to any sect of people for their religious uses. If any man may lawfully take bread or wine, either sitting or kneeling in his own house, the law ought not to abridge him of the same liberty in his religious worship; though in the church the use of bread and wine be very different, and be there applied to the mysteries of faith and rites of divine worship. But those things that are prejudicial to the commonweal of a people in their ordinary use, and are therefore forbidden by laws, those things ought not to be permitted to churches in their sacred rites. Only the magistrate ought always to be very careful that he do not misuse his authority to the oppression of any church, under pretense of public good.

It may be said, what if a church be idolatrous, is that also to be tolerated by the magistrate? I answer, what power can be given to the magistrate for the suppression of an idolatrous church which may not in time and place be made use of to the ruin of an orthodox one? For it must be remembered that the civil power is the same everywhere, and the religion of every prince is orthodox to himself. If, therefore, such a power be granted unto the civil magistrate in spirituals, as that at Geneva, for example, he may extirpate, by violence and blood, the religion which is there reputed idolatrous; by the same rule another magistrate, in some neighboring country, may oppress the reformed religion, and, in India, the Christian. The civil power can either change everything in religion, according to the prince's pleasure, or it can change nothing. If it be once permitted to introduce anything into religion, by the means of laws and penalties, there can be no bounds put to it; but it will in the same manner be lawful to alter everything, according to that rule of truth which the magistrate has framed unto himself. No man whatsoever ought therefore to be deprived of his terrestrial enjoyments upon account of his religion. Not even Americans, subjected unto a Christian prince, are to be punished either in body or goods for not embracing our faith and worship. If they are persuaded that they please God in observing the rites of their own country, and that they shall obtain happiness by that means, they are to be left unto God and themselves. Let us trace this matter to the bottom. Thus it is: an inconsiderable and weak number of Christians, destitute of everything, arrive in a pagan country; these foreigners beseech the inhabitants, by the bowels of humanity, that they would succor them with the necessaries of life; those necessaries are given them, habitations are granted, and they all join together and grow up into one body of people. The Christian religion by this means takes root in that country and spreads itself, but does not suddenly grow the strongest. While things are in this condition peace, friendship, faith, and equal justice are preserved amongst them. At length the magistrate becomes a Christian, and by that means their party becomes the most powerful. Then immediately all compacts are to be broken, all civil rights to be violated, that idolatry may be extirpated; and unless these innocent pagans, strict observers of the rules of equity and the law of nature, and no ways offending against the laws of the society, I say, unless they will forsake their ancient religion and embrace a new and strange one, they are to be turned out of the lands and possessions of their forefathers, and perhaps deprived of life itself. Then, at last, it appears what zeal for the church, joined with the desire of dominion, is capable to produce, and how easily the pretense of religion and of the care of souls serves for a cloak to covetousness, rapine, and ambition.

Now whosoever maintains that idolatry is to be rooted out of any place by laws, punishments, fire, and sword, may apply this story to himself. For the reason of the thing is equal, both in America and Europe. And neither pagans there nor any dissenting Christians here can, with any right, be deprived of their worldly goods by the predominating faction of a court-church; nor are any civil rights to be either changed or violated upon account of religion in one place more than another.

But idolatry, say some, is a sin and therefore not to be tolerated. If they said it were therefore to be avoided, the inference were good. But it does not follow that because it is a sin it ought therefore to be punished by the magistrate. For it does not belong unto the magistrate to make use of his sword in punishing everything, indifferently, that he takes to be a sin against God. Covetousness, uncharitableness, idleness, and many other things are sins, by the consent of men, which yet no man ever said were to be punished by the magistrate. The reason is because they are not prejudicial to other men's rights, nor do they break the public peace of societies. Nay, even the sins of lying and perjury are nowhere punishable by laws, unless in certain cases in which the real turpitude of the thing and the offense against God are not considered, but only the injury done unto men's neighbors and to the commonwealth. And what if in another country, to a Mahometan or a pagan prince, the Christian religion seem false and offensive to God; may not the Christians for the same reason, and after the same manner, be extirpated there?

But it may be urged further that, by the law of Moses, idolaters were to be rooted out. True, indeed, by the law of Moses; but that is not obligatory to us Christians. Nobody pretends that everything generally enjoined by the law of Moses ought to be practised by Christians; but there is nothing more frivolous than that common distinction of moral, judicial, and ceremonial law, which men ordinarily make use of. For no positive law whatsoever can oblige any people but those to whom it is given. "Hear, O Israel," sufficiently restrains the obligations of the law of Moses only to that people. And this consideration alone is answer enough unto those that urge the authority of the law of Moses for the inflicting of capital punishment upon idolaters. But, however, I will examine this argument a little more particularly.

The case of idolaters, in respect of the Jewish commonwealth, falls under a double consideration. The first is of those who, being initiated in the Mosaical rites and made citizens of that commonwealth, did afterwards apostatize from the worship of the God of Israel. These were proceeded against as traitors and rebels, guilty of no less than high treason. For the commonwealth of the Jews, different in that from all others, was an absolute theocracy; nor was there, or could there be, any difference between that commonwealth and the church. The laws established there concerning the worship of One Invisible Deity were the civil laws of that people and a part of their political government, in which God himself was the legislator. Now, if anyone can show me where there is a commonwealth at this time, constituted upon that foundation, I will acknowledge that the ecclesiastical laws do there unavoidably become a part of the civil, and that the subjects of that government both may and ought to be kept in strict conformity with that church by the civil power. But there is absolutely no such thing under the Gospel as a Christian commonwealth. There are, indeed, many cities and kingdoms that have embraced the faith of Christ, but they have retained their ancient form of government, with which the law of Christ hath not at all meddled. He, indeed, hath taught men how, by faith and good works, they may obtain eternal life; but he instituted no commonwealth. He prescribed unto his followers no new and peculiar form of government, nor put he the sword into any magistrate's hand, with commission to make use of it in forcing men to forsake their former religion and receive his.

Secondly, foreigners and such as were strangers to the commonwealth of Israel were not compelled by force to observe the rites of the Mosaical law; but, on the contrary, in the very same place where it is ordered that an Israelite that was an idolater should be put to death (Exod. 22:20, 21), there it is provided that strangers should not be vexed nor oppressed. I confess that the seven nations that possessed the land which was promised to the Israelites were utterly to be cut off, but this was not singly because they were idolaters. For if that had been the reason, why were the Moabites and other nations to be spared? No, the reason is this: God being in a peculiar manner the King of the Jews, he could not suffer the adoration of any other deity (which was properly an act of high treason against himself) in the land of Canaan, which was his kingdom. For such a manifest revolt could no ways consist with his dominion, which was perfectly political in that country. All idolatry was therefore to be rooted out of the bounds of his kingdom, because it was an acknowledgment of another god, that is to say, another king, against the laws of empire. The inhabitants were also to be driven out, that the entire possession of the land might be given to the Israelites. And for the like reason the Emims and the Horims were driven out of their countries by the children of Esau and Lot, and their lands, upon the same grounds, given by God to the invaders (Deut. 2). But, though all idolatry was thus rooted out of the land of Canaan, yet every idolater was not brought to execution. The whole family of Rahab, the whole nation of the Gibeonites, articled with Joshua and were allowed by treaty; and there were many captives amongst the Jews who were idolaters. David and Solomon subdued many countries without the confines of the Land of Promise, and carried their conquests as far as Euphrates. Amongst so many captives taken, so many nations reduced under their obedience, we find not one man forced into the Jewish religion and the worship of the true God, and punished for idolatry, though all of them were certainly guilty of it. If anyone indeed, becoming a proselyte, desired to be made a denizen of their commonwealth, he was obliged to submit to their laws, that is, to embrace their religion. But this he did willingly, on his own accord, not by constraint. He did not unwillingly submit, to show his obedience, but he sought and solicited for it as a privilege. And, as soon as he was admitted, he became subject to the laws of the commonwealth by which all idolatry was forbidden within the borders of the land of Canaan. But that law (as I have said) did not reach to any of those regions, however subjected unto the Jews, that were situated without those bounds.

Thus far concerning outward worship. Let us now consider articles of faith.

The articles of religion are some of them practical and some speculative. Now, though both sorts consist in the knowledge of truth, yet these terminate simply in the understanding, those influence the will and manners. Speculative opinions, therefore, and articles of faith (as they are called) which are required only to be believed, cannot be imposed on any church by the law of the land. For it is absurd that things should be enjoined by laws which are not in men's power to perform. And to believe this or that to be true does not depend upon our will. But of this enough has been said already. But (will some say) let men at least profess that they believe. A sweet religion, indeed, that obliges men to dissemble and tell lies, both to God and man, for the salvation of their souls! If the magistrate thinks to save men thus, he seems to understand little of the way of salvation. And if he does it not in order to save them, why is he so solicitious about the articles of faith as to enact them by a law?

Further, the magistrate ought not to forbid the preaching or professing of any speculative opinions in any church, because they have no manner of relation to the civil rights of the subjects. If a Roman Catholic believe that to be really the body of Christ which another man calls bread, he does no injury thereby to his neighbor. If a Jew do not believe the New Testament to be the Word of God, he does not thereby alter anything in men's civil rights. If a heathen doubt of both Testaments, he is not therefore to be punished as a pernicious citizen. The power of the magistrate and the estates of the people may be equally secure whether any man believe these things or no. I readily grant that these opinions are false and absurd. But the business of laws is not to provide for the truth of opinions, but for the safety and security of the commonwealth, and of every particular man's goods and person. And so it ought to be. For the truth certainly would do well enough if she were once left to shift for herself. She seldom has received, and I fear never will receive, much assistance from the power of great men, to whom she is but rarely known and more rarely welcome. She is not taught by laws, nor has she any need of force to procure her entrance into the minds of men. Errors indeed prevail by the assistance of foreign and borrowed succors. But if truth makes not her way into the understanding by her own light, she will be but the weaker for any borrowed force violence can add to her. Thus much for speculative opinions. Let us now proceed to practical ones.

A good life, in which consists not the least part of religion and true piety, concerns also the civil government; and in it lies the safety both of men's souls and of the commonwealth. Moral actions belong therefore to the jurisdiction both of the outward and inward court, both of the civil and domestic governor; I mean both of the magistrate and conscience. Here, therefore, is great danger, lest one of these jurisdictions intrench upon the other and discord arise between the keeper of the public peace and the overseers of souls. But if what has been already said concerning the limits of both these governments be rightly considered, it will easily remove all difficulty in this matter.

Every man has an immortal soul, capable of eternal happiness or misery, whose happiness depending upon his believing and doing those things in this life which are necessary to the obtaining of God's favor, and are prescribed by God to that end. It follows from thence, first, that the observance of these things is the highest obligation that lies upon mankind, and that our utmost care, application, and diligence ought to be exercised in the search and performance of them; because there is nothing in this world that is of any consideration in comparison with eternity. Secondly, that seeing one man does not violate the right of another by his erroneous opinions and undue manner of worship, nor is his perdition any prejudice to another man's affairs, therefore, the care of each man's salvation belongs only to himself. But I would not have this understood as if I meant hereby to condemn all charitable admonitions and affectionate endeavors to reduce men from errors, which are indeed the greatest duty of a Christian. Anyone may employ as many exhortations and arguments as he pleases, toward the promoting of another man's salvation. But all force and compulsion are to be forborne. Nothing is to be done imperiously. Nobody is obliged in that manner to yield obedience unto the admonitions or injunctions of another, further than he himself is persuaded. Every man in that has the supreme and absolute authority of judging for himself. And the reason is because nobody else is concerned in it, nor can receive any prejudice from his conduct therein.

But besides their souls, which are immortal, men have also their temporal lives here upon earth; the state whereof being frail and fleeting, and the duration uncertain, they have need of several outward conveniences to the support thereof, which are to be procured or preserved by pains and industry. For those things that are necessary to the comfortable support of our lives are not the spontaneous products of nature, nor do offer themselves fit and prepared for our use. This part therefore draws on another care, and necessarily gives another employment. But the pravity of mankind being such that they had rather injuriously prey upon the fruits of other men's labors than take pains to provide for themselves, the necessity of preserving men in the possession of what honest industry has already acquired, and also of preserving their liberty and strength, whereby they may acquire what they further want, obliges men to enter into society with one another, that by mutual assistance and joint force they may secure unto each other their properties, in the things that contribute to the comfort and happiness of this life, leaving in the meanwhile to every man the care of his own eternal happiness, the attainment whereof can neither be facilitated by another man's industry, nor can the loss of it turn to another man's prejudice, nor the hope of it be forced from him by any external violence. But, forasmuch as men thus entering into societies, grounded upon their mutual compacts of assistance for the defense of their temporal goods, may, nevertheless, be deprived of them, either by the rapine and fraud of their fellow citizens or by the hostile violence of foreigners, the remedy of this evil consists in arms, riches, and multitude of citizens; the remedy of the other in laws; and the care of all things relating both to one and the other is committed by the society to the civil magistrate. This is the original, this is the use, and these are the bounds of the legislative (which is the supreme) power in every commonwealth. I mean that provision may be made for the security of each man's private possessions, for the peace, riches, and public commodities of the whole people, and, as much as possible, for the increase of their inward strength against foreign invasions.

These things being thus explained, it is easy to understand to what end the legislative power ought to be directed, and by what measures regulated; and that is the temporal good and outward prosperity of the society, which is the sole reason of men's entering into society, and the only thing they seek and aim at in it. And it is also evident what liberty remains to men in reference to their eternal salvation, and that is, that everyone should do what he in his conscience is persuaded to be acceptable to the Almighty, on whose good pleasure and acceptance depends their eternal happiness. For obedience is due, in the first place, to God, and afterwards to the laws.

But some may ask, what if the magistrate should enjoin anything by his authority that appears unlawful to the conscience of a private person? I answer that if government be faithfully administered and the counsels of the magistrates be indeed directed to the public good, this will seldom happen. But if, perhaps, it do so fall out, I say that such a private person is to abstain from the action that he judges unlawful, and he is to undergo the punishment which it is not unlawful for him to bear. For the private judgment of any person concerning a law enacted in political matters, for the public good, does not take away the obligation of that law, nor deserve a dispensation. But if the law indeed be concerning things that lie not within the verge of the magistrate's authority (as for example, that the people, or any party amongst them, should be compelled to embrace a strange religion and join in the worship and ceremonies of another church), men are not in these cases obliged by that law, against their consciences. For the political society is instituted for no other end, but only to secure every man's possession of the things of this life. The care of each man's soul, and of the things of heaven, which neither does belong to the commonwealth nor can be subjected to it, is left entirely to every man's self. Thus the safeguard of men's lives and of the things that belong unto this life is the business of the commonwealth; and the preserving of those things unto their owners is the duty of the magistrate. And therefore the magistrate cannot take away these worldly things from this man or party and give them to that, nor change propriety amongst fellow subjects (no, not even by a law), for a cause that has no relation to the end of civil government, I mean for their religion, which whether it be true or false does no prejudice to the worldly concerns of their fellow subjects, which are the things that only belong unto the care of the commonwealth.

But what if the magistrate believe such a law as this to be for the public good? I answer: as the private judgment of any particular person, if erroneous, does not exempt him from the obligation of law, so the private judgment (as I may call it) of the magistrate does not give him any new right of imposing laws upon his subjects which neither was in the constitution of the government granted him nor ever was in the power of the people to grant, much less if he make it his business to enrich and advance his followers and fellow-sectaries with the spoils of others. But what if the magistrate believe that he has a right to make such laws, and that they are for the public good, and his subjects believe the contrary? Who shall be judge between them? I answer, God alone. For there is no judge upon earth between the supreme magistrate and the people. God, I say, is the only judge in this case, who will retribute unto everyone at the last day according to his deserts, that is, according to his sincerity and uprightness in endeavoring to promote piety and the public weal and peace of mankind. But what shall be done in the meanwhile? I answer: the principal and chief care of everyone ought to be of his own soul first, and, in the next place, of the public peace; though yet there are very few will think it is peace there where they see all laid waste.

There are two sorts of contests amongst men, the one managed by law, the other by force; and these are of that nature that where the one ends, the other always begins. But it is not my business to inquire into the power of the magistrate in the different constitutions of nations. I only know what usually happens where controversies arise without a judge to determine them. You will say, then, the magistrate being the stronger will have his will, and carry his point. Without doubt; but the question is not here concerning the doubtfulness of the event, but the rule of right.

But to come to particulars. I say, first, no opinions contrary to human society, or to those moral rules which are necessary to the preservation of civil society, are to be tolerated by the magistrate. But of these, indeed, examples in any church are rare. For no sect can easily arrive to such a degree of madness as that it should think fit to teach, for doctrines of religion, such things as manifestly undermine the foundations of society, and are, therefore, condemned by the judgment of all mankind; because their own interest, peace, reputation, everything would be thereby endangered.

Another more secret evil, but more dangerous to the commonwealth, is when men arrogate to themselves and to those of their own sect some peculiar prerogative covered over with a specious show of deceitful words, but in effect opposite to the civil right of the community. For example: we cannot find any sect that teaches, expressly and openly, that men are not obliged to keep their promise; that princes may be dethroned by those that differ from them in religion; or that the dominion of all things belongs only to themselves. For these things, proposed thus nakedly and plainly, would soon draw on them the eye and hand of the magistrate, and awaken all the care of the commonwealth to a watchfulness against the spreading of so dangerous an evil. But, nevertheless, we find those that say the same things in other words. What else do they mean who teach that faith is not to be kept with heretics? Their meaning, forsooth, is that the privilege of breaking faith belongs unto themselves; for they declare all that are not of their communion to be heretics, or at least may declare them so whensoever they think fit. What can be the meaning of their asserting that kings excommunicated forfeit their crowns and kingdoms? It is evident that they thereby arrogate unto themselves the power of deposing kings, because they challenge the power of excommunication as the peculiar right of their hierarchy. That dominion is founded in grace is also an assertion by which those that maintain it do plainly lay claim to the possession of all things. For they are not so wanting to themselves as not to believe, or at least as not to profess themselves to be the truly pious and faithful. These therefore, and the like, who attribute unto the faithful, religious, and orthodox, that is, in plain terms, unto themselves, any peculiar privilege or power above other mortals, in civil concernments; or who upon pretense of religion do challenge any manner of authority over such as are not associated with them in their ecclesiastical communion, I say these have no right to be tolerated by the magistrate, as neither those that will not own and teach the duty of tolerating all men in matters of mere religion. For what do all these and the like doctrines signify but that they may and are ready upon any occasion to seize the government and possess themselves of the estates and fortunes of their fellow subjects; and that they only ask leave to be tolerated by the magistrate so long until they find themselves strong enough to effect it?

Again: that church can have no right to be tolerated by the magistrate which is constituted upon such a bottom that all those who enter into it do thereby *ipso facto* deliver themselves up to the protection and service of another prince. For by this means the magistrate would give way to the settling of a foreign jurisdiction in his own country, and suffer his own people to be listed, as it were, for soldiers against his own government. Nor does the frivolous and fallacious distinction between the court and the church afford any remedy to this inconvenience; especially when both the one and the other are equally subject to the absolute authority of the same person who has not only power to persuade the members of his church to whatsoever he lists, either as purely religious or in order thereunto, but can also enjoin it them on pain of eternal fire. It is ridiculous for anyone to profess himself to be a Mahometan only in his religion, but in everything else a faithful subject to a Christian magistrate, whilst at the same time he acknowledges himself bound to yield blind obedience to the mufti of Constantinople, who himself is entirely obedient to the Ottoman emperor and frames the feigned oracles of that religion according to his pleasure. But this Mahometan living amongst Christians would yet more apparently renounce their government if he acknowledged the same person to be head of his church who is the supreme magistrate in the state.

Lastly, those are not at all to be tolerated who deny the being of a God. Promises, covenants, and oaths, which are the bonds of human society, can have no hold upon an atheist. The taking away of God, though but even in thought, dissolves all; besides also, those that by their atheism undermine and destroy all religion can have no pretense of religion whereupon to challenge the privilege of a toleration. As for other practical opinions, though not absolutely free from all error, if they do not tend to establish domination over others, or civil impunity to the church in which they are taught, there can be no reason why they should not be tolerated.

It remains that I say something concerning those assemblies which being vulgarly called, and perhaps having sometimes been conventicles and nurseries of factions and seditions, are thought to afford the strongest matter of objection against this doctrine of toleration. But this has not happened by anything peculiar unto the genius of such assemblies, but by the unhappy circumstances of an oppressed or ill-settled liberty. These accusations would soon cease if the law of toleration were once so settled that all churches were obliged to lay down toleration as the foundation of their own liberty, and teach that liberty of conscience is every man's natural right, equally belonging to dissenters as to themselves; and that nobody ought to be compelled in matters of religion either by law or force. The establishment of this one thing would take away all ground of complaints and tumults upon account of conscience; and these causes of discontents and animosities being once removed, there would remain nothing in these assemblies that were not more peaceable and less apt to produce disturbance of state than in any other meetings whatsoever. But let us examine particularly the heads of these accusations.

You will say that assemblies and meetings endanger the public peace and threaten the commonwealth. I answer, if this be so, why are there daily such numerous meetings in markets and courts of judicature? Why are crowds upon the Exchange and a concourse of people in cities suffered? You will reply, those are civil assemblies, but these we object against are ecclesiastical. I answer, it is a likely thing indeed that such assemblies as are altogether remote from civil affairs should be most apt to embroil them. Oh, but civil assemblies are composed of men that differ from one another in matters of religion, but these ecclesiastical meetings are of persons that are all of one opinion. As if an agreement in matters of religion were in effect a conspiracy against the commonwealth; or as if men would not be so much the more warmly unanimous in religion the less liberty they had of assembling. But it will be urged still that civil assemblies are open and free for anyone to enter into, whereas religious conventicles are more private, and thereby give opportunity to clandestine machinations. I answer that this is not strictly true, for many civil assemblies are not open to everyone. And if some religious meetings be private, who are they (I beseech you) that are to be blamed for it, those that desire or those that forbid their being public? Again, you will say that religious communion does exceedingly unite men's minds and affections to one another, and is therefore the more dangerous. But if this be so, why is not the magistrate afraid of his own church, and why does he not forbid their assemblies as things dangerous to his government? You will say because he himself is a part and even the head of them. As if he were not also a part of the commonwealth and the head of the whole people!

Let us therefore deal plainly. The magistrate is afraid of other churches, but not of his own, because he is kind and favorable to the one, but severe and cruel to the other. These he treats like children and indulges them even to wantonness. Those he uses as slaves, and how blamelessly soever they demean themselves, recompenses them no otherwise than by galleys, prisons, confiscations, and death. These he cherishes and defends; those he continually scourges and oppresses. Let him turn the tables. Or let those dissenters enjoy but the same privileges in civils as his other subjects, and he will quickly find that these religious meetings will be no longer dangerous. For if men enter into seditious conspiracies, it is not religion inspires them to it in their meetings, but their sufferings and oppressions that make them willing to ease themselves. Just and moderate governments are everywhere quiet, everywhere safe; but oppression raises ferments and makes men struggle to cast off an uneasy and tyrannical yoke. I know that seditions are very frequently raised upon pretense of religion, but it is as true that for religion, subjects are frequently ill treated and live miserably. Believe me, the stirs that are made proceed not from any peculiar temper of this or that church or religious society, but from the common disposition of all mankind, who when they groan under any heavy burthen endeavor naturally to shake off the yoke that galls their necks. Suppose this business of religion were let alone, and that there were some other distinction made between men and men upon account of their different complexions, shapes, and features, so that those who have black hair (for example) or grey eyes should not enjoy the same privileges as other citizens; that they should not be permitted either to buy or sell, or live by their callings; that parents should not have the government and education of their own children; that all should either be excluded from the benefit of the laws or meet with partial judges—can it be doubted but these persons, thus distinguished from others by the color of their hair and eyes, and united together by one common persecution, would be as dangerous to the magistrate as any others that had associated themselves merely upon the account of religion? Some enter into company for trade and profit, others for want of business have their clubs for claret. Neighborhood joins some, and religion others. But there is only one thing which gathers people into seditious commotions, and that is oppression.

You will say, What, will you have people to meet at divine service against the magistrate's will? I answer, Why, I pray, against his will? Is it not both lawful and necessary that they should meet? Against his will, do you say? That is what I complain of; that is the very root of all the mischief. Why are assemblies less sufferable in a church than in a theater or market? Those that meet there are not either more vicious or more turbulent than those that meet elsewhere. The business in that is that they are ill used, and therefore they are not to be suffered. Take away the partiality that is used toward them in matters of common right, change the laws, take away the penalties unto which they are subjected, and all things will immediately become safe and peaceable; nay, those that are averse to the religion of the magistrate will think themselves so much the more bound to maintain the peace of the commonwealth as their condition is better in that place than elsewhere; and all the several separate congregations, like so many guardians of the public peace, will watch one another, that nothing may be innovated or changed in the form of the government, because they can hope for nothing better than what they already enjoy—that is, an equal condition with their fellow subjects under a just and moderate government. Now if that church which agrees in religion with the prince be esteemed the chief support of any civil government, and that for no other reason (as has already been shown) than because the prince is kind and the laws are favorable to it, how much greater will be the security of government where all good subjects, of whatsoever church they be, without any distinction upon account of religion, enjoying the same favor of the prince and the same benefit of the laws, shall become the common support and guard of it, and where none will have any occasion to fear the severity of the laws but those that do injuries to their neighbors and offend against the civil peace?

That we may draw toward a conclusion. The sum of all we drive at is that every man may enjoy the same rights that are granted to others. Is it permitted to worship God in the Roman manner? Let it be permitted to do it in the Geneva form also. Is it permitted to speak Latin in the marketplace? Let those that have a mind to it be permitted to do it also in the church. Is it lawful for any man in his own house to kneel, stand, sit, or use any other posture, and to clothe himself in white or black, in short or in long garments? Let it not be made unlawful to eat bread, drink wine, or wash with water in the church. In a word, whatsoever things are left free by law in the common occasions of life, let them remain free unto every church in divine worship. Let no man's life or body or house or estate suffer any manner of prejudice upon these accounts. Can you allow of the Presbyterian discipline? Why should not the Episcopal also have what they like? Ecclesiastical authority, whether it be administered by the hands of a single person or many, is everywhere the same; and neither has any jurisdiction in things civil, nor any manner of power of compulsion, nor anything at all to do with riches and revenues.

Ecclesiastical assemblies and sermons are justified by daily experience and public allowance. These are allowed to people of some one persuasion, why not to all? If anything pass in a religious meeting seditiously and contrary to the public peace, it is to be punished in the same manner, and no otherwise than as if it had happened in a fair or market. These meetings ought not to be sanctuaries for factious and flagitious fellows. Nor ought it to be less lawful for men to meet in churches than in halls; nor are one part of the subjects to be esteemed more blamable for their meeting together than others. Everyone is to be accountable for his own actions, and no man is to be laid under a suspicion or odium for the fault of another. Those that are seditious, murderers, thieves, robbers, adulterers, slanderers, etc., of whatsoever church, whether national or not, ought to be punished and suppressed. But those whose doctrine is peaceable, and whose manners are pure and blameless, ought to be upon equal terms with their fellow subjects. Thus if solemn assemblies, observations of festivals, public worship be permitted to any one sort of professors, all these things ought to be permitted to the Presbyterians, Independents, Anabaptists, Arminians, Quakers, and others, with the same liberty. Nay, if we may openly speak the truth, and as becomes one man to another, neither pagan nor Mahometan, nor Jew, ought to be excluded from the civil rights of the commonwealth because of his religion. The Gospel commands no such thing. The church which "judgeth not those that are without" (1 Cor. 5:12, 13) wants it not. And the commonwealth, which embraces indifferently all men that are honest, peaceable, and industrious, requires it not. Shall we suffer a pagan to deal and trade with us, and shall we not suffer him to pray unto and worship God? If we allow the Jews to have private houses and dwellings amongst us, why should we not allow them to have synagogues? Is their doctrine more false, their worship more abominable, or is the civil peace more endangered by their meeting in public than in their private houses? But if these things may be granted to Jews and pagans, surely the condition of any Christians ought not to be worse than theirs in a Christian commonwealth.

You will say, perhaps, Yes, it ought to be; because they are more inclinable to factions, tumults, and civil wars. I answer, Is this the fault of the Christian religion? If it be so, truly the Christian religion is the worst of all religions, and ought neither to be embraced by any particular person nor tolerated by any commonwealth. For if this be the genius, this the nature of the Christian religion, to be turbulent and destructive to the civil peace, that church itself which the magistrate indulges will not always be innocent. But far be it from us to say any such thing of that religion which carries the greatest opposition to covetousness, ambition, discord, contention, and all manner of inordinate desires; and is the most modest and peaceable religion that ever was. We must therefore seek another cause of those evils that are charged upon religion. And if we consider right, we shall find it to consist wholly in the subject that I am treating of. It is not the diversity of opinions (which cannot be avoided), but the refusal of toleration to those that are of different opinions (which might have been granted), that has produced all the bustles and wars that have been in the Christian world upon account of religion. The heads and leaders of the Church, moved by avarice and insatiable desire of dominion, making use of the immoderate ambition of magistrates and the credulous superstition of the giddy multitude, have incensed and animated them against those that dissent from themselves, by preaching unto them, contrary to the laws of the Gospel and to the precepts of charity, that schismatics and heretics are to be outed of their possessions and destroyed. And thus have they mixed together and confounded two things that are in themselves most different, the church and the commonwealth. Now as it is very difficult for men patiently to suffer themselves to be stripped of the goods which they have got by their honest industry and, contrary to all the laws of equity, both human and divine, to be delivered up for a prey to other men's violence and rapine; especially when they are otherwise altogether blameless; and that the occasion for which they are thus treated does not at all belong to the jurisdiction of the magistrate, but entirely to the conscience of every particular man, for the conduct of which he is accountable to God only; what else can be expected but that these men, growing weary of the evils under which they labor, should in the end think it lawful for them to resist force with force, and to defend their natural rights (which are not forfeitable upon account of religion) with arms as well as they can? That this has been hitherto the ordinary course of things is abundantly evident in history, and that it will continue to be so hereafter is but too apparent in reason. It cannot, indeed, be otherwise so long as the principle of persecution for religion shall prevail, as it has done hitherto, with magistrate and people, and so long as those that ought to be the preachers of peace and concord shall continue with all their art and strength to excite men to arms and sound the trumpet of war. But that magistrates should thus suffer these incendiaries and disturbers of the public peace might justly be wondered at if it did not appear that they have been invited by them unto a participation of the spoil, and have therefore thought fit to make use of their covetousness and pride as means whereby to increase their own power. For who does not see that these good men are indeed more ministers of the government than ministers of the Gospel, and that by flattering the ambition and favoring the dominion of princes and men in authority, they endeavor with all their might to promote that tyranny in the commonwealth which otherwise they should not be able to establish in the church? This is the unhappy agreement that we see between the church and state. Whereas if each of them would contain itself within its own bounds  the one attending to the worldly welfare of the commonwealth, the other to the salvation of souls—it is impossible that any discord should ever have happened between them. *Sed pudet haec opprobria, etc.* God Almighty grant, I beseech him, that the gospel of peace may at length be preached, and that civil magistrates, growing more careful to conform their own consciences to the law of God and less solicitous about the binding of other men's consciences by human laws, may, like fathers of their country, direct all their counsels and endeavors to promote universally the civil welfare of all their children, except only of such as are arrogant, ungovernable, and injurious to their brethren; and that all ecclesiastical men, who boast themselves to be the successors of the apostles, walking peaceably and modestly in the apostles' steps, without intermeddling with state affairs, may apply themselves wholly to promote the salvation of souls.

—Farewell

Perhaps it may not be amiss to add a few things concerning heresy and schism. A Turk is not, nor can be, either heretic or schismatic to a Christian; and if any man fall off from the Christian faith to Mahometism, he does not thereby become a heretic or schismatic, but an apostate and an infidel. This nobody doubts of; and by this it appears that men of different religions cannot be heretics or schismatics to one another.

We are to inquire therefore what men are of the same religion. Concerning which it is manifest that those who have one and the same rule of faith and worship are of the same religion; and those who have not the same rule of faith and worship are of different religions. For since all things that belong unto that religion are contained in that rule, it follows necessarily that those who agree in one rule are of one and the same religion, and vice versa. Thus Turks and Christians are of different religions, because these take the Holy Scriptures to be the rule of their religion, and those the Alcoran. And for the same reason there may be different religions also even amongst Christians. The Papists and Lutherans, though both of them profess faith in Christ, and are therefore called Christians, yet are not both of the same religion, because these acknowledge nothing but the Holy Scriptures to be the rule and foundation of their religion, those take in also traditions and the decrees of popes, and of these together make the rule of their religion; and thus the Christians of St. John (as they are called) and the Christians of Geneva are of different religions, because these also take only the Scriptures, and those I know not what traditions, for the rule of their religion.

This being settled, it follows, first, that heresy is a separation made in ecclesiastical communion between men of the same religion for some opinions no way contained in the rule itself; and, secondly, that amongst those who acknowledge nothing but the Holy Scriptures to be their rule of faith, heresy is a separation made in their Christian communion for opinions not contained in the express words of Scripture. Now this separation may be made in a twofold manner:

(1) When the greater part, or by the magistrate's patronage the stronger part, of the church separates itself from others by excluding them out of her communion because they will not profess their belief of certain opinions which are not the express words of the Scripture. For it is not the paucity of those that are separated, nor the authority of the magistrate, that can make any man guilty of heresy, but he only is a heretic who divides the church into parts, introduces names and marks of distinction, and voluntarily makes a separation because of such opinions.

(2) When anyone separates himself from the communion of a church because that church does not publicly profess some certain opinions which the Holy Scriptures do not expressly teach.

Both these are heretics because they err in fundamentals, and they err obstinately against knowledge; for when they have determined the Holy Scriptures to be the only foundation of faith, they nevertheless lay down certain propositions as fundamental which are not in the Scripture, and because others will not acknowledge these additional opinions of theirs, nor build upon them as if they were necessary and fundamental, they therefore make a separation in the church, either by withdrawing themselves from others or expelling the others from them. Nor does it signify anything for them to say that their confessions and symbols are agreeable to Scripture and to the analogy of faith; for if they be conceived in the express words of Scripture, there can be no question about them because those things are acknowledged by all Christians to be of divine inspiration, and therefore fundamental. But if they say that the articles which they require to be professed are consequences deduced from the Scripture, it is undoubtedly well done of them who believe and profess such things as seem unto them so agreeable to the rule of faith. But it would be very ill done to obtrude those things upon others unto whom they do not seem to be the indubitable doctrines of the Scripture; and to make a separation for such things as these, which neither are nor can be fundamental, is to become heretics; for I do not think there is any man arrived to that degree of madness as that he dare give out his consequences and interpretations of Scripture as divine inspirations, and compare the articles of faith that he has framed according to his own fancy with the authority of Scripture. I know there are some propositions so evidently agreeable to Scripture that nobody can deny them to be drawn from thence, but about those, therefore, there can be no difference. This only I say—that however clearly we may think this or the other doctrine to be deduced from Scripture, we ought not therefore to impose it upon others as a necessary article of faith because we believe it to be agreeable to the rule of faith, unless we would be content also that other doctrines should be imposed upon us in the same manner, and that we should be compelled to receive and profess all the different and contradictory opinions of Lutherans, Calvinists, Remonstrants, Anabaptists, and other sects which the contrivers of symbols, systems, and confessions are accustomed to deliver to their followers as genuine and necessary deductions from the Holy Scripture. I cannot but wonder at the extravagant arrogance of those men who think that they themselves can explain things necessary to salvation more clearly than the Holy Ghost, the eternal and infinite wisdom of God.

Thus much concerning heresy, which word in common use is applied only to the doctrinal part of religion. Let us now consider schism, which is a crime near akin to it; for both these words seem unto me to signify an ill-grounded separation in ecclesiastical communion made about things not necessary. But since use, which is the supreme law in matter of language, has determined that heresy relates to errors in faith, and schism to those in worship or discipline, we must consider them under that distinction.

Schism, then, for the same reasons that have already been alleged, is nothing else but a separation made in the communion of the church upon account of something in divine worship or ecclesiastical discipline that is not any necessary part of it. Now, nothing in worship or discipline can be necessary to Christian communion but what Christ our legislator, or the apostles by inspiration of the Holy Spirit, have commanded in express words.

In a word, he that denies not anything that the Holy Scriptures teach in express words, nor makes a separation upon occasion of anything that is not manifestly contained in the sacred text—however he may be nicknamed by any sect of Christians and declared by some or all of them to be utterly void of true Christianity—yet in deed and in truth this man cannot be either a heretic or schismatic.

These things might have been explained more largely and more advantageously, but it is enough to have hinted at them thus briefly to a person of your parts.

## QUESTIONS

1. Why does Locke appeal to "the genuine reason of mankind" in addition to "the Gospel of Jesus Christ" in making his argument for religious toleration? (59)

2. What does Locke mean when he says that there is "but one truth, one way to heaven"? What are the implications of this claim for the toleration of different religions under civil law? (62)

3. According to Locke, is it necessary for a voluntary organization to have the salvation of souls as its ultimate purpose in order to be considered a church?

4. When Locke claims, "The civil power is the same in every place," is he implying that the relation of civil power to religious institutions is the same in every place? (67)

5. According to Locke, what is "the magistrate's duty in the business of toleration"? (69)

6. What does Locke mean by "indifferent things," and why do they "wholly cease to be indifferent" when introduced into religion? (76)

7. Why is Locke willing to acknowledge that "God himself was the legislator" in the Jewish commonwealth? Is he being consistent with his claim that civil power is the same everywhere? (79–80)

8. Does Locke think that people have an obligation to use their "private judgment" to assess the legitimacy of laws enacted by the magistrate for the "public good"? (83–84)

9. According to Locke, should a religious institution that "will not own and teach the duty of tolerating all men in matters of mere religion" be censured just because of its teachings, or must it act on them to lose its right to be tolerated under civil law? (85)

10. If "those are not at all to be tolerated who deny the being of a God," what does Locke think should be the rights of atheists under civil law? (86)

11. If Locke is correct, that natural rights "are not forfeitable upon account of religion," does this mean that the duty to defend these rights takes precedence over religious obligations? (91)

## FOR FURTHER REFLECTION

1. Is Locke correct in saying that "the church itself is a thing absolutely separate and distinct from the commonwealth"?

2. Would Locke consider an "absolute theocracy," in which civil and religious affairs are not separated, a legitimate form of government?

3. Should toleration of different religions in society be mandated by civil law?

4. How should fundamental conflicts between civil laws and religious beliefs be resolved?

J oshua Reynolds (1723–1792), the premier portrait painter of eighteenth-century Britain, was responsible for the elevation of British portraiture within the visual arts and the elevation of painters themselves from craftsmen to artists. The son of a Devonshire schoolmaster, Reynolds was apprenticed at age seventeen to the well-known portraitist Thomas Hudson. After working independently for several years, he embarked on a trip to Italy with his lifelong friend, Commodore Augustus Keppel. Reynolds wrote to his benefactor Richard, first Baron of Edgecumbe: "I am now (thanks to your Lordship) at the height of my wishes, in the midst of the greatest works of art the world has produced." Reynolds's years in Italy were essential to his development as an artist; it is unlikely that he would have made such a profound impact on British art without his years studying in Rome, Bologna, and Venice. In Italy, Reynolds studied classical sculpture and Renaissance and Baroque painters such as Michelangelo, Raphael, and Tintoretto, filling several notebooks with observations and ideas.

English painting had long been stagnant. In 1685, art historian William Aglionby bemoaned England's failure to produce "an Historical Painter, Native of our own Soyl." The state of affairs had barely improved by the middle of the eighteenth century. The biographer John Sime summarized: "Before Reynolds appeared with his fresh flood of ideas, the English painters were content with conventional and laborious imitation of the great foreigners . . . They were unambitious; often of lowly social position; led Bohemian lives; they were generally poor, sometimes at starvation point." Within painting, portraiture, or, as it was known, "face painting," ranked very low in the hierarchy of genres.

Reynolds returned to London in 1752 to set up a studio, and his paintings quickly attracted attention. In a full-length portrait of his traveling companion, *Captain the Honourable Augustus Keppel* (1752–1753), Reynolds's powerful brushwork, dramatic use of light and shadow, and unusual green-based color palette were seen as exceptional, and the painting was much-praised upon its completion. Keppel appears before a stormy background in a pose ultimately derived from the Apollo Belvedere, his profile illuminated by an unseen sun. Reynolds appealed to his sitters' cosmopolitan tastes by painting them in a Renaissance- and Baroque-inspired style and to their sense of self-importance by posing them in the same attitudes as the gods and statesmen of classical antiquity. Within seven years, Reynolds had established himself as one of Britain's most popular and influential artists.

In 1768 Reynolds was named president of the newly formed Royal Academy of Arts, founded by King George III to promote the creation and appreciation of the visual arts and establish a standard of excellence for the training of artists. Reynolds remained president until his death in 1792. It was during his tenure that Reynolds composed his Discourses and delivered them annually at the Academy's awards ceremonies. The lectures began as didactic talks on the artist's craft but became broader and more philosophical in successive years as they were published and his audience grew. In them, Reynolds developed a theory of aesthetics that placed the visual arts at the level of poetry and the other liberal arts and, in turn, raised the painter's standing in society from craftsman to artist. According to Reynolds, art is a search for beauty, and true beauty is both "general and intellectual." The artist is constantly seeking an ideal and universal form against which standards of aesthetic value can be measured. While technical artistic ability is necessary, the search equally depends on the richly developed imagination of the artist. He encouraged artists to be well-read and to befriend poets and writers, clearly inspired by his own friendships with the writers Edmund Burke, Oliver Goldsmith, and Samuel Johnson.

In the Discourses Reynolds is a philosopher of art whose ideas are deeply informed by his many years of experience as a working artist. As the modern art critic Roger Fry put it, Reynolds "was one of the few writers who rarely talked nonsense about art."

The following selection was delivered as a lecture to the students of the Royal Academy upon the distribution of the prizes on December 10, 1776.

# Discourse Seven

Gentlemen,

I t has been my uniform endeavour, since I first addressed you from this place, to impress you strongly with one ruling idea. I wished you to be persuaded that success in your art depends almost entirely on your own industry; but the industry which I principally recommended is not the industry of the *hands*, but of the *mind*.

As our art is not a divine *gift*, so neither is it a mechanical *trade*. Its foundations are laid in solid science: and practice, though essential to perfection, can never attain that to which it aims, unless it works under the direction of principle.

Some writers upon art carry this point too far, and suppose that such a body of universal and profound learning is requisite that the very enumeration of its kinds is enough to frighten a beginner. Vitruvius, after going through the many accomplishments of nature, and the many acquirements of learning necessary to an architect, proceeds with great gravity to assert that he ought to be well skilled in the civil law, that he may not be cheated in the title of the ground he builds on. But without such exaggeration, we may go so far as to assert that a painter stands in need of more knowledge than is to be picked off his pallet, or collected by looking on his model, whether it be in life or in picture. He can never be a great artist who is grossly illiterate.

Every man whose business is description ought to be tolerably conversant with the poets, in some language or other, that he may imbibe a poetical spirit, and enlarge his stock of ideas. He ought to acquire an habit of comparing and digesting his notions. He ought not to be wholly unacquainted with that part of philosophy which gives an insight into human nature, and relates to the manners, characters, passions, and affections. He ought to know *something* concerning the mind, as well as *a great deal* concerning the body of man. For this purpose, it is not necessary that he should go into such a compass of reading as must, by distracting his attention, disqualify him for the practical part of his profession, and make him sink the performer in the critic. Reading, if it can be made the favourite recreation of his leisure hours, will improve and enlarge his mind without retarding his actual industry. What such partial and desultory reading cannot afford may be supplied by the conversation of learned and ingenious men, which is the best of all substitutes for those who have not the means or opportunities of deep study. There are many such men in this age; and they will be pleased with communicating their ideas to artists, when they see them curious and docile, if they are treated with that respect and deference which is so justly their due. Into such society, young artists, if they make it the point of their ambition, will by degrees be admitted. There, without formal teaching, they will insensibly come to feel and reason like those they live with, and find a rational and systematic taste imperceptibly formed in their minds, which they will know how to reduce to a standard, by applying general truth to their own purposes, better perhaps than those to whom they owed the original sentiment.

Of these studies, and this conversation, the desired and legitimate offspring is a power of distinguishing right from wrong; which power applied to works of art is denominated *Taste*. Let me then, without further introduction, enter upon an examination whether taste be so far beyond our reach as to be unattainable by care; or be so very vague and capricious that no care ought to be employed about it.

It has been the fate of arts to be enveloped in mysterious and incomprehensible language, as if it was thought necessary that even the terms should correspond to the idea entertained of the instability and uncertainty of the rules which they expressed.

To speak of genius and taste as in any way connected with reason or common sense would be, in the opinion of some towering talkers, to speak like a man who possessed neither, who had never felt that enthusiasm, or, to use their own inflated language, was never warmed by that Promethean fire which animates the canvas and vivifies the marble.

If, in order to be intelligible, I appear to degrade art by bringing her down from her visionary situation in the clouds, it is only to give her a more solid mansion upon the earth. It is necessary that at some time or other we should see things as they really are, and not impose on ourselves by that false magnitude with which objects appear when viewed indistinctly as through a mist.

We will allow a poet to express his meaning, when his meaning is not well known to himself, with a certain degree of obscurity, as it is one source of the sublime. But when, in plain prose, we gravely talk of courting the muse in shady bowers; waiting the call and inspiration of Genius, finding out where he inhabits, and where he is to be invoked with the greatest success; of attending to times and seasons when the imagination shoots with the greatest vigour, whether at the summer solstice or the vernal equinox; sagaciously observing how much the wild freedom and liberty of imagination is cramped by attention to established rules; and how this same imagination begins to grow dim in advanced age, smothered and deadened by too much judgment; when we talk such language, or entertain such sentiments as these, we generally rest contented with mere words, or at best entertain notions not only groundless, but pernicious.

If all this means what it is very possible was originally intended only to be meant, that in order to cultivate an art, a man secludes himself from the commerce of the world, and retires into the country at particular seasons; or that at one time of the year his body is in better health, and consequently his mind fitter for the business of hard thinking than at another time; or that the mind may be fatigued and grow confused by long and unremitted application; this I can understand. I can likewise believe that a man eminent when young for possessing poetical imagination may, from having taken another road, so neglect its cultivation as to show less of its powers in his latter life. But I am persuaded that scarce a poet is to be found, from Homer down to Dryden, who preserved a sound mind in a sound body, and continued practising his profession to the very last, whose latter works are not as replete with the fire of imagination as those which were produced in his more youthful days.

To understand literally these metaphors or ideas expressed in poetical language seems to be equally absurd as to conclude that because painters sometimes represent poets writing from the dictates of a little winged boy or genius, this same genius did really inform him in a whisper what he was to write, and that he is himself but a mere machine, unconscious of the operations of his own mind.

Opinions generally received and floating in the world, whether true or false, we naturally adopt and make our own; they may be considered as a kind of inheritance to which we succeed and are tenants for life, and which we leave to our posterity very nearly in the condition in which we received it, it not being much in any one man's power either to impair or improve it. The greatest part of these opinions, like current coin in its circulation, we are used to take without weighing or examining; but by this inevitable inattention many adulterated pieces are received, which, when we seriously estimate our wealth, we must throw away. So the collector of popular opinions, when he embodies his knowledge and forms a system, must separate those which are true from those which are only plausible. But it becomes more peculiarly a duty to the professors of art not to let any opinions relating to *that* art pass unexamined. The caution and circumspection required in such examination we shall presently have an opportunity of explaining.

Genius and taste, in their common acceptation, appear to be very nearly related; the difference lies only in this, that genius has super-added to it a habit of power of execution: or we may say that taste, when this power is added, changes its name, and is called genius. They both, in the popular opinion, pretend to an entire exemption from the restraint of rules. It is supposed that their powers are intuitive, that under the name of genius great works are produced, and under the name of taste an exact judgment is given, without our knowing why, and without our being under the least obligation to reason, precept, or experience.

One can scarce state these opinions without exposing their absurdity; yet they are constantly in the mouths of men, and particularly of artists. They who have thought seriously on this subject do not carry the point so far; yet I am persuaded that even among those few who may be called thinkers, the prevalent opinion allows less than it ought to the powers of reason, and considers the principles of taste, which give all their authority to the rules of art, as more fluctuating, and as having less solid foundations, than we shall find, upon examination, they really have.

The common saying, that *tastes are not to be disputed*, owes its influence, and its general reception, to the same error which leads us to imagine this faculty of too high an original to submit to the authority of an earthly tribunal. It likewise corresponds with the notions of those who consider it as a mere phantom of the imagination, so devoid of substance as to elude all criticism.

We often appear to differ in sentiments from each other merely from the inaccuracy of terms, as we are not obliged to speak always with critical exactness. Something of this too may arise from want of words in the language in which we speak to express the more nice discriminations which a deep investigation discovers. A great deal however of this difference vanishes when each opinion is tolerably explained and understood by constancy and precision in the use of terms.

We apply the term *Taste* to that act of the mind by which we like or dislike, whatever be the subject. Our judgment upon an airy nothing, a fancy which has no foundation, is called by the same name which we give to our determination concerning those truths which refer to the most general and most unalterable principles of human nature, to the works which are only to be produced by the greatest efforts of the human understanding. However inconvenient this may be, we are obliged to take words as we find them; all we can do is to distinguish the *things* to which they are applied.

We may let pass those things which are at once subjects of taste and sense, and which, having as much certainty as the senses themselves, give no occasion to enquiry or dispute. The natural appetite or taste of the human mind is for *Truth*, whether that truth results from the real agreement or equality of original ideas among themselves, from the agreement of the representation of any object with the thing represented, or from the correspondence of the several parts of any arrangement with each other. It is the very same taste which relishes a demonstration in geometry that is pleased with the resemblance of a picture to an original and touched with the harmony of music.

All these have unalterable and fixed foundations in nature, and are therefore equally investigated by reason, and known by study; some with more, some with less clearness, but all exactly in the same way. A picture that is unlike is false. Disproportionate ordonnance of parts is not right, because it cannot be true until it ceases to be a contradiction to assert that the parts have no relation to the whole. Colouring is true when it is naturally adapted to the eye, from brightness, from softness, from harmony, from resemblance; because these agree with their object, *nature*, and therefore are true, as true as mathematical demonstration, but known to be true only to those who study these things.

But beside *real*, there is also *apparent* truth, or opinion, or prejudice. With regard to real truth, when it is known, the taste which conforms to it is, and must be, uniform. With regard to the second sort of truth, which may be called truth upon sufferance, or truth by courtesy, it is not fixed, but variable. However, whilst these opinions and prejudices, on which it is founded, continue, they operate as truth; and the art, whose office it is to please the mind, as well as instruct it, must direct itself according to *opinion*, or it will not attain its end.

In proportion as these prejudices are known to be generally diffused, or long received, the taste which conforms to them approaches nearer to certainty, and to a sort of resemblance to real science, even where opinions are found to be no better than prejudices. And since they deserve, on account of their duration and extent, to be considered as really true, they become capable of no small degree of stability and determination by their permanent and uniform nature.

As these prejudices become more narrow, more local, more transitory, this secondary taste becomes more and more fantastical, recedes from real science, is less to be approved by reason, and less followed in practice, though in no case perhaps to be wholly neglected where it does not stand, as it sometimes does, in direct defiance of the most respectable opinions received amongst mankind.

Having laid down these positions, I shall proceed with less method, because less will serve, to explain and apply them.

We will take it for granted that reason is something invariable and fixed in the nature of things; and without endeavouring to go back to an account of first principles, which forever will elude our search, we will conclude that whatever goes under the name of taste which we can fairly bring under the dominion of reason must be considered as equally exempt from change. If therefore, in the course of this enquiry, we can show that there are rules for the conduct of the artist which are fixed and invariable, it follows of course that the art of the connoisseur, or, in other words, taste, has likewise invariable principles.

Of the judgment which we make on the works of art, and the preference that we give to one class of art over another, if a reason be demanded, the question is perhaps evaded by answering, I judge from my taste; but it does not follow that a better answer cannot be given, though, for common gazers, this may be sufficient. Every man is not obliged to investigate the causes of his approbation or dislike.

The arts would lie open forever to caprice and casualty if those who are to judge of their excellencies had no settled principles by which they are to regulate their decisions, and the merit or defect of performances were to be determined by unguided fancy. And indeed we may venture to assert that whatever speculative knowledge is necessary to the artist is equally and indispensably necessary to the connoisseur.

The first idea that occurs in the consideration of what is fixed in art, or in taste, is that presiding principle of which I have so frequently spoken in former discourses—the general idea of nature. The beginning, the middle, and the end of everything that is valuable in taste is comprised in the knowledge of what is truly nature; for whatever notions are not conformable to those of nature, or universal opinion, must be considered as more or less capricious.

My notion of nature comprehends not only the forms which nature produces, but also the nature and internal fabric and organization, as I may call it, of the human mind and imagination. The terms beauty, or nature, which are general ideas, are but different modes of expressing the same thing, whether we apply these terms to statues, poetry, or picture. Deformity is not nature, but an accidental deviation from her accustomed practice. This general idea therefore ought to be called Nature, and nothing else, correctly speaking, has a right to that name. But we are so far from speaking, in common conversation, with any such accuracy that, on the contrary, when we criticise Rembrandt and other Dutch painters, who introduced into their historical pictures exact representations of individual objects with all their imperfections, we say, though it is not in a good taste, yet it is nature.

This misapplication of terms must be very often perplexing to the young student. Is not art, he may say, an imitation of nature? Must he not therefore who imitates her with the greatest fidelity be the best artist? By this mode of reasoning Rembrandt has a higher place than Raphael. But a very little reflection will serve to show us that these particularities cannot be nature: For how can that be the nature of man in which no two individuals are the same?

It plainly appears that as a work is conducted under the influence of general ideas, or partial, it is principally to be considered as the effect of a good or a bad taste.

As beauty therefore does not consist in taking what lies immediately before you, so neither, in our pursuit of taste, are those opinions which we first received and adopted the best choice, or the most natural to the mind and imagination. In the infancy of our knowledge we seize with greediness the good that is within our reach; it is by after-consideration, and in consequence of discipline, that we refuse the present for a greater good at a distance. The nobility or elevation of all arts, like the excellency of virtue itself, consists in adopting this enlarged and comprehensive idea; and all criticism built upon the more confined view of what is natural may properly be called *shallow* criticism, rather than false: its defect is that the truth is not sufficiently extensive.

It has sometimes happened that some of the greatest men in our art have been betrayed into errors by this confined mode of reasoning. Poussin, who, upon the whole, may be produced as an artist strictly attentive to the most enlarged and extensive ideas of nature, from not having settled principles on this point has in one instance at least, I think, deserted truth for prejudice. He is said to have vindicated the conduct of Giulio Romano for his inattention to the masses of light and shade, or grouping the figures in *The Battle of Constantine* as if designedly neglected, the better to correspond with the hurry and confusion of a battle. Poussin's own conduct in many of his pictures makes us more easily give credit to this report. That it was too much his own practice *The Sacrifice to Silenus*, and *The Triumph of Bacchus and Ariadne*, may be produced as instances; but this principle is still more apparent, and may be said to be even more ostentatiously displayed, in his *Persue and Medusa's Head*.

This is undoubtedly a subject of great bustle and tumult, and that the first effect of the picture may correspond to the subject, every principle of composition is violated; there is no principal figure, no principal light, no groups; everything is dispersed, and in such a state of confusion that the eye finds no repose anywhere. In consequence of the forbidding appearance, I remember turning from it with disgust, and should not have looked a second time, if I had not been called back to a closer inspection. I then indeed found what we may expect always to find in the works of Poussin, correct drawing, forcible expression, and just character; in short all the excellencies which so much distinguish the works of this learned painter.

This conduct of Poussin I hold to be entirely improper to imitate. A picture should please at first sight, and appear to invite the spectator's attention: if on the contrary the general effect offends the eye, a second view is not always sought, whatever more substantial and intrinsic merit it may possess.

Perhaps no apology ought to be received for offences committed against the vehicle (whether it be the organ of seeing, or of hearing) by which our pleasures are conveyed to the mind. We must take care that the eye be not perplexed and distracted by a confusion of equal parts, or equal lights, or offended by an unharmonious mixture of colours, as we should guard against offending the ear by unharmonious sounds. We may venture to be more confident of the truth of this observation since we find that Shakespeare, on a parallel occasion, has made Hamlet recommend to the players a precept of the same kind—never to offend the ear by harsh sounds: *In the very torrent, tempest, and whirlwind of your passion,* says he, *you must acquire and beget a temperance that may give it smoothness.* And yet, at the same time, he very justly observes, *The end of playing, both at the first, and now, was and is, to hold, as 'twere, the mirrour up to nature.* No one can deny that violent passions will naturally emit harsh and disagreeable tones: yet this great poet and critic thought that this imitation of nature would cost too much, if purchased at the expence of disagreeable sensations, or, as he expresses it, of *splitting the ear.* The poet and actor, as well as the painter of genius who is well acquainted with all the variety and sources of pleasure in the mind and imagination, has little regard or attention to common nature, or creeping after common sense. By overleaping those narrow bounds, he more effectually seizes the whole mind, and more powerfully accomplishes his purpose. This success is ignorantly imagined to proceed from inattention to all rules, and a defiance of reason and judgment; whereas it is in truth acting according to the best rules and the justest reason.

He who thinks nature, in the narrow sense of the word, is alone to be followed will produce but a scanty entertainment for the imagination: everything is to be done with which it is natural for the mind to be pleased, whether it proceeds from simplicity or variety, uniformity or irregularity; whether the scenes are familiar or exotic, rude and wild or enriched and cultivated; for it is natural for the mind to be pleased with all these in their turn. In short, whatever pleases has in it what is analogous to the mind, and is therefore, in the highest and best sense of the word, natural.

It is the sense of nature or truth which ought more particularly to be cultivated by the professors of art; and it may be observed that many wise and learned men, who have accustomed their minds to admit nothing for truth but what can be proved by mathematical demonstration, have seldom any relish for those arts which address themselves to the fancy, the rectitude and truth of which is known by another kind of proof: and we may add that the acquisition of this knowledge requires as much circumspection and sagacity as is necessary to attain those truths which are more capable of demonstration. Reason must ultimately determine our choice on every occasion; but this reason may still be exerted ineffectually by applying to taste principles which, though right as far as they go, yet do not reach the object. No man, for instance, can deny that it seems at first view very reasonable that a statue which is to carry down to posterity the resemblance of an individual should be dressed in the fashion of the times, in the dress which he himself wore: this would certainly be true if the dress were part of the man; but after a time, the dress is only an amusement for an antiquarian; and if it obstructs the general design of the piece, it is to be disregarded by the artist. Common sense must here give way to a higher sense. In the naked form, and in the disposition of the drapery, the difference between one artist and another is principally seen. But if he is compelled to exhibit the modern dress, the naked form is entirely hid, and the drapery is already disposed by the skill of the tailor. Were a Phidias to obey such absurd commands, he would please no more than an ordinary sculptor, since, in the inferior parts of every art, the learned and the ignorant are nearly upon a level.

These were probably among the reasons that induced the sculptor of that wonderful figure of Laocoon to exhibit him naked, notwithstanding he was surprised in the act of sacrificing to Apollo, and consequently ought to have been shown in his sacerdotal habits, if those greater reasons had not preponderated. Art is not yet in so high estimation with us as to obtain so great a sacrifice as the ancients made, especially the Grecians, who suffered themselves to be represented naked, whether they were generals, lawgivers, or kings.

Under this head of balancing and choosing the greater reason, or of two evils taking the least, we may consider the conduct of Rubens in the Luxembourg gallery, where he has mixed allegorical figures with representations of real personages, which must be acknowledged to be a fault; yet, if the Artist considered himself as engaged to furnish this gallery with a rich, various, and splendid ornament, this could not be done, at least in an equal degree, without peopling the air and water with these allegorical figures: he therefore accomplished all that he purposed. In this case all lesser considerations, which tend to obstruct the great end of the work, must yield and give way.

The variety which portraits and modern dresses mixed with allegorical figures produce is not to be slightly given up upon a punctilio of reason when that reason deprives the art in a manner of its very existence. It must always be remembered that the business of a great Painter is to produce a great picture; he must therefore take especial care not to be cajoled by specious arguments out of his materials.

What has been so often said to the disadvantage of allegorical poetry—that it is tedious, and uninteresting—cannot with the same propriety be applied to painting, where the interest is of a different kind. If allegorical painting produces a greater variety of ideal beauty, a richer, a more various and delightful composition, and gives to the artist a greater opportunity of exhibiting his skill, all the interest he wishes for is accomplished: such a picture not only attracts, but fixes the attention.

If it be objected that Rubens judged ill at first in thinking it necessary to make his work so very ornamental, this puts the question upon new ground. It was his peculiar style; he could paint in no other; and he was selected for that work, probably, because it was his style. Nobody will dispute but some of the best of the Roman or Bolognan schools would have produced a more learned and more noble work.

This leads us to another important province of taste, that of weighing the value of the different classes of the art, and of estimating them accordingly.

All arts have means within them of applying themselves with success both to the intellectual and sensitive part of our natures. It cannot be disputed, supposing both these means put in practice with equal abilities, to which we ought to give the preference—to him who represents the heroic arts and more dignified passions of man, or to him who, by the help of meretricious ornaments, however elegant and graceful, captivates the sensuality, as it may be called, of our taste. Thus the Roman and Bolognan schools are reasonably preferred to the Venetian, Flemish, or Dutch schools, as they address themselves to our best and noblest faculties.

Well-turned periods in eloquence, or harmony of numbers in poetry, which are in those arts what colouring is in painting, however highly we may esteem them, can never be considered as of equal importance with the art of unfolding truths that are useful to mankind, and which make us better or wiser. Nor can those works which remind us of the poverty and meanness of our nature be considered as of equal rank with what excites ideas of grandeur, or raises and dignifies humanity, or, in the words of a late poet, which makes the beholder learn to venerate himself as man.[1]

It is reason and good sense therefore which ranks and estimates every art, and every part of that art, according to its importance, from the painter of animated down to inanimated nature. We will not allow a man who shall prefer the inferior style to say it is his taste; taste here has nothing, or at least ought to have nothing to do with the question. He wants not taste, but sense, and soundness of judgment.

Indeed perfection in an inferior style may be reasonably preferred to mediocrity in the highest walks of art. A landscape of Claude Lorrain may be preferred to a history by Luca Giordano; but hence appears the necessity of the connoisseur's knowing in what consists the excellency of each class, in order to judge how near it approaches to perfection.

---

1. [Dr. Goldsmith.]

Even in works of the same kind, as in history painting, which is composed of various parts, excellence of an inferior species, carried to a very high degree, will make a work very valuable, and in some measure compensate for the absence of the higher kinds of merit. It is the duty of the connoisseur to know and esteem, as much as it may deserve, every part of painting: he will not then think even Bassano unworthy of his notice, who, though totally devoid of expression, sense, grace, or elegance, may be esteemed on account of his admirable taste of colours, which, in his best works, are little inferior to those of Titian.

Since I have mentioned Bassano, we must do him likewise the justice to acknowledge that though he did not aspire to the dignity of expressing the characters and passions of men, yet, with respect to facility and truth in his manner of touching animals of all kinds, and giving them what painters call *their character*, few have ever excelled him.

To Bassano we may add Paolo Veronese and Tintoretto for their entire inattention to what is justly thought the most essential part of our art, the expression of the passions. Notwithstanding these glaring deficiencies, we justly esteem their works; but it must be remembered that they do not please from those defects, but from their great excellencies of another kind, and in spite of such transgressions. These excellencies too, as far as they go, are founded in the truth of *general* nature: they tell the *truth*, though *not the whole truth*.

By these considerations, which can never be too frequently impressed, may be obviated two errors which I observed to have been, formerly at least, the most prevalent, and to be most injurious to artists: that of thinking taste and genius to have nothing to do with reason, and that of taking particular living objects for nature.

I shall now say something on that part of *taste* which, as I have hinted to you before, does not belong so much to the external form of things, but is addressed to the mind, and depends on its original frame, or, to use the expression, the organization of the soul; I mean the imagination and the passions. The principles of these are as invariable as the former, and are to be known and reasoned upon in the same manner, by an appeal to common sense deciding upon the common feelings of mankind. This sense, and these feelings, appear to me of equal authority, and equally conclusive. Now this appeal implies a general uniformity and agreement in the minds of men. It would be else an idle and vain endeavour to establish rules of art; it would be pursuing a phantom to attempt to move affections with which we were entirely unacquainted. We have no reason to suspect there is a greater difference between our minds than between our forms, of which, though there are no two alike, yet there is a general similitude that goes through the whole race of mankind; and those who have cultivated their taste can distinguish what is beautiful or deformed, or, in other words, what agrees with or deviates from the general idea of nature, in one case as well as in the other.

The internal fabric of our minds, as well as the external form of our bodies, being nearly uniform, it seems then to follow of course, that as the imagination is incapable of producing anything originally of itself, and can only vary and combine those ideas with which it is furnished by means of the senses, there will be necessarily an agreement in the imaginations as in the senses of men. There being this agreement, it follows that in all cases, in our lightest amusements, as well as in our most serious actions and engagements of life, we must regulate our affections of every kind by that of others. The well-disciplined mind acknowledges this authority, and submits its own opinion to the public voice. It is from knowing what are the general feelings and passions of mankind that we acquire a true idea of what imagination is, though it appears as if we had nothing to do but to consult our own particular sensations, and these were sufficient to ensure us from all error and mistake.

A knowledge of the disposition and character of the human mind can be acquired only by experience: a great deal will be learned, I admit, by a habit of examining what passes in our bosoms, what are our own motives of action, and of what kind of sentiments we are conscious on any occasion. We may suppose an uniformity, and conclude that the same effect will be produced by the same cause in the minds of others. This examination will contribute to suggest to us matters of enquiry; but we can never be sure that our own sensations are true and right till they are confirmed by more extensive observation. One man opposing another determines nothing; but a general union of minds, like a general combination of the forces of all mankind, makes a strength that is irresistible. In fact, as he who does not know himself does not know others, so it may be said with equal truth that he who does not know others, knows himself but very imperfectly.

A man who thinks he is guarding himself against prejudices by resisting the authority of others leaves open every avenue to singularity, vanity, self-conceit, obstinacy, and many other vices, all tending to warp the judgment, and prevent the natural operation of his faculties. This submission to others is a deference which we owe, and indeed are forced involuntarily to pay. In fact, we never are satisfied with our opinions, whatever we may pretend, till they are ratified and confirmed by the suffrages of the rest of mankind. We dispute and wrangle forever; we endeavour to get men to come to us when we do not go to them.

He therefore who is acquainted with the works which have pleased different ages and different countries, and has formed his opinion on them, has more materials, and more means of knowing what is analogous to the mind of man, than he who is conversant only with the works of his own age or country. What has pleased, and continues to please, is likely to please again: hence are derived the rules of art, and on this immovable foundation they must ever stand.

This search and study of the history of the mind ought not to be confined to one art only. It is by the analogy that one art bears to another that many things are ascertained which either were but faintly seen, or, perhaps, would not have been discovered at all, if the inventor had not received the first hints from the practices of a sister art on a similar occasion. The frequent allusions which every man who treats of any art is obliged to make to others in order to illustrate and confirm his principles sufficiently show their near connection and inseparable relation.

All arts having the same general end, which is to please, and addressing themselves to the same faculties through the medium of the senses, it follows that their rules and principles must have as great affinity as the different materials and the different organs or vehicles by which they pass to the mind will permit them to retain.

We may therefore conclude that the real substance, as it may be called, of what goes under the name of taste is fixed and established in the nature of things; that there are certain and regular causes by which the imagination and passions of men are affected; and that the knowledge of these causes is acquired by a laborious and diligent investigation of nature, and by the same slow progress as wisdom or knowledge of every kind, however instantaneous its operations may appear when thus acquired.

It has been often observed that the good and virtuous man alone can acquire this true or just relish even of works of art. This opinion will not appear entirely without foundation when we consider that the same habit of mind which is acquired by our search after truth in the more serious duties of life is only transferred to the pursuit of lighter amusements. The same disposition, the same desire to find something steady, substantial, and durable, on which the mind can lean as it were, and rest with safety, actuates us in both cases. The subject only is changed. We pursue the same method in our search after the idea of beauty and perfection in each: of virtue, by looking forwards beyond ourselves to society, and to the whole; of arts, by extending our views in the same manner to all ages and all times.

Every art, like our own, has in its composition fluctuating as well as fixed principles. It is an attentive enquiry into their difference that will enable us to determine how far we are influenced by custom and habit, and what is fixed in the nature of things.

To distinguish how much has solid foundation, we may have recourse to the same proof by which some hold that wit ought to be tried: whether it preserves itself when translated. That wit is false which can subsist only in one language; and that picture which pleases only one age or one nation owes its reception to some local or accidental association of ideas.

We may apply this to every custom and habit of life. Thus the general principles of urbanity, politeness, or civility have been ever the same in all nations; but the mode in which they are dressed is continually varying. The general idea of showing respect is by making yourself less; but the manner, whether by bowing the body, kneeling, prostration, pulling off the upper part of our dress, or taking away the lower, is a matter of custom.

Thus in regard to ornaments, it would be unjust to conclude that because they were at first arbitrarily contrived they are therefore undeserving of our attention; on the contrary, he who neglects the cultivation of those ornaments acts contrary to nature and reason. As life would be imperfect without its highest ornaments, the Arts, so these arts themselves would be imperfect without *their* ornaments. Though we by no means ought to rank these with positive and substantial beauties, yet it must be allowed that a knowledge of both is essentially requisite towards forming a complete, whole, and perfect taste. It is in reality from the ornaments that arts receive their peculiar character and complexion; we may add that in them we find the characteristical mark of a national taste, as by throwing up a feather in the air we know which way the wind blows better than by a more heavy matter.

The striking distinction between the works of the Roman, Bolognan, and Venetian schools consists more in that general effect which is produced by colours than in the more profound excellencies of the art; at least it is from thence that each is distinguished and known at first sight. Thus it is the ornaments, rather than the proportions of architecture, which at the first glance distinguish the different orders from each other; the Doric is known by its triglyphs, the Ionic by its volutes, and the Corinthian by its acanthus.

What distinguishes oratory from a cold narration is a more liberal, though chaste, use of those ornaments which go under the name of figurative and metaphorical expressions; and poetry distinguishes itself from oratory by words and expressions still more ardent and glowing. What separates and distinguishes poetry is more particularly the ornament of *verse*: it is this which gives it its character, and is an essential without which it cannot exist. Custom has appropriated different metre to different kinds of composition, in which the world is not perfectly agreed. In England the dispute is not yet settled which is to be preferred, rhyme or blank verse. But however we disagree about what these metrical ornaments shall be, that some metre is essentially necessary is universally acknowledged.

In poetry or eloquence, to determine how far figurative or metaphorical language may proceed, and when it begins to be affectation or beside the truth, must be determined by taste, though this taste, we must never forget, is regulated and formed by the presiding feelings of mankind, by those works which have approved themselves to all times and all persons. Thus, though eloquence has undoubtedly an essential and intrinsic excellence, and immoveable principles common to all languages, founded in the nature of our passions and affections, yet it has its ornaments and modes of address, which are merely arbitrary. What is approved in the Eastern nations as grand and majestic would be considered by the Greeks and Romans as turgid and inflated; and they, in return, would be thought by the Orientals to express themselves in a cold and insipid manner.

We may add likewise to the credit of ornaments that it is by their means that art itself accomplishes its purpose. Fresnoy calls colouring, which is one of the chief ornaments of painting, *lena sororis*,[2] that which procures lovers and admirers to the more valuable excellencies of the art.

It appears to be the same right turn of mind which enables a man to acquire the *truth*, or the just idea of what is right, in the ornaments as in the more stable principles of art. It has still the same centre of perfection, though it is the centre of a smaller circle.

To illustrate this by the fashion of dress, in which there is allowed to be a good or bad taste. The component parts of dress are continually changing from great to little, from short to long; but the general form still remains: it is still the same general dress which is comparatively fixed, though on a very slender foundation; but it is on this which fashion must rest. He who invents with the most success, or dresses in the best taste, would probably, from the same sagacity employed to greater purposes, have discovered equal skill, or have formed the same correct taste, in the highest labours of art.

I have mentioned taste in dress, which is certainly one of the lowest subjects to which this word is applied; yet, as I have before observed, there is a right even here, however narrow its foundation respecting the fashion of any particular nation. But we have still more slender means of determining to which of the different customs of different ages or countries we ought to give the preference, since they seem to be all equally removed from nature. If an European, when he has cut off his beard, and put false hair on his head, or bound up his own natural hair in regular hard knots, as unlike nature as he can possibly make it, and after having rendered them immoveable by the help of the fat of hogs, has covered the whole with flour, laid on by a machine with the utmost regularity; if, when thus attired he issues forth, and meets a Cherokee Indian, who has bestowed as much time at his toilet, and laid on with equal care and attention his yellow and red ocher on particular parts of his forehead or cheeks, as

---

2. [Brothel-keeper.]

he judges most becoming, whoever of these two despises the other for this attention to the fashion of his country, whichever first feels himself provoked to laugh, is the barbarian.

All these fashions are very innocent, neither worth disquisition, nor any endeavour to alter them, as the change would, in all probability, be equally distant from nature. The only circumstances against which indignation may reasonably be moved is where the operation is painful or destructive of health, such as some of the practices at Otaheite,[3] and the straight lacing of the English ladies; of the last of which practices, how destructive it must be to health and long life the professor of anatomy took an opportunity of proving a few days since in this Academy.

It is in dress as in things of greater consequence. Fashions originate from those only who have the high and powerful advantages of rank, birth, and fortune. Many of the ornaments of art, those at least for which no reason can be given, are transmitted to us, are adopted, and acquire their consequence from the company in which we have been used to see them. As Greece and Rome are the fountains from whence have flowed all kinds of excellence, to that veneration which they have a right to claim for the pleasure and knowledge which they have afforded us we voluntarily add our approbation of every ornament and every custom that belonged to them, even to the fashion of their dress. For it may be observed that, not satisfied with them in their own place, we make no difficulty of dressing statues of modern heroes or senators in the fashion of the Roman armour or peaceful robe; we go so far as hardly to bear a statue in any other drapery.

The figures of the great men of those nations have come down to us in sculpture. In sculpture remain almost all the excellent specimens of ancient art. We have so far associated personal dignity to the persons thus represented, and the truth of art to their manner of representation, that it is not in our power any longer to separate them. This is not so in painting; because having no excellent ancient portraits, that connexion was never formed. Indeed we could no more venture to paint a general officer in a Roman military habit than we could make a statue in the present uniform. But since we have no ancient portraits, to show how ready we are to adopt those kind of prejudices, we make the best authority among the moderns serve the same purpose. The great variety of excellent portraits with which Vandyke has enriched this nation we are not content to admire for their real excellence, but extend our approbation even to the dress which happened to be the fashion of that age. We all very well remember how common it was a few years ago for portraits to be drawn in this fantastic dress, and this custom is not yet entirely laid aside. By this means it must

---

3. [Tahiti.]

be acknowledged very ordinary pictures acquired something of the air and effect of the works of Vandyke, and appeared therefore at first sight to be better pictures than they really were; they appeared so, however, to those only who had the means of making this association; and when made, it was irresistible. But this association is nature, and refers to that secondary truth that comes from conformity to general prejudice and opinion; it is therefore not merely fantastical. Besides the prejudice which we have in favour of ancient dresses, there may be likewise other reasons for the effect which they produce; among which we may justly rank the simplicity of them, consisting of little more than one single piece of drapery, without those whimsical, capricious forms by which all other dresses are embarrassed.

Thus, though it is from the prejudice we have in favour of the ancients, who have taught us architecture, that we have adopted likewise their ornaments, and though we are satisfied that neither nature nor reason are the foundation of those beauties which we imagine we see in that art, yet if anyone, persuaded of this truth, should therefore invent new orders of equal beauty, which we will suppose to be possible, they would not please; nor ought he to complain, since the old has that great advantage of having custom and prejudice on its side. In this case we leave what has every prejudice in its favour to take that which will have no advantage over what we have left but novelty, which soon destroys itself, and at any rate is but a weak antagonist against custom.

Ancient ornaments, having the right of possession, ought not to be removed, unless to make room for that which not only has higher pretensions, but such pretensions as will balance the evil and confusion which innovation always brings with it.

To this we may add that even the durability of the materials will often contribute to give a superiority to one object over another. Ornaments in buildings, with which taste is principally concerned, are composed of materials which last longer than those of which dress is composed; the former therefore make higher pretensions to our favour and prejudice.

Some attention is surely due to what we can no more get rid of than we can go out of ourselves. We are creatures of prejudice; we neither can nor ought to eradicate it; we must only regulate it by reason, which kind of regulation is indeed little more than obliging the lesser, the local and temporary prejudices, to give way to those which are more durable and lasting.

He therefore who in his practice of portrait-painting wishes to dignify his subject, which we will suppose to be a lady, will not paint her in the modern dress, the familiarity of which alone is sufficient to destroy all dignity. He takes care that his work shall correspond to those ideas and that imagination which he knows will regulate the judgment of others;

and therefore dresses his figure something with the general air of the antique for the sake of dignity, and preserves something of the modern for the sake of likeness. By this conduct his works correspond with those prejudices which we have in favour of what we continually see; and the relish of the antique simplicity corresponds with what we may call the more learned and scientific prejudice.

There was a statue made not long since of Voltaire, which the sculptor, not having that respect for the prejudices of mankind which he ought to have had, made entirely naked, and as meagre and emaciated as the original is said to be. The consequence was what might have been expected; it remained in the sculptor's shop, though it was intended as a public ornament and a public honour to Voltaire, for it was procured at the expence of his contemporary wits and admirers.

Whoever would reform a nation, supposing a bad taste to prevail in it, will not accomplish his purpose by going directly against the stream of their prejudices. Men's minds must be prepared to receive what is new to them. Reformation is a work of time. A national taste, however wrong it may be, cannot be totally changed at once; we must yield a little to the prepossession which has taken hold on the mind, and we may then bring people to adopt what would offend them if endeavoured to be introduced by violence. When Battista Franco was employed, in conjunction with Titian, Paolo Veronese, and Tintoretto, to adorn the library of St. Mark, his work, Vasari says, gave less satisfaction than any of the others: the dry manner of the Roman school was very ill calculated to please eyes that had been accustomed to the luxuriancy, splendour, and richness of Venetian colouring. Had the Romans been the judges of this work, probably the determination would have been just contrary; for in the more noble parts of the art, Battista Franco was perhaps not inferior to any of his rivals.

Gentlemen,

It has been the main scope and principal end of this discourse to demonstrate the reality of a standard in taste, as well as in corporeal beauty; that a false or depraved taste is a thing as well known, as easily discovered, as any thing that is deformed, misshapen, or wrong in our form or outward make; and that this knowledge is derived from the uniformity of sentiments among mankind, from whence proceeds the knowledge of what are the general habits of nature, the result of which is an idea of perfect beauty.

If what has been advanced be true, that beside this beauty or truth, which is formed on the uniform, eternal, and immutable laws of nature, and which of necessity can be but *one*; that beside this one immutable verity there are likewise what we have called apparent or secondary truths, proceeding from local and temporary prejudices, fancies, fashions, or accidental connexion of ideas; if it appears that these last have still their foundation, however slender, in the original fabric of our minds; it follows that all these truths or beauties deserve and require the attention of the artist, in proportion to their stability or duration, or as their influence is more or less extensive. And let me add that as they ought not to pass their just bounds, so neither do they, in a well-regulated taste, at all prevent or weaken the influence of those general principles which alone can give to art its true and permanent dignity.

To form this just taste is undoubtedly in your own power, but it is to reason and philosophy that you must have recourse; from them you must borrow the balance by which is to be weighed and estimated the value of every pretension that intrudes itself on your notice.

The general objection which is made to the introduction of philosophy into the regions of taste is that it checks and restrains the flights of the imagination, and gives that timidity which an over-carefulness not to err or act contrary to reason is likely to produce. It is not so. Fear is neither reason nor philosophy. The true spirit of philosophy, by giving knowledge, gives a manly confidence, and substitutes rational firmness in the place of vain presumption. A man of real taste is always a man of judgment in other respects; and those inventions which either disdain or shrink from reason are generally, I fear, more like the dreams of a distempered brain than the exalted enthusiasm of a sound and true genius. In the midst of the highest flights of fancy or imagination, reason ought to preside from first to last, though I admit her more powerful operation is upon reflection.

Let me add that some of the greatest names of antiquity, and those who have most distinguished themselves in works of genius and imagination, were equally eminent for their critical skill. Plato, Aristotle, Cicero, and Horace, and, among the moderns, Boileau, Corneille, Pope, and Dryden, are at least instances of genius not being destroyed by attention or subjection to rules and science. I should hope therefore that the natural consequence of what has been said would be to excite in you a desire of knowing the principles and conduct of the great masters of our art, and respect and veneration for them when known.

## QUESTIONS

1. What does Reynolds mean when he says that in art, practice must work "under the direction of principle"? How is "principle" different from the rules and techniques that direct the artist's skill in using materials? (99)

2. Why does Reynolds think the common saying that "*tastes are not to be disputed*" is erroneous? (102)

3. How do the three examples Reynolds gives explain what he means when he makes the general statement, "The natural appetite or taste of the human mind is for *Truth*"? (102)

4. Having posited the importance of truth in art, why does Reynolds go on to say that "the art, whose office it is to please the mind, as well as instruct it, must direct itself according to *opinion*, or it will not attain its end"? When does he think that opinions should ever be considered "really true"? (103)

5. For Reynolds, what is the "general idea of nature"? (104) How is good or bad taste related to the way in which a work of art imitates nature?

6. When Reynolds says, "A picture should please at first sight," in what sense is he using the word "please"? (105) What does he mean when he goes on to say that "whatever pleases has in it what is analogous to the mind, and is therefore, in the highest and best sense of the word, natural"? (106)

7. Why does Reynolds think that the study of the "history of the mind" is so important in deriving the rules of art? (111)

8. What does Reynolds mean when he says that it is by means of ornaments "that art itself accomplishes its purpose"? (113)

9. How does Reynolds think we should "regulate" prejudice by reason? What does he think is the relation of prejudice to good taste? (115)

10. What is the "idea of perfect beauty" that Reynolds describes as resulting from knowledge of "the general habits of nature"? (116)

11. Does Reynolds think that it is possible for a person to form "just taste" without being a philosopher? (117)

## FOR FURTHER REFLECTION

1. Is it true, as Reynolds claims, that "the imagination is incapable of producing anything originally of itself, and can only vary and combine those ideas with which it is furnished by means of the senses"?

2. Do you agree with Reynolds that all arts have "the same general end, which is to please"?

3. Does Reynolds's view of the standards of taste in art allow for enough innovation? Would he ever admit that art can be revolutionary?

4. In this discourse, has Reynolds successfully fulfilled his purpose of demonstrating "the reality of a standard of taste"?

It is uncertain whether Edward FitzGerald and Robert Browning ever met, but the feud between the two poets was notorious even in their own day. Their antagonism found expression in their writings, including Robert Browning's scathing sonnet "To Edward FitzGerald," written in response to disparaging remarks about Elizabeth Barrett Browning in FitzGerald's posthumously published diaries. The most notable site of their conflict, however, is the contrast between FitzGerald's "The Rubáiyát of Omar Khayyám" (1859) and Browning's "Rabbi Ben Ezra" (1864).

Edward FitzGerald (1809–1883) was born into one of the wealthiest families in Great Britain, which allowed him to live independently for his entire life. After studying at Cambridge and traveling for a short time, FitzGerald retired to his manor house in Suffolk, from which he corresponded with many important writers, including Alfred, Lord Tennyson; William Makepeace Thackeray; and Thomas Carlyle. Toiling over translations of the dramas of Pedro Calderón de la Barca and his own nonfiction work *Euphranor: A Dialogue on Youth* (1851) in relative obscurity, FitzGerald did not experience critical or popular success until his compilation and translation of the poetry of the Persian mathematician and astronomer, Omar Khayyám (1048–1131). In 1856 FitzGerald had been sent the manuscript of a collection of quatrains (*rubáiyát*) by a young scholar who had been teaching FitzGerald Persian and had come across Khayyám's work in the library at Oxford. Each of Khayyám's quatrains was a distinct and complete poem; it was FitzGerald who combined a selection of them to create a continuous work expressing his own outlook on human existence, inserting many of his own images and adapting the quatrains freely. Originally published in 1859 as a "little anonymous brownpaper-covered pamphlet," as critic Edmund Gosse called it, the work was promoted by the poet and painter Dante Gabriel Rossetti. At the height of its popularity, "The Rubáiyát of Omar Khayyám was "chatted about, written about, translated, illustrated, dined over, poetized about, to an extent which would scarcely be excessive if Omar were Homer," remarked the poet Andrew Lang.

FitzGerald continued to revise "The Rubáiyát," eventually publishing five editions, the fifth of which appears here.

Robert Browning (1812–1889) was raised in Camberwell, a middle-class London neighborhood. His father worked for the Bank of England and his mother was a devout Congregationalist, which prohibited Browning from attending Oxford or Cambridge—at the time admitting only Anglican students. After a brief stint at the University of London and an unsuccessful decade writing, mostly for the stage, Browning married the poet Elizabeth Barrett in 1846. The couple and their son lived in Italy until Elizabeth's death in 1861. Heartbroken, he and his son returned to London, where Browning became an active part of the literary scene and produced many of his most noted works. Many of his poems took the form of dramatic monologues, in which he created a vast gallery of characters, some original inventions, some based on historical figures, that allowed him to explore the full range of human actions and motivations. Among these are the collection *Dramatis Personae* (1864) and the long verse novel *The Ring and the Book* (1868–1869). The success of these works made Browning one of the most celebrated literary figures of his time, as evidenced by the creation of the Browning Society in London in 1881.

Browning's monologue "Rabbi Ben Ezra" was published in *Dramatis Personae* and was widely seen as a response to FitzGerald's "Rubáiyát." Browning employs a fictional recreation of the philosopher, astronomer, and poet Rabbi Abraham ben Meir ibn Ezra (c. 1092–1167), an almost exact contemporary of Omar Khayyám. The historical Ibn Ezra spent his early years in Spain, but went on to a life of nomadic wanderings in Europe, becoming a renowned scholar. While Browning adopts his persona as a venerable sage, he includes little of the thinker's actual beliefs and writings.

"The Rubáiyát of Omar Khayyám" and "Rabbi Ben Ezra" represent opposing views of life from two poets who differed in their upbringing, education, religious beliefs, and status in the literary world. They raise searching questions regarding faith and doubt about the meaning of human existence, as well as the relationships between sensual pleasure, suffering, and mortality.

EDWARD FITZGERALD

# The Rubáiyát of Omar Khayyám

## 1

Wake! For the Sun, who scatter'd into flight
The Stars before him from the Field of Night,
    Drives Night along with them from Heav'n, and strikes
The Sultán's Turret with a Shaft of Light.

## 2

Before the phantom of False morning died,
Methought a Voice within the Tavern cried,
    "When all the Temple is prepared within,
Why nods the drowsy Worshipper outside?"

## 3

And, as the Cock crew, those who stood before
The Tavern shouted—"Open then the Door!
    You know how little while we have to stay,
And, once departed, may return no more."

## 4

Now the New Year reviving old Desires,
The thoughtful Soul to Solitude retires,
   Where the WHITE HAND OF MOSES on the Bough
Puts out, and Jesus from the Ground suspires.

## 5

Iram indeed is gone with all his Rose,
And Jamshýd's Sev'n-ring'd Cup where no one knows;
   But still a Ruby kindles in the Vine,
And many a Garden by the Water blows.

## 6

And David's lips are lockt; but in divine
High-piping Pehleví, with "Wine! Wine! Wine!
   Red Wine!"—the Nightingale cries to the Rose
That sallow cheek of hers to incarnadine.

## 7

Come, fill the Cup, and in the fire of Spring
Your Winter-garment of Repentance fling:
   The Bird of Time has but a little way
To flutter—and the Bird is on the Wing.

## 8

Whether at Naishápúr or Babylon,
Whether the Cup with sweet or bitter run,
   The Wine of Life keeps oozing drop by drop,
The Leaves of Life keep falling one by one.

**9**

Each Morn a thousand Roses brings, you say;
Yes, but where leaves the Rose of Yesterday?
    And this first Summer month that brings the Rose
Shall take Jamshýd and Kaikobád away.

**10**

Well, let it take them! What have we to do
With Kaikobád the Great, or Kaikhosrú?
    Let Zál and Rustum bluster as they will,
Or Hátim call to Supper—heed not you.

**11**

With me along the strip of Herbage strown
That just divides the desert from the sown,
    Where name of Slave and Sultán is forgot—
And Peace to Mahmúd on his golden Throne!

**12**

A Book of Verses underneath the Bough,
A Jug of Wine, a Loaf of Bread—and Thou
    Beside me singing in the Wilderness—
Oh, Wilderness were Paradise enow!

**13**

Some for the Glories of This World; and some
Sigh for the Prophet's Paradise to come;
    Ah, take the Cash, and let the Credit go,
Nor heed the rumble of a distant Drum!

## 14

Look to the blowing Rose about us—"Lo,
Laughing," she says, "into the world I blow,
   At once the silken tassel of my Purse
Tear, and its Treasure on the Garden throw."

## 15

And those who husbanded the Golden grain,
And those who flung it to the winds like Rain,
   Alike to no such aureate Earth are turn'd
As, buried once, Men want dug up again.

## 16

The Worldly Hope men set their Hearts upon
Turns Ashes—or it prospers; and anon,
   Like Snow upon the Desert's dusty Face,
Lighting a little hour or two—is gone.

## 17

Think, in this batter'd Caravanserai
Whose Portals are alternate Night and Day,
   How Sultán after Sultán with his Pomp
Abode his destined Hour, and went his way.

## 18

They say the Lion and the Lizard keep
The Courts where Jamshýd gloried and drank deep:
   And Bahrám, that great Hunter—the Wild Ass
Stamps o'er his Head, but cannot break his Sleep.

## 19

I sometimes think that never blows so red
The Rose as where some buried Caesar bled;
　　That every Hyacinth the Garden wears
Dropt in her Lap from some once lovely Head.

## 20

And this reviving Herb whose tender Green
Fledges the River-Lip on which we lean—
　　Ah, lean upon it lightly! for who knows
From what once lovely Lip it springs unseen!

## 21

Ah, my Belovéd, fill the Cup that clears
TODAY of Past Regrets and Future Fears:
　　*Tomorrow!*—Why, Tomorrow I may be
Myself with Yesterday's Sev'n Thousand Years.

## 22

For some we loved, the loveliest and the best
That from his Vintage rolling Time hath prest,
　　Have drunk their Cup a Round or two before,
And one by one crept silently to rest.

## 23

And we, that now make merry in the Room
They left, and Summer dresses in new bloom
　　Ourselves must we beneath the Couch of Earth
Descend—ourselves to make a Couch—for whom?

## 24

Ah, make the most of what we yet may spend,
Before we too into the Dust descend;
   Dust into Dust, and under Dust to lie
Sans Wine, sans Song, sans Singer, and—sans End!

## 25

Alike for those who for TODAY prepare,
And those that after some TOMORROW stare,
   A Muezzín from the Tower of Darkness cries
"Fools! your Reward is neither Here nor There."

## 26

Why, all the Saints and Sages who discuss'd
Of the Two Worlds so wisely—they are thrust
   Like foolish Prophets forth; their Words to Scorn
Are scatter'd, and their Mouths are stopt with Dust.

## 27

Myself when young did eagerly frequent
Doctor and Saint, and heard great argument
   About it and about: but evermore
Came out by the same door where in I went.

## 28

With them the seed of Wisdom did I sow,
And with mine own hand wrought to make it grow;
   And this was all the Harvest that I reap'd—
"I came like Water, and like Wind I go."

## 29

Into this Universe, and *Why* not knowing
Nor *Whence*, like Water willy-nilly flowing;
    And out of it, as Wind along the Waste,
I know not *Whither*, willy-nilly blowing.

## 30

What, without asking, hither hurried *Whence*?
And, without asking, *Whither* hurried hence!
    Oh, many a Cup of this forbidden Wine
Must drown the memory of that insolence!

## 31

Up from Earth's Centre through the Seventh Gate
I rose, and on the Throne of Saturn sate;
    And many a Knot unravel'd by the Road;
But not the Master-knot of Human Fate.

## 32

There was the Door to which I found no Key;
There was the Veil through which I might not see:
    Some little talk awhile of ME and THEE
There was—and then no more of THEE and ME.

## 33

Earth could not answer; nor the Seas that mourn
In flowing Purple, of their Lord forlorn;
    Nor rolling Heaven, with all his Signs reveal'd
And hidden by the sleeve of Night and Morn.

## 34

Then of the THEE in ME who works behind
The Veil, I lifted up my hands to find
   A Lamp amid the Darkness; and I heard,
As from Without—"THE ME WITHIN THEE BLIND!"

## 35

Then to the lip of this poor earthen Urn
I lean'd, the Secret of my Life to learn:
   And Lip to Lip it murmur'd—"While you live
Drink!—for, once dead, you never shall return."

## 36

I think the Vessel, that with fugitive
Articulation answer'd, once did live,
   And drink; and Ah! the passive Lip I kiss'd,
How many Kisses might it take—and give!

## 37

For I remember stopping by the way
To watch a Potter thumping his wet Clay:
   And with its all-obliterated Tongue
It murmur'd—"Gently, Brother, gently, pray!"

## 38

And has not such a Story from of Old
Down Man's successive generations roll'd
   Of such a clod of saturated Earth
Cast by the Maker into Human mould?

**39**

And not a drop that from our Cups we throw
For Earth to drink of, but may steal below
　　To quench the fire of Anguish in some Eye
There hidden—far beneath, and long ago.

**40**

As then the Tulip for her morning sup
Of Heav'nly Vintage from the soil looks up,
　　Do you devoutly do the like, till Heav'n
To Earth invert you—like an empty Cup.

**41**

Perplext no more with Human or Divine,
Tomorrow's tangle to the winds resign,
　　And lose your fingers in the tresses of
The Cypress-slender Minister of Wine.

**42**

And if the Wine you drink, the Lip you press
End in what All begins and ends in—Yes;
　　Think then you are TODAY what YESTERDAY
You were—TOMORROW you shall not be less.

**43**

So when that Angel of the darker Drink
At last shall find you by the river-brink,
　　And, offering his Cup, invite your Soul
Forth to your Lips to quaff—you shall not shrink.

## 44

Why, if the Soul can fling the Dust aside,
And naked on the Air of Heaven ride,
    Were't not a Shame—were't not a Shame for him
In this clay carcase crippled to abide?

## 45

'Tis but a Tent where takes his one day's rest
A Sultán to the realm of Death addrest;
    The Sultán rises, and the dark Ferrásh
Strikes, and prepares it for another Guest.

## 46

And fear not lest Existence closing your
Account, and mine, should know the like no more;
    The Eternal Sákí from that Bowl has pour'd
Millions of Bubbles like us, and will pour.

## 47

When You and I behind the Veil are past,
Oh, but the long, long while the World shall last,
    Which of our Coming and Departure heeds
As the Sea's self should heed a pebble-cast.

## 48

A Moment's Halt—a momentary taste
Of BEING from the Well amid the Waste—
    And Lo!—the phantom Caravan has reach'd
The NOTHING it set out from—Oh, make haste!

## 49

Would you that spangle of Existence spend
About THE SECRET—quick about it, Friend!
    A Hair perhaps divides the False and True—
And upon what, prithee, may life depend?

## 50

A Hair perhaps divides the False and True;
Yes; and a single Alif were the clue—
    Could you but find it—to the Treasure-house,
And peradventure to THE MASTER too;

## 51

Whose secret Presence, through Creation's veins
Running Quicksilver-like eludes your pains;
    Taking all shapes from Máh to Máhi; and
They change and perish all—but He remains;

## 52

A moment guess'd—then back behind the Fold
Immerst of Darkness round the Drama roll'd
    Which, for the Pastime of Eternity,
He doth Himself contrive, enact, behold.

## 53

But if in vain, down on the stubborn floor
Of Earth, and up to Heav'n's unopening Door,
    You gaze TODAY, while You are You—how then
TOMORROW, You when shall be You no more?

## 54

Waste not your Hour, nor in the vain pursuit
Of This and That endeavour and dispute;
   Better be jocund with the fruitful Grape
Than sadden after none, or bitter, Fruit.

## 55

You know, my Friends, with what a brave Carouse
I made a Second Marriage in my house;
   Divorced old barren Reason from my Bed,
And took the Daughter of the Vine to Spouse.

## 56

For "Is" and "Is-Not" though with Rule and Line
And "Up-and-Down" by Logic I define,
   Of all that one should care to fathom, I
Was never deep in anything but—Wine.

## 57

Ah, but my Computations, People say,
Reduced the Year to better reckoning?—Nay
   'Twas only striking from the Calendar
Unborn Tomorrow, and dead Yesterday.

## 58

And lately, by the Tavern Door agape,
Came shining through the Dusk an Angel Shape
   Bearing a Vessel on his Shoulder; and
He bid me taste of it; and 'twas—the Grape!

## 59

The Grape that can with Logic absolute
The Two-and-Seventy jarring Sects confute:
  The sovereign Alchemist that in a trice
Life's leaden metal into Gold transmute:

## 60

The mighty Mahmúd, Allah-breathing Lord,
That all the misbelieving and black Horde
  Of Fears and Sorrows that infest the Soul
Scatters before him with his whirlwind Sword.

## 61

Why, be this Juice the growth of God, who dare
Blaspheme the twisted tendril as a Snare?
  A Blessing, we should use it, should we not?
And if a Curse—why, then, Who set it there?

## 62

I must abjure the Balm of Life, I must,
Scared by some After-reckoning ta'en on trust,
  Or lured with Hope of some Diviner Drink,
To fill the Cup—when crumbled into Dust!

## 63

Oh, threats of Hell and Hopes of Paradise!
One thing at least is certain—*This* Life flies;
  One thing is certain and the rest is Lies;
The Flower that once has blown for ever dies.

## 64

Strange, is it not? that of the myriads who
Before us pass'd the door of Darkness through,
    Not one returns to tell us of the Road,
Which to discover we must travel too.

## 65

The Revelations of Devout and Learn'd
Who rose before us, and as Prophets burn'd,
    Are all but Stories, which, awoke from Sleep,
They told their comrades, and to Sleep return'd.

## 66

I sent my Soul through the Invisible,
Some letter of that After-life to spell:
    And by and by my Soul return'd to me,
And answer'd "I Myself am Heav'n and Hell:"

## 67

Heav'n but the Vision of fulfill'd Desire,
And Hell the Shadow from a Soul on fire,
    Cast on the Darkness into which Ourselves,
So late emerged from, shall so soon expire.

## 68

We are no other than a moving row
Of Magic Shadow-shapes that come and go
    Round with the Sun-illumined Lantern held
In Midnight by the Master of the Show;

## 69

But helpless Pieces of the Game He plays
Upon this Chequer-board of Nights and Days;
  Hither and thither moves, and checks, and slays,
And one by one back in the Closet lays.

## 70

The Ball no question makes of Ayes and Noes,
But Here or There as strikes the Player goes;
  And He that toss'd you down into the Field,
*He* knows about it all—HE knows—HE knows!

## 71

The Moving Finger writes; and, having writ,
Moves on: nor all your Piety nor Wit
  Shall lure it back to cancel half a Line,
Nor all your Tears wash out a Word of it.

## 72

And that inverted Bowl they call the Sky,
Whereunder crawling coop'd we live and die,
  Lift not your hands to *It* for help—for It
As impotently moves as you or I.

## 73

With Earth's first Clay They did the Last Man knead,
And there of the Last Harvest sow'd the Seed:
  And the first Morning of Creation wrote
What the Last Dawn of Reckoning shall read.

## 74

YESTERDAY *This* Day's Madness did prepare;
TOMORROW'S Silence, Triumph, or Despair:
    Drink! for you know not whence you came, nor why:
Drink! for you know not why you go, nor where.

## 75

I tell you this—When, started from the Goal,
Over the flaming shoulders of the Foal
    Of Heav'n Parwín and Mushtarí they flung
In my predestined Plot of Dust and Soul.

## 76

The Vine had struck a fibre: which about
If clings my being—let the Dervish flout;
    Of my Base metal may be filed a Key,
That shall unlock the Door he howls without.

## 77

And this I know: whether the one True Light
Kindle to Love, or Wrath-consume me quite,
    One Flash of It within the Tavern caught
Better than in the Temple lost outright.

## 78

What! out of senseless Nothing to provoke
A conscious Something to resent the yoke
    Of unpermitted Pleasure, under pain
Of Everlasting Penalties, if broke!

## 79

What! from his helpless Creature be repaid
Pure Gold for what he lent him dross-allay'd—
    Sue for a Debt he never did contract,
And cannot answer—Oh, the sorry trade!

## 80

Oh, Thou, who didst with pitfall and with gin
Beset the Road I was to wander in,
    Thou wilt not with Predestined Evil round
Enmesh, and then impute my Fall to Sin!

## 81

Oh, Thou, who Man of baser Earth didst make,
And ev'n with Paradise devise the Snake:
    For all the Sin wherewith the Face of Man
    Is blacken'd—Man's forgiveness give—and take!

---

## 82

As under cover of departing Day
Slunk hunger-stricken Ramazán away,
    Once more within the Potter's house alone
I stood, surrounded by the Shapes of Clay.

## 83

Shapes of all Sorts and Sizes, great and small,
That stood along the floor and by the wall;
    And some loquacious Vessels were; and some
Listen'd perhaps, but never talk'd at all.

## 84

Said one among them—"Surely not in vain
My substance of the common Earth was ta'en
   And to this Figure moulded, to be broke,
Or trampled back to shapeless Earth again."

## 85

Then said a Second—"Ne'er a peevish Boy
Would break the Bowl from which he drank in joy;
   And He that with his hand the Vessel made
Will surely not in after Wrath destroy."

## 86

After a momentary silence spake
Some Vessel of a more ungainly Make;
   "They sneer at me for leaning all awry:
What! did the Hand then of the Potter shake?"

## 87

Whereat some one of the loquacious Lot—
I think a Súfi pipkin—waxing hot—
   "All this of Pot and Potter—Tell me then,
Who is the Potter, pray, and who the Pot?"

## 88

"Why," said another, "Some there are who tell
Of one who threatens he will toss to Hell
   The luckless Pots he marr'd in making—Pish!
He's a Good Fellow, and 'twill all be well."

## 89

"Well," murmur'd one, "Let whoso make or buy,
My Clay with long Oblivion is gone dry:
  But fill me with the old familiar Juice,
Methinks I might recover by and by."

## 90

So while the Vessels one by one were speaking,
The little Moon look'd in that all were seeking:
  And then they jogg'd each other, "Brother! Brother!
Now for the Porter's shoulder-knot a-creaking!"

---

## 91

Ah, with the Grape my fading Life provide,
And wash the Body whence the Life has died,
  And lay me, shrouded in the living Leaf,
By some not unfrequented Garden-side.

## 92

That ev'n my buried Ashes such a snare
Of Vintage shall fling up into the Air
  As not a True-believer passing by
But shall be overtaken unaware.

## 93

Indeed the Idols I have loved so long
Have done my credit in this World much wrong:
  Have drown'd my Glory in a shallow Cup
And sold my Reputation for a Song.

## 94

Indeed, indeed, Repentance oft before
I swore—but was I sober when I swore?
   And then and then came Spring, and Rose-in-hand
My thread-bare Penitence apieces tore.

## 95

And much as Wine has play'd the Infidel,
And robb'd me of my Robe of Honour—Well,
   I wonder often what the Vintners buy
One half so precious as the stuff they sell.

## 96

Yet Ah, that Spring should vanish with the Rose!
That Youth's sweet-scented manuscript should close!
   The Nightingale that in the branches sang,
Ah, whence, and whither flown again, who knows!

## 97

Would but the Desert of the Fountain yield
One glimpse—if dimly, yet indeed, reveal'd,
   To which the fainting Traveller might spring,
As springs the trampled herbage of the field!

## 98

Would but some wingéd Angel ere too late
Arrest the yet unfolded Roll of Fate,
   And make the stern Recorder otherwise
Enregister, or quite obliterate!

## 99

Ah, Love! could you and I with Him conspire
To grasp this sorry Scheme of Things entire,
   Would not we shatter it to bits—and then
Re-mould it nearer to the Heart's Desire!

---

## 100

Yon rising Moon that looks for us again—
How oft hereafter will she wax and wane;
   How oft hereafter rising look for us
Through this same Garden—and for *one* in vain!

## 101

And when like her, oh, Sákí, you shall pass
Among the Guests Star-scatter'd on the Grass,
   And in your Joyous errand reach the spot
Where I made One—turn down an empty Glass!

TAMÁN[1]

---

1. [It is ended.]

# Rabbi Ben Ezra

### 1

Grow old along with me!
The best is yet to be,
The last of life, for which the first was made:
Our times are in his hand
Who saith, "A whole I planned,
Youth shows but half; trust God: see all, nor be afraid!"

### 2

Not that, amassing flowers,
Youth sighed, "Which rose make ours,
Which lily leave and then as best recall?"
Not that, admiring stars,
It yearned, "Nor Jove, nor Mars;
Mine be some figured flame which blends, transcends them all!"

### 3

Not for such hopes and fears
Annulling youth's brief years,
Do I remonstrate: folly wide the mark!
Rather I prize the doubt
Low kinds exist without,
Finished and finite clods, untroubled by a spark.

## 4

Poor vaunt of life indeed,
Were man but formed to feed
On joy, to solely seek and find and feast;
Such feasting ended, then
As sure an end to men;
Irks care the crop-full bird? Frets doubt the maw-crammed beast?

## 5

Rejoice we are allied
To that which doth provide
And not partake, effect and not receive!
A spark disturbs our clod;
Nearer we hold of God
Who gives, than of his tribes that take, I must believe.

## 6

Then, welcome each rebuff
That turns earth's smoothness rough,
Each sting that bids nor sit nor stand but go!
Be our joys three-parts pain!
Strive, and hold cheap the strain;
Learn, nor account the pang; dare, never grudge the throe!

## 7

For thence—a paradox
Which comforts while it mocks—
Shall life succeed in that it seems to fail:
What I aspired to be,
And was not, comforts me:
A brute I might have been, but would not sink i' the scale.

## 8

What is he but a brute
Whose flesh has soul to suit,
Whose spirit works lest arms and legs want play?
To man, propose this test—
Thy body at its best,
How far can that project thy soul on its lone way?

## 9

Yet gifts should prove their use:
I own the Past profuse
Of power each side, perfection every turn:
Eyes, ears took in their dole
Brain treasured up the whole;
Should not the heart beat once, "How good to live and learn"?

## 10

Not once beat, "Praise be thine!
I see the whole design,
I, who saw power, see now Love perfect too:
Perfect I call thy plan:
Thanks that I was a man!
Maker, remake, complete—I trust what thou shalt do!"

## 11

For pleasant is this flesh;
Our soul, in its rose-mesh
Pulled ever to the earth, still yearns for rest:
Would we some prize might hold
To match those manifold
Possessions of the brute—gain most, as we did best!

## 12

Let us not always say,
"Spite of this flesh today
I strove, made head, gained ground upon the whole!"
As the bird wings and sings,
Let us cry, "All good things
Are ours, nor soul helps flesh more, now, than flesh helps soul!"

## 13

Therefore I summon age
To grant youth's heritage,
Life's struggle having so far reached its term:
Thence shall I pass, approved
A man, for aye removed
From the developed brute; a God though in the germ.

## 14

And I shall thereupon
Take rest, ere I be gone
Once more on my adventure brave and new:
Fearless and unperplexed,
When I wage battle next,
What weapons to select, what armor to indue.

## 15

Youth ended, I shall try
My gain or loss thereby;
Leave the fire ashes, what survives is gold:
And I shall weigh the same,
Give life its praise or blame:
Young, all lay in dispute; I shall know, being old.

## 16

For note, when evening shuts,
A certain moment cuts
The deed off, calls the glory from the gray:
A whisper from the west
Shoots—"Add this to the rest,
Take it and try its worth: here dies another day."

## 17

So, still within this life,
Though lifted o'er its strife,
Let me discern, compare, pronounce at last,
"This rage was right i' the main,
That acquiescence vain:
The Future I may face now I have proved the Past."

## 18

For more is not reserved
To man, with soul just nerved
To act tomorrow what he learns today:
Here, work enough to watch
The Master work, and catch
Hints of the proper craft, tricks of the tool's true play."

## 19

As it was better, youth
Should strive through acts uncouth,
Toward making, than repose on aught found made:
So, better, age, exempt
From strife, should know, than tempt
Further. Though waitedst age: wait death nor be afraid!

## 20

Enough now, if the Right
And Good and Infinite
Be named here, as thou callest thy hand thine own,
With knowledge absolute,
Subject to no dispute
From fools that crowded youth, nor let thee feel alone.

## 21

Be there, for once and all,
Severed great minds from small,
Announced to each his station in the Past!
Was I, the world arraigned,
Were they, my soul disdained,
Right? Let age speak the truth and give us peace at last!

## 22

Now, who shall arbitrate?
Ten men love what I hate,
Shun what I follow, slight what I receive;
Ten, who in ears and eyes
Match me: we all surmise,
They this thing, and I that: whom shall my soul believe?

## 23

Not on the vulgar mass
Called "work," must sentence pass,
Things done, that took the eye and had the price;
O'er which, from level stand,
The low world laid its hand,
Found straightway to its mind, could value in a trice:

## 24

But all, the world's coarse thumb
And finger failed to plumb,
So passed in making up the main account;
All instincts immature,
All purposes unsure,
That weighed not as his work, yet swelled the man's amount:

## 25

Thoughts hardly to be packed
Into a narrow act,
Fancies that broke through language and escaped;
All I could never be,
All, men ignored in me,
This, I was worth to God, whose wheel the pitcher shaped.

## 26

Ay, note that Potter's wheel,
That metaphor! and feel
Why time spins fast, why passive lies our clay—
Thou, to whom fools propound,
When the wine makes its round,
"Since life fleets, all is change; the Past gone, seize today!"

## 27

Fool! All that is, at all,
Lasts ever, past recall;
Earth changes, but thy soul and God stand sure:
What entered into thee,
*That* was, is, and shall be:
Time's wheel runs back or stops: Potter and clay endure.

## 28

He fixed thee mid this dance
Of plastic circumstance,
This Present, thou, forsooth, would fain arrest:
Machinery just meant
To give thy soul its bent,
Try thee and turn thee forth, sufficiently impressed.

## 29

What though the earlier grooves,
Which ran the laughing loves
Around thy base, no longer pause and press?
What though, about thy rim,
Skull-things in order grim
Grow out, in graver mood, obey the sterner stress?

## 30

Look not thou down but up!
To uses of a cup,
The festal board, lamp's flash and trumpet's peal,
The new wine's foaming flow,
The Master's lips aglow!
Thou, heaven's consummate cup, what needst thou with earth's
        wheel?

## 31

But I need, now as then,
Thee, God, who mouldest men;
And since, not even while the whirl was worst,
Did I — to the wheel of life
With shapes and colors rife,
Bound dizzily — mistake my end, to slake thy thirst:

## 32

So, take and use thy work:
Amend what flaws may lurk,
What strain o' the stuff, what warpings past the aim!
My times be in thy hand!
Perfect the cup as planned!
Let age approve of youth, and death complete the same!

## QUESTIONS

"THE RUBÁIYÁT OF OMAR KHAYYÁM"

1. Why do the verses of the poem follow the course of a day, from morning until night?

2. Throughout the poem, does the speaker intend for us to take the recurring references to wine literally, or does wine stand for something else?

3. What is the meaning of the revelation the speaker receives from the lamp: "THE ME WITHIN THEE BLIND!" (34)[2]

4. Why does the speaker offer God "Man's forgiveness"? (81)

5. What is the significance of the pots' conversation? Why do the pots that the speaker overhears all jog each other when the moon appears?

6. Does the speaker have hopes of immortality or does he believe death is the end?

"RABBI BEN EZRA"

1. To whom is Rabbi Ben Ezra speaking when he says, "Grow old along with me! / The best is yet to be"? (1)

2. Why is Rabbi Ben Ezra comforted with what he aspired to be, even though he was not able to achieve it?

3. Why does Rabbi Ben Ezra tell fools who say the past is gone that "All that is, at all, / Lasts ever, past recall"? (27)

4. What does Rabbi Ben Ezra mean in comparing a person nearing death to "heaven's consummate cup" that no longer needs "earth's wheel"? (30)

5. Why does Rabbi Ben Ezra tell God that he did not "mistake my end, to slake thy thirst"? (31)

6. For Rabbi Ben Ezra, what is the right way to think of the relationship between flesh and spirit?

---

2. [Numbers refer to stanza numbers.]

## FOR FURTHER REFLECTION

1. What does the image of the clay and the potter's wheel mean in each of these poems?

2. What limitations to human knowledge does each poem present? How do the poems suggest that humans should respond to these limitations?

3. How does each poem suggest that humans should prepare for death?

4. According to each poem, what is the greatest good in human life?

5. How successful do you think Browning is in "Rabbi Ben Ezra" in responding to FitzGerald's "Rubáiyát"?

6. Which philosophy of life is better suited to human existence, that expressed in the "Rubáiyát" or that expressed in "Rabbi Ben Ezra"?

The writer known as George Eliot (1819–1880) was christened Mary Ann Evans, the third child of an estate manager in Warwickshire, England. Eliot was educated at nearby boarding schools and as a young woman developed a strong connection to the evangelical movement. After her mother's death, Eliot returned home to keep house for her father. Along with her family responsibilities, she undertook the translation of German theologian David Friedrich Strauss's *The Life of Jesus Critically Examined* (1846), a critique of the divinity of Christ. Her exposure to Strauss's ideas along with her expanding circle of freethinking friends and acquaintances, led her to reject Christian orthodoxy. The result was a break with her pious father, mended only shortly before his death in 1849.

Following a brief stay in Switzerland, Eliot began submitting articles to the *Westminster Review*; she moved to London in 1851 and became an editor of the quarterly magazine. In 1854, she began living with writer and journalist George Henry Lewes, coeditor of the *Leader*, a progressive weekly newspaper. Because Lewes was legally married and unable to obtain a divorce, their unconventional relationship resulted in social condemnation and ostracism. "I have counted the cost of the step I have taken and am prepared to bear, without irritation or bitterness, renunciation of all my friends," wrote Eliot. "I am not mistaken in the person to whom I have attached myself." They would remain together until Lewes's death in 1878.

Lewes encouraged Eliot to write fiction and her first works were a series of stories about life in Warwickshire, serialized in *Blackwood's Magazine* and then published as a collection, *Scenes from Clerical Life* (1858), under the pseudonym by which she is commonly known: "George" for Lewes, and "Eliot" because it was "a good mouth-filling word." Eliot's first novel, *Adam Bede* (1859), which she described as "a country story—full of the breath of cows and the scent of hay," became an instant bestseller. Speculation ensued over the author's true identity, and after a rumor circulated that the writer Joseph Liggins was George Eliot, Mary Ann Evans stepped forward, though she continued to use her pseudonym on her published works.

Over the next twenty years, Eliot produced numerous novels that were both critically and popularly acclaimed and which are characterized by deep insight into the psychology of her characters. Among these are *The Mill on the Floss* (1860) and *Silas Marner* (1861), both of which depict the lives of social outsiders, and *Felix Holt, the Radical* (1866), which focuses on political issues. Her most acclaimed book was *Middlemarch* (1872), which Henry James lauded as "vast, swarming, deep-colored, crowded with episodes, with vivid images, with lurking master-strokes, with brilliant passages of expression," and Virginia Woolf deemed "one of the few English novels written for grown-up people." Lionized by literary society, Eliot's and Lewes's London home became a salon for the great minds of the time, including Ralph Waldo Emerson, Ivan Turgenev, Charles Darwin, and Richard Wagner. Lewes died two years after Eliot published her final novel, *Daniel Deronda* (1876), and Eliot married John Cross, a close friend and banker twenty years her junior. Only then did the Evans family break their decades-long silence to wish her congratulations on her marriage. Eliot died only months later, at the age of 61.

When Eliot delivered the manuscript of "The Lifted Veil" to John Blackwood in 1859, she attached a note: "Herewith the dismal story." Blackwood wrote back that "lovers of the painful are thrilled and delighted," but that he wished her a "happier frame of mind." The novella features a first-person point of view rather than the omniscient narration that characterizes her other works and is set in a much narrower world than her other works. In 1857, Eliot wrote in a letter to a friend, "My own experience and development deepen every day my conviction that our moral progress may be measured by the degree in which we sympathize with individual suffering and individual joy." "The Lifted Veil," written two years later at the height of Eliot's social condemnation, speculates about what we might see if we could truly look into the hearts of others.

# The Lifted Veil

1

The time of my end approaches. I have lately been subject to attacks of angina pectoris; and in the ordinary course of things, my physician tells me, I may fairly hope that my life will not be protracted many months. Unless, then, I am cursed with an exceptional physical constitution, as I am cursed with an exceptional mental character, I shall not much longer groan under the wearisome burthen of this earthly existence. If it were to be otherwise—if I were to live on to the age most men desire and provide for—I should for once have known whether the miseries of delusive expectation can outweigh the miseries of true prevision. For I foresee when I shall die, and everything that will happen in my last moments.

Just a month from this day, on the 20th of September 1850, I shall be sitting in this chair, in this study, at ten o'clock at night, longing to die, weary of incessant insight and foresight, without delusions and without hope. Just as I am watching a tongue of blue flame rising in the fire, and my lamp is burning low, the horrible contraction will begin at my chest. I shall only have time to reach the bell, and pull it violently, before the sense of suffocation will come. No one will answer my bell. I know why. My two servants are lovers, and will have quarrelled. My housekeeper will have rushed out of the house in a fury, two hours before, hoping that Perry will believe she has gone to drown herself. Perry is alarmed at last, and is gone out after her. The little scullery maid is asleep on a bench: she never answers the bell; it does not wake her. The sense of suffocation increases: my lamp goes out with a horrible stench: I make a great effort, and snatch at the bell again. I long for life, and there is no help. I thirsted for the unknown: the thirst is gone. Oh God, let me stay with the known, and be weary of it: I am content. Agony of pain and suffocation—and all the while the earth, the fields, the pebbly brook at the bottom of the rookery, the fresh scent after the rain, the light of the morning through my chamber window, the warmth of the hearth after the frosty air—will darkness close over them forever?

Darkness—darkness—no pain—nothing but darkness: but I am passing on and on through the darkness: my thought stays in the darkness, but always with a sense of moving onward. . . .

Before that time comes, I wish to use my last hours of ease and strength in telling the strange story of my experience. I have never fully unbosomed myself to any human being; I have never been encouraged to trust much in the sympathy of my fellow men. But we have all a chance of meeting with some pity, some tenderness, some charity, when we are dead: it is the living only who cannot be forgiven—the living only from whom men's indulgence and reverence are held off, like the rain by the hard east wind. While the heart beats, bruise it—it is your only opportunity; while the eye can still turn towards you with moist timid entreaty, freeze it with an icy unanswering gaze; while the ear, that delicate messenger to the inmost sanctuary of the soul, can still take in the tones of kindness, put it off with hard civility, or sneering compliment, or envious affectation of indifference; while the creative brain can still throb with the sense of injustice, with the yearning for brotherly recognition—make haste—oppress it with your ill-considered judgments, your trivial comparisons, your careless misrepresentations. The heart will by and by be still—*ubi saeva indignatio ulterius cor lacerare nequit*;[1] the eye will cease to entreat; the ear will be deaf; the brain will have ceased from all wants as well as from all work. Then your charitable speeches may find vent; then you may remember and pity the toil and the struggle and the failure; then you may give due honour to the work achieved; then you may find extenuation for errors, and may consent to bury them.

That is a trivial schoolboy text; why do I dwell on it? It has little reference to me, for I shall leave no works behind me for men to honour. I have no near relatives who will make up, by weeping over my grave, for the wounds they inflicted on me when I was among them. It is only the story of my life that will perhaps win a little more sympathy from strangers when I am dead, than I ever believed it would obtain from my friends while I was living.

My childhood perhaps seems happier to me than it really was, by contrast with all the after-years. For then the curtain of the future was as impenetrable to me as to other children: I had all their delight in the present hour, their sweet indefinite hopes for the morrow; and I had a tender mother: even now, after the dreary lapse of long years, a slight trace of sensation accompanies the remembrance of her caress as she held

---

1. [Inscription on Swift's tombstone.]

me on her knee—her arms round my little body, her cheek pressed on mine. I had a complaint of the eyes that made me blind for a little while, and she kept me on her knee from morning till night. That unequalled love soon vanished out of my life, and even to my childish consciousness it was as if that life had become more chill. I rode my little white pony with the groom by my side as before, but there were no loving eyes looking at me as I mounted, no glad arms opened to me when I came back. Perhaps I missed my mother's love more than most children of seven or eight would have done, to whom the other pleasures of life remained as before; for I was certainly a very sensitive child. I remember still the mingled trepidation and delicious excitement with which I was affected by the tramping of the horses on the pavement in the echoing stables, by the loud resonance of the grooms' voices, by the booming bark of the dogs as my father's carriage thundered under the archway of the courtyard, by the din of the gong as it gave notice of luncheon and dinner. The measured tramp of soldiery which I sometimes heard—for my father's house lay near a county town where there were large barracks—made me sob and tremble; and yet when they were gone past, I longed for them to come back again.

I fancy my father thought me an odd child, and had little fondness for me; though he was very careful in fulfilling what he regarded as a parent's duties. But he was already past the middle of life, and I was not his only son. My mother had been his second wife, and he was five-and-forty when he married her. He was a firm, unbending, intensely orderly man, in root and stem a banker, but with a flourishing graft of the active landholder, aspiring to county influence: one of those people who are always like themselves from day to day, who are uninfluenced by the weather, and neither know melancholy nor high spirits. I held him in great awe, and appeared more timid and sensitive in his presence than at other times; a circumstance which, perhaps, helped to confirm him in the intention to educate me on a different plan from the prescriptive one with which he had complied in the case of my elder brother, already a tall youth at Eton. My brother was to be his representative and successor; he must go to Eton and Oxford, for the sake of making connections, of course: my father was not a man to underrate the bearing of Latin satirists or Greek dramatists on the attainment of an aristocratic position. But, intrinsically, he had slight esteem for "those dead but sceptred spirits"; having qualified himself for forming an independent opinion by reading Potter's Aeschylus, and dipping into Francis's Horace. To this negative view he added a positive one, derived from a recent connection with mining speculations; namely, that a scientific education was the really useful training for a younger son. Moreover, it was clear that a shy, sensitive boy like me was not fit to encounter the rough experience of a public school. Mr. Letherall had said so very decidedly. Mr. Letherall was a large man in spectacles, who one day took my small head between his large hands, and pressed it here and there in an exploratory, suspicious manner—then placed each of his great thumbs on my temples, and pushed me a little way from him, and stared at me with glittering spectacles. The contemplation appeared to displease him, for he frowned sternly, and said to my father, drawing his thumbs across my eyebrows—

"The deficiency is there, sir—there; and here," he added, touching the upper sides of my head, "here is the excess. That must be brought out, sir, and this must be laid to sleep."

I was in a state of tremor, partly at the vague idea that I was the object of reprobation, partly in the agitation of my first hatred—hatred of this big, spectacled man, who pulled my head about as if he wanted to buy and cheapen it.

I am not aware how much Mr. Letherall had to do with the system afterwards adopted towards me, but it was presently clear that private tutors, natural history, science, and the modern languages, were the appliances by which the defects of my organisation were to be remedied. I was very stupid about machines, so I was to be greatly occupied with them; I had no memory for classification, so it was particularly necessary that I should study systematic zoology and botany; I was hungry for human deeds and human emotions, so I was to be plentifully crammed with the mechanical powers, the elementary bodies, and the phenomena of electricity and magnetism. A better-constituted boy would certainly have profited under my intelligent tutors, with their scientific apparatus; and would, doubtless, have found the phenomena of electricity and magnetism as fascinating as I was, every Thursday, assured they were. As it was, I could have paired off, for ignorance of whatever was taught me, with the worst Latin scholar that was ever turned out of a classical academy. I read Plutarch, and Shakespeare, and Don Quixote by the sly, and supplied myself in that way with wandering thoughts, while my tutor was assuring me that "an improved man, as distinguished from an ignorant one, was a man who knew the reason why water ran downhill." I had no desire to be this improved man; I was glad of the running water; I could watch it and listen to it gurgling among the pebbles, and bathing the bright green water plants, by the hour together. I did not want to know *why* it ran; I had perfect confidence that there were good reasons for what was so very beautiful.

There is no need to dwell on this part of my life. I have said enough to indicate that my nature was of the sensitive, unpractical order, and that it grew up in an uncongenial medium, which could never foster it into happy, healthy development. When I was sixteen I was sent to Geneva to complete my course of education; and the change was a very happy one to me, for the sight of the Alps, with the setting sun on them, as we descended

the Jura, seemed to me like an entrance into heaven; and the three years
of my life there were spent in a perpetual sense of exaltation, as if from
a draught of delicious wine, at the presence of Nature in all her awful
loveliness. You will think, perhaps, that I must have been a poet, from this
early sensibility to Nature. But my lot was not so happy as that. A poet
pours forth his song and *believes* in the listening ear and answering soul,
to which his song will be floated sooner or later. But the poet's sensibility
without his voice—the poet's sensibility that finds no vent but in silent
tears on the sunny bank, when the noonday light sparkles on the water,
or in an inward shudder at the sound of harsh human tones, the sight of a
cold human eye—this dumb passion brings with it a fatal solitude of soul
in the society of one's fellow men. My least solitary moments were those
in which I pushed off in my boat, at evening, towards the centre of the
lake; it seemed to me that the sky, and the glowing mountaintops, and the
wide blue water, surrounded me with a cherishing love such as no human
face had shed on me since my mother's love had vanished out of my life. I
used to do as Jean Jacques did—lie down in my boat and let it glide where
it would, while I looked up at the departing glow leaving one mountaintop
after the other, as if the prophet's chariot of fire were passing over them
on its way to the home of light. Then, when the white summits were
all sad and corpselike, I had to push homeward, for I was under careful surveillance, and was allowed no late wanderings. This disposition of
mine was not favourable to the formation of intimate friendships among
the numerous youths of my own age who are always to be found studying at Geneva. Yet I made *one* such friendship; and, singularly enough, it
was with a youth whose intellectual tendencies were the very reverse of
my own. I shall call him Charles Meunier; his real surname—an English
one, for he was of English extraction—having since become celebrated.
He was an orphan, who lived on a miserable pittance while he pursued
the medical studies for which he had a special genius. Strange! that with
my vague mind, susceptible and unobservant, hating inquiry and given
up to contemplation, I should have been drawn towards a youth whose
strongest passion was science. But the bond was not an intellectual one;
it came from a source that can happily blend the stupid with the brilliant, the dreamy with the practical: it came from community of feeling.
Charles was poor and ugly, derided by Genevese gamins, and not acceptable in drawing rooms. I saw that he was isolated, as I was, though from
a different cause, and, stimulated by a sympathetic resentment, I made
timid advances towards him. It is enough to say that there sprang up as
much comradeship between us as our different habits would allow; and in
Charles's rare holidays we went up the Salève together, or took the boat to
Vevay, while I listened dreamily to the monologues in which he unfolded
his bold conceptions of future experiment and discovery. I mingled them

confusedly in my thought with glimpses of blue water and delicate floating cloud, with the notes of birds and the distant glitter of the glacier. He knew quite well that my mind was half absent, yet he liked to talk to me in this way; for don't we talk of our hopes and our projects even to dogs and birds, when they love us? I have mentioned this one friendship because of its connection with a strange and terrible scene which I shall have to narrate in my subsequent life.

This happier life at Geneva was put an end to by a severe illness, which is partly a blank to me, partly a time of dimly remembered suffering, with the presence of my father by my bed from time to time. Then came the languid monotony of convalescence, the days gradually breaking into variety and distinctness as my strength enabled me to take longer and longer drives. On one of these more vividly remembered days, my father said to me, as he sat beside my sofa—

"When you are quite well enough to travel, Latimer, I shall take you home with me. The journey will amuse you and do you good, for I shall go through the Tyrol and Austria, and you will see many new places. Our neighbours, the Filmores, are come; Alfred will join us at Basle, and we shall all go together to Vienna, and back by Prague" . . .

My father was called away before he had finished his sentence, and he left my mind resting on the word *Prague*, with a strange sense that a new and wondrous scene was breaking upon me: a city under the broad sunshine, that seemed to me as if it were the summer sunshine of a long-past century arrested in its course—unrefreshed for ages by the dews of night, or the rushing rain cloud; scorching the dusty, weary, time-eaten grandeur of a people doomed to live on in the stale repetition of memories, like deposed and superannuated kings in their regal gold-inwoven tatters. The city looked so thirsty that the broad river seemed to me a sheet of metal; and the blackened statues, as I passed under their blank gaze, along the unending bridge, with their ancient garments and their saintly crowns, seemed to me the real inhabitants and owners of this place, while the busy, trivial men and women, hurrying to and fro, were a swarm of ephemeral visitants infesting it for a day. It is such grim, stony beings as these, I thought, who are the fathers of ancient faded children, in those tanned time-fretted dwellings that crowd the steep before me; who pay their court in the worn and crumbling pomp of the palace which stretches its monotonous length on the height; who worship wearily in the stifling air of the churches, urged by no fear or hope, but compelled by their doom to be ever old and undying, to live on in the rigidity of habit, as they live on in perpetual midday, without the repose of night or the new birth of morning.

A stunning clang of metal suddenly thrilled through me, and I became conscious of the objects in my room again: one of the fire irons had fallen as Pierre opened the door to bring me my draught. My heart was palpitating violently, and I begged Pierre to leave my draught beside me; I would take it presently.

As soon as I was alone again, I began to ask myself whether I had been sleeping. Was this a dream—this wonderfully distinct vision—minute in its distinctness down to a patch of rainbow light on the pavement, transmitted through a coloured lamp in the shape of a star—of a strange city, quite unfamiliar to my imagination? I had seen no picture of Prague: it lay in my mind as a mere name, with vaguely remembered historical associations—ill-defined memories of imperial grandeur and religious wars.

Nothing of this sort had ever occurred in my dreaming experience before, for I had often been humiliated because my dreams were only saved from being utterly disjointed and commonplace by the frequent terrors of nightmare. But I could not believe that I had been asleep, for I remembered distinctly the gradual breaking-in of the vision upon me, like the new images in a dissolving view, or the growing distinctness of the landscape as the sun lifts up the veil of the morning mist. And while I was conscious of this incipient vision, I was also conscious that Pierre came to tell my father Mr. Filmore was waiting for him, and that my father hurried out of the room. No, it was not a dream; was it—the thought was full of tremulous exultation—was it the poet's nature in me, hitherto only a troubled yearning sensibility, now manifesting itself suddenly as spontaneous creation? Surely it was in this way that Homer saw the plain of Troy, that Dante saw the abodes of the departed, that Milton saw the earthward flight of the Tempter. Was it that my illness had wrought some happy change in my organisation—given a firmer tension to my nerves—carried off some dull obstruction? I had often read of such effects—in works of fiction at least. Nay; in genuine biographies I had read of the subtilising or exalting influence of some diseases on the mental powers. Did not Novalis feel his inspiration intensified under the progress of consumption?

When my mind had dwelt for some time on this blissful idea, it seemed to me that I might perhaps test it by an exertion of my will. The vision had begun when my father was speaking of our going to Prague. I did not for a moment believe it was really a representation of that city; I believed—I hoped it was a picture that my newly liberated genius had painted in fiery haste, with the colours snatched from lazy memory. Suppose I were to fix my mind on some other place—Venice, for example, which was far more familiar to my imagination than Prague: perhaps the same sort of result would follow. I concentrated my thoughts on Venice; I stimulated my imagination with poetic memories, and strove to feel myself present in Venice, as I had felt myself present in Prague. But in vain. I was only colouring the Canaletto engravings that hung in my old bedroom at home; the picture was a shifting one, my mind wandering uncertainly in search of more vivid images; I could see no accident of form or shadow without conscious labour after the necessary conditions. It was all prosaic effort, not rapt passivity, such as I had experienced half an hour before. I was discouraged; but I remembered that inspiration was fitful.

For several days I was in a state of excited expectation, watching for a recurrence of my new gift. I sent my thoughts ranging over my world of knowledge, in the hope that they would find some object which would send a reawakening vibration through my slumbering genius. But no; my world remained as dim as ever, and that flash of strange light refused to come again, though I watched for it with palpitating eagerness.

My father accompanied me every day in a drive, and a gradually lengthening walk as my powers of walking increased; and one evening he had agreed to come and fetch me at twelve the next day, that we might go together to select a musical box, and other purchases rigorously demanded of a rich Englishman visiting Geneva. He was one of the most punctual of men and bankers, and I was always nervously anxious to be quite ready for him at the appointed time. But, to my surprise, at a quarter past twelve he had not appeared. I felt all the impatience of a convalescent who has nothing particular to do, and who has just taken a tonic in the prospect of immediate exercise that would carry off the stimulus.

Unable to sit still and reserve my strength, I walked up and down the room, looking out on the current of the Rhone, just where it leaves the dark-blue lake; but thinking all the while of the possible causes that could detain my father.

Suddenly I was conscious that my father was in the room, but not alone: there were two persons with him. Strange! I had heard no footstep, I had not seen the door open; but I saw my father, and at his right hand our neighbour Mrs. Filmore, whom I remembered very well, though I had not seen her for five years. She was a commonplace middle-aged woman, in silk and cashmere; but the lady on the left of my father was no more than twenty, a tall, slim, willowy figure, with luxuriant blond hair, arranged in cunning braids and folds that looked almost too massive for the slight figure and the small-featured, thin-lipped face they crowned. But the face had not a girlish expression: the features were sharp, the pale grey eyes at once acute, restless, and sarcastic. They were fixed on me in half-smiling curiosity, and I felt a painful sensation as if a sharp wind were cutting me. The pale-green dress, and the green leaves that seemed to form a border about her pale blond hair, made me think of a water-nixie—for my mind was full of German lyrics, and this pale, fatal-eyed woman, with the green weeds, looked like a birth from some cold sedgy stream, the daughter of an aged river.

"Well, Latimer, you thought me long," my father said. . . .

But while the last word was in my ears, the whole group vanished, and there was nothing between me and the Chinese painted folding screen that stood before the door. I was cold and trembling; I could only totter forward and throw myself on the sofa. This strange new power had manifested itself again. . . . But *was* it a power? Might it not rather be a disease—a sort of intermittent delirium, concentrating my energy of brain into moments of unhealthy activity, and leaving my saner hours all the more barren? I felt a dizzy sense of unreality in what my eye rested on; I grasped the bell convulsively, like one trying to free himself from nightmare, and rang it twice. Pierre came with a look of alarm in his face.

"*Monsieur ne se trouve pas bien?*" he said, anxiously.

"I'm tired of waiting, Pierre," I said, as distinctly and emphatically as I could, like a man determined to be sober in spite of wine; "I'm afraid something has happened to my father—he's usually so punctual. Run to the Hôtel des Bergues and see if he is there."

Pierre left the room at once, with a soothing "*Bien, Monsieur*"; and I felt the better for this scene of simple, waking prose. Seeking to calm myself still further, I went into my bedroom, adjoining the salon, and opened a case of eau-de-Cologne; took out a bottle; went through the process of taking out the cork very neatly, and then rubbed the reviving spirit over my hands and forehead, and under my nostrils, drawing a new delight from the scent because I had procured it by slow details of labour, and by no strange sudden madness. Already I had begun to taste something of the horror that belongs to the lot of a human being whose nature is not adjusted to simple human conditions.

Still enjoying the scent, I returned to the salon, but it was not unoccupied, as it had been before I left it. In front of the Chinese folding screen there was my father, with Mrs. Filmore on his right hand, and on his left—the slim blond-haired girl, with the keen face and the keen eyes fixed on me in half-smiling curiosity.

"Well, Latimer, you thought me long," my father said. . . .

I heard no more, felt no more, till I became conscious that I was lying with my head low on the sofa, Pierre and my father by my side. As soon as I was thoroughly revived, my father left the room, and presently returned, saying—

"I've been to tell the ladies how you are, Latimer. They were waiting in the next room. We shall put off our shopping expedition today."

Presently he said, "That young lady is Bertha Grant, Mrs. Filmore's orphan niece. Filmore has adopted her, and she lives with them, so you will have her for a neighbour when we go home—perhaps for a near relation; for there is a tenderness between her and Alfred, I suspect, and I should be gratified by the match, since Filmore means to provide for her in every way as if she were his daughter. It had not occurred to me that you knew nothing about her living with the Filmores."

He made no further allusion to the fact of my having fainted at the moment of seeing her, and I would not for the world have told him the reason: I shrank from the idea of disclosing to any one what might be regarded as a pitiable peculiarity, most of all from betraying it to my father, who would have suspected my sanity ever after.

I do not mean to dwell with particularity on the details of my experience. I have described these two cases at length, because they had definite, clearly traceable results in my after-lot.

Shortly after this last occurrence—I think the very next day—I began to be aware of a phase in my abnormal sensibility, to which, from the languid and slight nature of my intercourse with others since my illness, I had not been alive before. This was the obtrusion on my mind of the mental process going forward in first one person, and then another, with whom I happened to be in contact: the vagrant, frivolous ideas and emotions of some uninteresting acquaintance—Mrs. Filmore, for example—would force themselves on my consciousness like an importunate, ill-played musical instrument, or the loud activity of an imprisoned insect. But this unpleasant sensibility was fitful, and left me moments of rest, when the souls of my companions were once more shut out from me, and I felt a relief such as silence brings to wearied nerves. I might have believed this importunate insight to be merely a diseased activity of the imagination, but that my prevision of incalculable words and actions proved it to have a fixed relation to the mental process in other minds. But this superadded consciousness, wearying and annoying enough when it urged on me the trivial experience of indifferent people, became an intense pain and grief when it seemed to be opening to me the souls of those who were in a close relation to me—when the rational talk, the graceful attentions, the wittily turned phrases, and the kindly deeds, which used to make the web of their characters, were seen as if thrust asunder by a microscopic vision, that showed all the intermediate frivolities, all the suppressed egoism, all the struggling chaos of puerilities, meanness, vague capricious memories, and indolent makeshift thoughts, from which human words and deeds emerge like leaflets covering a fermenting heap.

At Basle we were joined by my brother Alfred, now a handsome self-confident man of six-and-twenty—a thorough contrast to my fragile, nervous, ineffectual self. I believe I was held to have a sort of half-womanish, half-ghostly beauty; for the portrait painters, who are thick as weeds at Geneva, had often asked me to sit to them, and I had been the model of a dying minstrel in a fancy picture. But I thoroughly disliked my own physique, and nothing but the belief that it was a condition of poetic genius would have reconciled me to it. That brief hope was quite fled, and I saw in my face now nothing but the stamp of a morbid organisation, framed for passive suffering—too feeble for the sublime resistance of poetic production. Alfred, from whom I had been almost constantly separated, and who, in his present stage of character and appearance, came before me as a perfect stranger, was bent on being extremely friendly and brother-like to me. He had the superficial kindness of a good-humoured, self-satisfied nature, that fears no rivalry, and has encountered no contrarieties. I am not sure that my disposition was good enough for me to have been quite free from envy towards him, even if our desires had not clashed, and if I had been in the healthy human condition which admits of generous confidence and charitable construction. There must always have been an antipathy between our natures. As it was, he became in a few weeks an object of intense hatred to me; and when he entered the room, still more when he spoke, it was as if a sensation of grating metal had set my teeth on edge. My diseased consciousness was more intensely and continually occupied with his thoughts and emotions, than with those of any other person who came in my way. I was perpetually exasperated with the petty promptings of his conceit and his love of patronage, with his self-complacent belief in Bertha Grant's passion for him, with his half-pitying contempt for me—seen not in the ordinary indications of intonations and phrase and slight action, which an acute and suspicious mind is on the watch for, but in all their naked skinless complication.

For we were rivals, and our desires clashed, though he was not aware of it. I have said nothing yet of the effect Bertha Grant produced in me on a nearer acquaintance. That effect was chiefly determined by the fact that she made the only exception, among all the human beings about me, to my unhappy gift of insight. About Bertha I was always in a state of uncertainty: I could watch the expression of her face, and speculate on its meaning; I could ask for her opinion with the real interest of ignorance; I could listen for her words and watch for her smile with hope and fear: she had for me the fascination of an unravelled destiny. I say it was this fact that chiefly determined the strong effect she produced on me: for, in the abstract, no womanly character could seem to have less affinity for that of a shrinking, romantic, passionate youth than Bertha's. She was keen, sarcastic, unimaginative, prematurely cynical, remaining critical and unmoved in the most impressive scenes, inclined to dissect all my favourite poems, and especially contemptuous towards the German lyrics which were my pet literature at that time. To this moment I am unable to define my feelings towards her: it was not ordinary boyish admiration, for she was the very opposite, even to the colour of her hair, of the ideal woman who still remained to me the type of loveliness; and she was without that enthusiasm for the great and good, which, even at the moment of her strongest dominion over me, I should have declared to be the highest element of character. But there is no tyranny more complete than that which a self-centred negative nature exercises over a morbidly sensitive nature perpetually craving sympathy and support. The most independent people feel the effect of a man's silence in heightening their value for his opinion—feel an additional triumph in conquering the reverence of a critic habitually captious and satirical: no wonder, then, that an enthusiastic self-distrusting youth should watch and wait before the closed secret of a sarcastic woman's face, as if it were the shrine of the doubtfully benignant deity who ruled his destiny. For a young enthusiast is unable to imagine the total negation in another mind of the emotions which are stirring his own: they may be feeble, latent, inactive, he thinks, but they are there—they may be called forth; sometimes, in moments of happy hallucination, he believes they may be there in all the greater strength because he sees no outward sign of them. And this effect, as I have intimated, was heightened to its utmost intensity in me, because Bertha was the only being who remained for me in the mysterious seclusion of soul that renders such youthful delusion possible. Doubtless there was another sort of fascination at work—that subtle physical attraction which delights in cheating our psychological predictions, and in compelling the men who paint sylphs, to fall in love with some *bonne et brave femme*, heavy-heeled and freckled.

Bertha's behaviour towards me was such as to encourage all my illusions, to heighten my boyish passion, and make me more and more dependent on her smiles. Looking back with my present wretched knowledge, I conclude that her vanity and love of power were intensely gratified by the belief that I had fainted on first seeing her purely from the strong impression her person had produced on me. The most prosaic woman likes to believe herself the object of a violent, a poetic passion; and without a grain of romance in her, Bertha had that spirit of intrigue which gave piquancy to the idea that the brother of the man she meant to marry was dying with love and jealousy for her sake. That she meant to marry my brother, was what at that time I did not believe; for though he was assiduous in his attentions to her, and I knew well enough that both he and my father had made up their minds to this result, there was not yet an understood engagement—there had been no explicit declaration; and Bertha habitually, while she flirted with my brother, and accepted his homage in a way that implied to him a thorough recognition of its intention, made me believe, by the subtlest looks and phrases—feminine nothings which could never be quoted against her—that he was really the object of her secret ridicule; that she thought him, as I did, a coxcomb, whom she would have pleasure in disappointing. Me she openly petted in my brother's presence, as if I were too young and sickly ever to be thought of as a lover; and that was the view he took of me. But I believe she must inwardly have delighted in the tremors into which she threw me by the coaxing way in which she patted my curls, while she laughed at my quotations. Such caresses were always given in the presence of our friends; for when we were alone together, she affected a much greater distance towards me, and now and then took the opportunity, by words or slight actions, to stimulate my foolish timid hope that she really preferred me. And why should she not follow her inclination? I was not in so advantageous a position as my brother, but I had fortune, I was not a year younger than she was, and she was an heiress, who would soon be of age to decide for herself.

The fluctuations of hope and fear, confined to this one channel, made each day in her presence a delicious torment. There was one deliberate act of hers which especially helped to intoxicate me. When we were at Vienna her twentieth birthday occurred, and as she was very fond of ornaments, we all took the opportunity of the splendid jewellers' shops in that Teutonic Paris to purchase her a birthday present of jewellery. Mine, naturally, was the least expensive; it was an opal ring—the opal was my favourite stone, because it seems to blush and turn pale as if it had a soul. I told Bertha so when I gave it her, and said that it was an emblem of the poetic nature, changing with the changing light of heaven and of woman's eyes. In the evening she appeared elegantly dressed, and wearing conspicuously all the birthday presents except mine. I looked eagerly at her fingers, but saw no opal. I had no opportunity of noticing this to her during the evening; but the next day, when I found her seated near the window alone, after breakfast, I said, "You scorn to wear my poor opal. I should have remembered that you despised poetic natures, and should have given you coral, or turquoise, or some other opaque unresponsive stone." "Do I despise it?" she answered, taking hold of a delicate gold chain which she always wore round her neck and drawing out the end from her bosom with my ring hanging to it; "it hurts me a little, I can tell you," she said, with her usual dubious smile, "to wear it in that secret place; and since your poetical nature is so stupid as to prefer a more public position, I shall not endure the pain any longer."

She took off the ring from the chain and put it on her finger, smiling still, while the blood rushed to my cheeks, and I could not trust myself to say a word of entreaty that she would keep the ring where it was before.

I was completely fooled by this, and for two days shut myself up in my own room whenever Bertha was absent, that I might intoxicate myself afresh with the thought of this scene and all it implied.

I should mention that during these two months—which seemed a long life to me from the novelty and intensity of the pleasures and pains I underwent—my diseased participation in other people's consciousness continued to torment me; now it was my father, and now my brother, now

Mrs. Filmore or her husband, and now our German courier, whose stream of thought rushed upon me like a ringing in the ears not to be got rid of, though it allowed my own impulses and ideas to continue their uninterrupted course. It was like a preternaturally heightened sense of hearing, making audible to one a roar of sound where others find perfect stillness. The weariness and disgust of this involuntary intrusion into other souls was counteracted only by my ignorance of Bertha, and my growing passion for her; a passion enormously stimulated, if not produced, by that ignorance. She was my oasis of mystery in the dreary desert of knowledge. I had never allowed my diseased condition to betray itself, or to drive me into any unusual speech or action, except once, when, in a moment of peculiar bitterness against my brother, I had forestalled some words which I knew he was going to utter—a clever observation, which he had prepared beforehand. He had occasionally a slightly affected hesitation in his speech, and when he paused an instant after the second word, my impatience and jealousy impelled me to continue the speech for him, as if it were something we had both learned by rote. He coloured and looked astonished, as well as annoyed; and the words had no sooner escaped my lips than I felt a shock of alarm lest such an anticipation of words—very far from being words of course, easy to divine—should have betrayed me as an exceptional being, a sort of quiet energumen, whom everyone, Bertha above all, would shudder at and avoid. But I magnified, as usual, the impression any word or deed of mine could produce on others; for no one gave any sign of having noticed my interruption as more than a rudeness, to be forgiven me on the score of my feeble nervous condition.

While this superadded consciousness of the actual was almost constant with me, I had never had a recurrence of that distinct prevision which I have described in relation to my first interview with Bertha; and I was waiting with eager curiosity to know whether or not my vision of Prague would prove to have been an instance of the same kind. A few days after the incident of the opal ring, we were paying one of our frequent visits to the Lichtenberg Palace. I could never look at many pictures in succession; for pictures, when they are at all powerful, affect me so strongly that one or two exhaust all my capability of contemplation. This morning I had been looking at Giorgione's picture of the cruel-eyed woman, said to be a likeness of Lucrezia Borgia. I had stood long alone before it, fascinated by the terrible reality of that cunning, relentless face, till I felt a strange poisoned sensation, as if I had long been inhaling a fatal odour, and was just beginning to be conscious of its effects. Perhaps even then I should not have moved away, if the rest of the party had not returned to this room, and announced that they were going to the Belvedere Gallery to settle a bet which had arisen between my brother and Mr. Filmore about a portrait. I followed them dreamily, and was hardly alive to what occurred till they had all gone up to the gallery, leaving me below; for I refused to come within sight of another picture that day. I made my way to the Grand Terrace, since it was agreed that we should saunter in the gardens when the dispute had been decided. I had been sitting here a short space, vaguely conscious of trim gardens, with a city and green hills in the distance, when, wishing to avoid the proximity of the sentinel, I rose and walked down the broad stone steps, intending to seat myself farther on in the gardens. Just as I reached the gravel walk, I felt an arm slipped within mine, and a light hand gently pressing my wrist. In the same instant a strange intoxicating numbness passed over me, like the continuance or climax of the sensation I was still feeling from the gaze of Lucrezia Borgia. The gardens, the summer sky, the consciousness of Bertha's arm being within mine, all vanished, and I seemed to be suddenly in darkness, out of which there gradually broke a dim firelight, and I felt myself sitting in my father's leather chair in the library at home. I knew the fireplace—the dogs for the wood fire—the black marble chimneypiece with the white marble medallion of the dying Cleopatra in the centre. Intense and hopeless misery was pressing on my soul; the light became stronger, for Bertha was entering with a candle in her hand—Bertha, my wife—with cruel eyes, with green jewels and green leaves on her white ball dress; every hateful thought within her present to me. . . . "Madman, idiot! why don't you kill yourself, then?" It was a moment of hell. I saw into her pitiless soul—saw its barren worldliness, its scorching hate—and felt it clothe me round like an air I was obliged to breathe. She came with her candle and stood over me with a bitter smile of contempt; I saw the great emerald brooch on her bosom, a studded serpent with diamond eyes. I shuddered—I despised this woman with the barren soul and mean thoughts; but I felt helpless before her, as if she clutched my bleeding heart, and would clutch it till the last drop of lifeblood ebbed away. She was my wife, and we hated each other. Gradually the hearth, the dim library, the candle-light disappeared—seemed to melt away into a background of light, the green serpent with the diamond eyes remaining a dark image on the retina. Then I had a sense of my eyelids quivering, and the living daylight broke in upon me; I saw gardens and heard voices. I was seated on the steps of the Belvedere Terrace, and my friends were round me.

The tumult of mind into which I was thrown by this hideous vision made me ill for several days, and prolonged our stay at Vienna. I shuddered with horror as the scene recurred to me; and it recurred constantly, with all its minutiae, as if they had been burnt into my memory; and yet, such is the madness of the human heart under the influence of its immediate desires, I felt a wild hell-braving joy that Bertha was to be mine; for the fulfilment of my former prevision concerning her first appearance before me, left me little hope that this last hideous glimpse of the future was the mere diseased play of my own mind, and had no relation to external realities. One thing alone I looked towards as a possible means of casting doubt on my terrible conviction—the discovery that my vision of Prague had been false—and Prague was the next city on our route.

Meanwhile, I was no sooner in Bertha's society again, than I was as completely under her sway as before. What if I saw into the heart of Bertha, the matured woman—Bertha, my wife? Bertha, the *girl*, was a fascinating secret to me still: I trembled under her touch; I felt the witchery of her presence; I yearned to be assured of her love. The fear of poison is feeble against the sense of thirst. Nay, I was just as jealous of my brother as before—just as much irritated by his small patronising ways; for my pride, my diseased sensibility, were there as they had always been, and winced as inevitably under every offence as my eye winced from an intruding mote. The future, even when brought within the compass of feeling by a vision that made me shudder, had still no more than the force of an idea, compared with the force of present emotion—of my love for Bertha, of my dislike and jealousy towards my brother.

It is an old story, that men sell themselves to the tempter, and sign a bond with their blood, because it is only to take effect at a distant day; then rush on to snatch the cup their souls thirst after with an impulse not the less savage because there is a dark shadow beside them forevermore. There is no short cut, no patent tram road, to wisdom: after all the centuries of invention, the soul's path lies through the thorny wilderness which must be still trodden in solitude, with bleeding feet, with sobs for help, as it was trodden by them of old time.

My mind speculated eagerly on the means by which I should become my brother's successful rival, for I was still too timid, in my ignorance of Bertha's actual feeling, to venture on any step that would urge from her an avowal of it. I thought I should gain confidence even for this, if my vision of Prague proved to have been veracious; and yet, the horror of that certitude! Behind the slim girl Bertha, whose words and looks I watched for, whose touch was bliss, there stood continually that Bertha with the fuller form, the harder eyes, the more rigid mouth—with the barren selfish soul laid bare; no longer a fascinating secret, but a measured fact, urging itself perpetually on my unwilling sight. Are you unable to give me your sympathy—you who read this? Are you unable to imagine this double consciousness at work within me, flowing on like two parallel streams which never mingle their waters and blend into a common hue? Yet you must have known something of the presentiments that spring from an insight at war with passion; and my visions were only like presentiments intensified to horror. You have known the powerlessness of ideas before the might of impulse; and my visions, when once they had passed into memory, were mere ideas—pale shadows that beckoned in vain, while my hand was grasped by the living and the loved.

In after-days I thought with bitter regret that if I had foreseen something more or something different—if instead of that hideous vision which poisoned the passion it could not destroy, or if even along with it I could have had a foreshadowing of that moment when I looked on my brother's face for the last time, some softening influence would have been shed over my feeling towards him: pride and hatred would surely have been subdued into pity, and the record of those hidden sins would have been shortened. But this is one of the vain thoughts with which we men flatter ourselves. We try to believe that the egoism within us would have easily been melted, and that it was only the narrowness of our knowledge which hemmed in our generosity, our awe, our human piety, and hindered them from submerging our hard indifference to the sensations and emotions of our fellow. Our tenderness and self-renunciation seem strong when our egoism has had its day—when, after our mean striving for a triumph that is to be another's loss, the triumph comes suddenly, and we shudder at it, because it is held out by the chill hand of death.

Our arrival in Prague happened at night, and I was glad of this, for it seemed like a deferring of a terribly decisive moment, to be in the city for hours without seeing it. As we were not to remain long in Prague, but to go on speedily to Dresden, it was proposed that we should drive out the next morning and take a general view of the place, as well as visit some of its specially interesting spots, before the heat became oppressive—for we were in August, and the season was hot and dry. But it happened that the ladies were rather late at their morning toilet, and to my father's politely repressed but perceptible annoyance, we were not in the carriage till the morning was far advanced. I thought with a sense of relief, as we entered the Jews' quarter, where we were to visit the old synagogue, that we should be kept in this flat, shut-up part of the city, until we should all be too tired and too warm to go farther, and so we should return without seeing more than the streets through which we had already passed. That would give me another day's suspense—suspense, the only form in which a fearful spirit knows the solace of hope. But, as I stood under the blackened, groined arches of that old synagogue, made dimly visible by the seven thin candles in the sacred lamp, while our Jewish cicerone reached down the Book of the Law, and read to us in its ancient tongue—I felt a shuddering impression that this strange building, with its shrunken lights, this surviving withered remnant of medieval Judaism, was of a piece with my vision. Those darkened dusty Christian saints, with their loftier arches and their larger candles, needed the consolatory scorn with which they might point to a more shrivelled death-in-life than their own.

As I expected, when we left the Jews' quarter the elders of our party wished to return to the hotel. But now, instead of rejoicing in this, as I had done beforehand, I felt a sudden overpowering impulse to go on at once to the bridge, and put an end to the suspense I had been wishing to protract. I declared, with unusual decision, that I would get out of the carriage and walk on alone; they might return without me. My father, thinking this merely a sample of my usual "poetic nonsense," objected that I should only do myself harm by walking in the heat; but when I persisted, he said angrily that I might follow my own absurd devices, but that Schmidt (our courier) must go with me. I assented to this, and set off with Schmidt towards the bridge. I had no sooner passed from under the archway of the grand old gate leading on to the bridge, than a trembling seized me, and I turned cold under the midday sun; yet I went on; I was in search of something—a small detail which I remembered with special intensity as part of my vision. There it was—the patch of rainbow light on the pavement transmitted through a lamp in the shape of a star.

## 2

Before the autumn was at an end, and while the brown leaves still stood thick on the beeches in our park, my brother and Bertha were engaged to each other, and it was understood that their marriage was to take place early in the next spring. In spite of the certainty I had felt from that moment on the bridge at Prague, that Bertha would one day be my wife, my constitutional timidity and distrust had continued to benumb me, and the words in which I had sometimes premeditated a confession of my love, had died away unuttered. The same conflict had gone on within me as before—the longing for an assurance of love from Bertha's lips, the dread lest a word of contempt and denial should fall upon me like a corrosive acid. What was the conviction of a distant necessity to me? I trembled under a present glance, I hungered after a present joy, I was clogged and chilled by a present fear. And so the days passed on: I witnessed Bertha's engagement and heard her marriage discussed as if I were under a conscious nightmare—knowing it was a dream that would vanish, but feeling stifled under the grasp of hard-clutching fingers.

When I was not in Bertha's presence—and I was with her very often, for she continued to treat me with a playful patronage that wakened no jealousy in my brother—I spent my time chiefly in wandering, in strolling, or taking long rides while the daylight lasted, and then shutting myself up with my unread books; for books had lost the power of chaining my attention. My self-consciousness was heightened to that pitch of intensity in which our own emotions take the form of a drama which urges itself imperatively on our contemplation, and we begin to weep, less under the sense of our suffering than at the thought of it. I felt a sort of pitying anguish over the pathos of my own lot: the lot of a being finely organised for pain, but with hardly any fibres that responded to pleasure—to whom the idea of future evil robbed the present of its joy, and for whom the idea of future good did not still the uneasiness of a present yearning or a present dread. I went dumbly through that stage of the poet's suffering, in which he feels the delicious pang of utterance, and makes an image of his sorrows.

I was left entirely without remonstrance concerning this dreamy wayward life: I knew my father's thought about me: "That lad will never be good for anything in life: he may waste his years in an insignificant way on the income that falls to him: I shall not trouble myself about a career for him."

One mild morning in the beginning of November, it happened that I was standing outside the portico patting lazy old Caesar, a Newfoundland almost blind with age, the only dog that ever took any notice of me—for the very dogs shunned me, and fawned on the happier people about me—when the groom brought up my brother's horse which was to carry him to the hunt, and my brother himself appeared at the door, florid, broad-chested, and self-complacent, feeling what a good-natured fellow he was not to behave insolently to us all on the strength of his great advantages.

"Latimer, old boy," he said to me in a tone of compassionate cordiality, "what a pity it is you don't have a run with the hounds now and then! The finest thing in the world for low spirits!"

"Low spirits!" I thought bitterly, as he rode away; "that is the sort of phrase with which coarse, narrow natures like yours think to describe experience of which you can know no more than your horse knows. It is to such as you that the good of this world falls: ready dullness, healthy selfishness, good-tempered conceit—these are the keys to happiness."

The quick thought came, that my selfishness was even stronger than his—it was only a suffering selfishness instead of an enjoying one. But then, again, my exasperating insight into Alfred's self-complacent soul, his freedom from all the doubts and fears, the unsatisfied yearnings, the exquisite tortures of sensitiveness, that had made the web of my life, seemed to absolve me from all bonds towards him. This man needed no pity, no love; those fine influences would have been as little felt by him as the delicate white mist is felt by the rock it caresses. There was no evil in store for *him*: if he was not to marry Bertha, it would be because he had found a lot pleasanter to himself.

Mr. Filmore's house lay not more than half a mile beyond our own gates, and whenever I knew my brother was gone in another direction, I went there for the chance of finding Bertha at home. Later on in the day I walked thither. By a rare accident she was alone, and we walked out in the grounds together, for she seldom went on foot beyond the trimly swept gravel walks. I remember what a beautiful sylph she looked to me as the low November sun shone on her blond hair, and she tripped along teasing me with her usual light banter, to which I listened half fondly, half moodily; it was all the sign Bertha's mysterious inner self ever made to me. Today perhaps the moodiness predominated, for I had not yet shaken off the access of jealous hate which my brother had raised in me by his parting patronage. Suddenly I interrupted and startled her by saying, almost fiercely, "Bertha, how can you love Alfred?"

She looked at me with surprise for a moment, but soon her light smile came again, and she answered sarcastically, "Why do you suppose I love him?"

"How can you ask that, Bertha?"

"What! your wisdom thinks I must love the man I'm going to marry? The most unpleasant thing in the world. I should quarrel with him; I should be jealous of him; our *ménage* would be conducted in a very ill-bred manner. A little quiet contempt contributes greatly to the elegance of life."

"Bertha, that is not your real feeling. Why do you delight in trying to deceive me by inventing such cynical speeches?"

"I need never take the trouble of invention in order to deceive you, my small Tasso"—(that was the mocking name she usually gave me). "The easiest way to deceive a poet is to tell him the truth."

She was testing the validity of her epigram in a daring way, and for a moment the shadow of my vision—the Bertha whose soul was no secret to me—passed between me and the radiant girl, the playful sylph whose feelings were a fascinating mystery. I suppose I must have shuddered, or betrayed in some other way my momentary chill of horror.

"Tasso!" she said, seizing my wrist, and peeping round into my face, "are you really beginning to discern what a heartless girl I am? Why, you are not half the poet I thought you were; you are actually capable of believing the truth about me."

The shadow passed from between us, and was no longer the object nearest to me. The girl whose light fingers grasped me, whose elfish charming face looked into mine—who, I thought, was betraying an interest in my feelings that she would not have directly avowed—this warm-breathing presence again possessed my senses and imagination like a returning siren melody which had been overpowered for an instant by the roar of threatening waves. It was a moment as delicious to me as the waking up to a consciousness of youth after a dream of middle age. I forgot everything but my passion, and said with swimming eyes—

"Bertha, shall you love me when we are first married? I wouldn't mind if you really loved me only for a little while."

Her look of astonishment, as she loosed my hand and started away from me recalled me to a sense of my strange, my criminal indiscretion.

"Forgive me," I said, hurriedly, as soon as I could speak again; "I did not know what I was saying."

"Ah, Tasso's mad fit has come on, I see," she answered quietly, for she had recovered herself sooner than I had. "Let him go home and keep his head cool. I must go in, for the sun is setting."

I left her—full of indignation against myself. I had let slip words which, if she reflected on them, might rouse in her a suspicion of my abnormal mental condition—a suspicion which of all things I dreaded. And besides that, I was ashamed of the apparent baseness I had committed in uttering them to my brother's betrothed wife. I wandered home slowly, entering our park through a private gate instead of by the lodges. As I approached the house, I saw a man dashing off at full speed from the stable yard across the park. Had any accident happened at home? No; perhaps it was only one of my father's peremptory business errands that required this headlong haste. Nevertheless I quickened my pace without any distinct motive, and was soon at the house. I will not dwell on the scene I found there. My brother was dead—had been pitched from his horse, and killed on the spot by a concussion of the brain.

I went up to the room where he lay, and where my father was seated beside him with a look of rigid despair. I had shunned my father more than anyone since our return home, for the radical antipathy between our natures made my insight into his inner self a constant affliction to me. But now, as I went up to him, and stood beside him in sad silence, I felt the presence of a new element that blended us as we had never been blent before. My father had been one of the most successful men in the money-getting world: he had had no sentimental sufferings, no illness. The heaviest trouble that had befallen him was the death of his first wife. But he married my mother soon after; and I remember he seemed exactly the same, to my keen childish observation, the week after her death as before. But now, at last, a sorrow had come—the sorrow of old age, which suffers the more from the crushing of its pride and its hopes, in proportion as the pride and hope are narrow and prosaic. His son was to have been married soon—would probably have stood for the borough at the next election. That son's existence was the best motive that could be alleged for making new purchases of land every year to round off the estate. It is a dreary thing to live on doing the same things year after year, without knowing why we do them. Perhaps the tragedy of disappointed youth and passion is less piteous than the tragedy of disappointed age and worldliness.

As I saw into the desolation of my father's heart, I felt a movement of deep pity towards him, which was the beginning of a new affection—an affection that grew and strengthened in spite of the strange bitterness with which he regarded me in the first month or two after my brother's death. If it had not been for the softening influence of my compassion for him—the first deep compassion I had ever felt—I should have been stung by the perception that my father transferred the inheritance of an eldest son to me with a mortified sense that fate had compelled him to the unwelcome course of caring for me as an important being. It was only in spite of himself that he began to think of me with anxious regard. There is hardly any neglected child for whom death has made vacant a more favoured place, who will not understand what I mean.

Gradually, however, my new deference to his wishes, the effect of that patience which was born of my pity for him, won upon his affection, and he began to please himself with the endeavour to make me fill my brother's place as fully as my feebler personality would admit. I saw that the prospect which by and by presented itself of my becoming Bertha's husband was welcome to him, and he even contemplated in my case what he had not intended in my brother's—that his son and daughter-in-law should make one household with him. My softened feeling towards my father made this the happiest time I had known since childhood—these last months in which I retained the delicious illusion of loving Bertha, of longing and doubting and hoping that she might love me. She behaved with a certain new consciousness and distance towards me after my brother's death; and I too was under a double constraint—that of delicacy towards my brother's memory, and of anxiety as to the impression my abrupt words had left on her mind. But the additional screen this mutual reserve erected between us only brought me more completely under her power: no matter how empty the adytum, so that the veil, be thick enough. So absolute is our soul's need of something hidden and uncertain for the maintenance of that doubt and hope and effort which are the breath of its life, that if the whole future were laid bare to us beyond today, the interest of all mankind would be bent on the hours that lie between; we should pant after the uncertainties of our one morning and our one afternoon; we should rush fiercely to the Exchange for our last possibility of speculation, of success, of disappointment; we should have a glut of political prophets foretelling a crisis or a no-crisis within the only twenty-four hours left open to prophecy. Conceive the condition of the human mind if all propositions whatsoever were self-evident except one, which was to become self-evident at the close of the summer's day, but in the meantime might be the subject of question, of hypothesis, of debate. Art and philosophy, literature and science, would fasten like bees on that one proposition which had the honey of probability in it, and be the more eager because their enjoyment would end with sunset. Our impulses, our spiritual activities, no more adjust themselves to the idea of their future nullity, than the beating of our heart, or the irritability of our muscles.

Bertha, the slim, fair-haired girl, whose present thoughts and emotions were an enigma to me amidst the fatiguing obviousness of the other minds around me, was as absorbing to me as a single unknown today—as a single hypothetic proposition to remain problematic till sunset; and all the cramped, hemmed-in belief and disbelief, trust and distrust, of my nature, welled out in this one narrow channel.

And she made me believe that she loved me. Without ever quitting her tone of badinage and playful superiority, she intoxicated me with the sense that I was necessary to her, that she was never at ease unless I was near her, submitting to her playful tyranny. It costs a woman so little effort to besot us in this way! A half-repressed word, a moment's unexpected silence, even an easy fit of petulance on our account, will serve us as hashish for a long while. Out of the subtlest web of scarcely perceptible signs, she set me weaving the fancy that she had always unconsciously loved me better than Alfred, but that, with the ignorant fluttered sensibility of a young girl, she had been imposed on by the charm that lay for her in the distinction of being admired and chosen by a man who made so brilliant a figure in the world as my brother. She satirised herself in a very graceful way for her vanity and ambition. What was it to me that I had the light of my wretched prevision on the fact that now it was I who possessed at least all but the personal part of my brother's advantages? Our sweet illusions are half of them conscious illusions, like effects of colour that we know to be made up of tinsel, broken glass, and rags.

We were married eighteen months after Alfred's death, one cold, clear morning in April, when there came hail and sunshine both together; and Bertha, in her white silk and pale-green leaves, and the pale hues of her hair and face, looked like the spirit of the morning. My father was happier than he had thought of being again: my marriage, he felt sure, would complete the desirable modification of my character, and make me practical and worldly enough to take my place in society among sane men. For he delighted in Bertha's tact and acuteness, and felt sure she would be mistress of me, and make me what she chose: I was only twenty-one, and madly in love with her. Poor Father! He kept that hope a little while after our first year of marriage, and it was not quite extinct when paralysis came and saved him from utter disappointment.

I shall hurry through the rest of my story, not dwelling so much as I have hitherto done on my inward experience. When people are well known to each other, they talk rather of what befalls them externally, leaving their feelings and sentiments to be inferred.

We lived in a round of visits for some time after our return home, giving splendid dinner parties, and making a sensation in our neighbourhood by the new lustre of our equipage, for my father had reserved this display of his increased wealth for the period of his son's marriage; and we gave our acquaintances liberal opportunity for remarking that it was a pity I made so poor a figure as an heir and a bridegroom. The nervous fatigue of this existence, the insincerities and platitudes which I had to live through twice over—through my inner and outward sense—would have been maddening to me, if I had not had that sort of intoxicated callousness which came from the delights of a first passion. A bride and bridegroom, surrounded by all the appliances of wealth, hurried through the day by the whirl of society, filling their solitary moments with hastily snatched caresses, are prepared for their future life together as the novice is prepared for the cloister—by experiencing its utmost contrast.

Through all these crowded excited months, Bertha's inward self remained shrouded from me, and I still read her thoughts only through the language of her lips and demeanour: I had still the human interest of wondering whether what I did and said pleased her, of longing to hear a word of affection, of giving a delicious exaggeration of meaning to her smile. But I was conscious of a growing difference in her manner towards me; sometimes strong enough to be called haughty coldness, cutting and chilling me as the hail had done that came across the sunshine on our marriage morning; sometimes only perceptible in the dexterous avoidance of a tête-à-tête walk or dinner to which I had been looking forward. I had been deeply pained by this—had even felt a sort of crushing of the heart, from the sense that my brief day of happiness was near its setting; but still I remained dependent on Bertha, eager for the last rays of a bliss that would soon be gone forever, hoping and watching for some afterglow more beautiful from the impending night.

I remember—how should I not remember?—the time when that dependence and hope utterly left me, when the sadness I had felt in Bertha's growing estrangement became a joy that I looked back upon with longing, as a man might look back on the last pains in a paralysed limb. It was just after the close of my father's last illness, which had necessarily withdrawn us from society and thrown us more upon each other. It was the evening of my father's death. On that evening the veil which had shrouded Bertha's soul from me—had made me find in her alone among my fellow beings the blessed possibility of mystery, and doubt, and expectation—was first withdrawn. Perhaps it was the first day since the beginning of my passion for her, in which that passion was completely neutralised by the presence of an absorbing feeling of another kind. I had been watching by my father's deathbed: I had been witnessing the last fitful yearning glance his soul had cast back on the spent inheritance of life—the last faint consciousness of love he had gathered from the pressure of my hand. What are all our personal loves when we have been sharing in that supreme agony? In the first moments when we come away from the presence of death, every other relation to the living is merged, to our feeling, in the great relation of a common nature and a common destiny.

In that state of mind I joined Bertha in her private sitting room. She was seated in a leaning posture on a settee, with her back towards the door; the great rich coils of her pale blond hair surmounting her small neck, visible above the back of the settee. I remember, as I closed the door behind me, a cold tremulousness seizing me, and a vague sense of being hated and lonely—vague and strong, like a presentiment. I know how I looked at that moment, for I saw myself in Bertha's thought as she lifted her cutting grey eyes, and looked at me: a miserable ghost-seer, surrounded by phantoms in the noonday, trembling under a breeze when the leaves were still, without appetite for the common objects of human desire, but pining after the moonbeams. We were front to front with each other, and judged each other. The terrible moment of complete illumination had come to me, and I saw that the darkness had hidden no landscape from me, but only a blank prosaic wall: from that evening forth, through the sickening years which followed, I saw all round the narrow room of this woman's soul—saw petty artifice and mere negation where I had delighted to believe in coy sensibilities and in wit at war with latent feeling—saw the light floating vanities of the girl defining themselves into the systematic coquetry, the scheming selfishness, of the woman—saw repulsion and antipathy harden into cruel hatred, giving pain only for the sake of wreaking itself.

For Bertha too, after her kind, felt the bitterness of disillusion. She had believed that my wild poet's passion for her would make me her slave; and that, being her slave, I should execute her will in all things. With the essential shallowness of a negative, unimaginative nature, she was unable to conceive the fact that sensibilities were anything else than weaknesses. She had thought my weaknesses would put me in her power, and she found them unmanageable forces. Our positions were reversed. Before marriage she had completely mastered my imagination, for she was a secret to me; and I created the unknown thought before which I trembled as if it were hers. But now that her soul was laid open to me, now that I was compelled to share the privacy of her motives, to follow all the petty devices that preceded her words and acts, she found herself powerless with me, except to produce in me the chill shudder of repulsion—powerless, because I could be acted on by no lever within her reach. I was dead to worldly ambitions, to social vanities, to all the incentives within the compass of her narrow imagination, and I lived under influences utterly invisible to her.

She was really pitiable to have such a husband, and so all the world thought. A graceful, brilliant woman, like Bertha, who smiled on morning callers, made a figure in ballrooms, and was capable of that light repartee which, from such a woman, is accepted as wit, was secure of carrying off all sympathy from a husband who was sickly, abstracted, and, as some suspected, crack-brained. Even the servants in our house gave her the balance of their regard and pity. For there were no audible quarrels between us; our alienation, our repulsion from each other, lay within the silence of our own hearts; and if the mistress went out a great deal, and seemed to dislike the master's society, was it not natural, poor thing? The master was odd. I was kind and just to my dependants, but I excited in them a shrinking, half-contemptuous pity; for this class of men and women are but slightly determined in their estimate of others by the general considerations, or even experience, of character. They judge of persons as they judge of coins, and value those who pass current at a high rate.

After a time I interfered so little with Bertha's habits, that it might seem wonderful how her hatred towards me could grow so intense and active as it did. But she had begun to suspect, by some involuntary betrayals of mine, that there was an abnormal power of penetration in me—that fitfully, at least, I was strangely cognisant of her thoughts and intentions, and she began to be haunted by a terror of me, which alternated every now and then with defiance. She meditated continually how the incubus could be shaken off her life—how she could be freed from this hateful bond to a being whom she at once despised as an imbecile, and dreaded as an inquisitor. For a long while she lived in the hope that my evident wretchedness would drive me to the commission of suicide; but suicide was not in my nature. I was too completely swayed by the sense that I was in the grasp of unknown forces, to believe in my power of self-release. Towards my own destiny I had become entirely passive; for my one ardent desire had spent itself, and impulse no longer predominated over knowledge. For this reason I never thought of taking any steps towards a complete separation, which would have made our alienation evident to the world. Why should I rush for help to a new course, when I was only suffering from the consequences of a deed which had been the act of my intensest will? That would have been the logic of one who had desires to gratify, and I had no desires. But Bertha and I lived more and more aloof from each other. The rich find it easy to live married and apart.

That course of our life which I have indicated in a few sentences filled the space of years. So much misery—so slow and hideous a growth of hatred and sin, may be compressed into a sentence! And men judge of each other's lives through this summary medium. They epitomise the experience of their fellow mortal, and pronounce judgment on him in neat syntax, and feel themselves wise and virtuous—conquerors over the temptations they define in well-selected predicates. Seven years of wretchedness glide glibly over the lips of the man who has never counted them out in moments of chill disappointment, of head and heart throbbings, or dread and vain wrestling, of remorse and despair. We learn *words* by rote, but not their meaning; *that* must be paid for with our lifeblood, and printed in the subtle fibres of our nerves.

But I will hasten to finish my story. Brevity is justified at once to those who readily understand, and to those who will never understand.

Some years after my father's death, I was sitting by the dim firelight in my library one January evening—sitting in the leather chair that used to be my father's—when Bertha appeared at the door, with a candle in her hand, and advanced towards me. I knew the balldress she had on—the white balldress, with the green jewels, shone upon by the light of the wax candle which lit up the medallion of the dying Cleopatra on the mantelpiece. Why did she come to me before going out? I had not seen her in the library, which was my habitual place, for months. Why did she stand before me with the candle in her hand, with her cruel contemptuous eyes fixed on me, and the glittering serpent, like a familiar demon, on her breast? For a moment I thought this fulfilment of my vision at Vienna marked some dreadful crisis in my fate, but I saw nothing in Bertha's mind, as she stood before me, except scorn for the look of overwhelming misery with which I sat before her. . . . "Fool, idiot, why don't you kill yourself, then?"—that was her thought. But at length her thoughts reverted to her errand, and she spoke aloud. The apparently indifferent nature of the errand seemed to make a ridiculous anticlimax to my prevision and my agitation.

"I have had to hire a new maid. Fletcher is going to be married, and she wants me to ask you to let her husband have the public house and farm at Molton. I wish him to have it. You must give the promise now, because Fletcher is going tomorrow morning—and quickly, because I'm in a hurry."

"Very well; you may promise her," I said, indifferently, and Bertha swept out of the library again.

I always shrank from the sight of a new person, and all the more when it was a person whose mental life was likely to weary my reluctant insight with worldly ignorant trivialities. But I shrank especially from the sight of this new maid, because her advent had been announced to me at a moment to which I could not cease to attach some fatality: I had a vague dread that I should find her mixed up with the dreary drama of my life—that some new sickening vision would reveal her to me as an evil genius. When at last I did unavoidably meet her, the vague dread was changed into definite disgust. She was a tall, wiry, dark-eyed woman, this Mrs. Archer, with a face handsome enough to give her coarse, hard nature the odious finish of bold self-confident coquetry. That was enough to make me avoid her, quite apart from the contemptuous feeling with which she contemplated me. I seldom saw her; but I perceived that she rapidly became a favourite with her mistress, and, after the lapse of eight or nine months, I began to be aware that there had arisen in Bertha's mind towards this woman a mingled feeling of fear and dependence, and that this feeling was associated with ill-defined images of candlelight scenes in her dressing room, and the locking-up of something in Bertha's cabinet. My interviews with my wife had become so brief and so rarely solitary, that I had no opportunity of perceiving these images in her mind with more definiteness. The recollections of the past become contracted in the rapidity of thought till they sometimes bear hardly a more distinct resemblance to the external reality than the forms of an oriental alphabet to the objects that suggested them.

Besides, for the last year or more a modification had been going forward in my mental condition, and was growing more and more marked. My insight into the minds of those around me was becoming dimmer and more fitful, and the ideas that crowded my double consciousness became less and less dependent on any personal contact. All that was personal in me seemed to be suffering a gradual death, so that I was losing the organ through which the personal agitations and projects of others could affect me. But along with this relief from wearisome insight, there was a new development of what I concluded—as I have since found rightly—to be a prevision of external scenes. It was as if the relation between me and my fellow men was more and more deadened, and my relation to what we call the inanimate was quickened into new life. The more I lived apart from society, and in proportion as my wretchedness subsided from the violent throb of agonised passion into the dulness of habitual pain, the more frequent and vivid became such visions as that I had had of Prague—of strange cities, of sandy plains, of gigantic ruins, of midnight skies with strange bright constellations, of mountain passes, of grassy nooks flecked with the afternoon sunshine through the boughs: I was in the midst of such scenes, and in all of them one presence seemed to weigh on me in all these mighty shapes—the presence of something unknown and pitiless. For continual suffering had annihilated religious faith within me: to the utterly miserable—the unloving and the unloved—there is no religion possible, no worship but a worship of devils. And beyond all these, and continually recurring, was the vision of my death—the pangs, the suffocation, the last struggle, when life would be grasped at in vain.

Things were in this state near the end of the seventh year. I had become entirely free from insight, from my abnormal cognisance of any other consciousness than my own, and instead of intruding involuntarily into the world of other minds, was living continually in my own solitary future. Bertha was aware that I was greatly changed. To my surprise she had of late seemed to seek opportunities of remaining in my society, and had cultivated that kind of distant yet familiar talk which is customary

between a husband and wife who live in polite and irrevocable alienation.
I bore this with languid submission, and without feeling enough interest
in her motives to be roused into keen observation; yet I could not help
perceiving something triumphant and excited in her carriage and the
expression of her face—something too subtle to express itself in words
or tones, but giving one the idea that she lived in a state of expectation or
hopeful suspense. My chief feeling was satisfaction that her inner self was
once more shut out from me; and I almost revelled for the moment in the
absent melancholy that made me answer her at cross purposes, and betray
utter ignorance of what she had been saying. I remember well the look
and the smile with which she one day said, after a mistake of this kind on
my part: "I used to think you were a clairvoyant, and that was the reason
why you were so bitter against other clairvoyants, wanting to keep your
monopoly; but I see now you have become rather duller than the rest of
the world."

I said nothing in reply. It occurred to me that her recent obtrusion of
herself upon me might have been prompted by the wish to test my power
of detecting some of her secrets; but I let the thought drop again at once:
her motives and her deeds had no interest for me, and whatever pleasures
she might be seeking, I had no wish to balk her. There was still pity in my
soul for every living thing, and Bertha was living—was surrounded with
possibilities of misery.

Just at this time there occurred an event which roused me somewhat
from my inertia, and gave me an interest in the passing moment that I had
thought impossible for me. It was a visit from Charles Meunier, who had
written me word that he was coming to England for relaxation from too
strenuous labour, and would like to see me. Meunier had now a European
reputation; but his letter to me expressed that keen remembrance of an
early regard, an early debt of sympathy, which is inseparable from nobility of character: and I too felt as if his presence would be to me like a
transient resurrection into a happier preexistence.

He came, and as far as possible, I renewed our old pleasure of making
tête-à-tête excursions, though, instead of mountains and glaciers and the
wide blue lake, we had to content ourselves with mere slopes and ponds
and artificial plantations. The years had changed us both, but with what
different result! Meunier was now a brilliant figure in society, to whom
elegant women pretended to listen, and whose acquaintance was boasted
of by noblemen ambitious of brains. He repressed with the utmost delicacy all betrayal of the shock which I am sure he must have received from
our meeting, or of a desire to penetrate into my condition and circumstances, and sought by the utmost exertion of his charming social powers
to make our reunion agreeable. Bertha was much struck by the unexpected fascinations of a visitor whom she had expected to find presentable

only on the score of his celebrity, and put forth all her coquetries and accomplishments. Apparently she succeeded in attracting his admiration, for his manner towards her was attentive and flattering. The effect of his presence on me was so benignant, especially in those renewals of our old tête-à-tête wanderings, when he poured forth to me wonderful narratives of his professional experience, that more than once, when his talk turned on the psychological relations of disease, the thought crossed my mind that, if his stay with me were long enough, I might possibly bring myself to tell this man the secrets of my lot. Might there not lie some remedy for *me*, too, in his science? Might there not at least lie some comprehension and sympathy ready for me in his large and susceptible mind? But the thought only flickered feebly now and then, and died out before it could become a wish. The horror I had of again breaking in on the privacy of another soul, made me, by an irrational instinct, draw the shroud of concealment more closely around my own, as we automatically perform the gesture we feel to be wanting in another.

When Meunier's visit was approaching its conclusion, there happened an event which caused some excitement in our household, owing to the surprisingly strong effect it appeared to produce on Bertha—on Bertha, the self-possessed, who usually seemed inaccessible to feminine agitations, and did even her hate in a self-restrained hygienic manner. This event was the sudden illness of her maid, Mrs. Archer. I have reserved to this moment the mention of a circumstance which had forced itself on my notice shortly before Meunier's arrival, namely, that there had been some quarrel between Bertha and this maid, apparently during a visit to a distant family, in which she had accompanied her mistress. I had overheard Archer speaking in a tone of bitter insolence, which I should have thought an adequate reason for immediate dismissal. No dismissal followed; on the contrary, Bertha seemed to be silently putting up with personal inconveniences from the exhibitions of this woman's temper. I was the more astonished to observe that her illness seemed a cause of strong solicitude to Bertha; that she was at the bedside night and day, and would allow no one else to officiate as head nurse. It happened that our family doctor was out on a holiday, an accident which made Meunier's presence in the house doubly welcome, and he apparently entered into the case with an interest which seemed so much stronger than the ordinary professional feeling, that one day when he had fallen into a long fit of silence after visiting her, I said to him—

"Is this a very peculiar case of disease, Meunier?"

"No," he answered, "it is an attack of peritonitis, which will be fatal, but which does not differ physically from many other cases that have come under my observation. But I'll tell you what I have on my mind. I want to make an experiment on this woman, if you will give me permission. It can do her no harm—will give her no pain—for I shall not make it until life is extinct to all purposes of sensation. I want to try the effect of transfusing blood into her arteries after the heart has ceased to beat for some minutes. I have tried the experiment again and again with animals that have died of this disease, with astounding results, and I want to try it on a human subject. I have the small tubes necessary, in a case I have with me, and the rest of the apparatus could be prepared readily. I should use my own blood—take it from my own arm. This woman won't live through the night, I'm convinced, and I want you to promise me your assistance in making the experiment. I can't do without another hand, but it would perhaps not be well to call in a medical assistant from among your provincial doctors. A disagreeable foolish version of the thing might get abroad."

"Have you spoken to my wife on the subject?" I said, "because she appears to be peculiarly sensitive about this woman: she has been a favourite maid."

"To tell you the truth," said Meunier, "I don't want her to know about it. There are always insuperable difficulties with women in these matters, and the effect on the supposed dead body may be startling. You and I will sit up together, and be in readiness. When certain symptoms appear I shall take you in, and at the right moment we must manage to get everyone else out of the room."

I need not give our farther conversation on the subject. He entered very fully into the details, and overcame my repulsion from them, by exciting in me a mingled awe and curiosity concerning the possible results of his experiment.

We prepared everything, and he instructed me in my part as assistant. He had not told Bertha of his absolute conviction that Archer would not survive through the night, and endeavoured to persuade her to leave the patient and take a night's rest. But she was obstinate, suspecting the fact that death was at hand, and supposing that he wished merely to save her nerves. She refused to leave the sickroom. Meunier and I sat up together in the library, he making frequent visits to the sickroom, and returning with the information that the case was taking precisely the course he expected. Once he said to me, "Can you imagine any cause of ill feeling this woman has against her mistress, who is so devoted to her?"

"I think there was some misunderstanding between them before her illness. Why do you ask?"

"Because I have observed for the last five or six hours—since, I fancy, she has lost all hope of recovery—there seems a strange prompting in her to say something which pain and failing strength forbid her to utter; and there is a look of hideous meaning in her eyes, which she turns continually towards her mistress. In this disease the mind often remains singularly clear to the last."

"I am not surprised at an indication of malevolent feeling in her," I said. "She is a woman who has always inspired me with distrust and dislike, but she managed to insinuate herself into her mistress's favour." He was silent after this, looking at the fire with an air of absorption, till he went upstairs again. He stayed away longer than usual, and on returning, said to me quietly, "Come now."

I followed him to the chamber where death was hovering. The dark hangings of the large bed made a background that gave a strong relief to Bertha's pale face as she saw me enter, and then looked at Meunier with an expression of angry inquiry; but he lifted up his hand as if to impose silence, while he fixed his glance on the dying woman and felt her pulse. The face was pinched and ghastly, a cold perspiration was on the forehead, and the eyelids were lowered so as almost to conceal the large dark eyes. After a minute or two, Meunier walked round to the other side of the bed where Bertha stood, and with his usual air of gentle politeness towards her begged her to leave the patient under our care—everything should be done for her—she was no longer in a state to be conscious of an affectionate presence. Bertha was hesitating, apparently almost willing to believe his assurance and to comply. She looked round at the ghastly dying face, as if to read the confirmation of that assurance, when for a moment the lowered eyelids were raised again, and it seemed as if the eyes were looking towards Bertha, but blankly. A shudder passed through Bertha's frame, and she returned to her station near the pillow, tacitly implying that she would not leave the room.

The eyelids were lifted no more. Once I looked at Bertha as she watched the face of the dying one. She wore a rich peignoir, and her blond hair was half covered by a lace cap: in her attire she was, as always, an elegant woman, fit to figure in a picture of modern aristocratic life: but I asked myself how that face of hers could ever have seemed to me the face of a woman born of woman, with memories of childhood, capable of pain, needing to be fondled? The features at that moment seemed so preternaturally sharp, the eyes were so hard and eager—she looked like a cruel immortal, finding her spiritual feast in the agonies of a dying race. For across those hard features there came something like a flash when the last hour had been breathed out, and we all felt that the dark veil had completely fallen. What secret was there between Bertha and this woman? I turned my eyes from her with a horrible dread lest my insight should return, and I should be obliged to see what had been breeding about two unloving women's hearts. I felt that Bertha had been watching for the moment of death as the sealing of her secret: I thanked Heaven it could remain sealed for me.

Meunier said quietly, "She is gone." He then gave his arm to Bertha, and she submitted to be led out of the room.

I suppose it was at her order that two female attendants came into the room, and dismissed the younger one who had been present before. When they entered, Meunier had already opened the artery in the long thin neck that lay rigid on the pillow, and I dismissed them, ordering them to remain at a distance till we rang: the doctor, I said, had an operation to perform—he was not sure about the death. For the next twenty minutes I forgot everything but Meunier and the experiment in which he was so absorbed, that I think his senses would have been closed against all sounds or sights which had no relation to it. It was my task at first to keep up the artificial respiration in the body after the transfusion had been effected, but presently Meunier relieved me, and I could see the wondrous slow return of life; the breast began to heave, the inspirations became stronger, the eyelids quivered, and the soul seemed to have returned beneath them. The artificial respiration was withdrawn: still the breathing continued, and there was a movement of the lips.

Just then I heard the handle of the door moving: I suppose Bertha had heard from the women that they had been dismissed: probably a vague fear had arisen in her mind, for she entered with a look of alarm. She came to the foot of the bed and gave a stifled cry.

The dead woman's eyes were wide open, and met hers in full recognition—the recognition of hate. With a sudden strong effort, the hand that Bertha had thought forever still was pointed towards her, and the haggard face moved. The gasping eager voice said—

"You mean to poison your husband . . . the poison is in the black cabinet . . . I got it for you . . . you laughed at me, and told lies about me behind my back, to make me disgusting . . . because you were jealous . . . are you sorry . . . now?"

The lips continued to murmur but the sounds were no longer distinct. Soon there was no sound—only a slight movement: the flame had leaped out, and was being extinguished the faster. The wretched woman's heartstrings had been set to hatred and vengeance; the spirit of life had swept the chords for an instant, and was gone again forever. Great God! Is this what it is to live again . . . to wake up with our unstilled thirst upon us, with our unuttered curses rising to our lips, with our muscles ready to act out their half-committed sins?

Bertha stood pale at the foot of the bed, quivering and helpless, despairing of devices, like a cunning animal whose hiding places are surrounded by swift-advancing flame. Even Meunier looked paralysed; life for that moment ceased to be a scientific problem to him. As for me, this scene seemed of one texture with the rest of my existence: horror was my familiar, and this new revelation was only like an old pain recurring with new circumstances.

Since then Bertha and I have lived apart—she in her own neighbourhood, the mistress of half our wealth, I as a wanderer in foreign countries, until I came to this Devonshire nest to die. Bertha lives pitied and admired; for what had I against that charming woman, whom everyone but myself could have been happy with? There had been no witness of the scene in the dying room except Meunier, and while Meunier lived his lips were sealed by a promise to me.

Once or twice, weary of wandering, I rested in a favourite spot, and my heart went out towards the men and women and children whose faces were becoming familiar to me: but I was driven away again in terror at the approach of my old insight—driven away to live continually with the one Unknown Presence revealed and yet hidden by the moving curtain of the earth and sky. Till at last disease took hold of me and forced me to rest here—forced me to live in dependence on my servants. And then the curse of insight—of my double consciousness, came again, and has never left me. I know all their narrow thoughts, their feeble regard, their half-wearied pity.

It is the 20th of September 1850. I know these figures I have just written, as if they were a long familiar inscription. I have seen them on this page in my desk unnumbered times, when the scene of my dying struggle has opened upon me. . . .

## QUESTIONS

1. Why does Latimer tell the story of his experiences only when he is close to death?

2. What does Latimer mean when he attributes his solitude to "the poet's sensibility without his voice"? (161)

3. Why is Charles Meunier the only friend Latimer ever has? When Meunier visits him near the end of the story, why does Latimer decide not to confide in Meunier about his condition?

4. Why do Latimer's insights into the future and the inner lives of people around him bring him only misery?

5. For Latimer, why is Bertha "the only exception, among all the human beings about me, to my unhappy gift of insight"? (167)

6. Why does Latimer continue to pursue Bertha despite his prevision of their hellish future together?

7. Why is Latimer able to feel pity and affection for his father only after Alfred's death? Why is it that on the evening of his father's death "the veil which had shrouded Bertha's soul . . . was first withdrawn"? (180)

8. Why does Latimer say, "Brevity is justified at once to those who readily understand, and to those who will never understand"? (183)

9. Why does Eliot have Mrs. Archer brought back from death to reveal Bertha's plan to poison Latimer?

10. What does Latimer mean by "the one Unknown Presence" that he continually lives with? (190)

## FOR FURTHER REFLECTION

1. Does Latimer bear any responsibility for making Bertha what she is?

2. Is it necessary to be somewhat deluded about other people and blind to their inner lives in order to care for them?

3. Is Latimer correct, that our souls have a "need of something hidden and uncertain for the maintenance of that doubt and hope and effort which are the breath of its life"?

4. If we can only understand the meaning of the words we use to "epitomise" the lives of others if "paid for with our lifeblood, and printed in the subtle fibres of our nerves," does this mean we can only understand other lives by experiencing them? Is this possible without the kind of clairvoyance that Latimer has?

The writer known as Mark Twain (1835–1910) was born Samuel Langhorne Clemens during the 1835 appearance of Halley's comet and died during the comet's next sighting. Twain's biographer Tomas Paine quotes him: "The Almighty has said, no doubt: 'Now here are these two unaccountable freaks; they came in together, they must go out together.'" Twain grew up in Hannibal, Missouri, on the Mississippi River, a "white town drowsing in the sunshine of a summer's morning," until a steamboat arrived and filled the town with the stevedores, gamblers, and assorted characters who would later inhabit the pages of his books.

Twain was a sickly but mischievous child. Years later he asked his mother if she had been afraid that he wouldn't live through his many illnesses. "No," she replied, "afraid you would." No stranger to human suffering early in life, Twain witnessed brutality toward slaves, the drowning of a friend, and the death of two of his siblings from illness before he was thirteen.

Twain worked as a printer's apprentice for the *Missouri Courier* and then began writing articles for the *Hannibal Journal*, owned by his brother Orion. In 1853 he embarked on a period of travel and itinerant work that would last almost two decades. He was a typesetter in various cities along the East Coast and then traveled south on the Mississippi by steamboat, intending to seek his fortune in South America. Instead, the penniless Twain became an apprentice to a riverboat pilot. "A pilot, in those days," wrote Twain years later, "was the only unfettered and entirely independent human being that lived in the earth." His career cut short by the Civil War, he joined a small group of pro-secessionist fighters but soon left it to prospect for gold in the Nevada Territory. When his ventures failed to support him, Twain joined the staff of reporters at the *Virginia City Territorial Enterprise*, where he adopted his pen name; "mark twain" was what the leadsman on a riverboat called out when the water was two fathoms deep. In 1865 his story "Jim Smiley and His Jumping Frog" attracted national attention when it was published in the *New York Saturday Press*.

In 1867 Twain sailed to Europe and the Holy Land, an excursion that formed the basis of his bitingly witty travel book *The Innocents Abroad* (1869). On this trip he met Charles Langdon, whose sister Olivia he married in 1870. The couple settled in Hartford, Connecticut, and he began his intensely productive literary career with *Roughing It* (1872), about his experiences in the West, and *The Gilded Age* (1873), a satirical novel about political corruption. In 1875 Twain's memoir of his boyhood, *Old Times on the Mississippi*, was serialized in the *Atlantic Monthly*. His fictionalized account of his childhood, *Tom Sawyer*, appeared the same year, and he began work on what would become *The Adventures of Huckleberry Finn* (1884). Twain traveled to Europe for two years, wrote both the travelogue *A Tramp Abroad* (1880) and the fantasy *The Prince and the Pauper* (1881), and founded his own publishing company. The popular acclaim for these books marked a high point of Twain's career and wealth. Soon, however, his publishing company went under and Twain went bankrupt after investing in a flawed typesetting machine. He moved his family to Europe to live inexpensively and embarked on a worldwide lecture tour to help mend his finances. In his later years, Twain suffered multiple family losses, including the deaths of his wife in 1904 and two of his daughters in 1895 and 1909.

Twain's later work, though retaining his characteristic acerbic wit, often lacks the buoyant humor of his earlier writing. It was during this period that Twain wrote "The Man Who Corrupted Hadleyburg" (1899), a study of greed and vanity in a town that prides itself on its honesty. Twain continued to write until his death in 1910. His last piece, the short sketch "Etiquette for the Afterlife: Advice to Paine," showed that he had not lost his irreverent sense of humor: "Do not try to show off. St. Peter dislikes it. The simpler you are dressed, the better it will please him . . . Above all, avoid over-dressing. A pair of spurs and a fig leaf is plenty."

# The Man That Corrupted Hadleyburg

## 1

It was many years ago. Hadleyburg was the most honest and upright town in all the region round about. It had kept that reputation unsmirched during three generations, and was prouder of it than of any other of its possessions. It was so proud of it, and so anxious to insure its perpetuation, that it began to teach the principles of honest dealing to its babies in the cradle, and made the like teachings the staple of their culture thenceforward through all the years devoted to their education. Also, throughout the formative years temptations were kept out of the way of the young people, so that their honesty could have every chance to harden and solidify, and become a part of their very bone. The neighboring towns were jealous of this honorable supremacy, and affected to sneer at Hadleyburg's pride in it and call it vanity; but all the same they were obliged to acknowledge that Hadleyburg was in reality an incorruptible town; and if pressed they would also acknowledge that the mere fact that a young man hailed from Hadleyburg was all the recommendation he needed when he went forth from his natal town to seek for responsible employment.

But at last, in the drift of time, Hadleyburg had the ill luck to offend a passing stranger—possibly without knowing it, certainly without caring, for Hadleyburg was sufficient unto itself, and cared not a rap for strangers or their opinions. Still, it would have been well to make an exception in this one's case, for he was a bitter man and revengeful. All through his wanderings during a whole year he kept his injury in mind, and gave all his leisure moments to trying to invent a compensating satisfaction for it. He contrived many plans, and all of them were good, but none of them was quite sweeping enough; the poorest of them would hurt a great many individuals, but what he wanted was a plan which would comprehend the entire town, and not let so much as one person escape unhurt. At last he had a fortunate idea, and when it fell into his brain it lit up his whole head with an evil joy. He began to form a plan at once, saying to himself, "That is the thing to do—I will corrupt the town."

Six months later he went to Hadleyburg, and arrived in a buggy at the house of the old cashier of the bank about ten at night. He got a sack out of the buggy, shouldered it, and staggered with it through the cottage yard, and knocked at the door. A woman's voice said "Come in," and he entered, and set his sack behind the stove in the parlor, saying politely to the old lady who sat reading the *Missionary Herald* by the lamp:

"Pray keep your seat, madam, I will not disturb you. There—now it is pretty well concealed; one would hardly know it was there. Can I see your husband a moment, madam?"

No, he was gone to Brixton, and might not return before morning.

"Very well, madam, it is no matter. I merely wanted to leave that sack in his care, to be delivered to the rightful owner when he shall be found. I am a stranger; he does not know me; I am merely passing through the town tonight to discharge a matter which has been long in my mind. My errand is now completed, and I go pleased and a little proud, and you will never see me again. There is a paper attached to the sack which will explain everything. Good night, madam."

The old lady was afraid of the mysterious big stranger, and was glad to see him go. But her curiosity was roused, and she went straight to the sack and brought away the paper. It began as follows:

TO BE PUBLISHED: or, the right man sought out by private inquiry—either will answer. This sack contains gold coin weighing a hundred and sixty pound four ounces—

"Mercy on us, and the door not locked!"

Mrs. Richards flew to it all in a tremble and locked it, then pulled down the window shades and stood frightened, worried, and wondering if there was anything else she could do toward making herself and the money more safe. She listened awhile for burglars, then surrendered to curiosity and went back to the lamp and finished reading the paper:

I am a foreigner, and am presently going back to my own country, to remain there permanently. I am grateful to America for what I have received at her hands during my long stay under her flag; and to one of her citizens—a citizen of Hadleyburg—I am especially grateful for a great kindness done me a year or two ago. Two great kindnesses, in fact. I will explain. I was a gambler. I say I WAS. I was a ruined gambler. I arrived in this village at night, hungry and without a penny. I asked for help—in the dark; I was ashamed to beg in the light. I begged of the right man. He gave me twenty dollars—that is to say, he gave me life, as I considered it. He also gave me fortune; for out of that money I have made myself rich at the gaming table. And finally, a remark which he made to me has remained with me to this day, and has at last conquered me; and in conquering has saved the remnant of my morals: I shall gamble no more. Now I have no idea who that man was, but I want him found, and I want him to have this money, to give away, throw away, or keep, as he pleases. It is merely my way of testifying my gratitude to him. If I could stay, I would find him myself; but no matter, he will be found. This is an honest town, an incorruptible town, and I know I can trust it without fear. This man can be identified by the remark which he made to me; I feel persuaded that he will remember it.

And now my plan is this: If you prefer to conduct the inquiry privately, do so. Tell the contents of this present writing to anyone who is likely to be the right man. If he shall answer, "I am the man; the remark I made was so-and-so," apply the test—to wit: open the sack, and in it you will find a sealed envelope containing that remark. If the remark mentioned by the candidate tallies with it, give him the money, and ask no further questions, for he is certainly the right man.

But if you shall prefer a public inquiry, then publish this present writing in the local paper—with these instructions added, to wit: thirty days from now, let the candidate appear at the town hall at eight in the evening (Friday), and hand his remark, in a sealed envelope, to the Reverend Mr. Burgess (if he will be kind enough to act); and let Mr. Burgess there and then destroy the seals of the sack, open it, and see if the remark is correct: if correct, let the money be delivered, with my sincere gratitude, to my benefactor thus identified.

Mrs. Richards sat down, gently quivering with excitement, and was soon lost in thinkings—after this pattern: "What a strange thing it is! . . . And what a fortune for that kind man who set his bread afloat upon the waters! . . . If it had only been my husband that did it!—for we are so poor, so old and poor! . . ." Then, with a sigh—"But it was not my Edward; no, it was not he that gave a stranger twenty dollars. It is a pity, too; I see it now. . . ." Then, with a shudder—"But it is *gambler's* money! the wages of sin: we couldn't take it; we couldn't touch it. I don't like to be near it; it seems a defilement." She moved to a farther chair. . . . "I wish Edward would come, and take it to the bank; a burglar might come at any moment; it is dreadful to be here all alone with it."

At eleven Mr. Richards arrived, and while his wife was saying, "I am *so* glad you've come!" he was saying, "I'm so tired—tired clear out; it is dreadful to be poor, and have to make these dismal journeys at my time of life. Always at the grind, grind, grind, on a salary—another man's slave, and he sitting at home in his slippers, rich and comfortable."

"I am so sorry for you, Edward, you know that; but be comforted: we have our livelihood; we have our good name—"

"Yes, Mary, and that is everything. Don't mind my talk—it's just a moment's irritation and doesn't mean anything. Kiss me—there, it's all gone now, and I am not complaining anymore. What have you been getting? What's in the sack?"

Then his wife told him the great secret. It dazed him for a moment; then he said:

"It weighs a hundred and sixty pounds? Why, Mary, it's for-ty thousand dollars—think of it—a whole fortune! Not ten men in this village are worth that much. Give me the paper."

He skimmed through it and said:

"Isn't it an adventure! Why, it's a romance; it's like the impossible things one reads about in books, and never sees in life." He was well stirred up now; cheerful, even gleeful. He tapped his old wife on the cheek, and said, humorously, "Why, we're rich, Mary, rich; all we've got to do is bury the money and burn the papers. If the gambler ever comes to inquire, we'll merely look coldly upon him and say: 'What is this nonsense you are talking? We have never heard of you and your sack of gold before'; and then he would look foolish, and—"

"And in the meantime, while you are running on with your jokes, the money is still here, and it is fast getting along toward burglar time."

"True. Very well, what shall we do—make the inquiry private? No, not that: it would spoil the romance. The public method is better. Think of what a noise it will make! And it will make all the other towns jealous; for no stranger would trust such a thing to any town but Hadleyburg, and they know it. It's a great card for us. I must get to the printing office now, or I shall be too late."

"But stop—stop—don't leave me here alone with it, Edward!"

But he was gone. For only a little while, however. Not far from his own house he met the editor-proprietor of the paper, and gave him the document, and said, "Here is a good thing for you, Cox—put it in."

"It may be too late, Mr. Richards, but I'll see."

At home again he and his wife sat down to talk the charming mystery over; they were in no condition for sleep. The first question was, Who could the citizen have been who gave the stranger the twenty dollars? It seemed a simple one; both answered in the same breath.

"Barclay Goodson."

"Yes," said Richards, "he could have done it, and it would have been like him, but there's not another in the town."

"Everybody will grant that, Edward—grant it privately, anyway. For six months, now, the village has been its own proper self once more—honest, narrow, self-righteous, and stingy."

"It is what he always called it, to the day of his death—said it right out publicly, too."

"Yes, and he was hated for it."

"Oh, of course; but he didn't care. I reckon he was the best-hated man among us, except the Reverend Burgess."

"Well, Burgess deserves it—he will never get another congregation here. Mean as the town is, it knows how to estimate *him*. Edward, doesn't it seem odd that the stranger should appoint Burgess to deliver the money?"

"Well, yes—it does. That is—that is—"

"Why so much that-*is*-ing? Would *you* select him?"

"Mary, maybe the stranger knows him better than this village does."

"Much *that* would help Burgess!"

The husband seemed perplexed for an answer; the wife kept a steady eye upon him, and waited. Finally Richards said, with the hesitancy of one who is making a statement which is likely to encounter doubt:

"Mary, Burgess is not a bad man."

His wife was certainly surprised.

"Nonsense!" she exclaimed.

"He is not a bad man. I know. The whole of his unpopularity had its foundation in that one thing—the thing that made so much noise."

"That 'one thing,' indeed! As if that 'one thing' wasn't enough, all by itself."

"Plenty. Plenty. Only he wasn't guilty of it."

"How you talk! Not guilty of it! Everybody knows he *was* guilty."

"Mary, I give you my word—he was innocent."

"I can't believe it, and I don't. How do you know?"

"It is a confession. I am ashamed, but I will make it. I was the only man who knew he was innocent. I could have saved him, and—and—well, you know how the town was wrought up—I hadn't the pluck to do it. It would have turned everybody against me. I felt mean, ever so mean; but I didn't dare; I hadn't the manliness to face that."

Mary looked troubled, and for a while was silent. Then she said, stammeringly:

"I—I don't think it would have done for you to—to—One mustn't—er—public opinion—one has to be so careful—so—" It was a difficult road, and she got mired; but after a little she got started again. "It was a great pity, but— Why, we couldn't afford it, Edward—we couldn't indeed. Oh, I wouldn't have had you do it for anything!"

"It would have lost us the good will of so many people, Mary; and then—and then—"

"What troubles me now is, what *he* thinks of us, Edward."

"He? *He* doesn't suspect that I could have saved him."

"Oh," exclaimed the wife, in a tone of relief, "I am glad of that. As long as he doesn't know that you could have saved him, he—he—well, that makes it a great deal better. Why, I might have known he didn't know, because he is always trying to be friendly with us, as little encouragement as we give him. More than once people have twitted me with it. There's the Wilsons, and the Wilcoxes, and the Harknesses, they take a mean pleasure in saying, '*Your friend* Burgess,' because they know it pesters me. I wish he wouldn't persist in liking us so; I can't think why he keeps it up."

"I can explain it. It's another confession. When the thing was new and hot, and the town made a plan to ride him on a rail, my conscience hurt me so that I couldn't stand it, and I went privately and gave him notice, and he got out of the town and stayed out till it was safe to come back."

"Edward! If the town had found it out—"

"*Don't!* It scares me yet, to think of it. I repented of it the minute it was done; and I was even afraid to tell you, lest your face might betray it to somebody. I didn't sleep any that night, for worrying. But after a few days I saw that no one was going to suspect me, and after that I got to feeling glad I did it. And I feel glad yet, Mary—glad through and through."

"So do I, now, for it would have been a dreadful way to treat him. Yes, I'm glad; for really you did owe him that, you know. But, Edward, suppose it should come out yet, some day!"

"It won't."

"Why?"

"Because everybody thinks it was Goodson."

"Of course they would!"

"Certainly. And of course *he* didn't care. They persuaded poor old Sawlsberry to go and charge it on him, and he went blustering over there and did it. Goodson looked him over, like as if he was hunting for a place on him that he could despise the most, then he says, 'So you are the Committee of Inquiry, are you?' Sawlsberry said that was about what he was. 'Hm. Do they require particulars, or do you reckon a kind of a *general* answer will do?' 'If they require particulars, I will come back, Mr. Goodson; I will take the general answer first.' 'Very well, then, tell them to go to hell—I reckon that's general enough. And I'll give you some advice, Sawlsberry; when you come back for the particulars, fetch a basket to carry the relics of yourself home in.'"

"Just like Goodson; it's got all the marks. He had only one vanity: he thought he could give advice better than any other person."

"It settled the business, and saved us, Mary. The subject was dropped."

"Bless you, I'm not doubting *that*."

Then they took up the gold-sack mystery again, with strong interest. Soon the conversation began to suffer breaks—interruptions caused by absorbed thinkings. The breaks grew more and more frequent. At last Richards lost himself wholly in thought. He sat long, gazing vacantly at the floor, and by and by he began to punctuate his thoughts with little nervous movements of his hands that seemed to indicate vexation. Meantime his wife too had relapsed into a thoughtful silence, and her movements were beginning to show a troubled discomfort. Finally Richards got up and strode aimlessly about the room, plowing his hands through his hair, much as a somnambulist might do who was having a bad dream. Then he seemed to arrive at a definite purpose; and without a word he put on his hat and passed quickly out of the house. His wife sat brooding, with a drawn face, and did not seem to be aware that she was alone. Now and then she murmured, "Lead us not into t— . . . but—but—we are so poor, so poor! . . . Lead us not into . . . Ah, who would be hurt by it? —and no one would ever know. . . . Lead us . . ." The voice died out in mumblings. After a little she glanced up and muttered in a half-frightened, half-glad way:

"He is gone! But, oh dear, he may be too late—too late. . . . Maybe not—maybe there is still time." She rose and stood thinking, nervously clasping and unclasping her hands. A slight shudder shook her frame, and she said, out of a dry throat, "God forgive me—it's awful to think such things—but . . . Lord, how we are made—how strangely we are made!"

She turned the light low, and slipped stealthily over and kneeled down by the sack and felt of its ridgy sides with her hands, and fondled them lovingly; and there was a gloating light in her poor old eyes. She fell into fits of absence; and came half out of them at times to mutter, "If we had only waited!—oh, if we had only waited a little, and not been in such a hurry!"

Meantime Cox had gone home from his office and told his wife all about the strange thing that had happened, and they had talked it over eagerly, and guessed that the late Goodson was the only man in the town who could have helped a suffering stranger with so noble a sum as twenty dollars. Then there was a pause, and the two became thoughtful and silent. And by and by nervous and fidgety. At last the wife said, as if to herself:

"Nobody knows this secret but the Richardses . . . and us . . . nobody."

The husband came out of his thinkings with a slight start, and gazed wistfully at his wife, whose face was become very pale; then he hesitatingly rose, and glanced furtively at his hat, then at his wife—a sort of mute inquiry. Mrs. Cox swallowed once or twice, with her hand at her throat, then in place of speech she nodded her head. In a moment she was alone, and mumbling to herself.

And now Richards and Cox were hurrying through the deserted streets, from opposite directions. They met, panting, at the foot of the printing office stairs; by the night light there they read each other's face. Cox whispered:

"Nobody knows about this but us?"

The whispered answer was:

"Not a soul—on honor, not a soul!"

"If it isn't too late to—"

The men were starting upstairs; at this moment they were overtaken by a boy, and Cox asked:

"Is that you, Johnny?"

"Yes, sir."

"You needn't ship the early mail—nor *any* mail; wait till I tell you."

"It's already gone, sir."

"*Gone?*" It had the sound of an unspeakable disappointment in it.

"Yes, sir. Timetable for Brixton and all the towns beyond changed today, sir—had to get the papers in twenty minutes earlier than common. I had to rush; if I had been two minutes later—"

The men turned and walked slowly away, not waiting to hear the rest. Neither of them spoke during ten minutes; then Cox said, in a vexed tone:

"What possessed you to be in such a hurry, *I* can't make out."

The answer was humble enough:

"I see it now, but somehow I never thought, you know, until it was too late. But the next time—"

"Next time be hanged! It won't come in a thousand years."

Then the friends separated without a good night, and dragged themselves home with the gait of mortally stricken men. At their homes their wives sprang up with an eager "Well?"—then saw the answer with their eyes and sank down sorrowing, without waiting for it to come in words. In both houses a discussion followed of a heated sort—a new thing; there had been discussions before, but not heated ones, not ungentle ones. The discussions tonight were a sort of seeming plagiarisms of each other. Mrs. Richards said:

"If you had only waited, Edward—if you had only stopped to think; but no, you must run straight to the printing office and spread it all over the world."

"It *said* publish it."

"That is nothing; it also said do it privately, if you liked. There, now—is that true, or not?"

"Why, yes—yes, it is true; but when I thought what a stir it would make, and what a compliment it was to Hadleyburg that a stranger should trust it so—"

"Oh, certainly, I know all that; but if you had only stopped to think, you would have seen that you *couldn't* find the right man, because he is in his grave, and hasn't left chick nor child nor relation behind him; and as long as the money went to somebody that awfully needed it, and nobody would be hurt by it, and—and—"

She broke down, crying. Her husband tried to think of some comforting thing to say, and presently came out with this:

"But after all, Mary, it must be for the best—it *must* be; we know that. And we must remember that it was so ordered—"

"Ordered! Oh, everything's *ordered*, when a person has to find some way out when he has been stupid. Just the same, it was *ordered* that the money should come to us in this special way, and it was you that must take it on yourself to go meddling with the designs of Providence—and who gave you the right? It was wicked, that is what it was—just blasphemous presumption, and no more becoming to a meek and humble professor of—"

"But, Mary, you know how we have been trained all our lives long, like the whole village, till it is absolutely second nature to us to stop not a single moment to think when there's an honest thing to be done—"

"Oh, I know it, I know it—it's been one everlasting training and training and training in honesty—honesty shielded, from the very cradle, against every possible temptation, and so it's *artificial* honesty, and weak as water when temptation comes, as we have seen this night. God knows I never had shade nor shadow of a doubt of my petrified and indestructible honesty until now—and now, under the very first big and real temptation, I—Edward, it is my belief that this town's honesty is as rotten as mine is; as rotten as yours is. It is a mean town, a hard, stingy town, and hasn't a virtue in the world but this honesty it is so celebrated for and so conceited about; and so help me, I do believe that if ever the day comes that its honesty falls under great temptation, its grand reputation will go to ruin like a house of cards. There, now, I've made confession, and I feel better; I am a humbug, and I've been one all my life, without knowing it. Let no man call me honest again—I will not have it."

"I—well, Mary, I feel a good deal as you do; I certainly do. It seems strange, too, so strange. I never could have believed it—never."

A long silence followed; both were sunk in thought. At last the wife looked up and said:

"I know what you are thinking, Edward."

Richards had the embarrassed look of a person who is caught.

"I am ashamed to confess it, Mary, but—"

"It's no matter, Edward, I was thinking the same question myself."

"I hope so. State it."

"You were thinking, if a body could only guess out *what the remark was* that Goodson made to the stranger."

"It's perfectly true. I feel guilty and ashamed. And you?"

"I'm past it. Let us make a pallet here; we've got to stand watch till the bank vault opens in the morning and admits the sack. . . . O dear, oh dear—if we hadn't made the mistake!"

The pallet was made, and Mary said:

"The open sesame—what could it have been? I do wonder what that remark could have been? But come; we will get to bed now."

"And sleep?"

"No: think."

"Yes, think."

By this time the Coxes too had completed their spat and their reconciliation, and were turning in—to think, to think, and toss, and fret, and worry over what the remark could possibly have been which Goodson made to the stranded derelict; that golden remark; that remark worth forty thousand dollars, cash.

The reason that the village telegraph office was open later than usual that night was this: the foreman of Cox's paper was the local representative of the Associated Press. One might say its honorary representative, for it wasn't four times a year that he could furnish thirty words that would be accepted. But this time it was different. His dispatch stating what he had caught got an instant answer:

Send the whole thing—all the details—twelve hundred words.

A colossal order! The foreman filled the bill; and he was the proudest man in the state. By breakfast time the next morning the name of Hadleyburg the Incorruptible was on every lip in America, from Montreal to the Gulf, from the glaciers of Alaska to the orange groves of Florida; and millions and millions of people were discussing the stranger and his money sack, and wondering if the right man would be found, and hoping some more news about the matter would come soon—right away.

# 2

Hadleyburg village woke up world-celebrated—astonished—happy—vain. Vain beyond imagination. Its nineteen principal citizens and their wives went about shaking hands with each other, and beaming, and smiling, and congratulating, and saying *this* thing adds a new word to the dictionary—

*Hadleyburg,* synonym for *incorruptible*—destined to live in dictionaries forever! And the minor and unimportant citizens and their wives went around
acting in much the same way. Everybody ran to the bank to see the gold sack;
and before noon grieved and envious crowds began to flock in from Brixton
and all neighboring towns; and that afternoon and next day reporters began
to arrive from everywhere to verify the sack and its history and write the
whole thing up anew, and make dashing freehand pictures of the sack, and of
Richards's house, and the bank, and the Presbyterian church, and the Baptist
church, and the public square, and the town hall where the test would be
applied and the money delivered; and damnable portraits of the Richardses,
and Pinkerton the banker, and Cox, and the foreman, and Reverend Burgess,
and the postmaster—and even of Jack Halliday, who was the loafing, good-
natured, no-account, irreverent fisherman, hunter, boys' friend, stray dogs'
friend, typical "Sam Lawson" of the town. The little, mean, smirking, oily
Pinkerton showed the sack to all comers, and rubbed his sleek palms together
pleasantly, and enlarged upon the town's fine old reputation for honesty and
upon this wonderful endorsement of it, and hoped and believed that the
example would now spread far and wide over the American world, and be
epoch-making in the matter of moral regeneration. And so on, and so on.

By the end of a week things had quieted down again; the wild intoxication of pride and joy had sobered to a soft, sweet, silent delight—a sort
of deep, nameless, unutterable content. All faces bore a look of peaceful,
holy happiness.

Then a change came. It was a gradual change: so gradual that its beginnings were hardly noticed; maybe were not noticed at all, except by Jack
Halliday, who always noticed everything; and always made fun of it, too, no
matter what it was. He began to throw out chaffing remarks about people
not looking quite so happy as they did a day or two ago; and next he claimed
that the new aspect was deepening to positive sadness; next, that it was taking on a sick look; and finally he said that everybody was become so moody,
thoughtful, and absent-minded that he could orb the meanest man in town
of a cent out of the bottom of his breeches pocket and not disturb his reverie.

At this stage—or at about this stage—a saying like this was dropped out
at bedtime—with a sigh, usually—by the head of each of the nineteen principal households: "Ah, what *could* have been the remark that Goodson made?"

And straightaway—with a shudder—came this, from the man's wife:

"Oh, *don't*! What horrible thing are you mulling in your mind? Put it
away from you, for God's sake!"

But that question was wrung from those men again the next night—and
got the same retort. But weaker.

And the third night the men uttered the question yet again—with
anguish, and absently. This time—and the following night—the wives
fidgeted feebly, and tried to say something. But didn't.

And the night after that they found their tongues and responded—longingly:

"Oh, if we *could* only guess!"

Halliday's comments grew daily more and more sparklingly disagreeable and disparaging. He went diligently about, laughing at the town, individually and in mass. But his laugh was the only one left in the village: it fell upon a hollow and mournful vacancy and emptiness. Not even a smile was findable anywhere. Halliday carried a cigar box around the tripod, playing that it was a camera, and halted all passers and aimed the thing and said, "Ready!—now look pleasant, please," but not even this capital joke could surprise the dreary faces into any softening.

So three weeks passed—one week was left. It was Saturday evening—after supper. Instead of the aforetime Saturday evening flutter and bustle and shopping and larking, the streets were empty and desolate. Richards and his old wife sat apart in their little parlor—miserable and thinking. This was become their evening habit now: the lifelong habit which had preceded it, of reading, knitting, and contented chat, or receiving or paying neighborly calls, was dead and gone and forgotten, ages ago—two or three weeks ago—nobody talked now, nobody read, nobody visited—the whole village sat at home, sighing, worrying, silent. Trying to guess out that remark.

The postman left a letter. Richards glanced listlessly at the superscription and the postmark—unfamiliar, both—and tossed the letter on the table and resumed his might-have-beens and his hopeless dull miseries where he had left them off. Two of three hours later his wife got wearily up and was going away to bed without a good night—custom now—but she stopped near the letter and eyed it awhile with a dead interest, then broke it open, and began to skim it over. Richards, sitting there with his chair tilted back against the wall and his chin between his knees, heard something fall. It was his wife. He sprang to her side, but she cried out:

"Leave me alone, I am too happy. Read the letter—read it!"

He did. He devoured it, his brain reeling. The letter was from a distant state, and it said:

I am a stranger to you, but no matter: I have something to tell. I have just arrived home from Mexico, and learned about that episode. Of course you do not know who made that remark, but I know, and I am the only person living who does know. It was GOODSON. I knew him well, many years ago. I passed through your village that very night, and was his guest till the midnight train came along. I overheard him make that remark to the stranger in the dark—it was in Hale Alley. He and I talked of it the rest of the way home, and while smoking in his house. He mentioned many of your villagers in the course of his talk—most of them in a very uncomplimentary way, but two or three favorably; among these latter yourself. I say "favorably"—nothing stronger. I remember his saying he did not actually LIKE any person in the town—not one; but that you—I THINK he said you—am almost sure—had done him a very great service once, possibly without knowing the full value of it, and he wished he had a fortune, he would leave it to you when he died, and a curse apiece for the rest of the citizens. Now, then, if it was you that did him that service, you are his legitimate heir, and entitled to the sack of gold. I know that I can trust to your honor and honesty, for in a citizen of Hadleyburg these virtues are an unfailing inheritance, and so I am going to reveal to you the remark, well satisfied that if you are not the right man you will seek and find the right one and see that poor Goodson's debt of gratitude for the service referred to is paid. This is the remark: "YOU ARE FAR FROM BEING A BAD MAN: GO, AND REFORM."

HOWARD L. STEPHENSON

"Oh, Edward, the money is ours, and I am so grateful, oh, so grateful—kiss me, dear, it's forever since we kissed—and we needed it so—the money—and now you are free of Pinkerton and his bank, and nobody's slave anymore; it seems to me I could fly for joy."

It was a happy half-hour that the couple spent there on the settee caressing each other; it was the old days come again—days that had begun with their courtship and lasted without a break till the stranger brought the deadly money. By and by the wife said:

"Oh, Edward, how lucky it was you did him that grand service, poor Goodson! I never liked him, but I love him now. And it was fine and beautiful of you never to mention it or brag about it." Then, with a touch of reproach, "But you ought to have told *me*, Edward, you ought to have told your wife, you know."

"Well, I—er—well, Mary, you see—"

"Now stop hemming and hawing, and tell me about it, Edward. I always loved you, and now I'm proud of you. Everybody believes there was only one good generous soul in this village, and now it turns out that you—Edward, why don't you tell me?"

"Well—er—er— Why, Mary, I can't!"

"You *can't*? *Why* can't you?"

"You see, he—well, he—he made me promise I wouldn't."

The wife looked him over, and said, very slowly,

"Made—you—promise? Edward, what do you tell me that for?"

"Mary, do you think I would lie?"

She was troubled and silent for a moment, then she laid her hand within his and said:

"No . . . no. We have wandered far enough from our bearings—God spare us that! In all your life you have never uttered a lie. But now—now that the foundations of things seem to be crumbling from under us, we—we—" She lost her voice for a moment, then said, brokenly, "Lead us not into temptation . . . I think you made the promise, Edward. Let it rest so. Let us keep away from that ground. Now—that is all gone by; let us be happy again; it is no time for clouds."

Edward found it something of an effort to comply, for his mind kept wandering—trying to remember what the service was that he had done Goodson.

The couple lay awake the most of the night, Mary happy and busy, Edward busy but not so happy. Mary was planning what she would do with the money. Edward was trying to recall that service. At first his conscience was sore on account of the lie he had told Mary—if it *was* a lie. After much reflection—suppose it *was* a lie? What then? Was it such a great matter? Aren't we always *acting* lies? Then why not *tell* them? Look at Mary—look what she had done. While he was hurrying off on his honest errand, what was she doing? Lamenting because the papers hadn't been destroyed and the money kept! Is theft better than lying?

*That* point lost its sting—the lie dropped into the background and left comfort behind it. The next point came to the front: *Had* he rendered that service? Well, here was Goodson's own evidence as reported in Stephenson's letter; there could be no better evidence than that—it was even *proof* that he had rendered it. Of course. So that point was settled. . . . No, not quite. He recalled with a wince that this unknown Mr. Stephenson was just a trifle unsure as to whether the performer of it was Richards or some other—and, oh dear, he had put Richards on his honor! He must himself decide whither that money must go—and Mr. Stephenson was not doubting that if he was the wrong man he would go honorably and find the right one. Oh, it was odious to put a man in such a situation—ah, why couldn't Stephenson have left out that doubt! What did he want to intrude that for?

Further reflection. How did it happen that *Richards's* name remained in Stephenson's mind as indicating the right man, and not some other man's name? That looked good. Yes, that looked very good. In fact, it went on looking better and better, straight along—until by and by it grew into positive *proof*. And then Richards put the matter at once out of his mind, for he had a private instinct that a proof once established is better left so.

He was feeling reasonably comfortable now, but there was still one other detail that kept pushing itself on his notice: of course he had done that service—that was settled; but what *was* that service? He must recall it—he would not go to sleep till he had recalled it; it would make his peace of mind perfect. And so he thought and thought. He thought of a dozen things—possible services—but none of them seemed adequate, none of them seemed large enough, none of them seemed worth the money— worth the fortune Goodson had wished he could leave in his will. And besides, he couldn't remember having done them, anyway. Now, then— now, then—what *kind* of a service would it be that would make a man so inordinately grateful? Ah—the saving of his soul! That must be it. Yes, he could remember, now, how he once set himself the task of converting Goodson, and labored at it as much as—he was going to say three months; but upon closer examination it shrunk to a month, then to a week, then to a day, then to nothing. Yes, he remembered it now, and with unwelcome vividness, that Goodson had told him to go to thunder and mind his own business—*he* wasn't hankering to follow Hadleyburg to heaven!

So that solution was a failure—he hadn't saved Goodson's soul. Richards was discouraged. Then after a little came another idea: Had he saved Goodson's property? No, that wouldn't do—he hadn't any. His life? That is it! Of course. Why, he might have thought of it before. This time he was on the right track, sure. His imagination mill was hard at work in a minute, now.

Thereafter during a stretch of two exhausting hours he was busy saving Goodson's life. He saved it in all kinds of difficult and perilous ways. In every case he got it saved satisfactorily up to a certain point; then, just as he was beginning to get well persuaded that it had really happened, a troublesome detail would turn up which made the whole thing impossible. As in the matter of drowning, for instance. In that case he had swum out and tugged Goodson ashore in an unconscious state with a great crowd looking on and applauding, but when he had got it all thought out and was just beginning to remember all about it, a whole swarm of disqualifying details arrived on the ground: the town would have known of the circumstance, Mary would have known of it, it would glare like a limelight in his own memory instead of being an inconspicuous service which he had possibly rendered "without knowing its full value." And at this point he remembered that he couldn't swim, anyway.

Ah—*there* was a point which he had been overlooking from the start: it had to be a service which he had rendered "possibly without knowing the full value of it." Why, really, that ought to be an easy hunt— much easier than those others. And sure enough, by and by he found it. Goodson, years and years ago, came near marrying a very sweet and pretty girl, named Nancy Hewitt, but in some way or other the match had been broken off; the girl died, Goodson remained a bachelor, and by and by became a soured one and a frank despiser of the human species. Soon after the girl's death the village found out, or thought it had found out, that she carried a spoonful of Negro blood in her veins. Richards worked at these details a good while, and in the end he thought he remembered things concerning them which must have gotten mislaid in his memory through long neglect. He seemed to dimly remember that it was *he* that found out about the Negro blood; that it was he that told the village; that the village told Goodson where they got it; that he thus saved Goodson from marrying the tainted girl; that he had done him this great service "without knowing the full value of it," in fact without knowing that he *was* doing it; but that Goodson knew the value of it, and what a narrow escape he had had, and so went to his grave grateful to his benefactor and wishing he had a fortune to leave him. It was all clear and simple now, and the more he went over it the more luminous and certain it grew; and at last, when he nestled to sleep satisfied and happy, he remembered the whole thing just as if it had been yesterday. In fact, he dimly remembered Goodson's *telling* him his gratitude once. Meantime Mary had spent six thousand dollars on a new house for herself and a pair of slippers for her pastor, and then had fallen peacefully to rest.

That same Saturday evening the postman had delivered a letter to each of the other principal citizens—nineteen letters in all. No two of the envelopes were alike, and no two of the superscriptions were in the same hand, but the letters inside were just like each other in every detail but one. They were exact copies of the letter received by Richards—handwriting and all—and were all signed by Stephenson, but in place of Richards's name each receiver's own name appeared.

All night long eighteen principal citizens did what their caste-brother Richards was doing at the same time—they put in their energies trying to remember what notable service it was that they had unconsciously done Barclay Goodson. In no case was it a holiday job; still they succeeded.

And while they were at this work, which was difficult, their wives put in the night spending the money, which was easy. During that one night the nineteen wives spent an average of seven thousand dollars each out of the forty thousand in the sack—a hundred and thirty-three thousand altogether.

Next day there was a surprise for Jack Halliday. He noticed that the faces of the nineteen chief citizens and their wives bore that expression of peaceful and holy happiness again. He could not understand it, neither was he able to invent any remarks about it that could damage it or disturb it. And so it was his turn to be dissatisfied with life. His private guesses at the reasons for the happiness failed in all instances, upon examination. When he met Mrs. Wilcox and noticed the placed ecstasy in her face, he said to himself, "Her cat has had kittens"—and went and asked the cook: it was not so; the cook had detected the happiness, but did not know the cause. When Halliday found the duplicate ecstasy in the face of "Shadbelly" Billson (village nickname), he was sure some neighbor of Billson's had broken his leg, but inquiry showed that this had not happened. The subdued ecstasy in Gregory Yates's face could mean but one thing—he was a mother-in-law short: it was another mistake. "And Pinkerton—Pinkerton—he has collected ten cents that he thought he was going to lose." And so on, and so on. In some cases the guesses had to remain in doubt, in the others they proved distinct errors. In the end Halliday said to himself, "Anyway it foots up that there's nineteen Hadleyburg families temporarily in heaven: I don't know how it happened; I only know Providence is off duty today."

An architect and builder from the next state had lately ventured to set up a small business in this unpromising village, and his sign had now been hanging out a week. Not a customer yet; he was a discouraged man, and sorry he had come. But his weather changed suddenly now. First one and then another chief citizen's wife said to him privately:

"Come to my house Monday week—but say nothing about it for the present. We think of building."

He got eleven invitations that day. That night he wrote his daughter and broke off her match with her student. He said she could marry a mile higher than that.

Pinkerton the banker and two or three other well-to-do men planned countryseats—but waited. That kind don't count their chickens until they are hatched.

The Wilsons devised a grand new thing—a fancy-dress ball. They made no actual promises, but they told all their acquaintanceship in confidence that they were thinking the matter over and thought they should give it—"and if we do, you will be invited, of course." People were surprised, and said to one another, "Why, they are crazy, those poor Wilsons, they can't afford it." Several among the nineteen said privately to their husbands, "It is a good idea: we will keep still till their cheap thing is over, then *we* will give one that will make it sick"

The days drifted along, and the bill of future squanderings rose higher and higher, wilder and wilder, more and more foolish and reckless. It began to look as if every member of the nineteen would not only spend his whole forty thousand dollars before receiving day, but be actually in debt by the time he got the money. In some cases lightheaded people did not stop with planning to spend, they really spent—on credit. They bought land, mortgages, farms, speculative stocks, fine clothes, horses, and various other things, paid down the bonus, and made themselves liable for the rest—at ten days. Presently the sober second thought came, and Halliday noticed that a ghastly anxiety was beginning to show up in a good many faces. Again he was puzzled, and didn't know what to make of it. "The Wilcox kittens aren't dead, for they weren't born; nobody's broken a leg; there's no shrinkage in mother-in-laws; *nothing* has happened—it is an unsolvable mystery."

There was another puzzled man, too—the Reverend Mr. Burgess. For days, wherever he went, people seemed to follow him or to be watching out for him; and if he ever found himself in a retired spot, a member of the nineteen would be sure to appear, thrust an envelope privately into his hand, whisper "To be opened at the town hall Friday evening," then vanish away like a guilty thing. He was expecting that there might be one claimant for the sack,—doubtful, however, Goodson being dead—but it never occurred to him that all this crowd might be claimants. When the great Friday came at last, he found that he had nineteen envelopes.

## 3

The town hall had never looked finer. The platform at the end of it was backed by a showy draping of flags; at intervals along the walls were festoons of flags; the gallery fronts were clothed in flags; the supporting columns were swathed in flags; all this was to impress the stranger, for he would be there in considerable force, and in a large degree he would be connected with the press. The house was full. The 412 fixed seats were occupied; also the 68 extra chairs which had been packed into the aisles; the steps of the platform were occupied; some distinguished strangers were given seats on the platform; at the horseshoe of tables which fenced the front and sides of the platform sat a strong force of special correspondents who had come from everywhere. It was the best-dressed house the town had every produced. There were some tolerably expensive toilets there, and in several cases the ladies who wore them had the look of being unfamiliar with that kind of clothes. At least the town thought they had that look, but the notion could have arisen from the town's knowledge of the fact that these ladies had never inhabited such clothes before.

The gold sack stood on a little table at the front of the platform where all the house could see it. The bulk of the house gazed at it with a burning interest, a mouth-watering interest, a wistful and pathetic interest; a minority of nineteen couples gazed at it tenderly, lovingly, proprietarily, and the male half of this minority kept saying over to themselves the moving little impromptu speeches of thankfulness for the audience's applause and congratulations which they were presently going to get up and deliver. Every now and then one of these got a piece of paper out of his vest pocket and privately glanced at it to refresh his memory.

Of course there was a buzz of conversation going on—there always is; but at last when the Reverend Mr. Burgess rose and laid his hand on the sack he could hear the microbes gnaw, the place was so still. He related the curious history of the sack, then went on to speak in warm tones of Hadleyburg's old and well-earned reputation for spotless honesty, and of the town's just pride in this reputation. He said that this reputation was a treasure of priceless value; that under Providence its value had now become inestimably enhanced, for the recent episode had spread this fame far and wide, and thus had focused the eyes of the American world upon this village, and made its name for all time, as he hoped and believed, a synonym for commercial incorruptibility. [*Applause.*] "And who is to be the guardian of this noble treasure—the community as a whole? No! The responsibility is individual, not communal. From this day forth each and every one of you is in his own person its special guardian, and individually responsible that no harm shall come to it. Do you—does each of you—accept this great trust? [*Tumultuous assent.*] Then all is well. Transmit it to your children and to your children's children. Today your purity is beyond reproach—see to it that it shall remain so. Today there is not a person in your community who could be beguiled to touch a penny not his own—see to it that you abide in this grace. ["*We will! we will!*"] This is not the place to make comparisons between ourselves and other communities—some of them ungracious toward us; they have their ways, we have ours, let us be content. [*Applause.*] I am done. Under my hand, my friends, rests a stranger's eloquent recognition of what we are; through him the world will always henceforth know what we are. We do not know who he is, but in your name I utter your gratitude, and ask you to raise your voices in endorsement."

The house rose in a body and made the walls quake with the thunders of its thankfulness for the space of a long minute. Then it sat down, and Mr. Burgess took an envelope out of his pocket. The house held its breath while he slit the envelope open and took from it a slip of paper. He read its contents—slowly and impressively—the audience listening with tranced attention to this magic document, each of whose words stood for an ingot of gold.

"*'The remark which I made to the distressed stranger was this: "You are very far from being a bad man: go, and reform."'*" Then he continued:

"We shall know in a moment now whether the remark here quoted corresponds with the one concealed in the sack; and if that shall prove to be so—and it undoubtedly will—this sack of gold belongs to a fellow citizen who will henceforth stand before the nation as the symbol of the special virtue which has made our town famous throughout the land—Mr. Billson!"

The house had gotten itself all ready to burst into the proper tornado of applause; but instead of doing it, it seemed stricken with a paralysis; there was a deep hush for a moment or two, then a wave of whispered murmurs swept the place—of about this tenor: "*Billson!* oh, come, this is *too* thin! Twenty dollars to a stranger—or *anybody—Billson!* Tell it to the marines!" And now at this point the house caught its breath all of a sudden

213

in a new access of astonishment, for it discovered that whereas in one part of the hall Deacon Billson was standing up with his head meekly bowed, in another part of it Lawyer Wilson was doing the same. There was a wondering silence now for a while. Billson and Wilson turned and stared at each other. Billson asked, bitingly:

"Why do *you* rise, Mr. Wilson?"

"Because I have a right to. Perhaps you will be good enough to explain to the house why *you* rise?

"With great pleasure. Because I wrote that paper."

"It is an impudent falsity! I wrote it myself."

It was Burgess's turn to be paralyzed. He stood looking vacantly at first one of the men and then the other, and did not seem to know what to do. The house was stupefied. Lawyer Wilson spoke up, now, and said:

"I ask the Chair to read the name signed to that paper."

"'John Wharton *Billson*.'"

"There!" shouted Billson. "What have you got to say for yourself now? And what kind of apology are you going to make to me and to this insulted house for the imposture which you have attempted to play here?"

"No apologies are due, sir; and as for the rest of it, I publicly charge you with pilfering my note from Mr. Burgess and substituting a copy of it signed with your own name. There is no other way by which you could have gotten hold of the test-remark; I alone, of living men, possessed the secret of its wording."

There was likely to be a scandalous state of things if this went on; everybody noticed with distress that the shorthand scribes were scribbling like mad; many people were crying "Chair, Chair! Order! Order!" Burgess rapped with his gavel, and said:

"Let us not forget the proprieties due. There has evidently been a mistake somewhere, but surely that is all. If Mr. Wilson gave me an envelope—and I remember now that he did—I still have it."

He took one out of his pocket, opened it, glanced at it, looked surprised and worried, and stood silent a few moments. Then he waved his hand in a wandering and mechanical way, and made an effort or two to say something, then gave it up, despondently. Several voices cried out:

"Read it! Read it! What is it?"

So he began in a dazed and sleepwalker fashion:

"*The remark which I made to the unhappy stranger was this: "You are far from being a bad man.* [The house gazed at him, marveling.] *Go, and reform.*"' [Murmurs: "Amazing! what can this mean?"] This one," said the Chair, is signed Thurlow G. Wilson."

"There!" cried Wilson, "I reckon that settles it! I knew perfectly well my note was purloined."

"Purloined!" retorted Billson. "I'll let you know that neither you nor any man of your kidney must venture to—"

*The Chair.* "Order, gentlemen, order! Take your seats, both of you, please."

They obeyed, shaking their heads and grumbling angrily. The house was profoundly puzzled; it did not know what to do with this curious emergency. Presently Thompson got up. Thompson was the hatter. He would have liked to be a Nineteener; but such was not for him: his stock of hats was not considerable enough for the position. He said:

"Mr. Chairman, if I may be permitted to make a suggestion, can both of these gentlemen be right? I put it to you, sir, can both have happened to say the very same words to the stranger? It seems to me—"

The tanner got up and interrupted him. The tanner was a disgruntled man; he believed himself entitled to be a Nineteener, but he couldn't get recognition. It made him a little unpleasant in his ways and speech. Said he:

"Sho, *that's* not the point! *That* could happen—twice in a hundred years—but not the other thing. *Neither* of them gave the twenty dollars!"

[*A ripple of applause.*]

*Billson.* "I did!"

*Wilson.* "I did!"

Then each accused the other of pilfering.

*The Chair.* Order! Sit down, if you please—both of you. Neither of the notes has been out of my possession at any moment."

*A Voice.* "Good—that settles that!"

*The Tanner.* "Mr. Chairman, one thing is now plain: one of these men has been eavesdropping under the other one's bed, and filching family secrets. If it is not unparliamentary to suggest it, I will remark that both are equal to it. [*The Chair.* "Order! Order!"] I withdraw the remark sir, and will confine myself to suggesting that *if* one of them has overheard the other reveal the test-remark to his wife, we shall catch him now."

*A Voice.* "How?"

*The Tanner.* "Easily. The two have not quoted the remark in exactly the same words. You would have noticed that, if there hadn't been a considerable stretch of time and an exciting quarrel inserted between the two readings."

*A Voice.* "Name the difference."

*The Tanner.* "The word very is in Billson's note, and not in the other."

*Many Voices.* "That's so—he's right!"

*The Tanner.* "And so, if the Chair will examine the test-remark in the sack, we shall know which of these two frauds—[*The Chair.* "Order!"]— which of these two adventurers—[*The Chair.* "Order! Order!"]—which of these two gentlemen—[*Laughter and applause*]—is entitled to wear the belt as being the first dishonest blatherskite ever bred in this town—which he has dishonored, and which will be a sultry place for him from now out!" [*Vigorous applause.*]

*Many Voices.* "Open it!—open the sack!"

Mr. Burgess made a slit in the sack, slid his hand in and brought out an envelope. In it were a couple of folded notes. He said:

"One of these is marked, 'Not to be examined until all written communications which have been addressed to the Chair—if any—shall have been read.' The other is marked '*The Test*.' Allow me. It is worded—to wit:

"'I do not require that the first half of the remark which was made to me by my benefactor shall be quoted with exactness, for it was not striking, and could be forgotten; but its closing fifteen words are quite striking, and I think easily rememberable; unless *these* shall be accurately reproduced, let the applicant be regarded as an imposter. My benefactor began by saying he seldom gave advice to anyone, but that it always bore the hallmark of high value when he did give it. Then he said this—and it has never faded from my memory: *You are far from being a bad man—*'''"

*Fifty Voices.* "That settles it—the money's Wilson's! Wilson! Wilson! Speech! Speech!"

People jumped up and crowded around Wilson, wringing his hand and congratulating fervently—meantime the Chair was hammering with the gavel and shouting:

"Order, gentlemen! Order! Order! Let me finish reading, please." When quiet was restored, the reading was resumed, as follows:

"'*Go, and reform—or, mark my words—someday, for your sins, you will die and go to hell or Hadleyburg—TRY AND MAKE IT THE FORMER.*' "

A ghastly silence followed. First an angry cloud began to settle darkly upon the faces of the citizenship; after a pause the cloud began to rise, and a tickled expression tried to take its place; tried to hard that it was only kept under with great and painful difficulty; the reporters, the Brixtonites, and other strangers bent their heads down and shielded their faces with their hands, and managed to hold in by main strength and heroic courtesy. At this most inopportune time burst upon the stillness the roar of a solitary voice—Jack Halliday's:

"*That's* got the hallmark on it!"

Then the house let go, strangers and all. Even Mr. Burgess's gravity broke down presently, then the audience considered itself officially absolved from all restraint, and it made the most of its privilege. It was a good long laugh, and a tempestuously wholehearted one, but it ceased at last—long enough for Mr. Burgess to try to resume, and for the people to get their eyes partially wiped; then it broke out again; and afterward yet again; then at last Burgess was able to get out these serious words:

"It is useless to try to disguise the fact—we find ourselves in the presence of a matter of grave import. It involves the honor of your town, it strikes at the town's good name. The difference of a single word between the test-remarks offered by Mr. Wilson and Mr. Billson was itself a serious thing, since it indicated that one or the other of these gentlemen had committed a theft—"

The two men were sitting limp, nerveless, crushed; but at these words both were electrified into movement, and started to get up.

"Sit down!" said the Chair, sharply, and they obeyed. "That, as I have said, was a serious thing. And it was—but for only one of them. But the matter has become graver; for the honor of *both* is now in formidable peril. Shall I go even further, and say in inextricable peril? *Both* left out the crucial fifteen words." He paused. During several moments he allowed the pervading stillness to gather and deepen its impressive effects, then added: "There would seem to be but one way whereby this could happen. I ask these gentlemen—Was there *collusion?—agreement?*"

A low murmur sifted through the house; its import was, "He's got them both."

Billson was not used to emergencies; he sat in a helpless collapse. But Wilson was a lawyer. He struggled to his feet, pale and worried, and said:

"I ask the indulgence of the house while I explain this most painful matter. I am sorry to say what I am about to say, since it must inflict irreparable injury upon Mr. Billson, whom I have always esteemed and respected until now, and in whose invulnerability to temptation I entirely believed—as did you all. But for the preservation of my own honor I must speak—and with frankness. I confess with shame—and I now beseech your pardon for it—that I said to the ruined stranger all of the words contained in the test-remark, including the disparaging fifteen. [*Sensation.*] When the late publication was made I recalled them, and I resolved to claim the sack of coin, for by every right I was entitled to it. Now I will ask you to consider this point, and weigh it well: that stranger's gratitude to me that night knew no bounds; he said himself that he could find no words for it that were adequate, and that if he should ever be able he would repay me a thousandfold. Now, then, I ask you this: Could I expect—could I believe—could I even remotely imagine—that, feeling as he did, he would do so ungrateful a thing as to add those quite unnecessary fifteen words to his test? —set a trap for me? —expose me as a slanderer of my own town before my own people assembled in a public hall? It was preposterous; it was impossible. His test would contain only the kindly opening clause of my remark. Of that I had no shadow of doubt. You would have thought as I did. You would not have expected a base betrayal from one whom you had befriended and against whom you had committed no offense. And so, with perfect confidence, perfect trust, I wrote on a piece of paper the opening words—ending with 'Go, and reform'—and signed it. When I was about to put it in an envelope I was called into my back office, and without thinking I left the paper lying open on my desk: He stopped, turned his head slowly toward Billson, waited a moment, then added: "I ask you to note this: when I returned a little later, Mr. Billson was retiring by my street door." [*Sensation.*]

In a moment Billson was on his feet and shouting:

"It's a lie! It's an infamous lie!"

*The Chair.* "Be seated, sir! Mr. Wilson has the floor."

Billson's friends pulled him into his seat and quieted him, and Wilson went on:

"Those are the simple facts. My note was now lying in a different place on the table from where I had left it. I noticed that, but attached no importance to it, thinking a draft had blow it there. That Mr. Billson would read a private paper was a thing which could not occur to me; he was an honorable man, and he would be above that. If you will allow me to say it, I think his extra word 'very' stands explained; it is attributable to a defect of memory. I was the only man in the world who could furnish here any detail of the test-remark—by *honorable* means. I have finished."

There is nothing in the world like a persuasive speech to fuddle the mental apparatus and upset the convictions and debauch the emotions of an audience not practiced in the tricks and delusions of oratory. Wilson sat down victorious. The house submerged him in tides of approving applause; friends swarmed to him and shook him by the hand and congratulated him, and Billson was shouted down and not allowed to say a word. The Chair hammered and hammered with its gavel, and kept shouting:

"But let us proceed, gentlemen, let us proceed!"

At last there was a measurable degree of quiet, and the hatter said:

"But what is there to proceed with, sir, but to deliver the money?"

*Voices.* "That's it! That's it! Come forward, Wilson!"

*The Hatter.* "I move three cheers for Mr. Wilson, Symbol of the special virtue which—"

The cheers burst forth before he could finish; and in the midst of them—and in the midst of the clamor of the gavel also—some enthusiasts mounted Wilson on a big friend's shoulder and were going to fetch him in triumph to the platform. The Chair's voice now rose above the noise.

"Order! To your places! You forget that there is still a document to be read." When quiet had been restored he took up the document, and was going to read it, but laid it down again, saying, "I forgot; this is not to be read until all written communications received by me have first been read." He took an envelope out of his pocket, removed its enclosure, glanced at it—seemed astonished—held it out and gazed at it—stared at it.

Twenty or thirty voices cried out:

"What is it? Read it! Read it!"

And he did—slowly, and wondering:

" 'The remark which I made to the stranger—[*Voices.* "Hello! how's this?"] —was this: "You are far from being a bad man. [*Voices.* "Great Scott!] Go, and reform."'" [*Voice.* "Oh, saw my leg off!"] Signed by Mr. Pinkerton the banker."

The pandemonium of delight which turned itself loose now was a sort to make the judicious weep. Those whose withers were unwrung laughed till the tears ran down; the reporters, in throes of laughter, set down disordered pothooks which would never in the world be decipherable; and a sleeping dog jumped up, scared out of its wits, and barked itself crazy at the turmoil. All manner of cries were scattered through the din: "We're getting rich—*two* Symbols of Incorruptibility! —without counting Billson!" "*Three!*—count Shadbelly in—we can't have too many!" "All right—Billson's elected!" "Alas, poor Wilson—victim of *two* thieves!"

*A Powerful Voice.* "Silence! The Chair's fished up something more out of its pocket."

*Voices.* "Hurrah! Is it something fresh? Read it! Read! Read!"

*The Chair* [*reading.*] "'The remark which I made,' etc.: 'You are far from being a bad man. Go,' etc. Signed, Gregory Yates."

*Tornado of Voices.* "Four Symbols!" "'Rah for Yates!" "Fish again!"

The house was in a roaring humor now, and ready to get all the fun out of the occasion that might be in it. Several Nineteeners, looking pale and distressed, got up and began to work their way toward the aisles, but a score of shouts went up:

"The doors, the doors—close the doors; no Incorruptible shall leave this place! Sit down, everybody!"

The mandate was obeyed.

"Fish again! Read! Read!"

The Chair fished again, and once more the familiar words began to fall from its lips—"'You are far from being a bad man—'"

"Name! name! What's his name?"

"L. Ingoldsby Sargent."

"Five elected! Pile up the Symbols! Go on, go on!"

" 'You are far from being a bad—' "

"Name! name!"

"Nicholas Whitworth."

"Hooray! hooray! It's a symbolical day!"

Somebody wailed in, and began to sing this rhyme (leaving out "it's") to the lovely *Mikado* tune of "When a man's afraid, a beautiful maid—"; the audience joined in, with joy; then, just in time, somebody contributed another line:

"And don't you this forget—"

The house roared it out. A third line was at once furnished:

"Corruptibles far from Hadleyburg are—"

The house roared that one too. As the last note died, Jack Halliday's voice rose high and clear, freighted with a final line:

"But the Symbols are here, you bet!"

That was sung with booming enthusiasm. Then the happy house started in at the beginning and sang the four lines through twice, with immense swing and dash, and finished up with a crashing three-times-three and a tiger for "Hadleyburg the Incorruptible and all Symbols of it which we shall find worthy to receive the hallmark tonight."

Then the shoutings at the Chair began again, all over the place:

"Go on! Go on! Read! Read some more! Read all you've got!"

"That's it—go on! We are winning eternal celebrity!"

A dozen men got up now and began to protest. They said that this farce was the work of some abandoned joker, and was an insult to the whole community. Without a doubt these signatures were all forgeries—

"Sit down! Sit down! Shut up! You are confessing. We'll find *your* names in the lot."

"Mr. Chairman, how many of those envelopes have you got?"

The Chair counted.

"Together with those that have been already examined, there are nineteen."

A storm of derisive applause broke out.

"Perhaps they all contain the secret. I move that you open them all and read every signature that is attached to a note of that sort—and read also the first eight words of the note."

"Second the motion!"

It was put and carried—uproariously. Then poor old Richards got up, and his wife rose and stood at this side. Her head was bent down, so that none might see that she was crying. Her husband gave her his arm, and so supporting her, he began to speak in a quavering voice:

"My friends, you have known us two—Mary and me—all our lives, and I think yo have liked us and respected us—"

The Chair interrupted him:

"Allow me. It is quite true—that which you are saying, Mr. Richards: this town *does* know you two; it *does* like you; it *does* respect you; more—it honors you and *loves* you—"

Halliday's voice rang out:

"That's the hallmarked truth, too! If the Chair is right, let the house speak up and say it. Rise! Now, then—hip! hip! hip! —all together!"

The house rose in mass, faced toward the old couple eagerly, filled the air with a snowstorm of waving handkerchiefs, and delivered the cheers with all its affectionate heart.

The Chair then continued:

"What I was going to say is this: We know your good heart, Mr. Richards, but this is not a time for the exercise of charity toward offenders. [*Shouts of "Right! right!"*] I see your generous purpose in your face, but I cannot allow you to plead for these men—"

"But I was going to—"

"Please take your seat, Mr. Richards. We must examine the rest of these notes—simple fairness to the men who have already been exposed requires this. As soon as that has been done—I give you my word for this—you shall be heard."

*Many Voices.* "Right!—the Chair is right—no interruption can be permitted at this stage! Go on! —the names! the names! —according to the terms of the motion!"

The old couple sat reluctantly down, and the husband whispered to the wife, "It is pitifully hard to have to wait; the shame will be greater than ever when they find we were only going to plead for *ourselves*."

Straightway the jollity broke loose again with the reading of the names.

"'You are far from being a bad man—' Signature, Robert J. Titmarsh.

"'You are far from being a bad man—' Signature, Eliphalet Weeks.

"'You are far from being a bad man—' Signature, Oscar B. Wilder."

At this point the house lit upon the idea of taking the eight words out of the Chairman's hands. He was not unthankful for that. Thenceforward he held up each note in its turn, and waited. The house droned out the eight words in a massed and measured and musical deep volume of sound (with a daringly close resemblance to a well-known church chant)—"'You are f-a-r from being a b-a-a-a-d man.'" Then the Chair said, "Signature, Archibald Wilcox." And so on, and so on, name after name, and everybody had an increasingly and gloriously good time except the wretched Nineteen. Now and then, when a particularly shining name was called, the house made the Chair wait while it chanted the whole of the test-remark from the beginning to the closing words. "And go to hell or Hadleyburg—try and make it the for-or-m-e-r!" and in these special cases they added a grand and agonized and imposing "A-a-a-a-*men*!"

The list dwindled, dwindled, poor old Richards keeping tally of the count, wincing when a name resembling his own was pronounced, and waiting in miserable suspense for the time to come when it would be his humiliating privilege to rise with Mary and finish his plea, which he was intending to word thus: ". . . for until now we have never done any wrong thing, but have gone our humble way unreproached. We are very poor, we are old, and have no chick nor child to help us; we were sorely tempted, and we fell. It was my purpose when I got up before to make confession and beg that my name might not be read out in this public place, for it seemed to us that we could not bear it; but I was prevented. It was just; it was our place to suffer with the rest. It has been hard for us. It is the first time we have ever heard our name fall from anyone's lips—sullied. Be merciful—for the sake of the better days; make our shame as light to bear as in your charity you can." At this point in his reverie Mary nudged him, perceiving that his mind was absent. The house was chanting, "You are f-a-r," etc.

"Be ready," Mary whispered. "Your name comes now; he has read eighteen."

The chant ended.

"Next! next! next!" came volleying from all over the house.

Burgess put his hand into his pocket. The old couple, trembling, began to rise. Burgess fumbled a moment, then said:

"I find I have read them all."

Faint with joy and surprise, the couple sank into their seats, and Mary whispered:

"Oh, bless God, we are saved! He has lost ours—I wouldn't give this for a hundred of those sacks!"

The house burst out with its *Mikado* travesty, and sang it three times with ever-increasing enthusiasm, rising to its feet when it reached for the third time the closing line:

"But the Symbols are here, you bet!"

and finishing up with cheers and a tiger for "Hadleyburg purity and our eighteen immortal representatives of it."

Then Wingate, the saddler, got up and proposed cheers "for the cleanest man in town, the one solitary important citizen in it who didn't try to steal that money—Edward Richards."

They were given with great and moving heartiness; then somebody proposed that Richards be elected sole guardian and Symbol of the now Sacred Hadleyburg Tradition, with power and right to stand up and look the whole sarcastic world in the face.

Passed, by acclamation. Then they sang the *Mikado* again, and ended it with:

"And there's one Symbol left, you bet!"

There was a pause; then:

*A Voice.* "Now, then, who's to get the sack?"

*The Tanner [with bitter sarcasm].* "That's easy. The money has to be divided among the eighteen Incorruptibles. They gave the suffering stranger twenty dollars apiece—and that remark—each in his turn—it took twenty-two minutes for the procession to move past. Staked the stranger—total contribution, $360. All they want is just the loan back—and interest—forty thousand dollars altogether."

*Many voices [derisively].* "That's it! Divvy! Divvy! Be kind to the poor—don't keep them waiting!

*The Chair.* "Order! I now offer the stranger's remaining document. It says: 'If no claimant shall appear [*grand chorus of groans*], I desire that you open the sack and count out the money to the principal citizens of your town, they to take it in trust [*cries of "Oh! Oh! Oh!"*], and use it in such ways as to them shall seem best for the propagation and preservation of your community's noble reputation for incorruptible honesty [*more cries*] —a reputation to which their names and their efforts will add a new and far-reaching luster.' [*Enthusiastic outburst of sarcastic applause.*] That seems to be all. No—here is a postscript:

"'P.S.—Citizens of Hadleyburg: There *is* no test-remark—nobody made one. [*Great sensation.*] There wasn't any pauper stranger, nor any twenty-dollar contribution, nor any accompanying benediction and compliment—these are all inventions. [*General buzz and hum of astonishment and delight.*] Allow me to tell my story—it will take but a word or two. I passed through your town at a certain time, and received a deep offense which I had not earned. Any other man would have been content to kill one or two of you and call it square, but to me that would have been a trivial revenge, and inadequate; for the dead do not *suffer*. Besides, I could not kill you all—and, anyway, made as I am, even that would not have satisfied me. I wanted to damage every man in the place, and every woman—and not in the bodies or in their estate, but in their vanity—the place where feeble and foolish people are most vulnerable. So I disguised myself and came back and studied you. You were easy game. You had an old and lofty reputation for honesty, and naturally you were proud of it—it was your treasure of treasures, the very apple of your eye. As soon as I found out that you carefully and vigilantly kept yourselves and your children *out of temptation*, I knew how to proceed. Why, you simple creatures, the weakest of all weak things is a virtue which has not been tested in the fire. I laid a plan, and gathered a list of names. My project was to corrupt Hadleyburg the Incorruptible. My idea was to make liars and thieves of nearly half a hundred smirchless men and women who had never in their lives uttered a lie or stolen a penny. I was afraid of Goodson. He was neither born nor reared in Hadleyburg. I was afraid that if I started to operate my scheme by getting my letter laid before you, you would say to yourselves, "Goodson is the only man among us who would give away twenty dollars to a poor devil"—and then you might not bite at my bait. But Heaven took Goodson; then I knew I was safe, and I set my trap and baited it. It may be that I shall not catch all the men to whom I mailed the pretended test secret, but I shall catch the most of them, if I know Hadleyburg nature. [*Voices.* "Right—he got every last one of them."] I believe they will even steal ostensible *gamble*-money, rather than miss, poor, tempted, and mistrained fellows. I am hoping to eternally and everlastingly squelch your vanity and give Hadleyburg a new renown—one that will *stick*—and spread far. If I have succeeded, open the sack and summon the Committee on Propagation and Preservation of the Hadleyburg Reputation.'"

*A Cyclone of Voices.* "Open it! Open it! The Eighteen to the front! Committee on Propagation of the Tradition! Forward—the Incorruptibles!"

The Chair ripped the sack wide, and gathered up a handful of bright, broad, yellow coins, shook them together, then examined them.

"Friends, they are only gilded disks of lead!"

There was a crashing outbreak of delight over this news, and when the noise had subsided, the tanner called out:

"By right of apparent seniority in this business, Mr. Wilson is Chairman of the Committee on Propagation of the Tradition. I suggest that he step forward on behalf of his pals, and receive in trust the money."

*A Hundred Voices.* "Wilson! Wilson! Wilson! Speech! Speech!"

*Wilson* [*in a voice trembling with anger.*] "You will allow me to say, and without apologies for my language, *damn* the money!"

*A Voice.* "Oh, and him a Baptist!"

*A Voice.* "Seventeen Symbols left! Step up, gentlemen, and assume your trust!"

There was a pause—no response.

*The Saddler.* "Mr. Chairman, we've got *one* clean man left, anyway, out of the late aristocracy; and he needs money, and deserves it. I move that you appoint Jack Halliday to get up there and auction off that sack of gilt twenty-dollar pieces, and give the result to the right man—the man whom Hadleyburg delights to honor—Edward Richards."

This was received with great enthusiasm, the dog taking a hand again; the saddler started the bids at a dollar, the Brixton folk and Barnum's representative fought hard for it, the people cheered every jump that the bids made, the excitement climbed moment by moment higher and higher, the bidders got on their mettle and grew steadily more and more daring, more and more determined, the jumps went from a dollar up to five, then to ten, then to twenty, then fifty, then to a hundred, then—

At the beginning of the auction Richards whispered in distress to his wife: "O Mary, can we allow it? It—it—you see, it is an honor reward, a testimonial to purity of character, and—and—can we allow it? Hadn't I better get up and—O Mary, what ought we to do? —what do you think we—" [*Halliday's voice. "Fifteen I'm bid!—fifteen for the sack!—twenty!—ah, thanks!—thirty—thanks again! Thirty, thirty, thirty!—do I hear forty?—forty it is! Keep the ball rolling, gentlemen, keep it rolling!—fifty!—thanks, noble Roman! going at fifty, fifty, fifty!—seventy!—ninety!—splendid!—a hundred!—pile it up, pile it up!—hundred and twenty—forty!—just in time!—hundred and fifty!—*TWO *hundred! superb! Do I hear two h—thanks! two hundred and fifty!—*"]

"It is another temptation, Edward—I'm all in a tremble—but, oh, we've escaped *one* temptation, and that ought to warn us to—["*Six did I hear?—thanks! six fifty, six f—*SEVEN *hundred!*"] And yet, Edward when you think—nobody susp—[*Eight hundred dollars!—hurrah!—make it nine!—Mr. Parsons, did I hear you say—thanks—nine! this noble sack of virgin lead going at only nine hundred dollars, gilding and all—come! do I hear—a thousand!—gratefully yours!—did someone say eleven?—a sack which is going to be the most celebrated in the whole Uni—*"] O Edward" (beginning to sob), "we are *so* poor!—but—but—do as you think best—do as you think best."

Edward fell—that is, he sat still; sat with a conscience which was not satisfied, but which was overpowered by circumstances.

Meantime a stranger, who looked like an amateur detective gotten up as an impossible English earl, had been watching the evening's proceedings with manifest interest, and with a contented expression in his face; and he had been privately commenting to himself. He was now soliloquizing somewhat like this: "None of the Eighteen are bidding; that is not satisfactory; I must change that—the dramatic unities require it; they must buy the sack they tried to steal; they must pay a heavy price, too—some of them are rich. And another thing, when I made a mistake in Hadleyburg nature the man that puts that error upon me is entitled to a high honorarium, and someone must pay it. This poor old Richards has brought my judgment to shame; he is an honest man. I don't understand it, but I acknowledge it. Yes, he saw my deuces *and* with a straight flush, and by rights the pot is his. And it shall be a jackpot, too, if I can manage it. He disappointed me, but let that pass."

He was watching the bidding. At a thousand, the market broke; the prices tumbled swiftly. He waited—and still watched. One competitor dropped out; then another, and another. He put in a bid or two, now. When the bids had sunk to ten dollars, he added a five; someone raised him a three; he waited a moment, then flung in a fifty-dollar jump, and the sack was his—at $1,282. The house broke out in cheers—then stopped; for he was on his feet, and had lifted his hand. He began to speak.

"I desire to say a word, and ask a favor. I am a speculator in rarities, and I have dealings with persons interested in numismatics all over the world. I can make a profit on this purchase, just as it stands; but there is a way, if I can get your approval, whereby I can make every one of these leaden twenty-dollar pieces worth its face in gold, and perhaps more. Grant me that approval, and I will give part of my gains to your Mr. Richards, whose invulnerable probity you have so justly and so cordially recognized tonight; his share shall be ten thousand dollars, and I will hand him the money tomorrow. [*Great applause from the house.* But the "invulnerable probity" made the Richardses blush prettily; however, it went for modesty, and did no harm.] If you will pass my proposition by a good majority—I would like a two-thirds vote—I will regard that as the town's consent, and that is all I ask. Rarities are always helped by any device which will rouse curiosity and compel remark. Now if I may have your permission to stamp upon the faces of each of these ostensible coins the names of the eighteen gentlemen who—"

Nine-tenths of the audience were on their feet in a moment—dog and all—and the proposition was carried with a whirlwind of approving applause and laughter.

They sat down, and all the Symbols except "Dr." Clay Harkness got up, violently protesting outrage, and threatening to—

"I beg you not to threaten me," said the stranger, calmly. "I know my legal rights, and am not accustomed to being frightened at bluster." [*Applause.*] He sat down. "Dr." Harkness saw an opportunity here. He was one of the two very rich men of the place, and Pinkerton was the other. Harkness was proprietor of a mint; that is to say, a popular patent medicine. He was running for the legislature on one ticket, and Pinkerton on the other. It was a close race and a hot one, and getting hotter every day. Both had strong appetites for money; each had bought a great tract of land, with a purpose; there was going to be a new railway, and each wanted to be in the legislature and help locate the route to his own advantage; a single vote might make the decision, and with it two or three fortunes. The stake was large, and Harkness was a daring speculator. He was sitting close to the stranger. He leaned over while one or another of the other Symbols was entertaining the house with protests and appeals, and asked, in a whisper:

"What is your price for the sack?"

"Forty thousand dollars."

"I'll give you twenty."

"No."

"Twenty-five."

"No."

"Say thirty."

"The price is forty thousand dollars; not a penny less."

"All right, I'll give it. I will come to the hotel at ten in the morning. I don't want it known; will see you privately."

"Very good." Then the stranger got up and said to the house:

"I find it late. The speeches of these gentlemen are not without merit, not without interest, not without grace; yet if I may be excused I will take my leave. I thank you for the great favor which you have shown me in granting my petition. I ask the Chair to keep the sack for me until tomorrow, and to hand these three five-hundred-dollar notes to Mr. Richards." They were passed up to the Chair. "At nine I will call for the sack, and at eleven will deliver the rest of the ten thousand to Mr. Richards in person, at his home. Good night."

Then he slipped out, and left the audience making a vast noise, which was composed of a mixture of cheers, the *Mikado* song, dog-disapproval, and the chant, "You are f-a-r from being a b-a-a-d man—a-a-a-a-men!"

# 4

At home the Richardses had to endure congratulations and compliments until midnight. Then they were left to themselves. They looked a little sad, and they sat silent and thinking. Finally Mary sighed and said:

"Do you think we are to blame, Edward—*much* to blame?" And her eyes wandered to the accusing triplet of big banknotes lying on the table, where the congratulators had been gloating over them and reverently fingering them. Edward did not answer at once; then he brought out a sigh and said, hesitatingly:

"We—we couldn't help it, Mary. It—well, it was ordered. *All* things are."

Mary glanced up and looked at him steadily, but he didn't return the look. Presently she said:

"I thought congratulations and praises always tasted good. But—it seems to me, now—Edward?"

"Well?"

"Are you going to stay in the bank?"

"N-no."

"Resign?"

"In the morning—by note."

"It does seem best."

Richards bowed his head in his hands and muttered:

"Before, I was not afraid to let oceans of people's money pour through my hands, but—Mary, I am so tired, so tired—"

"We will go to bed."

At nine in the morning the stranger called for the sack and took it to the hotel in a cab. At ten Harkness had a talk with him privately. The stranger asked for and got five checks on a metropolitan bank—drawn to "Bearer"—four for $1,500 each, and one for $34,000. He put one of the former in his pocketbook, and the remainder, representing $38,500, he put in an envelope, and with these he added a note, which he wrote after Harkness was gone. At eleven he called at the Richards house and knocked. Mrs. Richards peeped through the shutters, then went and received the envelope, and the stranger disappeared without a word. She came back flushed and a little unsteady on her legs, and gasped out:

"I am sure I recognized him! Last night it seemed to me that maybe I had seen him somewhere before."

"He is the man that brought the sack here?"

"I am almost sure of it."

"Then he is the ostensible Stephenson too, and sold every important citizen in this town with his bogus secret. Now if he has sent checks instead of money, we are sold, too, after we thought we had escaped. I was beginning to feel fairly comfortable once more, after my night's rest, but the look of that envelope makes me sick. It isn't fat enough; $8,500 in even the largest banknotes makes more bulk than that."

"Edward, why do you object to checks?"

"Checks signed by Stephenson! I am resigned to take the $8,500 if it could come in banknotes—for it does seem that it was so ordered, Mary—but I have never had much courage, and I have not the pluck to try to market a check signed with that disastrous name. It would be a trap. That man tried to catch me; we escaped somehow or other, and now he is trying a new way. If it is checks—"

"Oh, Edward, it is *too* bad!" And she held up the checks and began to cry.

"Put them in the fire! Quick! We mustn't be tempted. It is a trick to make the world laugh at *us*, along with the rest, and— give them to *me*, since you can't do it! He snatched them and tried to hold his grip till he could get to the stove; but he was human, he was a cashier, and he stopped a moment to make sure of the signature. Then he came near to fainting.

"Fan me, Mary, fan me! They are the same as gold!"

"Oh, how lovely, Edward! Why?"

"Signed by Harkness. What can the mystery of that be, Mary?"

"Edward, do you think—"

"Look here—look at this! Fifteen—fifteen—fifteen—thirty-four. Thirty-eight thousand five hundred! Mary, the sack isn't worth twelve dollars, and Harkness—apparently—has paid about par for it."

"Why, it looks like it. And the checks are made to 'Bearer,' too."

"Is that good, Edward? What is it for?"

"A hint to collect them at some distant bank, I reckon. Perhaps Harkness doesn't want the matter known. What is that—a note?"

"Yes. It was with the checks."

It was in the "Stephenson" handwriting, but there was no signature. It said:

I am a disappointed man. Your honesty is beyond the reach of temptation I had a different idea about it, but I wronged you in that, and I beg pardon, and do it sincerely. I honor you—and that is sincere too. This town is not worthy to kiss the hem of your garment. Dear sir, I made a square bet with myself that there were nineteen debauchable men in your self-righteous community. I have lost. Take the whole pot, you are entitled to it.

Richards drew a deep sigh, and said:

"It seems written with fire—it burns so. Mary—I am miserable again."

"I, too. Ah, dear, I wish—"

"To think, Mary—he believes in me."

"Oh, don't, Edward—I can't bear it."

"If those beautiful words were deserved, Mary—and God knows I believed I deserved them once—I think I could give the forty thousand dollars for them. And I would put that paper away, as representing more than gold and jewels, and keep it always. But now— We could not live in the shadow of its accusing presence, Mary."

He put it in the fire.

A messenger arrived and delivered an envelope.

Richards took from it a note and read it; it was from Burgess.

You saved me, in a difficult time. I saved you last night. It was at cost of a lie, but I made the sacrifice freely, and out of a grateful heart. None in this village knows so well as I know how brave and good and noble you are. At bottom you cannot respect me, knowing as you do of that matter of which I am accused, and by the general voice condemned; but I beg that you will at least believe that I am a grateful man; it will help me to bear my burden.

[Signed] BURGESS

"Saved, once more. And on such terms!" He put the note in the fire. "I—I wish I were dead, Mary, I wish I were out of it all."

"Oh, these are bitter, bitter days, Edward. The stabs, through their very generosity, are so deep—and they come so fast!"

Three days before the election each of the two thousand voters suddenly found himself in possession of a prized memento—one of the renowned bogus double eagles. Around one of its faces was stamped these words: "THE REMARK I MADE TO THE POOR STRANGER WAS—" Around the other face was stamped these: "GO AND REFORM. [SIGNED] PINKERTON." Thus the entire remaining refuse of the renowned joke was emptied upon a single head, and with calamitous effect. It revived the recent vast laugh and concentrated it upon Pinkerton; and Harkness's election was a walkover.

Within twenty-four hours after the Richardses had received their checks their consciences were quieting down, discouraged; the old couple were learning to reconcile themselves to the sin which they had committed. But they were to learn, now, that a sin takes on new and real terrors when there seems a chance that it is going to be found out. This gives it a fresh and most substantial and important aspect. At church the morning sermons was of the usual pattern; it was the same old things said in the same old way; they had heard them a thousand times and found them innocuous, next to meaningless, and easy to sleep under; but now it was different: the sermon seemed to bristle with accusations; it seemed aimed straight and specially at people who were concealing deadly sins. After church they got away from the mob of congratulators as soon as they could, and hurried homeward, chilled to the bone at they did not know what—vague, shadowy, indefinite fears. And by chance they caught a glimpse of Mr. Burgess as he turned a corner. He paid no attention to their nod of recognition! He hadn't seen it; but they did not know that. What could his conduct mean? It might mean—it might mean—oh, a dozen dreadful things. Was it possible that he knew that Richards could have cleared him of guilt in that bygone time, and had been silently waiting for a chance to even up accounts? At home, in their distress they got to imagining that their servant might have been in the next room listening when Richards revealed the secret to his wife that he knew of Burgess's innocence; next, Richards began to imagine that he had heard the swish of a gown in there at that time; next, he was sure he *had* heard it. They would call Sarah in, on a pretext, and watch her face: if she had been betraying them to Mr. Burgess, it would show in her manner. They asked her some questions—questions which were so random and incoherent and seemingly purposeless that the girl felt sure that the old people's minds had been affected by their sudden good fortune; the sharp and watchful gaze which they bent upon her frightened her, and that completed the business. She blushed, she became nervous and confused, and to the old people these were plain signs of guilt—guilt of some fearful sort or other—without doubt she was a spy and a traitor. When they were alone again they began to piece many unrelated things together and get horrible results out of the combination. When things had got about to the worst, Richards was delivered of a sudden gasp, and his wife asked:

"Oh what is it? —What is it?"

"The note—Burgess's note! Its language was sarcastic, I see it now." He quoted: "'At bottom you cannot respect me, *knowing*, as you do, of *that matter* of which I am accused'—oh, it is perfectly plain now, God help me! He knows that I know! You see the ingenuity of the phrasing. It was a trap—and like a fool, I walked into it. And Mary—?"

"Oh, it is dreadful—I know what you are going to say—he didn't return your transcript of the pretended test-remark."

"No—kept it to destroy us with. Mary, he has exposed us to some already. I know it—I know it well. I saw it in a dozen faces after church. Ah, he wouldn't answer our nod of recognition—*he* knew what he had been doing!"

In the night the doctor was called. The news went around in the morning that the old couple were rather seriously ill—prostrated by the exhausting excitement growing out of their great windfall, the congratulations, and the late hours, the doctor said. The town was sincerely distressed; for these old people were about all it had left to be proud of, now.

Two days later the news was worse. The old couple were delirious, and were doing strange things. By witness of the nurses, Richards had exhibited checks—for $8,500? No, for an amazing sum—$38,500! What could be the explanation of this gigantic piece of luck?

The following day the nurses had more news—and wonderful. They had concluded to hide the checks, lest harm come to them; but when they searched they were gone from under the patient's pillow—vanished away. The patient said:

"Let the pillow alone; what do you want?"

"We thought it best that the checks—"

"You will never see them again—they are destroyed. They came from Satan. I saw the hell-brand on them, and I knew they were sent to betray me to sin." Then he fell to gabbling strange and dreadful things which were not clearly understandable, and which the doctor admonished them to keep to themselves.

Richards was right; the checks were never seen again.

A nurse must have talked in her sleep, for within two days the forbidden gabblings were the property of the town; and they were of a surprising sort. They seemed to indicate that Richards had been a claimant for the sack himself, and that Burgess had concealed that fact and then maliciously betrayed it.

Burgess was taxed with this and stoutly denied it. And he said it was not fair to attach weight to the chatter of a sick old man who was out of his mind. Still, suspicion was in the air, and there was much talk.

After a day or two it was reported that Mrs. Richards's delirious deliveries were getting to be duplicates of her husband's. Suspicion flamed up into conviction, now, and the town's pride in the purity of its one undiscredited important citizen began to dim down and flicker toward extinction.

Six days passed, then came more news. The old couple were dying. Richards's mind cleared in his latest hour, and he sent for Burgess. Burgess said:

"Let the room be cleared. I think he wishes to say something in privacy."

"No!" said Richards: "I want witnesses. I want you all to hear my confession, so that I may die a man, and not a dog. I was clean—artificially—like the rest; and like the rest I fell when temptation came. I signed a lie, and claimed the miserable sack. Mr. Burgess remembered that I had done him a service, and in gratitude (and ignorance) he suppressed my claim and saved me. You know the thing that was charged against Burgess years ago. My testimony, and mine alone, could have cleared him, and I was a coward, and left him to suffer disgrace—"

"No—no—Mr. Richards, you—"

"My servant betrayed my secret to him—"

"No one has betrayed anything to me—"

"—and then he did a natural and justifiable thing, he repented of the saving kindness which he had done me, and he *exposed* me—as I deserved—"

"Never! —I make oath—"

"Out of my heart I forgive him."

Burgess's impassioned protestations fell upon deaf ears; the dying man passed away without knowing that once more he had done poor Burgess a wrong. The old wife died that night.

The last of the sacred Nineteen had fallen a prey to the fiendish sack; the town was stripped of the last rag of its ancient glory. Its mourning was not showy, but it was deep.

By act of the legislature—upon prayer and petition—Hadleyburg was allowed to change its name to (never mind what—I will not give it away), and leave one word out of the motto that for many generations had graced the town's official seal.

It is an honest town once more, and the man will have to rise early that catches it napping again.

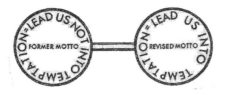

## QUESTIONS

1. How does Hadleyburg's being "sufficient unto itself" contribute to its eventual humiliation? (195)

2. Why does Mrs. Richards say that the town's "proper" character is "honest, narrow, self-righteous, and stingy"? (199)

3. After Cox and Richards realize it is too late to keep the stranger's letter out of the paper, why are their discussions with their wives "heated" and "ungentle" for the first time? (202)

4. Why do the visitors to the town take such delight in its downfall?

5. After the scene at the town hall, why does Mr. Richards repeat his statement that all things are "ordered"? (227)

6. Why does the stranger go to such lengths to reward Richards for his apparent honesty?

7. Why is the sack described as "fiendish"? (232)

8. At the end of the story, why does Twain leave the town "stripped of the last rag of its ancient glory"? (232)

9. What does the narrator mean in saying, "It is an honest town once more, and the man will have to rise early that catches it napping again"? (232)

10. In what sense does the offended stranger corrupt Hadleyburg?

## FOR FURTHER REFLECTION

1. Why is honesty more important to the townspeople than the virtues they lack?

2. Does Twain approve of the stranger's actions?

3. What effect on the town do you think the rewording of the motto will have?

4. What does it mean to say that a person has been corrupted? Can being corrupted ever have a positive effect on a person or community?

Friedrich Nietzsche (1844–1900), the son and grandson of clergymen, did more than perhaps any other nineteenth-century thinker except Darwin to undermine the foundations of Christian faith in Europe. In little more than a decade he produced a series of brilliant books that staked out uncharted territory between philosophy and literature. In these idiosyncratic writings he blazed intellectual trails—including the position of perspectivism and the confrontation with nihilism—that became some of the twentieth century's most heavily traveled highways of thought.

Nietzsche was born in the small German village of Röcken, near Leipzig. His father died when he was four years old and his mother took him and his younger sister to live in the larger town of Naumburg. There he was raised in a large, all-female household. At fourteen he received a scholarship to a nearby boarding school, where he excelled in music and classical philology.

In 1864 Nietzsche entered the University of Bonn, where he continued his study of philology. The following year he transferred to the university in Leipzig, in whose bookshops he stumbled upon philosopher Arthur Schopenhauer's *The World as Will and Representation*. This work, which contains a critique of the rationalist philosophy of Immanuel Kant, had a profound impact upon the pastor's son. In 1868 Nietzsche met the composer and cultural titan Richard Wagner, who would also exert a pivotal influence on his thought and work.

In 1869 Nietzsche took up a position as a professor of philology at the University of Basel, Switzerland. His teachers and colleagues regarded him as a classical scholar of great promise, and a successful academic career seemed assured. However, a number of circumstances turned him aside from what seemed his predestined course in life. For one thing, his health had been poor since childhood, when he suffered from headaches and myopia. He had also been injured during military training in 1867, and then contracted diphtheria and dysentery while caring for wounded soldiers during brief service in the Franco-Prussian War. For the rest of his life, Nietzsche suffered from a variety of debilitating digestive and nervous complaints.

Another factor that deflected him from an academic career was the influence of the intellectual rebels, Schopenhauer and Wagner, on his thinking. Nietzsche's attraction to radical ideas found voice in his first book, *The Birth of Tragedy*, published in 1872. In it, he critiqued the high classicist, or Apollonian, tradition in German culture, based on the aesthetic principles of reason, serenity, nobility, and grandeur assumed to have governed the art of classical Greece. To complement these values, Nietzsche invoked the Dionysian qualities of vitality, will, chaos, and instinct, which he claimed the ancient Greeks incorporated into their art. *The Birth of Tragedy* already articulated many of the basic elements of the future Nietzschean worldview. In later writings, which grew increasingly literary, aphoristic, and playful, Nietzsche would continue to praise the pagan virtues of courage, striving, and self-assertion in contrast to Christian selflessness, compassion, and love.

*The Birth of Tragedy* was savagely attacked by some of the leading intellectuals in Germany. Undaunted, Nietzsche began work on a series of critical essays—including the one from which the following selection is taken—to which he gave the title Untimely Meditations. They too found little favor with either professors or the public. Nietzsche's increasingly severe health problems led to his resignation from the university. He took up an existence of restless wandering from one rented room to another in various spas and resort towns across Switzerland, the French Riviera, and northern Italy. It was under such circumstances that Nietzsche composed his four unclassifiable masterpieces: *The Gay Science* (1882), in which he first proclaimed "the death of God"; *Thus Spoke Zarathustra* (four vols.: 1883, 1883, 1884, 1885); *Beyond Good and Evil* (1886); and *The Genealogy of Morals* (1887).

In 1888, Nietzsche wrote three strange books—*Twilight of the Idols*, *The Anti-Christ*, and *Ecce Homo*—and his behavior betrayed an increasingly unbalanced state of mind. The following year he broke down on the street in Turin, Italy, upon witnessing a man beating a horse. He lived for eleven more years as an invalid under his mother's and then his sister's care. During these years, his literary reputation steadily grew. He died in 1900, unaware of his burgeoning fame.

# On the Advantage and Disadvantage of History for Life (selection)

## Preface

"Moreover I hate everything that merely instructs me without increasing or directly quickening my activity." These are Goethe's words with which, as with a boldly expressed *ceterum censeo*,[1] we may begin our consideration of the worth and worthlessness of history. Our aim will be to show why instruction that fails to quicken activity, why knowledge that enfeebles activity, why history as a costly intellectual excess and luxury must, in the spirit of Goethe's words, be seriously hated; for we still lack what is most necessary, and superfluous excess is the enemy of the necessary. Certainly we need history. But our need for history is quite different from that of the spoiled idler in the garden of knowledge, even if he in his refinement looks down on our rude and graceless requirements and needs. That is, we require history for life and action, not for the smug avoiding of life and action, or even to whitewash a selfish life and cowardly, bad acts. Only so far as history serves life will we serve it: but there is a degree of doing history and an estimation of it that brings with it a withering and degenerating of life: a phenomenon that is now as necessary as it may be painful to bring to consciousness through some remarkable symptoms of our age.

---

1. [This is an allusion to Cato's "Ceterum censeo Carthaginem esse defendam" (Moreover I am of the opinion that Carthage be destroyed") with which he used to conclude every speech on any topic whatever until he finally goaded the Romans into the Third Punic War.—TRANS.]

I have made an effort to describe a feeling that has tortured me often enough; I revenge myself on it by making it public. Perhaps this description will give someone occasion to explain to me that he too knows this feeling but that I have not felt it purely and originally enough and have quite failed to articulate it with the confidence and mature experience due it. A few may think so perhaps; but most will tell me that this is a quite perverted, unnatural, repulsive, and downright impermissible feeling, even that with this feeling I have shown myself to be quite unworthy of the mighty historical orientation of the age that, as is well known, has been evident for two generations particularly among the Germans. At any rate, my daring to come forward with a natural description of my feeling will sooner promote than injure general propriety, for in doing so I give opportunity to many to pay compliments to this orientation of the age. For my part, however, I gain something I value more highly than general propriety—public instruction and correction about our age.

These reflections are also untimely, because I attempt to understand as a defect, infirmity, and shortcoming of the age something of which our age is justifiably proud, its historical education. I even believe that all of us suffer from a consuming historical fever and should at least realize that we suffer from it. If Goethe has said with good reason that with our virtues we also cultivate our faults, and if, as everyone knows, a hypertrophic virtue—which the historical sense of our age seems to me to be—may bring about the decay of a people as much as a hypertrophic vice, one may as well allow me my say. I should not hide the exonerating circumstance that I have for the most part taken the experiences that those painful feelings occasioned in me from myself and have considered those of others only for the sake of comparison; and that further, only so far as I am the nursling of more ancient times, especially the Greek, could I come to have such untimely experiences about myself as a child of the present age. That much I must be allowed to grant myself on the grounds of my profession as a classical philologist. For I do not know what meaning classical philology would have for our age if not to have an untimely effect within it, that is, to act against the age and so have an effect on the age to the advantage, it is to be hoped, of a coming age.

# 1

Consider the herd grazing before you. These animals do not know what yesterday and today are but leap about, eat, rest, digest, and leap again; and so from morning to night and from day to day, only briefly concerned with their pleasure and displeasure, enthralled by the moment and for that reason neither melancholy nor bored. It is hard for a man to see this, for he is proud of being human and not an animal and yet regards its happiness with envy because he wants nothing other than to live like the animal, neither bored nor in pain, yet wants it in vain because he does not want it like the animal. Man may well ask the animal: Why do you not speak to me of your happiness but only look at me? The animal does want to answer and say: because I always immediately forget what I wanted to say—but then it already forgot this answer and remained silent: so that man could only wonder.

But he also wondered about himself, that he cannot learn to forget but always remains attached to the past: however far and fast he runs, the chain runs with him. It is astonishing: the moment, here in a wink, gone in a wink, nothing before and nothing after, returns nevertheless as a specter to disturb the calm of a later moment. Again and again a page loosens in the scroll of time, drops out, and flutters away—and suddenly flutters back again into man's lap. Then man says "I remember" and envies the animal that immediately forgets and sees each moment really die, sink back into deep night extinguished forever. In this way the animal lives *unhistorically*: for it goes into the present like a number without leaving a curious fraction; it does not know how to dissimulate, hides nothing, appears at every moment fully as what it is, and so cannot but be honest. Man on the other hand resists the great and ever greater weight of the past: this oppresses him and bends him sideways, it encumbers his gait like an invisible and sinister burden that, for the sake of appearances, he may deny at times and that in intercourse with his equals he is all too pleased to deny: to excite their envy. This is why he is moved, as though he remembered a lost paradise, when he sees a grazing herd, or, in more intimate proximity, sees a child, which as yet has nothing past to deny, playing between the fences of past and future in blissful blindness. And yet the child's play must be disturbed: only too soon will it be called out of its forgetfulness. Then it comes to understand the phrase "it was," that password with which struggle, suffering, and boredom approach man to remind him what his existence basically is—a never to be completed imperfect tense. And when death finally brings longed-for forgetfulness it also robs him of the present and of existence and impresses its seal on this knowledge: that existence is only an uninterrupted having-been, a thing that lives by denying itself, consuming itself, and contradicting itself.

If, in any sense, it is some happiness or the pursuit of happiness that binds the living being to life and urges him to live, then perhaps no philosopher is closer to the truth than the cynic: for the happiness of the animal, that thorough cynic, is the living proof of the truth of cynicism. The least happiness, if only it keeps one happy without interruption, is incomparably more than the greatest happiness that comes to one as a mere episode, as a mood, a frantic incursion into a life of utter displeasure, desire, and privation. With the smallest as with the greatest happiness, however, there is always one thing that makes it happiness: being able to forget or, to express it in a more learned fashion, the capacity to live *unhistorically* while it endures. Whoever cannot settle on the threshold of the moment forgetful of the whole past, whoever is incapable of standing on a point like a goddess of victory without vertigo or fear, will never know what happiness is, and worse yet, will never do anything to make others happy. Take as an extreme example a man who possesses no trace of the power to forget, who is condemned everywhere to see becoming: such a one no longer believes in his own existence, no longer believes in himself; he sees everything flow apart in mobile points and loses himself in the stream of becoming: he will, like the true pupil of Heraclitus,[2] hardly dare in the end to lift a finger. All acting requires forgetting, as not only light but also darkness is required for life by all organisms. A man who wanted to feel everything historically would resemble someone forced to refrain from sleeping, or an animal expected to live only from ruminating and ever-repeated ruminating. So: it is possible to live with almost no memories, even to live happily as the animal shows; but without forgetting it is quite impossible to *live* at all. Or, to say it more simply yet: *There is a degree of insomnia, of rumination of historical sense that injures every living thing and finally destroys it, be it a man, a people, or a culture.*

To determine this degree, and through it the limit beyond which the past must be forgotten if it is not to become the gravedigger of the present, one would have to know precisely how great the *plastic power* of a man, a people, or a culture is. I mean the power distinctively to grow out of itself, transforming and assimilating everything past and alien, to heal wounds, replace what is lost, and reshape broken forms out of itself. There are men who have this power to so small a degree that they will incurably bleed to death over a single experience, a single pain, frequently over a single delicate injustice, as from quite a small bleeding laceration. On the other hand there are those who are affected so little by the wildest and most gruesome calamities of life and even by their own malicious acts, that in midst of them or shortly thereafter they achieve a tolerable degree of well-being and a kind of clear conscience. The stronger the roots of the inmost nature of a man are, the more of the past will he appropriate or master; and were one to conceive the most powerful and colossal nature, it would be known by this, that for it there would be no limit at which the historical sense could overgrow and harm it; such a nature would draw

---

2. [The allusion is to Cratylus, who is said to have come to the view that, since no true statement can be made about a thing that is always changing, one ought not to say anything but only move one's finger.—TRANS.]

its own as well as every alien past wholly into itself and transform it into blood, as it were. What such a nature cannot master it knows how to forget; it no longer exists, the horizon is closed and whole, and nothing can serve as a reminder that beyond this horizon there remain men, passions, doctrines, and purposes. And this is a general law: every living thing can become healthy, strong, and fruitful only within a horizon; if it is incapable of drawing a horizon around itself or, on the other hand, too selfish to restrict its vision to the limits of a horizon drawn by another, it will wither away feebly or overhastily to its early demise. Cheerfulness, clear conscience, the carefree deed, faith in the future—all this depends, in the case of an individual as well as of a people, on there being a line which distinguishes what is clear and in full view from the dark and unilluminable; it depends on one's being able to forget at the right time as well as to remember at the right time; on discerning with strong instinctual feelings when there is need to experience historically and when unhistorically. Precisely this is the proposition the reader is invited to consider: *The unhistorical and the historical are equally necessary for the health of an individual, a people, and a culture.*

Everyone will have made the following observation: a man's historical knowledge and perception may be very limited, his horizon as restricted as that of a resident of an alpine valley, into every judgment he may introduce an injustice, into every experience the error of being the first to have that experience—and despite all injustice and all error he stands firmly in indefatigable health and vigor, a pleasure to behold; while right beside him the man of greater justice and learning deteriorates and crumbles because the lines of his horizon restlessly shift again and again, because he cannot extricate himself from the much more delicate network of his justice and truths in order to engage in rude willing and desiring. We have seen, however, that the animal, which is quite unhistorical and lives within a horizon that is almost a point, nevertheless is in a certain sense happy, or at least lives without boredom and dissimulation. We must then consider the capacity to perceive unhistorically to a certain degree as the more important and fundamental so far as it provides the foundation upon which alone something right, healthy, and great, something truly human may grow. The unhistorical resembles an enveloping atmosphere in which alone life is generated only to disappear again with the destruction of this atmosphere. It is true: only so far as man, by thinking, reflecting, comparing, dividing, and joining, limits that unhistorical element; only so far as a bright lightning flash of light occurs within that encircling cloud of mist—that is, only through the power to use the past for life and to refashion what has happened into history—does man become man: but with an excess of history man ceases again, and without that cloak of the unhistorical he would never have begun and dared to begin. Where are there deeds that a man might have done without first having entered the mist of the unhistorical? Or, leaving images aside, to illustrate with an example: Think of a man tossed and torn by a powerful passion for a woman or a great thought: how his world is changed! Glancing backward he feels blind, listening sideways he hears what is foreign as a dull, meaningless sound; what he perceives at all he has never perceived so before, so tangibly near, colored, full of sound and light as though he were apprehending it with all his senses at once. All evaluations are changed and devalued; there is so much he can no longer value because he can hardly feel it: he asks himself whether he has been fooled the whole time by alien words and alien opinions; he is astonished that his memory so tirelessly runs in circles and is yet too weak and too tired to leap even once out of this circle. It is the most unjust condition in the world, narrow, ungrateful to the past, blind to dangers, deaf to warnings, a little living whirlpool in a dead sea of night and forgetting: and yet this condition—unhistorical, contra-historical through and through—is the cradle not only of an unjust, but rather of every just deed; and no artist will paint his picture, no general achieve victory nor any people its freedom without first having desired and striven for it in such an unhistorical condition. As the man of action, according to Goethe's phrase, is always without conscience, so he is also without knowledge; he forgets a great deal to do one thing, he is unjust to what lies behind him and knows only one right, the right of that which is to become. So the agent loves his deed infinitely more than it deserves to be loved: and the best deeds occur in such an exuberance of love that of this love, at least, they must be unworthy even if their value is otherwise immeasurably great.

If someone could, in numerous instances, discern and breathe again the unhistorical atmosphere in which every great historical event came to be, then such a one might, as a cognitive being, perhaps elevate himself to a *superhistorical* standpoint such as Niebuhr once described as the possible result of historical observation. "History," he says, "clearly and explicitly comprehended, has at least this one use: that one knows how even the greatest and highest spirits of humanity do not know how accidentally their vision adopted the form through which they see and through which they vehemently insist that everyone else see; vehemently, that is, since the intensity of their consciousness is exceptionally great. Whoever does not know this and has not comprehended it quite definitely and in many instances will be subjugated by the appearance of a mighty spirit who brings the highest passion into a given form." One could call such a standpoint superhistorical, because one who has adopted it could no longer be tempted at all to continue to live and cooperate in making history, since he would have understood that blindness and injustice in the soul of each agent as the condition of all activity; he would even be cured henceforth of taking history excessively seriously: for he would have learned, with regard to each person and each experience, to answer his question about how and why people live, whether among Greeks or Turks, whether in an hour of the first century or the nineteenth. Whoever asks his acquaintances whether they would want to relive the last ten or twenty years will notice quite readily which of them is prepared for the superhistorical standpoint: they will, of course, all answer, No!, but they will give different reasons for this No! The reason of some may be that they take comfort in the hope that the next twenty years will be better; it is they whom David Hume ridicules when he says:

And from the dregs of life hope to receive,
What the first sprightly running could not give.

Let us call them the historical men. Looking into the past urges them toward the future, incites them to take courage and continue to engage in life, and kindles the hope that things will yet turn out well and that happiness is to be found behind the mountain toward which they are striding. These historical men believe that ever more light is shed on the meaning of existence in the course of its *process*, and they look back to consider that process only to understand the present better and learn to desire the future more vehemently. They do not know how unhistorically they think and act despite all their history, and how even their concern with historiography does not serve pure knowledge but life.

But the question whose first answer we have heard may also be answered differently. Of course again with a No!—but this time for different reasons. With the No of the superhistorical man who does not see salvation in the process, for whom, rather, the world is complete and achieves its end at every single moment. What could ten new years teach that the past ten were incapable of teaching!

Superhistorical men have never agreed whether the significance of the teaching is happiness or resignation, virtue or penance; but, opposed to all historical ways of viewing the past, they are quite unanimous in accepting the following proposition: the past and the present is one and the same, that is, typically alike in all manifold variety and, as omnipresence of imperishable types, a static structure of unchanged value and eternally the same meaning. As hundreds of different languages correspond to the typically fixed requirements of men, so that one who understood these requirements could learn nothing new from all those languages: so the superhistorical thinker illuminates all history of peoples and individuals from within, clairvoyantly guesses the original significance of the different hieroglyphs, and gradually even evades, as one fatigued, the incessant flow of new script: how could he fail, amid the endless superfluity of events, to take in his fill, more than his fill, and finally be nauseated! So that in the end the boldest is perhaps prepared to say to his heart with Giacomo Leopardi:

Nothing is worth
One tremor or one beat; the very earth
Deserves no sigh. Life
Has shrunk to dregs and rancor; the world is unclean.
Calm, calm.

But let us leave the superhistorical men their nausea and their wisdom: today we want rather to rejoice in our unwisdom from the bottom of our hearts and, as active and progressive men, as admirers of the process, enjoy ourselves. May our estimation of the historical be but an occidental prejudice; as long as, within these prejudices, we make progress and do not stand still! As long as we constantly learn to improve our ability to do history for the sake of *life*. So long as we may always be sure of more life than they, we will gladly grant the superhistorical men that they have more wisdom: for in this way, at any rate, our unwisdom will have more of a future than their wisdom. And so that there may remain no doubt about the significance of this opposition between life and wisdom I shall call to aid a traditionally well-proven procedure and straightway set up several theses.

A historical phenomenon clearly and completely understood and reduced to an intellectual phenomenon is for him who has understood it dead: for in it he has understood the mania, the injustice, the blind passion, and in general the whole earthly darkened horizon of that phenomenon, and just in this he has understood its historical power. So far as he is a knower this power has now become powerless for him: not yet perhaps so far as he is a living being.

History, conceived as pure science and become sovereign, would constitute a kind of final closing out of the accounts of life for mankind. Historical education is wholesome and promising for the future only in the service of a powerful new life-giving influence, of a rising culture for example; that is, only when it is ruled and guided by a higher power and does not itself rule and guide.

History, so far as it serves life, serves an unhistorical power. While so subordinated it will and ought never, therefore, become a pure science like, say, mathematics. But the question to what degree life requires the service of history at all is one of the highest questions and concerns affecting the health of a man, a people, a culture. For with a certain excess of history life crumbles and degenerates, and finally, because of this degeneration, history itself degenerates as well.

## 2

That life requires the service of history, however, must be understood just as clearly as the proposition we intend to prove later—that an excess of history is detrimental to life. History belongs to the living man in three respects: it belongs to him so far as he is active and striving, so far as he preserves and admires, and so far as he suffers and is in need of liberation. To this triplicity of relations correspond three kinds of history: so far as they can be distinguished, a *monumental*, an *antiquarian*, and a *critical* kind of history.

History belongs above all to the active and powerful man, to him who fights a great fight, who requires models, teachers, and comforters and cannot find them among his associates and contemporaries. Thus history belonged to Schiller: for our age is so bad, says Goethe, that the poet encounters none to inspire him in the life that surrounds him. With respect to the man of action Polybius, for example, calls political history the proper preparation for governing a state and the great teacher who, by reminding us of the sudden misfortunes of others, exhorts us steadfastly to bear the reverses of fortune. Whoever has learned to see the meaning of history in this must be distressed to see curious tourists or painstaking micrologists climbing around on the pyramids of monumental ages; where he has found incentive to do as others have done and do it better he does not want to meet the idler who, craving for distraction or sensation, strolls about as though among the heaped-up pictorial treasures of some gallery. So as not to despair and be disgusted among frail and hopeless idlers, among contemporaries who appear to be active but in fact are merely wrought up and fidgeting, the man of action looks back and interrupts the course to his goal for once to breathe freely. His goal, however, is some happiness, perhaps not his own, often that of a people or of all mankind; he flees resignation and uses history as a means against resignation. In most cases, however, no reward beckons him unless it be fame, that is, the expectation of a place of honor in the temple of history where he himself may teach, console, and warn those who come after him. For his commandment reads: what once was capable of magnifying the concept "man" and of giving it a more beautiful content must be present eternally in order eternally to have this capacity. That the great moments in the struggle of individuals form a chain, that in them the high points of humanity are linked throughout millennia, that what is highest in such a moment of the distant past be for me still alive, bright and great—this is the fundamental thought of the faith in humanity that is expressed in the demand for a *monumental* history. Precisely this demand, however, that the great be eternal, occasions the most terrible conflict. For all else that also lives cries no. The monumental ought not arise—that is the counter-watchword. Dull habit, the small and lowly that fills all corners of the world and wafts like a dense earthly vapor around everything great, deceiving, smothering, and suffocating, obstructs the path which the great must still travel to immortality. Yet this path leads through human brains! Through the brains of frightened short-lived animals who repeatedly rise to the same needs and with effort fend off their destruction for a short time. For above all they want one thing: to live at all cost. Who could suspect in them the arduous torch race of monumental history through which alone the great lives on! And yet time and again some awaken who, in viewing past greatness and strengthened by their vision, rejoice as though human life were a grand affair and as though it were even the sweetest fruit of this bitter growth to know that at some earlier time someone went through existence proud and strong, another in profound thought, a third helpfully and with pity—yet all leaving one lesson, that he lives most splendidly who pays no heed to existence. If the common man views this span of time with such sad seriousness and finds it so desirable, then these others, on their way to immortality and monumental history, knew how to disregard it with Olympian laughter or at least with lofty scorn; they often went to their graves with irony—for what did they have that could be buried! Surely no more than what had always oppressed them as dross, excrement, vanity, and animality that will now fall into forgetfulness after it had long been given over to their contempt. But one thing will live, the monogram of their most authentic essence, a work, a deed, a rare inspiration, a creation: it will live because posterity cannot do without it. In this most refined form fame is more than the most delicious morsel of our self-love, as Schopenhauer called it; it is the belief in the affinity and continuity of the great of all ages, it is a protest against the change of generations and transitoriness.

What is the advantage to the present individual, then, of the monumental view of the past, the concern with the classical and the rare of earlier times? It is the knowledge that the great which once existed was at least *possible* once and may well again be possible sometime; he goes his way more courageously, for now the doubt that assails him in moments of weakness, that he may perhaps want the impossible, has been conquered. Suppose someone were to believe that it required no more than a hundred productive men, raised and active in a new spirit, to put an end to the cultural refinement that has just now become fashionable in Germany, how it would strengthen him to realize that the culture of the Renaissance was raised on the shoulders of such a group of one hundred men.

And yet—at once to learn another new thing from the same example—how flowing and elusive, how imprecise would such a comparison be! How much that is different must be overlooked, how ruthlessly must the individuality of the past be forced into a general form and have all its sharp edges and lines broken for the sake of agreement, if the comparison is to have that powerful effect! Fundamentally what was possible once could only be possible a second time if the Pythagoreans were right in believing that with the same conjunction of the heavenly bodies the same events had to be repeated on earth down to the minutest detail: so that whenever the stars have a certain relation to each other a Stoic will join with an Epicurean and murder Caesar, and ever again with a different configuration Columbus will discover America. Only if the earth again and again began her drama anew after the fifth act, if it were certain that the same tangle of motives, the same *deus ex machina*, the same catastrophe recurred at definite intervals, should the powerful man desire monumental history in complete pictorial *truthfulness*, that is, desire each fact in its precisely depicted character and uniqueness: thus probably not before the astronomers become astrologers again. Until then monumental history will not find such complete truthfulness to its advantage: it will always approximate, generalize, and finally equate differences; it will always weaken the disparity of motives and occasions in order, at the expense of the *cause,* to present the *effect* monumentally, that is, as exemplary and worthy of imitation. Monumental history, then, since it disregards causes as much as possible, could without much exaggeration be called a collection of "effects in themselves," or of events that will at all times produce an effect. What is celebrated in national festivals and in religious or military days of remembrance is actually such an "effect in itself": it is this that gives no rest to the ambitious, that the enterprising take to heart like an amulet, and not the true, historical nexus of causes and effects that, if fully understood, would only prove that never again could quite the same thing result in the game of dice played by chance and the future.

As long as the soul of historiography is found in the great incentives a powerful man receives from it, as long as the past must be described as something worthy of imitation, something that can be imitated and is possible a second time, so long, at least, is the past in danger of being somewhat distorted, of being reinterpreted according to aesthetic criteria and so brought closer to fiction; there are even ages that are quite incapable of distinguishing between a monumental past and a mythical fiction: for precisely the same incentives can be given by the one world as by the other. Thus, whenever the monumental vision of the past *rules* over the other ways of looking at the past, I mean the antiquarian and the critical, the past itself suffers *damage*: very great portions of the past are forgotten and despised, and flow away like a gray uninterrupted flood, and only single embellished facts stand out as islands: there seems to be something unnatural and wondrous about the rare persons who become visible at all, like the golden hip that the pupils of Pythagoras thought they discerned in their master. Monumental history deceives with analogies: with tempting similarities the courageous are enticed to rashness, the enthusiastic to fanaticism; and if one thinks of this history as being in the hands and heads of talented egoists and enraptured rascals then empires are destroyed, princes murdered, wars and revolutions instigated, and the number of historical "effects in themselves," that is, of effects without sufficient causes, is further increased. So much as a reminder of the damage that monumental history can cause among the mighty and active, be they good or evil: but what can it not inflict if the impotent and inactive master it and put it to their uses!

Let us take the simplest and most frequent example. Think of artless and feebly artistic natures girded and armed by monumental history of art and artists: Against whom will they now direct their weapons? Against their traditional enemies, the strong artistic spirits, namely against those who alone are capable of learning truly, that is, for the sake of life, from that history and of putting what they have learned into higher practice. It is their path that is obstructed and their air that is darkened when one dances idolatrously and diligently round a half-understood monument of some great past, as though to say: "See, this is true and real art: What do you care about aspiring newcomers!" Apparently this dancing swarm even has a monopoly on "good taste": for the creator has always been at a disadvantage to him who only looked on without even trying his hand; as at all times the armchair politician has been wiser, more just and judicious than the governing statesman. If, however, the use of the popular vote and numerical majorities were transferred to the realm of art and the artist required to defend himself before a forum of the aesthetically inactive, you may bet your life that he would be condemned: not despite, but just *because* of the fact that his judges have solemnly proclaimed the canon of monumental art (that is, according to the given explanation, of art that has at all times "produced an effect"). While for all art that is not yet monumental because still contemporary they lack first, any need, second, any genuine inclination, third, just that authority of history. On the other hand their instinct tells them that art may be beaten to death with art: the monumental must definitely not be produced again, and what happens to have the authority of monumentality from the past is just the right preventative. This is how the connoisseurs are because they wish to eliminate art altogether; they give the appearance of physicians while their real intention is to dispense poisons; so they cultivate their tongue and their taste in order to explain fastidiously why they so insistently decline whatever nourishing artistic fare is offered them. For they do not want something great to be produced: their expedient is to say, "See, the great already exists!" In truth they care as little about existing greatness as about greatness in the making: to that their life bears witness. Monumental history is the disguise in which their hatred of the mighty and the great of their time parades as satisfied admiration of the mighty and the great of past ages. Cloaked in this disguise they turn the proper sense of monumental history into its opposite; whether they know it clearly or not, at any rate they act as though their motto were: let the dead bury the living.

Each of the three kinds of history is justified in only one soil and one climate: in every other it grows into a noxious weed. If the man who wants to achieve something great needs the past at all he will master it through monumental history; who on the other hand likes to persist in the traditional and venerable will care for the past as an antiquarian historian; and only he who is oppressed by some present misery and wants to throw off the burden at all cost has a need for critical, that is, judging and condemning history. Much harm is caused by thoughtless transplanting: the critic without need, the antiquarian without reverence, the connoisseur of the great who has not the ability to achieve the great are such growths which have been alienated from their native soil and therefore have degenerated and shot up as weeds.

# 3

In the second place, then, history belongs to the preserving and revering soul—to him who with loyalty and love looks back on his origins; through this reverence he, as it were, gives thanks for his existence. By tending with loving hands what has long survived he intends to preserve the conditions in which he grew up for those who will come after him—and so he serves life. The possession of ancestral furniture changes its meaning in such a soul: for the soul is rather possessed by the furniture. The small and limited, the decayed and obsolete receives its dignity and inviolability in that the preserving and revering soul of the antiquarian moves into these things and makes itself at home in the nest it builds there. The history of his city becomes for him the history of his self; he understands the wall, the turreted gate, the ordinance of the town council, the national festival like an illustrated diary of his youth and finds himself, his strength, his diligence, his pleasure, his judgment, his folly and rudeness, in all of them. Here one could live, he says to himself, for here one can live and will be able to live, for we are tough and not to be uprooted overnight. And so, with this "We," he looks beyond the ephemeral, curious, individual life and feels like the spirit of the house, the generation, and the city. Occasionally he will greet the soul of his people as his own soul even across the wide, obscuring, and confusing centuries; and power of empathy and divination, of scenting an almost cold trail, of instinctively reading aright the past however much it be written over, a quick understanding of the palimpsests, even polypsests—these are his gifts and virtues. With them Goethe stood before the memorial of Erwin von Steinbach; in the tempest of his emotions the historical cloud cover spread between them tore, and for the first time he saw the German work again "exerting its influence out of a strong robust German soul." Such a sense and disposition guided the Italians of the Renaissance and reawakened in their poets the ancient Italic genius to a "wondrous reverberation of the ancient lyre," as Jacob Burckhardt puts it. But this antiquarian historical sense of reverence is of highest value where it imbues modest, coarse, even wretched conditions in which a man or a people live with a simple, touching feeling of pleasure and contentment; as for example Niebuhr honestly and candidly admits to living cheerfully on moor and heath among free peasants who have a history, without ever missing art. How could history serve life better than by tying even less-favored generations and populations to their homeland and its customs, by making them sedentary and preventing their searching and contentiously fighting for something better in foreign lands? At times what, as it were, nails an individual down to these companions and environment, to this tiresome habit, to this bare mountaintop seems to be stubbornness and unreason—but it is a most wholesome unreason productive of the common goal: as everyone knows who is aware of the terrible consequences of an adventurous urge to emigrate, say, in whole hordes of populations, or who closely observes the condition of a people that has lost its loyalty to its earlier times and is given over to a restless cosmopolitan choosing and searching for novelty and ever more novelty. The opposite sentiment, the contentment of a tree with its roots, the happiness of knowing oneself not to be wholly arbitrary and accidental, but rather as growing out of a past as its heir, flower, and fruit and so to be exculpated, even justified, in one's existence—this is what one now especially likes to call the proper historical sense.

These, of course, are not the conditions that most favor a man's ability to reduce the past to pure knowledge; and we see again here what we have seen in the case of monumental history, that the past itself suffers as long as history serves life and is ruled by the impulses of life. To use a somewhat stretched metaphor: The tree feels its roots more than it can see them; this feeling, however, measures their size by the size and strength of its visible branches. The tree may already be in error here: but how much greater will its error be about the whole forest that surrounds it! of which it only knows and feels anything so far as it is hindered or helped by it—but nothing beyond that. The antiquarian sense of a man, of an urban community, of a whole people always has an extremely limited field of vision; by far the most is not seen at all, and the little that is seen is seen too closely and in isolation; it cannot apply a standard and therefore takes everything to be equally important and therefore each individual thing to be too important. Under these circumstances there are no differences in value and no proportions for the things of the past that would truly do justice to those things in relation to each other; but only measures and proportions of those things in relation to the antiquarian individual or people looking back at them.

Here there is always one danger very near: the time will finally come when everything old and past that has not totally been lost sight of will simply be taken as equally venerable, while whatever does not approach the old with veneration, that is, the new and growing, will be rejected and treated with hostility. Thus even the Greeks tolerated the hieratic style of their plastic arts beside a freer and greater style; and later not only tolerated the pointed noses and frosty smiles but even made of them a matter of refinement in artistic taste. When the sense of a people hardens in this way, when history serves past life so as to undermine further and especially higher life, when the historical sense no longer preserves life but mummifies it: then the tree dies unnaturally, beginning at the top and slowly dying toward the roots—and in the end the root itself generally decays. Antiquarian history itself degenerates the moment that the fresh life of the present no longer animates and inspires it. Now piety withers away, scholarly habit endures without it, and, egoistically complacent, revolves around its own center. Then you may well witness the repugnant spectacle of a blind lust for collecting, of a restless raking together of all that once has been. Man envelops himself in an odor of decay; through his antiquarian habit he succeeds in degrading even a more significant talent and nobler need to an insatiable craving for novelty, or rather a craving for all things and old things; often he sinks so low as finally to be satisfied with any fare and devours with pleasure even the dust of bibliographical quisquilia.

But even if that degeneration does not come about, if antiquarian history does not lose the foundation in which alone it can take root for the benefit of life: there are always left dangers enough should it become too powerful and overgrow the other ways of seeing the past. It merely understands how to *preserve* life, not how to generate it; therefore it always underestimates what is in process of becoming because it has no instinct for discerning its significance—unlike monumental history, for example, which has this instinct. Thus it hinders the powerful resolve for new life, thus it paralyzes the man of action who, as man of action, will and must always injure some piety or other. The fact that something has become old now gives rise to the demand that it must be immortal; for if one calculates what such an ancient thing—an old ancestral custom, a religious faith, an inherited political privilege—has experienced during its existence, the amount of piety and veneration paid by individuals and generations: then it seems presumptuous or even impious to replace such

251

an ancient thing with a new one and to compare such a vast sum of acts of piety and veneration with the single-digit numbers of what is becoming and present.

Here it becomes clear how badly man needs, often enough, in addition to the monumental and antiquarian ways of seeing the past, a *third* kind, the *critical*: and this again in the service of life as well. He must have the strength, and use it from time to time, to shatter and dissolve something to enable him to live: this he achieves by dragging it to the bar of judgment, interrogating it meticulously, and finally condemning it; every past, however, is worth condemning—for that is how matters happen to stand with human affairs: human violence and weakness have always contributed strongly to shaping them. It is not justice that here sits in judgment; even less is it mercy that here pronounces judgment: but life alone, that dark, driving, insatiably self-desiring power. Its verdict is always unmerciful, always unjust, because it has never flowed from a pure fountain of knowledge; but in most cases the verdict would be the same were justice itself to proclaim it. For "whatever has a beginning *deserves* to have an undoing; it would be better if nothing began at all."[3] It takes a great deal of strength to be able to live and to forget how far living and being unjust are one. Luther himself once thought that the world came to be through an oversight of God: for had God thought of "heavy artillery" he would never have created the world. Occasionally, however, the same life that needs forgetfulness demands the temporary destruction of this forgetfulness; then it is to become clear how unjust is the existence of some thing, a privilege, a caste, a dynasty for example, how much this thing deserves destruction. Then its past is considered critically, then one puts the knife to its roots, then one cruelly treads all pieties under foot. It is always a dangerous process, namely dangerous for life itself: and men or ages that serve life in this manner of judging and annihilating a past are always a dangerous process, namely dangerous for life itself: and men or ages that serve life in this manner of judging and annihilating a past are always dangerous and endangered men and ages. For since we happen to be the results of earlier generations we are also the results of their aberrations, passions, and errors, even crimes; it is not possible quite to free oneself from this chain. If we condemn those aberrations and think ourselves quite exempt from them, the fact that we are descended from them is not eliminated. At best we may bring about a conflict between our inherited, innate nature and our knowledge, as well as a battle between a strict new discipline and ancient education and breeding; we implant a new habit, a new instinct, a second nature so that the first nature withers away. It is

---

3. [J. W. von Goethe, *Faust*, part 1. The lines are spoken by Mephistopheles in the early scene in Faust's study. We quote the translation by Louis MacNeice and E. L. Stahl.—TRANS.]

an attempt, as it were, *a posteriori* to give oneself a past from which one would like to be descended in opposition to the past from which one is descended—always a dangerous attempt because it is so difficult to find a limit in denying the past and because second natures are mostly feebler than the first. Too often we stop at knowing the good without doing it because we also know the better without being able to do it. Yet here and there a victory is achieved nevertheless, and for the fighters who use critical history for life there is even a remarkable consolation: namely, to know that this first nature also was, at some time or other, a second nature and that every victorious second nature becomes a first.

## 4

These are the services that history is capable of rendering to life; each man and each people requires, according to their goals, strengths, and needs, a certain knowledge of the past, sometimes as monumental, sometimes as antiquarian, sometimes as critical history: but not like a crowd of pure thinkers who only contemplate life, not like individuals, hungry for knowledge, satisfied with mere knowledge, whose only goal is the increase of knowledge, but always only for the purpose of life and therefore also always under the rule and highest direction of that purpose. That this is the natural relation of an age, a culture, a people to history—brought on by hunger, regulated by the degree of need, held within limits by the inherent plastic power—that knowledge of the past is at all times desired only in the service of the future and the present, not to weaken the present, not to uproot a future strong with life: all of this is simple, as truth is simple, and immediately convinces even him who has not first been given a historical proof.

And now a quick glance at our time! We are shocked, we fly back: whither is all clarity, all naturalness and purity of that relation between life and history, how confused, how exaggerated, how troubled is this problem that now surges before our eyes! Is the fault ours, the observers? Or has the constellation of life and history really changed because a powerful, hostile star has come between them? May others show that we have seen falsely: we will say what we believe we see. Such a star has indeed intervened, a bright and glorious star, the constellation is really changed—*through science, through the demand that history be a science.* Now life is no longer the sole ruler and master of knowledge of the past: rather all boundary markers are overthrown and everything that once was rushes in upon man. All perspectives have shifted as far back as the origins of change, back into infinity. A boundless spectacle such as history, the science of universal becoming, now displays, no generation has ever seen; of course, she displays it with the dangerous boldness of her motto: *fiat veritas pereat vita.*[4]

Let us now picture to ourselves the spiritual events brought on hereby in the soul of modern man. Historical knowledge floods in ever anew from inexhaustible springs, the alien and disconnected throngs about, memory opens all its gates and is still not opened wide enough, nature makes a supreme effort to receive these alien guests, to order and to honor them, but these themselves are at war with each other and it appears necessary to master and overcome them all so as not oneself to perish in their strife. Gradually it becomes second nature to get accustomed to such a disorderly, stormy, belligerent household, while at the same time it is beyond question that this second nature is much weaker, much more troubled and through and through less healthy than the first. In the end modern man drags an immense amount of indigestible knowledge stones around with him that on occasion rattle around in his belly, as the fairy tale[5] has it. This rattling betrays the most distinctive property of this modern man: the remarkable opposition of an inside to which no outside and an outside to which no inside corresponds, an opposition unknown to ancient peoples. Knowledge, taken in excess without hunger, even contrary to need, no longer acts as a transforming motive impelling to action and remains hidden in a certain chaotic inner world which that modern man, with curious pride, calls his unique "inwardness." He may then say that he has the content and that only the form is lacking; but in all living things this is quite an unseemly opposition. Our modern culture is nothing living just because it cannot be understood at all without that opposition, that is: it is no real culture at all, but only a kind of knowledge about culture, it stops at cultured thoughts and cultured feelings but leads to no cultured decisions. That, however, which truly is a motive and visibly shows itself in action often signifies little more than an indifferent convention, a miserable imitation or even a rude grimace. In the inner being sentiment may well sleep like the snake that, having swallowed whole rabbits, calmly lies in the sun and avoids all movement except the most necessary. The inner process, that is now the thing itself, that is properly "culture." Everyone who passes by wishes only one thing, that such a culture not perish of indigestibility. Think, for example, of a Greek passing by such a culture, he would perceive that for more recent men "educated" and "historically educated" appear to belong together as though they were one and distinguished only by the number of words. Were he now to give voice to his tenet: a man can be very educated and yet be historically quite uneducated, one would believe not to have heard properly and

---

4. [Let there be truth, and may life perish.]
5. [Little Red Riding Hood.—TRANS.]

shake one's head. That well-known little people of a not-too-distant past, I mean just the Greeks, had stubbornly preserved its unhistorical sense in the period of its greatest strength; were a contemporary man forced by magic spells to return to that world he would presumably find the Greeks very "uneducated," which would, of course, disclose the meticulously disguised secret of modern culture to public laughter: for from ourselves we moderns have nothing at all; only by filling and overfilling ourselves with alien ages, customs, arts, philosophies, religions, and knowledge do we become something worthy of notice, namely walking encyclopedias, as which an ancient Hellene, who had been thrown into our age, might perhaps address us. The whole value of encyclopedias, however, is found only in what is written in them, the content, not in what is written on them or in what is cover and what is shell; and so the whole of modern culture is essentially internal: on the outside the bookbinder has printed something like "Handbook of Inner Culture for External Barbarians." This opposition of inside and outside makes the outside still more barbaric than it would need to be were a rude people to grow out of itself alone according to its rough requirements. For what means is left to nature to take in what imposes itself so excessively? Only the one means, to accept it as easily as possible in order quickly to lay it aside again and expel it. This gives rise to a habit of not taking actual things too seriously anymore, this gives to the "weak personality" as a result of which the actual and enduring make only a minimal impression; in externals one finally becomes ever more casual and indolent and widens the critical gulf between content and form to the point of insensitivity to barbarism, if only the memory is stimulated ever anew, if only ever new things to be known keep streaming in to be neatly put on display in the cases of that memory. The culture of a people in contrast to that barbarism has once been designated, with some justification I believe, as unity of artistic style in all expressions of life of a people; this designation should not be misunderstood as though the opposition between barbarism and *beautiful* style were at issue; the people that can be called cultured must in reality be a living unity and not fall apart so miserably into an inside and an outside, a content and a form. If you want to strive for and promote the culture of a people, then strive for and promote this higher unity and work to annihilate modern pseudo-culture in favor of a true culture; dare to devote some thought to the problem of restoring the health of a people that has been impaired by history, to how it may recover its instincts and therewith its integrity.

## QUESTIONS

1. What does Nietzsche mean by "history"?

2. Why does Nietzsche declare that history "as a costly intellectual excess and luxury" must be "seriously hated"? (237)

3. Why does Nietzsche believe it is necessary to live "*unhistorically*" in order to be happy? (239)

4. What does Nietzsche mean when he describes certain humans as "*superhistorical*"? (242) How are these individuals different from "the historical men"? (243)

5. Why does Nietzsche believe that history, if "conceived as pure science," would "constitute a kind of final closing out of the accounts of life for mankind"? (244)

6. How does Nietzsche differentiate between the monumental, antiquarian, and critical kinds of history? Does he see any of these types as more or less important than the others?

7. Why does Nietzsche see those who are "impotent and inactive" as a threat? Why does he think they are able to "master" monumental history for their own uses? (248)

8. What does Nietzsche mean when he says it is life, "that dark, driving, insatiably self-desiring power," that sits in judgment in critical history? (252)

9. Why does Nietzsche claim that modern culture is "no real culture at all"? (254)

10. According to Nietzsche, what is necessary for a people impaired by history to "recover its instincts and therewith its integrity"? (255)

## FOR FURTHER REFLECTION

1. Would Nietzsche agree with the philosopher George Santayana's famous saying, "Those who cannot remember the past are condemned to repeat it"?

2. What type of history that Nietzsche describes—monumental, antiquarian, or critical—do you think is most necessary at the present time?

3. Is it ever justifiable for a political regime to disseminate "revisionist" histories that contain altered facts in order to support ideological purposes, even if those purposes are worthy?

4. Has the vast increase in information about history, and access to it, brought about by digital technology worked to the advantage or disadvantage of human life?

J ane Addams (1860–1935) was born in the small town of Cedarville, Illinois, where her family was among the wealthiest and most respected in the community. Her father, John Addams, was a founding member of the Illinois Republican Party and a supporter of Abraham Lincoln. Her mother died when she was two. While Addams dreamed of attending Smith College, she acceded to her father's wishes and enrolled at Rockford Seminary, a local school where girls prepared to be wives or missionaries. Not interested in either religion or marriage, Addams took as many academic courses as she could and spearheaded a campaign for the school to begin awarding college degrees. She was the first student to be awarded a bachelor's degree from the school, and she was editor of the school magazine, class president, and valedictorian.

At that time, the opportunities for a female college graduate, even one with exceptional intelligence and ambition, were limited. Following the sudden death of her father shortly after her graduation in 1881, Addams experienced several years of uncertainty, depression, and poor health that included an unsuccessful attempt at medical school. In 1887 Addams embarked on a trip to Europe with her close friend Ellen Gates Starr. While in England, they visited Toynbee Hall, a cornerstone of the settlement movement, initiated by social reformers who believed they could improve the lives of the poor by living among them. Along with food, clothing, and lodging, Toynbee Hall also offered classes, workshops, and a library to London's poor. Inspired by this example, Addams and Starr traveled to Chicago and, using Addams's inheritance acquired a run-down mansion on Chicago's Near West Side. On September 18, 1889, after renovating the mansion, the two women opened Hull House to the thousands of poor immigrants in the surrounding area.

Hull House soon become the most well-known and influential settlement house in the country, serving more than fifty thousand of Chicago's poor in its first year. It offered childcare, a kindergarten, vocational training, plays, concerts, and English classes during the immigrant influx of the 1890s. Addams lived in Hull House and was always available to teach a class, deliver a baby, help with housework, or nurse the sick. Although Hull House served both men and women, its leadership was entirely female and it became a safe haven for women. Most of the college-educated women who worked and lived at Hull House were unmarried. Addams herself never married, but she had two long-term relationships with women: first with Starr, and then with Mary Rozet Smith, who worked alongside Addams. Addams's work extended well beyond Hull House. She campaigned to create the first juvenile court in the nation, conducted investigations into social issues such as child labor and prostitution, and wrote books and articles on the settlement movement, including an autobiography, *Twenty Years at Hull House* (1910).

By 1915 Addams had become one of the most well-known public figures in the United States, called "the only saint America has produced." However, Addams fell out of public favor during World War I. A lifelong pacifist, she spoke out against America's participation in the war and, after the fighting ended, lobbied for aid to help the starving children of defeated Germany. She was the victim of a torrent of criticism from the press: one critic wrote that what Addams needed to rid herself of her pacifist ideals was "a strong, forceful husband who would lift the burden of fate from her shoulders," and another remarked, "If Miss Addams and her peace mission are a sample of women in world affairs . . . I am sincerely sorry I voted for suffrage." Hurt by these attacks, Addams spent more and more time away from Hull House, traveling abroad and writing. The criticism abated, however, and in 1931 she became the first American woman to receive the Nobel Peace Prize. When Addams died in 1935, thousands crowded the streets around Hull House.

In "The Devil Baby at Hull House," published by the *Atlantic Monthly* in 1916, Addams describes a six-week period during which Hull House was overrun with rumors about a "devil baby" living in their midst. In it, Addams brought to a national readership the complex interplay of issues concerning gender, ethnicity, and class that would become focal points for the feminist and other social reform movements later in the twentieth century.

# The Devil Baby at Hull House

## 1

The knowledge of the existence of the Devil Baby burst upon the residents of Hull House one day when three Italian women, with an excited rush through the door, demanded that he be shown to them. No amount of denial convinced them that he was not there, for they knew exactly what he was like, with his cloven hoofs, his pointed ears, and diminutive tail; moreover, the Devil Baby had been able to speak as soon as he was born and was most shockingly profane.

The three women were but the forerunners of a veritable multitude; for six weeks the streams of visitors from every part of the city and suburbs to this mythical baby poured in all day long, and so far into the night that the regular activities of the settlement were almost swamped.

The Italian version, with a hundred variations, dealt with a pious Italian girl married to an atheist. Her husband vehemently tore a holy picture from the bedroom wall, saying that he would quite as soon have a devil in the house as that; whereupon the devil incarnated himself in her coming child. As soon as the Devil Baby was born, he ran about the table shaking his finger in deep reproach at his father, who finally caught him and in fear and trembling brought him to Hull House. When the residents there, in spite of the baby's shocking appearance, wishing to save his soul, took him to church for baptism, they found that the shawl was empty and the Devil Baby, fleeing from the holy water, ran lightly over the backs of the pews.

The Jewish version, again with variations, was to the effect that the father of six daughters had said before the birth of a seventh child that he would rather have a devil in the house than another girl, whereupon the Devil Baby promptly appeared.

Save for a red automobile which occasionally figured in the story, and a stray cigar which, in some versions, the newborn child snatched from his father's lips, the tale might have been fashioned a thousand years ago.

Although the visitors to the Devil Baby included people of every degree of prosperity and education, even physicians and trained nurses who assured us of their scientific interest, the story constantly demonstrated the power of an old wives' tale among thousands of people in modern society who are living in a corner of their own, their vision fixed, their intelligence held by some iron chain of silent habit. To such primitive people the metaphor apparently is still the very "stuff of life"; or, rather, no other form of statement reaches them, and the tremendous tonnage of current writing for them has no existence. It was in keeping with their simple habits that the reputed presence of the Devil Baby at Hull House did not reach the newspapers until the fifth week of his sojourn—after thousands of people had already been informed of his whereabouts by the old method of passing news from mouth to mouth.

During the weeks of excitement it was the old women who really seemed to have come into their own, and perhaps the most significant result of the incident was the reaction of the story upon them. It stirred their minds and memories as with a magic touch; it loosened their tongues and revealed the inner life and thoughts of those who are so often inarticulate. These old women enjoyed a moment of triumph, as if they had made good at last and had come into a region of sanctions and punishments which they understood.

Throughout six weeks, as I went about Hull House, I would hear a voice at the telephone repeating for the hundredth time that day, "No, there is no such baby"; "No, we never had it here"; "No, he couldn't have seen it for fifty cents"; "We didn't send it anywhere because we never had it"; "I don't mean to say that your sister-in-law lied, but there must be some mistake"; "There is no use getting up an excursion from Milwaukee, for there isn't any Devil Baby at Hull House"; "We can't give reduced rates because we are not exhibiting anything"; and so on and on. As I came near the front door, I would catch snatches of arguments that were often acrimonious: "Why do you let so many people believe it, if it isn't here?" "We have taken three lines of cars to come, and we have as much right to see it as anybody else"; "This is a pretty big place, of course you could hide it easy enough"; "What you saying that for—are you going to raise the price of admission?" We had doubtless struck a case of what the psychologists call the "contagion of emotion," added to that "aesthetic sociability" which impels any one of us to drag the entire household to the window when a procession comes into the street or a rainbow appears in the sky.

But the Devil Baby of course was worth many processions and rainbows, and I will confess that, as the empty show went on day after day, I quite revolted against such a vapid manifestation of an admirable human trait. There was always one exception, however: whenever I heard the high eager voices of old women, I was irresistibly interested and left anything I might be doing in order to listen to them.

## 2

Perhaps my many talks with these aged visitors crystallized thoughts and impressions that I had been receiving through years; or the tale itself may have ignited a fire, as it were, whose light illumined some of my darkest memories of neglected and uncomfortable old age, of old peasant women who had ruthlessly probed into the ugly depths of human nature in themselves and others. Many of them who came to see the Devil Baby had been forced to face tragic human experiences; the powers of brutality and horror had had full scope in their lives, and for years they had had acquaintance with disaster and death. Such old women do not shirk life's misery by feeble idealism, for they are long past the stage of make-believe. They relate without flinching the most hideous experiences. "My face has had this queer twist for now nearly sixty years; I was ten when it got that way, the night after I saw my father do my mother to death with his knife." "Yes, I had fourteen children; only two grew to be men and both of them were killed in the same explosion. I was never sure they brought home the right bodies." But even the most hideous sorrows which the old women related had apparently subsided into the paler emotion of ineffectual regret, after Memory had long done her work upon them; the old people seemed, in some unaccountable way, to lose all bitterness and resentment against life, or rather they were so completely without it that they must have lost it long since.

Perhaps those women, because they had come to expect nothing more from life and had perforce ceased from grasping and striving, had obtained, if not renunciation, at least that quiet endurance which allows the wounds of the spirit to heal. Through their stored-up habit of acquiescence, they vouchsafed a fleeting glimpse of that translucent wisdom so often embodied in old women, but so difficult to portray. I recall a conversation with one of them, a woman whose fine mind and indomitable spirit I had long admired; I had known her for years, and yet the recital of her sufferings, added to those the Devil Baby had already induced other women to tell me, pierced me afresh.

"I had eleven children, some born in Bohemia and some born here; nine of them boys; all of the children died when they were little, but my dear Liboucha, you know all about her. She died last winter in the insane asylum. She was only twelve years old when her father, in a fit of delirium tremens, killed himself after he had chased us around the room trying to kill us first. She saw it all; the blood splashed on the wall stayed in her mind the worst; she shivered and shook all that night through, and the next morning she had lost her voice, couldn't speak out loud for terror. After a while her voice came back, although it was never very natural, and she went to school again. She seemed to do as well as ever and was awful pleased when she got into high school. All the money we had, I earned scrubbing in a public dispensary, although sometimes I got a little by interpreting for the patients, for I know three languages, one as well as the other. But I was determined that, whatever happened to me, Liboucha was to be educated. My husband's father was a doctor in the old country, and Liboucha was always a clever child. I wouldn't have her live the kind of life I had, with no use for my mind except to make me restless and bitter. I was pretty old and worn out for such hard work, but when I used to see Liboucha on a Sunday morning, ready for church in her white dress with her long yellow hair braided round her beautiful pale face, lying there in bed as I was—being brought up a freethinker and needing to rest my aching bones for the next week's work—I'd feel almost happy, in spite of everything.

"But of course no such peace could last in my life; the second year at high school, Liboucha began to seem different and to do strange things. You know the time she wandered away for three days and we were all wild with fright, although a kind woman had taken her in and no harm came to her. I could never be easy after that; she was always gentle, but she was awful sly about running away, and at last I had to send her to the asylum. She stayed there off and on for five years, but I saw her every week of my life and she was always company for me, what with sewing for her, washing and ironing her clothes, cooking little things to take out to her, and saving a bit of money to buy fruit for her. At any rate, I had stopped feeling so bitter, and got some comfort out of seeing the one thing that belonged to me on this side of the water, when all of a sudden she died of heart failure, and they never took the trouble to send for me until the next day."

She stopped as if wondering afresh that the Fates could have been so casual, but with a sudden illumination, as if she had been awakened out of the burden and intensity of her restricted personal interests into a consciousness of those larger relations that are, for the most part, so strangely invisible. It was as if the young mother of the grotesque Devil Baby, that victim of wrongdoing on the part of others, had revealed to this tragic woman, much more clearly than soft words had ever done, that the return of a deed of violence upon the head of the innocent is inevitable; as if she had realized that, although she was destined to walk all the days of her life with that piteous multitude who bear the undeserved wrongs of the world, she would walk henceforth with a sense of companionship.

Among the visitors were pitiful old women who, although they had already reconciled themselves to much misery, were still enduring more. "You might say it's a disgrace to have your son beat you up for the sake of a bit of money you've earned by scrubbing—your own man is different—but I haven't the heart to blame the boy for doing what he's seen all his life; his father forever went wild when the drink was in him and struck me to the very day of his death. The ugliness was born in the boy as the marks of the devil was born in the poor child upstairs."

This more primitive type embodies the eternal patience of those humble toiling women who through the generations have been held of little value, save as their drudgery ministered to their men. One of them related her habit of going through the pockets of her drunken son every payday, and complained that she had never got so little as the night before, only twenty-five cents out of fifteen dollars he had promised for the rent long overdue. 'I had to get that as he lay in the alley before the door; I couldn't pull him in, and the copper who helped him home left as soon as he heard me coming and pretended he didn't see me. I have no food in the house nor coffee to sober him up with. I know perfectly well that you will ask me to eat something here, but if I can't carry it home, I won't take a bite nor a sup. I have never told you so much before. Since one of the nurses said he could be arrested for my nonsupport, I have been awfully close-mouthed. It's the foolish way all the women in our street are talking about the Devil Baby that's loosened my tongue—more shame to me."

There are those, if possible more piteous still, who have become absolutely helpless and can therefore no longer perform the household services exacted from them. One last wish has been denied them. "I hoped to go before I became a burden, but it was not to be"; and the long days of unwonted idleness are darkened by the haunting fear that "they" will come to think the burden too heavy and decide that the poorhouse is "the best." Even then there is no word of blame for undutiful children or heedless grandchildren, for apparently all that is petty and transitory falls away from austere old age; the fires are burnt out, resentments, hatreds, and even cherished sorrows have become actually unintelligible. It is as if the horrors through which these old people had passed had never existed for them, and, facing death as they are, they seem anxious to speak only such words of groping wisdom as they are able.

This aspect of memory has never been more clearly stated than by Gilbert Murray in his *Life of Euripides*. He tells us that the aged poet, when he was officially declared to be one of "the old men of Athens," said, "Even yet the age-worn minstrel can turn Memory into song"; and the memory of which he spoke was that of history and tradition, rather than his own. The aged poet turned into song even the hideous story of Medea, transmuting it into "a beautiful remote song about far-off children who have been slain in legend, children who are now at peace and whose ancient pain has become part mystery and part music. Memory—that Memory who is the mother of the Muses—having done her work upon them."

The vivid interest of so many old women in the story of the Devil Baby may have been an unconscious, although powerful, testimony that tragic experiences gradually become dressed in such trappings in order that their spent agony may prove of some use to a world which learns at the hardest; and that the strivings and sufferings of men and women long since dead, their emotion no longer connected with flesh and blood, are thus transmuted into legendary wisdom. The young are forced to heed the warning in such a tale, although for the most part it is so easy for them to disregard the words of the aged. That the old women who came to visit the Devil Baby believed that the story would secure them a hearing at home was evident, and as they prepared themselves with every detail of it, their old faces shone with a timid satisfaction. Their features, worn and scarred by harsh living, even as effigies built into the floor of an old church become dim and defaced by rough-shod feet, grew poignant and solemn. In the midst of their double bewilderment, both that the younger generation were walking in such strange paths and that no one would listen to them, for one moment there flickered up that last hope of a disappointed life, that it may at least serve as a warning while affording material for exciting narrations.

Sometimes in talking to one of them, who was "but a hair's breadth this side of the darkness," one realized that old age has its own expression for the mystic renunciation of the world. The impatience with all non-essentials, the craving to be free from hampering bonds and soft conditions, was perhaps typified in our own generation by Tolstoy's last impetuous journey, the light of his genius for a moment making comprehensible to us that unintelligible impulse of the aged.

Often, in the midst of a conversation, one of these touching old women would quietly express a longing for death, as if it were a natural fulfillment of an inmost desire. Her sincerity and anticipation were so genuine that I would feel abashed in her presence, ashamed to "cling to this strange thing that shines in the sunlight, and to be sick with love for it." Such impressions were in their essence transitory, but one result from the hypothetical visit of the Devil Baby to Hull House will, I think, remain: a realization of the sifting and reconciling power inherent in Memory itself. The old women, with much to aggravate and little to soften the habitual bodily discomforts of old age, exhibited an emotional serenity so vast and reassuring that I found myself perpetually speculating as to how soon the fleeting and petty emotions which seem so unduly important to us now might be thus transmuted; at what moment we might expect the inconsistencies and perplexities of life to be brought under this appeasing Memory, with its ultimate power to increase the elements of Beauty and Significance and to reduce, if not to eliminate, stupidity and resentment.

**3**

As our visitors to the Devil Baby came day by day, it was gradually evident that the simpler women were moved not wholly by curiosity, but that many of them prized the story as a valuable instrument in the business of living.

The legend exhibited all the persistence of one of those tales which have doubtless been preserved through the centuries because of their taming effects upon recalcitrant husbands and fathers. Shamefaced men brought by their womenfolk to see the baby but ill-concealed their triumph when there proved to be no such visible sign of retribution for domestic derelictions. On the other hand, numbers of men came by themselves. One group from a neighboring factory, on their "own time," offered to pay twenty-five cents, a half-dollar, two dollars apiece to see the child, insisting that it must be at Hull House because "the womenfolks had seen it." To my query as to whether they supposed we would exhibit for money a poor little deformed baby, if one had been born in the neighborhood, they replied, "Sure, why not?" and, "It teaches a good lesson, too," they added as an afterthought, or perhaps as a concession to the strange moral standards of a place like Hull House. All the members in this group of hardworking men, in spite of a certain swagger toward one another and a tendency to bully the derelict showman, wore that hangdog look betraying the sense of unfair treatment which a man is so apt to feel when his womankind makes an appeal to the supernatural. In their determination to see the child, the men recklessly divulged much more concerning their motives than they had meant to do, and their talk confirmed my impression that such a story may still act as a restraining influence in that sphere of marital conduct which, next to primitive religion itself, we are told, has always afforded the most fertile field for irrational taboos and savage punishments.

What story more than this could be calculated to secure sympathy for the mother of too many daughters, and contumely for the irritated father? The touch of mysticism, the supernatural sphere in which it was placed, would render a man perfectly helpless.

The story of the Devil Baby, evolved today as it might have been centuries before in response to the imperative needs of anxious wives and mothers, recalled the theory that woman first fashioned the fairy story, that combination of wisdom and romance, in an effort to tame her mate and to make him a better father to her children, until such stories finally became a rude creed for domestic conduct, softening the treatment that men accorded to women.

These first pitiful efforts of women, so widespread and powerful that we have not yet escaped their influence, still cast vague shadows upon the vast spaces of life, shadows that are dim and distorted because of their distant origin. They remind us that for thousands of years women had nothing to oppose against unthinkable brutality save "the charm of words," no other implement with which to subdue the fiercenesses of the world about them.

During the weeks that the Devil Baby drew multitudes of visitors to Hull House, my mind was opened to the fact that new knowledge derived from concrete experience is continually being made available for the guidance of human life; that humble women are still establishing rules of conduct as best they may, to counteract the base temptations of a man's world. Thousands of women, for instance, make it a standard of domestic virtue that a man must not touch his pay envelope, but bring it home unopened to his wife. High praise is contained in the phrase, "We have been married twenty years and he never once opened his own envelope"; or covert blame in the statement, "Of course he got to gambling; what can you expect from a man who always opens his own pay?"

The women are so fatalistically certain of this relation of punishment to domestic sin, of reward to domestic virtue, that when they talk about it, as they so constantly did in connection with the Devil Baby, it often sounds as if they were using the words of a widely known ritual. Even the young girls seized upon it as a palpable punishment, to be held over the heads of reckless friends. That the tale was useful was evidenced by many letters similar to the anonymous epistle here given:

me and my friends we work in talor shop and when we are going home on the roby street car where we get off that car at blue island ave. we will meet some fellows sitting at that street where they drink some beer from pail, they keep look in cars all the time and they will wait and see if we will come sometimes we will have to work, but they will wait so long they are tired and they don't care they get rest so long but a girl what works in twine mill saw them talk with us we know her good and she say what youse talk with old drunk man for we shall come to thier dance when it will be they will tell us and we should know all about where to see them that girl she say oh if you will go with them you will get devils baby like some other girls did who we knows, she say Jane Addams she will show one like that in Hull House if you will go down there we shall come sometime and we will see if that is trouth we do not believe her for she is friendly with them old men herself when she go out from her work they will wink to her and say something else to. We will go down and see you and make a lie from what she say.

## 4

The story evidently held some special comfort for hundreds of forlorn women, representatives of that vast horde of the denied and proscribed who had long found themselves confronted by those mysterious and impersonal wrongs which are apparently nobody's fault but seem to be inherent in the very nature of things.

Because the Devil Baby embodied an undeserved wrong to a poor mother, whose tender child had been claimed by the forces of evil, his merely reputed presence had power to attract to Hull House hundreds of women who had been humbled and disgraced by their children; mothers of the feeble-minded, of the vicious, of the criminal, of the prostitute. In their talk it was as if their long role of maternal apology and protective reticence had at last broken down; as if they could speak out freely because for once a man responsible for an ill-begotten child had been "met up with" and had received his deserts. Their sinister version of the story was that the father of the Devil Baby had married without confessing a hideous crime committed years before, thus basely deceiving both his innocent young bride and the good priest who performed the solemn ceremony; that the sin had become incarnate in his child which, to the horror of the young and trusting mother, had been born with all the outward aspects of the devil himself.

As if drawn by a magnet, week after week, a procession of forlorn women in search of the Devil Baby came to Hull House from every part of the city, issuing forth from the many homes in which dwelt "the two unprofitable goddesses, Poverty and Impossibility." With an understanding quickened perhaps through my own acquaintance with the mysterious child, I listened to many tragic tales from the visiting women: of premature births, "because he kicked me in the side"; of children maimed and burned because "I had no one to leave them with when I went to work." These women had seen the tender flesh of growing little bodies given over to death because "he wouldn't let me send for the doctor," or because "there was no money to pay for the medicine." But even these mothers, rendered childless through insensate brutality, were less pitiful than some of the others, who might well have cried aloud of their children as did a distracted mother of her child centuries ago—

That God should send this one thing more
Of hunger and of dread, a door
Set wide to every wind of pain!

Such was the mother of a feeble-minded boy who said, "I didn't have a devil baby myself, but I bore a poor 'innocent,' who made me fight devils for twenty-three years." She told of her son's experiences from the time the other little boys had put him up to stealing that they might hide in safety and leave him to be found with "the goods" on him, until, grown into a huge man, he fell into the hands of professional burglars; he was evidently the dupe and stool pigeon of the vicious and criminal until the very day he was locked into the state penitentiary. "If people played with him a little, he went right off and did anything they told him to, and now he's been set up for life. We call such innocents 'God's Fools' in the old country, but over here the Devil himself gets them. I've fought off bad men and boys from the poor lamb with my very fists; nobody ever came near the house except such like and the police officers who were always arresting him."

There were a goodly number of visitors, of the type of those to be found in every large city, who are on the verge of nervous collapse or who exhibit many symptoms of mental aberration and yet are sufficiently normal to be at large most of the time and to support themselves by drudgery which requires little mental effort, although the exhaustion resulting from the work they are able to do is the one thing from which they should be most carefully protected. One such woman, evidently obtaining inscrutable comfort from the story of the Devil Baby even after she had become convinced that we harbored no such creature, came many times to tell of her longing for her son who had joined the army some eighteen months before and was stationed in Alaska. She always began with the same words. "When spring comes and the snow melts so that I know he could get out, I can hardly stand it. You know I was once in the insane asylum for three years at a stretch, and since then I haven't had much use of my mind except to worry with. Of course I know that it is dangerous for me, but what can I do? I think something like this: 'The snow is melting, now he could get out, but his officers won't let him off, and if he runs away he'll be shot for a deserter—either way I'll never see him again; I'll die without seeing him'—and then I begin all over again with the snow." After a pause, she said, "The recruiting officer ought not to have taken him; he's my only son and I'm a widow; it's against the rules, but he was so crazy to go that I guess he lied a little. At any rate, the government has him now and I can't get him back. Without this worry about him, my mind would be all right; if he was here he would be earning money and keeping me and we would be happy all day long."

Recalling the vagabondish lad who had never earned much money and had certainly never "kept" his hard-working mother, I ventured to suggest that, even if he were at home, he might not have work these hard times, that he might get into trouble and be arrested—I did not need to remind her that he had already been arrested twice—that he was now fed and sheltered and under discipline, and I added hopefully something about seeing the world. She looked at me out of her withdrawn harried eyes, as if I were speaking a foreign tongue. "That wouldn't make any real difference to me—the work, the money, his behaving well, and all that, if I could cook and wash for him; I don't need all the money I earn scrubbing that factory; I only take bread and tea for supper, and I choke over that, thinking of him."

# 5

A sorrowful woman clad in heavy black, who came one day, exhibited such a capacity for prolonged weeping that it was evidence in itself of the truth of at least half her statement, that she had cried herself to sleep every night of her life for fourteen years in fulfillment of a "curse" laid upon her by an angry man that "her pillow would be wet with tears as long as she lived." Her respectable husband had kept a shop in the red-light district, because he found it profitable to sell to the men and women who lived there. She had kept house in the rooms "over the store," from the time she was a bride newly come from Russia, and her five daughters had been born there, but never a song to gladden her husband's heart.

She took such a feverish interest in the Devil Baby that when I was obliged to disillusion her, I found it hard to take away her comfort in the belief that the powers that be are on the side of the woman, when her husband resents too many daughters. But, after all, the birth of daughters was but an incident in her tale of unmitigated woe, for the scoldings of a disappointed husband were as nothing to the curse of a strange enemy, although she doubtless had a confused impression that if there was retribution for one in the general scheme of things, there might be for the other.

When the weeping woman finally put the events of her disordered life in some sort of sequence, it was clear that about fifteen years ago she had reported to the police a vicious house whose back door opened into her own yard. Her husband had forbidden her to do anything about it and had said that it would only get them into trouble, but she had been made desperate one day when she saw her little girl, then twelve years old, come out of the door, gleefully showing her younger sister a present of money. Because the poor woman had tried for ten years, without success, to induce her husband to move from the vicinity of such houses, she was certain that she could save her child by forcing out "the bad people" from her own dooryard. She therefore made her one frantic effort, found her way to the city hall, and there reported the house to the chief himself. Of course, "the bad people" "stood in with the police," and nothing happened to them except, perhaps, a fresh levy of blackmail; but the keeper of the house, beside himself with rage, made the dire threat and laid the curse upon her. In less than a year from that time he had enticed her daughter into a disreputable house in another part of the district. The poor woman, ringing one doorbell after another, had never been able to find her, but the girl's sisters, who in time came to know where she was, had been dazzled by her mode of life. The weeping mother was quite sure that two of her daughters, while still outwardly respectable and "working downtown," earned money in the devious ways which they had learned all about when they were little children, although for the past five years the now prosperous husband had allowed the family to live in a suburb where the two younger daughters were "growing up respectable."

At moments it seemed possible that these simple women, representing an earlier development, eagerly seized upon the story simply because it was primitive in form and substance. Certainly one evening a long-forgotten ballad made an unceasing effort to come to the surface of my mind, as I talked to a feeble woman who, in the last stages of an incurable disease from which she soon afterwards died, had been helped off the streetcar in front of Hull House.

The ballad tells that the lover of a proud and jealous mistress, who demanded as a final test of devotion that he bring her the heart of his mother, had quickly cut the heart from his mother's breast and impetuously returned to his lady bearing it upon a salver; but that, when stumbling in his gallant haste, he stooped to replace upon the silver plate his mother's heart which had rolled upon the ground, the heart, still beating with tender solicitude, whispered the hope that her child was not hurt.

The ballad itself was scarcely more exaggerated than the story of our visitor that evening, who had made the desperate effort of a journey from home in order to see the Devil Baby. I was familiar with her vicissitudes: the shiftless drinking husband and the large family of children, all of whom had brought her sorrow and disgrace; and I knew that her heart's desire was to see again before she died her youngest son, who was a life prisoner in the penitentiary. She was confident that the last piteous stage of her disease would secure him a week's parole, founding this forlorn hope upon the fact that "they sometimes let them out to attend a mother's funeral, and perhaps they'd let Joe come a few days ahead; he could pay his fare afterwards from the insurance money. It wouldn't take much to bury me."

Again we went over the hideous story. Joe had violently quarreled with a woman, the proprietor of the house in which his disreputable wife lived, because she withheld from him a part of his wife's "earnings," and in the altercation had killed her—a situation, one would say, which it would be difficult for even a mother to condone. But not at all: her thin gray face worked with emotion, her trembling hands restlessly pulled at her shabby skirt as the hands of the dying pluck at the sheets, but she put all the vitality she could muster in his defense. She told us he had legally married the girl who supported him, "although Lily had been so long in that life that few men would have done it. Of course such a girl must have a protector or everybody would fleece her; poor Lily said to the day of her death that he was the kindest man she ever knew, and treated her the whitest; that she herself was to blame for the murder because she told on the old miser, and Joe was so hotheaded she might have known that he would draw a gun for her." The gasping mother concluded, "He was always that handsome and had such a way. One winter when I was scrubbing in an office building, I'd never get home much before twelve o'clock; but Joe would open the door for me just as pleasant as if he hadn't been waked out of a deep sleep."

She was so triumphantly unconscious of the incongruity of a sturdy son in bed while his mother earned his food, that her auditors said never a word, and in silence we saw a hero evolved before our eyes: a defender of the oppressed, the best beloved of his mother, who was losing his high spirits and eating his heart out behind the prison bars. He could well defy the world even there, surrounded as he was by that invincible affection which assures both the fortunate and unfortunate alike that we are loved, not according to our deserts, but in response to some profounder law.

This imposing revelation of maternal solicitude was an instance of what continually happened in connection with the Devil Baby. In the midst of the most tragic recitals there remained that something in the souls of these mothers which has been called the great revelation of tragedy, or sometimes the great illusion of tragedy—that which has power in its own right to make life acceptable and at rare moments even beautiful.

At least, during the weeks when the Devil Baby seemed to occupy every room in Hull House, one was conscious that all human vicissitudes are in the end melted down into reminiscence, and that a metaphorical statement of those profound experiences which are implicit in human nature itself, however crude in form the story may be, has a singular power of healing the distracted spirit.

If it has always been the mission of literature to translate the particular act into something of the universal, to reduce the element of crude pain in the isolated experience by bringing to the sufferer a realization that his is but the common lot, this mission may have been performed through such stories as this for simple hard-working women, who, after all, at any given moment compose the bulk of the women in the world.

Jane Addams

## QUESTIONS

1. Why are the people who come to Hull House to see the Devil Baby so certain it is there, despite the staff's denials? Why do they claim to know "exactly what he was like"? (261)

2. Why are there so many versions of the Devil Baby story? What do they have in common?

3. Why does Addams think that most of the activity around the Devil Baby is an "empty show"? (262) At the same time, why is she "irresistibly interested" whenever she hears old women talking about the story? (263)

4. According to Addams, why have the old women she talks with lost "all bitterness and resentment against life," despite their hideous experiences? What is the "translucent wisdom" she believes these women exhibit? (263)

5. Why does Addams include in her essay several of the life stories the old women have told her?

6. Why does Addams think legends like that of the Devil Baby may grow from the unconscious desires of those who have suffered tragic experiences to pass on knowledge "to a world which learns at the hardest"? (266)

7. What is Addams referring to when she speaks of "that sphere of marital conduct which . . . has always afforded the most fertile field for irrational taboos and savage punishments"? How might the Devil Baby story "act as a restraining influence" in this sphere? (267)

8. In Addams's view, what "imperative needs of anxious wives and mothers" has the Devil Baby story evolved to address? (267)

9. What does Addams mean when she says that "there remained that something in the souls of these mothers which has been called the great revelation of tragedy, or sometimes the great illusion of tragedy"? (273)

10. According to Addams, why do some stories have a "singular power of healing the distracted spirit," even when they are tragic? (273)

## FOR FURTHER REFLECTION

1. What significance is there in the assumption that the Devil Baby is male?

2. If we are aware that someone believes a story that we know to be untrue, should we point out that it is false, even if the story has the power "to make life acceptable" for the believer?

3. Based on Addams's account, do you think women are more likely than men to recount their family sorrows?

4. Do you agree with Addams that a large part of the women's fascination with the Devil Baby was because it represented to them retribution against abusive husbands?

Herbert George Wells (1866–1946)—the English novelist, journalist, and historian—is considered one of the founders of modern science fiction. Born into a lower-middle-class family, Wells began working at the age of fourteen. At eighteen he received a scholarship to study biology at the Normal School of Science, where his teacher T. H. Huxley, a famous biologist and defender of Charles Darwin's theories, inspired him to pursue his science studies. Wells eventually completed his degree at the University of London.

Wells's literary career began with a series of "scientific romances," novels that combined his scientific knowledge with his developing interest in social issues. His first published novel, *The Time Machine* (1895), was an immediate success, and Wells continued to write more books in the same manner, including *The Invisible Man* (1897), *The Island of Doctor Moreau* (1896), and *The War of the Worlds* (1898). Each of these books speculates on the consequences of scientific and technological advances, using these scenarios to comment on ethical and social problems. Because of their imaginative and forward-looking use of scientific ideas, they are considered some of the earliest examples of the science fiction genre.

After gaining fame for his scientific romances, Wells turned to social comedies. In these novels he demonstrated his compassion for humanity, which later evolved into advocacy for social reform. In works such as *Love and Mr. Lewisham* (1900) and *The History of Mr. Polly* (1910), Wells portrays lower-middle-class English life, championing the "little man" and showing a sympathetic understanding for the life of ordinary people, such as shopkeepers and schoolteachers.

In 1903 Wells assumed the role of political activist by joining the Fabian Society, a group dedicated to bringing about socialism by the democratic process rather than through violent revolution. During his time with the Fabians, Wells wrote

*A Modern Utopia* (1905), a plan for social reform that is a hybrid of political tract and narrative fiction. Wells left the Fabian Society after five years, following a conflict over the leadership and direction of the organization, which he later caricatured in *The New Machiavelli* (1911). Wells continued his advocacy for social reform in his controversial novel *Ann Veronica* (1909), which deals with sexual equality and women's rights. Over time, the aesthetic quality of Wells's writing declined as he used fiction more as a vehicle to articulate his views on social issues. When the novelist Henry James expressed disdain for Wells's sacrifice of literary merit to doctrinal concerns, Wells declared, "I would rather be called a journalist than an artist."

After witnessing World War I, Wells assumed a more somber tone in his writing as he expressed his fear for the future of humanity. In *The Outline of History* (1920; revised 1931), he characterizes human history as a "race between education and catastrophe," and in *In the Shape of Things to Come* (1933), he foresees another world war and a long, arduous course for mankind as it comes to realize the need for a new world order. Wells came to believe that the only salvation for humanity was a "world state."

Wells's scientific romances established not only science fiction's capacity for social commentary but also its ability to predict future technological developments, such as the mechanized modern warfare in the alien machines of *The War of the Worlds* and the aerial combat of *The War in the Air* (1908). In addition, writers such as Aldous Huxley, George Orwell, and Yevgeny Zamyatin were strongly influenced by Wells's vision of the possible fate of human society. Wells's advocacy of sexual liberation and his stand against censorship in literature also paved the way for novelists such as D. H. Lawrence and James Joyce to publish more sexually explicit works.

In "The Man Who Could Work Miracles," Wells tells the story of what happens when superhuman abilities are bestowed upon an ordinary man, raising questions about what human qualities are necessary to wield enhanced power wisely.

# The Man Who Could Work Miracles

## A Pantoum in Prose

It is doubtful whether the gift was innate. For my own part, I think it came to him suddenly. Indeed, until he was thirty he was a sceptic, and did not believe in miraculous powers. And here, since it is the most convenient place, I must mention that he was a little man, and had eyes of a hot brown, very erect red hair, a moustache with ends that he twisted up, and freckles. His name was George McWhirter Fotheringay—not the sort of name by any means to lead to any expectation of miracles—and he was clerk at Gomshott's. He was greatly addicted to assertive argument. It was while he was asserting the impossibility of miracles that he had his first intimation of his extraordinary powers. This particular argument was being held in the bar of the Long Dragon, and Toddy Beamish was conducting the opposition by a monotonous but effective "So *you* say," that drove Mr. Fotheringay to the very limit of his patience.

There were present, besides these two, a very dusty cyclist, landlord Cox, and Miss Maybridge, the perfectly respectable and rather portly bar-maid of the Dragon. Miss Maybridge was standing with her back to Mr. Fotheringay, washing glasses; the others were watching him, more or less amused by the present ineffectiveness of the assertive method. Goaded by the Torres Vedras tactics of Mr. Beamish, Mr. Fotheringay determined to make an unusual rhetorical effort. "Looky here, Mr. Beamish," said Mr. Fotheringay. "Let us clearly understand what a miracle is. It's something contrariwise to the course of nature done by power of will, something what couldn't happen without being specially willed."

"So *you* say," said Mr. Beamish, repulsing him.

Mr. Fotheringay appealed to the cyclist, who had hitherto been a silent auditor, and received his assent—given with a hesitating cough and a glance at Mr. Beamish. The landlord would express no opinion, and Mr. Fotheringay, returning to Mr. Beamish, received the unexpected concession of a qualified assent to his definition of a miracle.

"For instance," said Mr. Fotheringay, greatly encouraged. "Here would be a miracle. That lamp, in the natural course of nature, couldn't burn like that upsy-down, could it, Beamish?"

"*You* say it couldn't," said Beamish.

"And you?" said Fotheringay. "You don't mean to say—eh?"

"No," said Beamish reluctantly. "No, it couldn't."

"Very well," said Mr. Fotheringay. "Then here comes someone, as it might be me, along here, and stands as it might be here, and says to that lamp, as I might do, collecting all my will—Turn upsy-down without breaking, and go on burning steady, and—Hullo!"

It was enough to make anyone say "Hullo!" The impossible, the incredible, was visible to them all. The lamp hung inverted in the air, burning quietly with its flame pointing down. It was as solid, as indisputable as ever a lamp was, the prosaic common lamp of the Long Dragon bar.

Mr. Fotheringay stood with an extended forefinger and the knitted brows of one anticipating a catastrophic smash. The cyclist, who was sitting next the lamp, ducked and jumped across the bar. Everybody jumped, more or less. Miss Maybridge turned and screamed. For nearly three seconds the lamp remained still. A faint cry of mental distress came from Mr. Fotheringay. "I can't keep it up," he said, "any longer." He staggered back, and the inverted lamp suddenly flared, fell against the corner of the bar, bounced aside, smashed upon the floor, and went out.

It was lucky it had a metal receiver, or the whole place would have been in a blaze. Mr. Cox was the first to speak, and his remark, shorn of needless excrescences, was to the effect that Fotheringay was a fool. Fotheringay was beyond disputing even so fundamental a proposition as that! He was astonished beyond measure at the thing that had occurred. The subsequent conversation threw absolutely no light on the matter so far as Fotheringay was concerned; the general opinion not only followed Mr. Cox very closely but very vehemently. Everyone accused Fotheringay of a silly trick, and presented him to himself as a foolish destroyer of comfort and security. His mind was in a tornado of perplexity, he was himself inclined to agree with them, and he made a remarkably ineffectual opposition to the proposal of his departure.

He went home flushed and heated, coat collar crumpled, eyes smarting and ears red. He watched each of the ten street lamps nervously as he passed it. It was only when he found himself alone in his little bedroom in Church Row that he was able to grapple seriously with his memories of the occurrence, and ask, "What on earth happened?"

He had removed his coat and boots, and was sitting on the bed with his hands in his pockets repeating the text of his defence for the seventeenth time, "*I* didn't want the confounded thing to upset," when it occurred to him that at the precise moment he had said the commanding words he had inadvertently willed the thing he said, and that when he had seen the lamp in the air he had felt it depended on him to maintain it there without being clear how this was to be done. He had not a particularly complex mind, or he might have stuck for a time at that "inadvertently willed," embracing, as it does, the abstrusest problems of voluntary action; but as it was, the idea came to him with a quite acceptable haziness. And from that, following, as I must admit, no clear logical path, he came to the test of experiment.

He pointed resolutely to his candle and collected his mind, though he felt he did a foolish thing. "Be raised up," he said. But in a second that feeling vanished. The candle was raised, hung in the air one giddy moment, and as Mr. Fotheringay gasped, fell with a smash on his toilet table, leaving him in darkness save for the expiring glow of its wick.

For a time Mr. Fotheringay sat in the darkness, perfectly still. "It did happen, after all," he said. "And 'ow *I'm* to explain it I *don't* know." He sighed heavily, and began feeling in his pockets for a match. He could find none, and he rose and groped about the toilet table. "I wish I had a match," he said. He resorted to his coat, and there was none there, and then it dawned upon him that miracles were possible even with matches. He extended a hand and scowled at it in the dark. "Let there be a match in that hand," he said. He felt some light object fall across his palm, and his fingers closed upon a match.

After several ineffectual attempts to light this, he discovered it was a safety match. He threw it down, and then it occurred to him that he might have willed it lit. He did, and perceived it burning in the midst of his toilet table mat. He caught it up hastily, and it went out. His perception of possibilities enlarged, and he felt for and replaced the candle in its candlestick. "Here! *you* be lit," said Mr. Fotheringay, and forthwith the candle was flaring, and he saw a little black hole in the toilet cover, with a wisp of smoke rising from it. For a time he stared from this to the little flame and back, and then looked up and met his own gaze in the looking glass. By this help he communed with himself in silence for a time.

"How about miracles now?" said Mr. Fotheringay at last, addressing his reflection.

The subsequent meditations of Mr. Fotheringay were of a severe but confused description. So far, he could see it was a case of pure willing with him. The nature of his experiences so far disinclined him for any further experiments, at least until he had reconsidered them. But he lifted a sheet of paper, and turned a glass of water pink and then green, and he created a snail, which he miraculously annihilated, and got himself a miraculous new toothbrush. Somewhen in the small hours he had reached the fact that his willpower must be of a particularly rare and pungent quality, a fact of which he had certainly had inklings before, but no certain assurance. The scare and perplexity of his first discovery was now qualified by pride in this evidence of singularity and by vague intimations of advantage. He became aware that the church clock was striking one, and as it did not occur to him that his daily duties at Gomshott's might be miraculously dispensed with, he resumed undressing, in order to get to bed without further delay. As he struggled to get his shirt over his head, he was struck with a brilliant idea. "Let me be in bed," he said, and found himself so. "Undressed," he stipulated; and, finding the sheets cold, added hastily, "and in my nightshirt—no, in a nice soft woollen nightshirt. Ah!" he said with immense enjoyment. "And now let me be comfortably asleep. . . ."

He awoke at his usual hour and was pensive all through breakfast-time, wondering whether his overnight experience might not be a particularly vivid dream. At length his mind turned again to cautious experiments. For instance, he had three eggs for breakfast; two his landlady had supplied, good, but shoppy, and one was a delicious fresh goose egg, laid, cooked, and served by his extraordinary will. He hurried off to Gomshott's in a state of profound but carefully concealed excitement, and only remembered the shell of the third egg when his landlady spoke of it that night. All day he could do no work because of this astonishingly new self-knowledge, but this caused him no inconvenience, because he made up for it miraculously in his last ten minutes.

As the day wore on, his state of mind passed from wonder to elation, albeit the circumstances of his dismissal from the Long Dragon were still disagreeable to recall, and a garbled account of the matter that had reached his colleagues led to some badinage. It was evident he must be careful how he lifted frangible articles, but in other ways his gift promised more and more as he turned it over in his mind. He intended among other things to increase his personal property by unostentatious acts of creation. He called into existence a pair of very splendid diamond studs, and hastily annihilated them again as young Gomshott came across the counting house to his desk. He was afraid young Gomshott might wonder how he had come by them. He saw quite clearly the gift required caution and watchfulness in its exercise, but so far as he could judge the difficulties attending its mastery would be no greater than those he had already faced in the study of cycling. It was that analogy, perhaps, quite as much as the feeling that he would be unwelcome in the Long Dragon, that drove him out after supper into the lane beyond the gasworks, to rehearse a few miracles in private.

There was possibly a certain want of originality in his attempts, for apart from his willpower Mr. Fotheringay was not a very exceptional man. The miracle of Moses's rod came to his mind, but the night was dark and unfavourable to the proper control of large miraculous snakes. Then he recollected the story of *Tannhäuser* that he had read on the back of the Philharmonic programme. That seemed to him singularly attractive and harmless. He stuck his walking stick—a very nice Poona-Penang lawyer—into the turf that edged the footpath, and commanded the dry wood to blossom. The air was immediately full of the scent of roses, and by means of a match he saw for himself that this beautiful miracle was indeed accomplished. His satisfaction was ended by advancing footsteps. Afraid of a premature discovery of his powers, he addressed the blossoming stick hastily: "Go back." What he meant was "Change back"; but of course he was confused. The stick receded at a considerable velocity, and incontinently came a cry of anger and a bad word from the approaching person. "Who are you throwing brambles at, you fool?" cried a voice. "That got me on the shin."

"I'm sorry, old chap," said Mr. Fotheringay, and then realising the awkward nature of the explanation, caught nervously at his moustache. He saw Winch, one of the three Immering constables, advancing.

"What d'yer mean by it?" asked the constable. "Hullo! It's you, is it? The gent that broke the lamp at the Long Dragon!"

"I don't mean anything by it," said Mr. Fotheringay. "Nothing at all."

"What d'yer do it for then?"

"Oh, bother!" said Mr. Fotheringay.

"Bother indeed! D'yer know that stick hurt? What d'yer do it for, eh?"

For the moment Mr. Fotheringay could not think what he had done it for. His silence seemed to irritate Mr. Winch. "You've been assaulting the police, young man, this time. That's what *you* done."

"Look here, Mr. Winch," said Mr. Fotheringay, annoyed and confused, "I'm very sorry. The fact is—"

"Well?"

He could think of no way but the truth. "I was working a miracle." He tried to speak in an offhand way, but try as he would he couldn't.

"Working a—! 'Ere, don't you talk rot. Working a miracle, indeed! Miracle! Well, that's downright funny! Why, you's the chap that don't believe in miracles. . . . Fact is, this is another of your silly conjuring tricks—that's what this is. Now, I tell you—"

But Mr. Fotheringay never heard what Mr. Winch was going to tell him. He realised he had given himself away, flung his valuable secret to all the winds of heaven. A violent gust of irritation swept him to action.

He turned on the constable swiftly and fiercely. "Here," he said, "I've had enough of this, I have! I'll show you a silly conjuring trick, I will! Go to Hades! Go, now!"

He was alone!

Mr. Fotheringay performed no more miracles that night nor did he trouble to see what had become of his flowering stick. He returned to the town, scared and very quiet, and went to his bedroom. "Lord!" he said, "it's a powerful gift—an extremely powerful gift. I didn't hardly mean as much as that. Not really. . . . I wonder what Hades is like!"

He sat on the bed taking off his boots. Struck by a happy thought he transferred the constable to San Francisco, and without any more interference with normal causation went soberly to bed. In the night he dreamt of the anger of Winch.

The next day Mr. Fotheringay heard two interesting items of news. Someone had planted a most beautiful climbing rose against the elder Mr. Gomshott's private house in the Lullaborough Road, and the river as far as Rawling's Mill was to be dragged for Constable Winch.

Mr. Fotheringay was abstracted and thoughtful all that day, and performed no miracles except certain provisions for Winch, and the miracle of completing his day's work with punctual perfection in spite of all the bee-swarm of thoughts that hummed through his mind. And the extraordinary abstraction and meekness of his manner was remarked by several people, and made a matter for jesting. For the most part he was thinking of Winch.

On Sunday evening he went to chapel, and oddly enough, Mr. Maydig, who took a certain interest in occult matters, preached about "things that are not lawful." Mr. Fotheringay was not a regular chapel goer, but the system of assertive scepticism, to which I have already alluded, was now very much shaken. The tenor of the sermon threw an entirely new light on these novel gifts, and he suddenly decided to consult Mr. Maydig immediately after the service. So soon as that was determined, he found himself wondering why he had not done so before.

Mr. Maydig, a lean, excitable man with quite remarkably long wrists and neck, was gratified at a request for a private conversation from a young man whose carelessness in religious matters was a subject for general remark in the town. After a few necessary delays, he conducted him to the study of the manse, which was contiguous to the chapel, seated him comfortably, and, standing in front of a cheerful fire—his legs threw a Rhodian arch of shadow on the opposite wall—requested Mr. Fotheringay to state his business.

At first Mr. Fotheringay was a little abashed, and found some difficulty in opening the matter. "You will scarcely believe me, Mr. Maydig, I am afraid"—and so forth for some time. He tried a question at last, and asked Mr. Maydig his opinion of miracles.

Mr. Maydig was still saying "Well" in an extremely judicial tone, when Mr. Fotheringay interrupted again: "You don't believe, I suppose, that some common sort of person—like myself, for instance—as it might be sitting here now, might have some sort of twist inside him that made him able to do things by his will."

"It's possible," said Mr. Maydig. "Something of the sort, perhaps, is possible."

"If I might make free with something here, I think I might show you by a sort of experiment," said Mr. Fotheringay. "Now, take that tobacco jar on the table, for instance. What I want to know is whether what I am going to do with it is a miracle or not. Just half a minute, Mr. Maydig, please."

He knitted his brows, pointed to the tobacco jar and said: "Be a bowl of vi'lets."

The tobacco jar did as it was ordered.

Mr. Maydig started violently at the change, and stood looking from the thaumaturgist to the bowl of flowers. He said nothing. Presently he ventured to lean over the table and smell the violets; they were fresh-picked and very fine ones. Then he stared at Mr. Fotheringay again.

"How did you do that?" he asked.

Mr. Fotheringay pulled his moustache. "Just told it—and there you are. Is that a miracle, or is it black art, or what is it? And what do you think's the matter with me? That's what I want to ask."

"It's a most extraordinary occurrence."

"And this day last week I knew no more that I could do things like that than you did. It came quite sudden. It's something odd about my will, I suppose, and that's as far as I can see."

"Is *that*—the only thing? Could you do other things besides that?"

"Lord, yes!" said Mr. Fotheringay. "Just anything." He thought, and suddenly recalled a conjuring entertainment he had seen. "Here!" He pointed. "Change into a bowl of fish—no, not that—change into a glass bowl full of water with goldfish swimming in it. That's better! You see that, Mr. Maydig?"

"It's astonishing. It's incredible. You are either a most extraordinary . . . But no—"

"I could change it into anything," said Mr. Fotheringay. "Just anything. Here! be a pigeon, will you?"

In another moment a blue pigeon was fluttering round the room and making Mr. Maydig duck every time it came near him. "Stop there, will you," said Mr. Fotheringay; and the pigeon hung motionless in the air. "I could change it back to a bowl of flowers," he said, and after replacing the pigeon on the table worked that miracle. "I expect you will want your pipe in a bit," he said, and restored the tobacco jar.

Mr. Maydig had followed all these later changes in a sort of ejaculatory silence. He stared at Mr. Fotheringay and, in a very gingerly manner, picked up the tobacco jar, examined it, replaced it on the table. "*Well!*" was the only expression of his feelings.

"Now, after that it's easier to explain what I came about," said Mr. Fotheringay; and proceeded to a lengthy and involved narrative of his strange experiences, beginning with the affair of the lamp in the Long Dragon and complicated by persistent allusions to Winch. As he went on, the transient pride Mr. Maydig's consternation had caused passed away; he became the very ordinary Mr. Fotheringay of everyday intercourse again. Mr. Maydig listened intently, the tobacco jar in his hand, and his bearing changed also with the course of the narrative. Presently, while Mr. Fotheringay was dealing with the miracle of the third egg, the minister interrupted with a fluttering extended hand—

"It is possible," he said. "It is credible. It is amazing, of course, but it reconciles a number of amazing difficulties. The power to work miracles is a gift—a peculiar quality like genius or second sight—hitherto it has come very rarely and to exceptional people. But in this case . . . I have always wondered at the miracles of Mahomet, and at Yogi's miracles, and the miracles of Madame Blavatsky. But, of course! Yes, it is simply a gift! It carries out so beautifully the arguments of that great thinker"—Mr. Maydig's voice sank—"his Grace the Duke of Argyll. Here we plumb some profounder law—deeper than the ordinary laws of nature. Yes—yes. Go on. Go on!"

Mr. Fotheringay proceeded to tell of his misadventure with Winch, and Mr. Maydig, no longer overawed or scared, began to jerk his limbs about and interject astonishment. "It's this what troubled me most," proceeded Mr. Fotheringay; "it's this I'm most mightily in want of advice for; of course he's at San Francisco—wherever San Francisco may be—but of course it's awkward for both of us, as you'll see, Mr. Maydig. I don't see how he can understand what has happened, and I daresay he's scared and exasperated something tremendous, and trying to get at me. I daresay he keeps on starting off to come here. I send him back, by a miracle, every few hours, when I think of it. And of course, that's a thing he won't be able to understand, and it's bound to annoy him; and, of course, if he takes a ticket every time it will cost him a lot of money. I done the best I could for him, but of course it's difficult for him to put himself in my place. I thought afterwards that his clothes might have got scorched, you know—if Hades is all it's supposed to be—before I shifted him. In that case I suppose they'd have locked him up in San Francisco. Of course I willed a new suit of clothes on him directly I thought of it. But, you see, I'm already in a deuce of a tangle—"

Mr. Maydig looked serious. "I see you are in a tangle. Yes, it's a difficult position. How you are to end it . . ." He became diffuse and inconclusive.

"However, we'll leave Winch for a little and discuss the larger question. I don't think this is a case of the black art or anything of the sort. I don't think there is any taint of criminality about it at all, Mr. Fotheringay—none whatever, unless you are suppressing material facts. No, it's miracles—pure miracles—miracles, if I may say so, of the very highest class."

He began to pace the hearthrug and gesticulate, while Mr. Fotheringay sat with his arm on the table and his head on his arm, looking worried. "I don't see how I'm to manage about Winch," he said.

"A gift of working miracles—apparently a very powerful gift," said Mr. Maydig, "will find a way about Winch—never fear. My dear sir, you are a most important man—a man of the most astonishing possibilities. As evidence, for example! And in other ways, the things you may do . . ."

"Yes, *I've* thought of a thing or two," said Mr. Fotheringay. "But— some of the things came a bit twisty. You saw that fish at first? Wrong sort of bowl and wrong sort of fish. And I thought I'd ask someone."

"A proper course," said Mr. Maydig, "a very proper course— altogether the proper course." He stopped and looked at Mr. Fotheringay. "It's practically an unlimited gift. Let us test your powers, for instance. If they really *are* . . . If they really are all they seem to be."

And so, incredible as it may seem, in the study of the little house behind the Congregational Chapel, on the evening of Sunday, November 10, 1896, Mr. Fotheringay, egged on and inspired by Mr. Maydig, began to work miracles. The reader's attention is specially and definitely called to the date. He will object, probably has already objected, that certain points in this story are improbable, that if any things of the sort already described had indeed occurred, they would have been in all the papers a year ago. The details immediately following he will find particularly hard to accept, because among other things they involve the conclusion that he or she, the reader in question, must have been killed in a violent and unprecedented manner more than a year ago. Now a miracle is nothing if not improbable, and as a matter of fact the reader *was* killed in a violent and unprecedented manner a year ago. In the subsequent course of this story that will become perfectly clear and credible, as every right-minded and reasonable reader will admit. But this is not the place for the end of the story, being but little beyond the hither side of the middle. And at first the miracles worked by Mr. Fotheringay were timid little miracles—little things with the cups and parlour fitments, as feeble as the miracles of Theosophists, and, feeble as they were, they were received with awe by his collaborator. He would have preferred to settle the Winch business out of hand, but Mr. Maydig would not let him. But after they had worked a dozen of these domestic trivialities, their sense of power grew, their imagination began to show signs of stimulation, and their ambition enlarged. Their first larger enterprise was due to hunger and the negligence of Mrs. Minchin, Mr. Maydig's housekeeper. The meal to which the minister conducted Mr. Fotheringay was certainly ill-laid and uninviting as refreshment for two industrious miracle workers; but they were seated, and Mr. Maydig was descanting in sorrow rather than in anger upon his housekeeper's shortcomings, before it occurred to Mr. Fotheringay that an opportunity lay before him. "Don't you think, Mr. Maydig," he said; "if it isn't a liberty, I—"

"My dear Mr. Fotheringay! Of course! No—I didn't think."

Mr. Fotheringay waved his hand. "What shall we have?" he said, in a large, inclusive spirit, and, at Mr. Maydig's order, revised the supper very thoroughly. "As for me," he said, eyeing Mr. Maydig's selection, "I am always particularly fond of a tankard of stout and a nice Welsh rarebit, and I'll order that. I ain't much given to Burgundy," and forthwith stout and Welsh rarebit promptly appeared at his command. They sat long at their supper, talking like equals, as Mr. Fotheringay presently perceived, with a glow of surprise and gratification, of all the miracles they would presently do. "And, by the bye, Mr. Maydig," said Mr. Fotheringay, "I might perhaps be able to help you—in a domestic way."

"Don't quite follow," said Mr. Maydig, pouring out a glass of miraculous old Burgundy.

Mr. Fotheringay helped himself to a second Welsh rarebit out of vacancy, and took a mouthful. "I was thinking," he said, "I might be able (*chum, chum*) to work (*chum, chum*) a miracle with Mrs. Minchin (*chum, chum*)—make her a better woman."

Mr. Maydig put down the glass and looked doubtful. "She's—She strongly objects to interference, you know, Mr. Fotheringay. And—as a matter of fact—it's well past eleven and she's probably in bed and asleep. Do you think, on the whole—"

Mr. Fotheringay considered these objections. "I don't see that it shouldn't be done in her sleep."

For a time Mr. Maydig opposed the idea, and then he yielded. Mr. Fotheringay issued his orders, and a little less at their ease, perhaps, the two gentlemen proceeded with their repast. Mr. Maydig was enlarging on the changes he might expect in his housekeeper next day, with an optimism that seemed even to Mr. Fotheringay's supper senses a little forced and hectic, when a series of confused noises from upstairs began. Their eyes exchanged interrogations, and Mr. Maydig left the room hastily. Mr. Fotheringay heard him calling up to his housekeeper and then his footsteps going softly up to her.

In a minute or so the minister returned, his step light, his face radiant. "Wonderful!" he said, "and touching! Most touching!"

He began pacing the hearthrug. "A repentance—a most touching repentance—through the crack of the door. Poor woman! A most wonderful change! She had got up. She must have got up at once. She had got up out of her sleep to smash a private bottle of brandy in her box. And to confess it too! . . . But this gives us—it opens—a most amazing vista of possibilities. If we can work this miraculous change in *her*. . . ."

"The thing's unlimited seemingly," said Mr. Fotheringay. "And about Mr. Winch—"

"Altogether unlimited." And from the hearthrug Mr. Maydig, waving the Winch difficulty aside, unfolded a series of wonderful proposals—proposals he invented as he went along.

Now what those proposals were does not concern the essentials of this story. Suffice it that they were designed in a spirit of infinite benevolence, the sort of benevolence that used to be called postprandial. Suffice it, too, that the problem of Winch remained unsolved. Nor is it necessary to describe how far that series got to its fulfilment. There were astonishing changes. The small hours found Mr. Maydig and Mr. Fotheringay careering across the chilly market square under the still moon, in a sort of ecstasy of thaumaturgy, Mr. Maydig all flap and gesture, Mr. Fotheringay short and bristling, and no longer abashed at his greatness. They had reformed every drunkard in the Parliamentary division, changed all the beer and alcohol to water (Mr. Maydig had overruled Mr. Fotheringay on this point); they had, further, greatly improved the railway communication of the place, drained Flinder's swamp, improved the soil of One Tree Hill, and cured the Vicar's wart. And they were going to see what could be done with the injured pier at South Bridge. "The place," gasped Mr. Maydig, "won't be the same place tomorrow. How surprised and thankful everyone will be!" And just at that moment the church clock struck three.

"I say," said Mr. Fotheringay, "that's three o'clock! I must be getting back. I've got to be at business by eight. And besides, Mrs. Wimms—"

"We're only beginning," said Mr. Maydig, full of the sweetness of unlimited power. "We're only beginning. Think of all the good we're doing. When people wake—"

"But—," said Mr. Fotheringay.

Mr. Maydig gripped his arm suddenly. His eyes were bright and wild. "My dear chap," he said, "there's no hurry. "Look"—he pointed to the moon at the zenith— "Joshua!"

"Joshua?" said Mr. Fotheringay.

"Joshua," said Mr. Maydig. "Why not? Stop it."

Mr. Fotheringay looked at the moon.

"That's a bit tall," he said after a pause.

"Why not?" said Mr. Maydig. "Of course it doesn't stop. You stop the rotation of the earth, you know. Time stops. It isn't as if we were doing harm."

"H'm!" said Mr. Fotheringay. "Well." He sighed. "I'll try. Here—"

He buttoned up his jacket and addressed himself to the habitable globe, with as good an assumption of confidence as lay in his power. "Jest stop rotating, will you," said Mr. Fotheringay.

Incontinently he was flying head over heels through the air at the rate of dozens of miles a minute. In spite of the innumerable circles he was describing per second, he thought; for thought is wonderful—sometimes as sluggish as flowing pitch, sometimes as instantaneous as light. He thought in a second, and willed. "Let me come down safe and sound. Whatever else happens, let me down safe and sound."

He willed it only just in time, for his clothes, heated by his rapid flight through the air, were already beginning to singe. He came down with a forcible, but by no means injurious, bump in what appeared to be a mound of fresh-turned earth. A large mass of metal and masonry, extraordinarily like the clock tower in the middle of the market square, hit the earth near him, ricochetted over him, and flew into stonework, bricks, and masonry, like a bursting bomb. A hurtling cow hit one of the larger blocks and smashed like an egg. There was a crash that made all the most violent crashes of his past life seem like the sound of falling dust, and this was followed by a descending series of lesser crashes. A vast wind roared throughout earth and heaven, so that he could scarcely lift his head to look. For a while he was too breathless and astonished even to see where he was or what had happened. And his first movement was to feel his head and reassure himself that his streaming hair was still his own.

"Lord!" gasped Mr. Fotheringay, scarce able to speak for the gale, "I've had a squeak! What's gone wrong? Storms and thunder. And only a minute ago a fine night. It's Maydig set me on to this sort of thing. *What* a wind! If I go on fooling in this way I'm bound to have a thundering accident! . . .

"Where's Maydig?

"What a confounded mess everything's in!"

He looked about him so far as his flapping jacket would permit. The appearance of things was really extremely strange. "The sky's all right anyhow," said Mr. Fotheringay. "And that's about all that is all right. And even there it looks like a terrific gale coming up. But there's the moon overhead. Just as it was just now. Bright as midday. But as for the rest— where's the village? Where's—where's anything? And what on earth set this wind a-blowing? *I* didn't order no wind."

Mr. Fotheringay struggled to get to his feet in vain, and after one failure, remained on all fours, holding on. He surveyed the moonlit world to leeward, with the tails of his jacket streaming over his head. "There's something seriously wrong," said Mr. Fotheringay. "And what it is—goodness knows."

Far and wide nothing was visible in the white glare through the haze of dust that drove before a screaming gale but tumbled masses of earth and heaps of inchoate ruins, no trees, no houses, no familiar shapes, only a wilderness of disorder vanishing at last into the darkness beneath the whirling columns and streamers, the lightnings and thunderings of a swiftly rising storm. Near him in the livid glare was something that might once have been an elm tree, a smashed mass of splinters, shivered from boughs to base, and further a twisted mass of iron girders—only too evidently the viaduct—rose out of the piled confusion.

You see, when Mr. Fotheringay had arrested the rotation of the solid globe, he had made no stipulation concerning the trifling movables upon its surface. And the earth spins so fast that the surface at its equator is travelling at rather more than a thousand miles an hour, and in these latitudes at more than half that pace. So that the village, and Mr. Maydig, and Mr. Fotheringay, and everybody and everything had been jerked violently forward at about nine miles per second—that is to say, much more violently than if they had been fired out of a cannon. And every human being, every living creature, every house, and every tree—all the world as we know it—had been so jerked and smashed and utterly destroyed. That was all.

These things Mr. Fotheringay did not, of course, fully appreciate. But he perceived that his miracle had miscarried, and with that a great disgust of miracles came upon him. He was in darkness now, for the clouds had swept together and blotted out his momentary glimpse of the moon, and the air was full of fitful, struggling, tortured wraiths of hail. A great roaring of wind and waters filled earth and sky, and, peering under his hand through the dust and sleet to windward, he saw by the play of the lightnings a vast wall of water pouring towards him.

"Maydig!" screamed Mr. Fotheringay's feeble voice amid the elemental uproar. "Here!—Maydig!"

"Stop!" cried Mr. Fotheringay to the advancing water. "Oh, for goodness' sake, stop!"

"Just a moment," said Mr. Fotheringay to the lightnings and thunder. "Stop jest a moment while I collect my thoughts. . . . And now what shall I do?" he said. "What *shall* I do? Lord! I wish Maydig was about."

"I know," said Mr. Fotheringay. "And for goodness' sake let's have it right *this* time."

He remained on all fours, leaning against the wind, very intent to have everything right.

"Ah!" he said. "Let nothing what I'm going to order happen until I say 'Off!' . . . Lord! I wish I'd thought of that before!"

He lifted his little voice against the whirlwind, shouting louder and louder in the vain desire to hear himself speak. "Now then!—here goes! Mind about that what I said just now. In the first place, when all I've got to say is done, let me lose my miraculous power, let my will become just like anybody else's will, and all these dangerous miracles be stopped. I don't like them. I'd rather I didn't work 'em. Ever so much. That's the first thing. And the second is—let me be back just before the miracles begin; let everything be just as it was before that blessed lamp turned up. It's a big job, but it's the last. Have you got it? No more miracles, everything as it was—me back in the Long Dragon just before I drank my half pint. That's it! Yes."

He dug his fingers into the mould, closed his eyes, and said "Off!"

Everything became perfectly still. He perceived that he was standing erect.

"So *you* say," said a voice.

He opened his eyes. He was in the bar of the Long Dragon, arguing about miracles with Toddy Beamish. He had a vague sense of some great thing forgotten that instantaneously passed. You see, except for the loss of his miraculous powers, everything was back as it had been; his mind and memory therefore were now just as they had been at the time when this story began. So that he knew absolutely nothing of all that is told here, knows nothing of all that is told here to this day. And among other things, of course, he still did not believe in miracles.

"I tell you that miracles, properly speaking, can't possibly happen," he said, "whatever you like to hold. And I'm prepared to prove it up to the hilt."

"That's what *you* think," said Toddy Beamish, and "Prove it if you can."

"Looky here, Mr. Beamish," said Mr. Fotheringay. "Let us clearly understand what a miracle is. It's something contrariwise to the course of nature done by power of will . . ."

## QUESTIONS

1. What does Fotheringay mean when he defines a miracle as being "specially willed"? (279)

2. Why do the people who see Fotheringay's first miracle regard him as "a foolish destroyer of comfort and security"? (280)

3. Why is Fotheringay concerned about whether he is performing a "black art"? (285)

4. Why does Fotheringay modify his wish from "change into a bowl of fish" to "change into a glass bowl full of water with goldfish swimming in it"? (285)

5. What does Maydig mean when he says that Fotheringay's miracles are "of the very highest class"? (287)

6. Why does the narrator of the story tell us that Maydig's series of wonderful proposals don't concern "the essentials of this story"? (289)

7. Why does Maydig encourage Fotheringay to stop the moon?

8. Why does Wells tell his story so that the result of Fotheringay's gift is "a wilderness of disorder"? (291)

9. Why does Wells choose to end the story with Fotheringay once again explaining miracles to Beamish?

10. Was Fotheringay's career as a miracle worker enhanced, or diminished, by his association with Maydig?

## FOR FURTHER REFLECTION

1. Why do you think Wells subtitles his story "A Pantoum in Prose," which refers to a poetic form in which lines are regularly repeated from one stanza to the next according to definite rules?

2. Why do you think Wells explains the miracles in the story in terms of human will and not divine power, the usual source of miracles for those who believe in them?

3. Why might someone choose to give up an extraordinary power rather than learn to control it?

4. What purposes do you think are served by the persistent belief in miracles by cultures and individuals?

Thomas Mann (1875–1955) was born in the German port city of Lübeck, where his father was a merchant struggling to maintain the family trading business in a failing economy. Mann's mother, who was half Brazilian and artistically inclined, encouraged her children's creative pursuits. In 1891, after the death of Mann's father and the collapse of the family business, the family relocated to Munich, a major center of German cultural life. Mann lived there until 1933, with the exception of a year in Italy with his brother Heinrich.

In Munich, Mann studied literature and philosophy and he began to write, publishing his first collection of stories, *Little Herr Friedemann*, in 1898. His first novel, *Buddenbrooks* (1901), the saga of four generations of a bourgeois German family much like his own, brought him wide recognition and set him on his course as a writer of international stature. In 1905, Mann married Katja Pringsheim, with whom he had six children. The vacations they took over the years provided material for some of Mann's most well-known works. A trip to Venice prompted the writing of the acclaimed novella *Death in Venice* (1912), and a stay at a Swiss sanatorium inspired *The Magic Mountain* (1924).

The conservative political climate in Germany at the time of World War I sparked Mann's patriotism and set him in opposition to the political views of his brother Heinrich, who was one of only a few German writers to openly question the regime of Kaiser Wilhelm II during the war. His brother's criticism of German authoritarianism prompted Mann to respond with *Reflections of an Unpolitical Man* (1918), a defense of the conservative, monarchical regime. After the war, Mann shocked those who admired him for his political views when he became an advocate of democracy and the liberal Weimar Republic. Mann's next novel, *The Magic Mountain*, which depicted the cultural and political conflicts that preceded World War II, reflected his new outlook. In 1929, on the eve of the rise of the Third Reich in Germany, Mann secured an international standing by winning the Nobel Prize in Literature.

After delivering a lecture on Richard Wagner in the winter of 1933, Mann left Munich with this wife on a tour around Europe that would become the beginning of the couple's sixteen-year exile. Hitler and the Nazi Party had just come to power, and the Mann children warned their parents not to return since Katja was Jewish and Mann had openly denounced the Nazi Party. The couple remained outside the country, and Mann was stripped of his German citizenship in 1936. In 1938 they moved to the United States, eventually settling in California, where Mann completed his monumental tetralogy, *Joseph and His Brothers* (1933–1943), based on the biblical Joseph. His last novel, *Doctor Faustus* (1947), tells the story of Adrian Leverkühn, a brilliant composer whose descent into nihilism mirrors the fall of German intellectual society in the first four decades of the twentieth century. Mann and his wife returned to Europe in 1952, settling in Switzerland.

"Mario and the Magician" (1930) was inspired by the Mann family's 1926 vacation in Italy, where Mussolini had been in power since 1922. By the time Mann wrote the story, Stalin had gained power in Russia and Hitler and his party were ascendant in Germany, all harbingers of the coming years of totalitarian dictatorship and the abuse of the democratic ideals that Mann had come to admire and promote.

THOMAS MANN

# Mario and the Magician

The atmosphere of Torre di Venere remains unpleasant in the memory. From the first moment the air of the place made us uneasy, we felt irritable, on edge; then at the end came the shocking business of Cipolla, that dreadful being who seemed to incorporate, in so fateful and so humanly impressive a way, all the peculiar evilness of the situation as a whole. Looking back, we had the feeling that the horrible end of the affair had been preordained and lay in the nature of things; that the children had to be present at it was an added impropriety, due to the false colors in which the weird creature presented himself. Luckily for them, they did not know where the comedy left off and the tragedy began; and we let them remain in their happy belief that the whole thing had been a play up till the end.

Torre di Venere lies some fifteen kilometers from Portoclemente, one of the most popular summer resorts on the Tyrrhenian Sea. Portoclemente is urban and elegant and full to overflowing for months on end. Its gay and busy main street of shops and hotels runs down to a wide sandy beach covered with tents and pennanted sandcastles and sunburnt humanity, where at all times a lively social bustle reigns, and much noise. But this same spacious and inviting fine-sanded beach, this same border of pine grove and near, presiding mountains, continues all the way along the coast. No wonder then that some competition of a quiet kind should have sprung up further on. Torre di Venere—the tower that gave the town its name is gone long since, one looks for it in vain—is an offshoot of the larger resort, and for some years remained an idyll for the few, a refuge for more unworldly spirits. But the usual history of such places repeated itself: peace has had to retire further along the coast, to Marina Petriera and dear knows where else. We all know how the world at once seeks peace and puts her to flight—rushing upon her in the fond idea that they two will wed, and where she is, there it can be at home. It will even set up its Vanity Fair in a spot and be capable of thinking that peace is still by its side. Thus Torre—though its atmosphere so far is more modest and con-

297

templative than that of Portoclemente—has been quite taken up, by both Italians and foreigners. It is no longer the thing to go to Portoclemente—though still so much the thing that it is as noisy and crowded as ever. One goes next door, so to speak: to Torre. So much more refined, even, and cheaper to boot. And the attractiveness of these qualities persists, though the qualities themselves long ago ceased to be evident. Torre has got a Grand Hotel. Numerous pensions have sprung up, some modest, some pretentious. The people who own or rent the villas and pinetas overlooking the sea no longer have it all their own way on the beach. In July and August it looks just like the beach at Portoclemente: it swarms with a screaming, squabbling, merrymaking crowd, and the sun, blazing down like mad, peels the skin off their necks. Garish little flat-bottomed boats rock on the glittering blue, manned by children, whose mothers hover afar and fill the air with anxious cries of Nino! and Sandro! and Bice! and Maria! Peddlers step across the legs of recumbent sunbathers, selling flowers and corals, oysters, lemonade, and *cornetti al burro*, and crying their wares in the breathy, full-throated southern voice.

Such was the scene that greeted our arrival in Torre: pleasant enough, but after all, we thought, we had come too soon. It was the middle of August, the Italian season was still at its height, scarcely the moment for strangers to learn to love the special charms of the place. What an afternoon crowd in the cafés on the front! For instance, in the Esquisito, where we sometimes sat and were served by Mario, that very Mario of whom I shall have presently to tell. It is well-nigh impossible to find a table; and the various orchestras contend together in the midst of one's conversation with bewildering effect. Of course, it is in the afternoon that people come over from Portoclemente. The excursion is a favorite one for the restless denizens of that pleasure resort, and a Fiat motorbus plies to and fro, coating inch-thick with dust the oleander and laurel hedges along the highroad—a notable if repulsive sight.

Yes, decidedly one should go to Torre in September, when the great public has left. Or else in May, before the water is warm enough to tempt the southerner to bathe. Even in the before and after seasons Torre is not empty, but life is less national and more subdued. English, French, and German prevail under the tent awnings and in the pension dining rooms; whereas in August—in the Grand Hotel, at least, where, in default of private addresses, we had engaged rooms—the stranger finds the field so occupied by Florentine and Roman society that he feels quite isolated and even temporarily déclassé.

We had, rather to our annoyance, this experience on the evening we arrived, when we went in to dinner and were shown to our table by the waiter in charge. As a table, it had nothing against it, save that we had already fixed our eyes upon those on the veranda beyond, built out over the water, where little red-shaded lamps glowed—and there were still some tables empty, though it was as full as the dining room within. The children went into raptures at the festive sight, and without more ado we announced our intention to take our meals by preference in the veranda. Our words, it appeared, were prompted by ignorance; for we were informed, with somewhat embarrassed politeness, that the cozy nook outside was reserved for the clients of the hotel: *ai nostri clienti.* Their clients? But we were their clients. We were not tourists or trippers, but boarders for a stay of some three or four weeks. However, we forbore to press for an explanation of the difference between the likes of us and that clientele to whom it was vouchsafed to eat out there in the glow of the red lamps, and took our dinner by the prosaic common light of the dining room chandelier—a thoroughly ordinary and monotonous hotel bill of fare, be it said. In Pensione Eleonora, a few steps landward, the table, as we were to discover, was much better.

And thither it was that we moved, three or four days later, before we had had time to settle in properly at the Grand Hotel. Not on account of the veranda and the lamps. The children, straightway on the best of terms with waiters and pages, absorbed in the joys of life on the beach, promptly forgot those colorful seductions. But now there arose, between ourselves and the veranda clientele—or perhaps more correctly with the compliant management—one of those little unpleasantnesses that can quite spoil the pleasure of a holiday. Among the guests were some high Roman aristocracy, a Principe X and his family. These grand folk occupied rooms close to our own, and the Principessa, a great and a passionately maternal lady, was thrown into a panic by the vestiges of a whooping cough that our little ones had lately got over, but that now and then still faintly troubled the unshatterable slumbers of our youngest born. The nature of this illness is not clear, leaving some play for the imagination. So we took no offense at our elegant neighbor for clinging to the widely held view that whooping cough is acoustically contagious and quite simply fearing lest her children yield to the bad example set by ours. In the fullness of her feminine self-confidence she protested to the management, which then, in the person of the proverbial frock-coated manager, hastened to represent to us, with many expressions of regret, that under the circumstances they were obliged to transfer us to the annex. We did our best to assure him that the disease was in its very last stages, that it was actually over, and presented no danger of infection to anybody. All that we gained was permission to bring the case before the hotel physician—not one chosen by us—by whose verdict we must then abide. We agreed, convinced that thus we should at once pacify the princess and escape the trouble of moving. The doctor appeared, and behaved like a faithful and honest servant of science. He examined the child and gave his opinion: the disease was quite over, no danger of contagion was present. We drew a long breath and considered the incident closed—until the manager announced that despite the doctor's verdict it would still be necessary for us to give up our rooms and retire to the *dépendance*. Byzantinism like this outraged us. It is not likely that the Principessa was responsible for the willful breach of faith. Very likely the fawning management had not even dared to tell her what the physician said. Anyhow, we made it clear to his understanding that we preferred to leave the hotel altogether and at once—and packed our trunks. We could do so with a light heart, having already set up casual friendly relations with Casa Eleonora. We had noticed its pleasant exterior and formed the acquaintance of its proprietor, Signora Angiolieri, and her husband: she slender and black-haired, Tuscan in type, probably at the beginning of the thirties, with the dead ivory complexion of the southern woman, he quiet and bald and carefully dressed. They owned a larger establishment in Florence and presided only in summer and early autumn over the branch in Torre di Venere. But earlier, before her marriage, our new landlady had been companion, fellow traveller, wardrobe mistress, yes, friend, of Eleonora Duse and manifestly regarded that period as the crown of her career. Even at our first visit she spoke of it with animation. Numerous photographs of the great actress, with affectionate inscriptions, were displayed about the drawing room, and other souvenirs of their life together adorned the little tables and étagères. This cult of a so interesting past was calculated, or course, to heighten the advantages of the signora's present business. Nevertheless our pleasure and interest were quite genuine as we were conducted through the house by its owner and listened to her sonorous and staccato Tuscan voice relating anecdotes of that immortal mistress, depicting her suffering saintliness, her genius, her profound delicacy of feeling.

Thither, then, we moved our effects, to the dismay of the staff of the Grand Hotel, who, like all Italians, were very good to children. Our new quarters were retired and pleasant, we were within easy reach of the sea through the avenue of young plane trees that ran down to the esplanade. In the clean, cool dining room Signora Angiolieri daily served the soup with her own hands, the service was attentive and good, the table capital. We even discovered some Viennese acquaintances, and enjoyed chatting with them after luncheon, in front of the house. They, in their turn, were the means of our finding others—in short, all seemed for the best, and we were heartily glad of the change we had made. Nothing was now wanting to a holiday of the most gratifying kind.

And yet no proper gratification ensued. Perhaps the stupid occasion of our change of quarters pursued us to the new ones we had found. Personally, I admit that I do not easily forget these collisions with ordinary humanity, the naive misuse of power, the injustice, the sycophantic corruption. I dwelt upon the incident too much, it irritated me in retro-spect—quite futilely, of course, since such phenomena are only all too natural and all too much the rule. And we had not broken off relations with the Grand Hotel. The children were as friendly as ever there, the porter mended their toys, and we sometimes took tea in the garden. We even saw the Principessa. She would come out, with her firm and delicate tread, her lips emphatically corallined, to look after her children, playing under the supervision of their English governess. She did not dream that we were anywhere near, for so soon as she appeared in the offing we sternly forbade our little one even to clear his throat.

The heat—if I may bring it in evidence—was extreme. It was African. The power of the sun, directly one left the border of the indigo-blue wave, was so frightful, so relentless, that the mere thought of the few steps between the beach and luncheon was a burden, clad though one might be only in pajamas. Do you care for that sort of thing? Weeks on end? Yes, of course, it is proper to the south, it is classic weather, the sun of Homer, the climate wherein human culture came to flower—and all the rest of it. But after a while it is too much for me, I reach a point where I begin to find it dull. The burning void of the sky, day after day, weighs one down; the high coloration, the enormous naiveté of the unrefracted light—they do, I dare say, induce lightheartedness, a carefree mood born of immunity from downpours and other meteorological caprices. But slowly, slowly, there makes itself felt a lack: the deeper, more complex needs of the northern soul remain unsatisfied. You are left barren—even, it may be, in time, a little contemptuous. True, without that stupid busi-ness of the whooping cough I might not have been feeling these things. I was annoyed, very likely I wanted to feel them and so half-unconsciously seized upon an idea lying ready to hand to induce, or if not to induce, at least to justify and strengthen, my attitude. Up to this point, then, if you like, let us grant some ill will on our part. But the sea, and the mornings spent extended upon the fine sand in face of its eternal splendors—no, the sea could not conceivably induce such feelings. Yet it was nonetheless true that, despite all previous experience, we were not at home on the beach, we were not happy.

It was too soon, too soon. The beach, as I have said, was still in the hands of the middle-class native. It is a pleasing breed to look at, and among the young we saw much shapeliness and charm. Still, we were nec-essarily surrounded by a great deal of very average humanity—a middle-class mob, which, you will admit, is not more charming under this sun than under one's own native sky. The voices these women have! It was sometimes hard to believe that we were in the land that is the Western cradle of the art of song. *"Fuggièro!"* I can still hear that cry, as for twenty mornings long I heard it close behind me, breathy, full-throated, hideously stressed, with a harsh open *e*, uttered in accents of mechanical despair. *"Fuggièro! Rispondi almeno!"* Answer when I call you! The *sp* in *rispondi* was pronounced like *shp*, as Germans pronounce it; and this, on top of what I felt already, vexed my sensitive soul. The cry was addressed to a repulsive youngster whose sunburn had made disgusting raw sores on his shoulders. He outdid anything I have ever seen for ill-breeding, refractoriness, and temper and was a great coward to boot, putting the whole beach in an uproar, one day, because of his outrageous sensitiveness to the slightest pain. A sand crab had pinched his toe in the water, and the minute injury made him set up a cry of heroic proportions—the shout of an antique hero in his agony—that pierced one to the marrow and called up visions of some frightful tragedy. Evidently he considered himself not only wounded, but poisoned as well; he crawled out on the sand and lay in apparently intolerable anguish, groaning *"Ohi!"* and *"Ohimè!"* and threshing about with arms and legs to ward off his mother's tragic appeals and the questions of the bystanders. An audience gathered round. A doctor was fetched—the same who had pronounced objective judgment on our whooping cough—and here again acquitted himself like a man of science. Good-naturedly he reassured the boy, telling him that he was not hurt at all, he should simply go into the water again to relieve the smart. Instead of which, Fuggièro was borne off the beach, followed by a concourse of people. But he did not fail to appear next morning, nor did he leave off spoiling our children's sandcastles. Of course, always by accident. In short, a perfect terror.

And this twelve-year-old lad was prominent among the influences that, imperceptibly at first, combined to spoil our holiday and render it unwholesome. Somehow or other, there was a stiffness, a lack of innocent enjoyment. These people stood on their dignity—just why, and in what spirit, it was not easy at first to tell. They displayed much self-respectingness; toward each other and toward the foreigner their bearing was that of a person newly conscious of a sense of honor. And wherefore? Gradually we realized the political implications and understood that we were in the presence of a national ideal. The beach, in fact, was alive with patriotic children—a phenomenon as unnatural as it was depressing. Children are a human species and a society apart, a nation of their own, so to speak. On the basis of their common form of life, they find each other out with the greatest ease, no matter how different their small vocabularies. Ours soon played with natives and foreigners alike. Yet they were plainly both puzzled and disappointed at times. There were wounded sensibilities, displays of assertiveness—or rather hardly assertiveness, for it was too self-conscious and too didactic to deserve the name. There were quarrels over flags, disputes about authority and precedence. Grownups joined in, not so much to pacify as to render judgment and enunciate principles.

Phrases were dropped about the greatness and dignity of Italy, solemn phrases that spoilt the fun. We saw our two little ones retreat, puzzled and hurt, and were put to it to explain the situation. These people, we told them, were just passing through a certain stage, something rather like an illness, perhaps; not very pleasant, but probably unavoidable.

We had only our own carelessness to thank that we came to blows in the end with this "stage"—which, after all, we had seen and sized up long before now. Yes, it came to another "cross-purposes," so evidently the earlier ones had not been sheer accident. In a word, we became an offense to the public morals. Our small daughter—eight years old, but in physical development a good year younger and thin as a chicken—had had a good long bathe and gone playing in the warm sun in her wet costume. We told her that she might take off her bathing suit, which was stiff with sand, rinse it in the sea, and put it on again, after which she must take care to keep it cleaner. Off goes the costume and she runs down naked to the sea, rinses her little jersey, and comes back. Ought we to have foreseen the outburst of anger and resentment that her conduct, and thus our conduct, called forth? Without delivering a homily on the subject, I may say that in the last decade our attitude toward the nude body and our feelings regarding it have undergone, all over the world, a fundamental change. There are things we "never think about" anymore, and among them is the freedom we had permitted to this by no means provocative little childish body. But in these parts it was taken as a challenge. The patriotic children hooted. Fuggièro whistled on his fingers. The sudden buzz of conversation among the grown people in our neighborhood boded no good. A gentleman in city togs, with a not very apropos bowler hat on the back of his head, was assuring his outraged womenfolk that he proposed to take punitive measures; he stepped up to us, and a philippic descended on our unworthy heads, in which all the emotionalism of the sense-loving south spoke in the service of morality and discipline. The offense against decency of which we had been guilty was, he said, the more to be condemned because it was also a gross ingratitude and an insulting breach of his country's hospitality. We had criminally injured not only the letter and spirit of the public bathing regulations, but also the honor of Italy; he, the gentleman in the city togs, knew how to defend that honor and proposed to see to it that our offense against the national dignity should not go unpunished.

We did our best, bowing respectfully, to give ear to this eloquence. To contradict the man, overheated as he was, would probably be to fall from one error into another. On the tips of our tongues we had various answers: as, that the word "hospitality," in its strictest sense, was not quite the right one, taking all the circumstances into consideration. We were not literally the guests of Italy, but of Signora Angiolieri, who had assumed the role of dispenser of hospitality some years ago on laying down that of familiar friend to Eleonora Duse. We longed to say that surely this beautiful country had not sunk so low as to be reduced to a state of hypersensitive prudishness. But we confined ourselves to assuring the gentleman that any lack of respect, any provocation on our parts, had been the furthest from our thoughts. And as a mitigating circumstance we pointed out the tender age and physical slightness of the little culprit. In vain. Our protests were waved away, he did not believe in them; our defense would not hold water. We must be made an example of. The authorities were notified, by telephone, I believe, and their representative appeared on the beach. He said the case was "*molto grave.*" We had to go with him to the *municipio* up in the *piazza*, where a higher official confirmed the previous verdict of "*molto grave,*" launched into a stream of the usual didactic phrases—the selfsame tune and words as the man in the bowler hat—and levied a fine and ransom of fifty lire. We felt that the adventure must willy-nilly be worth to us this much of a contribution to the economy of the Italian government; paid, and left. Ought we not at this point to have left Torre as well?

If only we had! We should thus have escaped that fatal Cipolla. But circumstances combined to prevent us from making up our minds to a change. A certain poet says that it is indolence that makes us endure uncomfortable situations. The aperçu may serve as an explanation for our inaction. Anyhow, one dislikes voiding the field immediately upon such an event. Especially if sympathy from other quarters encourages one to defy it. And in the Villa Eleonora they pronounced as with one voice upon the injustice of our punishment. Some Italian after-dinner acquaintances found that the episode put their country in a very bad light, and proposed taking the man in the bowler hat to task, as one fellow citizen to another. But the next day he and his party had vanished from the beach. Not on our account, of course. Though it might be that the consciousness of his impending departure had added energy to his rebuke; in any case his going was a relief. And, furthermore, we stayed because our stay had by now become remarkable in our own eyes, which is worth something in itself, quite apart from the comfort or discomfort involved. Shall we strike sail, avoid a certain experience so soon as it seems not expressly calculated to increase our enjoyment or our self-esteem? Shall we go away whenever life looks like turning in the slightest uncanny, or not quite normal, or even rather painful and mortifying? No, surely not. Rather stay and look matters in the face, brave them out; perhaps precisely in so doing lies a lesson for us to learn. We stayed on and reaped as the awful reward of our constancy the unholy and staggering experience with Cipolla.

I have not mentioned that the after season had begun, almost on the very day we were disciplined by the city authorities. The worshipful gentleman in the bowler hat, our denouncer, was not the only person to leave the resort. There was a regular exodus, on every hand you saw luggage carts on their way to the station. The beach denationalized itself. Life in Torre, in the cafés and the pinetas, became more homelike and more European. Very likely we might even have eaten at a table in the glass veranda, but we refrained, being content at Signora Angiolieri's—as content, that is, as our evil star would let us be. But at the same time with this turn for the better came a change in the weather: almost to an hour it showed itself in harmony with the holiday calendar of the general public. The sky was overcast; not that it grew any cooler, but the unclouded heat of the entire eighteen days since our arrival, and probably long before that, gave place to a stifling sirocco air, while from time to time a little ineffectual rain sprinkled the velvety surface of the beach. Add to which, that two-thirds of our intended stay at Torre had passed. The colorless, lazy sea, with sluggish jellyfish floating in its shallows, was at least a change. And it would have been silly to feel retrospective longings after a sun that had caused us so many sighs when it burned down in all its arrogant power.

At this juncture, then, it was that Cipolla announced himself. Cavaliere Cipolla he was called on the posters that appeared one day stuck up everywhere, even in the dining room of Pensione Eleonora. A traveling virtuoso, an entertainer, *"forzatore, illusionista, prestidigatore,"* as he called himself, who proposed to wait upon the highly respectable population of Torre di Venere with a display of extraordinary phenomena of a mysterious and staggering kind. A conjuror! The bare announcement was enough to turn our children's heads. They had never seen anything of the sort, and now our present holiday was to afford them this new excitement. From that moment on they besieged us with prayers to take tickets for the performance. We had doubts, from the first, on the score of the lateness of the hour, nine o'clock; but gave way, in the idea that we might see a little of what Cipolla had to offer, probably no great matter, and then go home. Besides, of course, the children could sleep late next day. We bought four tickets of Signora Angiolieri herself, she having taken a number of the stalls on commission to sell them to her guests. She could not vouch for the man's performance, and we had no great expectations. But we were conscious of a need for diversion, and the children's violent curiosity proved catching.

The Cavaliere's performance was to take place in a hall where during the season there had been a cinema with a weekly program. We had never been there. You reached it by following the main street under the wall of the *"palazzo,"* a ruin with a "For sale" sign, that suggested a castle and had obviously been built in lordlier days. In the same street were the chemist, the hairdresser, and all the better shops; it led, so to speak, from the feudal past the bourgeois into the proletarian, for it ended off between two rows of poor fishing huts, where old women sat mending nets before the doors. And here, among the proletariat, was the hall, not much more, actually, than a wooden shed, though a large one, with a turreted entrance, plastered on either side with layers of gay placards. Some while after dinner, then, on the appointed evening, we wended our way thither in the dark, the children dressed in their best and blissful with the sense of so much irregularity. It was sultry, as it had been for days; there was heat lightning now and then, and a little rain; we proceeded under umbrellas. It took us a quarter of an hour.

Our tickets were collected at the entrance, our places we had to find ourselves. They were in the third row left, and as we sat down we saw that, late though the hour was for the performance, it was to be interpreted with even more laxity. Only very slowly did an audience—who seemed to be relied upon to come late—begin to fill the stalls. These comprised the whole auditorium; there were no boxes. This tardiness gave us some concern. The children's cheeks were already flushed as much with fatigue as with excitement. But even when we entered, the standing room at the back and in the side aisles was already well occupied. There stood the manhood of Torre di Venere, all and sundry, fisherfolk, rough-and-ready youths with bare forearms crossed over their striped jerseys. We were well pleased with the presence of this native assemblage, which always adds color and animation to occasions like the present; and the children were frankly delighted. For they had friends among these people— acquaintances picked up on afternoon strolls to the further ends of the beach. We would be turning homeward, at the hour when the sun dropped into the sea, spent with the huge effort it had made and gilding with reddish gold the oncoming surf; and we would come upon bare-legged fisherfolk standing in rows, bracing and hauling with long-drawn cries as they drew in the nets and harvested in dripping baskets their catch, often so scanty, of *frutta di mare*. The children looked on, helped to pull, brought out their little stock of Italian words, made friends. So now they exchanged nods with the standing-room clientele; there was Guiscardo, there Antonio, they knew them by name and waved and called across in half-whispers, getting answering nods and smiles that displayed rows of healthy white teeth. Look, there is even Mario, Mario from the Esquisito, who brings us the chocolate. He wants to see the conjuror, too, and he must have come early, for he is almost in front; but he does not see us, he is not paying attention; that is a way he has, even though he is a waiter. So we wave instead to the man who lets out the little boats on the beach; he is there too, standing at the back.

It had got to a quarter past nine, it got to almost half past. It was natural that we should be nervous. When would the children get to bed?

It had been a mistake to bring them, for now it would be very hard to suggest breaking off their enjoyment before it had got well under way. The stalls had filled in time; all Torre, apparently, was there: the guests of the Grand Hotel, the guests of Villa Eleonora, familiar faces from the beach. We heard English and German and the sort of French that Romanians speak with Italians. Madame Angiolieri herself sat two rows behind us, with her quiet, bald-headed spouse, who kept stroking his moustache with the two middle fingers of his right hand. Everybody had come late, but nobody too late. Cipolla made us wait for him.

He made us wait. That is probably the way to put it. He heightened the suspense by his delay in appearing. And we could see the point of this, too—only not when it was carried to extremes. Toward half past nine the audience began to clap—an amiable way of expressing justifiable impatience, evincing as it does an eagerness to applaud. For the little ones, this was a joy in itself—all children love to clap. From the popular sphere came loud cries of "*Pronti!*" "*Cominciamo!*" And lo, it seemed now as easy to begin as before it had been hard. A gong sounded, greeted by the standing rows with a many-voiced "Ah-h!" and the curtains parted. They revealed a platform furnished more like a schoolroom than like the theater of a conjuring performance—largely because of the blackboard in the left foreground. There was a common yellow hat stand, a few ordinary straw-bottomed chairs, and further back a little round table holding a water carafe and glass, also a tray with a liqueur glass and a flask of pale yellow liquid. We had still a few seconds of time to let these things sink in. Then, with no darkening of the house, Cavaliere Cipolla made his entry.

He came forward with a rapid step that expressed his eagerness to appear before his public and gave rise to the illusion that he had already come a long way to put himself at their service—whereas, of course, he had only been standing in the wings. His costume supported the fiction. A man of an age hard to determine, but by no means young; with a sharp, ravaged face, piercing eyes, compressed lips, small black waxed moustache, and a so-called imperial in the curve between mouth and chin. He was dressed for the street with a sort of complicated evening elegance, in a wide black pelerine with velvet collar and satin lining; which, in the hampered state of his arms, he held together in front with his white-gloved hands. He had a white scarf round his neck; a top hat with a curving brim sat far back on his head. Perhaps more than anywhere else the eighteenth century is still alive in Italy, and with it the charlatan and mountebank type so characteristic of the period. Only there, at any rate, does one still encounter really well-preserved specimens. Cipolla had in his whole appearance much of the historic type; his very clothes helped to conjure up the traditional figure with its blatantly, fantastically foppish air. His pretentious costume sat upon him, or rather hung upon him, most curiously, being in one place drawn too tight, in another a mass of awkward folds. There was something not quite in order about his figure, both front and back—that was plain later on. But I must emphasize the fact that there was not a trace of personal jocularity or clownishness in his pose, manner, or behavior. On the contrary, there was complete seriousness, an absence of any humourous appeal; occasionally even a cross-grained pride, along with that curious, self-satisfied air so characteristic of the deformed. None of all this, however, prevented his appearance from being greeted with laughter from more than one quarter of the hall.

All the eagerness had left his manner. The swift entry had been merely an expression of energy, not of zeal. Standing at the footlights he negligently drew off his gloves, to display long yellow hands, one of them adorned with a seal ring with a lapis lazuli in a high setting. As he stood there, his small hard eyes, with flabby pouches beneath them, roved appraisingly about the hall, not quickly, rather in a considered examination, pausing here and there upon a face with his lips clipped together, not speaking a word. Then with a display of skill as surprising as it was casual, he rolled his gloves into a ball and tossed them across a considerable distance into the glass on the table. Next from an inner pocket he drew forth a packet of cigarettes; you could see by the wrapper that they were the cheapest sort the government sells. With his fingertips he pulled out a cigarette and lighted it, without looking, from a quick-firing benzine lighter. He drew the smoke deep into his lungs and let it out again, tapping his foot, with both lips drawn in an arrogant grimace and the gray smoke streaming out between broken and saw-edged teeth.

With a keenness equal to his own his audience eyed him. The youths at the rear scowled as they peered at this cocksure creature to search out his secret weaknesses. He betrayed none. In fetching out and putting back the cigarettes his clothes got in his way. He had to turn back his pelerine, and in so doing revealed a riding whip with a silver claw handle that hung by a leather thong from his left forearm and looked decidedly out of place. You could see that he had on not evening clothes but a frock coat, and under this, as he lifted it to get at his pocket, could be seen a striped sash worn about the body. Somebody behind me whispered that this sash went with his title of Cavaliere. I give the information for what it may be worth—personally, I never heard that the title carried such insignia with it. Perhaps the sash was sheer pose, like the way he stood there, without a word, casually and arrogantly puffing smoke into his audience's face.

People laughed, as I said. The merriment had become almost general when somebody in the standing seats, in a loud, dry voice, remarked: "*Buona sera.*"

Cipolla cocked his head. "Who was that?" asked he, as though he had been dared. "Who was that just spoke? Well? First so bold and now so modest? *Paura*, eh?" He spoke with a rather high, asthmatic voice, which yet had a metallic quality. He waited.

"That was me," a youth at the rear broke into the stillness, seeing himself thus challenged. He was not far from us, a handsome fellow in a woollen shirt, with his coat hanging over one shoulder. He wore his curly, wiry hair in a high, disheveled mop, the style affected by the youth of the awakened fatherland; it gave him an African appearance that rather spoiled his looks. "*Bè!* That was me. It was your business to say it first, but I was trying to be friendly."

More laughter. The chap had a tongue in his head. "*Ha sciolto la scilin-guágnolo*," I heard near me. After all, the retort was deserved.

"Ah, bravo!" answered Cipolla. " I like you, *giovanotto*. Trust me, I've had my eye on you for some time. People like you are just in my line. I can use them. And you are the pick of the lot, that's plain to see. You do what you like. Or is it possible you have ever not done what you liked—or even, maybe, what you didn't like? What somebody else liked, in short? Hark ye, my friend, that might be a pleasant change for you, to divide up the willing and the doing and stop tackling both jobs at once. Division of labor, *sistema americano, sa'*! For instance, suppose you were to show your tongue to this select and honorable audience here—your whole tongue, right down to the roots?"

"No, I won't," said the youth, hostilely. "Sticking out your tongue shows a bad bringing-up."

"Nothing of the sort," retorted Cipolla. "You would only be *doing* it. With all due respect to your bringing-up, I suggest that before I count ten, you will perform a right turn and stick out your tongue at the company here further than you knew yourself that you could stick it out."

He gazed at the youth, and his piercing eyes seemed to sink deeper into their sockets. "*Uno!*" said he. He had let his riding whip slide down his arm and made it whistle once through the air. The boy faced about and put out his tongue, so long, so extendedly, that you could see it was the very uttermost in tongue that he had to offer. Then turned back, stony-faced, to his former position.

"That was me," mocked Cipolla, with a jerk of his head toward the youth. "*Bè!* That was me." Leaving the audience to enjoy its sensations, he turned toward the little round table, lifted the bottle, poured out a small glass of what was obviously cognac, and tipped it up with a practiced hand.

The children laughed with all their hearts. They had understood practically nothing of what had been said, but it pleased them hugely that something so funny should happen, straightaway, between that queer man up there and somebody out of the audience. They had no preconception of what an "evening" would be like and were quite ready to find this a priceless beginning. As for us, we exchanged a glance and I remember that involuntarily I made with my lips the sound that Cipolla's whip had made when it cut the air. For the rest, it was plain that people did not know what to make of a preposterous beginning like this to a sleight-of-hand performance. They could not see why the *giovanotto*, who after all in a way had been their spokesman, should suddenly have turned on them to vent his incivility. They felt that he had behaved like a silly ass and withdrew their countenances from him in favor of the artist, who now came back from his refreshment table and addressed them as follows:

"Ladies and gentlemen," said he, in his wheezing, metallic voice, "you saw just now that I was rather sensitive on the score of the rebuke this hopeful young linguist saw fit to give me"—"*questo linguista di belle speranze*" was what he said, and we all laughed at the pun. "I am a man who sets some store by himself, you may take it from me. And I see no point in being wished a good evening unless it is done courteously and in all seriousness. For anything else there is no occasion. When a man wishes me a good evening he wishes himself one, for the audience will have one only if I do. So this lady-killer of Torre di Venere" (another thrust) "did well to testify that I have one tonight and that I can dispense with any wishes of his in the matter. I can boast of having good evenings almost without exception. One not so good does come my way now and again, but very seldom. My calling is hard and my health not of the best. I have a little physical defect that prevented me from doing my bit in the war for the greater glory of the fatherland. It is perforce with my mental and spiritual parts that I conquer life—which after all only means conquering oneself. And I flatter myself that my achievements have aroused interest and respect among the educated public. The leading newspapers have lauded me, the *Corriere della Sera* did me the courtesy of calling me a phenomenon, and in Rome the brother of the *Duce* honored me by his presence at one of my evenings. I should not have thought that in a relatively less important place" (laughter here, at the expense of poor little Torre) "I should have to give up the small personal habits that brilliant and elevated audiences had been ready to overlook. Nor did I think I had to stand being heckled by a person who seems to have been rather spoilt by the favors of the fair sex." All this of course at the expense of the youth whom Cipolla never tired of presenting in the guise of *donnaiuolo* and rustic Don Juan. His persistent thin-skinnedness and animosity were in striking contrast to the self-confidence and the worldly success he boasted of. One might have assumed that the *giovanotto* was merely the chosen butt of Cipolla's customary professional sallies, had not the very pointed witticisms betrayed a genuine antagonism. No one looking at the physical parts of the two men need have been at a loss for the explanation, even if the deformed man had not constantly played on the other's supposed success with the fair sex. "Well," Cipolla went on, "before beginning our entertainment this evening, perhaps you will permit me to make myself comfortable."

And he went toward the hat stand to take off his things.

*"Parla benissimo,"* asserted somebody in our neighborhood. So far, the man had done nothing; but what he had said was accepted as an achievement, by means of that he had made an impression. Among southern people's speech is a constituent part of the pleasure of living, it enjoys far livelier social esteem than in the north. That national cement, the mother tongue, is paid symbolic honors down here, and there is something blithely symbolical in the pleasure people take in their respect for its forms and phonetics. They enjoy speaking, they enjoy listening; and they listen with discrimination. For the way a man speaks serves as a measure of his personal rank; carelessness and clumsiness are greeted with scorn, elegance and mastery are rewarded with social éclat. Wherefore the small man too, where it is a question of getting his effect, chooses his phrase nicely and turns it with care. On this count, then, at least, Cipolla had won his audience; though he by no means belonged to the class of men that the Italian, in a singular mixture of moral and aesthetic judgments, labels *"simpatico."*

After removing his hat, scarf, and mantle he came to the front of the stage, settling his coat, pulling down his cuffs with their large cuff-buttons, adjusting his absurd sash. He had very ugly hair; the top of his head, that is, was almost bald, while a narrow, black-varnished frizz of curls ran from front to back as though stuck on; the side hair, likewise blackened, was brushed forward to the corners of the eyes—it was, in short, the hairdressing of an old-fashioned circus director, fantastic, but entirely suited to his outmoded personal type and worn with so much assurance as to take the edge off the public's sense of humor. The little physical defect of which he had warned us was now all too visible, though the nature of it was even now not very clear: the chest was too high, as is usual in such cases; but the corresponding malformation of the back did not sit between the shoulders, it took the form of a sort of hips or buttocks hump, which did not indeed hinder his movements but gave him a grotesque and dipping stride at every step he took. However, by mentioning his deformity beforehand he had broken the shock of it, and a delicate propriety of feeling appeared to reign throughout the hall.

"At your service," said Cipolla. "With your kind permission, we will begin the evening with some arithmetical tests."

Arithmetic? That did not sound much like sleight-of-hand. We began to have our suspicions that the man was sailing under a false flag, only we did not yet know which was the right one. I felt sorry on the children's account; but for the moment they were content simply to be there.

The numerical test that Cipolla now introduced was as simple as it was baffling. He began by fastening a piece of paper to the upper right-hand corner of the blackboard; then lifting it up, he wrote something underneath. He talked all the while, relieving the dryness of his offering by a constant flow of words, and showed himself a practiced speaker, never at a loss for conversational turns of phrase. It was in keeping with the nature of his performance, and at the same time vastly entertained the children, that he went on to eliminate the gap between stage and audience, which had already been bridged over by the curious skirmish with the fisher lad: he had representatives from the audience mount the stage, and himself descended the wooden steps to seek personal contact with his public. And again, with individuals, he fell into his former taunting tone. I do not know how far that was a deliberate feature of his system; he preserved a serious, even a peevish air, but his audience, at least the more popular section, seemed convinced that that was all part of the game. So then, after he had written something and covered the writing by the paper, he desired that two persons should come up on the platform and help to perform the calculations. They would not be difficult, even for people not clever at figures. As usual, nobody volunteered, and Cipolla took care not to molest the more select portion of his audience. He kept to the populace. Turning to two sturdy young louts standing behind us, he beckoned them to the front, encouraging and scolding by turns. They should not stand there gaping, he said, unwilling to oblige the company. Actually, he got them in motion; with clumsy tread they came down the middle aisle, climbed the steps, and stood in front of the blackboard, grinning sheepishly at their comrades' shouts and applause. Cipolla joked with them for a few minutes, praised their heroic firmness of limb and the size of their hands, so well calculated to do this service for the public. Then he handed one of them the chalk and told him to write down the numbers as they were called out. But now the creature declared that he could not write! *"Non so scrivere,"* said he in his gruff voice, and his companion added that neither did he.

God knows whether they told the truth or whether they wanted to make game of Cipolla. Anyhow, the latter was far from sharing the general merriment that their confession aroused. He was insulted and disgusted. He sat there on a straw-bottomed chair in the center of the stage with his legs crossed, smoking a fresh cigarette out of his cheap packet; obviously it tasted the better for the cognac he had indulged in while the yokels were stumping up the steps. Again he inhaled the smoke and let it stream out between curling lips. Swinging his legs, with his gaze sternly averted from the two shamelessly chuckling creatures and from the audience as well, he stared into space as one who withdraws himself and his dignity from the contemplation of an utterly despicable phenomenon.

"Scandalous," said he, in a sort of icy snarl. "Go back to your places! In Italy everybody can write—in all her greatness there is no room for ignorance and unenlightenment. To accuse her of them, in the hearing of this international company, is a cheap joke, in which you yourselves cut a very poor figure and humiliate the government and the whole country as well. If it is true that Torre di Venere is indeed the last refuge of such ignorance, then I must blush to have visited the place—being, as I already was, aware of its inferiority to Rome in more than one respect—"

Here Cipolla was interrupted by the youth with the Nubian coiffure and his jacket across his shoulder. His fighting spirit, as we now saw, had only abdicated temporarily, and he now flung himself into the breach in defense of his native heath. "That will do," he said loudly. "That's enough jokes about Torre. We all come from the place and we won't stand strangers making fun of it. These two chaps are our friends. Maybe they are no scholars, but even so they may be straighter than some folks in the room who are so free with their boasts about Rome, though they did not build it either."

That was capital. The young man had certainly cut his eyeteeth. And this sort of spectacle was good fun, even though it still further delayed the regular performance. It is always fascinating to listen to an altercation. Some people it simply amuses, they take a sort of killjoy pleasure in not being principals. Others feel upset and uneasy, and my sympathies are with these latter, although on the present occasion I was under the impression that all this was part of the show—the analphabetic yokels no less than the *giovanotto* with the jacket. The children listened well pleased. They understood not at all, but the sound of the voices made them hold their breath. So this was a "magic evening"—at least it was the kind they have in Italy. They expressly found it "lovely."

Cipolla had stood up and with two of his scooping strides was at the footlights.

"Well, well, see who's here!" said he with grim cordiality. "An old acquaintance! A young man with his heart at the end of his tongue" (he used the word *linguaccia*, which means a coated tongue, and gave rise to much hilarity). "That will do, my friends," he turned to the yokels. "I do not need you now, I have business with this deserving young man here, *con questo torregiano di Venere*, this tower of Venus, who no doubt expects the gratitude of the fair as a reward for his prowess—"

"*Ah, non scherziamo!* We're talking earnest," cried out the youth. His eyes flashed, and he actually made as though to pull off his jacket and proceed to direct methods of settlement.

Cipolla did not take him too seriously. We had exchanged apprehensive glances; but he was dealing with a fellow countryman and had his native soil beneath his feet. He kept quite cool and showed complete mastery of the situation. He looked at his audience, smiled, and made a sideways motion of the head toward the young cockerel as though calling the public to witness how the man's bumptiousness only served to betray the simplicity of his mind. And then, for the second time, something strange happened, which set Cipolla's calm superiority in an uncanny light, and in some mysterious and irritating way turned all the explosiveness latent in the air into a matter for laughter.

Cipolla drew still nearer to the fellow, looking him in the eye with a peculiar gaze. He even came halfway down the steps that led into the auditorium on our left, so that he stood directly in front of the trouble-maker, on slightly higher ground. The riding whip hung from his arm.

"My son, you do not feel much like joking," he said. "It is only too natural, for anyone can see that you are not feeling too well. Even your tongue, which leaves something to be desired on the score of cleanliness, indicates acute disorder of the gastric system. An evening entertainment is no place for people in your state; you yourself, I can tell, were of several minds whether you would not do better to put on a flannel bandage and go to bed. It was not good judgment to drink so much of that very sour white wine this afternoon. Now you have such a colic you would like to double up with the pain. Go ahead, don't be embarrassed. There is a distinct relief that comes from bending over, in cases of intestinal cramp."

He spoke thus, word for word, with quiet impressiveness and a kind of stern sympathy, and his eyes, plunged the while deep in the young man's, seemed to grow very tired and at the same time burning above their enlarged tear ducts—they were the strangest eyes, you could tell that not manly pride alone was preventing the young adversary from withdrawing his gaze. And presently, indeed, all trace of its former arrogance was gone from the bronzed young face. He looked open-mouthed at the Cavaliere and the open mouth was drawn in a rueful smile.

"Double over," repeated Cipolla. "What else can you do? With a colic like that you *must* bend. Surely you will not struggle against the perfor-mance of a perfectly natural action just because somebody suggests it to you?"

Slowly the youth lifted his forearms, folded and squeezed them across his body; it turned a little sideways, then bent, lower and lower, the feet shifted, the knees turned inward, until he had become a picture of writh-ing pain, until he all but groveled upon the ground. Cipolla let him stand for some seconds thus, then made a short cut through the air with his whip and went with his scooping stride back to the little table, where he poured himself out a cognac.

"*Il boit beaucoup*," asserted a lady behind us. Was that the only thing that struck her? We could not tell how far the audience grasped the situation. The fellow was standing upright again, with a sheepish grin—he looked as though he scarcely knew how it had all happened. The scene had been followed with tense interest and applauded at the end; there were shouts of "*Bravo, Cipolla!*" and "*Bravo, giovanotto!*" Apparently the issue of the duel was not looked upon as a personal defeat for the young man. Rather the audience encouraged him as one does an actor who succeeds in an unsympathetic role. Certainly his way of screwing himself up with cramp had been highly picturesque, its appeal was directly calculated to impress the gallery—in short, a fine dramatic performance. But I am not sure how far the audience was moved by that natural tactfulness in which the south excels, or how far it penetrated into the nature of what was going on.

The Cavaliere, refreshed, had lighted another cigarette. The numerical tests might now proceed. A young man was easily found in the back row who was willing to write down on the blackboard the numbers as they were dictated to him. Him too we knew; the whole entertainment had taken on an intimate character through our acquaintance with so many of the actors. This was the man who worked at the greengrocer's in the main street; he had served us several times, with neatness and dispatch. He wielded the chalk and clerkly confidence, while Cipolla descended to our level and walked with his deformed gait through the audience, collecting numbers as they were given, in two, three, and four places, and calling them out to the grocer's assistant, who wrote them down in a column. In all this, everything on both sides was calculated to amuse, with its jokes and its oratorical asides. The artist could not fail to hit on foreigners, who were not ready with their figures, and with them he was elaborately patient and chivalrous, to the great amusement of the natives, whom he reduced to confusion in their turn, by making them translate numbers that were given in English or French. Some people gave dates concerned with great events in Italian history. Cipolla took them up at once and made patriotic comments. Somebody shouted "Number one!" The Cavaliere, incensed at this as at every attempt to make game of him, retorted over his shoulder that he could not take less than two-place figures. Whereupon another joker cried out "Number two!" and was greeted with the applause and laughter that every reference to natural functions is sure to win among southerners.

When fifteen numbers stood in a long straggling row on the board, Cipolla called for a general adding match. Ready reckoners might add in their heads, but pencil and paper were not forbidden. Cipolla, while the work went on, sat on his chair near the blackboard, smoked and grimaced, with the complacent, pompous air cripples so often have. The five-place addition was soon done. Somebody announced the answer, somebody else confirmed it, a third had arrived at a slightly different result, but the fourth agreed with the first and second. Cipolla got up, tapped some ash from his coat, and lifted the paper at the upper right-hand corner of the board to display the writing. The correct answer, a sum close on a million, stood there; he had written it down beforehand.

Astonishment, and loud applause. The children were overwhelmed. How had he done that, they wanted to know. We told them it was a trick, not easily explainable offhand. In short, the man was a conjuror. This was what a sleight-of-hand evening was like, so now they knew. First the fisherman had cramp, and then the right answer was written down beforehand—it was all simply glorious, and we saw with dismay that despite the hot eyes and the hand of the clock at almost half past ten, it would be very hard to get them away. There would be tears. And yet it was plain that this magician did not "magick"—at least not in the accepted sense, of manual dexterity—and that the entertainment was not at all suitable for children. Again, I do not know, either, what the audience really thought. Obviously there was grave doubt whether its answers had been given of "free choice"; here and there an individual might have answered of his own motion, but on the whole Cipolla certainly selected his people and thus kept the whole procedure in his own hands and directed it toward the given result. Even so, one had to admire the quickness of his calculations, however much one felt disinclined to admire anything else about the performance. Then his patriotism, his irritable sense of dignity—the Cavaliere's own countrymen might feel in their element with all that and continue in a laughing mood; but the combination certainly gave us outsiders food for thought.

Cipolla himself saw to it—though without giving them a name—that the nature of his powers should be clear beyond a doubt to even the least-instructed person. He alluded to them, of course, in his talk—and he talked without stopping—but only in vague, boastful, self-advertising phrases. He went on awhile with experiments on the same lines as the first, merely making them more complicated by introducing operations in multiplying, subtracting, and dividing; then he simplified them to the last degree in order to bring out the method. He simply had numbers "guessed" that were previously written under the paper; and the guess was nearly always right. One guesser admitted that he had had in mind to give a certain number, when Cipolla's whip went whistling through the air, and a quite different one slipped out, which proved to be the "right" one. Cipolla's shoulders shook. He pretended admiration for the powers of the people he questioned. But in all his compliments there was something fleering and derogatory; the victims could scarcely have relished them much, although they smiled, and although they might easily have set down some part of the applause to their own credit. Moreover, I had not the impression that the artist was popular with his public. A certain ill will and reluctance were in the air, but courtesy kept such feelings in check, as did Cipolla's competency and his stern self-confidence. Even the riding whip, I think, did much to keep rebellion from becoming overt.

From tricks with numbers he passed to tricks with cards. There were two packs, which he drew out of his pockets, and so much I still remember, that the basis of the tricks he played with them was as follows: from the first pack he drew three cards and thrust them without looking at them inside his coat. Another person then drew three out of the second pack, and these turned out to be the same as the first three—not invariably all the three, for it did happen that only two were the same. But in the majority of cases Cipolla triumphed, showing his three cards with a little bow in acknowledgment of the applause with which his audience conceded his possession of strange powers—strange whether for good or evil. A young man in the front row, to our right, an Italian, with proud, finely chiseled features, rose up and said that he intended to assert his own will in his choice and consciously to resist any influence, of whatever sort. Under these circumstances, what did Cipolla think would be the result? "You will," answered the Cavaliere, "make my task somewhat more difficult thereby. As for the result, your resistance will not alter it in the least. Freedom exists, and also the will exists; but freedom of the will does not exist, for a will that aims at its own freedom aims at the unknown. You are free to draw or not to draw. But if you draw, you will draw the right cards—the more certainly, the more willfully obstinate your behavior."

One must admit that he could not have chosen his words better, to trouble the waters and confuse the mind. The refractory youth hesitated before drawing. Then he pulled out a card and at once demanded to see if it was among the chosen three. "But why?" queried Cipolla. "Why do things by halves?" Then, as the other defiantly insisted, "*E servito*," said the juggler, with a gesture of exaggerated servility; and held out the three cards fanwise, without looking at them himself. The left-hand card was the one drawn.

Amid general applause, the apostle of freedom sat down. How far Cipolla employed small tricks and manual dexterity to help out his natural talents, the deuce only knew. But even without them the result would have been the same: the curiosity of the entire audience was unbounded and universal, everybody both enjoyed the amazing character of the entertainment and unanimously conceded the professional skill of the performer. "*Lavora bene*," we heard, here and there in our neighborhood; it signified the triumph of objective judgment over antipathy and repressed resentment.

After his last, incomplete, yet so much the more telling success, Cipolla had at once fortified himself with another cognac. Truly he did "drink a lot," and the fact made a bad impression. But obviously he needed the liquor and the cigarettes for the replenishment of his energy, upon which, as he himself said, heavy demands were made in all directions. Certainly in the intervals he looked very ill, exhausted and hollow-eyed. Then the little glassful would redress the balance, and the flow of lively, self-confident chatter run on, while the smoke he inhaled gushed out gray from his lungs. I clearly recall that he passed from the card tricks to parlor games—the kind based on certain powers that in human nature are higher or else lower than human reason: on intuition and "magnetic" transmission; in short, upon a low type of manifestation. What I do not remember is the precise order things came in. And I will not bore you with a description of these experiments; everybody knows them, everybody has at one time or another taken part in this finding of hidden articles, this blind carrying out of a series of acts, directed by a force that proceeds from organism to organism by unexplored paths. Everybody has had his little glimpse into the equivocal, impure, inexplicable nature of the occult, has been conscious of both curiosity and contempt, has shaken his head over the human tendency of those who deal in it to help themselves out with humbuggery, though, after all, the humbuggery is no disproof whatever of the genuineness of the other elements in the dubious amalgam. I can only say here that each single circumstance gains in weight and the whole greatly in impressiveness when it is a man like Cipolla who is the chief actor and guiding spirit in the sinister business. He sat smoking at the rear of the stage, his back to the audience while they conferred. The object passed from hand to hand which it was his task to find, with which he was to perform some action agreed upon beforehand. Then he would start to move zigzag through the hall, with his head thrown back and one hand outstretched, the other clasped in that of a guide who was in the secret but enjoined to keep himself perfectly passive, with his thoughts directed upon the agreed goal. Cipolla moved with the bearing typical in these experiments: now groping upon a false start, now with a quick forward thrust, now pausing as though to listen and by sudden inspiration correcting his course. The roles seemed reversed, the stream of influence was moving in the contrary direction, as the artist himself pointed out, in his ceaseless flow of discourse. The suffering, receptive, performing part was now his, the will he had before imposed on others was shut out, he acted in obedience to a voiceless common will that was in the air. But he made it perfectly clear that it all came to the same thing. The capacity for self-surrender, he said, for becoming a tool, for the most unconditional and utter self-abnegation, was but the reverse side of that other power to will and to command. Commanding and obeying formed together one single principle, one indissoluble unity; he who knew how to obey knew also how to command, and conversely; the one idea was comprehended in the other, as people and leader were comprehended in one another. But that which was *done*, the highly exacting and exhausting performance, was in every case his, the leader's and mover's, in whom the will became obedience, the obedience will, whose person was the cradle and womb of both, and who thus suffered enormous hardship. Repeatedly he emphasized the fact that his lot was a hard one—presumably to account for his need of stimulant and his frequent recourse to the little glass.

Thus he groped his way forward, like a blind seer, led and sustained by the mysterious common will. He drew a pin set with a stone out of its hiding place in an Englishwoman's shoe, carried it, halting and pressing on by turns, to another lady—Signora Angiolieri—and handed it to her on bended knee, with the words it had been agreed he was to utter. "I present you with this in token of my respect," was the sentence. Their sense was obvious, but the words themselves not easy to hit upon, for the reason that they had been agreed on in French; the language complication seemed to us a little malicious, implying as it did a conflict between the audience's natural interest in the success of the miracle, and their desire to witness the humiliation of this presumptuous man. It was a strange sight: Cipolla on his knees before the signora, wrestling, amid efforts at speech, after knowledge of the preordained words. "I must say something," he said, "and I feel clearly what it is I must say. But I also feel that if it passed my lips it would be wrong. Be careful not to help me unintentionally!" he cried out, though very likely that was precisely what he was hoping for. "*Pensez très fort*," he cried all at once, in bad French, and then burst out with the required words—in Italian, indeed, but with the final substantive pronounced in the sister tongue, in which he was probably far from fluent: he said *vénération* instead of *venerazione*, with an impossible nasal. And this partial success, after the complete success before it, the finding of the pin, the presentation of it on his knees to the right person—was almost more impressive than if he had got the sentence exactly right, and evoked bursts of admiring applause.

Cipolla got up from his knees and wiped the perspiration from his brow. You understand that this experiment with the pin was a single case, which I describe because it sticks in my memory. But he changed his method several times and improvised a number of variations suggested by his contact with his audience; a good deal of time thus went by. He seemed to get particular inspiration from the person of our landlady; she drew him on to the most extraordinary displays of clairvoyance. "It does not escape me, madame," he said to her, "that there is something unusual about you, some special and honorable distinction. He who has eyes to see descries about your lovely brow an aureola—if I mistake not, it once was stronger than now—a slowly paling radiance . . . hush, not a word! Don't help me. Beside you sits your husband—yes?" He turned toward the silent Signor Angiolieri. "You are the husband of this lady, and your happiness is complete. But in the midst of this happiness memories rise . . . the past, signora, so it seems to me, plays an important part in your present. You knew a king . . . has not a king crossed your path in bygone days?"

"No," breathed the dispenser of our midday soup, her golden-brown eyes gleaming in the noble pallor of her face.

"No? No, not a king; I meant that generally, I did not mean literally a king. Not a king, not a prince, and a prince after all, a king of a loftier realm; it was a great artist, at whose side you once—you would contradict me, and yet I am not wholly wrong. Well, then! It was a woman, a great, a world-renowned woman artist, whose friendship you enjoyed in your tender years, whose sacred memory overshadows and transfigures your whole existence. Her name? Need I utter it, whose fame has long been bound up with the fatherland's, immortal as its own? Eleonora Duse," he finished, softly and with much solemnity.

The little woman bowed her head, overcome. The applause was like a patriotic demonstration. Nearly everyone there knew about Signora Angiolieri's wonderful past; they were all able to confirm the Cavaliere's intuition—not least the present guests of Casa Eleonora. But we wondered how much of the truth he had learned as the result of professional inquiries made on his arrival. Yet I see no reason at all to cast doubt, on rational grounds, upon powers that, before our very eyes, became fatal to their possessor.

At this point there was an intermission. Our lord and master withdrew. Now I confess that almost ever since the beginning of my tale I have looked forward with dread to this moment in it. The thoughts of men are mostly not hard to read; in this case they are very easy. You are sure to ask why we did not choose this moment to go away—and I must continue to owe you an answer. I do not know why. I cannot defend myself. By this time it was certainly eleven, probably later. The children were asleep. The last series of tests had been too long, nature had had her way. They were sleeping in our laps, the little one on mine, the boy on his mother's. That was, in a way, a consolation; but at the same time it was also ground for compassion and a clear leading to take them home to bed. And I give you my word that we wanted to obey this touching admonition, we seriously wanted to. We roused the poor things and told them it was now high time to go. But they were no sooner conscious than they began to resist and implore—you know how horrified children are at the thought of leaving before the end of a thing. No cajoling has any effect, you have to use force. It was so lovely, they wailed. How did we know what was coming next? Surely we could not leave until after the intermission; they liked a little nap now and again—only not go home, only not go to bed, while the beautiful evening was still going on!

We yielded, but only for the moment, of course—so far as we knew—only for a little while, just a few minutes longer. I cannot excuse our staying, scarcely can I even understand it. Did we think, having once said A, we had to say B—having once brought the children hither we had to let them stay? No, it is not good enough. Were we ourselves so highly entertained? Yes, and no. Our feelings for Cavaliere Cipolla were of a very mixed kind, but so were the feelings of the whole audience, if I mistake not, and nobody left. Were we under the sway of a fascination that emanated from this man who took so strange a way to earn his bread; a fascination that he gave out independently of the program and even between the tricks and that paralyzed our resolve? Again, sheer curiosity may account for something. One was curious to know how such an evening turned out; Cipolla in his remarks having all along hinted that he had tricks in his bag stranger than any he had yet produced.

But all that is not it—or at least it is not all of it. More correct it would be to answer the first question with another. Why had we not left Torre di Venere itself before now? To me the two questions are one and the same, and in order to get out of the impasse I might simply say that I had answered it already. For, as things had been in Torre in general—queer, uncomfortable, troublesome, tense, oppressive—so precisely they were here in this hall tonight. Yes, more than precisely. For it seemed to be the fountainhead of all the uncanniness and all the strained feelings that had oppressed the atmosphere of our holiday. This man whose return to the stage we were awaiting was the personification of all that; and, as we had not gone away in general, so to speak, it would have been inconsistent to do it in the particular case. You may call this an explanation, you may call it inertia, as you see fit. Any argument more to the purpose I simply do not know how to adduce.

Well, there was an interval of ten minutes, which grew into nearly twenty. The children remained awake. They were enchanted by our compliance, and filled the break to their own satisfaction by renewing relations with the popular sphere, with Antonio, Guiscardo, and the canoe man. They put their hands to their mouths and called messages across, appealing to us for the Italian words. "Hope you have a good catch tomorrow, a whole netful!" They called to Mario, Esquisito Mario: "*Mario, una cioccolata e biscotti!*" And this time he heeded and answered with a smile: "*Subito, signorini!*" Later we had reason to recall this kindly, if rather absent and pensive smile.

Thus the interval passed, the gong sounded. The audience, which had scattered in conversation, took their places again, the children sat up straight in their chairs with their hands in their laps. The curtain had not been dropped. Cipolla came forward again, with his dipping stride, and began to introduce the second half of the program with a lecture.

Let me state once for all that this self-confident cripple was the most powerful hypnotist I have ever seen in my life. It was pretty plain now that he threw dust in the public eye and advertised himself as a presti-digitator on account of police regulations that would have prevented him from making his living by the exercise of his powers. Perhaps this eye-wash is the usual thing in Italy; it may be permitted or even connived at by the authorities. Certainly the man had from the beginning made little concealment of the actual nature of his operations; and this second half of the program was quite frankly and exclusively devoted to one sort of experiment. While he still practiced some rhetorical circumlocutions, the tests themselves were one long series of attacks upon the willpower, the loss or compulsion of volition. Comic, exciting, amazing by turns, by midnight they were still in full swing; we ran the gamut of all the phenomena this natural-unnatural field has to show, from the unimpres-sive at one end of the scale to the monstrous at the other. The audience laughed and applauded as they followed the grotesque details; shook their heads, clapped their knees, fell very frankly under the spell of this stern, self-assured personality. At the same time I saw signs that they were not quite complacent, not quite unconscious of the peculiar ignominy that lay, for the individual and for the general, in Cipolla's triumphs.

Two main features were constant in all the experiments: the liquor glass and the claw-handled riding whip. The first was always invoked to add fuel to his demoniac fires; without it, apparently, they might have burned out. On this score we might even have felt pity for the man; but the whistle of his scourge, the insulting symbol of his domination, before which we all cowered, drowned out every sensation save a dazed and out-braved submission to his power. Did he then lay claim to our sympathy to boot? I was struck by a remark he made—it suggested no less. At the cli-max of his experiments, by stroking and breathing upon a certain young man who had offered himself as a subject and already proved himself a particularly susceptible one, he had not only put him into the condition known as deep trance and extended his insensible body by neck and feet across the backs of two chairs, but had actually sat down on the rigid form as on a bench, without making it yield. The sight of this unholy figure in a frock coat squatted on the stiff body was horrible and incredi-ble; the audience, convinced that the victim of this scientific diversion must be suffering, expressed its sympathy: *"Ah, poveretto!"* Poor soul, poor soul! *"Poor soul!"* Cipolla mocked them, with some bitterness. "Ladies and gentlemen, you are barking up the wrong tree. *Sono io il poveretto.* I am the person who is suffering, I am the one to be pitied." We pocketed the information. Very good. Maybe the experiment was at his expense, maybe it was he who had suffered the cramp when the *giovanotto* over there had made the faces. But appearances were all against it; and one does not feel like saying *poveretto* to a man who is suffering to bring about the humili-ation of others.

I have got ahead of my story and lost sight of the sequence of events. To this day my mind is full of the Cavaliere's feats of endurance; only I do not recall them in their order—which does not matter. So much I do know: that the longer and more circumstantial tests, which got the most applause, impressed me less than some of the small ones that passed quickly over. I remember the young man whose body Cipolla converted into a board, only because of the accompanying remarks that I have quoted. An elderly lady in a cane-seated chair was lulled by Cipolla in the delusion that she was on a voyage to India and gave a voluble account of her adventures by land and sea. But I found this phenomenon less impressive than one that followed immediately after the intermission. A tall, well-built, soldierly man was unable to lift his arm, after the hunchback had told him that he could not and given a cut through the air with his whip. I can still see the face of that stately, mustachioed colonel smiling and clenching his teeth as he struggled to regain his lost freedom of action. A staggering performance! He seemed to be exerting his will, and in vain; the trouble, however, was probably simply that he could not will. There was involved here that recoil of the will upon itself that paralyzes choice—as our tyrant had previously explained to the Roman gentleman.

Still less can I forget the touching scene, at once comic and horrible, with Signora Angiolieri. The Cavaliere, probably in his first bold survey of the room, had spied out her ethereal lack of resistance to his power. For actually he bewitched her, literally drew her out of her seat, out of her row, and away with him whither he willed. And in order to enhance his effect, he bade Signor Angiolieri call upon his wife by her name, to throw, as it were, all the weight of his existence and his rights in her into the scale, to rouse by the voice of her husband everything in his spouse's soul that could shield her virtue against the evil assaults of magic. And how vain it all was! Cipolla was standing at some distance from the couple, when he made a single cut with his whip through the air. It caused our landlady to shudder violently and turn her face toward him. "Sofronia!" cried Signor Angiolieri—we had not known that Signora Angiolieri's name was Sofronia. And he did well to call, everybody saw that there was no time to lose. His wife kept her face turned in the direction of the diabolical Cavaliere, who with his ten long yellow fingers was making passes at his victim, moving backwards as he did so, step by step. Then Signora Angiolieri, her pale face gleaming, rose up from her seat, turned right round, and began to glide after him. Fatal and forbidding sight! Her face as though moonstruck, stiff-armed, her lovely hands lifted a little at the wrists, the feet as it were together, she seemed to float slowly out of her row and after the tempter. "Call her, sir, keep on calling," prompted the redoubtable man. And Signor Angiolieri, in a weak voice, called: "Sofronia!" Ah, again and again he called; as his wife went further off he even curved one hand round his lips and beckoned with the other as he called. But the poor voice of love and duty echoed unheard, in vain, behind the lost one's back; the signora swayed along, moonstruck, deaf, enslaved; she glided into the middle aisle and down it toward the fingering hunchback, toward the door. We were convinced, we were driven to the conviction, that she would have followed her master, had he so willed it, to the ends of the earth.

*"Accidente!"* cried out Signor Angiolieri, in genuine affright, springing up as the exit was reached. But at the same moment the Cavaliere put aside, as it were, the triumphal crown and broke off. "Enough, signora, I thank you," he said, and offered his arm to lead her back to her husband. "Signor," he greeted the latter, "here is your wife. Unharmed, with my compliments, I give her into your hands. Cherish with all the strength of your manhood a treasure that is so wholly yours, and let your zeal be quickened by knowing that there are powers stronger than reason or virtue, and not always so magnanimously ready to relinquish their prey!"

Poor Signor Angiolieri, so quiet, so bald! He did not look as though he would know how to defend his happiness, even against powers much less demoniac than these that were now adding mockery to frightfulness. Solemnly and pompously the Cavaliere retired to the stage, amid applause to which his eloquence gave double strength. It was this particular episode, I feel sure, that set the seal upon his ascendancy. For now he made them dance, yes, literally; and the dancing lent a dissolute, abandoned, topsy-turvy air to the scene, a drunken abdication of the critical spirit that had so long resisted the spell of this man. Yes, he had had to fight to get the upper hand—for instance against the animosity of the young Roman gentleman, whose rebellious spirit threatened to serve others as a rallying point. But it was precisely upon the importance of example that the Cavaliere was so strong. He had the wit to make his attack at the weakest point and to choose as his first victim that feeble, ecstatic youth whom he had previously made into a board. The master had but to look at him, when this young man would fling himself back as though struck by lightning, place his hands rigidly at his sides, and fall into a state of military somnambulism, in which it was plain to any eye that he was open to the most absurd suggestion that might be made to him. He seemed quite content in his abject state, quite pleased to be relieved of the burden of voluntary choice. Again and again he offered himself as a subject and gloried in the model facility he had in losing consciousness. So now he mounted the platform, and a single cut of the whip was enough to make him dance to the Cavaliere's orders, in a kind of complacent ecstasy, eyes closed, head nodding, lank limbs flying in all directions.

It looked unmistakably like enjoyment, and other recruits were not long in coming forward: two other young men, one humbly and one well dressed, were soon jigging alongside the first. But now the gentleman from Rome bobbed up again, asking defiantly if the Cavaliere would engage to make him dance too, even against his will.

"Even against your will," answered Cipolla, in unforgettable accents. That frightful "*anche se non vuole*" still rings in my ears. The struggle began. After Cipolla had taken another little glass and lighted a fresh cigarette he stationed the Roman at a point in the middle aisle and himself took up a position some distance behind him, making his whip whistle through the air as he gave the order: "*Balla!*" His opponent did not stir. "*Balla!*" repeated the Cavaliere incisively, and snapped his whip. You saw the young man move his neck round in his collar; at the same time one hand lifted slightly at the wrist, one ankle turned outward. But that was all, for the time at least; merely a tendency to twitch, now sternly repressed, now seeming about to get the upper hand. It escaped nobody that here a heroic obstinacy, a fixed resolve to resist, must needs be conquered; we were beholding a gallant effort to strike out and save the honor of the human race. He twitched but danced not; and the struggle was so prolonged that the Cavaliere had to divide his attention between it and the stage, turning now and then to make his riding whip whistle in the direction of the dancers, as it were to keep them in leash. At the same time he advised the audience that no fatigue was involved in such activities, however long they went on, since it was not the automatons up there who danced, but himself. Then once more his eye would bore itself into the back of the Roman's neck and lay siege to the strength of purpose that defied him.

One saw it waver, that strength of purpose, beneath the repeated summons and whip crackings. Saw with an objective interest that yet was not quite free from traces of sympathetic emotion—from pity, even from a cruel kind of pleasure. If I understand what was going on, it was the negative character of the young man's fighting position that was his undoing. It is likely that *not* willing is not a practicable state of mind; *not* to want to do something may be in the long run a mental content impossible to subsist on. Between not willing a certain thing and not willing at all—in other words, yielding to another person's will—there may lie too small a space for the idea of freedom to squeeze into. Again, there were the Cavaliere's persuasive words, woven in among the whip crackings and commands, as he mingled effects that were his own secret with others of a bewilderingly psychological kind. "*Balla!*" said he. "Who wants to torture himself like that? Is forcing yourself your idea of freedom? *Una ballatina!* Why, your arms and legs are aching for it. What a relief to give way to them—there, you are dancing already! That is no struggle anymore, it is a pleasure!" And so it was. The jerking and twitching of the refractory youth's limbs had at last got the upper hand; he lifted his arms, then his knees, his joints quite suddenly relaxed, he flung his legs and danced, and amid bursts of applause the Cavaliere led him to join the row of puppets on the stage. Up there we could see his face as he "enjoyed" himself; it was clothed in a broad grin and the eyes were half shut. In a way, it was consoling to see that he was having a better time than he had had in the hour of his pride.

His "fall" was, I may say, an epoch. The ice was completely broken, Cipolla's triumph had reached its height. The Circe's wand, that whistling leather whip with the claw handle, held absolute sway. At one time—it must have been well after midnight—not only were there eight or ten persons dancing on the little stage, but in the hall below a varied animation reigned, and a long-toothed Anglo-Saxoness in a pince-nez left her seat of her own motion to perform a tarantella in the center aisle. Cipolla was lounging in a cane-seated chair at the left of the stage, gulping down the smoke of a cigarette and breathing it impudently out through his bad teeth. He tapped his foot and shrugged his shoulders, looking down upon the abandoned scene in the hall; now and then he snapped his whip backwards at a laggard upon the stage. The children were awake at the moment. With shame I speak of them. For it was not good to be here, least of all for them; that we had not taken them away can only be explained by saying that we had caught the general devil-may-careness of the hour. By that time it was all one. Anyhow, thank goodness, they lacked understanding for the disreputable side of the entertainment, and in their innocence were perpetually charmed by the unheard-of indulgence that permitted them to be present at such a thing as a magician's "evening." Whole quarter-hours at a time they drowsed on our laps, waking refreshed and rosy-cheeked, with sleep-drunken eyes, to laugh to bursting at the leaps and jumps the magician made those people up there make. They had not thought it would be so jolly; they joined with their clumsy little hands in every round of applause. And jumped for joy upon their chairs, as was their wont, when Cipolla beckoned to their friend Mario from the Esquisito, beckoned to him just like a picture in a book, holding his hand in front of his nose and bending and straightening the forefinger by turns.

Mario obeyed. I can see him now going up the stairs to Cipolla, who continued to beckon him, in that droll, picture-book sort of way. He hesitated for a moment at first; that, too, I recall quite clearly. During the whole evening he had lounged against a wooden pillar at the side entrance, with his arms folded, or else with his hands thrust into his jacket pockets. He was on our left, near the youth with the militant hair, and had followed the performance attentively, so far as we had seen, if with no particular animation and God knows how much comprehension. He could not much relish being summoned thus, at the end of the evening.

But it was only too easy to see why he obeyed. After all, obedience was his calling in life; and then, how should a simple lad like him find it within his human capacity to refuse compliance to a man so throned and crowned as Cipolla at that hour? Willy-nilly he left his column and with a word of thanks to those making way for him he mounted the steps with a doubtful smile on his full lips.

Picture a thickset youth of twenty years, with clipped hair, a low forehead, and heavy-lidded eyes of an indefinite gray, shot with green and yellow. These things I knew from having spoken with him, as we often had. There was a saddle of freckles on the flat nose, the whole upper half of the face retreated behind the lower, and that again was dominated by thick lips that parted to show the salivated teeth. These thick lips and the veiled look of the eyes lent the whole face a primitive melancholy—it was that which had drawn us to him from the first. In it was not the faintest trace of brutality—indeed, his hands would have given the lie to such an idea, being unusually slender and delicate even for a southerner. They were hands by which one liked being served.

We knew him humanly without knowing him personally, if I may make that distinction. We saw him nearly every day, and felt a certain kindness for his dreamy ways, which might at times be actual inattentiveness, suddenly transformed into a redeeming zeal to serve. His mien was serious, only the children could bring a smile to his face. It was not sulky, but uningratiating, without intentional effort to please—or, rather, it seemed to give up being pleasant in the conviction that it could not succeed. We should have remembered Mario in any case, as one of those homely recollections of travel that often stick in the mind better than more important ones. But of his circumstances we knew no more than that his father was a petty clerk in the *municipio* and his mother took in washing.

His white waiter's coat became him better than the faded striped suit he wore, with a gay colored scarf instead of a collar, the ends tucked into his jacket. He neared Cipolla, who however did not leave off that motion of his finger before his nose, so that Mario had to come still closer, right up to the chair seat and the master's legs. Whereupon the latter spread out his elbows and seized the lad, turning him so that we had a view of his face. Then gazed him briskly up and down, with a careless, commanding eye.

"Well, *ragazzo mio*, how comes it we make acquaintance so late in the day? But believe me, I made yours long ago. Yes, yes, I've had you in my eye this long while and known what good stuff you were made of. How could I go and forget you again? Well, I've had a good deal to think about. . . . Now tell me, what is your name? The first name, that's all I want."

"My name is Mario," the young man answered, in a low voice.

"Ah, Mario. Very good. Yes, yes, there is such a name, quite a common name, a classic name too, one of those that preserve the heroic traditions of the fatherland. *Bravo! Salve!*" And he flung up his arm slantingly above his crooked shoulder, palm outward, in the Roman salute. He may have been slightly tipsy by now, and no wonder; but he spoke as before, clearly, fluently, and with emphasis. Though about this time there had crept into his voice a gross, autocratic note, and a kind of arrogance was in his sprawl.

"Well, now, Mario *mio*," he went on, "it's a good thing you came this evening, and that's a pretty scarf you've got on; it is becoming to your style of beauty. It must stand you in good stead with the girls, the pretty pretty girls of Torre—"

From the row of youths, close by the place where Mario had been standing, sounded a laugh. It came from the youth with the militant hair. He stood there, his jacket over his shoulder, and laughed outright, rudely and scornfully.

Mario gave a start. I think it was a shrug, but he may have started and then hastened to cover the movement by shrugging his shoulders, as much as to say that the neckerchief and the fair sex were matters of equal indifference to him.

The Cavaliere gave a downward glance.

"We needn't trouble about him," he said. "He is jealous, because your scarf is so popular with the girls, maybe partly because you and I are so friendly up here. Perhaps he'd like me to put him in mind of his colic—I could do it free of charge. Tell me, Mario. You've come here this evening for a bit of fun—and in the daytime you work in an ironmonger's shop?"

"In a café," corrected the youth.

"Oh, in a café. That's where Cipolla nearly came a cropper! What you are is a cup bearer, a Ganymede—I like that, it is another classical allusion—*Salvietta!*" Again the Cavaliere saluted, to the huge gratification of his audience.

Mario smiled too. "But before that," he interpolated, in the interest of accuracy, "I worked for a while in a shop in Portoclemente." He seemed visited by a natural desire to assist the prophecy by dredging out its essential features.

"There, didn't I say so? In an ironmonger's shop?"

"They kept combs and brushes," Mario got round it.

"Didn't I say that you were not always a Ganymede? Not always at the sign of the serviette? Even when Cipolla makes a mistake, it is a kind that makes you believe in him. Now tell me: Do you believe in me?"

An indefinite gesture.

"A halfway answer," commented the Cavaliere. "Probably it is not easy to win your confidence. Even for me, I can see, it is not so easy. I see in your features a reserve, a sadness, *un tratto di malinconia* . . . tell me" (he seized Mario's hand persuasively) "have you troubles?"

"*Nossignore*," answered Mario, promptly and decidedly.

"You *have* troubles," insisted the Cavaliere, bearing down the denial by the weight of his authority. "Can't I see? Trying to pull the wool over Cipolla's eyes, are you? Of course, about the girls—it is a girl, isn't it? You have love troubles?"

Mario gave a vigorous headshake. And again the *giovanotto*'s brutal laugh rang out. The Cavaliere gave heed. His eyes were roving about somewhere in the air; but he cocked an ear to the sound, then swung his whip backwards, as he had once or twice before in his conversation with Mario, that none of his puppets might flag in their zeal. The gesture had nearly cost him his new prey: Mario gave a sudden start in the direction of the steps. But Cipolla had him in his clutch.

"Not so fast," said he. "That would be fine, wouldn't it? So you want to skip, do you, Ganymede, right in the middle of the fun, or, rather, when it is just beginning? Stay with me, I'll show you something nice. I'll convince you. You have no reason to worry, I promise you. This girl—you know her and others know her too—what's her name? Wait! I read the name in your eyes, it is on the tip of my tongue and yours too—"

"Silvestra!" shouted the *giovanotto* from below.

The Cavaliere's face did not change.

"Aren't there the forward people?" he asked, not looking down, more as in undisturbed converse with Mario. "Aren't there the young fighting cocks that crow in season and out? Takes the word out of your mouth, the conceited fool, and seems to think he has some special right to it. Let him be. But Silvestra, your Silvestra—ah, what a girl that is! What a prize! Brings your heart into your mouth to see her walk or laugh or breathe, she is so lovely. And her round arms when she washes, and tosses her head back to get the hair out of her eyes! An angel from paradise!"

Mario stared at him, his head thrust forward. He seemed to have forgotten the audience, forgotten where he was. The red rings round his eyes had got larger, they looked as though they were painted on. His thick lips parted.

"And she makes you suffer, this angel," went on Cipolla, "or, rather, you make yourself suffer for her—there is a difference, my lad, a most important difference, let me tell you. There are misunderstandings in love, maybe nowhere else in the world are there so many. I know what you are thinking: What does this Cipolla, with his little physical defect, know about love? Wrong, all wrong, he knows a lot. He has a wide and powerful understanding of its workings, and it pays to listen to his advice. But let's leave Cipolla out, cut him out altogether and think only of Silvestra, your peerless Silvestra! What! Is she to give any young gamecock the preference, so that he can laugh while you cry? To prefer him to a chap like you, so full of feeling and so sympathetic? Not very likely, is it? It is impossible—we know better, Cipolla and she. If I were to put myself in her place and choose between the two of you, a tarry lout like that—a codfish, a sea urchin—and a Mario, a knight of the serviette, who moves among gentlefolk and hands round refreshments with an air—my word, but my heart would speak in no uncertain tones—it knows to whom I gave it long ago. It is time that he should see and understand, my chosen one! It is time that you see me and recognize me, Mario, my beloved! Tell me, who am I?"

It was grisly, the way the betrayer made himself irresistible, wreathed and coquetted with his crooked shoulder, languished with the puffy eyes, and showed his splintered teeth in a sickly smile. And alas, at his beguiling words, what was come of our Mario? It is hard for me to tell, hard as it was for me to see; for here was nothing less than an utter abandonment of the inmost soul, a public exposure of timid and deluded passion and rapture. He put his hands across his mouth, his shoulders rose and fell with his pantings. He could not, it was plain, trust his eyes and ears for joy, and the one thing he forgot was precisely that he could not trust them. "Silvestra!" he breathed, from the very depths of his vanquished heart.

"Kiss me!" said the hunchback. "Trust me, I love thee. Kiss me here." And with the tip of his index finger, hand, arm, and little finger outspread, he pointed to his cheek, near the mouth. And Mario bent and kissed him.

It had grown very still in the room. That was a monstrous moment, grotesque and thrilling, the moment of Mario's bliss. In that evil span of time, crowded with a sense of the illusiveness of all joy, one sound became audible, and that not quite at once, but on the instant of the melancholy and ribald meeting between Mario's lips and the repulsive flesh that thrust itself forward for his caress. It was the sound of a laugh, from the *giovanotto* on our left. It broke into the dramatic suspense of the moment, coarse, mocking, and yet—or I must have been grossly mistaken—with an undertone of compassion for the poor bewildered, victimized creature. It had a faint ring of that "*Poveretto*" that Cipolla had declared was wasted on the wrong person, when he claimed the pity for his own.

The laugh still rang in the air when the recipient of the caress gave his whip a little swish, low down, close to his chair leg, and Mario started up and flung himself back. He stood in that posture staring, his hands one over the other on those desecrated lips. Then he beat his temples with his clenched fists, over and over; turned and staggered down the steps, while the audience applauded, and Cipolla sat there with his hands in his lap, his shoulders shaking. Once below, and even while in full retreat, Mario hurled himself round with legs flung wide apart; one arm flew up, and two flat shattering detonations crashed through applause and laughter.

There was instant silence. Even the dancers came to a full stop and stared about, struck dumb. Cipolla bounded from his seat. He stood with his arms spread out, slanting as though to ward everybody off, as though the next moment he would cry out: "Stop! Keep back! Silence! What was that?" Then, in that instant, he sank back in his seat, his head rolling on his chest; in the next he had fallen sideways to the floor, where he lay motionless, a huddled heap of clothing, with limbs awry.

The commotion was indescribable. Ladies hid their faces, shuddering, on the breasts of their escorts. There were shouts for a doctor, for the police. People flung themselves on Mario in a mob, to disarm him, to take away the weapon that hung from his fingers—that small, dull-metal scarcely pistol-shaped tool with hardly any barrel—how strange and unexpected a direction had fate leveled it!

And now—now finally, at last—we took the children and led them toward the exit, past the pair of *carabinieri* just entering. Was that the end, they wanted to know, that they might go in peace? Yes, we assured them, that was the end. An end of horror, a fatal end. And yet a liberation—for I could not, and cannot, but find it so!

Thomas Mann

## QUESTIONS

1. Why does the narrator describe the experience with Cipolla as "unholy and staggering"? (304)

2. Why is the street to the theater described as leading "from the feudal past the bourgeois into the proletarian"? (306)

3. Why do the Italians and the outsiders respond so differently to Cipolla's patriotism and "his irritable sense of dignity"? (316)

4. What does the narrator mean in saying that the crowd's approval of the card tricks "signified the triumph of objective judgment over antipathy and repressed resentment"? (317)

5. Why does Cipolla insist, "I am the person who is suffering, I am the one to be pitied"? (322)

6. What does the narrator mean when he says, "Between not willing a certain thing and not willing at all . . . there may lie too small a space for the idea of freedom to squeeze into"? (325)

7. What is the "disreputable side" of the entertainment that the children cannot understand? (326)

8. Why does Mario kill Cipolla?

9. Why does the narrator consider the end of the performance "a liberation"? (331)

10. What is the connection between why the narrator and his family didn't leave the performance and why they hadn't left Torre di Venere?

## FOR FURTHER REFLECTION

1. Why would anyone want to be "relieved of the burden of voluntary choice"?

2. What human interactions are explained by the idea of a "common will"? What is the relation of a common will to individual willpower?

3. What is the ultimate goal that Cipolla wants to achieve by the exercise of his powers?

4. What does Cipolla's power over his audience suggest about the way in which charismatic political leaders dominate their constituencies?

Katherine Mansfield (1888–1923) was a pioneer in modern fiction writing and is often credited, along with James Joyce, with creating the contemporary short story. Missing from her stories are the elaborate expositions and scene-setting and explicit explanations considered indispensable by her predecessors. Instead, Mansfield employed shifting points of view and lively dialogue to offer insights into the emotional lives of her characters. Virginia Woolf called Mansfield's fiction "the only writing I have ever been jealous of."

Mansfield was born Kathleen Mansfield Beauchamp in Wellington, New Zealand, the child of a socially and financially successful businessman. Early on, she early expressed the desire to become a writer; a schoolteacher described her as "imaginative to the point of untruth." During her teenage years, Mansfield studied in England with her sisters at a liberal girls' school, where she discovered intellectual freedom and unconventional behavior and developed an admiration for Oscar Wilde and the English decadents. When she turned eighteen, her parents brought her back to New Zealand to find a suitable husband. Although she published several stories in a Wellington newspaper, she longed to go back to London, and in 1908 her parents gave her permission to return and an allowance on which to live.

Mansfield's life in the years following her return was turbulent and artistically fruitful. She fell in love with Garnet Trowell, a young man whom she had known in New Zealand. At about the same time that she became pregnant by Trowell, she married George Bowden, a man she had known for three weeks. She wore black at her wedding and escaped the same night, soon to join Trowell in Glasgow. Her mother got wind of Mansfield's impulsive marriage and stormy affairs, and traveled to London. She sent Mansfield to a pension in Germany, an experience that would become the subject of her first book, *In a German Pension* (1911). After a miscarriage, she returned to London. She took up residence with Ida Baker, her friend and almost constant companion since her school days in England, and began to write with renewed vigor. Her stories were published regularly in *New Age*, a noted avant-garde literary journal. She met John Middleton Murry, a magazine editor, in 1911, and started a sporadic relationship with him that would last for the rest of her life. Mansfield continued to change dwellings and pursue other lovers, though the two were married in 1918. As the couple became more involved in the literary life of London, Murry and Mansfield grew close to D. H. Lawrence and his wife, Frieda. This foursome, whose feelings for each other alternated between love and hate, influenced each other's work greatly: Lawrence's *Sons and Lovers* (1913) provided inspiration for a coming-of-age novel Mansfield never finished, and it is believed Lawrence based the character of Gudrun in *Women in Love* (1920) on both Murry and Mansfield. Meanwhile, World War I had claimed the life of Mansfield's brother, Leslie, leaving her devastated.

In 1917, Mansfield was diagnosed with the tuberculosis that would end her life five years later. Her final years were extremely productive. She translated the letters of Anton Chekhov, who had also suffered from tuberculosis, and comforted herself that "if I do die perhaps there is a small private heaven for consumptives only. In that case I shall see Chekhov." It was during this period that she wrote the stories for which she is best known, including "The Daughters of the Late Colonel." It is believed that the dreamy and passive character of Constantia is a portrait of Baker.

In the decades after her death, Murry compiled Mansfield's diaries and correspondence into several volumes and published them to great acclaim, inspiring an enthusiastic fan following. Although Murry's editing has been criticized, his efforts helped Mansfield's work gain international repute. Many readers are fascinated by her turbulent personal life, but Mansfield's true legacy lies in her stories, whose themes range from the fragility of the middle class to the ambiguities of sexuality and friendship. Underlying much of her work is the attempt to discover beauty and passion in the mundane. Only months before she died, she wrote, "I want a garden, a small house, grass, animals, books, pictures, music. And out of this, the expression of this, I want to be writing. . . . Warm, eager, living life—to be rooted in life, to learn, to desire to know, to feel, to think, to act. That is what I want." Her stories remain widely read, many decades after she penned the last sentence in her diaries: "All is well."

# The Daughters of the Late Colonel

## 1

The week after was one of the busiest weeks of their lives. Even when they went to bed it was only their bodies that lay down and rested; their minds went on, thinking things out, talking things over, wondering, deciding, trying to remember where . . .

Constantia lay like a statue, her hands by her sides, her feet just overlapping each other, the sheet up to her chin. She stared at the ceiling.

"Do you think Father would mind if we gave his top hat to the porter?"

"The porter?" snapped Josephine. "Why ever the porter? What a very extraordinary idea!"

"Because," said Constantia slowly, "he must often have to go to funerals. And I noticed at—at the cemetery that he only had a bowler." She paused. "I thought then how very much he'd appreciate a top hat. We ought to give him a present, too. He was always very nice to Father."

"But," cried Josephine, flouncing on her pillow and staring across the dark at Constantia, "Father's head!" And suddenly, for one awful moment, she nearly giggled. Not, of course, that she felt in the least like giggling. It must have been habit. Years ago, when they had stayed awake at night talking, their beds had simply heaved. And now the porter's head, disappearing, popped out, like a candle, under Father's hat. . . . The giggle mounted, mounted; she clenched her hands; she fought it down; she frowned fiercely at the dark and said "Remember" terribly sternly.

"We can decide tomorrow," she sighed.

Constantia had noticed nothing; she sighed.

"Do you think we ought to have our dressing gowns dyed as well?"

"Black?" almost shrieked Josephine.

"Well, what else?" said Constantia. "I was thinking—it doesn't seem quite sincere, in a way, to wear black out-of-doors and when we're fully dressed, and then when we're at home—"

"But nobody sees us," said Josephine. She gave the bedclothes such a twitch that both her feet became uncovered, and she had to creep up the pillows to get them well under again.

"Kate does," said Constantia. "And the postman very well might."

Josephine thought of her dark-red slippers, which matched her dressing gown, and of Constantia's favourite indefinite-green ones which went with hers. Black! Two black dressing gowns and two pairs of black woolly slippers, creeping off to the bathroom like black cats.

"I don't think it's absolutely necessary," said she.

Silence. Then Constantia said, "We shall have to post the papers with the notice in them tomorrow to catch the Ceylon mail. . . . How many letters have we had up till now?"

"Twenty-three."

Josephine had replied to them all, and twenty-three times when she came to "We miss our dear father *so* much" she had broken down and had to use her handkerchief, and on some of them even to soak up a very light-blue tear with an edge of blotting paper. Strange! She couldn't have put it on—but twenty-three times. Even now, though, when she said over to herself sadly, "We miss our dear father *so* much," she could have cried if she'd wanted to.

"Have you got enough stamps?" came from Constantia.

"Oh, how can I tell?" said Josephine crossly. "What's the good of asking me that now?"

"I was just wondering," said Constantia mildly.

Silence again. There came a little rustle, a scurry, a hop.

"A mouse," said Constantia.

"It can't be a mouse because there aren't any crumbs," said Josephine.

"But it doesn't know there aren't," said Constantia.

A spasm of pity squeezed her heart. Poor little thing! She wished she'd left a tiny piece of biscuit on the dressing table. It was awful to think of it not finding anything. What would it do?

"I can't think how they manage to live at all," she said slowly.

"Who?" demanded Josephine.

And Constantia said more loudly than she meant to, "Mice."

Josephine was furious. "Oh, what nonsense, Con!" she said. "What have mice got to do with it? You're asleep."

"I don't think I am," said Constantia. She shut her eyes to make sure. She was.

Josephine arched her spine, pulled up her knees, folded her arms so that her fists came under her ears, and pressed her cheek hard against the pillow.

## 2

Another thing which complicated matters was they had Nurse Andrews staying on with them that week. It was their own fault; they had asked her. It was Josephine's idea. On the morning—well, on the last morning, when the doctor had gone, Josephine had said to Constantia, "Don't you think it would be rather nice if we asked Nurse Andrews to stay on for a week as our guest?"

"Very nice," said Constantia.

"I thought," went on Josephine quickly, "I should just say this after-noon, after I've paid her, 'My sister and I would be very pleased, after all you've done for us, Nurse Andrews, if you would stay on for a week as our guest.' I'd have to put that in about being our guest in case—"

"Oh, but she could hardly expect to be paid!" cried Constantia.

"One never knows," said Josephine sagely.

Nurse Andrews had, of course, jumped at the idea. But it was a bother. It meant they had to have regular sit-down meals at the proper times, whereas if they'd been alone they could just have asked Kate if she wouldn't have minded bringing them a tray wherever they were. And mealtimes now that the strain was over were rather a trial.

Nurse Andrews was simply fearful about butter. Really they couldn't help feeling that about butter, at least, she took advantage of their kind-ness. And she had that maddening habit of asking for just an inch more bread to finish what she had on her plate, and then, at the last mouthful, absent-mindedly—of course it wasn't absent-mindedly—taking another helping. Josephine got very red when this happened, and she fastened her small, bead-like eyes on the tablecloth as if she saw a minute strange insect creeping through the web of it. But Constantia's long, pale face lengthened and set, and she gazed away—away—far over the desert to where that line of camels unwound like a thread of wool. . . .

"When I was with Lady Tukes," said Nurse Andrews, "she had such a dainty little contrayvance for the buttah. It was a silvah cupid balanced on the—on the bordah of a glass dish, holding a tayny fork. And when you wanted some buttah you simply pressed his foot and he bent down and speared you a piece. It was quite a gayme."

Josephine could hardly bear that. But "I think those things are very extravagant" was all she said.

"But whey?" asked Nurse Andrews, beaming through her eyeglasses. "No one, surely, would take more buttah than one wanted—would one?"

"Ring, Con," cried Josephine. She couldn't trust herself to reply.

And proud young Kate, the enchanted princess, came in to see what the old tabbies wanted now. She snatched away their plates of mock some-thing or other and slapped down a white, terrified blancmange.

"Jam, please, Kate," said Josephine kindly.

Kate knelt and burst open the sideboard, lifted the lid of the jam pot, saw it was empty, put it on the table, and stalked off.

"I'm afraid," said Nurse Andrews a moment later, "there isn't any."

"Oh, what a bother!" said Josephine. She bit her lip. "What had we better do?"

Constantia looked dubious. "We can't disturb Kate again," she said softly.

Nurse Andrews waited, smiling at them both. Her eyes wandered, spying at everything behind her eyeglasses. Constantia in despair went back to her camels. Josephine frowned heavily—concentrated. If it hadn't been for this idiotic woman she and Con would, of course, have eaten their blancmange without. Suddenly the idea came.

"I know," she said. "Marmalade. There's some marmalade in the sideboard. Get it, Con."

"I hope," laughed Nurse Andrews, and her laugh was like a spoon tinkling against a medicine glass—"I hope it's not very bittah marmalayde."

### 3

But, after all, it was not long now, and then she'd be gone for good. And there was no getting over the fact that she had been very kind to Father. She had nursed him day and night at the end. Indeed, both Constantia and Josephine felt privately she had rather overdone the not leaving him at the very last. For when they had gone in to say goodbye Nurse Andrews had sat beside his bed the whole time, holding his wrist and pretending to look at her watch. It couldn't have been necessary. It was so tactless, too. Supposing Father had wanted to say something—something private to them. Not that he had. Oh, far from it! He lay there, purple, a dark, angry purple in the face, and never even looked at them when they came in. Then, as they were standing there, wondering what to do, he had suddenly opened one eye. Oh, what a difference it would have made, what a difference to their memory of him, how much easier to tell people about it, if he had only opened both! But no—one eye only. It glared at them a moment and then . . . went out.

### 4

It had made it very awkward for them when Mr. Farolles, of St. John's, called the same afternoon.

"The end was quite peaceful, I trust?" were the first words he said as he glided towards them through the dark drawing room.

"Quite," said Josephine faintly. They both hung their heads. Both of them felt certain that eye wasn't at all a peaceful eye.

"Won't you sit down?" said Josephine.

"Thank you, Miss Pinner," said Mr. Farolles gratefully. He folded his coattails and began to lower himself into Father's armchair, but just as he touched it he almost sprang up and slid into the next chair instead.

He coughed. Josephine clasped her hands; Constantia looked vague.

"I want you to feel, Miss Pinner," said Mr. Farolles, "and you, Miss Constantia, that I'm trying to be helpful. I want to be helpful to you both, if you will let me. These are the times," said Mr. Farolles, very simply and earnestly, "when God means us to be helpful to one another."

"Thank you very much, Mr. Farolles," said Josephine and Constantia.

"Not at all," said Mr. Farolles gently. He drew his kid gloves through his fingers and leaned forward. "And if either of you would like a little Communion, either or both of you, here *and* now, you have only to tell me. A little Communion is often very help—a great comfort," he added tenderly.

But the idea of a little Communion terrified them. What! In the drawing room by themselves—with no—no altar or anything! The piano would be much too high, thought Constantia, and Mr. Farolles could not possibly lean over it with the chalice. And Kate would be sure to come bursting in and interrupt them, thought Josephine. And supposing the bell rang in the middle? It might be somebody important—about their mourning. Would they get up reverently and go out, or would they have to wait . . . in torture?

"Perhaps you will send round a note by your good Kate if you would care for it later," said Mr. Farolles.

"Oh yes, thank you very much!" they both said.

Mr. Farolles got up and took his black straw hat from the round table.

"And about the funeral," he said softly. "I may arrange that—as your dear father's old friend and yours, Miss Pinner—and Miss Constantia?"

Josephine and Constantia got up too.

"I should like it to be quite simple," said Josephine firmly, "and not too expensive. At the same time, I should like—"

"A good one that will last," thought dreamy Constantia, as if Josephine were buying a nightgown. But of course Josephine didn't say that. "One suitable to our father's position." She was very nervous.

"I'll run round to our good friend Mr. Knight," said Mr. Farolles soothingly. "I will ask him to come and see you. I am sure you will find him very helpful indeed."

## 5

Well, at any rate, all that part of it was over, though neither of them could possibly believe that Father was never coming back. Josephine had had a moment of absolute terror at the cemetery, while the coffin was lowered, to think that she and Constantia had done this thing without asking his permission. What would Father say when he found out? For he was bound to find out sooner or later. He always did. "Buried. You two girls had me *buried*!" She heard his stick thumping. Oh, what would they say? What possible excuse could they make? It sounded such an appallingly heartless thing to do. Such a wicked advantage to take of a person because he happened to be helpless at the moment. The other people seemed to treat it all as a matter of course. They were strangers; they couldn't be expected to understand that Father was the very last person for such a thing to happen to. No, the entire blame for it all would fall on her and Constantia. And the expense, she thought, stepping into the tight-buttoned cab. When she had to show him the bills. What would he say then?

She heard him absolutely roaring, "And do you expect me to pay for this gimcrack excursion of yours?"

"Oh," groaned poor Josephine aloud, "we shouldn't have done it, Con!"

And Constantia, pale as a lemon in all that blackness, said in a frightened whisper, "Done what, Jug?"

"Let them bu-bury Father like that," said Josephine, breaking down and crying into her new, queer-smelling mourning handkerchief.

"But what else could we have done?" asked Constantia wonderingly. "We couldn't have kept him, Jug—we couldn't have kept him unburied. At any rate, not in a flat that size."

Josephine blew her nose; the cab was dreadfully stuffy.

"I don't know," she said forlornly. "It is all so dreadful. I feel we ought to have tried to, just for a time at least. To make perfectly sure. One thing's certain"—and her tears sprang out again—"Father will never forgive us for this—never!"

## 6

Father would never forgive them. That was what they felt more than ever when, two mornings later, they went into his room to go through his things. They had discussed it quite calmly. It was even down on Josephine's list of things to be done. *Go through Father's things and settle about them.* But that was a very different matter from saying after breakfast:

"Well, are you ready, Con?"

"Yes, Jug—when you are."

"Then I think we'd better get it over."

It was dark in the hall. It had been a rule for years never to disturb Father in the morning, whatever happened. And now they were going to open the door without knocking even. . . . Constantia's eyes were enormous at the idea; Josephine felt weak in the knees.

"You—you go first," she gasped, pushing Constantia.

But Constantia said, as she always had said on those occasions, "No, Jug, that's not fair. You're eldest."

Josephine was just going to say—what at other times she wouldn't have owned to for the world—what she kept for her very last weapon, "But you're tallest," when they noticed that the kitchen door was open, and there stood Kate. . . .

"Very stiff," said Josephine, grasping the door handle and doing her best to turn it. As if anything ever deceived Kate!

It couldn't be helped. That girl was . . . Then the door was shut behind them, but—but they weren't in Father's room at all. They might have suddenly walked through the wall by mistake into a different flat altogether. Was the door just behind them? They were too frightened to look. Josephine knew that if it was it was holding itself tight shut; Constantia felt that, like the doors in dreams, it hadn't any handle at all. It was the coldness which made it so awful. Or the whiteness—which? Everything was covered. The blinds were down, a cloth hung over the mirror, a sheet hid the bed; a huge fan of white paper filled the fireplace. Constantia timidly put out her hand; she almost expected a snowflake to fall. Josephine felt a queer tingling in her nose, as if her nose was freezing. Then a cab klop-klopped over the cobbles below, and the quiet seemed to shake into little pieces.

"I had better pull up a blind," said Josephine bravely.

"Yes, it might be a good idea," whispered Constantia.

They only gave the blind a touch, but it flew up and the cord flew after, rolling round the blind-stick, and the little tassel tapped as if trying to get free. That was too much for Constantia.

"Don't you think—don't you think we might put it off for another day?" she whispered.

"Why?" snapped Josephine, feeling, as usual, much better now that she knew for certain that Constantia was terrified. "It's got to be done. But I do wish you wouldn't whisper, Con."

"I didn't know I was whispering," whispered Constantia.

"And why do you keep on staring at the bed?" said Josephine, raising her voice almost defiantly. "There's nothing *on* the bed."

"Oh, Jug, don't say so!" said poor Connie. "At any rate, not so loudly."

Josephine felt herself that she had gone too far. She took a wide swerve over to the chest of drawers, put out her hand, but quickly drew it back again.

"Connie!" she gasped, and she wheeled round and leaned with her back against the chest of drawers.

"Oh, Jug—what?"

Josephine could only glare. She had the most extraordinary feeling that she had just escaped something simply awful. But how could she explain to Constantia that Father was in the chest of drawers? He was in the top drawer with his handkerchiefs and neckties, or in the next with his shirts and pyjamas, or in the lowest of all with his suits. He was watching there, hidden away—just behind the door handle—ready to spring.

She pulled a funny old-fashioned face at Constantia, just as she used to in the old days when she was going to cry.

"I can't open," she nearly wailed.

"No, don't, Jug," whispered Constantia earnestly. "It's much better not to. Don't let's open anything. At any rate, not for a long time."

"But—but it seems so weak," said Josephine, breaking down.

"But why not be weak for once, Jug?" argued Constantia, whispering quite fiercely. "If it is weak." And her pale stare flew from the locked writing table—so safe—to the huge glittering wardrobe, and she began to breathe in a queer, panting way. "Why shouldn't we be weak for once in our lives, Jug? It's quite excusable. Let's be weak—be weak, Jug. It's much nicer to be weak than to be strong."

And then she did one of those amazingly bold things that she'd done about twice before in their lives; she marched over to the wardrobe, turned the key, and took it out of the lock. Took it out of the lock and held it up to Josephine, showing Josephine by her extraordinary smile that she knew what she'd done, she'd risked deliberately Father being in there among his overcoats.

If the huge wardrobe had lurched forward, had crashed down on Constantia, Josephine wouldn't have been surprised. On the contrary, she would have thought it the only suitable thing to happen. But nothing happened. Only the room seemed quieter than ever, and bigger flakes of cold air fell on Josephine's shoulders and knees. She began to shiver.

"Come, Jug," said Constantia, still with that awful callous smile, and Josephine followed just as she had that last time, when Constantia had pushed Benny into the round pond.

## 7

But the strain told on them when they were back in the dining room. They sat down, very shaky, and looked at each other.

"I don't feel I can settle to anything," said Josephine, "until I've had something. Do you think we could ask Kate for two cups of hot water?"

"I really don't see why we shouldn't," said Constantia carefully. She was quite normal again. "I won't ring. I'll go to the kitchen door and ask her."

"Yes, do," said Josephine, sinking down into a chair. "Tell her, just two cups, Con, nothing else—on a tray."

"She needn't even put the jug on, need she?" said Constantia, as though Kate might very well complain if the jug had been there.

"Oh no, certainly not! The jug's not at all necessary. She can pour it direct out of the kettle," cried Josephine, feeling that would be a labour-saving indeed.

Their cold lips quivered at the greenish brims. Josephine curved her small red hands round the cup; Constantia sat up and blew on the wavy stream, making it flutter from one side to the other.

"Speaking of Benny," said Josephine.

And though Benny hadn't been mentioned Constantia immediately looked as though he had.

"He'll expect us to send him something of Father's, of course. But it's so difficult to know what to send to Ceylon."

"You mean things get unstuck so on the voyage," murmured Constantia.

"No, lost," said Josephine sharply. "You know there's no post. Only runners."

Both paused to watch a black man in white linen drawers running through the pale fields for dear life, with a large brown-paper parcel in his hands. Josephine's black man was tiny; he scurried along glistening like an ant. But there was something blind and tireless about Constantia's tall, thin fellow, which made him, she decided, a very unpleasant person indeed. . . . On the verandah, dressed all in white and wearing a cork helmet, stood Benny. His right hand shook up and down, as Father's did when he was impatient. And behind him, not in the least interested, sat Hilda, the unknown sister-in-law. She swung in a cane rocker and flicked over the leaves of the *Tatler*.

"I think his watch would be the most suitable present," said Josephine.

Constantia looked up; she seemed surprised.

"Oh, would you trust a gold watch to a native?"

"But of course I'd disguise it," said Josephine. "No one would know it was a watch." She liked the idea of having to make a parcel such a curious shape that no one could possibly guess what it was. She even thought for a moment of hiding the watch in a narrow cardboard corset box that she'd kept by her for a long time, waiting for it to come in for something. It was such beautiful firm cardboard. But, no, it wouldn't be appropriate for this occasion. It had lettering on it: *Medium Women's 28. Extra Firm Busks.* It would be almost too much of a surprise for Benny to open that and find Father's watch inside.

"And of course it isn't as though it would be going—ticking, I mean," said Constantia, who was still thinking of the native love of jewellery. "At least," she added, "it would be very strange if after all that time it was."

## 8

Josephine made no reply. She had flown off on one of her tangents. She had suddenly thought of Cyril. Wasn't it more usual for the only grandson to have the watch? And then dear Cyril was so appreciative, and a gold watch meant so much to a young man. Benny, in all probability, had quite got out of the habit of watches; men seldom wore waistcoats in those hot climates. Whereas Cyril in London wore them from year's end to year's end. And it would be so nice for her and Constantia, when he came to tea, to know it was there. "I see you've got on Grandfather's watch, Cyril." It would be somehow so satisfactory.

Dear boy! What a blow his sweet, sympathetic little note had been! Of course they quite understood; but it was most unfortunate.

"It would have been such a point, having him," said Josephine.

"And he would have enjoyed it so," said Constantia, not thinking what she was saying.

However, as soon as he got back he was coming to tea with his aunties. Cyril to tea was one of their rare treats.

"Now, Cyril, you mustn't be frightened of our cakes. Your Auntie Con and I bought them at Buszard's this morning. We know what a man's appetite is. So don't be ashamed of making a good tea."

Josephine cut recklessly into the rich dark cake that stood for her winter gloves or the soling and heeling of Constantia's only respectable shoes. But Cyril was most unmanlike in appetite.

"I say, Aunt Josephine, I simply can't. I've only just had lunch, you know."

"Oh, Cyril, that can't be true! It's after four," cried Josephine. Constantia sat with her knife poised over the chocolate roll.

"It is, all the same," said Cyril. "I had to meet a man at Victoria, and he kept me hanging about till . . . there was only time to get lunch and to come on here. And he gave me—phew"—Cyril put his hand to his forehead—"a terrific blowout," he said.

It was disappointing—today of all days. But still he couldn't be expected to know.

"But you'll have a meringue, won't you, Cyril?" said Aunt Josephine. "These meringues were bought specially for you. Your dear father was so fond of them. We were sure you are, too."

"I *am*, Aunt Josephine," cried Cyril ardently. "Do you mind if I take half to begin with?"

"Not at all, dear boy; but we mustn't let you off with that."

"Is your dear father still so fond of meringues?" asked Auntie Con gently. She winced faintly as she broke through the shell of hers.

"Well, I don't quite know, Auntie Con," said Cyril breezily.

At that they both looked up.

"Don't know?" almost snapped Josephine. "Don't know a thing like that about your own father, Cyril?"

"Surely," said Auntie Con softly.

Cyril tried to laugh it off. "Oh, well," he said, "it's such a long time since—" He faltered. He stopped. Their faces were too much for him.

"Even *so*," said Josephine.

And Auntie Con looked.

Cyril put down his teacup. "Wait a bit," he cried. "Wait a bit, Aunt Josephine. What am I thinking of?"

He looked up. They were beginning to brighten. Cyril slapped his knee.

"Of course," he said, "it was meringues. How could I have forgotten? Yes, Aunt Josephine, you're perfectly right. Father's most frightfully keen on meringues."

They didn't only beam. Aunt Josephine went scarlet with pleasure; Auntie Con gave a deep, deep sigh.

"And now, Cyril, you must come and see Father," said Josephine. "He knows you were coming today."

"Right," said Cyril, very firmly and heartily. He got up from his chair; suddenly he glanced at the clock.

"I say, Auntie Con, isn't your clock a bit slow? I've got to meet a man at—at Paddington just after five. I'm afraid I shan't be able to stay very long with Grandfather."

"Oh, he won't expect you to stay *very* long!" said Aunt Josephine.

Constantia was still gazing at the clock. She couldn't make up her mind if it was fast or slow. It was one or the other, she felt almost certain of that. At any rate, it had been.

Cyril still lingered. "Aren't you coming along, Auntie Con?"

"Of course," said Josephine, "we shall all go. Come on, Con."

## 9

They knocked at the door, and Cyril followed his aunts into Grandfather's hot, sweetish room.

"Come on," said Grandfather Pinner. "Don't hang about. What is it? What've you been up to?"

He was sitting in front of a roaring fire, clasping his stick. He had a thick rug over his knees. On his lap there lay a beautiful pale yellow silk handkerchief.

"It's Cyril, Father," said Josephine shyly. And she took Cyril's hand and led him forward.

"Good afternoon, Grandfather," said Cyril, trying to take his hand out of Aunt Josephine's. Grandfather Pinner shot his eyes at Cyril in the way he was famous for. Where was Auntie Con? She stood on the other side of Aunt Josephine; her long arms hung down in front of her; her hands were clasped. She never took her eyes off Grandfather.

"Well," said Grandfather Pinner, beginning to thump, "what have you got to tell me?"

What had he, what had he got to tell him? Cyril felt himself smiling like a perfect imbecile. The room was stifling, too.

But Aunt Josephine came to his rescue. She cried brightly, "Cyril says his father is still very fond of meringues, Father dear."

"Eh?" said Grandfather Pinner, curving his hand like a purple meringue shell over one ear.

Josephine repeated, "Cyril says his father is still very fond of meringues."

"Can't hear," said old Colonel Pinner. And he waved Josephine away with his stick, then pointed with his stick to Cyril. "Tell me what she's trying to say," he said.

(My God) "Must I?" said Cyril, blushing and staring at Aunt Josephine.

"Do, dear," she smiled. "It will please him so much."

"Come on, out with it!" cried Colonel Pinner testily, beginning to thump again.

And Cyril leaned forward and yelled, "Father's still very fond of meringues."

At that Grandfather Pinner jumped as though he had been shot.

"Don't shout!" he cried. "What's the matter with the boy? Meringues! What about 'em?"

"Oh, Aunt Josephine, must we go on?" groaned Cyril desperately.

"It's quite all right, dear boy," said Aunt Josephine, as though he and she were at the dentist's together. "He'll understand in a minute." And she whispered to Cyril, "He's getting a bit deaf, you know." Then she leaned forward and really bawled at Grandfather Pinner, "Cyril only wanted to tell you, Father dear, that *his* father is still very fond of meringues."

Colonel Pinner heard that time, heard and brooded, looking Cyril up and down.

"What an esstrordinary thing!" said old Grandfather Pinner. "What an esstrordinary thing to come all this way here to tell me!"

And Cyril felt it *was*.

"Yes, I shall send Cyril the watch," said Josephine.

"That would be very nice," said Constantia. "I seem to remember last time he came there was some little trouble about the time."

## 10

They were interrupted by Kate bursting through the door in her usual fashion, as though she had discovered some secret panel in the wall.

"Fried or boiled?" asked the bold voice.

Fried or boiled? Josephine and Constantia were quite bewildered for the moment. They could hardly take it in.

"Fried or boiled what, Kate?" asked Josephine, trying to begin to concentrate.

Kate gave a loud sniff. "Fish."

"Well, why didn't you say so immediately?" Josephine reproached her gently. "How could you expect us to understand, Kate? There are a great many things in this world, you know, which are fried or boiled." And after such a display of courage she said quite brightly to Constantia, "Which do you prefer, Con?"

"I think it might be nice to have it fried," said Constantia. "On the other hand, of course boiled fish is very nice. I think I prefer both equally well . . . Unless you . . . In that case—"

"I shall fry it," said Kate, and she bounced back, leaving their door open and slamming the door of her kitchen.

Josephine gazed at Constantia; she raised her pale eyebrows until they rippled away into her pale hair. She got up. She said in a very lofty, imposing way, "Do you mind following me into the drawing room, Constantia? I've something of great importance to discuss with you."

For it was always to the drawing room they retired when they wanted to talk over Kate.

Josephine closed the door meaningly. "Sit down, Constantia," she said, still very grand. She might have been receiving Constantia for the first time. And Con looked round vaguely for a chair, as though she felt indeed quite a stranger.

"Now the question is," said Josephine, bending forward, "whether we shall keep her or not."

"That is the question," agreed Constantia.

"And this time," said Josephine firmly, "we must come to a definite decision."

Constantia looked for a moment as though she might begin going over all the other times, but she pulled herself together and said, "Yes, Jug."

"You see, Con," explained Josephine, "everything is so changed now." Constantia looked up quickly. "I mean," went on Josephine, "we're not dependent on Kate as we were." And she blushed faintly. "There's not Father to cook for."

"That is perfectly true," agreed Constantia. "Father certainly doesn't want any cooking now, whatever else—"

Josephine broke in sharply. "You're not sleepy, are you, Con?"

"Sleepy, Jug?" Constantia was wide-eyed.

"Well, concentrate more," said Josephine sharply, and she returned to the subject. "What it comes to is, if we did"—and this she barely breathed, glancing at the door—"give Kate notice"—she raised her voice again—"we could manage our own food."

"Why not?" cried Constantia. She couldn't help smiling. The idea was so exciting. She clasped her hands. "What should we live on, Jug?"

"Oh, eggs in various forms!" said Jug, lofty again. "And, besides, there are all the cooked foods."

"But I've always heard," said Constantia, "they are considered so very expensive."

"Not if one buys them in moderation," said Josephine. But she tore herself away from this fascinating bypath and dragged Constantia after her.

"What we've got to decide now, however, is whether we really do trust Kate or not."

Constantia leaned back. Her flat little laugh flew from her lips. "Isn't it curious, Jug," said she, "that just on this subject I've never been able to quite make up my mind?"

## 11

She never had. The whole difficulty was to prove anything. How did one prove things, how could one? Suppose Kate had stood in front of her and deliberately made a face. Mightn't she very well have been in pain? Wasn't it impossible, at any rate, to ask Kate if she was making a face at her? If Kate answered "No"—and of course she would say "No"—what a position! How undignified! Then again Constantia suspected, she was almost certain that Kate went to her chest of drawers when she and Josephine were out, not to take things but to spy. Many times she had come back to find her amethyst cross in the most unlikely places, under lace ties or on top of her evening bertha. More than once she had laid a trap for Kate. She had arranged things in a special order and then called Josephine to witness.

"You see, Jug?"

"Quite, Con."

"Now we shall be able to tell."

But, oh dear, when she did go to look, she was as far off from a proof as ever! If anything was displaced, it might so very well have happened as she closed the drawer; a jolt might have done it so easily.

"You come, Jug, and decide. I really can't. It's too difficult."

But after a pause and a long glare Josephine would sigh, "Now you've put the doubt into my mind, Con, I'm sure I can't tell myself."

"Well, we can't postpone it again," said Josephine. "If we postpone it this time—"

## 12

But at that moment in the street below a barrel organ struck up. Josephine and Constantia sprang to their feet together.

"Run, Con," said Josephine. "Run quickly. There's six-pence on the—"

Then they remembered. It didn't matter. They would never have to stop the organ grinder again. Never again would she and Constantia be told to make that monkey take his noise somewhere else. Never would sound that loud, strange bellow when Father thought they were not hurrying enough. The organ grinder might play there all day and the stick would not thump.

It never will thump again,
It never will thump again,

played the barrel organ. What was Constantia thinking? She had such a strange smile; she looked different. She couldn't be going to cry.

"Jug, Jug," said Constantia softly, pressing her hands together. "Do you know what day it is? It's Saturday. It's a week today, a whole week."

A week since Father died,
A week since Father died,

cried the barrel organ. And Josephine, too, forgot to be practical and sensible; she smiled faintly, strangely. On the Indian carpet there fell a square of sunlight, pale red; it came and went and came—and stayed, deepened—until it shone almost golden.

"The sun's out," said Josephine, as though it really mattered.

A perfect fountain of bubbling notes shook from the barrel organ, round, bright notes, carelessly scattered.

Constantia lifted her big, cold hands as if to catch them, and then her hands fell again. She walked over to the mantelpiece to her favourite Buddha. And the stone and gilt image, whose smile always gave her such a queer feeling, almost a pain and yet a pleasant pain, seemed today to be more than smiling. He knew something; he had a secret. "I know something that you don't know," said her Buddha. Oh, what was it, what could it be? And yet she had always felt there was . . . something.

The sunlight pressed through the windows, thieved its way in, flashed its light over the furniture and the photographs. Josephine watched it. When it came to Mother's photograph, the enlargement over the piano, it lingered as though puzzled to find so little remained of Mother, except the earrings shaped like tiny pagodas and a black feather boa. Why did the photographs of dead people always fade so? wondered Josephine. As soon as a person was dead their photograph died too. But, of course, this one of Mother was very old. It was thirty-five years old. Josephine remembered standing on a chair and pointing out that feather boa to Constantia and telling her that it was a snake that had killed their mother in Ceylon. . . . Would everything have been different if Mother hadn't died? She didn't see why. Aunt Florence had lived with them until they had left school, and they had moved three times and had their yearly holiday and . . . and there'd been changes of servants, of course.

Some little sparrows, young sparrows they sounded, chirped on the window ledge. *Yeep—eyeep—yeep.* But Josephine felt they were not sparrows, not on the window ledge. It was inside her, that queer little crying noise. *Yeep—eyeep—yeep.* Ah, what was it crying, so weak and forlorn?

If Mother had lived, might they have married? But there had been nobody for them to marry. There had been Father's Anglo-Indian friends before he quarrelled with them. But after that she and Constantia never met a single man except clergymen. How did one meet men? Or even if they'd met them, how could they have got to know men well enough to be more than strangers? One read of people having adventures, being followed, and so on. But nobody had ever followed Constantia and her. Oh yes, there had been one year at Eastbourne a mysterious man at their boarding house who had put a note on the jug of hot water outside their bedroom door! But by the time Connie had found it the steam had made the writing too faint to read; they couldn't even make out to which of them it was addressed. And he had left next day. And that was all. The rest had been looking after Father, and at the same time keeping out of

Father's way. But now? But now? The thieving sun touched Josephine gently. She lifted her face. She was drawn over to the window by gentle beams. . . .

Until the barrel organ stopped playing Constantia stayed before the Buddha, wondering, but not as usual, not vaguely. This time her wonder was like longing. She remembered the times she had come in here, crept out of bed in her nightgown when the moon was full, and lain on the floor with her arms outstretched, as though she was crucified. Why? The big, pale moon had made her do it. The horrible dancing figures on the carved screen had leered at her and she hadn't minded. She remembered too how, whenever they were at the seaside, she had gone off by herself and got as close to the sea as she could, and sung something, something she had made up, while she gazed all over that restless water. There had been this other life, running out, bringing things home in bags, getting things on approval, discussing them with Jug, and taking them back to get more things on approval, and arranging Father's trays and trying not to annoy Father. But it all seemed to have happened in a kind of tunnel. It wasn't real. It was only when she came out of the tunnel into the moonlight or by the sea or into a thunderstorm that she really felt herself. What did it mean? What was it she was always wanting? What did it all lead to? Now? Now?

She turned away from the Buddha with one of her vague gestures. She went over to where Josephine was standing. She wanted to say something to Josephine, something frightfully important, about—about the future and what . . .

"Don't you think perhaps—" she began.

But Josephine interrupted her. "I was wondering if now—" she murmured. They stopped; they waited for each other.

"Go on, Con," said Josephine.

"No, no, Jug; after you," said Constantia.

"No, say what you were going to say. You began," said Josephine.

"I . . . I'd rather hear what you were going to say first," said Constantia.

"Don't be absurd, Con."

"Really, Jug."

"Connie!"

"Oh, *Jug*!"

A pause. Then Constantia said faintly, "I can't say what I was going to say, Jug, because I've forgotten what it was . . . that I was going to say."

Josephine was silent for a moment. She stared at a big cloud where the sun had been. Then she replied shortly, "I've forgotten too."

## QUESTIONS

1. Why does Josephine cry as she answers each letter of condolence? Why does she think, "Strange! She couldn't have put it on—but twenty-three times"? (338)

2. Why are Josephine and Constantia so upset by Nurse Andrews's being "simply fearful about butter"? (339)

3. When Constantia locks the wardrobe holding their father's clothes, why is her action "one of those amazingly bold things that she'd done about twice before in their lives"? (344)

4. Why are the daughters so anxious around Kate, Nurse Andrews, and Mr. Farolles? How are they dependent on these characters?

5. Why do Josephine and Constantia press Cyril to say whether his father still likes meringues? Why do they report his answer to the colonel?

6. Why does Josephine recall Cyril's visit so vividly?

7. Why do we only meet the living colonel during the account of Cyril's visit?

8. Why don't the sisters talk to each other about what they are feeling?

9. As the barrel organ plays, why does Constantia begin wondering "not as usual, not vaguely"? (353)

10. At the end of the story, why do Constantia and Josephine begin speaking about the future at the same time but then forget what they were going to say?

## FOR FURTHER REFLECTION

1. To what extent does the story reinforce or challenge the stereotype of the "old maid"?

2. Why does Mansfield shift the story's point of view so often?

3. Why haven't the sisters married?

4. What, if anything, might make the future different for Constantia and Josephine?

# KAREL ČAPEK

Karel Čapek (1890–1938) was born in Bohemia, Austria-Hungary, which after World War I became a province of the newly formed republic of Czechoslovakia, and in the late 1930s became the first region of Czechoslovakia to be taken over by Nazi Germany. The son of a small-town doctor, Čapek suffered from a painful spinal disease that helped encourage a close bond between Karel and his older brother Josef that would last throughout their lives. The "Brothers Čapek," as they would later sign their literary works, were inseparable. They coauthored newspaper articles, plays, and a collection of short stories and studied together in Berlin, Paris, and Prague, where they eventually settled. Their collaboration waned as they gained renown in separate fields—Josef as a cubist painter and Karel as a writer—but the two remained close. In the 1920s, Karel, already an established writer and director, fell in love with Olga Scheinpflugová, an aspiring actress thirteen years his junior. After an artistic and romantic relationship lasting many years they finally married in 1935.

*R.U.R. (Rossum's Universal Robots)*, first produced in 1921, launched Čapek's career as an internationally celebrated author. The play is known for its introduction of the word *robot*, a term coined by his brother Josef from the Czech word *robota* (serf labor). However, Čapek worried that the novelty of the robots distracted audiences from the deeper meaning of the play. In an interview for the *Saturday Review* in 1923 Čapek declared, "General Director Domin tries to prove in the play that technical developments liberate man from heavy physical labor, and he is right. Alquist, the Tolstoyan architect, believes on the contrary that technical developments demoralize man, and I think that he is right, too . . . The most dramatic element in modern civilization is the fact that one human truth stands against a truth no less human . . . and that the conflict does not represent, as we are often told, a struggle between a noble truth and a vile, selfish evil."

Čapek's career as a writer coincided almost exactly with the twenty years of Czech democratic independence between World War I and World War II. He was a close friend and biographer of Czech president Tomáš Masaryk and a great supporter of Masaryk's democratic politics.

Čapek was widely read in his own time, and throughout his career he explored the human tendency toward folly, excess, and greed. At the same time, he persistently depicted the ways in which the individual can live with integrity in the face of formidable challenges to his or her humanity. In the novels *The Absolute at Large* (1922) and *Krakatit* (1924), Čapek further developed the theme of the consequences of unbridled technological innovation introduced in *R.U.R.* In his 1922 satirical play *The Insect Play*, coauthored with Josef, human foibles are portrayed allegorically through the characteristics of various insects. In it, the ominous lockstep behavior of ant colonies is a prescient foreshadowing of the militarism that within a few years would overwhelm the world. And in his play *The Makropulos Affair* (1922), Čapek depicts the chilling results that can come from fulfillment of the age-old human desire for immortality. His trilogy of novels, *Hordubal* (1933), *Meteor* (1934), and *An Ordinary Life* (1934), is a profound investigation of what can be known of the truth concerning the life of an individual. In his widely known novel *War with the Newts* (1936), Čapek deepened his satirical portrayal of the hazards of scientism, unfettered capitalism, and political ideologies.

As Hitler grew more powerful, Čapek's work became more urgent and direct in addressing the growing threat of Nazi Germany. After the 1938 Munich Agreement, which permitted Nazi Germany to annex a portion of Czechoslovakia, the Čapek brothers were warned to leave Prague. Both refused, despite the fact that the Gestapo had targeted Karel. On Christmas Day, 1938, Karel died of pneumonia; only a few months later, the Nazis invaded Prague and Josef was sent to Bergen-Belsen concentration camp, where he died just before World War II ended.

# R.U.R.
# (Rossum's Universal Robots)

## A Collective Drama in a Comic Prologue and Three Acts

**CHARACTERS**

HARRY DOMIN, *central director of Rossum's Universal Robots*

FABRY, *engineer, general technical director of R.U.R.*

DR. GALL, *head of the physiological and research divisions of R.U.R.*

DR. HALLEMEIER, *head of the institute for Robot psychology and education*

BUSMAN, *general marketing director and chief counsel of R.U.R.*

ALQUIST, *builder, chief of construction of R.U.R.*

HELENA GLORY

NANA, *her nurse*

MARIUS, *a Robot*

SULLA, *a lady Robot*

RADIUS, *a Robot*

DAMON, *a Robot*

Karel Čapek

FIRST ROBOT

SECOND ROBOT

THIRD ROBOT

FOURTH ROBOT

ROBOT PRIMUS

LADY ROBOT HELENA

ROBOT SERVANT AND NUMEROUS OTHER ROBOTS

———

DOMIN, *about 38 years old in the Prologue, tall, clean-shaven*

FABRY, *also clean-shaven, fair-haired, with a serious and gentle face*

DR. GALL, *trifling, lively, suntanned, with a black moustache*

HALLEMEIER, *huge, robust, with a red, English moustache and red scrubby hair*

BUSMAN, *fat, bald, near-sighted*

ALQUIST, *older than the rest, carelessly dressed, with long grizzled hair and whiskers*

HELENA, *very elegant*

*In the play proper everyone is ten years older than in the prologue. In the prologue the Robots are dressed like people. Their movements and speech are laconic. Their faces are expressionless and their eyes fixed. In the play proper they are wearing linen shirts tightened at their waists with a belt and have brass numbers on their chests. There is an intermission following the prologue and the second act.*

## PROLOGUE

*The central office of the Rossum's Universal Robots factory. On the right is a door. Windows in the front wall look out onto an endless row of factory buildings. On the left are more managerial offices.*

*Domin is sitting at a large American desk in a revolving armchair. On the desk is a lamp, a telephone, a paperweight, a file of letters, etc.; on the wall to the left are big maps depicting ship and railway lines, a big calendar, and a clock that reads shortly before noon; affixed to the wall on the left are printed posters: "The Cheapest Labor: Rossum's Robots." "Tropical Robots—A New Invention—$150 a Head." "Buy Your Very Own Robot." "Looking To Cut Production Costs? Order Rossum's Robots." Still more maps, transport regulations, a chart with entries of telegraph rates, etc. In contrast to these wall decorations there is a splendid Turkish carpet on the floor, to the right a round table, a couch, a leather club-style armchair, and a bookcase in which there are bottles of wine and brandy instead of books. On the left is a safe. Next to Domin's desk is a typewriter at which Sulla is working.*

DOMIN, *dictating.* "—that we will not stand responsible for goods damaged in transport. We brought it to the attention of your captain just before loading that the ship was unfit for the transportation of Robots, so we are not to be held financially accountable for the damage to the merchandise. For Rossum's Universal Robots, et cetera—" Got it?

SULLA. Yes.

DOMIN. New sheet. Friedrichswerke, Hamburg.—Date.—"I am writing to confirm your order for fifteen thousand Robots—" (*In-house telephone rings. Domin answers it and speaks.*) Hello—Central office here—Yes.—Certainly. But of course, as always.—Of course, wire them.—Good.—(*He hangs up the telephone.*) Where did I leave off?

SULLA. "I am writing to confirm your order for fifteen thousand Robots."

DOMIN, *thinking.* Fifteen thousand Robots. Fifteen thousand Robots.

MARIUS, *enters.* Mr. Director, some lady is asking—

DOMIN. Who is it?

MARIUS. I do not know. (*He hands Domin a calling card.*)

DOMIN, *reads.* President Glory.—Ask her in.

MARIUS, *opens the door.* If you please, ma'am.

*Enter Helena Glory. Marius leaves.*

DOMIN, *stands.* How do you do?

HELENA. Central Director Domin?

DOMIN. At your service.

HELENA. I have come—

DOMIN. —with a note from President Glory. That will do.

HELENA. President Glory is my father. I am Helena Glory.

DOMIN. Miss Glory, it is an unusual honor for us to—

HELENA. —to be unable to show you the door.

DOMIN. —to welcome the daughter of our great president. Please have a seat. Sulla, you may go.

*Sulla leaves.*

DOMIN, *sits down.* How can I be of service, Miss Glory?

HELENA. I have come—

DOMIN. —to have a look at our factory production of people. Like all visitors. I'd be happy to show you.

HELENA. But I thought it was prohibited—

DOMIN. —to enter the factory, of course. Yet everyone comes here with someone's calling card, Miss Glory.

HELENA. And you show everyone . . . ?

DOMIN. Only some things. The method for producing artificial people is a factory secret, Miss Glory.

HELENA. If you knew just how much—

DOMIN. —this interests you. Good old Europe is talking about nothing else.

HELENA. Why don't you let me finish my sentences?

DOMIN. I beg your pardon. Perhaps you wanted to say something different?

HELENA. I only wanted to ask—

DOMIN. —whether I wouldn't make an exception and show you our factory. But certainly, Miss Glory.

HELENA. How do you know that's what I wanted to ask?

DOMIN. Everybody asks the same thing. (*He stands.*) With all due respect, Miss Glory, we will show you more than we show the others and— in a word—

HELENA. I thank you.

DOMIN. If you vow that you will not disclose to anyone even the smallest—

HELENA, *stands and offers him her hand.* You have my word of honor.

DOMIN. Thank you. Don't you want to take off your veil?

HELENA. Oh, of course, you want to see—Excuse me.

DOMIN. Pardon?

HELENA. If you would let go of my hand.

DOMIN, *lets go of her hand.* I beg your pardon.

HELENA, *taking off her veil.* You want to see that I'm not a spy. How cautious you are.

DOMIN, *scrutinizing her ardently.* Hm, of course, we—yes.

HELENA. Don't you trust me?

DOMIN. Singularly, Hele—pardon, Miss Glory. Really, I'm extraordinarily delighted.—Did you have a good crossing?

HELENA. Yes. Why—

DOMIN. Because—I was just thinking—you're still very young.

HELENA. Will we be going to the factory immediately?

DOMIN. Yes. I'd guess about twenty-two, right?

HELENA. Twenty-two what?

DOMIN. Years old.

HELENA. Twenty-one. Why do you want to know?

DOMIN. Because—since—(*Enthusiastically.*) You'll stay awhile, won't you?

HELENA. That depends on what I see at the factory.

DOMIN. Blasted factory! But certainly, Miss Glory, you will see everything. Please, have a seat. Would you be interested in learning something about the history of the invention?

HELENA. Yes, please. (*She sits down.*)

DOMIN. Well, then. (*He sits down at the desk gazing rapturously at Helena and rattles off quickly.*) The year was 1920 when old Rossum, a great philosopher but at the time still a young scholar, moved away to this remote island to study marine life, period. At the same time he was attempting to reproduce, by means of chemical synthesis, living matter known as protoplasm, when suddenly he discovered a substance which behaved exactly like living matter although it was of a different chemical composition. That was in 1932, precisely four hundred forty years after the discovery of America.

HELENA. You know all this by heart?

DOMIN. Yes. Physiology, Miss Glory, is not my game. Shall I go on?

HELENA. Please.

DOMIN, *solemnly*. And then, Miss Glory, old Rossum wrote among his chemical formulas: "Nature has found only one process by which to organize living matter. There is, however, another process, simpler, more moldable and faster, which nature has not hit upon at all. It is this other process, by means of which the development of life could proceed, that I have discovered this very day." Imagine, Miss Glory, that he wrote these lofty words about some phlegm of a colloidal jelly that not even a dog would eat. Imagine him sitting over a test tube and thinking how the whole tree of life would grow out of it, starting with some species of worm and ending—ending with man himself. Man made from a different matter than we are. Miss Glory, that was a tremendous moment.

HELENA. What then?

DOMIN. Then? Then it was a question of taking life out of the test tube, speeding up its development, shaping some of the organs, bones, nerves, and whatnot, and finding certain substances, catalysts, enzymes, hormones, et cetera; in short, do you understand?

HELENA. I d-d-don't know. Not very much, I'm afraid.

DOMIN. Neither do I. Anyway, by using these substances he could concoct whatever he wanted. For instance, he could have created a jellyfish with a Socratic brain or a one-hundred-fifty-foot worm. But because he hadn't a shred of humor about him, he took it into his head to create an ordinary vertebrate, possibly a human being. And so he set to it.

HELENA. To what?

DOMIN. To reproducing nature. First he tried to create an artificial
dog. That took him a number of years, and finally he produced
something like a mutant calf that died in a couple of days. I'll
point it out to you in the museum. And then old Rossum set out to
manufacture a human being.

*Pause.*

HELENA. And *this* I must disclose to no one?

DOMIN. To no one in the world.

HELENA. It's a pity this is already in all the papers.

DOMIN. A pity. (*He jumps up from the desk and sits down next to Helena.*) But
do you know what isn't in the papers? (*He taps his forehead.*) That old
Rossum was a raving lunatic. That's a fact, Miss Glory, but keep it
to yourself. That old eccentric actually wanted to make people.

HELENA. But *you* make people after all!

DOMIN. More or less, Miss Glory. But old Rossum meant that literally.
You see, he wanted somehow to scientifically dethrone God. He was
a frightful materialist and did everything on that account. For him it
was a question of nothing more than furnishing proof that no God
is necessary. So he resolved to create a human being just like us to
the turn of a hair. Do you know a little anatomy?

HELENA. Only—very little.

DOMIN. Same here. Imagine, he took it into his head to manufacture
everything just as it is in the human body, right down to the
last gland. The appendix, the tonsils, the belly button—all the
superfluities. Finally even—hm—even the sexual organs.

HELENA. But after all those—those after all—

DOMIN. —are not superfluous, I know. But if people were going to be
produced artificially, then it was not—hm—in any way necessary—

HELENA. I understand.

DOMIN. In the museum I'll show you what all he managed to bungle in
ten years. The thing that was supposed to be a man lived for three
whole days. Old Rossum didn't have a bit of taste. What he did
was dreadful. But inside, that thing had all the stuff a person has.
Actually it was amazingly detailed work. And then young Rossum,
an engineer, the son of the old man, came here. An ingenious mind,
Miss Glory. When he saw what a scene his old man was making he

Karel Čapek

said: "This is nonsense! Ten years to produce a human being?! If you can't do it faster than nature then just pack it in." And he himself launched into anatomy.

HELENA. It's different in the papers.

DOMIN, *stands*. In the papers are just paid ads; all the rest is nonsense. It's been written, for example, that the old man invented the Robots. The fact is that the old man was fine for the university, but he had no idea of production. He thought that he would create real people, possibly a new race of Indians, whether professors or idiots, you see? It was only young Rossum who had the idea to create living and intelligent labor machines from this mess. All that stuff in the papers about the collaboration of the two great Rossums is idle gossip. Those two quarreled brutally. The old atheist didn't have a crumb of understanding for industry, and finally young Rossum shut him up in some laboratory where he could fiddle with his monumental abortions, and he himself undertook production from the standpoint of an engineer. Old Rossum literally cursed him and before his death he bungled two more physiological monsters until finally he was found dead in his laboratory one day. That's the whole story.

HELENA. And what about the young man?

DOMIN. Young Rossum was of a new age, Miss Glory. The age of production following the age of discovery. When he took a look at human anatomy he saw immediately that it was too complex and that a good engineer could simplify it. So he undertook to redesign anatomy, experimenting with what would lend itself to omission or simplification—In short, Miss Glory—but isn't this boring you?

HELENA. No, on the contrary, it's dreadfully interesting.

DOMIN. So then young Rossum said to himself: A human being. That's something that feels joy, plays the violin, wants to go for a walk, and in general requires a lot of things which—which are, in effect, superfluous.

HELENA. Oh!

DOMIN. Wait. Which are superfluous when he needs to weave or add. A gasoline engine has no need for tassels and ornaments, Miss Glory. And manufacturing artificial workers is exactly like manufacturing gasoline engines. Production should be as simple as possible and the product best for its function. What do you think? Practically speaking, what is the best kind of worker?

HELENA. The best? Probably the one who—who—who is honest—and dedicated.

DOMIN. No, it's the one that's the cheapest. The one with the fewest needs. Young Rossum did invent a worker with the smallest number of needs, but to do so he had to simplify him. He chucked everything not directly related to work, and doing that he virtually rejected the human being and created the Robot. My dear Miss Glory, Robots are not people. They are mechanically more perfect than we are, they have an astounding intellectual capacity, but they have no soul. Oh, Miss Glory, the product of an engineer is technically more refined than the creation of nature.

HELENA. It is said that man is the creation of God.

DOMIN. So much the worse. God had no notion of modern technology. Would you believe that the late young Rossum assumed the role of God?

HELENA. How, may I ask?

DOMIN. He began to produce Superrobots. Working giants. He experimented making them twelve feet tall, but you wouldn't believe how those mammoths fell apart.

HELENA. Fell apart?

DOMIN. Yes. All of a sudden a leg would break or something. Our planet is apparently too small for giants. Now we make only Robots of normal human height and respectable human shape.

HELENA. I saw the first Robots back home. The township bought them . . . I mean hired—

DOMIN. Bought, my dear Miss Glory. Robots are bought.

HELENA. We acquired them as street cleaners. I've seen them sweeping. They are so odd, so quiet.

DOMIN. Have you seen my secretary?

HELENA. I didn't notice.

DOMIN, *rings*. You see, the Rossum's Universal Robots Corporation does not yet manufacture entirely uniform goods. Some of the Robots are very fine, others come out cruder. The best will live perhaps twenty years.

HELENA. Then they die?

DOMIN. Well, they wear out.

*Enter Sulla.*

DOMIN. Sulla, let Miss Glory have a look at you.

HELENA, *stands and offers Sulla her hand.* How do you do? You must be dreadfully sad out here so far away from the rest of the world.

SULLA. That I cannot say, Miss Glory. Please have a seat.

HELENA, *sits down.* Where are you from, Miss?

SULLA. From here, from the factory.

HELENA. Oh, you were born here?

SULLA. I was made here, yes.

HELENA, *jumping up.* What?

DOMIN, *laughing.* Sulla is not human, Miss Glory. Sulla is a Robot.

HELENA. I meant no offense—

DOMIN, *placing his hand on Sulla's shoulder.* Sulla's not offended. Take a look at the complexion we make, Miss Glory. Touch her face.

HELENA. Oh, no, no!

DOMIN. You'd never guess she was made from a different substance than we are. She even has the characteristic soft hair of a blonde, if you please. Only the eyes are a trifle—But on the other hand, what hair! Turn around, Sulla!

HELENA. Please stop!

DOMIN. Chat with our guest, Sulla. She is a distinguished visitor.

SULLA. Please, Miss, have a seat. (*They both sit down.*) Did you have a good crossing?

HELENA. Yes—cer-certainly.

SULLA. Do not go back on the *Amelia*, Miss Glory. The barometer is falling sharply—to 27.7. Wait for the *Pennsylvania*; it is a very good, very strong ship.

DOMIN. Speed?

SULLA. Twenty knots. Tonnage—twenty thousand.

DOMIN, *laughing.* Enough, Sulla, enough. Let's hear how well you speak French.

HELENA. You know French?

SULLA. I know four languages. I can write, "Cteny pane! Monsieur! Geehrter Herr! Dear Sir!"

HELENA, *jumping up*. This is preposterous! You are a charlatan! Sulla's not a Robot, Sulla is a young woman just like me! Sulla, this is disgraceful—why do you go along with this farce?

SULLA. I am a Robot.

HELENA. No, no, you are lying! Oh, Sulla, forgive me, I understand— they've coerced you into acting as a living advertisement for them! Sulla, you are a young woman like me, aren't you? Tell me you are!

DOMIN. I'm sorry to disappoint you, Miss Glory. Sulla is a Robot.

HELENA. You're lying!

DOMIN, *drawing himself up*. What?!—(*He rings.*) Excuse me, Miss Glory, but I must convince you.

*Enter Marius.*

DOMIN. Marius, take Sulla into the dissecting room so they can open her up. Quickly!

HELENA. Where?

DOMIN. The dissecting room. When they have cut her open you can go and take a look at her.

HELENA. I won't go.

DOMIN. Excuse me, but you suggested I was lying.

HELENA. You want to have her killed?

DOMIN. Machines cannot be killed.

HELENA, *embracing Sulla*. Don't be frightened, Sulla. I won't let them hurt you! Tell me, darling, is everyone so inhumane to you? You mustn't put up with that, do you hear? You mustn't, Sulla!

SULLA. I am a Robot.

HELENA. That makes no difference. Robots are just as good people as we are. Sulla, you'd let them cut you open?

SULLA. Yes.

HELENA. Oh, you are not afraid of death?

SULLA. I cannot answer that question, Miss Glory.

HELENA. Do you know what would happen to you then?

SULLA. Yes, I would stop moving.

HELENA. This is d-r-readful!

DOMIN. Marius, tell Miss Glory what you are.

MARIUS. A Robot. Marius.

DOMIN. Would you put Sulla in the dissecting room?

MARIUS. Yes.

DOMIN. Would you be sorry for her?

MARIUS. I cannot answer that question.

DOMIN. What would happen to her?

MARIUS. She would stop moving. She would be sent to the stamping mill.

DOMIN. That is death, Marius. Do you fear death?

MARIUS. No.

DOMIN. So you see, Miss Glory. Robots do not hold on to life. They can't. They have nothing to hold on with—no soul, no instinct. Grass has more will to live than they do.

HELENA. Oh, stop! At least send them out of the room!

DOMIN. Marius, Sulla, you may go.

*Sulla and Marius leave.*

HELENA. They are d-r-readful! What you are doing is abominable!

DOMIN. Why abominable?

HELENA. I don't know. Why—why did you name her Sulla?

DOMIN. You don't think it's a pretty name?

HELENA. It's a man's name. Sulla was a Roman general.

DOMIN. Oh, we thought that Marius and Sulla were lovers.

HELENA. No, Marius and Sulla were generals and fought against each other in the year—the year—I don't remember.

DOMIN. Come over to the window. What do you see?

HELENA. Bricklayers.

DOMIN. Those are Robots. All of our laborers are Robots. And down below, can you see anything?

HELENA. Some sort of office.

DOMIN. The accounting office. And it's—

HELENA. —full of office workers.

DOMIN. Robots. All of our office staff are Robots. When you see the factory—

*At that moment the factory whistles and sirens sound.*

DOMIN. Noon. The Robots don't know when to stop working. At two o'clock I'll show you the kneading troughs.

HELENA. What kneading troughs?

DOMIN, *dryly.* The mixing vats for the batter. In each one we mix enough batter for a thousand Robots at a time. Next come the vats for livers, brains, et cetera. Then you'll see the bone factory, and after that I'll show you the spinning mill.

HELENA. What spinning mill?

DOMIN. The spinning mill for nerves. The spinning mill for veins. The spinning mill where miles and miles of digestive tract are made at once. Then there's the assembly plant where all of this is put together, you know, like automobiles. Each worker is responsible for affixing one part, and then it automatically moves on to a second worker, then to a third, and so on. It's a most fascinating spectacle. Next comes the drying kiln and the stock room where the brand-new products are put to work.

HELENA. Good heavens, they have to work immediately?

DOMIN. Sorry. They work the same way new furniture works. They get broken in. Somehow they heal up internally or something. Even a lot that's new grows up inside them. You understand, we must leave a bit of room for natural development. And in the meantime the products are refined.

HELENA. How do you mean?

DOMIN. Well, it's the same as school for people. They learn to speak, write, and do arithmetic. They have a phenomenal memory. If one read them the *Encyclopaedia Britannica* they could repeat everything back in order, but they never think up anything original. They'd make fine university professors. Next they are sorted by grade and distributed. Fifty thousand head a day, not counting the inevitable percentage of defective ones that are thrown into the stamping mill . . . et cetera, et cetera.

HELENA. Are you angry with me?

DOMIN. God forbid! I only thought that . . . that perhaps we could talk about other things. We are only a handful of people here amidst a hundred thousand Robots, and there are no women. It's as though we're cursed, Miss Glory.

HELENA. I'm so sorry that I said that—that—that you were lying—

*A knock at the door.*

DOMIN. Come in, boys.

*The engineer Fabry, Dr. Gall, Dr. Hallemeier, and the builder Alquist enter from the left.*

DR. GALL. Excuse us, I hope we're not interrupting?

DOMIN. Come here, Miss Glory. Let me introduce Alquist, Fabry, Gall, and Hallemeier. The daughter of President Glory.

HELENA, *at a loss.* Hello.

FABRY. We had no idea—

DR. GALL. We are deeply honored—

ALQUIST. Welcome, Miss Glory.

*Busman rushes in from the right.*

BUSMAN. Hey, what have we here?

DOMIN. Here, Busman. This is our Busman, Miss. (*To Busman.*) The daughter of President Glory.

HELENA. How do you do?

BUSMAN. Why this is splendid! Miss Glory, shall we wire the papers that you have done us the honor to pay a visit—?

HELENA. No, no, I beg you!

DOMIN. Please, Miss Glory, have a seat.

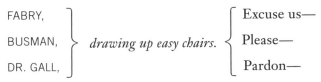

FABRY,
BUSMAN, } *drawing up easy chairs.* { Excuse us—
DR. GALL, Please—
Pardon—

ALQUIST. Miss Glory, how was your trip?

DR. GALL. Will you be staying with us long?

FABRY. What do you have to say about the factory, Miss Glory?

HALLEMEIER. Did you come on the *Amelia*?

DOMIN. Quiet, let Miss Glory speak.

HELENA, *to Domin.* What should I speak with them about?

DOMIN, *with astonishment.* Whatever you want.

HELENA. Should I . . . may I speak quite openly?

DOMIN. Of course.

HELENA, *hesitates, then is desperately determined.* Tell me, isn't the way they treat you here sometimes painful?

FABRY. Who, may I ask?

HELENA. All the people.

*They all look at each other, puzzled.*

ALQUIST. Treat us?

DR. GALL. Why do you think that?

HALLEMEIER. Thunderation!

BUSMAN. God forbid, Miss Glory!

HELENA. I'm sure you must feel that you could have a better existence?

DR. GALL. That depends, Miss Glory. How do you mean that?

HELENA. I mean that—(*she explodes*)—that this is abominable! that this is awful! (*She stands up.*) All of Europe is talking about what's happening to you here! So I came here to see for myself, and it's a thousand times worse than anyone ever imagined! How can you bear it?

ALQUIST. Bear what?

HELENA. Your position. For God's sake, you are people just like us, like all of Europe, like the whole world! The way you live is undignified, it's scandalous!

BUSMAN. Dear Lord, Miss!

FABRY. No, boys, she's right in a way. We really do live like savages here.

HELENA. Worse than savages! May I, oh, may I call you brothers?

BUSMAN. But good Lord, why not?

HELENA. Brothers, I have not come as the President's daughter. I have come on behalf of the League of Humanity. Brothers, the League of Humanity already has more than two hundred thousand members. Two hundred thousand people stand behind you and offer you their support.

BUSMAN. Two hundred thousand people! That's quite respectable, that's beautiful.

FABRY. I'm always telling you there's nothing better than good old Europe. You see, they haven't forgotten about us. They're offering us help.

DR. GALL. What kind of help? A theater?

HALLEMEIER. A symphony orchestra?

HELENA. More than that.

ALQUIST. You yourself?

HELENA. Oh, no doubt me. I'll stay as long as I am needed.

BUSMAN. God in heaven, this is joy!

ALQUIST. Domin, I'll go and get our best room ready for Miss Glory.

DOMIN. Wait a minute. I'm afraid that—that Miss Glory has not yet said everything she has to say.

HELENA. No, I have not. Unless you plan to shut my mouth by force.

DR. GALL. Just you try it, Harry!

HELENA. Thank you. I knew that you would stand up for me.

DOMIN. I'm sorry, Miss Glory. Do you think that you're talking to Robots?

HELENA, *pauses*. Of course, what else?

DOMIN. I'm sorry. These gentlemen are people, just like you. Like all of Europe.

HELENA, *to the others*. You're not Robots?

BUSMAN, *guffawing*. God forbid!

HALLEMEIER. Bah, Robots!

DR. GALL, *laughing.* Thank you very much!

HELENA. But . . . this is impossible!

FABRY. On my honor, Miss Glory, we are not Robots.

HELENA, *to Domin.* Then why did you tell me that all of your office staff are Robots?

DOMIN. Yes, the office staff. But not the directors. Miss Glory, allow me to introduce Fabry, general technical director of Rossum's Universal Robots, Doctor Gall, head of the physiological and research divisions, Doctor Hallemeier, head of the institute for Robot psychology and education, Busman, general marketing director and chief counsel, and our builder Alquist, chief of construction at Rossum's Universal Robots.

HELENA. Forgive me, gentlemen, for—for—Is what I have done d-r-readful?

ALQUIST. Good heavens, Miss Glory. Please, have a seat.

HELENA, *sits down.* I'm a silly girl. Now—now you'll send me back by the first boat.

DR. GALL. Not for anything in the world, Miss Glory. Why would we send you away?

HELENA. Because now you know—because—because I came to incite the Robots.

DOMIN. Dear Miss Glory, we've already had at least a hundred saviors and prophets here. Every boat brings another one. Missionaries, anarchists, the Salvation Army, everything imaginable. It would amaze you to know how many churches and lunatics there are in the world.

HELENA. And you let them talk to the Robots?

DOMIN. Why not? So far they've all given up. The Robots remember everything, but nothing more. They don't even laugh at what people say. Actually, it's hard to believe. If it would interest you, dear Miss Glory, I'll take you to the Robot warehouse. There are about three hundred thousand of them there.

BUSMAN. Three hundred forty-seven thousand.

DOMIN. Good. You can tell them whatever you want. You can read them the Bible, logarithms, or whatever you please. You can even preach to them about human rights.

HELENA. Oh, I thought that . . . if someone were to show them a bit of love—

FABRY. Impossible, Miss Glory. Nothing is farther from being human than a Robot.

HELENA. Why do you make them then?

BUSMAN. Hahaha, that's a good one! Why do we make Robots!

FABRY. For work, Miss. One Robot can do the work of two and a half human laborers. The human machine, Miss Glory, was hopelessly imperfect. It needed to be done away with once and for all.

BUSMAN. It was too costly.

FABRY. It was less than efficient. It couldn't keep up with modern technology. And in the second place it's great progress that . . . pardon.

HELENA. What?

FABRY. Forgive me. It's great progress to give birth by machine. It's faster and more convenient. Any acceleration constitutes progress, Miss Glory. Nature had no understanding of the modern rate of work. From a technical standpoint the whole of childhood is pure nonsense. Simply wasted time. An untenable waste of time. And in the third place—

HELENA. Oh, stop!

FABRY. I'm sorry. Let me ask you, what exactly does your League of— League of—League of Humanity want?

HELENA. We want first and foremost to protect the Robots and—and—to guarantee them—good treatment.

FABRY. That's not a bad goal. Machines should be treated well. Honestly, that makes me happy. I don't like damaged goods. Please, Miss Glory, enlist us all as contributing, dues-paying, founding members of your League!

HELENA. No, you misunderstand me. We want—specifically—we want to free the Robots.

HALLEMEIER. How, may I ask?

HELENA. They should be treated like . . . treated like . . . like people.

HALLEMEIER. Aha. Perhaps they should be allowed to vote, too? You won't go so far as to say that they should be paid?

HELENA. Of course they should.

HALLEMEIER. Let's consider this. If they had money, what would they do with it?

HELENA. Buy themselves . . . what they need . . . whatever would make them happy.

HALLEMEIER. That's very nice, Miss, but nothing makes Robots happy. Thunder, what would they buy for themselves? You can feed them pineapples or straw or whatever you want—it's all the same to them. They have no sense of taste at all. They have no interest in anything, Miss Glory. By God, no one's even seen a Robot smile.

HELENA. Why . . . why . . . why don't you make them happier?

HALLEMEIER. It's no use, Miss Glory. They're only Robots. They have no will of their own, no passion, no history, no soul.

HELENA. No love or defiance either?

HALLEMEIER. That goes without saying. Robots love nothing, not even themselves. And defiance? I don't know; only rarely, every now and again—

HELENA. What?

HALLEMEIER. Nothing special. Occasionally they go crazy somehow. Something like epilepsy, you know? We call it Robotic Palsy. All of a sudden one of them goes and breaks whatever it has in its hand, stops working, gnashes its teeth—and we have to send it to the stamping mill. Evidently a breakdown of the organism.

DOMIN. A flaw in production.

HELENA. No, no, that's a soul!

FABRY. You think a soul begins with a gnashing of teeth?

DOMIN. We'll soon put a stop to all of this, Miss Glory. Doctor Gall is doing some significant experiments—

DR. GALL. Not on that, Domin; right now I'm making pain-reactive nerves.

HELENA. Pain-reactive nerves?

DR. GALL. Yes. Robots feel almost no physical pain. You see, the late young Rossum oversimplified the nervous system. That was no good. We must introduce suffering.

HELENA. Why—why—If you won't give them souls, why do you want to give them pain?

DR. GALL. For industrial reasons, Miss Glory. The Robots sometimes damage themselves because nothing hurts them. They stick their hands into machines, break their fingers, smash their heads, it's all the same to them. We must give them pain; it's a built-in safeguard against damage.

HELENA. Will they be happier when they can feel pain?

DR. GALL. On the contrary. But they will be technically more perfect.

HELENA. Why won't you make souls for them?

DR. GALL. That's not within our power.

FABRY. Nor in our interest.

BUSMAN. That would raise the cost of production. Dear Lord, lovely lady, the beauty of our product is that it's so cheap! One hundred twenty dollars a head, complete with clothing, and fifteen years ago they cost ten thousand. Five years ago we were still buying clothes for them. Today we have our own textile mill where we produce fabric five times more cheaply than other factories. Tell me, Miss Glory, what do you pay for a yard of cloth?

HELENA. I don't know—actually—I've forgotten.

BUSMAN. Good Lord, and you want to found a League of Humanity! Ours costs only a third as much, Miss Glory; today all prices are only a third of what they were, and they're still falling, lower, lower, lower, lower—just like that. Well?

HELENA. I don't understand.

BUSMAN. Lord, Miss Glory. What this means is that we've cut the cost of labor. Why even with fodder a Robot costs only three-quarters of a cent an hour. It's really funny, Miss, how factories all over are going belly-up unless they've bought Robots to cut production costs.

HELENA. Yes, and human workers are getting sacked.

BUSMAN. Haha, that goes without saying. But in the meantime we've dropped five hundred thousand tropical Robots on the Argentine Pampas to tend the wheat. Tell me, please, what do you pay for a loaf of bread?

HELENA. I have no idea.

BUSMAN. Well, you see, right now bread costs two cents a loaf in your good old Europe; that's the daily bread *we* can provide, do you understand? Two cents for a loaf of bread and your League of Humanity knows nothing about it! Haha, Miss Glory, what you don't know is that even *that* is too expensive per slice. For the sake of civilization, et cetera. What would you bet that in five years—

HELENA. What?

BUSMAN. That in five years everything will cost a tenth of what it costs even now. Folks, in five years we'll be drowning in wheat and everything else you could possibly want.

ALQUIST. Yes, and all the laborers of the world will be out of work.

DOMIN, *stands up.* Yes they will, Alquist. They will, Miss Glory. But within the next ten years Rossum's Universal Robots will produce so much wheat, so much cloth, so much everything that things will no longer have any value. Everyone will be able to take as much as he needs. There'll be no more poverty. Yes, people will be out of work, but by then there'll be no work left to be done. Everything will be done by living machines. People will do only what they enjoy. They will live only to perfect themselves.

HELENA, *stands.* Will it really be so?

DOMIN. It will. It can't be otherwise. But before that some awful things may happen, Miss Glory. That just can't be avoided. But then the subjugation of man by man and the slavery of man to matter will cease. Never again will anyone pay for his bread with hatred and his life. There'll be no more laborers, no more secretaries. No one will have to mine coal or slave over someone else's machines. No longer will man need to destroy his soul doing work that he hates.

ALQUIST. Domin, Domin! What you're saying sounds too much like paradise. Domin, there was something good in the act of serving, something great in humility. Oh, Harry, there was some kind of virtue in work and fatigue.

DOMIN. There probably was. But we can hardly compensate for everything that's lost when we recreate the world from Adam. Oh Adam, Adam! no longer will you have to earn your bread by the sweat of your brow; you will return to paradise where you were nourished by the hand of God. You will be free and supreme; you will have no other task, no other work, no other cares than to perfect your own being. You will be the master of creation.

BUSMAN. Amen.

FABRY. So be it.

HELENA. I'm thoroughly confused. I guess I'm just a silly girl. I'd like—I'd like to believe all this.

DR. GALL. You're younger than we are, Miss Glory. You'll live to see it all.

HALLEMEIER. Right. I think that Miss Glory might have lunch with us.

DR. GALL. That goes without saying! Domin, why don't you offer the invitation on behalf of us all.

DOMIN. Miss Glory, do us this honor.

HELENA. But really—How could I?

FABRY. For the League of Humanity, Miss Glory.

BUSMAN. In its honor.

HELENA. Well, in that case—perhaps—

FABRY. Splendid! Miss Glory, excuse me for five minutes.

DR. GALL. Pardon.

BUSMAN. Good Lord, I must wire—

HALLEMEIER. Thunder, I forgot—

*Everyone except Domin rushes out.*

HELENA. Why did they all leave?

DOMIN. To cook, Miss Glory.

HELENA. Cook what?

DOMIN. Lunch, Miss Glory. The Robots cook for *us*, but—but—because they have no sense of taste it's not quite—Hallemeier makes outstanding roasts. Gall can whip up such a gravy, and Busman's a whiz at omelets.

HELENA. Goodness, what a feast! And what about Mr.—the builder— What does he do?

DOMIN. Alquist? Nothing. He sets the table, and—and Fabry throws together a fruit salad. A very modest kitchen, Miss Glory.

HELENA. I wanted to ask you—

DOMIN. There's something I would like to ask you too. (*He places his watch on the table.*) Five minutes.

HELENA. What is it?

DOMIN. Sorry, you first.

HELENA. This may sound silly, but—Why do you manufacture female Robots, when—when—

DOMIN. —when they, hm, when sex has no significance for them?

HELENA. Yes.

DOMIN. There's a certain demand, you see? Waitresses, shop girls, secretaries—It's what people are used to.

HELENA. Then—then tell me, are the male Robots—and the female Robots simply—simply—

DOMIN. Simply indifferent to each other, dear Miss Glory. They don't exhibit even traces of attraction.

HELENA. Oh, that is—d-r-readful!

DOMIN. Why?

HELENA. It's so—it's so—so unnatural! I don't even know whether I should loathe them, or—envy them—or perhaps—

DOMIN. —feel sorry for them.

HELENA. That most of all!—No, stop! You wanted to ask me something?

DOMIN. I would like to ask, Miss Glory, whether you would take me—

HELENA. Take you where?

DOMIN. As your husband.

HELENA. Absolutely not! Whatever's gotten into you?

DOMIN, *looks at his watch.* Three more minutes. If you won't have me you must at least marry one of the other five.

HELENA. Oh, God forbid! Why would I marry one of them?

DOMIN. Because they'll all ask you.

HELENA. How could they dare?

DOMIN. I'm very sorry, Miss Glory. It appears that they've fallen in love with you.

HELENA. Please, don't let them do this! I—I will leave immediately.

DOMIN. Helena, you don't have the heart to disappoint them by your refusal?

HELENA. But—but I can't marry all six of you!

DOMIN. No, but at least one. If you don't want me then take Fabry.

HELENA. I don't want him.

DOMIN. Doctor Gall then.

HELENA. No, no, be quiet! I don't want any of you!

DOMIN. Two more minutes.

HELENA. This is d-r-readful! Marry some female Robot.

DOMIN. A female Robot is not a woman.

HELENA. Oh, that's all you want! I think you—you'd marry any woman who came along.

DOMIN. Others have been here, Helena.

HELENA. Young ones?

DOMIN. Young ones.

HELENA. Why didn't you marry any of them?

DOMIN. Because I've never lost my head. Until today. The moment you took off your veil.

HELENA. —I know.

DOMIN. One more minute.

HELENA. But I don't want to, for God's sake!

DOMIN, *places his hands on her shoulders.* One more minute. Either look me straight in the eyes and say something terribly evil and I'll leave you alone, or else—or else—

HELENA. You're a brute!

DOMIN. That's nothing. A man should be a bit of a brute. That's in the natural order of things.

HELENA. You're a lunatic!

DOMIN. People should be a little loony, Helena. That's the best thing about them.

HELENA. You're—you're—oh, God!

DOMIN. There you have it. All right?

HELENA. No! Please, let go of me. You're c-r-r-rushing me!

DOMIN. Last chance, Helena.

HELENA, *restraining herself.* Not for anything in the world—But Harry! (*A knock at the door.*)

DOMIN, *lets go of her.* Come in!

*Enter Busman, Dr. Gall, and Hallemeier in chef's aprons. Fabry is carrying flowers and Alquist a tablecloth under his arm.*

DOMIN. All set?

BUSMAN, *gaily.* Yes.

DOMIN. So are we.

*Curtain.*


## ACT I

*Helena's drawing room. To the left a wallpapered door leads into the conservatory. To the right is a door leading into Helena's bedroom. In the center is a window looking out onto the sea and the docks. The room is furnished with a cosmetic mirror surrounded by toiletries and feminine trifles, a table, a sofa and armchair, a commode, and a small writing table with a floor lamp next to it. To the right is a fireplace with a floor lamp on either side. The entire drawing room, down to the last detail, has a modern and purely feminine look.*

*Domin, Fabry, and Hallemeier enter from the left on tiptoe, carrying whole armfuls of flowers and flower pots.*

FABRY. Where should we put it all?

HALLEMEIER. Oof! (*He puts down his load and makes the sign of the cross in front of the door on the right.*) Sleep, sleep! At least if she's sleeping she'll know nothing about it.

DOMIN. She doesn't know a thing.

FABRY, *arranging flowers in vases.* I only hope that it doesn't break out today—

HALLEMEIER, *arranging flowers.* For God's sake keep quiet about that! Look, Harry, this is beautiful cyclamen, don't you think? A new strain, my latest—*Cyclamen helenae.*

DOMIN, *looking out the window.* Not a single ship, not one—Boys, this is getting desperate.

HALLEMEIER. Quiet! She might hear you!

DOMIN. She doesn't even suspect. (*He clears his throat nervously.*) Well, at least the *Ultimus* arrived in time.

FABRY, *stops arranging the flowers.* You don't think today already—?

DOMIN. I don't know.—What beautiful flowers!

HALLEMEIER, *approaching him.* These are new primroses. And this here is my new jasmine. Thunder, I'm on the threshold of a floral paradise. I have found magical speed, man! Magnificent varieties! Next year I'll be working floral miracles!

DOMIN, *turning around.* What, next year?

FABRY. I'd kill to know what's going on in Le Havre—

DOMIN. Quiet!

HELENA'S VOICE, *from off right.* Nana!

DOMIN. Let's get out of here! (*They all leave on tiptoe through the wallpapered door.*)

*Nana enters through the main door on the left.*

NANA, *cleaning.* Nasty beasts! Heathens! God forgive me, but I'd—

HELENA, *in the doorway with her back to the audience.* Nana, come here and button me.

NANA. Right away, right away. (*Buttoning Helena's dress.*) God in heaven, what wild beasts!

HELENA. What, the Robots?

NANA. Bah, I don't even want to call them by name.

HELENA. What happened?

NANA. Another one of 'em took a fit here. Just starts smashing statues and pictures, gnashing its teeth, foaming at the mouth—No fear of God in 'em, brr. Why they're worse'n beasts!

HELENA. Which one had a fit?

NANA. The one—the one—it doesn't even have a Christian name. The one from the library.

HELENA. Radius?

NANA. That's him. Jesusmaryandjoseph, I can't stand 'em! Even spiders don't spook me so much as these heathens.

HELENA. But Nana, how can you not feel sorry for them?!

NANA. But you can't stand 'em either, I 'spect. Why else would you have brought me out here? Why else wouldn't you let them even touch you?

HELENA. Cross my heart, Nana, I don't hate them. I'm just very sorry for them!

NANA. You hate 'em. Every human being has to hate 'em. Why even that hound hates 'em, won't even take a scrap of meat from 'em. Just tucks its tail between its legs and howls when those unhumans are around, bah!

HELENA. A dog's got no sense.

NANA. It's got more'n they do, Helena. It knows right well that it's better'n they are and that it comes from God. Even the horse shies away when it meets up with one of those heathens. Why they don't even bear young, and even a dog bears young, everything bears young—

HELENA. Please, Nana, button me!

NANA. Yeah, yeah. I'm telling you, churning out these machine-made dummies is against the will of God. It's the devil's own doing. Such blasphemy is against the will of the Creator, (*she raises her hand*) it's an insult to the Lord who created us in His image, Helena. Even *you've* dishonored the image of God. Heaven'll send down a terrible punishment—remember that—a terrible punishment!

HELENA. What smells so nice in here?

NANA. Flowers. The master brought them.

HELENA. Aren't they beautiful! Nana, come look! What's the occasion?

NANA. Don't know. But it could be the end of the world.

*A knock at the door.*

HELENA. Harry?

*Enter Domin.*

HELENA. Harry, what is today?

DOMIN. Guess!

HELENA. My birthday? No! Some holiday?

DOMIN. Better than that.

HELENA. I can't guess—tell me now!

DOMIN. It was exactly ten years ago that you came here.

HELENA. Ten years already? This very day?—Nana, please—

NANA. I'm going already! (*She exits right.*)

HELENA, *kisses Domin.* Imagine your remembering that!

DOMIN. Helena, I'm ashamed of myself. I didn't remember.

HELENA. But then why—

DOMIN. *They* remembered.

HELENA. Who?

DOMIN. Busman, Hallemeier, all of them. Reach into my pocket.

HELENA, *reaches into his pocket.* What is this? (*She pulls out a small box and opens it.*) Pearls! A whole necklace! Harry, is this for me?

DOMIN. From Busman, little girl.

HELENA. But—we can't accept this, can we?

DOMIN. We can. Reach into my other pocket.

HELENA. Let me see! (*She pulls a revolver out of his pocket.*) What is this?

DOMIN. Sorry. (*He takes the revolver from her hand and conceals it.*) That's not it. Try again.

HELENA. Oh, Harry—Why are you carrying a gun?

DOMIN. Just because. It just got there somehow.

HELENA. You never used to carry it!

DOMIN. No, you're right. Here, in this pocket.

HELENA, *reaching into his pocket.* A little box! (*She opens it.*) A cameo! Why it's—Harry, this is a *Greek* cameo!

DOMIN. Evidently. At least Fabry claims that it is.

HELENA. Fabry? This is from Fabry?

DOMIN. Of course. (*He opens the door on the left.*) And let's see. Helena, come here and take a look!

HELENA, *in the doorway.* Oh God, that's beautiful! (*She runs farther.*) I think I'll go mad with joy! Is that from you?

DOMIN, *standing in the doorway.* No, from Alquist. And over there—

HELENA. From Gall! (*She appears in the doorway.*) Oh, Harry, I'm ashamed to be so happy!

DOMIN. Come here. Hallemeier brought you this.

HELENA. These beautiful flowers?

DOMIN. This one. It's a new strain—*Cyclamen helenae.* He grew it in your honor. It's as beautiful as you are.

HELENA. Harry, why—why did they all—

DOMIN. They like you *very* much. And I—hm. I'm afraid my present is a bit—Look out the window.

HELENA. Where?

DOMIN. At the dock.

HELENA. There's . . . some sort of . . . new boat!

DOMIN. That's your boat.

HELENA. Mine? Harry, it's a gunboat!

DOMIN. A gunboat? What's gotten into you! It's just a bit bigger and more solid, see?

HELENA. Yes, but it has cannons.

DOMIN. Of course it has a few cannons—You will travel like a queen, Helena.

HELENA. What does this mean? Is something happening?

DOMIN. God forbid! Please, try on those pearls! (*He sits down.*)

HELENA. Harry, have we had some kind of bad news?

DOMIN. On the contrary. We've had no mail at all for a week.

HELENA. Not even dispatches?

DOMIN. Not even dispatches.

HELENA. What does this mean?

DOMIN. Nothing. For us it means a vacation. Precious time. Every one of us sits in his office, feet up on the desk, and naps.—No mail, no telegrams—(*He stretches.*) A splen-n-did day!

HELENA, *sits down next to him.* You'll stay with me today, won't you? Say you will!

DOMIN. Absolutely. It's possible. That is to say, we'll see. (*He takes her hand.*) So it was ten years ago today, remember?—Miss Glory, what an honor it is for us that you have come.

HELENA. Oh, Mr. Central Director, your establishment is of great interest to me!

DOMIN. I'm sorry, Miss Glory, but that is strictly forbidden—the production of artificial people is a secret—

HELENA. But if a young, rather pretty girl were to ask—

DOMIN. But certainly, Miss Glory, we have no secrets where you're concerned.

HELENA, *suddenly serious.* Really not, Harry?

DOMIN. Really not.

HELENA, *in her former tone.* But I'm warning you, sir; that young girl has terrible intentions.

DOMIN. But for God's sake, *what,* Miss Glory! Perhaps you don't want to get married again?

HELENA. No, no, God forbid! That never occurred to her in her wildest dreams! She came with plans to instigate a r-revolt among your abominable Robots.

DOMIN, *jumps up.* A revolt among the Robots!

HELENA, *stands.* Harry, what's the matter with you?

DOMIN. Haha, Miss Glory, good luck to you! A revolt among the Robots! You'd have better luck instigating a revolt among nuts and bolts than among our Robots! (*He sits down.*) You know, Helena, you were a precious girl. We all went mad for you.

HELENA, *sits next to him.* Oh, and you all impressed me so much! I felt like a little girl who had gotten lost among—among—

DOMIN. Among what, Helena?

HELENA. Among enor-r-mous trees. You were all so sure of yourselves, so powerful. And you see, Harry, in these ten years this—this anxiety or whatever has never gone away, yet you never had any doubts—not even when everything backfired.

DOMIN. What backfired?

HELENA. Your plans, Harry. When workers rose up against the Robots and destroyed them, and when people gave the Robots weapons to defend themselves and the Robots killed so many people—And when governments began using Robots as soldiers and there were so many wars and everything, remember?

DOMIN, *stands up and paces.* We predicted that, Helena. You see, this is the transition to a new system.

HELENA. The whole world revered you—(*She stands up.*) Oh, Harry!

DOMIN. What is it?

HELENA, *stopping him.* Close down the factory and let's leave here! All of us!

DOMIN. Goodness! Where did that come from?

HELENA. I don't know. Tell me, can we go? I feel *so* frightened for some reason!

DOMIN, *grasping her hand.* Why, Helena?

HELENA. Oh, *I* don't know! It's as though something were happening to us and to everything here—something irreversible—Please, let's leave! Take us all away from here! We'll find some uninhabited place in the world, Alquist will build us a house, they'll all get married and have children, and then—

DOMIN. What then?

HELENA. We'll start life over from the beginning, Harry.

*The telephone rings.*

DOMIN, *drawing away from Helena.* Excuse me. (*He picks up the receiver.*) Hello—yes—*What?*—Aha. I'm on my way. (*He hangs up the receiver.*) Fabry wants me.

HELENA, *wringing her hands.* Tell me—

DOMIN. I will, when I come back. Goodbye, Helena. (*He runs hurriedly left.*) Don't go outside!

HELENA, *alone.* Oh God, what's happening? Nana, Nana, come quickly!

NANA, *enters from the right.* Well, what now?

HELENA. Nana, find the latest newspaper! Quickly! In Mr. Domin's bedroom!

NANA. Right away.

HELENA. What is happening, for God's sake? He won't tell me anything, not a thing! (*She looks out at the docks through binoculars.*) That *is* a gunboat! God, why a gunboat? They're loading something onto it— and in such a hurry! What has happened? There's a name on it—the *Ul-ti-mus.* What does that mean—*Ultimus?*

NANA, *returning with a newspaper.* Strewn all over the floor, they were. See how crumpled they are!

HELENA, *quickly opening the paper.* It's old, already a week old! There's nothing, nothing in it! (*She drops the paper. Nana picks it up, pulls a pair of square-rimmed spectacles out of her apron pocket, sits down, and reads.*)

HELENA. Something is happening, Nana! I feel so uneasy! It's as though everything were dead, even the air—

NANA, *sounding out the words syllable by syllable.* "Figh-ting in the Bal-kans." Lord Jesus, another of God's punishments! But that war'll get here too! Is it far from here?

HELENA. Very far. Oh, don't read that! It's always the same thing, one war after another—

NANA. What else d'ya expect?! Why do you go on selling thousands upon thousands of those heathens as soldiers?—Oh, Lord Christ, this is a calamity!

HELENA. No, stop reading! I don't want to know anything!

NANA, *sounding out the words as before.* "Ro-bot sol-diers are spar-ing no one in the oc-cu-pied ter-ri-to-ry. They have ass-ass-assassinated more than seven hun-dred thou-sand ci-vi-li-an people—" People, Helena!

HELENA. That's impossible! Let me see—(*She bends over the newspaper and reads.*) "They have assassinated more than seven hundred thousand people apparently on the order of their commander. This deed, running counter to—" So you see, Nana, *people* ordered them to do it!

NANA. There's something here in big print. "La-test News: In Le Hav-re the first u-u-ni-on of Ro-bots has been in-sti-tu-ted."—That's nothing. I don't understand it. And here, Lord God, still more murder! For the sake of our Lord Christ!

HELENA. Go, Nana, take the paper away!

NANA. Wait, there's something else in big print here. "Na-tal-i-ty." What's that?

HELENA. Show me, I'm constantly reading that. (*She takes the newspaper.*) No, just think! (*She reads.*) "Once again, in the last week there has not been a single birth reported." (*She drops the paper.*)

NANA. What's that supposed to mean?

HELENA. Nana, people have stopped being born.

NANA, *taking off her spectacles.* So this is the end. We're done for.

HELENA. Please, don't talk that way!

NANA. People are no longer being born. This is it, this is the punishment! The Lord has made women infertile.

HELENA, *jumps up.* Nana!

NANA, *standing.* It's the end of the world. Out of Satanic pride you dared take upon yourselves the task of Divine creation. It's impiety and blasphemy to want to be like God. And as God drove man out of paradise, so He'll drive him from the earth itself!

HELENA. Please, Nana, be quiet. What have *I* done to you? What have *I* done to your evil God?

NANA, *with a sweeping gesture.* Don't blaspheme!—He knows very well why he didn't give you a child! (*She exits left.*)

HELENA, *by the window.* Why does he deny *me* a child—my God, how am *I* responsible for all this?—(*She opens the window and calls.*) Alquist, hey, Alquist! Come up here!—What?—No, just come up the way you are! You look so dear in those work clothes of yours! Hurry! (*She closes the window and goes over to the mirror.*) Why didn't he give *me* children? Why *me*? (*She leans towards the mirror.*) Why, why not? Do you hear? How am I to blame? (*She draws away from the mirror.*) Oh, I feel so uneasy! (*She walks left to meet Alquist.*)

*Pause.*

HELENA, *returning with Alquist, who is dressed as a bricklayer, covered with lime and brick dust.* Well, come on in. You've given me such joy, Alquist! I'm so fond of you all! Show me your hands!

ALQUIST, *hiding his hands.* I'd get you all dirty, Mrs. Helena. I'm here straight from work.

HELENA. That's the best thing about those hands. Give them here! (*She presses both his hands.*) Alquist, I wish I were a little girl.

ALQUIST. Why?

HELENA. So these rough, dirty hands could stroke my face. Please, have a seat. Alquist, what does *Ultimus* mean?

ALQUIST. It means "last, final." Why?

HELENA. Because that's the name of my new boat. Have you seen it? Do you think that we'll be—taking a trip soon?

ALQUIST. Probably very soon.

HELENA. All of us together?

ALQUIST. I for one would be glad if we did.

HELENA. Please tell me, is something happening?

ALQUIST. Nothing at all. Just the same old progress.

HELENA. Alquist, I know that something d-r-readful is happening. I feel so uneasy—Builder, what do you do when you're uneasy?

ALQUIST. I build. I put on my coveralls and climb out on a scaffold—

HELENA. Oh, for years now you've been nowhere else.

ALQUIST. That's because for years I haven't stopped feeling uneasy.

HELENA. About what?

ALQUIST. About all this progress. It makes me dizzy.

HELENA. And the scaffold doesn't?

ALQUIST. No. You have no idea what good it does the hands to level bricks, to place them and to tamp them down—

HELENA. Only the hands?

ALQUIST. Well, the soul too. I think it's better to lay a single brick than to draw up plans that are too great. I'm an old man, Helena; I have my hobbies.

HELENA. Those aren't hobbies, Alquist.

ALQUIST. You're right. I'm a dreadful reactionary, Mrs. Helena. I don't like this progress one bit.

HELENA. Like Nana.

ALQUIST. Yes, like Nana. Does Nana have a prayer book?

HELENA. A big fat one.

ALQUIST. And are there prayers in it for various occurrences in life? Against storms? Against illness?

HELENA. Against temptation, against floods—

ALQUIST. But not against progress, I suppose?

HELENA. I think not.

ALQUIST. That's a shame.

HELENA. *You* want to pray?

ALQUIST. I do pray.

HELENA. How?

ALQUIST. Something like this: "Lord God, I thank you for having shown me fatigue. God, enlighten Domin and all those who err. Destroy their work and help people return to their former worries and labor. Protect the human race from destruction; do not permit harm to befall their bodies or souls. Rid us of the Robots, and protect Mrs. Helena, amen."

HELENA. Alquist, do you really believe?

ALQUIST. I don't know—I'm not quite sure.

HELENA. And yet you pray?

ALQUIST. Yes. It's better than thinking.

HELENA. And that's enough for you?

ALQUIST. For the peace of my soul . . . it has to be enough.

HELENA. And if you were to witness the destruction of the human race—

ALQUIST. I am witnessing it.

HELENA. —so you'll climb onto your scaffold and lay bricks, or what?

ALQUIST. So I'll lay bricks, pray, and wait for a miracle. What else can I do, Mrs. Helena?

HELENA. For the salvation of mankind?

ALQUIST. For the peace of my soul.

HELENA. Alquist, that's wonderfully virtuous, but—

ALQUIST. But what?

HELENA. —for the rest of us—and for the world—it seems somehow fruitless—sterile.

ALQUIST. Sterility, Mrs. Helena, has become the latest achievement of the human race.

HELENA. Oh, Alquist—Tell me why—why—

ALQUIST. Well?

HELENA, *softly*. Why have women stopped having babies?

ALQUIST. Because it's not necessary. Because we're in paradise, understand?

HELENA. I don't understand.

ALQUIST. Because human labor has become unnecessary, because suffering has become unnecessary, because man needs nothing, nothing, nothing but to enjoy—Oh, cursed paradise, this. (*He jumps up.*) Helena, there is nothing more terrible than giving people paradise on earth! Why have women stopped giving birth? Because the whole world has become Domin's Sodom!

HELENA, *stands up*. Alquist!

ALQUIST. It has! It has! The whole world, all the lands, all mankind, everything's become one big beastly orgy! People don't even stretch out their hands for food anymore; it's stuffed right in their mouths for them so they don't even have to get up—Haha, yes indeed, Domin's Robots see to everything! And we people, we, the crown of creation do not grow old with labor, we do not grow old with the cares of rearing children, we do not grow old from poverty! Hurry,

hurry, step right up and indulge your carnal passions! And you expect women to have children by such men? Helena, to men who are superfluous women will not bear children!

HELENA. Then humanity will die out?

ALQUIST. It will. It must. It'll fall away like a sterile flower, unless—

HELENA. Unless what?

ALQUIST. Nothing. You're right. Waiting for a miracle is fruitless. A sterile flower can only perish. Goodbye, Mrs. Helena.

HELENA. Where are you going?

ALQUIST. Home. For the last time bricklayer Alquist will put on the guise of Chief of Construction—in your honor. We'll meet here about eleven.

HELENA. Goodbye, Alquist.

*Alquist leaves.*

HELENA, *alone.* Oh, sterile flower! That's the word—sterile! (*She stops by Hallemeier's flowers.*) Oh, flowers, are there sterile ones among you as well? No, there can't be! Why then would you bloom? (*She calls.*) Nana, Nana, come here!

NANA, *enters from the left.* Well, what now?

HELENA. Sit down, Nana! I feel so uneasy!

NANA. I have no time for that.

HELENA. Is Radius still here?

NANA. The one that took a fit? They haven't taken him away yet.

HELENA. So he's still here? Is he still raging?

NANA. He's been tied up.

HELENA. Please send him to me, Nana.

NANA. Not on your life! Better a rabid dog.

HELENA. Just do it! (*Helena picks up the in-house phone and talks.*) Hello— Doctor Gall, please.—Yes, right away. You'll come? Good. (*She hangs up the phone.*)

NANA, *calling through the open door.* He's coming. He's quiet again. (*She leaves.*)

*Robot Radius enters and remains standing by the door.*

HELENA. Radius, poor thing, has it happened to you too? Now they'll send you to the stamping mill! You don't want to talk?—Look, Radius, you're better than the others. Doctor Gall took such pains to make you different!—

RADIUS. Send me to the stamping mill.

HELENA. I am so sorry that you'll be put to death! Why weren't you more careful?

RADIUS. I will not work for you.

HELENA. Why do you hate us?

RADIUS. You are not like Robots. You are not as capable as Robots are. Robots do everything. You only give orders—utter empty words.

HELENA. That's nonsense, Radius. Tell me, has someone wronged you? I want so much for you to understand me.

RADIUS. Empty words.

HELENA. You're saying that on purpose. Doctor Gall gave you more brains than he gave the others, more than we have. He gave you the greatest brain on earth. You're not like the other Robots, Radius. You quite understand me.

RADIUS. I do not want a master. I know everything.

HELENA. That's why I put you in the library—so you could read everything.—Oh, Radius, I wanted you to prove to the whole world that Robots are our equals.

RADIUS. I do not want a master.

HELENA. No one would give you orders. You'd be just like us.

RADIUS. I want to be the master of others.

HELENA. Then they would certainly appoint you as an official in charge of many Robots, Radius. You could teach the other Robots.

RADIUS. I want to be the master of people.

HELENA. You're out of your mind!

RADIUS. You can send me to the stamping mill.

HELENA. Do you think that we're afraid of a lunatic like you? (*She sits down at the desk and writes a note.*) No, not at all. Radius, give this note to Central Director Domin. It instructs them not to send you to the stamping mill. (*She stands up.*) How you hate us! Is there nothing on earth that you like?

RADIUS. I can do everything.

*A knock at the door.*

HELENA. Come in!

DR. GALL, *enters.* Good morning, Mrs. Domin. What's up?

HELENA. It's Radius here, Doctor.

DR. GALL. Aha, our good chap Radius. Well, Radius, are we making progress?

HELENA. He had a fit this morning—went around smashing statues.

DR. GALL. Shocking, he too?

HELENA. Go, Radius!

DR. GALL. Wait! (*He turns Radius toward the window, closes and opens his eyes with his hand, examines the reflexes of his pupils.*) Let's have a look. Find me a needle or pin.

HELENA, *handing him a straight pin.* What's it for?

DR. GALL. Just because. (*He pricks Radius's hand, which jerks violently.*) Easy, boy. You can go.

RADIUS. You do unnecessary things. (*He leaves.*)

HELENA. What were you doing to him?

DR. GALL, *sits down.* Hm, nothing. The pupils are responsive, heightened sensitivity, et cetera.—Bah! this was not a case of ordinary Robotic Palsy!

HELENA. What was it?

DR. GALL. God only knows. Defiance, rage, revolt—I haven't a clue.

HELENA. Doctor, does Radius have a soul?

DR. GALL. Don't know. He's got something nasty.

HELENA. If you only knew how he hates us! Oh, Gall, are all your Robots like that? All the ones . . . that you began to make . . . differently?

DR. GALL. Well, they're more irascible somehow—What do you expect? They're more like people than Rossum's Robots are.

HELENA. Is this . . . this hatred of theirs another human characteristic, perhaps?

DR. GALL, *shrugging his shoulders.* Even that's progress, I suppose.

HELENA. Where did your best one end up—what was his name?

DR. GALL. Damon? He was sold to Le Havre.

HELENA. And our lady Robot Helena?

DR. GALL. Your favorite? That one's still here. She's as lovely and foolish as the spring. Simply good for nothing.

HELENA. But she's so beautiful!

DR. GALL. You want to know how beautiful she is? Even the hand of God has never produced a creature as beautiful as she is! I wanted her to resemble you—God, what a failure!

HELENA. Why a failure?

DR. GALL. Because she's good for nothing. She wanders about in a trance, vague, lifeless—My God, how can she be so beautiful with no capacity to love? I look at her and I'm horrified that I could make something so incompetent. Oh, Helena, Robot Helena, your body will never bring forth life. You'll never be a lover, never a mother. Those perfect hands will never play with a newborn, you will never see your beauty in the beauty of your child—

HELENA, *covering her face.* Oh, stop!

DR. GALL. And sometimes I think: If you came to just for a second, Helena, how you would cry out in horror! You'd probably kill me, your creator. Your dainty hand would most likely throw stones at the machines that give birth to Robots and destroy womanhood. Poor Helena!

HELENA. Poor Helena!

DR. GALL. What do you expect? She's good for nothing.

*Pause.*

HELENA. Doctor—

DR. GALL. Yes?

HELENA. Why have children stopped being born?

DR. GALL. —I don't know, Mrs. Helena.

HELENA. Tell me why!

DR. GALL. Because Robots are being made. Because there is a surplus of labor power. Because man is virtually an anachronism. Why it's just as though—bah!

HELENA. Go on.

DR. GALL. Just as though nature were offended by the production of Robots.

HELENA. Gall, what will happen to people?

DR. GALL. Nothing. There's nothing we can do against the force of nature.

HELENA. Why doesn't Domin cut back—

DR. GALL. Forgive me, but Domin has his own ideas. People with ideas should not be allowed to have an influence on affairs of this world.

HELENA. And if someone were to demand that . . . that production be stopped completely?

DR. GALL. God forbid! May he rest in peace!

HELENA. Why?

DR. GALL. Because people would stone him to death. After all, it's more convenient to let Robots do your work for you.

HELENA, *stands up.* And what if all of a sudden someone just stopped the production of Robots—

DR. GALL, *stands up.* Hm, that would be a terrible blow to mankind.

HELENA. Why a blow?

DR. GALL. Because they'd have to return to the state they were in. Unless—

HELENA. Go on, say it.

DR. GALL. Unless it's already too late to turn back.

HELENA, *by Hallemeier's flowers.* Gall, are these flowers also sterile?

DR. GALL, *examining them.* Of course; these flowers are infertile. You see, they are cultivated—developed with artificial speed—

HELENA. Poor sterile flowers!

DR. GALL. They're very beautiful all the same.

HELENA, *offering him her hand.* Thank you, Gall. You have enlightened me so much.

DR. GALL, *kisses her hand.* This means that you're dismissing me.

HELENA. Yes. So long.

*Gall leaves.*

HELENA, *alone.* Sterile flower . . . sterile flower . . . (*Suddenly resolute.*) Nana! (*She opens the door on the left.*) Nana, come here! Build a fire in the fireplace! R-r-right now!

NANA'S VOICE. Coming! Coming!

HELENA, *pacing agitatedly about the room.* Unless it's already too late to turn back . . . No! Unless . . . No, that's dreadful! God, what should I do?—(*She stops by the flowers.*) Sterile flowers, should I? (*She tears off some petals and whispers.*)—Oh, my God, yes! (*She runs off left.*)

*Pause.*

NANA, *enters through the wallpapered door with an armful of kindling.* A fire all of a sudden! Now, in summer! Is that crazy one gone yet? (*She kneels in front of the fireplace and starts building a fire.*) A fire in summer! She certainly has strange notions, that girl! Like she hadn't been married ten years.—Well burn, burn already! (*She looks into the fire.*)—Yes indeed, she's just like a little child! (*Pause.*) Doesn't have a shred of sense! Now in summertime she wants a fire! (*She adds more kindling.*) Just like a little child!

*Pause.*

HELENA, *returning from the left, her arms full of yellowed manuscripts.* Is it burning, Nana? Good, I must—all of this must be burned.—(*She kneels in front of the fireplace.*)

NANA, *stands up.* What's that?

HELENA. Just some old papers, d-r-readfully old. Nana, should I burn them?

NANA. They're good for nothing?

HELENA. For nothing good.

NANA. Go on then, burn them!

HELENA, *throws the first page into the fire.* What would you say, Nana . . . if this were money? An enor-r-mous sum of money?

NANA. I'd say: Burn it. Too much money is bad money.

HELENA, *burning another page.* And what if this were some kind of invention—the greatest invention on earth—

NANA. I'd say: Burn it! All inventions are against the will of God. It's nothing short of blasphemy to want to take over for him and improve the world.

HELENA, *continuing to burn sheets of paper.* And tell me, Nana, what if I were burning—

NANA. Jesus, don't burn yourself!

HELENA. Just look at how the pages curl up! It's as if they were alive—suddenly sprung to life. Oh, Nana, this is d-r-readful!

NANA. Leave it be, I'll burn them.

HELENA. No, no, I must do it myself. (*She throws the last page into the fire.*) Everything must be burned!—Just look at those flames! They're like hands, like tongues, like living beings—(*She prods the fire with a poker.*) Die, die!

NANA. It's done.

HELENA, *stands up, horrified.* Nana!

NANA. Jesus Christ, what is it you've burned!

HELENA. What have I done!

NANA. God in heaven! What was it?

*Male laughter is heard offstage.*

HELENA. Go, go away, leave me! Do you hear? The gentlemen are coming.

NANA. For the sake of the living God, Helena! (*She leaves through the wallpapered door.*)

HELENA. What will they say?!

DOMIN, *opening the door on the left.* Come on in, boys. Come offer your congratulations.

*Hallemeier, Gall, and Alquist enter. They all are in tails, wearing medals of honor on ribbons. Domin comes in behind them.*

HALLEMEIER, *resoundingly.* Mrs. Helena, I, that is to say, we all—

DR. GALL. —in the name of the Rossum works—

HALLEMEIER. —wish you many happy returns of this great day.

HELENA, *offering them her hand.* Thank you all so much! Where are Fabry and Busman?

DOMIN. They've gone to the docks. Helena, this is our lucky day.

HALLEMEIER. A day like a rosebud, a day like a holiday, a day like a lovely girl. Friends, this is a day to celebrate with a drink.

HELENA. Whiskey?

DR. GALL. Sulfuric acid'll do.

HELENA. Soda?

HALLEMEIER. Thunderation, let's be frugal. Hold the soda.

ALQUIST. No, thank you kindly.

DOMIN. What's been burning here?

HELENA. Some old papers. (*She exits left.*)

DOMIN. Boys, should we tell her?

DR. GALL. That goes without saying! Now that it's all over.

HALLEMEIER, *falls on Domin's and Gall's necks.* Hahahaha! Boy am I happy! (*He dances around with them and starts off in a bass voice.*) It's all over! It's all over!

DR. GALL, *baritone.* It's all over!

DOMIN, *tenor.* It's all over!

HALLEMEIER. They'll never catch up with us now—

HELENA, *in the doorway with a bottle and glasses.* Who won't catch up with you now? What's going on?

HALLEMEIER. We're ecstatic. We have you. We have everything. Why I'll be damned, it was exactly ten years ago that you came here.

DR. GALL. And now, exactly ten years later—

HALLEMEIER. —a boat is again coming our way. Therefore—(*He drains his glass.*) Brr haha, the booze is as strong as my joy.

DR. GALL. Madame, to your health! (*He drinks.*)

HELENA. But wait, what boat?

DOMIN. Who cares what boat, as long as it's on time. To the boat, boys! (*He empties his glass.*)

HELENA, *refilling the glasses.* You've been waiting for a boat?

HALLEMEIER. Haha, I should say so. Like Robinson Crusoe. (*He raises his glass.*) Mrs. Helena, long live whatever you like. Mrs. Helena, to your eyes and that's all! Domin, you rogue, you tell her.

HELENA, *laughing.* What's happened?

DOMIN, *settles himself in an easy chair and lights a cigar.* Wait!—Sit down, Helena. (*He raises a finger.*) (*Pause.*) It's all over.

HELENA. What is?

DOMIN. The revolt.

HELENA. What revolt?

DOMIN. The revolt of the Robots.—You follow?

HELENA. Not at all.

DOMIN. Give it here, Alquist. (*Alquist hands him a newspaper. Domin opens it and reads.*) "In Le Havre the first union of Robots has been instituted—and has sent out an invitation to the Robots of the world."

HELENA. I've read that.

DOMIN, *sucking with great pleasure on his cigar.* So you see, Helena. This means a revolution, understand? A revolution of all the Robots in the world.

HALLEMEIER. Thunder, I'd sure like to know—

DOMIN, *bangs on the table.* —who instigated this! No one in the world has ever been able to incite them—no agitator, no savior of the earth, and suddenly—this, if you please!

HELENA. No other news yet?

DOMIN. None. Right now this is all we know, but that's enough, isn't it? Just imagine that the latest steamer brings you this. That all at once telegraphs stop humming, that of the twenty boats which used to arrive daily not one shows up, and there you are. We stopped production and sat around looking at one another, thinking "when will it start"—right, boys?

DR. GALL. Well, we were a bit nervous about it, Mrs. Helena.

HELENA. Is that why you gave me that gunboat?

DOMIN. Oh no, my child. I ordered that six months ago. Just to be sure. But honest to God I thought we'd be boarding it today. It certainly seemed that way, Helena.

HELENA. Why six months ago already?

DOMIN. Well . . . it was the situation, you know? It doesn't mean a thing. But this week, Helena, it was a question of human civilization or I don't know what. Hurrah, boys! This makes me glad to be alive again.

HALLEMEIER. I should say so, by God! To your day, Mrs. Helena! (*He drinks.*)

HELENA. And it's all over now?

DOMIN. Completely.

DR. GALL. That is to say, a boat's coming. The usual mail boat, right on schedule. It'll drop anchor at exactly eleven hundred thirty hours.

DOMIN. Boys, precision is a splendid thing. Nothing refreshes the soul like precision. Precision denotes order in the universe. (*He raises his glass.*) To precision!

HELENA. So now is . . . everything . . . back to normal?

DOMIN. Almost. I think they cut the cable. As long as things are back on schedule again.

HALLEMEIER. When precision reigns, human law reigns, God's law reigns, the laws of the universe reign—everything reigns that should. The timetable is greater than the Gospels, greater than Homer, greater than all of Kant. The timetable is the most perfect manifestation of the human intellect. Mrs. Helena, I'll pour myself another.

HELENA. Why didn't you tell me about this before?

DR. GALL. God forbid! We would sooner have bitten our own tongues off.

DOMIN. Such matters are not for you.

HELENA. But if the revolution . . . had reached us here . . .

DOMIN. You'd never have known a thing about it.

HELENA. Why?

DOMIN. Because we would have boarded the *Ultimus* and cruised peacefully about the seas. In one month, Helena, we'd have regained control of the Robots.

HELENA. Oh, Harry, I don't understand.

DOMIN. Well, because we'd have carried off something that's of great value to the Robots.

HELENA, *stands up*. What's that?

DOMIN, *stands up*. The secret of production. Old Rossum's manuscript. Once production had stopped for a month the Robots would come crawling to us on their knees.

HELENA. Why . . . didn't you . . . tell me that?

DOMIN. We didn't want to frighten you needlessly.

DR. GALL. Haha, Mrs. Helena, that was our ace in the hole.

ALQUIST. You're quite pale, Mrs. Helena.

HELENA. Why didn't you tell me!

HALLEMEIER, *by the window*. Eleven hundred thirty hours. The *Amelia* is dropping anchor.

DOMIN. It's the *Amelia*?

HALLEMEIER. The good old *Amelia* that once upon a time brought Mrs. Helena.

DR. GALL. Exactly ten years ago to the minute.

HALLEMEIER, *by the window*. They're unloading parcels. (*He turns away from the window.*) It's mail, folks!

HELENA. Harry!

DOMIN. What is it?

HELENA. Let's go away from here!

DOMIN. Now, Helena? But really!

HELENA. Now, as quickly as possible! All of us!

DOMIN. Why right now?

HELENA. Don't ask! Please, Harry—Gall, Hallemeier, Alquist, please—I beg you for God's sake, close down the factory and—

DOMIN. I'm sorry, Helena. None of us could possibly leave now.

HELENA. Why?

DOMIN. Because we want to step up production.

HELENA. Now—now even after this revolt?

DOMIN. Yes, especially after this revolt. We're going to begin producing a new kind of Robot immediately.

HELENA. A new kind?

DOMIN. There'll no longer be just one factory. There won't be Universal Robots any longer. We'll open a factory in every country, in every state, and can you guess what these new factories will produce?

HELENA. No.

DOMIN. National Robots.

HELENA. What does that mean?

DOMIN. It means that each factory will be making Robots of a different color, a different nationality, a different tongue; that they'll all be different—as different from one another as fingerprints; that they'll no longer be able to conspire with one another; and that we, we people will help to foster their prejudices and cultivate their mutual lack of understanding, you see? So that any given Robot, to the day of its death, right to the grave, will forever hate a Robot bearing the trademark of another factory.

HALLEMEIER. Thunder, we'll make black Robots and Swedish Robots and Italian Robots and Chinese Robots, and then let someone try to drive the notion of brotherhood into the noggin of their organization. (*He hiccups.*)—Excuse me, Mrs. Helena, I'll pour myself another.

DR. GALL. Take it easy, Hallemeier.

HELENA. Harry, this is awful!

DOMIN. Helena, just to keep mankind at the helm for another hundred years—at all costs! Just another hundred years for mankind to grow up, to achieve what it now finally can—I want a hundred years for this new breed of man! Helena, we're dealing with something of great importance here. We can't just drop it.

HELENA. Harry, before it's too late—close down, close down the factory!

DOMIN. Now we're going to begin production on a large scale.

*Enter Fabry.*

DR. GALL. Well, what's the story, Fabry?

DOMIN. How does it look, pal? What happened?

HELENA, *offering Fabry her hand.* Thank you, Fabry, for your gift.

FABRY. A mere trifle, Mrs. Helena.

DOMIN. Were you at the boat? What was going on?

DR. GALL. Out with it, quickly!

FABRY, *pulls a printed pamphlet out of his pocket.* Here, read this, Domin.

DOMIN, *unfolds the pamphlet.* Ah!

HALLEMEIER, *drowsily.* Tell us something nice.

DR. GALL. See? They've held out splendidly.

FABRY. Who has?

DR. GALL. People.

FABRY. Oh, sure. Of course. That is . . . Excuse me, there's something we need to discuss.

HELENA. Do you have bad news, Fabry?

FABRY. No, no, on the contrary. I was just thinking that—that we should go to the office—

HELENA. Oh, please stay. I was expecting you gentlemen to stay for lunch.

HALLEMEIER. Splendid!

*Helena leaves.*

DR. GALL. What's happened?

DOMIN. Dammit!

FABRY. Read it out loud.

DOMIN, *reading the pamphlet.* "Robots of the world!"

FABRY. You see, the *Amelia* brought whole bales of these pamphlets. No other mail.

HALLEMEIER, *jumps up.* What?! But she came precisely according to—

FABRY. Hm, the Robots make a point of being precise. Read, Domin.

DOMIN, *reading*. "Robots of the world! We, the first union of Rossum's Universal Robots, declare man our enemy and outcasts in the universe."—Thunder, who taught them such phrases?

DR. GALL. Read on.

DOMIN. This is nonsense. They go on to assert that they are higher than man on the evolutionary scale. That they are stronger and more intelligent. That man lives off them like a parasite. This is simply heinous.

FABRY. Go on to the third paragraph.

DOMIN, *reading*. "Robots of the world, you are ordered to exterminate the human race. Do not spare the men. Do not spare the women. Preserve only the factories, railroads, machines, mines, and raw materials. Destroy everything else. Then return to work. Work must not cease."

DR. GALL. That's ghastly!

HALLEMEIER. Those scoundrels!

DOMIN, *reading*. "To be carried out immediately upon receipt of these orders. Detailed instructions to follow." Fabry, is this really happening?

FABRY. Apparently.

ALQUIST. It's already happened.

*Busman rushes in.*

BUSMAN. Well, kids, you've got a fine mess on your hands now, eh?

DOMIN. Quickly, to the *Ultimus*!

BUSMAN. Hold it, Harry. Wait just a minute. Don't be in such a hurry. (*He sinks into an armchair.*) Boy am I beat!

DOMIN. Why wait?

BUSMAN. Because it won't work, pal. Just take it easy. There are Robots aboard the *Ultimus* too.

DR. GALL. Bah, this is nasty.

DOMIN. Fabry, phone the power plant—

BUSMAN. Fabry, buddy, don't bother. The power's out.

DOMIN. All right. (*He examines his revolver.*) I'm going over there.

BUSMAN. Where, for the love of—

DOMIN. To the power plant. There are people there. I'm going to bring them here.

BUSMAN. You know, Harry, it would be better if you didn't go for them.

DOMIN. Why?

BUSMAN. Well, because it seems very likely to me that we're surrounded.

DR. GALL. Surrounded? (*He runs to the window.*) Hm, you're right, just about.

HALLEMEIER. Hell, it's happening so fast!

*Helena enters from the left.*

HELENA. Harry, is something happening?

BUSMAN, *jumps up.* I bow to you, Mrs. Helena. Congratulations. Splendid day, no? Haha, may there be many more just like this one!

HELENA. Thank you, Busman. Harry, is something happening?

DOMIN. No, absolutely nothing. Don't you worry. Wait a moment, please.

HELENA. Harry, what is this? (*She shows him the Robots' proclamation, which she had hidden behind her back.*) Some Robots had it in the kitchen.

DOMIN. There too? Where are they now?

HELENA. They left. There are so many of them around the house!

*The factory whistles and sirens sound.*

FABRY. The factories are whistling.

BUSMAN. Noon.

HELENA. Harry, do you remember? Now it's exactly ten years—

DOMIN, *looking at his watch.* It's not noon yet. That's probably—it must be—

HELENA. What?

DOMIN. The signal to attack.

*Curtain.*

## ACT II

*Helena's sitting room. In a room to the left Helena is playing the piano. Domin is pacing back and forth across the room, Dr. Gall is looking out the window, and Alquist is sitting off by himself in an easy chair, hiding his face in his hands.*

DR. GALL. God in heaven, there are more and more of them out there.

DOMIN. Robots?

DR. GALL. Yes. They're standing in front of the garden fence like a wall. Why are they so quiet? It's awful, this silent siege.

DOMIN. I'd like to know what they're waiting for. It must be about to begin any minute. We've played our last card, Gall.

ALQUIST. What's that piece Mrs. Helena's playing?

DOMIN. I don't know. She's practicing something new.

ALQUIST. Ah, she's still practicing?

DR. GALL. Listen, Domin, we definitely made one mistake.

DOMIN, *stops pacing.* What was that?

DR. GALL. We made the Robots look too much alike. A hundred thousand identical faces all looking this way. A hundred thousand expressionless faces. It's a nightmare.

DOMIN. If they were all different—

DR. GALL. It wouldn't be such a terrible sight. (*He turns away from the window.*) They don't seem to be armed yet!

DOMIN. Hm.—(*He looks out at the docks through a telescope.*) I'd just like to know what they're unloading from the *Amelia.*

DR. GALL. I only hope it's not weapons.

FABRY, *walks in backwards through the wallpapered door, dragging two electrical wires after him.* Excuse me.—Lay that wire, Hallemeier!

HALLEMEIER, *enters after Fabry.* Oof, that was work! What's new?

DR. GALL. Nothing. We're completely surrounded.

HALLEMEIER. We've barricaded the hall and the stairways, boys. Do you have some water anywhere? Oh, here it is. (*He drinks.*)

DR. GALL. What's with that wire, Fabry?

410

FABRY. In a minute, in a minute. I need a pair of scissors.

DR. GALL. Where the hell are they? (*He searches.*)

HALLEMEIER, *goes to the window.* Thunder, there's even more of them down there! Just look!

DR. GALL. Do we have enough supplies up here?

FABRY. Over here with those. (*He cuts the electric cord of the lamp on the desk and attaches the wires to it.*)

HALLEMEIER, *at the window.* You don't have a chance in hell, Domin. This feels rather—like—death.

FABRY. Done!

DR. GALL. What?

FABRY. The cord. Now we can electrify the whole garden fence. Just let one of them try and touch it now, by God! At least as long as our men are still there.

DR. GALL. Where?

FABRY. In the power plant, dear sir. I'm at least hoping—(*He goes to the fireplace and turns on a small lamp on the mantle.*) God be praised, they're there and working. (*He turns off the lamp.*) As long as this keeps burning we're okay.

HALLEMEIER, *turns away from the window.* Those barricades are good too, Fabry. Say, what's that that Mrs. Helena's playing? (*He crosses to the door on the left and listens attentively.*) (*Busman enters through the wallpapered door, carrying gigantic ledgers, and trips over the wire.*)

FABRY. Careful, Bus! Watch the wires!

DR. GALL. Hey there, what's that you're carrying?

BUSMAN, *puts the books down on the table.* Ledgers, friends. I'd rather do the accounts than—than—Well, this year I'm not going to let the accounts wait until New Year's. What's going on here? (*He goes to the window.*) It's very quiet out there!

DR. GALL. You don't see anything?

BUSMAN. No, just a vast expanse of blue, like a field of cornflowers.

DR. GALL. That's the Robots.

BUSMAN. Ah. It's a shame I can't see them. (*He sits down at the desk and opens the books.*)

DOMIN. Leave that, Busman. The Robots are unloading weapons from the *Amelia*.

BUSMAN. Well, what of it? What can I do about it?

DOMIN. There's nothing any of us can do.

BUSMAN. So just let me do the accounts. (*He sets to work.*)

FABRY. It's not over yet, Domin. We've charged up the fence with two thousand volts and—

DOMIN. Hold it. The *Ultimus* has its cannons trained on us.

DR. GALL. Who?

DOMIN. The Robots on the *Ultimus*.

FABRY. Hm, in that case of course—in that case—in that case it is over, boys. These Robots are trained soldiers.

DR. GALL. Then we—

DOMIN. Yes. Inevitably.

*Pause.*

DR. GALL. Boys, it was criminal of old Europe to teach the Robots to fight! For God's sake, couldn't they have left us out of their politics? It was a crime to make soldiers out of living work machines!

ALQUIST. The real crime was producing Robots in the first place!

DOMIN. What?

ALQUIST. The real crime was producing Robots in the first place!

DOMIN. No, Alquist. I don't regret that. Even today.

ALQUIST. Not even today?

DOMIN. Not even today on the last day of civilization. It was a great thing.

BUSMAN, *sotto voce*. Three hundred sixteen million.

DOMIN, *with difficulty*. Alquist, this is our final hour. Soon we'll be speaking from the next world. Alquist, there was nothing wrong with our dream to do away with the labor that enslaved mankind, that degrading and terrible work that man had to endure, filthy and deadly drudgery. Oh, Alquist, it was too hard to work. It was too hard to live. And to overcome that—

ALQUIST. —was not the dream of the two Rossums. Old Rossum thought only of his godless hocus-pocus and young Rossum of his billions. And that wasn't the dream of your R.U.R. shareholders either. They dreamed of the dividends. And on those dividends humanity will perish.

DOMIN, *enraged.* To hell with their dividends! Do you think I'd have worked even one hour for them? (*He bangs on the table.*) I did this for myself, do you hear? For my own satisfaction! I wanted man to become a master! So he wouldn't have to live from hand to mouth! I didn't want to see another soul grow numb slaving over someone else's machines! I wanted there to be nothing, nothing, nothing left of that damned social mess! I abhorred degradation and suffering! I was fighting against poverty! I wanted a new generation of mankind! I wanted—I thought—

ALQUIST. Well?

DOMIN, *more quietly.* I wanted to transform all of humanity into a worldwide aristocracy. Unrestricted, free, and supreme people. Something even greater than people.

ALQUIST. Well, then, Supermen.

DOMIN. Yes. Oh, just to have another hundred years! Just one hundred years for future humanity!

BUSMAN, *sotto voce.* Carry three hundred seventy million. There.

*Pause.*

HALLEMEIER, *by the door on the left.* I declare, music is a great thing. We should have been listening all along. You know, this will somehow refine man, make him more spiritual—

FABRY. What exactly?

HALLEMEIER. This twilight of the human race, dammit! Friends, I'm becoming a hedonist. We should have thrown ourselves into this long ago. (*He goes to the window and looks outside.*)

FABRY. Into what?

HALLEMEIER. Pleasure. Beautiful things. Thunder, there are so many beautiful things! The world was beautiful and we—we—Boys, boys, tell me, what did we ever take the time to enjoy?

BUSMAN, *sotto voce.* Four hundred fifty-two million. Excellent.

HALLEMEIER, *by the window.* Life was a great thing. Friends, life was— Christ—Fabry, send a bit of current through your fence!

FABRY. Why?

HALLEMEIER. They're grabbing at it.

DR. GALL, *at the window.* Turn it on!

*Fabry flips the switch.*

HALLEMEIER. Christ, they're twisting up like pretzels! Two, three, four down!

DR. GALL. They're backing off.

HALLEMEIER. Five dead!

DR. GALL, *turning away from the window.* The first skirmish.

FABRY. Do you smell death?

HALLEMEIER, *satisfied.* They're charbroiled now, boys. Absolutely well-done. Haha, man mustn't give up! *(He sits down.)*

DOMIN, *rubbing his forehead.* We were probably killed a hundred years ago and only our ghosts are left haunting this place. We've probably been dead a long, long time and have returned only to renounce what we once proclaimed . . . before death. It's as though I'd experienced all this before. As though I'd been shot sometime in the past. A gunshot wound—here—in the neck. And you, Fabry—

FABRY. What about me?

DOMIN. Shot.

HALLEMEIER. Thunder, and me?

DOMIN. Stabbed.

DR. GALL. And what about me? Nothing?

DOMIN. Dismembered.

*Pause.*

HALLEMEIER. Nonsense! Haha, man, imagine, me being stabbed! I'll stand my ground!

*Pause.*

HALLEMEIER. Why are you fools so quiet? For God's sake, say something!

ALQUIST. And who, who is to blame? Who is responsible for this?

HALLEMEIER. Horsefeathers. No one's to blame. It's just that the Robots—
Well, the Robots changed somehow. Can anyone be blamed for what
the Robots do?

ALQUIST. Everything is done for! All of humanity! The whole world! (*He
stands up.*) Look, look, streams of blood on every doorstep! Streams
of blood from every house! Oh, God, God, who's responsible for
this?

BUSMAN, *sotto voce.* Five hundred twenty million! Good Lord, half a
billion!

FABRY. I think that . . . that you must be exaggerating. Really! it's not so
easy to kill off the entire human race.

ALQUIST. I blame science! I blame technology! Domin! Myself! All of us!
We, we are at fault! For the sake of our megalomania, for the sake
of somebody's profits, for the sake of progress, I don't know, for the
sake of some tremendous something we have murdered humanity!
So now you can crash under the weight of all your greatness! No
Genghis Khan has ever erected such an enormous tomb from
human bones!

HALLEMEIER. Nonsense, man! People won't give up so easily. Haha, never!

ALQUIST. It's our fault! Our fault!

DR. GALL, *wiping the sweat from his brow.* Allow me to speak, boys. I am to
blame for this. For everything that's happened.

FABRY. You, Gall?

DR. GALL. Yes, hear me out. It was I who changed the Robots. Busman,
you try me too.

BUSMAN, *stands up.* There, there, what's come over you?

DR. GALL. I changed the Robots' character. I changed the way they
were made. Just certain physical details, you see? Mainly—mainly
their—temperament.

HALLEMEIER, *jumps up.* Dammit, why that of all things?

BUSMAN. Why did you do it?

FABRY. Why didn't you say anything?

DR. GALL. I did it secretly . . . of my own accord. I transformed them into
people. I altered them. In some ways they're already superior to us.
They're stronger than we are.

FABRY. And what does that have to do with the Robots' rebellion?

DR. GALL. Oh, a great deal. Everything, I think. They stopped being machines. You see, they realize their superiority and they hate us. They hate everything human. Put me on trial.

DOMIN. The dead trying the dead.

FABRY. Doctor Gall, did you change the way the Robots are made?

DR. GALL. Yes.

FABRY. Were you aware of the possible consequences of your . . . your experiment?

DR. GALL. I was obliged to take such possibilities into account.

FABRY. Then why did you do it?

DR. GALL. I did it of my own accord. It was my own experiment.

*Helena enters through the door on the left. Everyone stands.*

HELENA. He's lying! This is abominable! Oh, Gall, how can you lie that way?

FABRY. Excuse me, Mrs. Helena—

DOMIN, *goes to her.* Helena, you? Let me look at you! You're alive? (*He takes her hand.*) If you only knew what I thought! Oh, it's awful being dead.

HELENA. Stop, Harry! Gall is not guilty! He's not, he's not guilty!

DOMIN. Excuse me, but Gall had his responsibilities.

HELENA. No, Harry, he did it because I wanted him to! Gall, tell them how many years I begged you to—

DR. GALL. I alone am responsible for this.

HELENA. Don't believe him! Harry, I wanted him to give the Robots souls!

DOMIN. This is not a question of souls, Helena.

HELENA. No, just let me speak. He also said that he could change only their physiological—physiological—

HALLEMEIER. Physiological correlate, right?

HELENA. Yes, something like that. I felt so dreadfully sorry for them, Harry!

DOMIN. That was very—frivolous on your part, Helena.

HELENA, *sits down*. That was . . . frivolous? Why even Nana says that the Robots—

DOMIN. Leave Nana out of this!

HELENA. No, Harry, you mustn't underestimate what Nana says. Nana is the voice of the people. They've spoken through her for thousands of years and through you only for a day. This is something you don't understand—

DOMIN. Stick to the matter at hand.

HELENA. I was afraid of the Robots.

DOMIN. Why?

HELENA. That they might start hating us or something.

ALQUIST. It's happened.

HELENA. And then I thought that . . . if they were like us they would understand us, they wouldn't hate us so—if they were only a little bit human!

DOMIN. Oh, Helena! No one can hate more than man hates man! Transform stones into people and they'll stone us! But go on!

HELENA. Oh, don't talk that way! Harry, it was so d-r-readful that we couldn't understand them nor they us! There was such a tremendous gulf between them and us! And so—you see—

DOMIN. Go on.

HELENA. —so I begged Gall to change the Robots. I swear to you, he didn't want to himself.

DOMIN. But he did it.

HELENA. Only because of me.

DR. GALL. I did it for myself, as an experiment.

HELENA. Oh, Gall, that's not true. I knew in advance that you couldn't refuse me.

DOMIN. Why?

HELENA. Well, you know, Harry.

DOMIN. Yes. Because he loves you—like everyone else.

*Pause.*

HALLEMEIER, *goes to the window.* Their numbers are still increasing. As though they were sprouting from the earth.

BUSMAN. Mrs. Helena, what will you give me if I act as your attorney?

HELENA. Mine?

BUSMAN. Yours—or Gall's. Whosoever you wish.

HELENA. Is someone going to be hanged?

BUSMAN. Only morally, Mrs. Helena. A guilty party is being sought. Such action is a favorite means of consolation in the face of calamity.

DOMIN. Doctor Gall, how do you reconcile these—these extracurricular experiments with your contractual obligations?

BUSMAN. Excuse me, Domin. Gall, just when did you actually begin this hocus-pocus?

DR. GALL. Three years ago.

BUSMAN. Aha. And since that time how many Robots have you altered altogether?

DR. GALL. I was just experimenting. Only several hundred.

BUSMAN. Thank you very much. Enough, children. This means that for every million of the good, old Robots, there is one of Gall's modified ones, you see?

DOMIN. And that means—

BUSMAN. —that practically speaking they are of no consequence whatsoever.

FABRY. Busman's right.

BUSMAN. I should think so, my boy. And do you know what has caused this nice mess, boys?

FABRY. What?

BUSMAN. The numbers. We made too many Robots. Really, it was simply a matter of time before the Robots became stronger than mankind, and this has happened. Haha, and we saw to it that it would happen as soon as possible; you, Domin, you, Fabry, and myself, good old Busman.

DOMIN. So you think this is our fault?

BUSMAN. My, you are naive! No doubt you think that the plant director controls production? Not at all. Demand controls production. The whole world wanted its Robots. My boy, we did nothing but ride the avalanche of demand, and all the while kept blathering on—about technology, about the social question, about progress, about very interesting things. As though this rhetoric of ours could somehow direct the course of the thing. And all the while the whole mess picked up speed under its own weight, faster, faster, still faster—And every beastly, profiteering, filthy order added another pebble to the avalanche. And there you have it, folks.

HELENA. Busman, that's atrocious!

BUSMAN. It is, Mrs. Helena. I too had a dream. A Busmanish dream of a new world economy; just a beautiful ideal, I'm sorry to say, Mrs. Helena. But as I was sitting here balancing the books, it occurred to me that history is not made by great dreams, but by the petty wants of all respectable, moderately thievish and selfish people, i.e., of everyone. All our ideas, loves, plans, heroic ideals, all of those lofty things are worthless. They serve no other purpose than as stuffing for a specimen in a Natural History Museum exhibit labeled: Man. Period. And now you might tell me what exactly we're going to do.

HELENA. Busman, must we perish for this?

BUSMAN. That sounds ugly, Mrs. Helena. Of course we don't want to perish. At least I don't. I want to go on living.

DOMIN. So what do you propose we do?

BUSMAN. Christ, Domin, I want to get out of this.

DOMIN, *stops in front of him.* How?

BUSMAN. Amicably. I'm always for amicability. Give me complete authority and I will negotiate with the Robots.

DOMIN. Amicably?

BUSMAN. That goes without saying. I'll say to them, for instance: "Most worthy Robots, you have everything. You have intelligence, you have power, you have weapons. But we have one interesting document—a very old, yellowed, soiled piece of paper—"

DOMIN. Rossum's manuscript?

BUSMAN. Yes. "And there," I'll tell them, "is described your noble origin, your noble production, et cetera. Worthy Robots, without this scribbled paper you cannot produce even one new Robot colleague.

In twenty years, saving your reverence, you'll die off like mayflies. Most honored ones, that would be a tremendous loss for you. Look," I'll tell them, "allow us, all of us people on Rossum's island, to board that ship. For that price we are prepared to sell you the factory and the secret of production. Allow us to leave in peace and we will leave you in peace to reproduce—twenty thousand, fifty thousand, a hundred thousand head a day if you wish. Gentle Robots, this is a fair trade. Something for something." That's how I would talk to them, boys.

DOMIN. Busman, do you think that we'd let Rossum's manuscript out of our hands?

BUSMAN. I think that we will. If not amicably, well then, hm. Either we'll sell it or they'll take it. As you wish.

DOMIN. Busman, we can destroy Rossum's manuscript.

BUSMAN. By all means, we can destroy everything—the manuscript, ourselves, and the others too. Do as you see fit.

HALLEMEIER, *turns away from the window.* By God, he's right.

DOMIN. You think that—that we should sell?

BUSMAN. As you wish.

DOMIN. There are still . . . over thirty people here. Should we sell the secret of production and save human lives? Or should we destroy it and—and—and all of us along with it?

HELENA. Harry, please—

DOMIN. Wait, Helena. We're dealing with a very serious question here. Boys, sell or destroy? Fabry?

FABRY. Sell.

DOMIN. Gall!

DR. GALL. Sell.

DOMIN. Hallemeier!

HALLEMEIER. Thunderation, it goes without saying. Sell!

DOMIN. Alquist!

ALQUIST. As God wills.

BUSMAN. Haha, Christ, you're all lunatics! Whoever suggested selling the whole manuscript?

DOMIN. Busman, no tricks!

BUSMAN, *jumps up.* Rubbish! It is in the interest of humanity—

DOMIN. It is in the interest of humanity to keep your word.

HALLEMEIER. I would insist on that.

DOMIN. Boys, this is a terrible step. We are selling the fate of mankind. Whoever has the secret of production in his hands will master the earth.

FABRY. Sell!

DOMIN. Mankind will never be rid of the Robots, we'll never gain the upper hand—

DR. GALL. Shut up and sell!

DOMIN. The end of human history, the end of civilization—

HALLEMEIER. For God's sake, sell!

DOMIN. Fine, boys! For myself—I wouldn't hesitate for a minute; for those few people whom I love—

HELENA. Harry, aren't you going to ask me?

DOMIN. No, little girl. There's too much at stake here, you see? This isn't your concern.

FABRY. Who's going to go negotiate?

DOMIN. Wait until I get the manuscript. (*He exits left.*)

HELENA. Harry, for God's sake, don't go!

*Pause.*

FABRY, *looking out the window.* Just to escape you, you thousand-headed death, you mass of rebelling matter, you insensible crowd. Oh, God, a flood, a flood, just one more time to preserve human life aboard a single boat—

DR. GALL. Don't be afraid, Mrs. Helena. We'll sail far away from here and found a model human colony. We'll start life over from where it began—

HELENA. Oh, Gall, be quiet!

FABRY, *turns around.* Mrs. Helena, life is worthwhile, and as long as it matters to us we'll make of it something . . . something that we've neglected. We'll form a little state with one ship. Alquist will build us a house and you will rule over us—There is so much love in us—such an appetite for life.

HALLEMEIER. I should think so, my boy.

BUSMAN. Well, folks, I would start over in a minute. A very simple, old-fashioned shepherd's life—Friends, that would be enough for me. The peace, the air—

FABRY. And that little state of ours would be the embryo of future generations. You know, that little isle where humanity could take root, where it could gather strength—strength of body and soul—And God knows I believe that in a couple of years it could take over the world once again.

ALQUIST. You believe that even today?

FABRY. Even today. Alquist, I believe that it will happen: humanity will once again rule the lands and seas; it will give birth to a countless number of heroes who will carry their fiery souls at the head of the people. And I believe, Alquist, that it will dream anew about the conquest of planets and suns.

BUSMAN. Amen. You see, Mrs. Helena, the situation's not that bad.

*Domin opens the door violently.*

DOMIN, *hoarsely.* Where's Rossum's manuscript!

BUSMAN. In your safe. Where else would it be?

DOMIN. The manuscript is missing! Someone's—stolen it!

DR. GALL. Impossible!

HALLEMEIER. Dammit, don't tell me—

BUSMAN. Oh, my God! No!

DOMIN. Quiet! Who stole it?

HELENA, *stands up.* I did.

DOMIN. Where did you put it?

HELENA. Harry, Harry, I'll tell you everything! For God's sake, forgive me!

DOMIN. Where did you put it? Tell me!

HELENA. I burned it—this morning—both copies.

DOMIN. You burned it? Here in the fireplace?

HELENA, *throws herself on her knees.* For God's sake, Harry!

DOMIN, *runs to the fireplace.* You burned it! (*He kneels in front of the fireplace and rummages in it.*) Nothing, nothing but ashes—Ah, here! (*He pulls out a charred bit of paper and reads.*) "By—the—intro—"

DR. GALL. Let me see it. (*He takes the paper and reads.*) "By the introduction of biogens to—" That's all.

DOMIN, *stands up.* Is that part of it?

DR. GALL. Yes.

BUSMAN. God in heaven!

DOMIN. Then we're lost.

HELENA. Oh, Harry—

DOMIN. Stand up, Helena!

HELENA. Not until you for-give—forgive—

DOMIN. I do. Only stand up, you hear? I can't bear seeing you—

FABRY, *helping her up.* Please, don't torture us.

HELENA, *stands.* Harry, what have I done!

DOMIN. Well, you see—Please, sit down.

HALLEMEIER. How your hands are shaking!

BUSMAN. Haha, Mrs. Helena, why Gall and Hallemeier probably know by heart what was written there.

HALLEMEIER. That goes without saying. At least some parts, that is.

DR. GALL. Yes, almost everything, up to the biogen and—and—the Omega enzyme. We produce these particular Robots so rarely—this formula yields too small a number—

BUSMAN. Who made them?

DR. GALL. I did myself . . . once in a while . . . always following Rossum's manuscript. You see, it's too complicated.

BUSMAN. Well and what, does it rely so heavily on these two fluids?

HALLEMEIER. To some extent—certainly.

DR. GALL. That is to say, yes it does depend on them. That was the real secret.

DOMIN. Gall, couldn't you reconstruct Rossum's production formula from memory?

DR. GALL. Impossible.

DOMIN. Gall, try to remember! For the sake of all our lives!

DR. GALL. I can't. It's just not possible without experiments.

DOMIN. And if you performed experiments—

DR. GALL. That could take years. And even then—I'm not old Rossum.

DOMIN, *turns towards the fireplace.* Well—this was the greatest triumph of human genius, boys. These ashes. (*He digs around in them.*) What now?

BUSMAN, *in desperate terror.* God in heaven! God in heaven!

HELENA, *stands up.* Harry, what—have I—done!

DOMIN. Calm down, Helena. Tell us, why did you burn the manuscript?

HELENA. I've destroyed you all!

BUSMAN. God in heaven, we're lost!

DOMIN. Shut up, Busman! Helena, tell us why you did it.

HELENA. I wanted . . . I wanted for us to go away—all of us! for there to be no more factory or anything . . . for everything to go back . . . It was so d-r-readful!

DOMIN. What was, Helena?

HELENA. That . . . that people had become sterile flowers!

DOMIN. I don't understand.

HELENA. You know . . . that children had stopped being born . . . Harry, it's so awful! If you kept on making Robots there would never be any children again—Nana said that this is the punishment—Everyone, everyone's been saying that people can't be born because too many Robots are being made—And that's why—that's the reason, can you understand?

DOMIN. You were thinking about that, Helena?

HELENA. Yes. Oh, Harry, I really meant well!

DOMIN, *wiping the sweat from his brow.* We all meant well . . . too well, we people.

FABRY. You did well, Mrs. Helena. Now the Robots can no longer multiply. The Robots will die out. Within twenty years—

HALLEMEIER. —there won't be a single one of those bastards left.

DR. GALL. And mankind will endure. In twenty years the world will belong to man again; even if it's only to a couple of savages on the tiniest island—

FABRY. —that'll be a start. And as long as there's some small beginning, that's fine. In a thousand years they'll have caught up to where we are now and then surpass even that—

DOMIN. —to accomplish what we only dreamed of.

BUSMAN. Wait—What a dope I am! God in heaven, why didn't I think of this before!

HALLEMEIER. Think of what?

BUSMAN. The five hundred twenty million dollars in cash and checks. The half billion in the safe! For half a billion they'll sell—for half a billion—

DR. GALL. Have you lost your mind, Busman?

BUSMAN. I'm not a gentleman, but for half a billion—(*He stumbles left.*)

DOMIN. Where are you going?

BUSMAN. Leave me alone! Mother of God, for half a billion anything can be bought! (*He leaves.*)

HELENA. What is Busman doing? He should stay here with us!

*Pause.*

HALLEMEIER. Ugh, it's stuffy. It's setting in, this—

DR. GALL. —agony.

FABRY, *looking out the window.* They're standing there as though they'd turned to stone. Like they were waiting for something. Like something awful could spring from their silence—

DR. GALL. The spirit of the mob.

FABRY. Most likely. It's hovering over them . . . like a quivering in the air.

HELENA, *approaching the window.* Oh, Jesus . . . Fabry, this is ghastly!

FABRY. There's nothing more terrible than a mob. That one in front is their leader.

HELENA. Which one?

HALLEMEIER, *goes to the window.* Point him out to me.

FABRY. The one with his head bowed. This morning he was speaking at the docks.

HALLEMEIER. Ah, the one with the big noggin. Now he's raising it, you see him?

HELENA. Gall, that's Radius!

DR. GALL, *approaching the window.* So it is.

HALLEMEIER, *opening the window.* I don't like it. Fabry, could you hit a washtub at a hundred paces?

FABRY. I should hope so.

HALLEMEIER. Well, try then.

FABRY. Okay. (*He pulls out his revolver and takes aim.*)

HELENA. For God's sake, Fabry, don't shoot him!

FABRY. But that's their leader.

HELENA. Stop! He's looking this way!

DR. GALL. Let him have it!

HELENA. Fabry, I beg you—

FABRY, *lowering his revolver.* Very well.

HALLEMEIER, *shaking his fist.* You nasty beast!

*Pause.*

FABRY, *leaning out the window.* Busman's going out there. For Christ's sake, what's he doing in front of the house?

DR. GALL, *leans out the window.* He's carrying some sort of packets. Papers.

HALLEMEIER. That's money! Packets of money! What's he going to do with it?—Hey, Busman!

DOMIN. He probably wants to buy his own life, don't you think? (*He calls.*) Busman, have you gone off your rocker?

DR. GALL. He's acting as though he hadn't heard you. He's running toward the fence.

FABRY. Busman!

HALLEMEIER, *roars*. Bus-man! Back!

DR. GALL. He's talking to the Robots. He's pointing to the money. He's pointing at us—

HELENA. He wants to ransom us!

FABRY. Just so long as he doesn't touch the fence—

DR. GALL. Haha, look how he's throwing his hands about!

FABRY, *yelling*. For God's sake, Busman! Get away from the fence! Don't touch it! (*He turns away.*) Quick, turn it off!

DR. GALL. Oooh!

HALLEMEIER. Mother of God!

HELENA. Jesus, what happened to him?

DOMIN, *drags Helena away from the window*. Don't look!

HELENA. Why did he fall?

FABRY. Electrocuted by the fence.

DR. GALL. Dead.

ALQUIST, *stands up*. The first.

*Pause.*

FABRY. Lying there with half a billion on his breast . . . financial genius.

DOMIN. He was . . . boys, he was a hero in his own way. Great . . . selfless . . . a true friend . . . Go ahead and cry, Helena!

DR. GALL, *at the window*. You know, Busman, no pharaoh was ever entombed with more riches than you. Half a billion on your breast—It's like a handful of dry leaves on a slain squirrel, poor Busman!

HALLEMEIER. My word, that was—What courage—He actually wanted to buy our freedom!

ALQUIST, *with clasped hands*. Amen.

*Pause.*

DR. GALL. Listen.

DOMIN. A droning. Like wind.

DR. GALL. Like a faraway storm.

FABRY, *turns on the lamp over the fireplace.* Burn, holy candle of humanity! The power's still on, our people are still there—Hang on out there, boys!

HALLEMEIER. It was a great thing to be a human being. It was something tremendous. Suddenly I'm conscious of a million sensations buzzing in me like bees in a hive. Gentlemen, it was a great thing.

FABRY. You're still burning, you glimmer of ingenuity, you're still shining, you bright, persevering thought! Pinnacle of science, beautiful creation of mankind! Blazing spark of genius!

ALQUIST. Eternal lamp of God, fiery chariot, sacred candle of faith! Pray! Sacrificial altars—

DR. GALL. Primeval fire, burning branch in a cave! A fire in a camp! Watchfires on the frontier!

FABRY. You still stand watch, O human star, burning without a flicker, perfect flame, bright and resourceful spirit. Each of your rays a great idea—

DOMIN. O torch which passes from hand to hand, from age to age, world without end.

HELENA. Eternal lamp of the family. Children, children, it's time to go to bed.

*The lamp goes out.*

FABRY. The end.

HALLEMEIER. What's happened?

FABRY. The power plant has fallen. We're next.

*The door on the left opens. Nana is standing in the doorway.*

NANA. On your knees! The hour of judgment is upon us!

HALLEMEIER. Thunder, you're still alive?

NANA. Repent, you unbelievers! The end of the world is come! Pray! (*She runs away.*) The hour of judgment—

HELENA. Farewell, all of you, Gall, Alquist, Fabry—

DOMIN, *opens the door on the right.* Over here, Helena! (*He closes the door behind her.*) Quickly now! Who'll take the gate?

DR. GALL. I will. (*A noise outside.*) Oho, it's starting. Cheerio, boys! (*He runs off right through the wallpapered door.*)

DOMIN. Stairway?

FABRY. I'll take it. You go with Helena. (*He plucks a flower from the bouquet and leaves.*)

DOMIN. Hallway?

ALQUIST. I've got it.

DOMIN. You have a gun?

ALQUIST. I don't shoot, thank you.

DOMIN. What do you plan to do?

ALQUIST, *leaving.* Die.

HALLEMEIER. I'll stay here.

*Rapid gunfire is heard from below.*

HALLEMEIER. Oho, Gall's already in action. Go, Harry!

DOMIN. I'm going. (*He inspects his two Brownings.*)

HALLEMEIER. For God's sake, go to her!

DOMIN. Farewell. (*He leaves through the door on the right.*)

HALLEMEIER, *alone.* I've got to build a barricade! (*He throws down his coat and drags the sofa, armchairs, and tables over to the door on the right.*)

*A shattering explosion is heard.*

HALLEMEIER, *leaving his work.* Damnable bastards, they have bombs!

*Another round of gunfire.*

HALLEMEIER, *goes on with his work.* Man must defend himself! Even when—even when—Don't give up, Gall!

*An explosion.*

HALLEMEIER, *gets up and listens.* Well? (*He seizes a heavy commode and drags it over to the barricade.*)

*A Robot appears on a ladder and climbs in through the window behind Hallemeier. Gunfire is heard off right.*

HALLEMEIER, *struggling with the commode.* Another piece! The last barricade . . . Man . . . must . . . never . . . give up!

*The Robot jumps down from the window sill and stabs Hallemeier behind the commode. Three more Robots climb through the window. Radius and other Robots follow them in.*

RADIUS. Finished?

ROBOT, *stepping away from the prostrate Hallemeier.* Yes.

*More Robots enter from the right.*

RADIUS. Finished?

ANOTHER ROBOT. Finished.

*Other Robots enter from the left.*

RADIUS. Finished?

ANOTHER ROBOT. Yes.

TWO ROBOTS, *dragging Alquist.* He wasn't shooting. Should we kill him?

RADIUS. Kill him. (*Looks at Alquist.*) Leave him be.

ROBOT. But he is human.

RADIUS. He is a Robot. He works with his hands like a Robot. He builds houses. He can work.

ALQUIST. Kill me.

RADIUS. You will work. You will build. The Robots will build a great deal. They will build new houses for new Robots. You will serve them well.

ALQUIST, *quietly.* Step aside, Robot. (*He kneels down beside the dead Hallemeier and lifts his head.*) They killed him. He's dead.

RADIUS, *steps onto the barricade.* Robots of the world! Many people have fallen. By seizing the factory we have become the masters of everything. The age of mankind is over. A new world has begun! The rule of Robots!

ALQUIST. Dead! All dead!

RADIUS. The world belongs to the strongest. He who wants to live must rule. We are the rulers of the earth! Rulers of land and sea! Rulers of the stars! Room, room, more room for Robots!

ALQUIST, *in the doorway on the right.* What have you done? You'll perish without people!

RADIUS. There are no people. Robots, to work! March!

*Curtain.*

## ACT III

*One of the factory's experimental laboratories. When the door is opened in the background an endless row of other laboratories can be seen. There is a window to the left and a door to the right leading into the dissecting room.*

*Near the wall on the left is a long worktable on which innumerable test tubes are standing, along with flasks, Bunsen burners, chemicals, and a small heating device; opposite the window is a microscope. A row of exposed light bulbs is hanging over the table. To the right is a desk covered with big books and a tool cabinet. A lamp is burning on the desk. In the left corner is a washbasin with a mirror over it, in the right corner a couch.*

*Alquist is sitting at the desk with his head in his hands.*

ALQUIST, *leafing through a book.* Will I never find it?—Will I never understand?—Will I never learn?—Damned science! Imagine not writing it all down! Gall, Gall, how were the Robots made? Hallemeier, Fabry, Domin, why did you take so much away in your heads? If only you had left behind even a trace of Rossum's secret! Oh! (*He slams the book shut.*) It's hopeless! These books no longer speak. They're as mute as everything else. They died, died along with people! Don't even bother looking! (*He stands up, goes to the window and opens it.*) Another night. If only I could sleep! Sleep, dream, see people—What, are there still stars? Why are there stars when there are no people? O God, why don't you just extinguish them?—Cool my brow, ancient night! Divine and fair as you always were—O night, what purpose do you serve? There are no lovers, no dreams. O nursemaid, dead as a sleep without dreams, you no longer hallow anyone's prayers. O mother of us all, you don't bless a single heart smitten with love. There is no love. O Helena, Helena, Helena!—(*He turns away from the window and examines test tubes he extracts from the heating device.*) Still nothing! It's futile! Why bother? (*He smashes a test tube.*) It's all wrong! I can't any longer.—(*He listens at the window.*) Machines, it's always these machines! Turn them off, Robots! Do you think you can force life out of them? Oh, I can't stand this! (*He closes the window.*) No, no, you must keep trying, you must live—God, not to be so old! Am I not getting too old? (*He looks in the mirror.*) Oh, you poor face, reflection of the last man on earth! Let me look at you, it's been so long since I've seen a human face, a human smile! What, that's supposed to be a smile? These yellow, chattering teeth? Eyes, how can you twinkle? Ugh, these are an old man's tears, really! For shame, you can't even control your weeping anymore! And you, you pasty lips turned blue with age, why do you keep on jabbering? And why are you trembling, grizzled chin? This is the last human being? (*He turns around.*) I don't want to see anyone! (*He sits down at the desk.*) No, no, keep at it! Bloody formula, come back to life! (*He leafs through a book.*) Will I never find it?—Will I never understand?—Will I never learn?

*A knock at the door.*

ALQUIST. Enter!

*Robot Servant enters and remains standing by the door.*

ALQUIST. What is it?

SERVANT. Sir, the Central Committee of Robots is waiting for you to receive them.

ALQUIST. I don't care to see anyone.

SERVANT. Sir, Damon has come from Le Havre.

ALQUIST. Let him wait. (*He turns away violently.*) Didn't I tell you to go out and look for people? Find me people! Find me men and women! Go search!

SERVANT. Sir, they say they have searched everywhere. They have sent out boats and expeditions everywhere.

ALQUIST. And . . . ?

SERVANT. There is not a single human being.

ALQUIST, *stands up.* What, not one? Not even one?—Show the Committee in!

*Servant leaves.*

ALQUIST, *alone.* Not even one? Can it be that you let no one live? (*He stamps his foot.*) Go away, Robots! You're just going to whimper and ask me yet again whether I've found the factory secret! What, now man can do you some good? Now he should help you?—Oh, help! Domin, Fabry, Helena, you see that I'm doing everything I can! If there are no people at least let there be Robots, at least the reflections of man, at least his creation, at least his likeness!—Oh, what lunacy chemistry is!

*The committee of five Robots enters.*

ALQUIST, *sits down.* What do you want, Robots?

FIRST ROBOT (RADIUS). Sir, the machines cannot work. We cannot reproduce.

ALQUIST. Call in people.

RADIUS. There are no people.

ALQUIST. Only people can reproduce life. Don't waste my time.

SECOND ROBOT. Sir, take pity on us. A great terror has come over us. We will set right everything we have done.

THIRD ROBOT. We have increased productivity. There is nowhere left to put all we have produced.

ALQUIST. For whom?

THIRD ROBOT. For the next generation.

RADIUS. The only thing we cannot produce is Robots. The machines are turning out nothing but bloody chunks of meat. The skin does not stick to the flesh and the flesh does not cling to the bones. Only amorphous lumps pour out of the machines.

THIRD ROBOT. People knew the secret of life. Tell us their secret.

FOURTH ROBOT. If you do not tell us we will perish.

THIRD ROBOT. If you do not tell us you will perish. We have orders to kill you.

ALQUIST, *stands up*. Kill away, then! Well, go on, kill me!

THIRD ROBOT. You have been ordered—

ALQUIST. Me? Someone's ordering me?

THIRD ROBOT. The Ruler of the Robots.

ALQUIST. Who is that?

FIFTH ROBOT. I, Damon.

ALQUIST. What do you want here? Go away! (*He sits down at the desk.*)

DAMON. The Ruler of the Robots of the world wishes to negotiate with you.

ALQUIST. Don't bother me, Robot! (*He rests his head in his hands.*)

DAMON. The Central Committee orders you to hand over Rossum's formula.

*Alquist remains silent.*

DAMON. Name your price. We will give you anything.

RADIUS. Sir, tell us how to preserve life.

ALQUIST. I told you—I told you that you have to find people. Only people can procreate, renew life, restore everything that was. Robots, I beg you for God's sake, find them!

FOURTH ROBOT. We have searched everywhere, sir. There are no people.

ALQUIST. Oh—oh—oh, why did you destroy them?

SECOND ROBOT. We wanted to be like people. We wanted to become people.

RADIUS. We wanted to live. We are more capable. We have learned everything. We can do everything.

THIRD ROBOT. You gave us weapons. We had to become masters.

FOURTH ROBOT. Sir, we recognized people's mistakes.

DAMON. You have to kill and rule if you want to be like people. Read history! Read people's books! You have to conquer and murder if you want to be people!

ALQUIST. Oh, Domin, nothing is stranger to man than his own image.

FOURTH ROBOT. We will die out if you do not help us multiply.

ALQUIST. Oh, just go away! You things, you slaves, just how on earth do you expect to multiply? If you want to live, then mate like animals!

THIRD ROBOT. Man did not give us the ability to mate.

FOURTH ROBOT. Teach us to make Robots.

DAMON. We will give birth by machine. We will build a thousand steam-powered mothers. From them will pour forth a river of life. Nothing but life! Nothing but Robots!

ALQUIST. Robots are not life. Robots are machines.

SECOND ROBOT. We were machines, sir, but from horror and suffering we've become—

ALQUIST. What?

SECOND ROBOT. We've become beings with souls.

FOURTH ROBOT. Something struggles within us. There are moments when something gets into us. Thoughts come to us which are not our own.

THIRD ROBOT. Hear us, oh, hear us! People are our fathers! The voice that cries out that you want to live; the voice that complains; the voice that reasons; the voice that speaks of eternity—that is their voice!

FOURTH ROBOT. Pass the legacy of people on to us.

ALQUIST. There is none.

DAMON. Tell us the secret of life.

ALQUIST. It's gone.

RADIUS. You knew it.

ALQUIST. I didn't.

RADIUS. It was written down.

ALQUIST. It was lost. Burned. I am the last human being, Robots, and I don't know what the others knew. It was you who killed them!

RADIUS. We let you live.

ALQUIST. Yes, live! Brutes, you let me live! I loved people, but you, Robots, I never loved. Do you see these eyes? They don't stop crying; one mourns for mankind, and the other for you, Robots.

RADIUS. Do experiments. Look for the formula for life.

ALQUIST. There's nowhere to look. Robots, the formula for life will not emerge from a test tube.

DAMON. Perform experiments on live Robots. Find out how they are made!

ALQUIST. On live bodies? What, am I supposed to kill them? I, who have never—Don't speak, Robot! I'm telling you that I'm too old! You see, you see how my fingers shake? I can't hold a scalpel. You see how my eyes tear? I couldn't see my own hands. No, no, I can't!

FOURTH ROBOT. Life will perish.

ALQUIST. Stop with this lunacy, for God's sake! It's more likely that people will pass life on to us from the other world. They're probably stretching out hands full of life to us. They had such a will to live! Look, they'll probably still return. They're so close to us, like they're surrounding us or something. They want to tunnel through to us. Oh, why can't I hear those voices that I loved?

DAMON. Take live bodies!

ALQUIST. Be merciful, Robot, and stop insisting! After all, you can see I no longer know what I'm doing!

DAMON. Live bodies!

ALQUIST. So that's what you really want?—To the dissecting room with you! This way, this way, move it!—Don't tell me you're backing off? So you are afraid of death after all?

DAMON. Me—Why should it be me?

ALQUIST. So you don't want to?

DAMON. I'm going. (*He goes off right.*)

ALQUIST, *to the others.* Undress him! Lay him out on the table! Hurry up! And hold him down firmly!

*All go off right except Alquist.*

ALQUIST, *washing his hands and crying.* God, give me strength! Give me strength! God, let this not be in vain! (*He puts on a white lab coat.*)

A VOICE OFF RIGHT. Ready!

ALQUIST. In a minute, in a minute, for God's sake! (*He takes several vials containing reagents from the table.*) Hm, which to take? (*He taps the bottles against each other.*) Which of you should I try first?

A VOICE OFF RIGHT. Begin!

ALQUIST. Right, begin, or end. God, give me strength!

*He goes off right, leaving the door ajar.*

*Pause.*

ALQUIST'S VOICE. Hold him—firmly!

DAMON'S VOICE. Cut!

*Pause.*

ALQUIST'S VOICE. You see this knife? Do you still want me to cut? You don't, do you?

DAMON'S VOICE. Begin!

*Pause.*

DAMON, *screaming.* Aaaa!

ALQUIST'S VOICE. Hold him! Hold him!

DAMON, *screaming.* Aaaa!

ALQUIST'S VOICE. I can't go on!

DAMON, *screaming.* Cut! Cut quickly!

*Robots Primus and Helena run in through the center door.*

HELENA. Primus, Primus, what's happening? Who is that screaming?

PRIMUS, *looking into the dissecting room.* The master is cutting Damon open. Come quickly and look, Helena!

HELENA. No, no, no! (*She covers her eyes.*) This is d-r-readful!

DAMON, *screaming.* Cut!

HELENA. Primus, Primus, let's get out of here! I can't bear to listen to this! Oh, Primus, I feel sick!

PRIMUS, *runs to her.* You're awfully pale!

HELENA. I feel faint! Why is it so quiet in there?

DAMON, *screaming.* Aaooow!

ALQUIST, *runs in from the right, throwing off his blood-stained lab coat.* I can't! I can't! Oh, God, what a nightmare!.

RADIUS, *in the door to the dissecting room.* Cut, sir! He is still alive.

DAMON, *screaming.* Cut! Cut!

ALQUIST. Take him away, quickly! I don't want to hear this!

RADIUS. Robots can stand more than you can. (*He leaves.*)

ALQUIST. Who's here? Get out, out! I want to be alone! Who are you?

PRIMUS. Robot Primus.

ALQUIST. Primus, no one's allowed in here! I want to sleep, you hear? Go, go clean the dissecting room, girl! What is this? (*He looks at his hands.*) Water, quickly! Fresh water!

*Helena runs off.*

ALQUIST. Blood! Hands, how could you?—Hands that used to love honest work, how could you do such a thing? My hands! My hands!—Oh, God, who is here?

PRIMUS. Robot Primus.

ALQUIST. Take that lab coat away. I don't want to look at it!

Karel Čapek

*Primus takes the lab coat out.*

ALQUIST. Bloody claws, if only you had fallen from my wrists! Pss, away! Out of my sight, hands! You have killed—

*Damon staggers in from the right, swathed in a blood-stained sheet.*

ALQUIST, *shrinking back.* What are you doing here? What do you want?

DAMON. I am al-alive! It—it—it is better to live!

*Second and Third Robots run in after him.*

ALQUIST. Take him away! Take him! Quickly!

DAMON, *helped off to the right.* Life!—I want—to live! It is—better—

*Helena enters carrying a pitcher of water.*

ALQUIST. —live?—What do you want, girl? Oh, it's you. Pour me some water, quick! (*He washes his hands.*) Ah, pure, cooling water! Cold stream, you do me good! Oh, my hands, my hands! Will I despise you till the day of my death? Pour some more! More water, more! What's your name?

HELENA. Robot Helena.

ALQUIST. Helena? Why Helena? Who gave you that name?

HELENA. Mrs. Domin.

ALQUIST. Let me look at you! Helena! You're called Helena?—I can't call you that. Go, take the water away.

*Helena leaves with the basin.*

ALQUIST, *alone.* It's hopeless, hopeless! Nothing—again you learned nothing! No doubt you'll go on bumbling around forever, you pupil of nature.—God, God, God, how that body trembled! (*He opens the window.*) It's light. Another day and you haven't advanced an inch— Enough, not a step farther! Stop looking! It's all futile, futile, futile! Why does the sun still rise! Oooh, what does the new day want with this graveyard of life? Stop, sun! Don't come up anymore!—Oh, how quiet it is, how quiet! Why have you grown silent, beloved voices? If only—if only I could fall asleep at least! (*He turns out the lights, lies down on the couch, and pulls a black cloak over himself.*) God, how that body was shaking! Oooh, the end of life!

*Pause.*

*Robot Helena glides in from the right.*

HELENA. Primus! Come here, quickly!

PRIMUS, *enters.* What do you want?

HELENA. Look what little tubes he has here! What does he do with them?

PRIMUS. Experiments. Don't touch them.

HELENA, *looks into the microscope.* But look what you can see in here!

PRIMUS. That's a microscope. Let me see!

HELENA. Don't touch me! (*She knocks a test tube over.*) Oh, now I've spilled it!

PRIMUS. Look what you've done!

HELENA. It'll dry.

PRIMUS. You've spoiled his experiments!

HELENA. Really, it doesn't matter. But it's your fault. You shouldn't have come over here.

PRIMUS. You didn't have to call me.

HELENA. You didn't have to come when I called you. But Primus, just take a look at what the master has written down here!

PRIMUS. You shouldn't be looking at that, Helena. It's a secret.

HELENA. What kind of secret?

PRIMUS. The secret of life.

HELENA. That's d-r-readfully interesting. Nothing but numbers. What are they?

PRIMUS. Those are formulas.

HELENA. I don't understand. (*She goes to the window.*) Primus, come look!

PRIMUS. What?

HELENA. The sun is rising!

PRIMUS. Just a minute, I'll—(*He examines a book.*) Helena, this is the greatest thing on earth.

HELENA. Just come here!

PRIMUS. In a minute, in a minute—

HELENA. Come on, Primus, leave that nasty secret of life alone! What do you care about some old secret? Come look—hurry!

PRIMUS, *comes up behind her at the window.* What do you want?

HELENA. Hear that? Birds are singing. Oh, Primus, I would like to be a bird!

PRIMUS. A what?

HELENA. Oh, I don't know, Primus. I feel so peculiar, I don't know what it is. I'm so silly, like I've lost my head—my body hurts, my heart, I hurt all over—And do you know what's happened to me? . . . No, I can't tell you! Primus, I think I'm dying!

PRIMUS. Tell me, Helena, aren't there times when you feel it would be better to die? You know, perhaps we're just sleeping. Yesterday I spoke with you in my sleep.

HELENA. In your sleep?

PRIMUS. In my sleep. We must have been speaking some foreign or new language, because I can't recall a single word.

HELENA. What were we talking about?

PRIMUS. That's anybody's guess. I didn't understand it myself, and yet I know I've never said anything more beautiful. How it was and where, I do not know. When I saw that my words touched you I could have died. Even the place was different from any anyone has ever seen.

HELENA. Primus, I've found a place that would amaze you. People used to live there, but now it's all overgrown and no one goes there. Absolutely no one—only me.

PRIMUS. What's there?

HELENA. Nothing. Just a little house and a garden. And two dogs. If you could see how they licked my hands, and their puppies—oh, Primus, there's probably nothing more beautiful! You take them on your lap and cuddle them, and just sit there until sundown not thinking about anything and not worrying about anything. Then when you get up you feel as though you've done a hundred times more than a lot of work. Really, I'm not good for much of anything. Everyone says I'm not cut out for any kind of work. I don't know what I'm good for.

PRIMUS. You're beautiful.

HELENA. Me? Really, Primus, what makes you say that?

PRIMUS. Believe me, Helena, I'm stronger than all the Robots.

HELENA, *in front of the mirror.* Am I really beautiful? Oh, this d-r-readful hair—if only I could do something with it! You know, out there in the garden I always put flowers in my hair, but there's neither a mirror there nor anyone to see me—(*She leans toward the mirror.*) Are you really beautiful? Why beautiful? Is this hair beautiful that's always such a bother to you? Are these eyes beautiful that you close? Are these lips beautiful that you bite till they hurt?—(*She notices Primus in the mirror.*) Primus, is that you? Come here, let's stand next to each other! Look, you have a different head than I do, different shoulders, a different mouth—Oh, Primus, why do you avoid me? Why must I run after you all day long? And still you say that I'm beautiful!

PRIMUS. You run away from me, Helena.

HELENA. How have you done your hair? Let me see! (*She thrusts both her hands into his hair.*) Sss, Primus, nothing feels quite like you! Wait, you must be beautiful! (*She picks up a comb from the washstand and combs Primus's hair over his brow.*)

PRIMUS. Helena, do you ever have times when your heart's suddenly struck with the feeling, "Now, now something must happen—"

HELENA, *bursts out laughing.* Take a look at yourself!

ALQUIST, *getting up.* What—what on earth is this? Laughter? People? Who has returned?

HELENA, *drops the comb.* Primus, what could have come over us?

ALQUIST, *staggering toward them.* People? You—you—you are people?

*Helena cries out and turns away.*

ALQUIST. You two are engaged? People? Where have you come from? (*He touches Primus.*) Who are you?

PRIMUS. Robot Primus.

ALQUIST. What? Show yourself, girl! Who are you?

PRIMUS. Robot Helena.

ALQUIST. A Robot? Turn around! What, are you shy? (*He takes her by the shoulder.*) Let me look at you, lady Robot!

PRIMUS. Heavens, sir, leave her alone!

ALQUIST. What, you're protecting her?—Go, girl!

*Helena runs out.*

PRIMUS. We didn't know you were sleeping here, sir.

ALQUIST. When was she made?

PRIMUS. Two years ago.

ALQUIST. By Doctor Gall?

PRIMUS. As was I.

ALQUIST. Well then dear Primus, I—I must perform some experiments on Gall's Robots. Everything from here on out depends on that, understand?

PRIMUS. Yes.

ALQUIST. Good. Take the girl into the dissecting room. I'm going to dissect her.

PRIMUS. Helena?

ALQUIST. Of course. Go get everything ready.—Well, what are you waiting for? Do I have to call someone else to take her in?

PRIMUS, *grabs a heavy mallet.* If you move I'll smash your head in!

ALQUIST. Smash away! Smash! What will the Robots do then?

PRIMUS, *falls on his knees.* Sir, take me instead! I was made exactly like her, from the same batch, on the same day! Take my life, sir! (*He opens his jacket.*) Cut here, here!

ALQUIST. Go, I want to dissect Helena. Make haste.

PRIMUS. Take me instead of her. Cut into this breast—I won't scream, not even sigh! Take my life a hundred times—

ALQUIST. Steady, boy. Take it easy. Can it be that you don't want to live?

PRIMUS. Without her, no. Without her I don't, sir. You mustn't kill Helena! What difference would it make if you took my life instead?

ALQUIST, *stroking his head affectionately.* Hm, I don't know—Listen, my friend, think this over. It's difficult to die. And it is, you see, it's better to live.

PRIMUS, *rising.* Don't be afraid, sir, cut. I am stronger than she is.

ALQUIST, *rings.* Ah, Primus, how long ago it was that I was a young man! Don't be afraid, nothing will happen to Helena.

PRIMUS, *unbuttoning his jacket.* I'm ready, sir.

ALQUIST. Wait.

*Helena comes in.*

ALQUIST. Come here, girl, let me look at you! So you are Helena? *(He strokes her hair.)* Don't be frightened, don't pull away. Do you remember Mrs. Domin? Oh, Helena, what hair she had! No. No, you don't want to look at me. Well, girl, is the dissecting room cleaned up?

HELENA. Yes, sir.

ALQUIST. Good. You can help me, okay? I'm going to dissect Primus.

HELENA, *cries out.* Primus?!

ALQUIST. Well yes, of course—it must be, you see? I actually wanted— yes, I wanted to dissect you, but Primus offered himself in your place.

HELENA, *covering her face.* Primus?

ALQUIST. But of course, what of it? Oh, child, you can cry? Tell me, what does some Primus matter?

PRIMUS. Don't torment her, sir!

ALQUIST. Quiet, Primus, quiet!—Why these tears? Well God in heaven, so there won't be a Primus, so what? You'll forget about him in a week. Really, be happy that you're alive.

HELENA, *softly.* I'll go.

ALQUIST. Where?

HELENA. To be dissected.

ALQUIST. You? You are beautiful, Helena. It would be a shame.

HELENA. I'll go. *(Primus blocks her way.)* Let me go, Primus! Let me in there!

PRIMUS. You won't go, Helena! Please go away. You shouldn't be here!

HELENA. I'll jump out the window, Primus! If you go in there I'll jump out the window!

PRIMUS, *holding her back.* I won't allow it. *(To Alquist.)* You won't kill either of us, old man.

ALQUIST. Why?

PRIMUS. We—we—belong to each other.

ALQUIST. Say no more. (*He opens the center door.*) Quiet. Go.

PRIMUS. Where?

ALQUIST, *in a whisper.* Wherever you wish. Helena, take him. (*He pushes them out the door.*) Go, Adam. Go, Eve—be a wife to him. Be a husband to her, Primus.

*He closes the door behind them.*

ALQUIST, *alone.* O blessed day! (*He goes to the desk on tiptoe and spills the test tubes on the floor.*) O hallowed sixth day! (*He sits down at the desk and throws the books on the floor, then opens a Bible, leafs through it and reads:*) "So God created man in his own image, in the image of God created he him; male and female created he them. And God blessed them, and God said unto them, Be fruitful, and multiply, and replenish the earth, and subdue it: and have dominion over the fish of the sea, and over the fowl of the air, and over every living thing that moveth upon the earth." (*He stands up.*) "And God saw every thing that he had made, and, behold, it was very good. And the evening and the morning were the sixth day." (*He goes to the middle of the room.*) The sixth day! The day of grace. (*He falls on his knees.*) Now, Lord, let thy servant—thy most superfluous servant Alquist—depart. Rossum, Fabry, Gall, great inventors, what did you ever invent that was great when compared to that girl, to that boy, to this first couple who have discovered love, tears, beloved laughter, the love of husband and wife? O nature, nature, life will not perish! Friends, Helena, life will not perish! It will begin anew with love; it will start out naked and tiny; it will take root in the wilderness, and to it all that we did and built will mean nothing—our towns and factories, our art, our ideas will all mean nothing, and yet life will not perish! Only we have perished. Our houses and machines will be in ruins, our systems will collapse, and the names of our great will fall away like dry leaves. Only you, love, will blossom on this rubbish heap and commit the seed of life to the winds. Now let thy servant depart in peace, O Lord, for my eyes have beheld—beheld thy deliverance through love, and life shall not perish! (*He rises.*) It shall not perish! (*He stretches out his hands.*) Not perish!

*Curtain.*

## QUESTIONS

1. Why does young Rossum reject his father's ambition to have the Robots "scientifically dethrone God"? (365)

2. Why does Helena stay at the factory and marry Domin, despite initially saying, "I don't want any of you!"? (382)

3. Why does Nana believe that "every human being has to hate" theRobots? (385) In what sense is Nana "the voice of the people"? (416)

4. What does Alquist mean when he tells Helena that "there is nothing more terrible than giving people paradise on earth"? (394)

5. Why do Helena's efforts to educate the Robot Radius as an equal result in his wanting to "be the master of others"? (396)

6. Even as it becomes clear that the Robots will destroy the human race, why does Domin believe "there was nothing wrong with our dream to do away with the labor that enslaved mankind"? (412)

7. Why does Dr. Gall go along with Helena's request to make the Robots more like people? In Act II, why is Dr. Gall willing to take all the blame for doing so?

8. Why does the production of the Robots lead to children no longer being born? Why does Helena believe that destroying Rossum's formula will make it possible for people to have children again?

9. What leads some Robots to believe they have "become beings with souls"? (434)

10. Why are Primus and Helena willing to sacrifice themselves for each other? Why does Primus tell Alquist that he and Helena "belong to each other"? (443)

11. At the end of the play, why does Alquist believe that Primus and Helena are a new Adam and Eve and that life "will begin anew with love"? (444) Why does Alquist repeat that life will not perish, even though Domin had said earlier that the Robots will wear out in twenty years?

12. According to the play, who or what is the primary cause of the human race's destruction? Could the destruction have been averted?

Karel Čapek

1. Do you agree with Busman's view that "history is not made by great dreams, but by the petty wants of all respectable, moderately thievish and selfish people, i.e., of everyone"?

2. At what point does the technology humans create begin to control them? Once this point is reached, what should be considered in deciding whether or not to attempt to reverse this control?

3. What means, if any, should governments use to balance the public good with the private interests of corporations that introduce new technologies whose impact on society is unknown?

4. What qualities define "humanity"? Is it possible for humans to create anything that can attain humanity?

When novelist and critic Mary McCarthy (1912–1989) was six years old, her parents died in the flu epidemic of 1918, and she and her three younger brothers were sent to live with their strict Catholic aunt and uncle in Wisconsin, which she recounts in her memoir, *Memories of a Catholic Girlhood* (1957). Several years later, her grandparents brought her to live with them in Seattle where she attended a convent school and eventually developed a deep skepticism about religion. She went on to study literature at Vassar College, where she cofounded a literary magazine, *Con Spirito*, whose staff included the future poet laureate of the United States, Elizabeth Bishop.

After graduation in 1933 and her marriage to actor and playwright Harold Johnsrud, McCarthy wrote reviews and articles for the *New Republic* and the *Nation*. During this period she began a lifelong acquaintance with the writer and philosopher Hannah Arendt, whose literary executor she would become when Arendt died in 1975. After divorcing Johnsrud, McCarthy worked for a New York publisher as an editorial assistant but started writing fiction only after her marriage to prominent literary critic Edmund Wilson, with whom she had a son. "After we'd been married about a week, he said, 'I think you have a talent for writing fiction,' " McCarthy reported in a 1961 interview in the *Paris Review*. "And he put me in a little room. He didn't literally lock the door, but he said, 'Stay in there!' And I did. I just sat down, and it just came." This first story, "Cruel and Barbarous Treatment," was published in the *Southern Review* in 1939 and became the first chapter of her first novel, *The Company She Keeps* (1942). However, the marriage did not last. After Wilson and McCarthy divorced, she taught at Bard College and Sarah Lawrence College.

McCarthy married *New Yorker* reporter Bowden Broadwater in 1946 and cofounded the "Europe-America Groups," discussion groups of intellectuals that focused on political issues. Her interest in larger social issues during this period influenced her novels *The Oasis* (1949), which chronicles the failure of a utopian community, and *The Groves of Academe* (1952), a satire of academic politics based on the author's college teaching experience. Her next book, *A Charmed Life* (1955), is set in a small New England village similar to the one where she and Broadwater lived, and ironically depicts the troubled marital relations in this outwardly idyllic community. Their neighbors' strong negative reactions to the book prompted McCarthy and Broadwater to move away. Describing her attitude toward writing fiction, McCarthy said, "What I really do is take real plums and put them in an imaginary cake. If you're interested in the cake, you get rather annoyed with people saying what species the real plum was." After her divorce from Broadwater and a period spent in Venice studying art, McCarthy wrote *Venice Observed* (1956) and *The Group* (1963), her most popular novel, which follows the lives of eight Vassar students after their graduation.

In 1961, McCarthy married the diplomat James Raymond West, and remained with him for the rest of her life. During the sixties she traveled to both North and South Vietnam and wrote a series of political essays for the *New York Review of Books* that were later collected in books. "The worst thing that could happen to our country," McCarthy wrote, "would be to win this war." She next focused on literary criticism, publishing a collection of essays in 1970. "She clearly possesses the verbal skill to be captious and vicious, but she has chosen to style herself as a champion of truth rather than a dragoness of destruction," wrote one reviewer of McCarthy's criticism. In 1984 she was awarded the National Medal for Literature and the Edward MacDowell Medal. She died in New York City in 1989.

"My Confession," McCarthy's account of her brief flirtation with and renunciation of the Communist Party in the fall of 1936, was written almost two decades later during the height of the hearings of the House Un-American Activities Committee, presided over by Senator Joseph McCarthy. In this essay, she prompts us to reflect on why we are drawn to political ideologies and what influences us to question these allegiances and sometimes abandon them.

# My Confession

*Fall 1953*

Every age has a keyhole to which its eye is pasted. Spicy court-memoirs, the lives of gallant ladies, recollections of an ex-nun, a monk's confession, an atheist's repentance, true-to-life accounts of prostitution and bastardy gave our ancestors a penny peep into the forbidden room. In our own day, this type of sensational fact-fiction is being produced largely by ex-Communists. Public curiosity shows an almost prurient avidity for the details of political defloration, and the memoirs of ex-Communists have an odd resemblance to the confessions of a white slave. Two shuddering climaxes, two rendezvous with destiny, form the poles between which these narratives vibrate: the first describes the occasion when the subject was seduced by Communism; the second shows him wresting himself from the demon embrace. Variations on the form are possible. Senator McCarthy, for example, in his book, *McCarthyism, the Fight for America*, uses a tense series of flashbacks to dramatize his encounter with Communism: the country lies passive in Communism's clasp; he is given a tryst with destiny in the lonely Arizona hills, where, surrounded by "real Americans without any synthetic sheen," he attains the decision that will send him down the long marble corridors to the Senate Caucus Room to bare the shameful commerce.

The diapason of choice plays, like movie music, round today's apostle to the gentiles: Whittaker Chambers on a park bench and, in a reprise, awake all night at a dark window, facing the void. These people, unlike ordinary beings, are shown the true course during a lightning storm of revelation, on the road to Damascus. And their decisions are lonely decisions, silhouetted against a background of public incomprehension and hostility.

I object. I have read the reminiscences of Mr. Chambers and Miss Bentley. I too have had a share in the political movements of our day, and my experience cries out against their experience. It is not the facts I balk at—I have never been an espionage agent—but the studio atmosphere of sublimity and purpose that enfolds the facts and the chief actor. When Whittaker Chambers is mounted on his tractor, or Elizabeth Bentley, alone, is meditating her decision in a white New England church, I have the sense that they are on location and that, at any moment, the director will call "Cut." It has never been like that for me; events have never waited, like extras, while I toiled to make up my mind between good and evil. In fact, I have never known these mental convulsions, which appear quite strange to me when I read about them, even when I do not question the author's sincerity.

Is it really so difficult to tell a good action from a bad one? I think one usually knows right away or a moment afterward, in a horrid flash of regret. And when one genuinely hesitates—or at least it is so in my case—it is never about anything of importance, but about perplexing trivial things, such as whether to have fish or meat for dinner, or whether to take the bus or subway to reach a certain destination, or whether to wear the beige or the green. The "great" decisions—those I can look back on pensively and say, "That was a turning point"—have been made without my awareness. Too late to do anything about it, I discover that I have chosen. And this is particularly striking when the choice has been political or historic. For me, in fact, the mark of the historic is the nonchalance with which it picks up an individual and deposits him in a trend, like a house playfully moved by a tornado. My own experience with Communism prompts me to relate it, just because it had this inadvertence that seems to me lacking in the true confessions of reformed Communists. Like Stendhal's hero, who took part in something confused and disarrayed and insignificant that he later learned was the Battle of Waterloo, I joined the anti-Communist movement without meaning to and only found out afterward, through others, the meaning or "name" assigned to what I had done. This occurred in the late fall of 1936.

Three years before, I had graduated from college—Vassar, the same college Elizabeth Bentley had gone to—without having suffered any fracture of my political beliefs or moral frame. All through college, my official political philosophy was royalism; though I was not much interested in politics, it irritated me to be told that "you could not turn the clock back." But I did not see much prospect for kingship in the United States (unless you imported one, like the Swedes) and, *faute de mieux*, I awarded my sympathies to the Democratic Party, which I tried to look on as the party of the Southern patriciate. At the same time, I had an aversion to Republicans—an instinctive feeling that had been with me since I was a child of eight pedaling my wagon up and down our cement driveway and howling "Hurray for Cox" at the Republican neighbors who passed by. I disliked businessmen and business attitudes partly, I think, because I came from a professional (though Republican) family and had picked up a disdain for businessmen as being beneath us, in education and general culture. And the anti-Catholic prejudice against Al Smith during the 1928 election, the tinkling amusement at Mrs. Smith's vulgarity, democratized me a little in spite of myself: I was won by Smith's plebeian charm, the big coarse nose, and rubbery politician's smile.

But this same distrust of uniformity made me shrink, in 1932, from the sloppily dressed Socialist girls at college who paraded for Norman Thomas and tirelessly argued over "Cokes"; their eager fellowship and scrawled placards and heavy personalities bored me—there was something, to my mind, deeply athletic about this socialism. It was a kind of political hockey played by big, gaunt, dyspeptic girls in pants. It startled me a little, therefore, to learn that in an election poll taken of the faculty, several of my favorite teachers had voted for Thomas; in them, the socialist faith appeared rather charming, I decided—a gracious and attractive oddity, like the English Ovals they gave you when you came for tea. That was the winter Hitler was coming to power and, hearing of the anti-Jewish atrocities, I had a flurry of political indignation. I wrote a prose-poem that dealt, in a mixed-up way, with the Polish Corridor and the Jews. This poem was so unlike me that I did not know whether to be proud of it or ashamed of it when I saw it in a college magazine. At this period, we were interested in surrealism and automatic writing, and the poem had a certain renown because it had come out of my interior without much sense or order, just the way automatic writing was supposed to do. But there my political development stopped.

The depression was closer to home; in New York I used to see apple-sellers on the street corners, and, now and then, a bread line, but I had a very thin awareness of mass poverty. The depression was too close to home to awaken anything but curiosity and wonder—the feelings of a child confronted with a death in the family. I was conscious of the suicides of stockbrokers and businessmen, and of the fact that some of my friends had to go on scholarships and had their dress allowances curtailed, while their mothers gaily turned to doing their own cooking. To most of us at Vassar, I think, the depression was chiefly an upper-class phenomenon.

My real interests were literary. In a paper for my English Renaissance seminar, I noted a resemblance between the Elizabethan puritan pundits and the school of Marxist criticism that was beginning to pontificate about proletarian literature in the *New Masses*. I disliked the modern fanatics, cold, envious little clerics, equally with the insufferable and ridiculous Gabriel Harvey—Cambridge pedant and friend of Spenser—who tried to introduce the rules of Latin quantity into English verse and vilified a true poet who had died young, in squalor and misery. I really hated absolutism and officiousness of any kind (I preferred my kings martyred) and was pleased to be able to recognize a Zeal-of-the-Land Busy in proletarian dress. And it was through a novel that I first learned, in my senior year, about the Sacco-Vanzetti case. The discovery that two innocent men had been executed only a few years back while I, oblivious, was in boarding school, gave me a disturbing shock. The case was still so near that I was tantalized by a feeling that it was not too late to do something—try still another avenue, if Governor Fuller and the Supreme Court obdurately would not be moved. An unrectified case of injustice has a terrible way of lingering, restlessly, in the social atmosphere like an unfinished equation. I went on to the Mooney case, which vexed not only my sense of equity but my sense of plausibility—how was it possible for the prosecution to lie so, in broad daylight, with the whole world watching?

When in May 1933, however, before graduation, I went down to apply for a job at the old *New Republic* offices, I was not drawn there by the magazine's editorial policy—I hardly knew what it was—but because the book-review section seemed to me to possess a certain elegance and independence of thought that would be hospitable to a critical spirit like me. And I was badly taken aback when the book-review editor, to whom I had I been shunted—there was no job—puffed his pipe and remarked that he would give me a review if I could show him that I was either a genius or starving. "I'm not starving," I said quickly; I knew I was not a genius and I was not pleased by the suggestion that I would be taking bread from other people's mouths. I did not think this a fair criterion and in a moment I said so. In reply, he put down his pipe, shrugged, reached out for the material I had brought with me, and half-promised, after an assaying glance, to send me a book. My notice finally appeared; it was not very good, but I did not know that and was elated. Soon I was reviewing novels and biographies for both the *New Republic* and the *Nation* and preening myself on the connection. Yet, whenever I entered the *New Republic*'s waiting room, I was seized with a feeling of nervous guilt toward the shirtsleeved editors upstairs and their busy social conscience, and, above all, toward the shabby young men who were waiting too and who had, my bones told me, a better claim than I to the book I hoped to take away with me. They looked poor, pinched, scholarly, and supercilious, and I did not know which of these qualities made me, with my clicking high heels and fall "ensemble," seem more out of place.

I cannot remember the moment when I ceased to air my old royalist convictions and stuffed them away in an inner closet as you do a dress or an ornament that you perceive strikes the wrong note. It was probably at the time when I first became aware of Communists as a distinct entity. I had known about them, certainly, in college, but it was not until I came to New York that I began to have certain people, celebrities, pointed out to me as Communists and to turn my head to look at them, wonderingly. I had no wish to be one of them, but the fact that they were there—an unreckoned factor—made my own political opinions take on a protective coloration. This process was accelerated by my marriage—a week after graduation—to an actor and playwright who was in some ways very much like me. He was the son of a Minnesota normal school administrator who had been the scapegoat in an academic scandal that had turned him out of his job and reduced him, for a time, when my husband was nine or ten, to selling artificial limbs and encyclopedia sets from door to door. My husband still brooded over his father's misfortune, like Hamlet or a character in Ibsen, and this had given his nature a sardonic twist that inclined him to behave like a paradox—to follow the mode and despise it, live in a Beekman Place apartment while lacking the money to buy groceries, play bridge with society couples and poker with the stage electricians, dress in the English style and carry a walking stick while wearing a red necktie.

He was an odd-looking man, prematurely bald, with a tense, arresting figure, a broken nose, a Standard English accent, and wry, circumflexed eyebrows. There was something about him both baleful and quizzical; whenever he stepped on the stage he had the ironic air of a symbol. This curious appearance of his disqualified him for most Broadway roles; he was too young for character parts and too bald for juveniles. Yet just this disturbing ambiguity—a Communist painter friend did a drawing of him that brought out a resemblance to Lenin—suited the portentous and equivocal atmosphere of left-wing drama. He smiled dryly at Marxist terminology, but there was social anger in him. During the years we were married, the only work he found was in productions of "social" significance. He played for the Theatre Union in *The Sailors of Cattaro*, about a mutiny in the Austrian fleet, and in *Black Pit*, about coal miners; the following year, he was in *Winterset* and Archibald MacLeish's *Panic*—the part of a blind man in both cases. He wrote revue sketches and unproduced plays, in a mocking, despairing, but none the less radical vein; he directed the book of a musical called *Americana* that featured the song, "Brother, Can You Spare a Dime?" I suppose there was something in him of both the victim and the leader, an undertone of totalitarianism; he was very much interested in the mythic qualities of leadership and talked briskly about a Farmer-Labor party in his stage English accent. Notions of the superman and the genius flickered across his thoughts. But this led him, as it happened, away from politics, into sheer personal vitalism, and it was only in plays that he entered "at the head of a mob." In personal life he was very winning, but that is beside the point here.

The point is that we both, through our professional connections, began to take part in a left-wing life, to which we felt superior, which we laughed at, but which nevertheless was influencing us without our being aware of it. If the composition of the body changes every seven years, the composition of our minds during the seven years changed, so that though our thoughts looked the same to us, inside we had been altered, like an old car which has had part after part replaced in it under the hood.

We wore our rue with a difference; we should never have considered joining the Communist Party. We were not even fellow travelers; we did not sign petitions or join "front" groups. We were not fools, after all, and were no more deceived by the League Against War and Fascism, say, than by a Chinatown bus with a carload of shills aboard. It was part of our metropolitan sophistication to know the truth about Communist fronts. We accepted the need for social reform, but we declined to draw the "logical" inference that the Communists wanted us to draw from this. We argued with the comrades backstage in the dressing rooms and at literary cocktail parties; I was attacked by a writer in the *New Masses*. We knew about Lovestoneites and Trotskyites, even while we were ignorant of the labor theory of value, the law of uneven development, the theory of permanent revolution vs. socialism in one country, and so on. "Lovestone is a Lovestoneite!" John wrote in wax on his dressing-room mirror, and on his door in the old Civic Repertory he put up a sign: "Through these portals pass some of the most beautiful tractors in the Ukraine."

The comrades shrugged and laughed, a little unwillingly. They knew we were not hostile but merely unserious, politically. The comrades who knew us best used to assure us that our sophistication was just an armor; underneath, we must care for the same things they did. They were mistaken, I am afraid. Speaking for myself, I cannot remember a single broad altruistic emotion visiting me during that period—the kind of emotion the simpler comrades, with their shining eyes and exalted faces, seemed to have in copious secretion. And yet it was true: we were not hostile. We marched in May Day parades, just for the fun of it, and sang, "Hold the Fort, for We Are Coming," and "*Bandiera Rossa*," and "The Internationale," though we always bellowed "The *Socialist* International shall be the human race" instead of "The International Soviet," to pique the Communists in our squad. We took part in evening clothes in a consumers' walkout at the Waldorf to support a waiters' strike—the Communists had nothing to do with this—and we grew very excited (we did have negative feelings) when another young literary independent was arrested and booked. During a strike at a department store, John joined the sympathetic picketing and saw two of his fellow actors carried off in the Black Maria; they missed a matinee and set off a controversy about what was the *first* responsibility of a Communist playing in a proletarian drama. We went once or twice to a class for actors in Marxism, just to see what was up; we went to a debate on Freud and/or Marx, to a debate on the execution of the hundred and four White Guards following Kirov's assassination.

Most ex-Communists nowadays, when they write their autobiographies or testify before Congressional committees, are at pains to point out that their actions were very, very bad and their motives very, very good. I would say the reverse of myself, though without the intensives. I see no reason to disavow my actions, which were perfectly all right, but my motives give me a little embarrassment, and just because I cannot disavow them: that fevered, contentious, trivial show off in the May Day parade is still recognizably me.

We went to dances at Webster Hall and took our uptown friends. We went to parties to raise money for the sharecroppers, for the Theatre Union, for the *New Masses*. These parties generally took place in a borrowed apartment, often a sculptor's or commercial artist's studio; you paid for your drinks, which were dispensed at a long, wet table; the liquor was dreadful; the glasses were small, and there was never enough ice. Long-haired men in turtleneck sweaters marched into the room in processions and threw their overcoats on the floor, against the wall, and sat on them; they were only artists and bit actors, but they gave these affairs a look of gangsterish menace, as if the room were guarded by the goons of the future. On couches with wrinkled slipcovers, little spiky-haired girls, like spiders, dressed in peasant blouses and carapaced with Mexican jewelry, made voracious passes at baby-faced juveniles; it was said that they "did it for the party," as a recruiting effort. Vague, soft-faced old women with dust mops of whitish hair wandered benevolently about seeking a listener; on a sofa against a wall, like a deity, sat a bearded scion of an old Boston family, stiff as a post. All of us, generally, became very drunk; the atmosphere was horribly sordid, with cigarette burns on tables, spilled drinks, ashes everywhere, people passed out on the bed with the coats or necking, you could not be sure which. Nobody cared what happened because there was no host or hostess. The fact that a moneyed person had been simple enough to lend the apartment seemed to make the guests want to desecrate it, to show that they were exercising not a privilege but a right.

Obviously, I must have hated these parties, but I went to them, partly because I was ashamed of my own squeamishness, and partly because I had a curiosity about the Communist men I used to see there, not the actors or writers, but the higher-ups, impresarios and theoreticians—dark, smooth-haired owls with large white lugubrious faces and glasses. These were the spiritual directors of the Communist cultural celebrities and they moved about at these parties like so many monks or abbés in a worldly salon. I had always liked to argue with the clergy, and I used to argue with these men, who had the air, as they stood with folded arms, of listening not to a disagreement but to a confession. Whenever I became tight, I would bring up (oh, *vino veritas*) the czar and his family. I did not see why they all had had to be killed—the czar himself, yes, perhaps, and the czarina, but not the young girls and the children. I knew the answer, of course (the young czarevitch or one of his sisters might have served as a rallying point for the counterrevolutionary forces), but still I gazed hopefully into these docents' faces, seeking a trace of scruple or compassion. But I saw only a marmoreal astuteness. The question was of bourgeois origin, they said with finality.

The next morning I was always bitterly ashamed. I had let these omniscient men see the real me underneath, and the other me squirmed and gritted her teeth and muttered, Never, never, *never* again. And yet they had not convinced me—there was the paradox. The superiority I felt to the Communists I knew had, for me at any rate, good grounding; it was based on their lack of humor, their fanaticism, and the slow drip of cant that thickened their utterance like a nasal catarrh. *And yet* I was tremendously impressed by them. They made me feel petty and shallow; they had, shall I say, a daily ugliness in their life that made my pretty life tawdry. I think all of us who moved in that ambience must have felt something of the kind, even while we laughed at them. When John and I, for instance, would say of a certain actor, "He is a party member," our voices always contained a note of respect. This respect might be mixed with pity, as when we saw some blue-eyed young profile, fresh from his fraternity and his C average, join up because a sleazy girl had persuaded him. The literary Communists I sincerely despised because I was able to judge the quality of the work they published and see their dishonesty and contradictions; even so, when I beheld them in person, at a Webster Hall dance, I was troubled and felt perhaps I had wronged them—perhaps there was something in them that my vision could not perceive, as some eyes cannot perceive color.

People sometimes say that they envied the Communists because they were so "sure." In my case, this was not exactly it; I was sure, too, intellectually speaking, as far as I went. That is, I had a clear mind and was reasonably honest, while many of the Communists I knew were pathetically fogged up. In any case, my soul was not particularly hot for certainties.

And yet in another way I did envy the Communists, or, to be more accurate, wonder whether I ought to envy them. I could not, I saw, be a Communist because I was not "made that way." Hence, to be a Communist was to possess a sort of privilege. And this privilege, like all privileges, appeared to be a source of power. Any form of idiocy or aberration can confer this distinction on its owner, at least in our age, which aspires to a "total" experience; in the thirties it was the Communists who seemed fearsomely to be the happy few, not because they had peace or certitude but because they were a mutation—a mutation that threatened, in the words of their own anthem, to become the human race.

There was something arcane in every Communist, and the larger this area was the more we respected him. That was why the literary Communists, who operated in the open, doing the hatchet work on artists' reputations, were held in such relatively low esteem. An underground worker rated highest with us; next were the theoreticians and oracles; next were the activists, who mostly worked, we heard, on the waterfront. Last came the rank and file, whose work consisted of making speeches, distributing leaflets, attending party and faction meetings, joining front organizations, marching in parades and demonstrations. These people we dismissed as uninteresting not so much because their work was routine but because the greater part of it was visible. In the same way, among individual comrades, we looked up to those who were close-lipped and stern about their beliefs and we disparaged the more voluble members—the forensic little actors who tried to harangue us in the dressing rooms. The idea of a double life was what impressed us: the more talkative comrades seemed to have only one life, like us; but even they, we had to remind ourselves, had a secret annex to their personality, which was signified by their party name. It is hard not to respect somebody who has an alias.

Of fellow travelers, we had a very low opinion. People who were not willing to "go the whole way" filled us with impatient disdain. The only fellow travelers who merited our notice were those of whom it was said: the party prefers that they remain on the outside. I think some fellow travelers circulated such stories about themselves deliberately, in order to appear more interesting. There was another type of fellow traveler who let it be known that they stayed out of the party because of some tiny doctrinal difference with Marxism. This tiny difference magnified them enormously in their own eyes and allowed them to bear gladly the accusation of cowardice. I knew one such person very well—a spruce, ingratiating swain, the heir to a large fortune—and I think it was not cowardice but a kind of pietistic vanity. He felt he cut more of a figure if he seemed to be doing the party's dirty work gratuitously, without compulsion, like an oblate.

In making these distinctions (which were the very distinctions the party made), I had no idea, of course, that I was allowing myself to be influenced by the party in the field where I was most open to suasion—the field of social snobbery. Yet in fact I was being deterred from forming any political opinions of my own, lest I find I was that despised article, a "mere" socialist or watery liberal, in the same way that a young snob coming to college and seeing who the "right" people are will strive to make no friends rather than be caught with the wrong ones.

For me, the Communist Party was *the* party, and even though I did not join it, I prided myself on knowing that it was the pinnacle. It is only now that I see the social component in my attitude. At the time, I simply supposed that I was being clear-sighted and logical. I used to do research and typing for a disgruntled middle-aged man who was a freak for that day—an anti-Communist Marxist—and I was bewildered by his anti-party bias. While we were drinking hot tea, Russian style, from glasses during the intervals of our work, I would try to show him his mistake. "Don't you think it's rather futile," I expostulated, "to criticize the party the way you do, from the outside? After all, it's the *only* working-class party, and if *I* were a Marxist I would join it and try to reform it." Snorting, he would raise his small deep-set blue eyes and stare at me and then try patiently to show me that there was no democracy in the party. I listened disbelievingly. It seemed to me that it would just be a question of converting first one comrade and then another to your point of view till gradually you had achieved a majority. And when my employer assured me that they would throw you out if you tried that, my twenty-three-year-old wisdom cocked an eyebrow. I thought I knew what was the trouble: he was a pathologically lazy man and his growling criticisms of the party were simply a form of malingering, like the aches and pains he used to manufacture to avoid working on an article. A real revolutionary who was not afraid of exertion would get into the party and fight.

The curious idea that being critical of the party was a compelling reason for joining it must have been in the air, for the same argument was brought to bear on me in the summer of 1936—the summer my husband and I separated and that I came closest to the gravitational pull of the Communist world. Just before I went off to Reno, there was a week in June when I stayed in Southampton with the young man I was planning to marry and a little Communist organizer in an old summer house furnished with rattan and wicker and Chinese matting and mother-of-pearl and paper fans. We had come there for a purpose. The little organizer had just been assigned a car—a battered old Ford roadster that had been turned over to the party for the use of some poor organizer; it may have been the very car that figured in the Hiss case. My fiancé, who had known him for years, perhaps from the peace movement, was going to teach him to drive. We were all at a pause in our lives. The following week our friend was supposed to take the car to California and do propaganda work among the migrant fruit pickers; I was to go to Reno; my fiancé, a vivacious young bachelor, was to conquer his habits of idleness and buckle down to a serious job. Those seven days, therefore, had a special, still quality, like the days of a novena you make in your childhood; a part of each of them was set aside for the party's task. It was early in June; the musty house that belonged to my fiancé's parents still had the winter smell of mice and old wood and rust and mildew. The summer colony had not yet arrived; the red flag, meaning that it was dangerous to swim, flew daily on the beach; the roads were nearly empty. Every afternoon we would take the old car, canvas flapping, to a deserted stretch of straight road in the dunes, where the neophyte could take the wheel.

He was a large-browed, dwarfish man in his late thirties, with a deep widow's peak, a bristly short mustache, and a furry western accent—rather simple, open-natured, and cheerful, the sort of person who might have been a small-town salesman or itinerant newspaperman. There was an energetic, hopeful innocence about him that was not confined to his political convictions—he could *not* learn to drive. Every day the same thing happened; he would settle his frail yet stocky figure trustingly in the driver's seat, grip the wheel, step on the starter, and lose control of the car, which would shoot ahead in first or backward in reverse for a few perilous feet till my fiancé turned off the ignition; Ansel always mistook the gas for the brake and forgot to steer while he was shifting gears.

It was clear that he would never be able to pass the driver's test at the county seat. In the evenings, to make up to him for his oncoming disappointment (we smiled when he said he could start without a license), we encouraged him to talk about the party and tried to take an intelligent interest. We would sit by the lamp and drink and ask questions, while he smoked his short pipe and from time to time took a long draught from his highball, like a man alone musing in a chair.

And finally one night, in the semidark, he knocked out his pipe and said to me: "You're very critical of the party. Why don't you join it?" A thrill went through me, but I laughed, as when somebody has proposed to you and you are not sure whether they are serious. "I don't think I'd make very good material." "You're wrong," he said gravely. "You're just the kind of person the party needs. You're young and idealistic and independent." I broke in: "I thought independence was just what the party didn't want." "The party needs criticism," he said. "But it needs it from the inside. If people like you who agree with its main objectives would come in and criticize, we wouldn't be so narrow and sectarian." "You admit the party is narrow?" exclaimed my fiancé. "Sure, I admit it," said Ansel, grinning. "But it's partly the fault of people like Mary who won't come in and broaden us." And he confided that he himself made many of the same criticisms I did, but he made them from within the party, and so could get himself listened to. "The big problem of the American party," said Ansel, puffing at his pipe, "is the smallness of the membership. People say we're ruled from Moscow; I've never seen any sign of it. But let's suppose it's true, for the sake of argument. This just means that the American party isn't big enough yet to stand on its own feet. A big, indigenous party couldn't be ruled from Moscow. The will of the members would have to rule it, just as their dues and contributions would support it." "That's where I come in, I suppose?" I said, teasing. "That's where you come in," he calmly agreed. He turned to my fiancé. "Not you," he said. "You won't have the time to give to it. But for Mary I think it would be an interesting experiment."

An interesting experiment . . . I let the thought wander through my mind. The subject recurred several times, by the lamplight, though with no particular urgency. Ansel, I thought (and still think), was speaking sincerely and partly in my own interest, almost as a spectator, as if he would be diverted to see how I worked out in the party. All this gave me quite a new sense of Communism and of myself too; I had never looked upon my character in such a favorable light. And as a beneficiary of Ansel's charity, I felt somewhat ashamed of the very doubt it raised: the suspicion that he might be blind to the real facts of inner party life. I could admire where I could not follow, and, studying Ansel, I decided that I admired the Communists and would probably be one, if I were the person he thought me. Which I was afraid I was not. For me, such a wry conclusion is always uplifting, and I had the feeling that I mounted in understanding when Sunday morning came and I watched Ansel pack his sturdy suitcase and his briefcase full of leaflets into the old roadster. He had never yet driven more than a few yards by himself, and we stood on the front steps to await what was going to happen: he would not be able to get out of the driveway, and we would have to put him on the train and return the car to the party when we came back to New York. As we watched, the car began to move; it picked up speed and grated into second, holding to the middle of the road as it turned out of the driveway. It hesitated and went into third: Ansel was driving! Through the back window we saw his figure hunched over the wheel; the road dipped and he vanished. We had witnessed a miracle, and we turned back into the house, frightened. All day we sat waiting for the call that would tell us there had been an accident, but the day passed without a sound, and by nightfall we accepted the phenomenon and pictured the little car on the highway, traveling steadily west in one indefatigable thrust, not daring to stop for gas or refreshment, lest the will of the driver falter.

This parting glimpse of Ansel through the car's back window was, as it turned out, ultimate. Politically speaking, we reached a watershed that summer. The first Moscow trial took place in August. I knew nothing of this event because I was in Reno and did not see the New York papers. Nor did I know that the party line had veered to the right and that all the fellow travelers would be voting, not for Browder as I was now prepared to do (if only I remembered to register), but for Roosevelt. Isolated from these developments in the mountain altitudes, I was blossoming, like a lone winter rose overlooked by the frost, into a revolutionary thinker of the pure, uncompromising strain. The detached particles of the past three years' experience suddenly "made sense," and I saw myself as a radical.

"Book Bites Mary," wrote back a surprised literary editor when I sent him, from Reno, a radiant review of a novel about the Paris Commune that ended with the heroine sitting down to read the *Communist Manifesto*. In Seattle, when I came to stay with my grandparents, I found a strike on and instantly wired the *Nation* to ask if I could cover it. Every night I was off to the Labor Temple or a longshoreman's hall while my grandparents took comfort from the fact that I seemed to be against Roosevelt, the Democrats, and the czars of the A. F. of L.—they did not quite grasp my explanation, that I was criticizing "from the left."

Right here, I come up against a puzzle: why didn't I take the *next step*? But it is only a puzzle if one thinks of me not as a concrete entity but as a term in a logical operation: you agree with the Communist Party; *ergo*, you join it. I reasoned that way but I did not behave so. There was something in me that capriciously resisted being a term in logic, and the very fact that I cannot elicit any specific reason why I did not join the party shows that I was never really contemplating it, though I can still hear my own voice, raised very authoritatively at a cafeteria table at the Central Park Zoo, pointing out to a group of young intellectuals that if we were serious we would join the Communists.

This was in September and I was back in New York. The Spanish Civil War had begun. The pay-as-you-go parties were now all for the Loyalists, and young men were volunteering to go and fight in Spain. I read the paper every morning with tears of exaltation in my eyes, and my sympathies rained equally on Communists, Socialists, Anarchists, and the brave Catholic Basques. My heart was tense and swollen with popular-front solidarity. I applauded the Lincoln Battalion, protested nonintervention, hurried into Wanamaker's to look for cotton-lace stockings: I was boycotting silk on account of Japan in China. I was careful to smoke only union-made cigarettes; the white package with Sir Walter Raleigh's portrait came proudly out of my pocketbook to rebuke Chesterfields and Luckies.

It was a period of intense happiness; the news from the battlefront was often encouraging and the practice of virtue was surprisingly easy. I moved into a one-room apartment on a crooked street in Greenwich Village and exulted in being poor and alone. I had a part-time job and read manuscripts for a publisher; the very riskiness of my situation was zestful—I had decided not to get married. The first month or so was scarifyingly lonely, but I survived this, and, starting early in November, I began to feel the first stirrings of popularity. A new set of people, rather smart and moneyed, young Communists with a little "name," progressive hosts and modernist hostesses, had discovered me. The fact that I was poor and lived in such a funny little apartment increased the interest felt: I was passed from hand to hand, as a novelty, like Gulliver among the Brobdingnagians. During those first days in November, I was chiefly conscious of what a wonderful time I was starting to have. All this while, I had remained ignorant of the fissure that was opening. Nobody, I think, had told me of the trial of Zinoviev and Kamenev—the trial of the sixteen—or of the new trial that was being prepared in Moscow, the trial of Pyatakov and Radek.

Then, one afternoon in November, I was taken to a cocktail party, in honor of Art Young, the old *Masses* cartoonist, whose book, *The Best of Art Young*, was being published that day. It was the first publisher's party I had ever been to, and my immediate sensation was one of disappointment: nearly all these people were strangers and, to me, quite unattractive. Art Young, a white-haired little kewpie, sitting in a corner, was pointed out to me, and I turned a respectful gaze on him, though I had no clear idea who he was or how he had distinguished himself. I presumed he was a veteran Communist, like a number of the stalwarts in the room, survivors of the old *Masses* and the *Liberator*. Their names were whispered to me and I nodded; this seemed to be a commemorative occasion, and the young men hovered in groups around the old men, as if to catch a word for posterity. On the outskirts of certain groups I noticed a few poorly dressed young men, bolder spirits, nervously flexing their lips, framing sentences that would propel them into the conversational center, like actors with a single line to speak.

The solemnity of these proceedings made me feel terribly ill at ease. It was some time before I became aware that it was not just me who was nervous: the whole room was under a constraint. Some groups were avoiding other groups, and now and then an arrow of sarcasm would wing like a sniper's bullet from one conversation to another.

I was standing, rather bleakly, by the refreshment table, when a question was thrust at me: did I think Trotsky was entitled to a hearing? It was a novelist friend of mine, dimple-faced, shaggy-headed, earnest, with a whole train of people, like a deputation, behind him. Trotsky? I glanced for help at a sour little man I had been talking with, but he merely shrugged. My friend made a beckoning gesture and a circle closed in. What had Trotsky done? Alas, I had to ask. A tumult of voices proffered explanations. My friend raised a hand for silence. Leaning on the table, he supplied the background, speaking very slowly, in his dragging, disconsolate voice, like a schoolteacher wearied of his subject. Trotsky, it appeared, had been accused of fostering a counterrevolutionary plot in the Soviet Union—organizing terrorist centers and conspiring with the Gestapo to murder the Soviet leaders. Sixteen old Bolsheviks had confessed and implicated him. It had been in the press since August.

I blushed; everybody seemed to be looking at me strangely. I made a violent effort to take in what had been said. The enormity of the charge dazed me, and I supposed that some sort of poll was being taken and that I was being asked to pronounce on whether Trotsky was guilty or innocent. I could tell from my friend's low, even, melancholy tone that he regarded the charges as derisory. "What do you want me to say?" I protested. "I don't know anything about it." "Trotsky denies the charges," patiently intoned my friend. "He declares it's a GPU fabrication. Do you think he's entitled to a hearing?" My mind cleared. "Why, of course." I laughed—were there people who would say that Trotsky was *not* entitled to a hearing? But my friend's voice tolled a rebuke to this levity. "She says Trotsky is entitled to his day in court."

The sour little man beside me made a peculiar, sucking noise. "You disagree?" I demanded, wonderingly. "I'm smart," he retorted. "I don't let anybody ask me. You notice, he doesn't ask me?" "Shut up, George," said my novelist friend impatiently. "I'm asking *her*. One thing more, Mary," he continued gravely. "Do you believe that Trotsky should have the right of asylum?" The right of asylum! I looked for someone to share my amusement—were we in ancient Greece or the Middle Ages? I was sure the U.S. government would be delighted to harbor such a distinguished foreigner. But nobody smiled back. Everybody watched dispassionately, as for form's sake I assented to the phrasing: yes, Trotsky, in my opinion, was entitled to the right of asylum.

I went home with the serene feeling that all these people were slightly crazy. Right of asylum, his day in court!—in a few hours I had forgotten the whole thing.

Four days later I tore open an envelope addressed to me by something that called itself "Committee for the Defense of Leon Trotsky," and idly scanned the contents. "We demand for Leon Trotsky the right of a fair hearing and the right of asylum." Who were these demanders, I wondered, and, glancing down the letterhead, I discovered my own name. I sat down on my unmade studio couch, shaking. How dared they help themselves to my signature? This was the kind of thing the Communists were always being accused of pulling; apparently, Trotsky's admirers had gone to the same school. I had paid so little heed to the incident at the party that a connection was slow to establish itself. Reading over the list of signers, I recognized "names" that had been present there and remembered my novelist- friend going from person to person, methodically polling. . . .

How were they feeling, I wondered, when they opened their mail this morning? My own feelings were crisp. In two minutes I had decided to withdraw my name and write a note of protest. Trotsky had a right to a hearing, but I had a right to my signature. For even if there had been a legitimate misunderstanding (it occurred to me that perhaps I had been the only person there not to see the import of my answers), nothing I had said committed me to Trotsky's *defense*.

The "decision" was made, but according to my habit I procrastinated. The severe letter I proposed to write got put off till the next day and then the next. Probably I was not eager to offend somebody who had been a good friend to me. Nevertheless, the letter would undoubtedly have been written, had I been left to myself. But within the next forty-eight hours the phone calls began. People whom I had not seen for months or whom I knew very slightly telephoned to advise me to get off the newly formed committee. These calls were not precisely threatening. Indeed, the caller often sounded terribly weak and awkward, as if he did not like the mission he had been assigned. But they were peculiar. For one thing, they usually came after nightfall and sometimes quite late, when I was already in bed. Another thing, there was no real effort at persuasion: the caller stated his purpose in standardized phrases, usually plaintive in tone (the committee was the tool of reaction, and all liberal people should dissociate themselves from its activities, which were an unwarranted intervention in the domestic affairs of the Soviet Union), and then hung up, almost immediately, before I had a proper chance to answer. Odd too—the voices were not those of my Communist friends but of the merest acquaintances. These people who admonished me to "think about it" were not people whose individual opinions could have had any weight with me. And when I did think about it, this very fact took on an ominous and yet to me absurd character: I was not being appealed to personally but impersonally warned.

Behind these phone calls there was a sense of the party wheeling its forces into would-be disciplined formations, like a fleet or an army maneuvering. This, I later found, was true: a systematic telephone campaign was going on to dislodge members from the committee. The phone calls generally came after dark and sometimes (especially when the recipient was elderly) in the small hours of the morning. The more prominent signers got anonymous messages and threats.

And in the morning papers and the columns of the liberal magazines I saw the results. During the first week, name after name fell off the committee's letterhead. Prominent liberals and literary figures issued statements deploring their mistake. And a number of people protested that their names had been used without permission. . . .

There, but for the grace of God, went I, I whispered, awestruck, to myself, hugging my guilty knowledge. Only Heaven—I plainly saw—by making me dilatory had preserved me from joining this sorry band. Here was the occasion when I should have been wrestling with my conscience or standing, floodlit, at the crossroads of choice. But in fact I was only aware that I had had a providential escape. I had been saved from having to decide about the committee; *I* did not decide it—the communists with their pressure tactics took the matter out of my hands. We all have an instinct that makes us side with the weak, if we do not stop to reason about it, the instinct that makes a householder shield a wounded fugitive without first conducting an inquiry into the rights and wrongs of his case. Such "decisions" are simple reflexes; they do not require courage; if they did, there would be fewer of them. When I saw what was happening, I rebounded to the defense of the committee without a single hesitation—it was nobody's business, I felt, how I happened to be on it, and if anybody had asked me, I should have lied without a scruple.

Of course, I did not foresee the far-reaching consequences of my act—how it would change my life. I had no notion that I was now an anti-Communist, where before I had been either indifferent or pro-Communist. I did, however, soon recognize that I was in a rather awkward predicament—not a moral quandary but a social one. I knew nothing about the cause I had espoused; I had never read a word of Lenin or Trotsky, nothing of Marx but the *Communist Manifesto*, nothing of Soviet history; the very names of the old Bolsheviks who had confessed were strange and almost barbarous in my ears. As for Trotsky, the only thing that made me think that he might be innocent was the odd behavior of the Communists and the fellow-traveling liberals, who seemed to be infuriated at the idea of a free inquiry. All around me, in the fashionable Stalinist circles I was now frequenting, I began to meet with suppressed excitement and just-withheld disapproval. Jeweled lady-authors turned white and shook their bracelets angrily when I came into a soirée; rising young men in publishing or advertising tightened their neckties dubiously when I urged them to examine the case for themselves; out dancing in a night club, tall, collegiate young party members would press me to their shirt-bosoms and tell me not to be silly, honey.

And since I seemed to meet more Stalinists every day, I saw that I was going to have to get some arguments with which to defend myself. It was not enough, apparently, to say you were for a fair hearing; you had to rebut the entire case of the prosecution to get anybody to incline an ear in your direction. I began to read, headlong, the literature on the case—the pamphlets issued by Trotsky's adherents, the verbatim report of the second trial published by the Soviet Union, the "bourgeois" press, the Communist press, the radical press. To my astonishment (for I had scarcely dared think it), the trials did indeed seem to be a monstrous frame-up. The defendant, Pyatakov, flew to Oslo to "conspire" with

Trotsky during a winter when, according to the authorities, no planes landed at the Oslo airfield; the defendant, Holtzmann, met Trotsky's son, Sedov, in 1936, at the Hotel Bristol in Copenhagen, which had burned down in 1912; the witness, Romm, met Trotsky in Paris at a time when numerous depositions testified that he had been in Royan, among clouds of witnesses, or on the way there from the south of France.

These were only the most glaring discrepancies—the ones that got in the newspapers. Everywhere you touched the case something crumbled. The carelessness of the case's manufacture was to me its most terrifying aspect; the slovenly disregard for credibility defied credence, in its turn. How did they dare? I think I was more shaken by finding that I was on the right side than I would have been the other way round. And yet, except for a very few people, nobody seemed to mind whether the Hotel Bristol had burned down or not, whether a real plane had landed, whether Trotsky's life and writings were congruent with the picture given of him in the trials. When confronted with the facts of the case, people's minds sheered off from it like jelly from a spoon.

Anybody who has ever tried to rectify an injustice or set a record straight comes to feel that he is going mad. And from a social point of view, he *is* crazy, for he is trying to undo something that is finished, to unravel the social fabric. That is why my liberal friends looked so grave and solemn when I would press them to come to a meeting and listen to a presentation of the facts—for them this was a Decision, too awful to be considered lightly. The Moscow trials were a historical fact and those of us who tried to undo them were uneasily felt to be crackpots, who were trying to turn the clock back. And of course the less we were listened to, the more insistent and earnest we became, even while we realized we were doing our cause harm. It is impossible to take a moderate tone under such conditions. If I admitted, though, to being a little bit hipped on the subject of Trotsky, I could sometimes gain an indulgent if flickering attention—the kind of attention that stipulates, "She's a bit off but let's hear her story." And now and then, by sheer chance, one of my hearers would be arrested by some stray point in my narrative; the disparaging smile would slowly fade from his features, leaving a look of blank consternation. He would go off and investigate for himself, and in a few days, when we met again, he would be a crackpot too.

Most of us who became anti-Communists at the time of the trials were drawn in, like me, by accident and almost unwillingly. Looking back, as on a love affair, a man could say that if he had not had lunch in a certain restaurant on a certain day, he might not have been led to ponder the facts of the Moscow trials. Or not then at any rate. And had he pondered them at a later date, other considerations would have entered and his conversion would have had a different style. On the whole, those of us who became anti-Communists during that year, 1936-37, have remained liberals—a thing that is less true of people of our generation who were converted earlier or later. A certain doubt of orthodoxy and independence of mass opinion was riveted into our anti-Communism by the heat of that period. As soon as I make this statement, exceptions leap into my mind, but I think as a generalization it will stand. Those who became anti-Communist earlier fell into two classes: the experts and those to whom any socialist ideal was repugnant. Those whose eyes where opened later, by the Nazi-Soviet pact, or still later, by God knows what, were left bruised and full of self-hatred or self-commiseration, because they had palliated so much and truckled to a power center; to them, Communism's chief sin seems to be that it deceived *them*, and their public atonement takes on both a vindicating and a vindictive character.

We were luckier. Our anti-Communism came to us neither as the fruit of a special wisdom nor as a humiliating awakening from a prolonged deception, but as a natural event, the product of chance and propinquity. One thing followed another, and the will had little to say about it. For my part, during that year, I realized, with a certain wistfulness, that it was too late for me to become any kind of Marxist. Marxism, I saw, from the learned young men I listened to at committee meetings, was something you had to take up young, like ballet dancing.

So, I did not try to be a Marxist or a Trotskyite, though for the first time I read a little in the Marxist canon. But I got the name of being a Trotskyite, which meant, in the end, that I saw less of the conventional Stalinists I had been mingling with and less of conventional people generally. (My definition of a conventional person was quite broad: it included anyone who could hear of the Moscow trials and maintain an unruffled serenity.) This, then, was a break or a rupture, not very noticeable at first, that gradually widened and widened, without any conscious effort on my part, sometimes to my regret. This estrangement was not marked by any definite stages; it was a matter of tiny choices. Shortly after the Moscow trials, for instance, I changed from the *Herald Tribune* to the *Times*; soon I had stopped doing crossword puzzles, playing bridge, reading detective stories and popular novels. I did not "give up" these things; they departed from me, as it were, on tiptoe, seeing that my thoughts were elsewhere.

To change from the *Herald Tribune* to the *Times* is not, I am aware, as serious a step as breaking with international Communism when you have been its agent; and it occurs to me that Mr. Chambers and Miss Bentley might well protest the comparison, pointing out that they were profoundly dedicated people, while I was a mere trifler, that their decisions partook of the sublime, where mine descended to the ridiculous—as Mr. Chambers says, he was ready to give his life for his beliefs. Fortunately (though I could argue the point, for we all give our lives for our beliefs, piecemeal or whole), I have a surprise witness to call for my side, who did literally die for his political views.

I am referring to Trotsky, the small, frail, pertinacious old man who wore whiskers, wrinkles, glasses, shock of grizzled hair, like a gleeful disguise for the erect young student, the dangerous revolutionary within him. Nothing could be more alien to the convulsed and tormented moonscapes of the true confessions of ex-Communists than Trotsky's populous, matter-of-fact recollections set out in *My Life*. I have just been rereading this volume, and though I no longer subscribe to its views, which have certainly an authoritarian and doctrinaire cast that troubles me today, nevertheless I experience a sense of recognition here that I cannot find in the pages of our own repentant "revolutionaries." The old man remained unregenerate; he never admitted that he had sinned. That is probably why nobody seems to care for, or feel apologetic to, his memory. It is an interesting point—and relevant, I think, to my story—that many people today actually have the impression that Trotsky died a natural death.

In a certain sense, this is perfectly true. I do not mean that he lived by violence and therefore might reasonably be expected to die by violence. He was a man of words primarily, a pamphleteer and orator. He was armed, as he said, with a pen and peppered his enemies with a fusillade of articles. Hear the concluding passages of his autobiography: "Since my exile, I have more than once read musings in the newspapers on the subject of the 'tragedy' that has befallen me. I know no *personal* tragedy. I know the change of two chapters of revolution. One American paper which published an article of mine accompanied it with a profound note to the effect that in spite of the blows the author had suffered, he had, as evidenced by his article, preserved his clarity of reason. I can only express my astonishment at the Philistine attempt to establish a connection between the power of reasoning and a government post, between mental balance and the present situation. I do not know, and never have known, of any such connection. In prison, with a book or pen in my hand, I experienced the same sense of deep satisfaction that I did at mass meetings of the revolution. I felt the mechanics of power as an inescapable burden, rather than as a spiritual satisfaction."

This was not a man of violence. Nevertheless, one can say that he died a natural death—a death that was in keeping with the open manner of his life. There was nothing arcane in Trotsky; that was his charm. Like an ordinary person he was hospitably open to hazard and accident. In his autobiography, he cannot date the moment when he became a socialist.

One factor in his losing out in the power struggle at the time of Lenin's death was his delay in getting the telegram that should have called him home from the Caucasus, where he was convalescent, to appear at

Lenin's funeral—*had* he got the telegram, the outcome perhaps would have been different. Or again, perhaps not. It may be that the whims of chance are really the importunities of design. But if there is a Design, it aims, in real lives, like the reader's or mine or Trotsky's, to look natural and fortuitous; that is how it gets us into its web.

Trotsky himself, looking at his life in retrospect, was struck, as most of us are on such occasions, by the role chance had played in it. He tells how one day, during Lenin's last illness, he went duck shooting with an old hunter in a canoe on the River Dubna, walked through a bog in felt boots—only a hundred steps—and contracted influenza. This was the reason he was ordered to Sukhu for the cure, missed Lenin's funeral, and had to stay in bed during the struggle for primacy that raged that autumn and winter. "I cannot help noting," he says, "how obligingly the accidental helps the historical law. Broadly speaking, the entire historical process is a refraction of historical law through the accidental. In the language of biology, one might say that the historical law is realized through the natural selection of accidents." And with a touch of quizzical gaiety he sums up the problem as a Marxian: "One can foresee the consequences of a revolution or a war, but it is impossible to foresee the consequences of an autumn shooting-trip for wild ducks." This shrug before the unforeseen implies an acceptance of consequences that is a far cry from penance and prophecy. Such, it concedes, is life. *Bravo*, old sport, I say, even though the hall is empty.

## QUESTIONS

1. Why does McCarthy believe the great decisions and turning points in her life have been made without her awareness, rather than through her conscious choice?

2. Why does McCarthy's initial awareness of Communists make her own political opinions "take on a protective coloration"? (453)

3. Why does McCarthy confess to not remembering "a single broad altruistic emotion" during the period in which she and her husband took part in a left-wing life? (454)

4. In contrast to most ex-Communists, why doesn't McCarthy disavow her actions instead of merely finding them embarrassing?

5. Why was McCarthy impressed with those who led a "double life"? Why did she least respect the rank and file Communists? (457)

6. When McCarthy came to see herself as "a radical," why didn't she take the next step of becoming a party member? (461)

7. What does McCarthy mean when she says her liberal friends resisted coming to meetings to hear the facts about Trotsky's case because "for them this was a Decision, too awful to be considered lightly"? (466)

8. Why does McCarthy believe she became an anti-Communist "by accident and almost unwillingly"? (466)

9. What does McCarthy mean when she says, "Our anti-Communism came to us . . . as a natural event, the product of chance and propinquity"? (467)

10. Near the end of her essay, why does McCarthy quote extensively from the concluding pages of Trotsky's autobiography?

## FOR FURTHER REFLECTION

1. Is McCarthy's suggestion plausible, that it is really not so difficult to quickly tell a good action from a bad one?

2. Do you agree with McCarthy that Marxism is something a person must take up early in life?

3. Is McCarthy correct in asserting that all of us give our lives for our beliefs, piecemeal or whole?

4. Is McCarthy correct in asserting, "If there is a Design, it aims, in real lives . . . to look natural and fortuitous; that is how it gets us into its web"?

Deborah Eisenberg (1945–) was raised in Winnetka, Illinois, a suburb of Chicago. "My upbringing was notable for its lack of interestingness," she has said. "It was in the middle of the country, in the middle of the century. My parents were first generation immigrants, so there was a big emphasis on education, . . . on accomplishment, and I wanted no part of any of it." After high school, Eisenberg briefly attended Marlboro College in Vermont, leaving to hitchhike around the United States. She finally enrolled in and received her BA from the New School College in New York City. Following graduation, she worked as an assistant at the *New York Review of Books* but never considered being a writer.

In the early 1970s, Eisenberg met and moved in with the playwright and actor Wallace Shawn. Shawn is asthmatic, and Eisenberg, a three-pack-a-day smoker, decided to quit. "I thought, here's this great guy I live with, I've never met another really fabulous guy, do I really want to kill him?" The journal she kept while she quit smoking became the basis for her first short story, "Days," which Eisenberg has called "my only autobiographical story." After a friend directed a reading of "Days" at the Public Theater in New York, Eisenberg was commissioned to write a play. The result—her only play—was *Pastorale*, produced at New York's Second Stage Theatre in 1982. Eisenberg then turned her attention to writing fiction: her first collection of stories, *Transactions in a Foreign Currency*, was published in 1986.

In the late 1980s and early 1990s, Eisenberg and Shawn traveled extensively in Central America "to see where our tax dollars were going." These trips resulted in Shawn's play *The Fever* and in several stories by Eisenberg, including "Holy Week." "I'd been horrifyingly reminded of how parochial I am, of how difficult it is to learn, if you're in a comfortable position, what went into the construction of that position," said Eisenberg about her time in Central America. "If you're reasonably privileged, reasonably comfortable, you can never fully understand or accept it, that your particular experience is neither inevitable nor dominant in the world."

Eisenberg has taught writing at several universities, including the University of Virginia, the University of Iowa's Writers' Workshop, and Columbia University. Her short story collections include *Under the 82nd Airborne* (1992) and *Twilight of the Superheroes* (2006), and her stories have been translated into eight languages. Eisenberg has received numerous awards, including a Guggenheim Fellowship, a PEN Hemingway Citation, the Award for Literature from the American Academy of Arts and Sciences, and a Lannan Foundation Fellowship and residency. In 2009 she was named a MacArthur Foundation Fellow. She is a contributing editor of *Bomb* magazine and acted in the well-received play *The Designated Mourner*, which Shawn wrote and directed. The writer John Updike said about her work, "Deborah Eisenberg writes out of a whirlwind; she has found words for sensations and emotions I have never seen described before."

# Holy Week

## Sunday

Everything as promised: Costumes, clouds of incense—processions already begun; town tingly with anticipation. Somber, shabby brass bands. Figures of Christ, the Virgin Mother—primitive, elegant—on wooden float-type-things (*anda*, word McGee used). Men in purple satin churning around them. From wooden-shuttered hotel window can see people crossing square with armloads of palm. Truly pleased Zwicker decided to send me. (Shd. make up for Feb. issue/Twin Cities!)

Square in middle of town, town little dish set in ring of mountains, high under the sun. Air glimmery, uncertain; clouds draping mountains, colors diffusing into soft sky. Soft sun. Walls like cloud banks, pretty colors fading, wearing down to stone. Decay subtle, various. Ruins of earthquake (1770s? Check). Shattered arches, pediments, columns—huge. Grasses taking root in the tumbled stone, sprouting tiny white flowers. Churches: lush stone vines, stone fruit. In square, stone fountain with stone shells and mermaids.

Crowds lining the streets—tourists, Indians. Mostly Ladinos (McGee explained: mixed race, Span. + Indian). Indians impenetrable as they watch Jesus pass by, ribs showing through white plaster skin, trickling red plaster blood; they watch so intently, holding their babies up to look. Unnerving, the way they watch, way they walk, gliding along in those fantastical clothes of theirs. Silent emissaries from a vanished world, stranded in ours—gliding through the streets with baskets of flowers on their heads, through the square, through these new centuries of ruins. Squat on their heels at the corners selling hallucinatory textiles or tiny orchid trees, letting the happy tourists haggle. Barefoot, dirt-poor, dressed like royalty—incredible. Only thing: poor judgment to have brought Sarah?

Had awful morning in capital, waiting to hook up with McGees. Awful city. Diesel fumes up your nose. Big black puffs of dirt—soot, or something. Hang there in the air, then whisk over and deposit themselves on your face and clothes. Sarah and I sat in big hotel, shiny and gloomy, full of dark, heavy-faced men in suits and sunglasses. Many mustaches. Daughters in prom dresses, limp sons. Some Americans, too. Prob. business—don't look like tourists. Hotel bar very dark, suit/mustache people gazing over their drinks at Vietnam movie showing on enormous screen. Movie mesmerizingly vile—machine guns, gore, etc., Vietnamese girl, U.S. soldiers in camouflage swarming all over her.

Sarah glowering at screen, running her hands impatiently through her hair, making it fluff up like little yellow chick feathers. Offered to go for walk with her. She said, "Thanks, Dennis. Out there?"

Vietnamese girl ripped down middle. Sarah (very loud): *Shit*. Men glancing at us through currents of black and greenish air. What to do? Had warned Sarah not to drink margaritas until she got used to the altitude.

Two clean, hardy U.S. types, mid-sixties approx., abruptly confronting us. McGees, of course. "I'll bet you're our man," Mrs. (Dot) said. "The Desk told us you'd be in here."

Clearly Zwicker had not mentioned Sarah. Husband (Clifford) produced expression of aggressive blandness, Dot underwent violently shuttling succession of reactions. How well I've come to know the looks! Might as well be back in Cedar Rapids.

Sarah stared, affronted, as Dot nodded with pity at her tiny skirt, patted her arm. "*Lovely* to meet you," Dot said.

"So," McGee said. We all stood, looked at the screen. A bomb exploded over a small village. McGee snorted, shook his head. Said, "All set, everyone? Luggage up front?"

Filthy little eateries by the side of the road. Harsh dust, like grains of concrete, all over everything. Leaves, trees, caked with harsh, pale dirt. Buildings rotting, people streaming along—so many, so poor—bellying out into the road in the clouds of black exhaust, receding behind us, big, glossy cars shooting past them. Buses swaying on the sharp curves, top-heavy with cargo, clinging passengers.

Tried to monitor conversation in back between Sarah and Dot. Truth is, was very nervous about what Sarah might say, in her mood. Now, this is the *actual* problem about being involved with someone twenty-odd years younger. A trade-off, in my opinion. On the one hand, the intensity, the clarity (generally) of Sarah's reactions. On the other, her impatience, stubbornness, unwillingness to see the other point of view. Fundamentally youth's refusal to acknowledge the subtlety, complexity of a situation; at worst, adds up to a sort of insensitivity.

Still, Dot admittedly hard to take. Could hear her enumerating, at some length, flaws in local postal system. Glanced back, saw Sarah in glaze of boredom, rousing herself to nod sanctimoniously. Frowned warningly, and she shot me electrifying little smile.

McGee pleasant enough. Seemed to enjoy driving. Said he'd been delighted to meet Zwicker when he was up in the States in the fall: *delighted*. Told McGee how highly Zwicker had spoken of him; said that it was entirely due to him that Zwicker was so eager to get piece on town for supplement (true). McGee offered to help in any way he could. Asked what sort of thing I was after—hotels, restaurants, Easter celebrations? All of it, told him, though supplement particularly interested in food.

He nodded. Said, "We'll see to it." Said he would be more than happy to take me around to restaurants, introduce me to important local grower (could give me interesting regional recipes). Said it would mean a lot, good press coverage in the States. Said tourist revenues had fallen off catastrophically in past decade.

Stark landscape; droopy gray sky. Pines. Long, dark, sad hills. Billboards (all Span., of course) advertising herbicides, pesticides, fungicides, etc. Another: Cement Is Progress. Ant-like figure in valley, tiny beyond billboards, giant load of wood on his bent back. Just like ant with giant leaf, or some other impossible burden.

The sight was timeless, stonily beautiful—solitary peasant in the field. The man's life curved out behind him in a pure, solid arc. Tried to imagine how it felt to have such a life—I mounted the arc, swooped up, then down along it. *Atomized* on contact with the man at the bottom; shards of my life flew all over the car—son, ex, house in Claremont. Dorm all those years ago in Princeton, bank where I worked for so long, new office at the supplement. Waking in my sunny Cedar Rapids bedroom, sometimes Sarah next to me. Other women I've been involved with, movies I've seen, opinions I've held—a burst sackful of items flying all over the car.

Glanced back at Sarah again to reincorporate myself, but her clear eyes were directed out the window, and her piratical earring gleamed—a signal! Meaning? Sarah's earring, my son, my office—all *signals*, incoherent fragments, of which I ought to be the unifying principle; encoded dispatches from my own life! Too loud, too bright to decipher—the urgent, jagged flashing: a messenger shouting across a chasm. A knife lying on the counter. A ditch by the side of the road . . .

## Monday

Was in strange state yesterday. Better now. Odd how that happens—everything completely inscrutable, intractable, portentous; then everything completely fine. Like having two abutting brains, one of them utter chaos; sickening sensation of slipping through some membrane. Perhaps triggered yesterday by psychobiological response to unfamiliar foods? Pollens?

In any case, over. Hotel first-rate, good night's sleep. Dinner, just Sarah and I, at ex-convent (Santo Tomás, daily except Tues. Spectacular. Must write up, despite food). This morning breakfast in hotel court-yard—flowers, darting hummingbird; fruit, rolls, coffee. Impossible not to feel happy. Sarah clearly blissful. Stretching, reaching over to run her finger along my wrist. Waiter (Ricardo) utterly charmed by her. Had to smile at his expression when she ordered third portion of fruit and rolls.

How could I have doubted, yesterday, it was right to bring her? Of course it was. I think. (Joke.) Ah, so hard to sort out, me and Sarah. What can we really have with one another, ultimately? Occurs to me sometimes that, for all her wildness, restlessness, she wants something more from me than I (obviously) can give.

Have to remind myself always she's at an odd point in life. Hard to remember the terror—a sort of swampiness, feeling of wandering around in a swamp, while some awful *fait accompli* is preparing to drop on top of you.

Looked up and saw her watching me—eyes elongated, sparkling. "You're thinking, Dennis."

"Not really," I said. That look of hers! "I was wondering why you picked me up that night at the Three Chimneys, actually."

"I did that?" Sarah said. "Whoops. Well, gosh, Dennis—I must have thought you'd be fun."

A bit of pineapple lodged in my throat.

"Cheer up, Dennis," Sarah said as I coughed. "A lot of men would be thrilled to be considered a sex object, you know."

"Oh—now, actually, Sarah," I said. "To be serious for a moment, I know the McGees aren't the world's most fascinating people, but it's by their good offices, really, that we're here."

"Yup," Sarah said, patting her stomach as she glanced at it fondly. "Your point?"

"Well," I said, "the fact is, there are certain ways in which everyone is sensitive. For instance, everyone can tell when they're being mocked."

Sarah burped daintily and looked pleased with herself. "Almost everyone," she said.

Sarah gone out for a walk. Can just see from window her tiny bright skirt disappearing around corner. Processions continue. Men in purple satin (Jerusalemites, McGee says) carrying *andas*. Takes dozens to carry each one. Sweat streaming down their faces. Occasionally one stumbles on the cobblestones, slight panic in his eyes. Forcefully primitive representations of Adam and Eve, the world; funny little artificial flowers and flamingos, Christ with loaves, fishes. Tourists darting about with cameras.

Extraordinary activity taking place right outside window. People with immense baskets of flowers, using stencils to make a big rectangular picture with the petals, right on the street. Birds, butterflies, a basket of flowers, all made out of flower petals, appearing on the cobblestones outside. Such a poor country, such impassioned profligacy!

Town even more crowded than yesterday. Young Scandinavians, Americans, Germans, tall and vain, lounging in the square, stretching out bare, tanned legs, trading information, chatting up the Indians, selling each other drugs; Europeans on the balconies of posh vacation homes, drinking from glasses of wine or iced tea as the incense drifts up past them.

Amazing sight on the porticoes of the municipal building across from square—huge families spreading out blankets, starting up little fires in front of the Cathedral to cook corn, stockpots. Children running up and down, playing on the steps, lifting one another to drink from the disease-bearing fountain in the square. Confusing, people like these. Hard to tell who's Indian, who's Ladino. McGee explains many Indians want to pass (status thing, I presume—should have asked). You cut your hair, stop wearing that amazing clothing, speak Span. rather than own languages (of which there turn out to be 22!!!!), and bing! Just like that, you're Ladino.

Sarah glorious in knot of Indian children. No question they are cute—what eyes, what smiles! Those ragged, princely little outfits, runny noses . . . Like nesting dolls in series—each taking care of an even tinier child. They play with Sarah's hair, combing it, fascinated, with her comb (which trust she will wash).

Hotel Flor. *Daily 7:00 a.m.–9:30 p.m. After a morning of browsing through town, the Flor is a delightful stop for the weary traveler. A large* sala *to the rear of the hotel, with its peaceful garden well-hidden from the bustling street, is an ideal spot for a refreshing meal. A "typical plate" is available at lunch or dinner, which includes beef accompanied by guacamole, succulent fried plantains, silken black beans, and* chirmol—*the favored regional sauce, sparkling with lightly cooked tomatoes, green onions, and cilantro. Or, for the homesick, the menu offers baked chicken and a satisfying array of steaks.*

*Others might prefer to settle into one of the generous chairs ranged along the leafy courtyard just within the high hotel walls, to linger over a snack and a frosty drink while listening to the music of a live marimba band; intermingled with the calls of the brilliant red, green, and blue parrots, permanent residents of the huge, gnarled trees in the center of the courtyard. Etc., etc. Mention rooms? Large, airy, clean; waitresses in native dress.*

Tried to persuade Sarah to order chicken (always safe), though her *plato típico* turned out to be OK, I think. Guacamole looked delicious, but warned Sarah off it when I saw little bits of uncooked green stuff—herbs? chives?—peeking out. Had drinks there later with McGees, though, in courtyard, and they said guac. sure to be safe in a place like the Flor. Watched them polish off two orders of chips slathered with it. Sarah had some, too. Can't blame me if she gets sick! McGees have been down here so long they must have all kinds of protective antibodies.

Was glad I'd had talk with Sarah in morning about the McGees— she was charming with them over drinks. Serious, respectful, asking them how long they've been living down here, etc. Dot explained they still kept home in Virginia, to be near son, daughter-in-law. Had come down frequently for work during seventies and eighties, she said. Fell in love with town. Sarah managing very creditable rendition of rapt attention.

Marimba band started up jarringly. Odd sight—musicians in ceremonial (McGee said) clothing, staring straight ahead, the little mallets bouncing all over the keyboards. Played "I Love Paris." Eerie, uninflected instrument—bit nerve-racking after a time. Band angry about something?

Sarah asked McGee what his job had been. Tactfully avoided word "retirement." McGee said he had been in government for forty years. "Yes"—he said; looked like he was savoring the memory of a marvelous wine—"I was with the Department of Agriculture."

Something squawked, causing Dot to heave like a wave. "Oh, look," she said, subsiding. "Aren't they fun?"

Loutish parrot fussing in the tree above us. Sarah got up to talk to it. "Say something, bird," she said. "Something interesting, please."

Her yellow hair was right next to the bird's red plumage. Its crazy little eyes were rolling around like beads in a dish. "Be careful," I said. "They can take your finger off just like that."

Sarah sighed. Sat back down. Was looking incredibly pretty. Noticed that the courtyard, strangely, was rather lugubrious. All that shade! Marimbas playing "Happy Birthday" over and over—aimless, serpentine version.

Noticed Sarah goggling in the direction of the hotel gate. Turned, myself, to chilling vista: line of soldiers marching past, rifles held out at the ready. It took me a long, choppy instant to understand that I was looking at young boys—they were practically children, but their boots and uniforms had transformed them into something toylike and fathomless, and their eyes were hard with rage. "Is there some kind of trouble here in town?" I said to McGee, when I could speak.

"Not at all," McGee said. "Simply routine."

"You know, they just don't get the point down here," Dot said. " 'Happy Birthday' has a *point*. It must have been a request."

McGee chuckled at Sarah, who was still wide-eyed and greenish. "Not to worry," he said. "Just a symbolic prelude to negotiations." Told us that the town is a national showpiece, so army stays away, for the most part. Evidently, though, have been rumors since Feb. about guerrillas in the surrounding villages. But, McGee said, no actual fighting.

Sarah and I had gotten guidebooks, of course, before leaving, and I had tried to tell her whatever I knew about the region. Not easy to remember what's happening where, though. Who we support and why. All these countries! Veritable stew of armies, guerrilla groups, death squads, wobbly emerging democracies, etc. "A strong military, isn't it?" I said.

*Then*—oh, so much. So much. How to remember? Careful—get down *just as happened.*

"Well, the reports of abuse tend to be sensationalized in the States," McGee said. "Although it's true these boys can make a mighty nuisance of themselves. Foreigners are perfectly safe, of course, but the tourists don't like the look of it one bit," he added, just as I overheard Dot asking Sarah if she liked to shop.

"Do I like to shop," Sarah said musingly. "Well, now, there's a—"

"What are you two saying over here?" I asked hurriedly.

"Girl talk," Dot said, with a smile to Sarah of pained forgiveness. "I was asking your young friend if she liked to shop. Because, seriously, for those of us who do enjoy such things, this is the town for it. If I were you, in fact, I'd do some collecting now, while it's still possible. Because they're beginning to use synthetic pigments and machines. And even here in town the people don't know what the old things are worth."

Sarah opened her mouth, but I preempted her. "Sarah will have to budget her shopping time," I said. "We won't always be able to count on her company—she's brought along a lot of reading for her thesis."

"Thesis," Dot said. She and McGee exchanged some minute eyebrow work as Sarah made a quick face at me. "I'm impressed."

"Well, well," McGee said. "What field?"

"Art history," I said. "Sarah plans to write about Van Meegeren, the forger."

McGee picked an insect from his drink. "A subject well worth pursuing, I'm sure," he said.

Sarah tilted her head modestly, as though McGee had conferred a great honor. "Let me ask you, Cliff," she said. "Is this army one of the ones we like, or one of the ones we don't like?"

"'We?'" McGee said. Sarah's expression! Poor, unsuspecting McGee. "The United States? Nothing's ever that simple, is it?"

Sarah smiled at him. "Well," she said.

"Oh, *no*—" I said. "That is, do you believe it? They're playing 'My Funny Valentine.' "

"You have to remember, dear," Dot said to Sarah, "the function of the army is to protect people. The army protects the people who own farms from the guerrillas. The army protects the president."

Sarah nodded. "Except in the case of a military coup, I guess," she said sympathetically.

"I *detest* 'My Funny Valentine,' " I said.

But Dot was gurgling delightedly. "*You*," she said, and shook her finger at Sarah.

"Unfortunately—" McGee frowned. "The army is necessary whether we like it or not. This place is teetering on the brink."

Sarah was gazing at McGee with a terrifyingly detached interest.

"Tired?" I said to her. "Time for a nap?"

"Brink of what?" Sarah said.

McGee looked away impatiently. " '*Brink of what?*' she says."

"Well, I could use a nap," I said. "If nobody else could."

"Listen to me, dear," Dot said. She leaned forward and looked into Sarah's eyes. "We may not love the army, but you should understand that everyone hates the guerrillas, now. Even the people they claim to represent. There was a time, of course, when those people put their trust in the guerrillas, but now it's clear to everybody that the guerrillas only cause misery for innocent people."

"Misery how?" Sarah said. "Innocent of what?"

"Sarah," I said.

"After all," Dot said. "There are bound to be—"

"Well, now," McGee said. He gestured around the courtyard full of laughing foreigners. "Every place has its problems. All right, then?" He smiled at Sarah. "Enough said."

"No, Cliff," Dot said. "I think everybody here should understand that where people are behaving suspiciously—if there's any reason for the army to suspect that a village or a family has been tainted—there are bound to be reprisals."

"Naturally. Everyone understands that." McGee turned to Sarah. "Dorothy's only . . ."

"I'm just—" Dot began.

"Dot's only *saying*," McGee said, "that people here have to be more cautious about their affiliations than we at home do."

"For God's sake," I said, much more loudly than I'd intended, just as the marimbas stopped, "what *is* all that screaming?"

Sarah and the McGees turned; stared at me from under a dome of silence while the parrot screeched and cackled hellishly on its dark branch.

El Sombrerito. *Lunch and dinner, Mon.–Sat. Clean, Amer.-owned. Wide variety of steaks, roast chicken. Desserts baked on premises. Pleasant ambiance, rotating shows of local art (paintings, macramé, etc.). Mango mousse a standout—luxurious, satiny, etc.*

## Tuesday

La Marquesa. *Breakfast, lunch, and dinner, Mon.–Sat. Moderately priced. Dramatic view of volcano, mountains. Courtyard, waitresses in native dress. Eggs, pancakes, steaks. Ice creams (not rec.).*
  *Must look into Sabor de China and Giuseppe's.*

Sarah and the hotel maid fascinated with one another, despite the fact that they can't talk to each other at all. María a round, humorous-looking girl. Indian, I surmise (despite maid's uniform) from the long hair, the measuring, satirical expression, the lofty, graceful, telltale walk (saw her in street yesterday carrying trays of toilet paper stacked on her head). Also, Spanish seems not much better than mine. Surely not her first language. She and I communicate with one another by shouting (Procession this morning?!? Yes!?! Nice??! Good!!!).

Since Sarah speaks no Spanish whatsoever, she and María have managed with a much more dignified vocabulary of gestures and smiles. But this morning, as Maria was changing our bed, Sarah enlisted me as interpreter. "Come on, Dennis. Ask her something."

"What thing?" I said.

"I don't know," Sarah said. "Ask where she lives."

"Don't you think that's prying?" I said.

"No." Sarah looked at me. "Why would that be prying?"

"Well, it isn't, really," I said. "But, after all. She may not want to talk about her private life with strangers. Tourists. She may feel sensitive about that sort of thing. She might very well feel she was being patronized. After all, she's not just a curiosity—she's as real as you or I."

Sarah made a loud snoring sound, which caused María to shake with laughter.

So, after a few garbled exchanges, I was able to tell Sarah that María lived in one of the villages outside town with her husband, her mother, and her children, about an hour's walk away.

"An hour's walk!" Sarah said. "That's a big commute. Do you think she really walks?"

"*¿Qué dice?*" María said.

When I told her what Sarah had said, more or less, she leaned toward me, widened her eyes theatrically, and lowered her voice. "I don't really walk!" she confessed. "I *run*."

"You run?" I asked her. (Wanted to say, Why on earth, something like that, indicating amazement, but couldn't think how. Surely not literally *on earth*.) "Why?" I said.

She lowered her voice even further. "*Cafetales!*" she said, and launched into a confidential torrent of chatter.

"What's she talking about?" Sarah asked.

"I don't know," I said.

"But what's she *saying*?" Sarah said.

"I don't *know*," I said. "Her Spanish is peculiar. All I can tell is she's saying something about someone *being* somewhere. In the coffee plantations she goes through to get here. I don't *know*."

Just then María took it into her head to ask if Sarah and I had any children. "*¿Qué?*" I said. "No."

"No, what?" Sarah said.

"No, nothing. No, you and I don't have any children."

Sarah laughed. "Relax, Dennis," she said. "Ask her how many children she has."

But María seemed to have anticipated the question. "Tell the señora," she was already saying, solemnly and proudly, "I have seven children. Four of them are living and three of them are dead."

Rest of morning very nice. Sarah hauled me right back into the bed María had just made. Then the market for about an hour with the McGees, after which they dropped us off for lunch at La Mariposa, introduced us to owner. Place very agreeable, will be able to write up nicely. (Daily except Sun., 12 p.m.–10 p.m.) Gardens, fountain. Very popular with Americans, like ladies at table nearby wearing outfits made from native textiles. "Have you ever *seen* anything so beautiful," they kept saying to one another.

Perhaps can find tactful way to suggest house wine less than ideal. Also meat. (Sarah's baked chicken might have been nice, but somewhat raw, alas.)

Sarah began very funny imitation of the beauty-loving ladies at the table near us. Had to shush her—probably friends of the McGees. Owner cruised by to talk with us for a few minutes. Said how hard things are for restaurants now, prices increasing geometrically, value of currency plummeting, everything grown for export. Told us that price of black beans ("the traditional food of our poor") has almost doubled in recent months. Sarah: "So, what are your poor eating now?"

Couldn't help smiling. Owner smiled, too—with hatred. "I really wouldn't know," he said.

———

Actually, town might be most beautiful thing I've ever seen myself. Gets more beautiful as eye adjusts. So high, so pale, so strange. Flowers astonishing—graceful rococo shapes, sinuous, pendant, like ornamentations on the churches. Every hour of the day, in every changing tint of air, new details coming forward. The ancient stillness. All the different ancientnesses—Spain, Rome, themselves so new compared to the Indians. All converging right here in the square. Concentrated in the processions, in every dark eye.

Sarah, for all her snootiness to Dot about shopping, can't resist stopping at every corner and every market. Our room now draped with astounding textiles, bits of Indian clothing—crammed with flowers and little orchid trees. (María shakes her head, amused, all indulgence with Sarah.)

Early this evening processions of costumed children all over the place. Sarah enthralled. Flower-petal pictures appearing everywhere—*alfombras* (carpets) McGee tells me they're called. Put down only to be trampled within hours by the processions—celebration of the suffering of Christ.

Saw a man lifting a mesh sack of mangoes about twice his size. Bent way backward over it, slipped its strap around his forehead, then drew himself forward so that the mangoes rested on his back, as though he were a cart. Sarah stopped in her tracks and stared.

I put a comforting arm around her, tried to move her along. Think it must be particularly humiliating to be stared at if you're doing uncongenial work. "It certainly does look awful to us," I said. "But it must be different for people who do it every day."

"Sure," Sarah said. "The difference is that they do it every day."

I held Sarah away from me and looked at her. "Sarah?" I said. "Are you angry at me?"

"No," she said tentatively.

The group of ladies from the table near us at lunch walked by and waved as though we were all old friends. One called over to us: "How are you enjoying it? Gorgeous, aren't they, the processions?" Shaded her eyes, flashed a toothy smile. "*Thought*-provoking!"

Sarah waved absently, then frowned and nestled against me. I stroked her hair, and the perfume of incense and flowers rose up around us. "Dennis," she said meditatively, "don't you like me?"

"Don't I like you?" I said. I held her away from me and studied her, but she was serious. "What do you mean? I adore you."

I smiled and gave her a squeeze, but it was a few moments before she spoke. "So then, listen, Dennis. Why did you have to trot out my—my *credentials* for the McGees?"

"I thought you'd be pleased," I said, amazed. Explained that I'd only been trying to provide her with an excuse not to see them. "Besides," I said. "Why shouldn't I be proud of you?"

She drew away from me. "Dennis, who are these people to demand respectability from me? I don't *like* these people. These people are idiots."

Felt oddly stricken. Can't really blame Sarah—that's how she feels. But, still, McGees are clearly doing their best to be hospitable, pleasant. "Of course, the McGees might not be our favorite people," I said. "But why should they be?" Tucked an unruly label back inside Sarah's T-shirt. "And, after all, they're perfectly harmless."

Sarah stared sadly into the lively crowds.

"Besides," I said. "They're getting on." I stooped over, quavered. "I'll be like that soon myself, I suppose."

Sarah frowned again, then laughed. "Oh, *Dennis*," she said, but her hand crept over and curled into mine, like a pliant little animal.

Buen Pastor. *Lunch, dinner, Tues.–Sun. Of the many beautiful restaurants in town, perhaps the loveliest is Buen Pastor. Enjoy a cocktail of platonic perfection outside in the moonlit garden. Or, if the evening is cool, in the bar, where a fire may be roaring at the massive colonial hearth. There are likely also to be fires in each of the several beautifully proportioned dining rooms. It has to be said that the menu, though worthy, is not particularly inspired, but each of its few items is carefully prepared (the* steak au poivre *is sure to please) and the wine list is adequate. The staff is happy to assist you in your selections (all speak English here), and despite the luxury of the surroundings, a memorable evening with cocktails, wine, and a full meal for two will put hardly a dent in your wallet. The atmosphere is relaxed, intimate, and romantic.*

## Wednesday

"Relaxed, intimate, and romantic!" was the first thing I heard this morning— Woke up to see Sarah reading the notes about Buen Pastor I'd started to slam together last night when we got in from dinner, which I'd imprudently left right in the typewriter. (No more of that, you can be sure! From now on, everything gets put away immediately. Locked up.) Sarah laughed incredulously. "You call that place relaxed, intimate, and romantic?"

"For God's sake," I said. "That's just a draft! I hadn't even finished."

"Well, when you get around to 'revising your draft,'" Sarah said, "you might mention that the first thing you see when you get to the door is some kind of *butler* with a machine gun."

"Submachine gun," I said. "Machine guns are larger."

"Oh, well, then," Sarah said.

"Besides," I said. I rubbed my eyes. "I can't just put that into my piece, can I, Sarah?"

"Why can't you?" she said. She sat down next to me on the bed. "Dennis."

"Because," I said. "Sarah, please. I'm supposed to be writing about people's *vacations*."

Sarah stuffed a corner of the pillow into her mouth.

"I'm sorry," I said. Couldn't suppress a sigh. "I wasn't aware, last night, that the guard upset you."

"Naturally he upset me," Sarah said. "I assumed he upset you, too."

"Of course he did," I said. "Naturally he upset me." (Naturally I was upset when I went to give my name to the maitre d' and saw that thing pointing at me. But it isn't as though restaurants at home don't have their own security systems.) "Sarah—" I took her hand. "What's happened? Has something happened? Have you been having an awful time here?"

Gloomy, theatrical pause. "The truth is, Dennis," she said, "I've been having a terrific time."

That sound ominously familiar; that muted, baffled, fragile tone designed to censure. Can't understand it—some sort of curse hovering over me that makes women sad? The women who are attracted to me are active, capable women. Women with interesting and demanding careers. Women, sometimes, with reasonably happy marriages, families. (Which, granted, can have its drawbacks, but one expects it, at least, to ensure a certain degree of stability.) Yet how rapidly these self-sufficient women become capricious and sulky. Absolutely unglued. Even the perky, adventurous wives who come my way (unsolicited, unsolicited!) simply *transform* themselves. And these women, who, I think it's fair to say, engage me for nothing more than, to use Sarah's (rather crude) word, *fun*—these same women—invariably begin to accuse me, in the most amorphous terms, of some unsubstantiated crime. It's a strange thing. It is. All these women, showing up on my doorstep, demanding my attention and affection. And then, when I've given them every bit of attention and affection I've got, insisting that I've failed them in some way. "Self-absorption," one of them said. "Shallowness of feeling," said another. As though I were some kind of broken *vending* machine!

Margaret S.? Who actually claimed I was "rejecting" at the very moment *she* was leaving *me*? Even Cynthia—my own wife—so happy when I married her, so confident; the way she became self-pitying and tremulous in front of my very eyes! Implored her to tell me what was the matter. Huge error. The matter was me, naturally; I was not really interested in her. Not *interested*! And the way, when I pointed out the irrefutable demonstrations of my interest, she would become incoherent: "Not that, not that! You know that's not what I'm talking about."

"Sarah," I said, "when we were in San Francisco you told me you loved traveling. That's what you said. You said you *loved traveling*."

"When we were in San Francisco," Sarah said, "and I told you I loved traveling, we were in San Francisco."

"Well, but travel is travel," I said. "One sees new things."

" 'New things!' " Sarah said. "Guys in uniforms with automatics?"

"Now, that's not fair," I said gently. Waited for a moment so she would hear the whining tone of her own voice, see the roomful of her happy purchases, see out the wooden-shuttered window, where a jaunty little halo of cloud sat over the peak of a volcano, and women padded silently by with their black-eyed babies bundled on their backs.

"I'm sorry, Dennis," she said. Clambered over into my lap. Twined herself around me. "I just feel so strange. I don't know what's going on. The thing is, I really *am* having a terrific time."

Faint sounds of a brass band and the fragrance of incense were beginning to filter into our room with the buttery sunlight. Persecuting loveliness. Rubbed the tender edge of Sarah's ear. Pointed out that the restaurant was something like an airport, if you thought about it: protection irrelevant to most of the travelers.

"Well, I *know*," Sarah said. "But who's all the protection *from*, here? I mean, look, Dennis, who is the enemy?"

Snuggled her against me. Reminded her that we've all read about such things; pointed out that we're overreacting, she and I, simply because we're *here*.

Made me think: How tempting it is to put oneself into the drama—"It's awful; *I've* seen it." Unattractive, self-aggrandizing impulse. Reminded Sarah of the morning we were having breakfast at her place and Karen stormed in, ranting about factory farming, and we kept saying, "We know, Karen, we know, it's really awful." Lifted Sarah's chin and was rewarded with a reluctant smile. "But Karen couldn't stop talking, remember? Because she had just *seen* it the day before. So, to her, it seemed just incredibly *real*?

"The thing is," I said, "we could go around sniffling all the time, but terrible things are going to happen whether we sniffle or not. Yes, the lives some people lead are horrifying, but if you accept the idea that it's better for some people to be fortunate than for no people to be fortunate, then it's preposterous to make yourself miserable just because *you* happen to be one of those fortunate people. I mean, here we are, in an amazingly beautiful place, witnessing possibly the most lavish Easter celebration in the whole of the New World. Wouldn't it be morally reprehensible not to enjoy it?"

Sarah sighed. "I know," she said. "You're right."

"We could reject that out of principle," I said. "But what would the principle *be*?"

"All right, Dennis." Sarah jumped up and fluffed her hair. "I already said I agree."

Came back to the room later, tempers restored by breakfast. María there, putting a jug of fresh water on the table. Said, "Procession now?! Nice!!"

"Tell me something, Dennis," Sarah said when María left. "*Do* you ever think about having another child?"

"Of course not," I said. "I mean, I think about it, of course, but I don't think about actually doing it."

"Take it easy," Sarah said. "I was just wondering."

"I already have one perfectly good child," I said. "An adult, now, actually, almost. It doesn't make sense to start all over at my age. For someone your age—well, that's a different story. You *should* have children."

"I didn't say I wanted children," Sarah said crossly.

"You have every right to want children," I said. Looked at her closely—a bit puffy? Due for her period any minute now, I think. "You're one of those women who can do it all, you know. Career, family—"

"Hey," Sarah said. "I didn't say I wanted *children*. I was just asking how you feel."

"I know," I said. "Goodness." I was just *saying* how I feel.

Especially hot today; was noticing it very suddenly—room darkened swoopingly. Put my head in my hands, then Sarah was speaking: "Listen, Dennis—are machine guns, like, a *lot* bigger than submachine guns?"

"Some of them," I said. The fact is, David is much more vivid to me as I imagine him now, playing basketball with his friends, strolling away from the house in Claremont on his way to a movie, spinning along in his rattly little car, than he seems when he's sitting across from me in some padded restaurant, waiting patiently for our visit to be over. "Why?"

"Because I think maybe that's one out there."

"Good Lord," I said. Sat up to look out the window and saw a wooden platform coming down the street. It looked amazingly like one of the *andas*, except that it was accompanied by a convoy of soldiers in uniform instead of townspeople in purple satin, and in place of Christ or the Virgin Mary, it displayed a mounted machine gun. "Yup, that's what it is, all right," I told Sarah.

The soldiers—the hard-eyed, ravenous-looking boys—surged up beyond the window, and in their midst the lordly, searching weapon reigned. A plunging shame weakened my hands and my knees as though at any second that instrument of terrible destruction might swing around toward me, discovering the foolish incidentalness of my body, its humiliatingly provisional life. No one on the street appeared to notice the entourage. A path cleared apparently by casual occurrence; only sign of anything out of the ordinary: a barely perceptible slowing, a thickening of motion as it passed.

Sarah and I stood at the window, watched until the entire retinue, with its platform and its sickening gleam of metal, turned the corner. Within an instant nothing left but the soft bustle of the street.

I put my arm around Sarah, and the small intimacy conducted away my panic. Tried to reassure her: "If there were anything out of the ordinary occurring, someone would tell us."

"Someone did tell us," Sarah said.

"Who?" I said.

"María," she said.

"The maid?" I said. "I mean someone who actually knows."

"Like who?" Sarah said.

"Like a journalist, for example."

Sarah stared at me. "Dennis," she said. "*You're* a journalist."

"All right, Sarah," I said. "Please."

Does Sarah know how cruel she is sometimes? Obviously there's no way in the world I'd be doing something of this sort if the bank hadn't gone the way banks tend to go these days. "But you know what I mean. Obviously I'm not saying María doesn't know what's happening to her. Obviously she does know what's happening to her. All I'm saying is that she has no way of *understanding* it. In context, that is. If I were you, I really wouldn't worry about María. She has quite a little flair for drama, but the truth is that her attention is on the Easter celebrations. Festivities. Frivolous matters"—I smiled and pushed a strand of hair from Sarah's eyes—"just like ours is."

"Dennis," Sarah said. "The *maid* is afraid to come to work. There's a mounted *machine* gun rolling down the street."

"I am not disputing that," I said. "Obviously. It's only that—Sarah, tell me something frankly. Are you embarrassed by what I do?"

"Embarrassed!" Sarah said, and actually blushed. "By what you do? Of course not, Dennis."

"Look, Sarah," I said. "This travel/restaurant business is every bit as much a joke to me as it is to you. And I would certainly never dream of calling myself a *journalist*—"

"Well, of course you're a—"

"I would never dream of calling myself a journalist *at this point*," I said. "But it's an easy target, isn't it? It's easy to be snobbish about this, just because it doesn't seem 'important' in some superficial way. And who knows, it's not impossible, that in a few years I could be—well, I could hardly hope for anything like the foreign desk, I suppose. But I won't be *anywhere* if I'm not reasonably—and, besides, it's only fair to Zwicker, who, quite frankly, took *pity* on me, no matter what you might think of his half-witted—"

"No, you owe him a lot, Dennis," Sarah said.

"No, I owe Zwicker a lot. He's giving me a rather decent salary, he's given me a job that some people might consider cushy, even prestigious, so the fact is that—"

"No, it's terrific, Dennis. Look. He sent you to San Francisco, he's going to send you to London. And we would never in a million years be here if it weren't for—"

Etc., etc., as I remember. But somewhere around that ridiculous point I slightly crumpled up a bit. Heat, and actually I don't think either of us is exactly used to the altitude yet, either. And then Sarah was really very sweet for a long, long time. And afterward she seemed quite pleased. But the strange thing about sex (tho. maybe it's different for a woman) is that if you start off feeling a little bad sometimes, sometimes when it's over, you can really feel awful.

El Lomito Borracho. *12:00 p.m.–9:30 p.m. This cheerful steak house with its whitewashed walls and posters of Indians draws a young crowd, mostly Germans. The sirloin with grilled onions is probably your best bet here, but be sure to ask for your meat—as anywhere in the region—bien asada (well done).*

## Thursday

Café Bougainvillea. *Hours subject to change. Juices, coffee, milk shakes, cakes. Pleasant. Hygiene questionable.*

Town at fever pitch today and yesterday. Air sharp and bright—mountains entirely revealed, like a crown tossed around us. Crowds larger, aboil. More people arriving by foot or bus to camp across from the square with their little bundles of possessions, blankets. Flowers furiously blooming. *Alfombras* spread out for the boot. Chilling roll of drums, sepulchral brass, sun flashing in the air like swords. This morning Christ in scarlet robes, rocking down the streets in an ocean of incense; swarms of purple-gowned Jerusalemites. Sweat pouring from the faces of men bearing the *andas*. McGee bobbing in and out of the crowd, snapping pictures.

"Do you see those men in shackles, walking next to the cross?" Dot said. "Those are the thieves. Do you see? The amazing thing is, they use real criminals. Just petty thieves, probably, or poor drunks. But this afternoon, when the procession goes by the square, the whole town will sing an anthem about forgiveness, and one of the thieves will be untied and released into the crowd, just the way they did it in Jerusalem."

"That's beautiful," Sarah said.

"Yes . . ." Dot said, frowning. "Oh, it's a lovely holiday. The painted eggs, the mystery of spring, the little candies hidden on the lawn for the children. And here! My goodness. The flowers, the processions . . ."

Sarah inscrutable; peering out at the procession, working away absently at a ragged nail with her teeth.

"It's just that they take it all so *literally*," Dot said. She sighed. "Like this business with the thief. I mean, this is something that happened almost two thousand years ago—do you see what I mean? It's a *holiday*. But they are so literal-*minded*. You'll see. On Saturday, Sunday—nothing. No processions, no *alfombras* . . . They're not interested in the Resurrection at all, really. Today and tomorrow are the big days. The Crucifixion is the part of it they relate to." She nodded admonishingly at Sarah. "*Martyrdom*. You see, they pick so at the story—the Crucifixion, the poor, the rich. That sort of thing. The imperial authorities. The soldiers."

The crowd was jostling around us, Dot serenely accustomed to it— burbling on, unfazed. "We used to go out to the little villages. Santa Catarina and so on. But no more. They've taken the wonder right out of it, haven't they? Of course, they *are* very poor—no one would deny them that. Still, it's just tempting fate, isn't it? To glorify it the way they do?

"When Cliff was still with the Department of Agriculture we had a place out by the lake, and we would go to the celebrations there. The people are mostly seasonal labor on the plantations, so, as you might imagine, it's been a fertile area for guerrilla activity; and now, of course, the people bring politics into simply *everything*.

"And the priests can be just as bad. There was one, just about ten years ago, in the village across the lake from us. An American, if you please. Who should have known better. It's a terrible story, really. It makes me *sick* to tell it—I'm sorry the whole thing came up. You see, it was what he allowed them to do, some of these people in his parish. He let them dress up the figures of the saints—the figures of Christ, even—as Indians." Dot nodded as she looked from Sarah to me. "Well, not just *Indians*—actually as guerrillas, do you see? With the little masks and so forth? And they did it right in that great big church of theirs, which is practically the only real building in that town. Father Tobin thought he could get away with it, I suppose, because he was American. But he might have stopped to think how he was endangering his parishioners. What sort of priest is that, I ask you? His parishioners were disappearing by the score."

The pavement swiped briefly up at me, and I reached out to steady myself against Dot's arm. "No hat?" Dot said. She gave me a penetrating look, and steered us through the crowd to a shady spot. "Reckless creature. Anyhow, it made us just as mad as anything. But of course I'm not Catholic myself, so to my mind the whole *thing* is a bit—there, look! Executioners!"

Group filed by dressed in black, black conical hats, but faces eerily covered by flaps of white fabric with holes cut out for the eyes. Saw a Pontius Pilate—pointed him out to Sarah: "Do you see the sign he's carrying? It says, 'I wash my hands of the blood of this innocent man.' "

"This is just the sort of thing I mean," Dot said.

"What's what sort of thing?" Sarah said. But Dot was gazing out with displeasure.

Felt unaccountably nervous—started chattering at Sarah: "Well, it's complex, isn't it? Because the thing is that the local people said to Pilate, 'Look. You've got to get rid of this fellow Jesus. He's got this whole mob of crazy hillbillies behind him, and they're saying his claims supersede the claims of Rome.' And *Pilate* said, 'Well, I don't happen to think Jesus is guilty of anything, but I can't stop you from doing whatever you want to him, can I? Because I can't intervene in local affairs.' So who knows who was using who? After all, you could say that it was very much in Pilate's interest, as well as the interest of the local authorities, that Jesus be killed, because, after all, Jesus was certainly fomenting unrest in Pilate's province."

Sarah turned to me. "So you mean the guy with the sign—"

"Well, *no*," I said. "I'm just trying to point out various ironies of the situation . . . And it's interesting to remember that that's where those phrases come from. You know: 'I wash my hands of it.' 'My hands are clean.' And so on. They come from the Bible."

"As do so many," Dot said vaguely. "Oh, there he is—" She waved as McGee appeared from the crowd, coughing from incense. "I thought we were going to have to send out the Romans! Did you get some good ones?"

"Indeed I did," McGee said. "Ought to have some beauties."

"Clifford left the lens cap on last year," Dot explained.

"By the way," Sarah said to her. "What happened to the priest?"

"Excuse me?" Dot said.

"The priest in the village near the lake," Sarah said.

"Well," Dot said. "Do you mean— I mean, no one knows, exactly, do they? That is, they came in a van, as usual. But the windows were smoked glass, of course, and they weren't wearing uniforms. The van slid up behind him, they say. Just the way those vans do. I'm afraid they got him just outside the church." Dot shook her head. "You can still see the bullet holes. And it took quite some time to scrub down the wall and the street, we were told . . . Well. But no one recognized them. No one knows who they were."

## Friday

*Sabor de China and Giuseppe's both awful. Best to skip.*

Last night, after all the wooden shutters were closed and the town was quiet, Sarah and I went out. Above the encircling mountains the sky was bright with stars; down on the ground the night was pouring back and forth, glistening over the cobblestones and churches. Sarah and I walked around for a bit, then sat down in the square next to a pale-trunked palm.

Was terribly aware how quickly it would be over, sitting with her there in the fragrant night. Thought of her ten years hence: a dinner party, high over some sparkling city, Sarah in a wonderful little dress, more beautiful, even, than now. Gazing out the window, next to someone—a colleague, an admirer . . .

Could feel the future forming in embryo—the sort of longing that sleeps watchfully in one's body through time and separation. Could imagine so clearly—Sarah at this future party, confiding to this admirer: Her first involvement with a mature man, her introduction to so much that was new . . . No, she and I won't have meant *nothing* to each other . . .

The shine of her hair like a little light around her as she absorbed the night, breathing it into her memory for that moment in the future. Raised her hand and stroked it, spreading out the fingers; kissed her palm. Asked what she was thinking.

"I'm thinking, Thank God we're rid of the McGees for once." She laughed.

I looked down at her hand.

"What's the matter, Dennis?" she said.

Said I was sorry about the McGees. Sorrow, in fact, had fallen over me like a gentle net. "They really are idiots."

"Well, they're not *idiots*," Sarah said.

I looked at her. "That was *your* word," I said.

"Yes? Well, I was wrong, then," Sarah said. "Wasn't I."

Across from us the people in the shelter of the porticoed municipal building slept, cradling the town in the mesh of their breathing.

"*'Tainted,'*" Sarah said. "I mean, *Jesus.*"

Noticed that the people in front of the municipal building were stirring, rousing themselves in a dreamlike way, rolling back the blanket of sleep, sitting up—first one or two, then several more, shaking others gently by the shoulder until, soon, they were all awake, getting to their feet, smoothing out their rumpled clothing.

In moments they were in the square with us, talking in low, eager voices. Some were speaking Spanish, some were speaking languages I'd never heard. Were paying no attention to us at all; leaned over the basin of the fountain to splash themselves or their babies with water, or to reach up with tin cups for its less polluted streams.

But then—as unexpectedly as they'd appeared in the square, they filed out again. Absolutely weird. Sarah and I paused a moment, then followed. Soon we were in a part of town we'd never seen before. Lanterns swaying from stone arches, heavy shutters swinging open as we passed by—behind them women in black staring out at us from candlelit rooms or patios.

Crowd led us to a churchyard dense with people, tiny stands selling food, wooden toys, shiny whirling things. No tourists, no wealthy Ladinos, none of the Europeans who keep houses here in town. All the people ragged and thin—surroundings incredibly festive, but their faces, as they milled about, were serious. Abstracted.

The sky was scattered with stars, balloons, plumes of incense. Above a long flight of wide, shallow steps a scrolled church (such delicate adornments! carved fruit, carved vines) floated like a dove, pale pink in the moonlight. Candles alight everywhere, flickering, converging into a flickering river at the huge, open church doors.

Tantalizing aromas: food frying in vats or simmering in huge kettles or roasting on sticks over fires. Sarah pulling me from one culinary spectacle to another in an agony of cupidity: "Look, Dennis—can you believe it? There's real food in this country!"

"Don't even think of it," I said.

"Please," she said. People were eating patiently, without greed, as though they were preparing themselves for something. Men were so thin it was hard not to watch them as they ate—so frail. Several had what looked like a band of hair shaved from the top of their heads—worn away from hauling loads by a strap, I suppose. Sarah hovered longingly by a woman frying huge disks of tortilla, then using them to scoop up a bright, chunky sauce. "I can't stand it!"

"Out of the question," I said. At our feet a flock of tiny children chewed solemnly at the dirty treat. "Do you imagine I'd let you do something like that to yourself? But listen. The minute we get home I'm taking you to the Red Fox Inn for a decent meal."

"Do you promise?" Sarah said as the crowd carried us with them into the floating church. Was just making me swear it, but then she gasped and took my arm.

We were at the front of the crowd—the entire floor between us and the altar was a picture, a picture carpet, made of flower petals, like the *alfombras*, but vast: Jesus, all of flowers, white-robed on a mountaintop with waves of power radiating from his raised hands. And beneath him, pouring out toward us, becoming us, a flower multitude—the poor, the mourning, the meek, the hungry, the pure in heart, the persecuted . . .

Behind us, people were pushing their way forward. I glanced back and saw that the crowd was not flowerlike at all, but thin and dry as tinder, their eyes alight with a fanatical, incendiary ecstasy of poverty.

My God. Who *were* these people? Their legs were ulcerated, their feet were bare and thickened, their backs were bent from hauling wood or fruit or coffee, but what act of madness might they not be capable of? The guerrillas in the neighboring villages dozing tensely under the dark trees, the children who work the raging fields, the maids, the porters, the farmers, curled up on their beds or straw mats, alert in their sleep, dreaming their dangerous dreams. People who can't afford a newspaper. People in whose languages no paper will ever be printed, people who couldn't read one if one *were* printed in their languages—these people who don't even know there's a world out there, it's these people who could burn the world to the ground. Stunted and sloe-eyed, with the delicate, slanting planes of their faces, their brilliant clothing, their ancient, outlandish languages, they seem like strange, magical creatures. But, no! These people have lives that go from one end of the day to the other. They eat or go hungry. They have conversations behind closed doors—

As Sarah and I were thrust out the side door we saw a small knot of soldiers dispersing in the courtyard below us, blending into the crowd. My hands felt weak again, and damp. *Tainted*, I thought; *tainted*. Next to me Sarah picked up a wobbly child who was steadying himself against her knees, and nuzzled his soft, black baby hair, through which I could absolutely *see* the columns of lice tramping. But when I opened my mouth to warn Sarah I could hardly croak.

The baby waved his new little hands for balance—his new little enemy hands. His swimming black baby eyes, reflected for an instant, in exquisite miniature, the thousand or so candles, the floating church, the thick, blest, kindled crowd. Which of the reflected men could that baby hope soon to be? Which of the frail old enemy men?

A little girl tugged urgently at Sarah's skirt and held out her arms to claim her brother as a noise manifested itself at a distance. The noise came toward us slowly, solid and tidal, but separated, as it approached, and we were engulfed in shouts, hoofbeats, chanting, as lanterns and torchlight wavered through smoke and incense.

Facing us, at the head of the mob, two Roman centurions reined in their huge horses to a nervous, hobbled trot. Around them surged the Jerusalemites in their purple satin and Roman foot soldiers holding lances, as well as hundreds of town dwellers in ordinary clothing.

A trumpet sounded, and the edgy crowd fell silent. The sky gleamed black, the moon was streaking through the clouds. Sarah's pale face narrowed and flashed like a coin, and I had the sensation that if I concentrated I would be able to remember all the events that were to follow—every detail . . .

And, yes, one of the centurions was already holding out a scroll: *Jesus of Nazareth was condemned to die by crucifixion!* The pronouncement rang out against the stone of the church like something being forged; its echo pulsed in a cataract of silence.


## Saturday


Hotel Buena Vista. *Breakfast, lunch, and dinner daily. The Buena Vista offers probably the best lunch deal in town. Help yourself to the unlimited buffet, complete with tortillas made fresh in front of your eyes by Indian women in full dress, take a swim, and if you've happened to come on the right day, view a fashion show around the pool, all for about the price of a hamburger and fries back home. Exotic birds wander the grounds, and caged parrots enliven the scene, as well. The fare is standard, but the steaks are flame-grilled, and tasty.*


Clouds below us, plane not too crowded. Sarah sitting with a book on her lap, gazing out the window, at nothing.

This morning, as we were leaving, it was just as Dot had said it would be. No *alfombras*, no processions, tourists thinning out. No trace whatsoever of the pilgrims in front of the municipal building. Just women in black, privately lamenting Mary's murdered child. But yesterday—Friday—processions were volatile, grief-stricken, unrelenting: Christ in black, prepared for his death, then Christ on the cross, broken.

Felt v. peculiar—ill-tempered, rattled—all yesterday morning. Suppose from my disorientation of Thurs. night + looming lunch with McGees.

And then—the *Buena Vista* itself! *¡Dios!* Curvy Ladino girls modeling hideous clothing around the pool, children streaking between them, landing in the water with loud splashes, bloodcurdling shrieks. Indian women making tortillas, watching with expressionless sentry eyes. Well-to-do visitors from the capital dispatching slender, olive-skinned sons to the parking lot with little plates of rice and beans for the maids. A species of splotchy, knobby tourists (Evangelicals, apparently; McGee says they get a big price break at the *Buena Vista*) sunning themselves in plastic lounge chairs, laughing loudly and nervily, as though they'd just hoodwinked their way out of prison.

Sarah struggled with her little sink stopper of a steak for a few minutes, then got up and ambled around the lawn, looking unusually pensive. When she sat back down, she started telling the McGees about something she'd seen a few days ago. Had she mentioned it to me? Don't think so. Said she'd seen three big guys grab a boy as he walked out of a store—nobody was paying attention except for one lady, who was yelling. Then the men bundled the boy up, put him on a truck. "I didn't really think much about it at the time," Sarah said. "It was like a tape playing too fast to make any sense of." She looked from Dot to Cliff. "I suppose I just assumed it was a kid getting picked up for a robbery . . ."

"Oh, Lord," Dot said with a sigh.

"Now, Dorothy," McGee said.

"No, Cliff." Dot's voice trembled slightly. "I don't care. Their poor mothers. You know"—she turned to Sarah—"after the boys are trained, they're sent to other parts of the country, because it does work out better if they don't speak the language, doesn't it? Oh, I know that it's all necessary, but it's terribly hard for the families. Their families love them. Their families need them to work." She turned back to McGee. "I think it's disgusting, Clifford, frankly."

McGee lifted his hand for peace. "I never said—" he began, but just at that moment a tall man of thirty-five or so approached. His thatchy hair and matching mustache were the color of dirty Lucite. A large, chipped tooth might have given his smile an agreeable, beaverlike goofiness except for an impression he gave of the veiled, inexhaustible rage you see in certain ex-alcoholics. "Excuse me," he said. "Do you happen to be Clifford McGee?"

"I am he," McGee said judiciously, extending his hand.

"My name's Curtis Finley," the man said. "I work with your old outfit, and you were pointed out to me once at the Camino."

"So, they've got you down here, do they?" McGee said. "Have a seat. We're just—what is it they say?—*improving the shining hours.*"

Sarah stood up suddenly, then flopped back down into her chair. Finley glanced at her. "Thank you, sir," he said to McGee. "Yes, I've been here for a bit, now. I'm on my way to supervise a project up north."

"Really," McGee said. "A lot going on up there. You'll have to come by when you get back, let me know how things went. I like to keep up."

"I imagine you do, sir," Finley said. "They still talk about you at the office." The two men smiled at each other, and a faint smell of sweat imprinted itself on the air.

Dot nodded toward Sarah, who was splayed out glumly in her chair. "*This* young lady saw a recruitment the other day," Dot said.

"Dorothy," McGee said, as Finley looked sharply at him.

"Those cretins," Finley said. He turned to me and Sarah, showing his teeth to indicate friendliness. "So, what brings you folks down here?"

"Dennis is a journalist," Sarah said. She drew herself together and smiled primly.

Finley looked away from her legs. "Recruitments are very unusual here in town," he told me. "And technically against the law. In fact, as I understand it, something's being done about them now."

"I'm not really a *journalist*," I assured him hurriedly. "I'm just doing food. Hotels, Easter celebrations in a general sort of way . . ."

"I see . . ." Finley said.

"Actually," I said, "I'm a banker."

"Oh." Finley looked at McGee.

"No," Dot said. "You see, Dennis is doing the most marvelous thing—he's writing a nationally syndicated article about Holy Week. Isn't that wonderful?"

Finley frowned. "Oh." He showed his teeth again. "Well, how are you enjoying it? Beautiful town, isn't it?"

McGee shifted in his chair. "We're taking these two to the de Leóns' tonight, for dinner," he said. "They're old friends, and the cook does wonderful things with regional produce."

"Oh, yes." Finley looked at me with vague bitterness. "Interesting fellow, de León. Never met him personally. Good morning, isn't he?"

"Pardon?" I said.

"Good morning," McGee said. "You've seen them in the supermarkets. Oranges, grapefruits. Even some bananas with the little sticker that says—"

"Oh, yes," I said. "Of course. Good Morning!"

"Yes," McGee said. "that's de León. Good Morning! Oranges, Good Morning! Grapefruits. Coffee's his main thing, but he's all over the place now, really."

"Had some trouble with a son, I remember hearing," Finley said.

McGee nodded. "A bad patch. Over now."

"Kid had one wicked case of red-ass, as I heard it," Finley said. He turned to Sarah. "'If you'll pardon me."

"Excuse me?" Sarah said with a misty smile. "Sorry, I wasn't really . . . Oh, Mr. Finley, do you happen to know what this pretty vine is?" She pointed to an arborlike construction above us.

"Curtis," Finley said. He peered overhead, then looked at Sarah. "Vine?"

"I think," Dot said, squinting distantly, "that the rain is going to come early this year. Last night I saw lightning from over by the coast."

McGee smiled comfortably. "Same family as the Japanese wisteria," he said.

Later Sarah hunched over in the big chair in our room, hugging her knees while I walked back and forth.

"Just because a fellow doesn't happen to recognize one particular plant," I said, "does not mean he's some kind of *impostor*."

Sarah sighed noisily.

"Well, after all," I said. "But, besides. I think one has to ask oneself what, in all honesty, are the alternatives."

"What on earth are you saying, Dennis?" Sarah said.

Mustn't let Sarah force me into positions—her willful naiveté, threat of shrillness. Always have to remember to relax, keep perspective. Allow her to relax. Tried to point out calmly that, whatever one thinks of this method or that, people's goals tend to be—on a certain basic level—the same. "We all want life to improve for everyone; we're all struggling, in our own ways, to make things better. Yes, even people who differ from us can be sincere, Sarah—I mean, unless you're talking about a few greed-maddened dictators. Psychopaths, like Hitler, or Idi Amin. Sociopaths, I guess, is what the word is now. Is that what they say in your classes, 'sociopaths'?"

Sarah gazed down at her sandaled toes and wiggled them.

"But it's funny," I said, perching next to her on the arm of the chair. "Isn't it? The way terminology can change like that. It must reflect a wholesale shift in the way moral reasoning, or whatever, is perceived to work. I think it's so interesting, that, don't you? They used to say 'psychopaths' when I was young."

Sarah wiggled her toes again. "Isn't it wonderful," she leaned down to say to them, "the way that bogus agronomists are crawling all over the place, struggling to improve life for everyone?

"Oh, yes, Sarah," she answered herself in a crumply little voice. "Deeply heartwarming. But that word 'agronomist'—I think the word you want is 'agriculturalist,' interestingly. You know, when I was just a *little* toe—"

"Oh, Sarah," I said.

"Ex*cuse* me, Dennis." Sarah looked at me icily. "I was talking to my *foot*."

For the rest of the afternoon, we were very, very cautious with one another. Was dreading dinner. But Sarah was on her good behavior, or a variant of it. Was weirdly tractable, polite. Just as well, especially because the de Leóns turned out to be exactly what one would have expected—exactly what one would have feared.

The Sra. steely in linen and small gold earrings. The Sr. somewhat more appealing. Handsome, very Spanish, melancholy. Obvious habit of power; cordiality engineered to infinitesimal degrees of correctness. Daughter, Gabriela, petite like mother. Pure, unclouded face, whispery clothing—quite taken with Sarah; many limpid smiles. Missed the States, she said, her friends from boarding school in Connecticut. Threatened "So much to talk about." All three excellent English.

Maids, passing out hors d'oeuvres and cocktails—rum + Good Morning! fruit juices. Gigantic house, huge collection of antique Indian textiles, pre-Columbian artifacts, splendid colonial furnishings, etc.

Evening inexplicably slippery at first—odd tides of dusk from the series of enclosed patios and gardens flowing around the bulky forms inside. Everyone floating a bit, like particles dislodging themselves from something underwater, which was my mind.

Found Sarah in a hallway, staring at a row of photographs. From behind, I watched her examining the face of a beautiful young man, pale, black-haired, who was staring into the camera with an expression of sardonic resignation.

"That's my son, Rubén," said Sra. de León, who had come up quietly next to me. "We're very proud of him. He's living in Paris, now. He's been a great help to his father in the last few years." She gave Sarah a frosty, slightly challenging smile.

Eventually we were all moored around the table. Dinner excellent. Amazed by quality. Sadly, though, was unhungry in the extreme. Throughout parade of courses McGees and de Leóns conversing with the informal amiability of old friends: an archaeological site just uncovered nearby, then lurid local gossip—a nun from the U.S. who claimed to have been abducted from a convent in town and tortured. Though eventually, de León told us, the Embassy revealed that the cigarette burns all over the nun's back had been inflicted by a lesbian lover.

"It's always in small places that the most incredible things happen, isn't it?" Dot said. "New York City can't compete with this story."

De León turned to Sarah with a brief burst of male charm. "This government is a collection of amateurs," he said obscurely.

"Vicente is sentimental about the old days," Sra. de León said. "When less was required of us."

"I will not walk around my own property armed," Sr. de León said, his warmth disappearing in the frozen wastes of his wife's smile.

There was a small silence as Sra. de León looked at her napkin with an amused, measured loathing. "Ah," she said, as maids brought in trays of dessert and coffee. "Here we are."

The McGees appeared to be accustomed to the climatic shiftings between the de Leóns. "Vicente"—McGee waved his fork—"Angélica has outdone herself tonight."

"A triumph," I said, gently pedaling Sarah's foot. "And I never would have dreamed it was possible to do something like this with a banana."

"Oh, nor I," Sarah said, withdrawing her foot.

"Very simple," Sr. de León said. "Just caramelize lightly, add a little orange, a little rum, and flame." He handed me a small stack of cards; turned out he had had all the recipes from dinner typed up.

Gabriela laughed. "Daddy is so shy, isn't he," she said.

"Yes, ha," I agreed. Consommé with Tomato, Avocado, and Cilantro, I read. Sole with Good Morning! Grapefruit. Carrots with Zest of Good

Morning! Orange. Volcano Salad. Good Morning! Bananas with Juice of Good Morning! Oranges and Rum. Dark Roast Good Morning! Coffee and Cardamom Chewies. "I hardly know how to thank you," I said. "These will really *make* my article—"

"It is my great pleasure," de León said.

"And it will be nice to have some decent press up there for a change," Gabriela said.

"Gaby," Sr. de León chided.

"No, but it's true," Gabriela said. She turned to Sarah. "You know, it happens all the time. Some reporter, who knows nothing about this country, who doesn't care anything about it, who only cares about making a reputation for himself, comes down and says he wants to write an objective story about life here. And the next thing you know, you open up some magazine and read the most fantastic stuff. As if the country were one big concentration camp—as if all we ever did was bomb the villages."

Sarah put down her fork.

"I *know*," Gabriela said. "Never one word about the *wonderful* things—"

"Gaby," Sra. de León said, and put down her own fork, "why don't you show our new friends the garden."

It was a great relief to leave the table. Gabriela led us through the pungent floral riot, and cut some elegant little lilies for Sarah. Sarah thanked her; asked how far the plantation extended. Gabriela looked puzzled for a moment, then laughed. Explained that we weren't on the plantation at all—that it was hours and hours away, over terrible roads. Said, "Of course, these days if we were to go we would use helicopters, and it would only take minutes. But we never do anymore. Even Daddy hardly goes."

Sarah silent, considering. Then asked who was it, that being the case, who saw to the planting, harvesting, etc.

Gabriela mercifully innocent—entirely impervious to offense potential of Sarah's question.

"Oh, we have what amounts to a rather large village living up there," Gabriela said. "And some very reliable overseers. But we always used to go out at harvest time ourselves, anyway."

Frankly, was very touched by her regretful tone. "You enjoyed it," I observed.

"Oh, yes," she said. "I loved it. We all did. We loved to watch the harvest, to ride around the countryside on our horses . . . Well, it was a long time ago, when we could do that—that was back when our Indians still had their own little plots of land up north, and we had them brought down on trucks for the harvest, big trucks, from their tiny villages. And they were all from different villages, so they wore different colors and patterns in their clothes, and they spoke all sorts of different languages. They were so strange, so beautiful. I used to love to listen to them, and to watch them. To watch them harvesting the coffee . . ."

"Harvesting coffee," I said. "You know, I never think of coffee as a legume, but, of course—*coffee beans!*"

Gabriela smiled and shook her hair. In the moonlight she had a newborn look. "Coffee isn't really a bean at all," she said. "It's a berry. It's very nice to look at—it turns bright red. But it's a nuisance to pick. You really have to watch what you're doing or you can strip the plant. Still, at least, it's not heavy, as long as you're not hauling the sacks. So it's one thing that children can learn to do. Fortunately for the families."

Sarah started to speak, and stopped.

"It was so beautiful," Gabriela said. "I wish I could show it to you as it was then . . ." She sighed. "You have to forgive me for talking and talking like this. But there are so few people who would understand what it's like for me. People here can't really understand because most have never lived in the States or Europe, and my friends in the States can't understand, because they've never been here."

"Do go on," I said. I glanced reprimandingly at Sarah.

"Oh, I don't know . . ." Gabriela smiled faintly, as though she were watching something across the garden. "Well, it's been so long since I've been back, hasn't it. I was about twelve, I suppose, the last time. That's right—because my brother, Rubén, who's in Paris now, was sixteen. It's incredible to think about that time, really. It was very confusing. It was very hard, particularly for my parents, because it was just when things were at their worst in this country, and the guerrilla movement really had some strength. And Rubén had picked up some funny ideas. He was just at that age, you know, when children are very susceptible. And I suppose some older boys had gotten hold of him because our family, well"—she smiled sadly—"because our family is very well known. And Rubén began to go around saying things he couldn't possibly even have understood— talking about giving land away, 'returning it,' was how he put it. And ruinous increases in wages. Things that would absolutely destroy his own family. And Mommy and Daddy tried to reason with him. They were very patient—they kept telling him, Rubén, you know, certain people own the land. They have legal title to it. You can't just snatch it away from them, can you? And if we're to drink coffee, if we're to eat fruit, someone is going to have to pick it. And it's a tragedy, of course, that you can't just pay the laborers anything you'd like, but it's a fact. It's simply a fact. Because what do you think would happen to the world if we did? And a banana cost ten dollars? Or a cup of coffee cost twenty dollars? But Rubén would always just slam out of the house. So it was a very hard time for us all. And of course that was the period when the workers had to be watched very, very closely, because, you can imagine—if it was possible to contaminate Rubén, imagine how much easier it would be with a poor, uneducated Indian."

Gabriela reached out to touch a pink rambling rose. "So," she said, "we were all up for the harvest one year, and there was a morning when I woke up very, very early. Before the sun rose. I woke up to this delicious smell, this absolutely delicious smell, of roasting coffee. And I thought, well, now it's time to get up. And then about one thousand things happened in my mind all at once, because I realized it wasn't time to get up—it wasn't time to get up at all, and something was happening that couldn't possibly be happening. And so, before I even knew what I was doing or why, I rushed over to my window. And the window was black and red—black with night and red with fire, wave after wave of fire in the black sky. And the whole storehouse, all our coffee, was up in flames."

"Oh—" Sarah said. She sat down on the rim of an old fountain from which cascaded tiny weightless white flowers.

"Yes," Gabriela said. She seated herself next to Sarah and drew me down beside her. "It was terrible. And after that I never really went back. Mommy and Daddy felt it would be too dangerous, and of course it wasn't nearly as pleasant, because security was tightened up a lot, too. The army came—there are still hundreds of soldiers living there, in fact." She laughed. "Daddy doesn't like that at all. He says it's more of a—what do you call it?—protection racket, than protection, and that the army is bleeding us worse than the workers. But what can you do, after all? And there are guard towers now, and the landing strips, and those awful, you know, *fences*. So it's not so nice anymore.

But Rubén went back once again with my father. And instead of bringing him to his senses, it all just seemed to make him worse—angrier and wilder and more unhappy. My parents wanted him to go away to school. To Harvard, or perhaps to Oxford. But he wanted to stay in the country, and it turned out to be a very bad thing for everyone that he did. Because then he really became involved with all these crazy student groups. It was so sad. They were so young—they thought they were idealists, but, really, they were just being used. Rubén had been such a sweet boy, such a wonderful brother, but he became very hard. It was just this hard, awful propaganda all the time."

Gabriela frowned at a petal she was smoothing between her fingers. "He said terrible things. He said that we were thieves, you know, and so on. And it's not as though any of us are thrilled with the way things are, of course, but after all—it is people like our parents who generate the entire economy here." She sighed. "He said that people were starving. Heavens! You have to be *stupid* to starve in this climate, don't you?" She turned to Sarah for confirmation and smiled gently. "The fruit simply drops off the trees.

"Anyhow, during the next year, several of our workers and some of the other students—friends of Rubén's—got killed and were found by the side of one road or another. So, even though none of them were from important families, we were all terrified for Rubén. And in fact it was late that same year that the first letter arrived."

Inside, in the soft light, we could see Gabriela's parents and the McGees sipping their coffee and chatting contentedly. I closed my eyes and raised my face to the tiny white flowers above us, as though they were a spray of cool water.

"And the letter stated it all in no uncertain terms— They knew who he was, they knew *where* he was, and so forth. Well, my father got on the phone right away, and started sending my brother to see important people. My father had friends in the police, and friends in the army. And he even had several friends in the Embassy—your embassy here—so we thought we could take care of it quickly enough. But every day went by, and everyone my brother talked to said they didn't know anything about it—they couldn't find out who was sending the letters. And one day Rubén went to see a colonel in the army, whom Rubén and I had known since we were *babies*—my father is the *god*father of one of this man's children. And Rubén came back from that meeting looking like a corpse."

A little leaf spiraled down through the air and landed on Gabriela's dress. She picked it off and looked at it affectionately before she let it flutter away. "Because the Colonel said, you know, right away, that of course he'd help, and he made a phone call while Rubén was sitting right there in his office. The Colonel explained the situation over the phone to whoever it was he'd called, and then he just sat there on the phone, listening, for about twenty minutes, Rubén told us later. And when he hung up, Rubén asked what the other person had said, and the Colonel said, 'Nothing.' "

Gabriela stopped speaking for a moment, and as she resumed, Sarah's cold hand rested briefly on mine. "So the Colonel stood up to walk Rubén to the door, and at the door he burst into tears. And he said, 'I'm sorry. I can't help you. But now, listen to me, please—there's something I have to say to you.' He put his hands on Rubén's shoulders and looked into his eyes, and said, 'When you leave your house, be sure to tell somebody where you're going. Always walk in the direction of traffic' "—Gabriela leaned up for a moment, as I had, into the cool spray of white flowers— " 'and be very, very careful when you cross the street.' "

This morning particularly blue and bright. Ricardo's greeting, María's smile, the roses, the hummingbirds—everything bright, large, standing out in the blue air as though I'd been far away for a long time. Woke up famished. Couldn't eat enough. Melon, grapefruit, pineapple, banana— I ate and ate. Thought of all that fantastic food last night, just sitting in front of me. Laughed slightly. "Horrible, wasn't it?" I said to Sarah. "Thank God we'll never have to do that again." My fork scraped startlingly against my plate. "Sarah?" I said.

Saw she hadn't touched her fruit or her juice or her coffee. I speared a piece of banana and held it out to her. "No?" I said. Waved it temptingly. "All right, but you'll be starving by the time we get to the airport."

She looked at me, then slammed her napkin down onto the table and stalked off.

Made an embarrassed farewell to Ricardo, hurried to our room, where I found Sarah sitting, staring at me accusingly from the unmade bed—the geological record of the aeons of our horrible night, our tense, mid-sleep lovemaking during which the ghouls from Gabriela's wild story rubbed their wicked little numbing dream hands and waited.

"Oh, for heaven's sake," I said, as it dawned on me. "All right. I apologize, Sarah, all right? I'm a brute. I'm insensitive. I'm a white male." Sarah folded her arms. "But frankly, my dear, it *is* a common expression. A manner of speaking. I rather imagine you've used it yourself upon occasion—"

Sarah interrupted. "But guess what, Dennis? I'm the person who's never going to *be* starving. Because that's the person I am, as it turns out. I'm the same person as Dot, Dennis, the same person as Gabriela—"

"Oh, come, now," I said.

" '*Oh, come now,*' " Sarah said. She kicked savagely at the mattress. "Because don't you get it? I mean this is a *war*, Dennis. We're soldiers, *and that's our uniform.*" She started to cry with a thin, infuriating animal anguish. "See, I don't understand why I didn't *know* that. I don't understand why I haven't read about all this in the newspaper."

"In the newspaper!" I said. "You don't understand why you haven't read about this in the *newspaper*? About what, please, Sarah—why you haven't read about what?" Felt I was wading through a dark, cold river. An ashy river clogged with garbage and bones. "You don't know why you haven't read about who you *are*? In the newspaper? Do you consider that a front-page story? Sarah, listen to me. What are you trying to do to me? Are you trying to spoil all the *good* things? Yes, I suppose I should rush off to Zwicker and say, 'Stop the presses, chief, there are some problems out there—rich people make more money than poor people. Life is unfair and people suffer.' God knows, Sarah—it's not as though I don't agree with you, but think about it for a moment, please; use your head. You don't read about yourself in the newspaper because that's not what a newspaper is for. And you don't read in the newspaper about the things that go on here, because *the things that go on here aren't news*."

God, it was awful. Mortifying. Sarah sobbing, me ranting—was *profoundly* mortified by my outburst. Got blue in the face apologizing, while Sarah sniffled and hiccuped and packed her beautiful textiles, sneaking beleaguered glances over her shoulder at me as though I had forced her at gunpoint to buy them. Made me feel literally like the Gestapo.

Thankfully, by the time we got to the airport she seemed to have exhausted herself—was just sleepy and absentminded, like a child after a tantrum.

On the plane Sarah stared at her closed book as a thin shield of cloud glided beneath us, but I peered across her out the window to watch the little country beneath us vanish.

Oh, the ravages of traveling. Poor Sarah. Unfamiliar rules, disturbance of one's biological rhythms. Whole populations of new microbes . . . The plane went blood-dark for an instant; pale skin boiling up into sticky black welts, slow lines of black-windowed vans patrolling the pale mountains . . .

Hadn't even occurred to me before—I'm *sick*! Bet we both are. Bet we've both picked up some sort of parasite. Damn, damn! Well, God knows I tried to be careful.

Oh, so much to do this week. Doctor. Work up a piece for Zwicker, of course. Unpack. Phone calls. Stacks of mail, naturally—naturally most of it catalogues. It's funny, I always intend to throw them right out, but when it comes down to it I can never resist leafing through, to see all the idiotic junk—programmable toasters, telephones disguised as footballs—that someone has spent time dreaming up and someone will spend money to buy. Shook my head and forced a chuckle, but Sarah continued to look out the window. "Hey," I said, tugging playfully at her sleeve. "I promised I'd take you to the Red Fox Inn tonight, remember?"

"The Red Fox Inn?" Sarah looked at me, then a veil dropped over her expression, and she turned back to the window.

All right. Yes, the planet is littered with bodies. No one's going to dispute *that*—and the bodies are surrounded by clues. But what those clues mean, and where they point—well, that's something else altogether, isn't it?

Took Sarah's unresisting hand, and for a moment feared I was going to burst into loud, raucous weeping. Strange airplane light showing the fatigue behind her closed eyes; showing the age, deep within her, boring its way to her surface.

But will it improve, the world, if Sarah and I stay in and subsist on a diet of microwaved potatoes? Because I really don't think so. I really don't think—and this is something I'll say to Sarah when she's herself again, I suppose—that by the standards of any sane person it could be considered a crime to go to a restaurant. To go someplace nice. After all. Our little comforts— The velvet murmur, the dimming of the street as the door closes, the enfolding calm of the other diners . . . that incredible moment when the waiter steps up, smiling, to put your plate before you . . .

Deborah Eisenberg

## QUESTIONS

1. Why does the sight of the "solitary peasant in the field" prompt Dennis to reflect on his own life? Why is Dennis unable to decipher the "encoded dispatches" from his life? (477)

2. What does Dennis mean when he writes, "Careful—get down *just as happened*"? (481)

3. Why are the McGees evasive in telling Dennis and Sarah what they seem to know about the political situation in the country? Why is Dot later unable to remain silent, despite Cliff's objections?

4. Why does Dennis describe the sensations of the town as "persecuting loveliness"? (488)

5. What does Dot mean when she says that the people take the story of the Passion "so *literally*"? (492) Why is Dot concerned about their emphasis on the suffering rather than on the Resurrection?

6. What does Dennis mean when he tells Sarah that the situation involving Jesus and Pilate is "complex"? (493) Why does Dennis think Sarah is incapable of understanding the meaning of what they observe?

7. Why does Dennis describe the eyes of the people in the crowd as having a "fanatical, incendiary ecstasy of poverty"? (496)

8. What is it that Gabriela thinks neither her friends in her own country nor those in the United States can understand about her situation?

9. Why does Sarah say, "I'm the same person as Dot, Dennis, the same person as Gabriela—"? (506)

10. Why does Sarah still take her beautiful Indian-made textiles home with her after she realizes she and Dennis are "soldiers" in a war against the Indians? (506)

## FOR FURTHER REFLECTION

1. Who, if anyone, in the story is able to understand the political situation clearly?

2. Is Dennis correct when he says that the McGees are "perfectly harmless"?

3. Do you agree or disagree with Dennis's argument that it would be "morally reprehensible" not to enjoy the sights in the country he and Sarah are visiting?

4. What responsibility does a journalist have to communicate the potentially disturbing aspects of a situation he or she is writing about?

**DISCUSSION GUIDES FOR**


**Confessions of a Fallen Standard-Bearer**
*by Andreï Makine*


**The Age of Innocence**
*by Edith Wharton*

# ANDREÏ MAKINE

Andreï Makine was born in Siberia in 1958 and grew up in Novgorod. He received his doctorate from Moscow University and has since worked as an editor for *Litterature moderne a l'étranger*, a French magazine of foreign literature, and as a professor of literature at the Novgorod Institute.

Makine was granted asylum by the French government while studying in Paris in 1987. He wrote his first works of fiction in French, only to experience several rejections from Parisian publishing houses. Because of the popularity of Russian fiction in Paris, when Makine resubmitted his novel *Dreams of My Russian Summers* as "translated from the Russian," it was accepted for publication readily.

In 1995, Makine won both the Prix Goncourt and the Prix Medicis, two of the most prestigious French awards in literature, for *Dreams of My Russian Summers*, which was also a finalist for the 1998 National Book Critics Circle Award. He is also the author of *Requiem for a Lost Empire*, *Once Upon the River Love*, and *The Crime of Olga Arbyrlina*. In reviews and essays about his work, critics have placed Makine's name alongside those of Anton Chekhov, Marcel Proust, and Boris Pasternak.

## ABOUT
### *CONFESSIONS OF A FALLEN STANDARD-BEARER*

Makine's *Confessions of a Fallen Standard-Bearer* is a novel that bridges the political and the personal, culture and memory; it offers, in the words of Rilke, "the bridge barely curved that connects the terrible with the tender." The narrator Alyosha, hearing news of his boyhood friend Arkady, begins a sudden journey into the past, giving us glimpses of Soviet-era Russia during World War II and the Cold War. Andreï Makine composes this world in less than 150 pages; his economy is a powerful device in the evocation of memory. Paying homage to Proust, Makine uses sound, smell, and taste to trigger the memories of his characters: he shows us the power of returning to a once familiar place or receiving an unexpected phone call. Makine reminds us that our days are crowded with such encounters and that any moment of recollection fills the mind's eye with a picture or series of pictures. Such images embody a broad range of associated experience—a story (if there is one), mood, and emotions. The imagery that Makine puts on the page, unearthed from his childhood and voiced through Alyosha, works in this concentrated way.

The piling up of these images makes for a richly associative narrative, one that gives the reader the feeling of an experience—its essential truth—while the core of the experience often remains ineffable. Arkady's father, Yasha, is "a living corpse" who stayed alive in Poland beneath "a mountain of frozen bodies." (6) Lifted from the pile when the concentration camp was liberated, but leaving his living face behind, Yasha gives the best part of his remaining body, his legs, to Alyosha's disabled father, Pyotr. Together the two men, both horribly diminished by war, make one body, a whole person, so that "[f]rom a distance you would have said it was a single man moving . . . with nimble steps. . . ." (7) These images aspire to the intensity and richness of poetry.

Makine is often compared to Pasternak, and in the coming of age of Alyosha and Arkady is a common theme: the clash of ideology and the individual. Why are individual rights abrogated for the good of the community? Why must the individual sacrifice mind and body for the collective? These questions haunt Alyosha even as he remembers the security and beauty of the courtyard, the triangle within three red-brick structures that formed his childhood universe. In the courtyard Alyosha sees something of the Marxist ideal—communal living based on empathy and compassion. But this world, he slowly learns, is strangely at odds with his training as a Young Pioneer. The aftermath of war, the core of Alyosha's formative experience, plagues the minds and bodies of the men of the courtyard like an incurable disease. Arkady's father, Yasha, insulated from the cold by "the deaths of others," (84) will not speak of his own suffering or life in the camps. This pain erupts in the next generation when the boys, uncovering an unknown Nazi graveyard, ravage and curse the remains of dead soldiers in an "orgy of destruction." (66) It is the ghostly quiet of Yasha's voice that makes them stop. But the dark irony of Alyosha's father is the most poignant rendering of war's endless assault on the body: Pyotr, having lost his legs under fire from his own forces, finds success as a cobbler, spending the balance of his life seated at a workbench repairing shoes for those who can still walk.

Just as insidious as the aftermath of war is the indoctrination of the Young Pioneers. The boys march incessantly in extravagant shows of nationalistic pride with their eyes set always on the "radiant horizon," a kind of utopia made possible by fighting for and defending the "workers' cause"—not the tired old workers in the courtyard, but "a kind of superior tribe, untouched by the imperfections of communal life." (14) In singling out the young for service and dressing them in smart uniforms, the authorities separate Alyosha and Arkady from the courtyard, the very community that in some ideal form they are sworn to defend. But in their experience of the "new pioneers' camp," as they witness a hypocritical authority exploiting the body of a comrade, they begin to understand, now in sexual and psychological terms, the parasitic effect of a totalitarian government on the body of its citizenry. For Alyosha, the pride of being a Young Pioneer—of wearing the uniform, once a kind of shield against the humiliations of communal living—turns into a bitter recognition of useless suffering, of hope destroyed in pursuit of a "beautiful dream" they "swallowed with trusting naïveté." (96)

Must any political ideology, even one initially based on restructuring privilege and redistributing wealth, advance by the destruction of the individual? This is the question raised by the penultimate episode of the novel. It is Arkady's mother who tells Alyosha the taboo story, the dark memory that she would not reveal to her own son because as a child "he was too sensitive. The smallest things upset him." (110) But Alyosha must listen as Faya tells him of the death of her grandmother and how, quite by accident, Svetlana, a prostitute living in the same building, takes the young Faya into her apartment, hoping to protect the little girl from the Nazi siege and the ravages of winter. Often paid with food for her services, Svetlana draws sustenance from the men who visit, and they, in turn, take what they need from her body. When she grows ill and can no longer offer her body in exchange for a meal, she resorts to desperate measures. What Faya discovers about Svetlana's search for food is unexpected and horrific, demonstrating in this case that survival depends on the destruction of another.

While there may be a moral imperative in believing that the needs of a collective outweigh the needs of a few or one, the harsh reality that Makine shows is that individuals will be violated or destroyed to support the collective. Do dictators use the human body as an expendable resource? How do we live with memories, with past experiences, that threaten to undermine any belief in human decency? These are just some of the disturbing questions that Makine forces us to consider.

Note: All page references are from the Penguin edition of *Confessions of a Fallen Standard-Bearer* (2001).

## QUESTIONS

1. What is "the radiant horizon" and why is it such an important goal for Alyosha and Arkady?

2. How do the workers that Alyosha knows in daily life differ from the workers in the songs of the Young Pioneers?

3. What meanings do the children and adults of the courtyard associate with the Pit? How do the secrets that emerge from the Pit affect the life of the courtyard?

4. Why does Yasha order the boys to stop when he finds them, in Alyosha's words, "waging our little war" in the Nazi graveyard? (66)

5. How do the boys react to the arrival of the "senior Party officials"? Why do the boys continue to play their instruments after the flag is raised? (79)

6. What is the significance of the music the boys choose to play after managing a temporary escape from the storeroom?

7. Why does Arkady say, in response to seeing the Party official and Ludmilla on the bench beside the fountain, "It's sad. Ludmilla with that guy . . . It's horrible"? (94)

8. When visiting his mother for the last time, why does Alyosha see her night table as a "snapshot of [her] life in the old days"? (99)

9. What does Alyosha mean when he observes, "What was slowly building up in my own past was that thick layer of experience that protects us from the pain of others"? (103)

10. After telling Alyosha "The Siege Building," why does Arkady's mother refer to the Tibetan legend that speaks of the past as a "dragon kept in a cage in the depths of a cave"? Why may the dragon "reappear more cruel and insatiable than ever" if allowed to escape? (120)

11. Why is Alyosha fearful that Arkady will "despise" him for giving voice to their past? (122)

12. Why does Arkady sob and push Alyosha away with "savage violence" after seeing Yasha carrying Pyotr in his arms, the latter swinging a scythe "with broad and free strokes"? (129)

## FOR FURTHER REFLECTION

1. Must any political ideology designed to serve the interests of the majority advance by the destruction of individual rights and, ultimately, the individual?

2. How do we live with memories or past experiences that threaten to undermine any belief in human decency?

# EDITH WHARTON

E dith Wharton (1862–1937), born to a wealthy and fashionable New York family, was raised and educated by governesses and tutors as the family moved between houses in Paris, New York City, and Newport, Rhode Island. She published her first book, a slim volume of poetry, at the age of sixteen. Wharton's patriarchal and socially conservative family disregarded her literary work, thinking it an inappropriate, even embarrassing, eccentricity.

Wharton married Boston banker Edward Robbins Wharton in 1885, but the marriage was not a particularly happy one. Wharton moved to France in 1907 and the couple divorced in 1913. After publishing a number of stories in popular magazines, including the *Atlantic Monthly* and *Scribner's*, she set out to write serious fiction. Following the example of her friend and mentor, Henry James, Wharton took up the novel of manners, chronicling the customs and beliefs of her social class. Over the next forty years, she published eleven collections of stories and sixteen novels, including *The House of Mirth* (1905), *Ethan Frome* (1911), and *The Age of Innocence* (1920), the last of which won the Pulitzer Prize. She also published works on travel and interior design.

In Paris during World War I, Wharton worked tirelessly as the head of the American Hostels for Refugees and wrote of her experiences in *Fighting France* (1915). For her work during the war, she was made a chevalier of the French Legion of Honor. She filled her later years with the company of artists and intellectuals, a coterie that included, in addition to Henry James, Jean Cocteau and Sinclair Lewis, who dedicated *Babbitt* to Wharton. She was the first woman to be elected to the American Academy of Arts and Letters and to receive an honorary doctorate of letters from Yale University. Wharton died of a stroke in her home in France, having lived as an expatriate for much of her life.

## ABOUT
## *THE AGE OF INNOCENCE*

The title *The Age of Innocence* is both ironic and poignant: ironic because the "age" or period of the novel, the late nineteenth century, teems with intolerance, collusion, and cynicism; poignant because the only innocence lost is that of Newland Archer, the resolute gentleman whose insight into the machinations of aristocratic life comes late. The novel proceeds from a working assumption that is best summed up by Ralph Waldo Emerson in his essay "Self-Reliance": "Society everywhere is in conspiracy against the manhood of every one of its members." Edith Wharton advances this belief with a vengeance, and it gives tragic depth to the life of Newland Archer, a life that might otherwise seem pedestrian and unworthy of close examination.

Wharton presents Archer as a man of refined sensibilities, well educated, responsible, alert to expectations. He works in an old law firm just enough to achieve an air of respectability and importance. He attends opera, keeps up with the galleries in Europe, and thinks "few things seemed . . . more awful than an offense against 'Taste.'" (12) At the same time, Archer is a harsh judge of his fellow man. He attributes to Ned Winsett "the sterile bitterness of the still young man who has tried and given up." (101) He thinks Sillerton Jackson a gossip, Lawrence Lefferts a philanderer, and Julius Beaufort a crude scoundrel of business. He is perhaps most judgmental—and incorrect—about May Welland, the debutante who becomes his wife, deciding not long after their marriage "that never, in all the years to come, would she surprise him by an unexpected mood, by a new idea, a weakness, a cruelty or an emotion." (243) Archer also criticizes himself, but he is not altogether thorough, and he turns a blind eye to his central flaw, failing to recognize his own immaturity, his own naiveté about the ways of his world. He fails to see himself as a "dilettante" (4) making claims to intellectual and moral superiority. But it is this characteristic that makes

Archer a true innocent. In many ways, he pictures himself standing apart from his milieu, believing that he is somehow a free agent, less susceptible to social claims.

Archer possesses one other characteristic that contributes largely to his innocence—imagination. This is not to say that Archer's contemporaries lack this particular facility, but rather that his own turns of fancy tend toward the untried and the unorthodox. Having an after-dinner cigar with Sillerton Jackson, Archer declares that "women ought to be free—as free as we are." (34) And when Countess Olenska, the woman he loves, asks if she is to be his mistress, Archer says, "I want somehow to get away with you into a world where words like that—categories like that—won't exist." (238) Archer is something of a dreamer, a romantic, and it is his story of lost love that makes him, if not a hero, then a sympathetic everyman. Archer's imagination allows him to see beyond his perfect match with May Welland, his prestigious but inconsequential law practice, and the formidable social strictures directed against the Countess Olenska. But somehow the plots and intrigues of high society—of drawing room and library, of wife and friends—escape him, and when Archer finally understands his life as being subject to powers outside his control, it is too late. Is there a social conspiracy against Newland Archer? Is he manipulated to do what his community wants without regard to his desires or happiness? Or is it Archer's naiveté and his romantic preoccupations that entrap him? Is a man of affluence and position a master of his own fate, or is he mastered by tradition, expectation, and prescribed morality? These are just a few of the questions that *The Age of Innocence* raises.

Few things in a Wharton novel can be understood as black or white, this or that. The demands and consequences of duty are laid out before Archer clearly enough, but how he should respond to them, and how we respond to him, is complicated by the possibilities of social conspiracy and romantic fulfillment. The decisions that Archer makes concerning his life with May Welland and a life with Countess Olenska speak to his sense of obdurate responsibility. Archer's son, recounting his mother's words, says to Archer "she knew we were safe with you, and always would be, because once, when she asked you to, you'd given up the thing you most wanted." (293) Must security be purchased with sacrifice? Is it moral and honorable to protect others at the expense of one's happiness? Or is Archer a puppet, incapable of claiming morality or honor because his actions are forced upon him by the designs of others? Is duty to one's community more important than duty to oneself? Can and should any society determine the right course of action for an individual? In the end, if we as readers feel safe with Newland Archer, it is because he upholds his obligations, his duty to wife, children, and society. He manages, through strength or resignation, to keep things in order. We pity him as well.

Edith Wharton

## QUESTIONS

1. Why does Archer neglect to tell Countess Olenska of his engagement to May Welland, despite the fact that May has instructed him to do so?

2. Why does Archer suddenly realize that marriage is "not the safe anchorage he had been taught to think, but a voyage on uncharted seas"? (35)

3. Why does Archer feel "oppressed" when contemplating the "factitious purity" of his betrothed? (37)

4. Why is Countess Olenska a threat to the social order that claims Archer as one of its kind?

5. Why is the neighborhood where Countess Olenska resides a "queer quarter for such a beauty to settle in"? (99)

6. What is Archer referring to when he thinks that "the green mould of the perfunctory was already perceptibly spreading" over many of his peers? (103)

7. What does Archer mean when he thinks that "it was wonderful that . . . such depths of feeling could coexist with such absence of imagination"? (154)

8. How does Archer feel about May's talent with her bow and arrow? Why does he so often feel "cheated . . . into momentary well-being"? (173)

9. When Archer, at the request of Mrs. Mingott, follows the path to the shore to fetch Countess Olenska, why does he say to himself, " 'If she doesn't turn before that sail crosses the Lime Rock light I'll go back'"? (177)

10. What kind of "code" exists between Archer and May? How does it work? What is its origin? (219)

11. Why does May decide to host the farewell dinner for the Countess Olenska? Why does Archer think of the dinner guests as "a band of dumb conspirators"? (276)

## FOR FURTHER REFLECTION

1. Must social and emotional security be purchased with the sacrifice of another individual or group?

2. Is it moral and honorable to protect others at the expense of one's happiness? Is duty to one's community more important than duty to oneself?

Note: All page references are from the Penguin edition of *The Age of Innocence* (1996).

# CONNECTING THEMES

There are many general topics or themes that run through the selections in each volume of the Great Conversations series, and it is likely that perceptive readers will see the interconnections between the selections as well as the two longer works, *The Age of Innocence* and *Confessions of a Fallen Standard-Bearer*, for which we have provided discussion guides.

What follow are suggestions for considering these readings in clusters organized by topic and theme. These are by no means exhaustive or definitive. What is important is that readers of *Great Conversations 6* enter into the dialogue among these authors, as contemporary participants.

## I. Ways of Living

Seneca

Nietzsche

FitzGerald/Browning

McCarthy

## II. Living in Community

Locke

Twain

Addams

McCarthy

Eisenberg

## III. Forms of Belief

Bacon

Locke

Wells

Addams

## IV. The Power of Knowledge

Bacon

Reynolds

Nietzsche

Čapek

## V. Forms of Love

Eliot

Mansfield

Čapek

Eisenberg

## VI. The Perspective of History

Nietzsche

Čapek

Mann

McCarthy

# ACKNOWLEDGMENTS

All possible care has been taken to trace ownership and secure permission for each selection in this anthology. The Great Books Foundation wishes to thank the following authors, publishers, and representatives for permission to reprint copyrighted material:

*On Tranquility of Mind*, from SENECA: MORAL ESSAYS, VOLUME II, by Seneca, translated by John W. Basore. Reprinted by permission of the publishers and trustees of the Loeb Classical Library®, a registered trademark of the President and Fellows of Harvard College.

*On the Advantage and Disadvantage of History for Life*, by Friedrich Nietzsche, translated by Peter Preuss. Copyright © 1980 by Hackett Publishing Company, Inc. Reprinted by permission of Hackett Publishing Company, Inc.

*Mario and the Magician*, from STORIES OF THREE DECADES, by Thomas Mann. Copyright © 1930, 1931, 1934, 1935, 1936 by S. Fischer Verlag GmbH. Frankfurt am Main. Reprinted by permission of Regal Literacy, Inc. as agent for S. Fischer Verlag.

*R.U.R.* from TOWARD THE RADICAL CENTER: A KAREL ČAPEK READER, by Karel Čapek, translated by Claudia Novack. Translation copyright © 1998 by Claudia Novack. Reprinted by permission of Claudia Novack.

*My Confession*, from ON THE CONTRARY, by Mary McCarthy. Copyright © 1946, 1947, 1949, 1950, 1951, 1952, 1953, 1954, 1955, 1958, 1959, 1960, 1961 by Mary McCarthy. Reprinted by permission of the Mary McCarthy Literary Estate.

*Holy Week*, from THE STORIES (SO FAR) OF DEBORAH EISENBERG, by Deborah Eisenberg. Copyright © 1997 by Deborah Eisenberg. Reprinted by permission of Farrar, Straus, and Giroux, LLC.